lonely planet

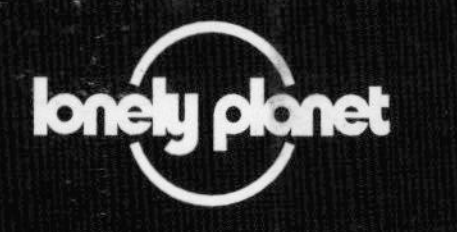

Tasmania

Carolyn Bain
Gina Tsarouhas, Paul Smitz

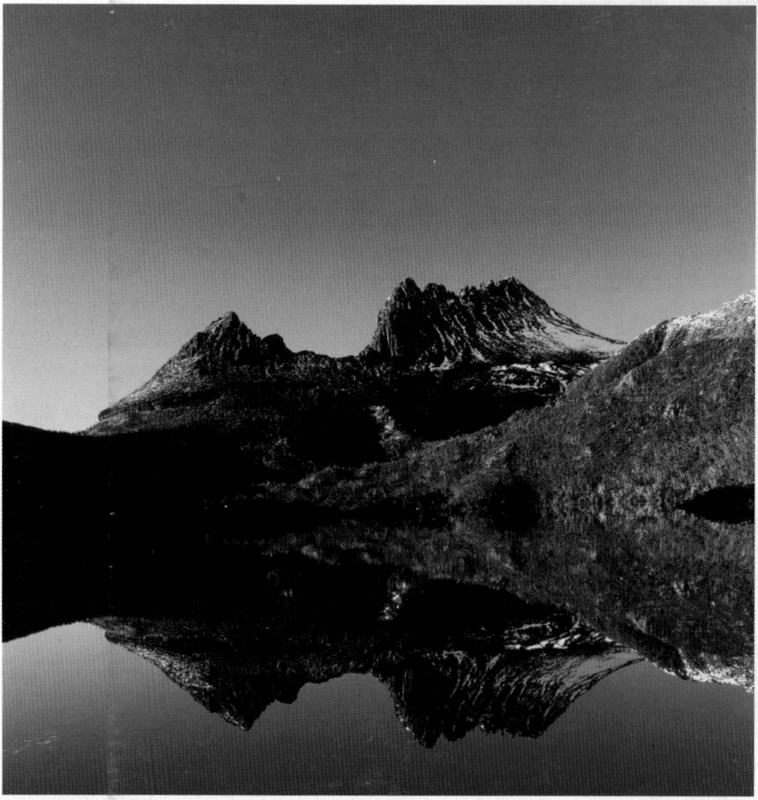

Destination Tasmania

Tasmania's diversity and relatively compact size make it a perfect holiday destination: in the space of a week you can take in dazzling coastal and mountain scenery, explore absorbing colonial history, eat your way through some of the best seafood in the country, and still have time to visit Hobart's Salamanca Market and spend a day wine-tasting in the Tamar Valley. Although you can see a lot in a short space of time, resist the urge to zoom around cramming everything in. Stop to smell the roses, as they say – or in Tasmania's case, the cheeses, apples, wines, fresh air, forests…

One quarter of this outlandishly beautiful state is made up of wildlife-saturated national parks, with most of that awarded the status of World Heritage area. Tasmania is justly famous for its wilderness, which ranges from the wildest of ocean dunes and satellite islets to near-impenetrable rainforest, rugged mountain ranges, soaring sea cliffs and fragile alpine moorlands.

But Tasmania is also an exuberant human habitat. The main cities of Hobart and Launceston might be engaged in a cosmopolitan face-off across the length of the island, but smaller towns are also getting in on the act, continually adding to their urban inventories a mixture of plush new accommodation, funky cafés, festive occasions, and restaurants that prepare the splendid local produce with creative culinary fervour.

Those with a yen for the great outdoors, gourmet produce, friendly locals or an intriguing history (but especially all of the above) will be hard-pressed to find a more rewarding destination than Australia's island state of Tasmania.

Highlights

JOHN HAY

Taste the beer of Tasmania's south at Cascade Brewery (p74), Hobart

RICHARD I'ANSON

Browse the stalls at Salamanca Market (p69), Hobart

OTHER HIGHLIGHTS

- Inspecting the galleries, restaurants and cafés of Salamanca Place (p69)
- Seeing the sun rise over Wineglass Bay (p169), Freycinet National Park
- Fishing the trout-filled lakes of the Central Plateau (p152)
- Sampling the cool-climate wines of the Tamar Valley (p206)

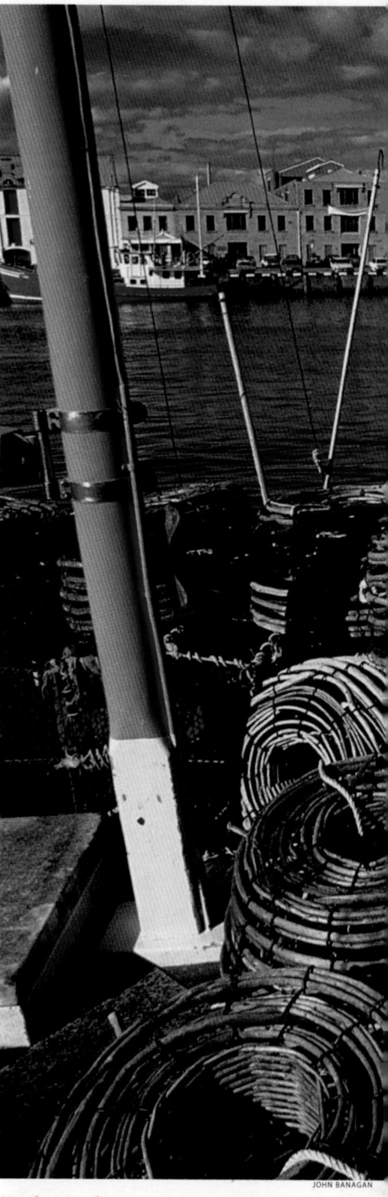

JOHN BANAGAN

Watch your dinner arrive in a lobster pot at Victoria Dock (p65), Hobart

Stock up on fresh local produce at Salamanca Market (p96)

SALLY DILLON

JOHN HAY

Consume renowned Tasmanian-made cheeses (p59)

Meet the ferocious Tasmanian devil (p38)

JOHN BANAG

CHRIS KLEP

Seek some thrills white-water rafting (p46)

GRANT DIXON

Climb magnificent formations on the Tasman Peninsula (p48)

See the coastline from a sea kayak (p47)

GRANT DIXON

PAUL SINCLAIR

Feel the spray of Horseshoe Falls at Mt Field National Park (p107)

GRANT DIXON

Cross-country ski around Mt Field National Park (p107)

Surf or swim at the beaches of Mt William National Park (p188)

ROB BLAKERS

ROB BLAKERS

Stroll beneath deciduous beech at Cradle Mountain–Lake St Clair National Park (p284)

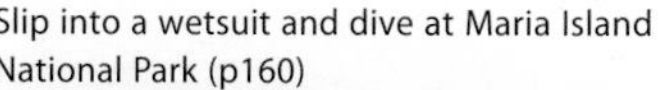

Slip into a wetsuit and dive at Maria Island National Park (p160)

ROB BLAKERS

Climb challenging Mt Anne in Southwest National Park (p298)

GRANT DIXON

GLENN BEANL

Stand atop Richmond Bridge (p108), the oldest road bridge in Australia, built over the Coal River in Richmond

Marvel at towering sand dunes in the Tarkine Wilderness (p263)

PAUL SINC

LINDSAY BROWN

Soak up the history at Port Arthur's convict church (p119)

Contents

Lonely Planet books provide independent advice. Lonely Planet does not accept advertising in guidebooks, nor do we accept payment in exchange for listing or endorsing any place or business. Lonely Planet writers do not accept discounts or payments in exchange for positive coverage of any sort.

Regional Map Contents

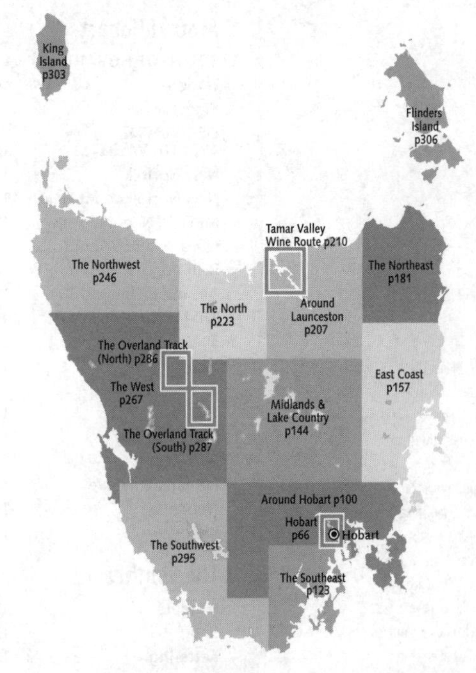

The Authors

CAROLYN BAIN

Coordinating Author, Hobart, Southern & Eastern Tasmania, Bass Strait Islands

Melbourne-born Carolyn has spent 15 years studying, travelling and researching guidebooks in far-flung corners of the world, and on her first trip to Tasmania was thrilled to discover a first-class destination so close to home. Later trips across stormy Bass Strait have given her the chance to yak with the friendly locals while exploring Tassie's scenic coastline, blissful national parks, sleepy historic villages, and – most importantly – excellent tearooms and wineries. She is currently based in Melbourne, getting her regular fix of Tassie heaven through King Island cheese, Tasmanian salmon and Boag's Draught beer.

My Tasmania

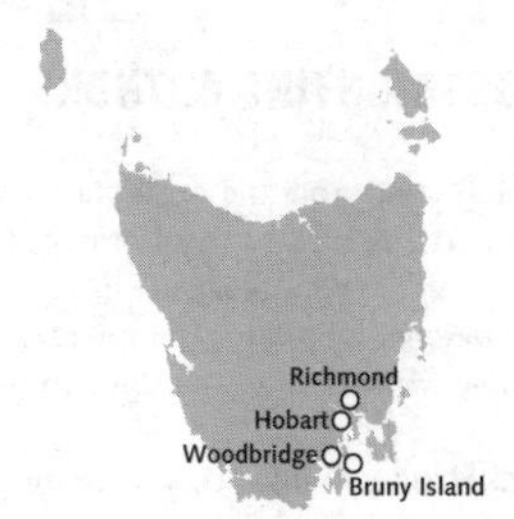

One of the highlights of my Tassie trips involves a handful of friends from Melbourne winging their way south for a long weekend, to help me with my Hobart 'research'. The itinerary includes Friday evening at Salamanca for the free live music and party atmosphere (p95), Saturday brunch and pottering at Salamanca Market (p69), caffeine fixes at my favourite cafés (please, Jackman & McRoss, open a branch in Melbourne!), and salivating over the local produce in at least one swanky restaurant: Lickerish in North Hobart (p92), maybe Peppermint Bay to the south in Woodbridge (p132) or possibly Meadowbank Estate near Richmond (p111). We'll check out local real-estate prices and marvel at the bargains (and I'll kick myself again for not buying on Bruny Island, p125 – a pristine island paradise – before the boom), then we'll visit a couple of wineries and/or bars and swoon over the local tipples.

GINA TSAROUHAS

Northern & Western Tasmania

Born in Melbourne with Greek blood flowing through her veins, Gina packed her little suitcase at the tender age of four and took off for Greece. Infected with a constant yearning for travel, Gina flitted between continents over the years until she decided to stay put for a while and she now works as an editor at Lonely Planet. Itching to get out of the office, she packed her suitcase once more to explore Tasmania – this time as an author. Gina spent a joyous few weeks hugging the northern and western coastlines, finding a new religion in the wilderness and scrambling over the state's craggy mountain peaks searching for the ultimate view.

LONELY PLANET AUTHORS

Why is our travel information the best in the world? It's simple: our authors are independent, dedicated travellers. They don't research using just the Internet or phone, and they don't take freebies in exchange for positive coverage. They travel widely, to all the popular spots and off the beaten track. They personally visit thousands of hotels, restaurants, cafés, bars, galleries, palaces, museums and more – and they take pride in getting all the details right, and telling it how it is. For more, see the authors section on www.lonelyplanet.com.

PAUL SMITZ

According to Paul's lemon juice–soaked résumé, he escaped from a test tube in Canberra and in some early wanderings collected gold bullion in Mexico, cruised the Panama Canal, tottered around Europe, and navigated Africa's west coast (he was only six at the time but reckoned it still counted). After other travels, he left Canberra for a round-Oz odyssey but ran out of petrol in Melbourne, where he joined Lonely Planet and ruined lives as an editor, map publishing manager and Web writer. He lives just outside Melbourne with an enigmatic woman who has an unfortunate spiritual connection with Ute Lemper.

CONTRIBUTING AUTHORS

Bob Brown wrote the boxed text 'Simple Steps for Saving the Forests' (p35) in the Environment chapter. Bob was elected to the Tasmanian parliament on the day after his release from Risdon Prison, during the Franklin dam blockade in 1983. He was first elected to the Senate in 1996. His books include *Memo for a Saner World* (Penguin, 2004) and a guide to the Styx River forests with Vica Bayley, entitled *The Valley of the Giants* (The Wilderness Society, 2005).

Tim Flannery wrote the Environment chapter (p34). Tim's a naturalist, explorer and writer. He is the author of a number of award-winning books, including *Country* (an account of Tim's personal experience of Australia), *The Future Eaters* (an ecological history of Australia), *Throwim Way Leg* (an account of his adventures as a biologist in Papua New Guinea) and *The Eternal Frontier* (a landmark ecological history of North America). Tim Flannery lives in Adelaide where he is director of the South Australian Museum and a professor at the University of Adelaide.

Dr David Millar wrote the Health chapter (p342). Dr Millar is a travel medicine specialist, diving doctor and lecturer in wilderness medicine who graduated in Hobart, Tasmania. He has worked in all states of Australia and as an expedition doctor with the Maritime Museum of Western Australia, accompanying a variety of expeditions around the country, including the Pandora wreck in Far North Queensland and Rowley Shoals off the northwest coast. Dr Millar is currently a medical director with the Travel Doctor in Auckland.

Getting Started

Tasmania is a traveller-friendly, tourism-conscious state that provides options for visitors on all budgets, and despite its small size (relative to other Australian states) it allows for surprising diversity – you can explore early Australian history, lose yourself (hopefully not literally!) in unspoilt natural wilderness, or undertake a waistline-expanding expedition to sample the first-rate local produce.

Tassie is an excellent family-holiday destination, and is ideally suited to a self-drive trip. It's important, however, that visitors avoid trying to cover too much ground in a short period of time. Distances might appear to be short on a map but it may take longer than you expect to drive them due to narrow, winding roads. You might wish to concentrate your touring in a specific region rather than darting from one coast to the other; otherwise you could find yourself spending most of your holiday in the car.

See Climate Chart (p317) for more information.

WHEN TO GO

Tasmania is most popular during summer, when it's warm enough for swimming and it's great to be outdoors. December, January and February are the busiest times for tourism. Accommodation is heavily booked (and often more expensive) and the popular restaurants are more crowded, but as compensation you can expect to see a variety of festivals and events, including the finish of the Sydney to Hobart Yacht Race (p82).

The winter months are generally cold, wet and cloudy, but days are capable of bucking this trend and can be clear, crisp and sunny – ideal for sightseeing and short bushwalks. The great advantage of visiting in winter is that tourist numbers and prices are low, and it can seem as if you have parts of the island to yourself.

Spring is the windiest time in Tasmania. Temperatures in early September are quite cold, the weather can be changeable and snowfalls can still occur, but by spring's end the weather is improving and the blooming gardens look and smell magnificent. Autumn is often pleasant, with mild temperatures, but towards the end of the season, the days (even sunny ones) are usually quite cold and windy.

Unless you want to be competing with hordes of grimly determined local holiday-makers for road space, hotel rooms, camp sites, restaurant tables and the better vantage points for every major attraction, avoid Tasmania's prime destinations during school holidays. Tasmanians are predisposed to holidaying in their own state; camping in national parks is particularly

DON'T LEAVE HOME WITHOUT...

- Strong sunscreen – Tasmania has long had an undeserved reputation for bleak weather, but even with overcast skies UV radiation down here is *high*
- Comfy, sturdy walking shoes so you can explore all those excellent national parks and walking tracks
- Good waterproof gear, and warm clothing (even in midsummer)
- A relaxed frame of mind – unwind, switch to 'Tassie time', and don't try to rush things
- A hearty appetite for sampling the local food and wine

popular at such times. Holidays vary from year to year, but the main period is from mid-December to late January, and again at Easter; see p321 for more information, and for a useful list of school holidays in all Australian states, check out www.dest.gov.au/schools/dates.htm. During these times, you're also likely to encounter mysterious, spontaneous rises in the price of everything from accommodation to petrol.

TOP TENS

Top Reads

The following page-turners have a rich Tasmanian flavour that evokes the state's people and places, its unique wilderness and complex history. Many have won critical acclaim in Australia and abroad. For reviews of these and other books, see p30.

- *The Alphabet of Light and Dark* Danielle Wood
- *The Boys in the Island* Christopher Koch
- *A Child's Book of True Crime* Chloe Hooper
- *Death of a River Guide* Richard Flanagan
- *English Passengers* Matthew Kneale
- *For the Term of His Natural Life* Marcus Clarke
- *Gould's Book of Fish* Richard Flanagan
- *The Hunter* Julia Leigh
- *The Sooterkin* Tom Gilling
- *The Sound of One Hand Clapping* Richard Flanagan

Top Festivals & Events

Australians will seize on just about any excuse for a celebration, and Tasmanians are no exception. Here are our top reasons to get festive (see p320 for more information):

- Finish of the Sydney to Hobart Yacht Race – Hobart, late December to early January (p82)
- Hobart Summer Festival – Hobart, late December to early January (p82)
- Cygnet Folk Festival – Cygnet, January (p132)
- Festivale – Launceston, February (p199)
- Ten Days on the Island – Statewide, March (every two years) (p320)
- Three Peaks Race – starts from Beauty Point, Easter (p199)
- Antarctic Midwinter Festival – Hobart, June (p82)
- Tastings at the Top – Cradle Mountain, June (p285)
- Wynyard Tulip Festival – Wynyard, October (p251)
- Tasmanian Craft Fair – Deloraine, October (p225)

Top Outdoor Activities

There are countless ways to get up close and personal with Tassie's renowned coastline, national parks and pristine wilderness areas. Here's our list of fave activities (see p44):

- Trekking the famed Overland Track through Cradle Mountain–Lake St Clair National Park (p285)
- Making a two-wheeled dash down Mt Wellington into Hobart (p77)
- Flying over and into the remote southwest wilderness (p299)
- White-water rafting down the magnificent Franklin River (p282)
- Taking the soft option – relaxing on a Gordon River cruise out of Strahan (p274)
- Fishing for trout in the serene beauty of the Lake Country (p151)
- Having a beach to yourself – surfing at remote Marrawah (p260)
- Exploring the gorgeous D'Entrecasteaux Channel by kayak (p125)
- Joining an eco-cruise out of Bruny Island to view great coastline and wildlife (p128)
- Walking to (and swimming in) stunning Wineglass Bay on the beautiful Freycinet Peninsula (p169)

COSTS

Overseas travellers should find Tasmania generally cheap to travel around. Manufactured goods tend to be relatively expensive, but daily living costs such as food and accommodation are relatively cheap. The biggest expense in visiting Tasmania is transport, both in terms of getting there – your options are restricted to planes and ferries – and getting around.

How much you should budget for depends on how you travel and how you'll be occupying yourself. If you regard sightseeing and having a good time as integral parts of the travel experience, prefer to stay in at least midrange hotels, motels or B&Bs, and have a stomach that demands regular restaurant visits, then $80 to $100 per day (per person travelling as a couple) should do it, though you can easily spend more by regularly taking tours and staying in top-end guesthouses.

At the low-cost end, if you camp or stay in hostels, cook your own meals, restrain your urge for entertainment and sightseeing, and travel around by bus (or in your own vehicle), you could probably eke out an existence on $45 per day; for a budget that realistically enables you to have a good time, raise the stakes to $60 per day. Staying in places for longer periods and/or travelling in a group will allow you to lower your costs.

LONELY PLANET INDEX

One litre of petrol
$1.00 to $1.20

One litre of bottled water
$2 to $3

Glass of beer (Cascade in the south, Boag's in the north)
$2.50

Souvenir T-shirt
$20

Street treat (meat pie)
$2.50 to $3.50

PRE-DEPARTURE READING

From the Sea: Images of Tasmania's Glorious Sailing Waters, Seafood and Wines, by Rob and Rosemary Peterswald, will certainly whet your appetite for a visit to Tassie. It's a glossy book containing beautiful photographs, recipes (utilising local seafood and other regional produce, often from well-known Tasmanian chefs), and personal reflections on the state's beguiling coastal regions.

English writer and biographer Nicholas Shakespeare visited Tasmania in 1999 and decided on a whim to stay. He soon discovered that he had family connections in Tassie and, like any writer with a nose for a good story, he went exploring. The resulting tale, *In Tasmania,* tells of his search, interspersed with fascinating tales of his adopted home state.

Down Home: Revisiting Tasmania (also known as *Behind the Mountain: Revisiting Tasmania*), by Tasmanian-born academic, journalist and critic Peter Conrad, combines autobiography, history and travelogue in a penetrating account of his return to the island after a 20-year absence. It describes the island's cultural isolation and the ensuing sense of displacement of its people; it's a contemplative book that will appeal particularly to those with a love of language.

The *Australian Geographic Book of Tasmania* by Lindsay Simpson photographs by Bruce Miller) is the author's personal account of her travels around the state and features her partner's stunning photographs.

INTERNET RESOURCES

Discover Tasmania (www.discovertasmania.com) The official site of Tourism Tasmania, with comprehensive details of key destinations, festivals, tours and accommodation.

Leatherwood Online (www.leatherwoodonline.com) Online magazine with great articles and excellent photography.

Lonely Planet (www.lonelyplanet.com) Succinct summaries, links to related sites and travellers trading information on the Thorn Tree.

Parks & Wildlife (www.parks.tas.gov.au) Excellent site for information on Tasmania's national parks, World Heritage areas, flora and fauna.

Tasmania Online (www.tas.gov.au) Huge site with links to almost every Tasmanian website.

Itineraries

CLASSIC ROUTES

THE NORTH & WEST

Two Weeks/Launceston–Cradle Mountain–Strahan–Stanley

Roll off the Devonport ferry or pick up a car at **Launceston** (p193), then take a stroll through Lonnie's Cataract Gorge. Enjoy an eclectic mix of attractions (seahorses, mining monuments, lighthouses and wineries) around the **Tamar Valley** (p206), and if wine's your thing, be sure to make a side trip to the **Pipers River region** (p213). Take in the historic towns of **Evandale** (p218) and **Westbury** (p216) before drifting west to **Deloraine** (p224) and the caves at **Mole Creek** (p227). A roundabout route (via Moina) takes you to iconic **Cradle Mountain–Lake St Clair National Park** (p284), one of Australia's finest national parks. From here, drive southwest to the sparse landscape of **Queenstown** (p278), where you can ride the West Coast Wilderness Railway. At **Strahan** (p272) you can experience more wilderness in comfort on a boat trip on the Gordon River. From Strahan, head north through the vast, empty **Arthur Pieman Conservation Area** (p263), stop to catch a wave in **Marrawah** (p260), then unwind in the Nutty **Stanley** (p255). A dip in the ocean at idyllic **Boat Harbour Beach** (p252) is the perfect end to your 800km journey before you head back to Devonport or Launceston.

Exercise all your senses on this trip from Tassie's second city into its famed western wilderness. It's an all-round feast for the eyes, plus you'll breathe some of the world's cleanest air, give your tastebuds a thrill on the Tamar and give your legs a workout on Cradle Mountain.

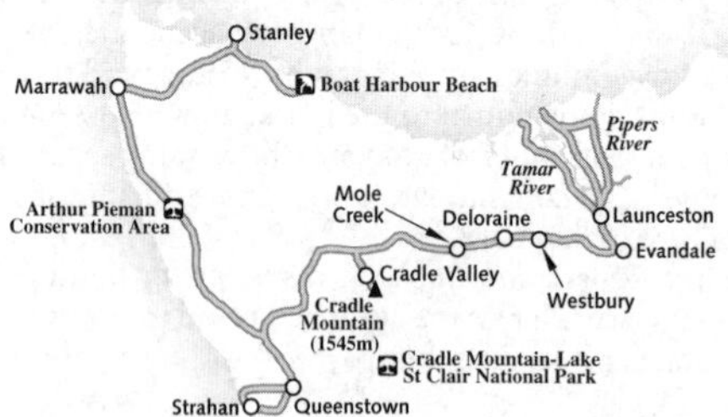

THE SOUTH & EAST

Two Weeks/Hobart–Port Arthur–Freycinet Peninsula

Spend a few days getting acquainted with Australia's smallest, southernmost state capital, the delightful **Hobart** (p65) – and if you want to cover some real southern territory, consider a scenic flight from here over the awe-inspiring **southwest wilderness** (p294); be sure to choose one that lands at **Melaleuca** (p300) and gives you time to take it all in. Back in civilisation, load up the car and set off on a loop taking in the southeast coast's many bucolic charms: unspoiled **Bruny Island** (p125), arty **Cygnet** (p132) and picturesque **Dover** (p139), with a detour to tiptoe through the treetops at **Tahune AirWalk** (p138). You'll need to retrace your path back to Hobart before making your way out to the rocky, dramatic **Tasman Peninsula** (p112), where you can visit **Port Arthur** (p117) and marvel at the existence of such a cruel and tragic place in such a beautiful location. History lesson over, wend your way north again, stopping at attractions (both natural and constructed) in **Taranna** (p116) and **Eaglehawk Neck** (p115) en route. In the Copping area, look out for the shortcut to the east coast via the scenic **Wielangta Forest Drive** (p159). Hit the beaches of **Orford** (p157), take a boat out to **Maria Island** (p160), unwind in **Swansea** (p162), and save the best until last – the breathtaking **Freycinet Peninsula** (p166), in all its glory.

Get a feel for the southern treasures of Tassie with this 800km trip through its past (Port Arthur's penal settlement) and present (surprisingly cosmopolitan Hobart), then see for yourself what all the fuss is about on the gorgeous east coast.

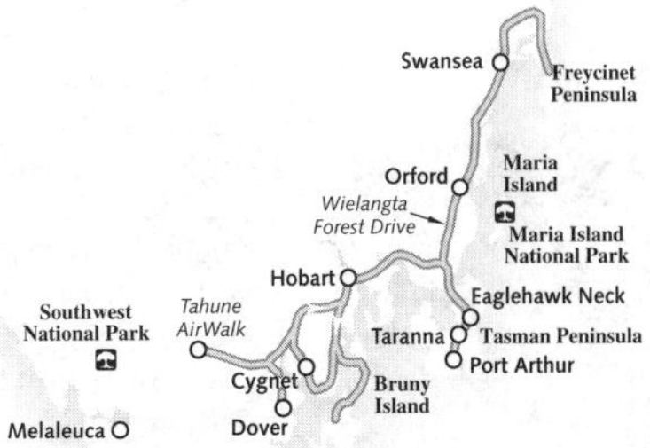

TAILORED TRIPS

NATURAL WONDERS

'Australia's natural state' has 19 national parks offering dazzling diversity and countless treats for nature-lovers. Start by enjoying the stupendous views over the capital from **Mt Wellington** (p76). South from here and a ferry-ride away, wonderful **Bruny Island** (p125) offers empty beaches, scenic drives and wildlife-spotting, and further south you can go underground at **Hastings Caves** (p141). West of Hobart is the family-friendly **Mt Field National Park** (p106), where you can enjoy wildlife, walks and waterfalls; it's worth a detour from Mt Field to see the tallest trees in the southern hemisphere in the **Styx Valley** (p297). Cut north to the Lyell Hwy and west to **Lake St Clair**, part of the incredible **Cradle Mountain–Lake St Clair National Park** (p284). Loop around the park and you'll reach Cradle Valley, where visitors soak up the splendour of **Cradle Mountain**. You're not far away from more caving action at **Mole Creek Karst National Park** (p229) and following the A3 highway from here takes you to Launceston, home to **Cataract Gorge** (p194), and on to the northeast coast. From St Helens, head north to the **Bay of Fires** (p187) or south to glorious national parks at **Freycinet Peninsula** (p166), **Maria Island** (p160) and the **Tasman Peninsula** (p112).

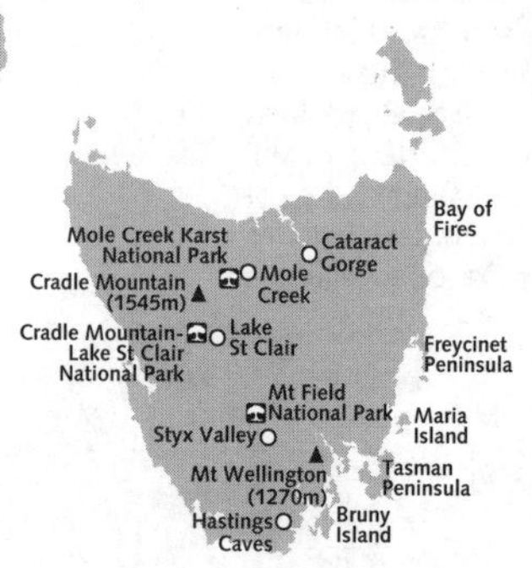

GOURMET DELIGHTS

Tasmania has a deserved reputation for fine, home-grown gastronomic goodies. Start your feasting in the restaurants of **Hobart** (p89) and check out the ace take-home gourmet products in the stalls of Saturday's **Salamanca Market** (p69). While in the capital, visit the **Cadbury Factory** (p74; for chocolate, der), **Cascade brewery** (p74; beer) and the **Cascades Female Factory** (p76; fudge). Next, head to the slick new **Peppermint Bay** (p132) restaurant in Woodbridge for tantalising tastes of the southeast, and visit the wineries and cheesemakers in the neighbourhood. **Richmond** (p108) is the next stop, near the winemakers along the **Coal River** (p111), and you're not far from the fresh-fruit and fresh-oyster heaven of **Sorell** (p113). The east coast offers up more seafood – oysters at the Marine Farm (p170 on the Freycinet Peninsula and crayfish in **St Helens** (p182). Waddle west to **Pyengana** (p184) for moreish cheese, then get someone else to do the driving around the vineyard-rich **Pipers River region** (p213) and **Tamar Valley** (p206). A restaurant ramble in **Launceston** (p203) should further tingle the tastebuds, and here you can pledge your (informed) allegiance to a Tassie beer after visiting **Boag's Brewery** (p197). Finally, if you can fit anything else in, the area around **Deloraine** (p224) and **Mole Creek** (p227) is home to honey producers, a raspberry farm and a cheese factory.

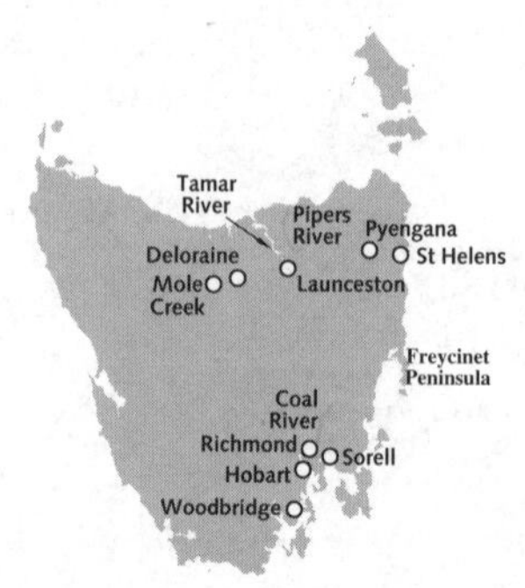

Snapshot

Interesting things are afoot in the island state, with Tasmania experiencing a renaissance unlike any other Australian state. Tasmania's era of economic decline and population decrease (p26) appears to have recently come to an end, and the locals are revelling in the chance to shake off the label of Australia's backwater and show off their assets to a more receptive audience.

Tasmania is gaining a reputation as a friendly, unhurried and safe holiday destination. The significant increase in tourist numbers in recent years indicates that Tassie has become a more popular travel destination for mainlanders, thanks in no small part to high-profile advertising campaigns from tourism authorities, the two ferries crossing Bass Strait between Devonport and Melbourne (and the less successful ferry chugging to and from Sydney), plus the recent explosion of low-cost airlines offering bargain prices for flights into Hobart and Launceston.

Tasmania is getting more attention in mainland newspapers, too – witness the coverage in 2004 of the inelegant downfall of Richard Butler, Tasmania's controversial state governor; the keenly felt death of former premier Jim Bacon from lung cancer; and newspaper columns devoted to the logging debate in the lead-up to Australia's federal election. Note, too, the positive spotlight cast by Tasmania's home-grown royalty, Crown Princess Mary of Denmark.

A welcome feeling of optimism is in the air, and visitors can witness and partake in the state's rejuvenation, especially at venues such as Launceston's redeveloped seaport, the glossy Henry Jones Art Hotel in Hobart, and sleek new restaurants such as Peppermint Bay in Woodbridge that lure diners with fine, locally sourced produce. On our most recent trip, it seemed that every second hospitality establishment (guesthouse, motel, pub, tearoom) had just changed hands and had recently undergone, or was in the midst of, renovations – often by mainlanders moving south for a 'sea change' of sorts. For these new residents, Tasmania's allure varies: a change of climate for overheated Queenslanders, a lifestyle change for empty-nesters or burnt-out city folk, a chance for many to take advantage of some of the cheapest real-estate prices in the country, or ex-Tasmanians returning home now that things are on the up. The locals can't be too thrilled with being priced out of some areas, but the breath of fresh air passing through the tourism industry in Tasmania is very welcome. And visitors will still see plenty of 'Property For Sale' signs, as more locals cash in on the rising property prices.

Still, no-one can turn a blind eye to the division that cuts through the state. Car bumper stickers tell some of the story, wanting to 'Save our Forests' and 'Save the Styx/Tarkine/South Sister/Ralphs Bay' from logging or development. 'Ban 1080' refers to a chemical poison used in agriculture and forestry to protect newly planted seedlings from being eaten by the local wildlife; it results in the deaths of tens of thousands of native animals annually. In the other corner of the ring, a succinct sticker proclaims 'Greens Tell Lies'.

Pro-environment locals are asking some tough questions, such as how can the state government continue to stand idly by while forestry concerns devastate some of the state's finest assets in the interests of corporate profit? No doubt about it, it's a charged debate, and sadly it's unlikely to be resolved any time soon.

FAST FACTS

Population: 482,000

Area: 68,332 sq km

Size of Wilderness World Heritage Area: 1.38 million hectares

Number of national parks: 19

Unemployment rate: 6.5%

Gross state product growth (GSP): 3% (2003–04)

Number of tourists: approx 745,000 in 2003 (15% from overseas)

Number of Tasmanian-born queens-to-be: 1 (Mary Donaldson, now crown princess of Denmark)

Number of surviving Tasmanian tigers: 0 (but we can't be sure)

Size of apple crop: approx 52,500 tonnes in 2003

History

TASMANIAN ABORIGINES

Since European settlement, the story of the Tasmanian Aborigines has had a terribly unhappy theme. The Aboriginal people were subjected to an attempted genocide, during which they were dispossessed of their land so quickly and thoroughly that it's remarkable any traces of their history, culture or language survive. Survive they do, though, in carvings and paintings in once-inhabited caves, in coastal middens of shells that yielded meals, in quarries where stone tools were fashioned, and, most importantly, in the form of the Tasmanian Aborigines themselves and their persisting cultural identity and reasserted sovereignty. Good places to learn about their art and culture are Tiagarra (p235; the Aboriginal cultural centre and museum in Devonport); the new Living History Museum of Aboriginal Cultural Heritage outside Cygnet in the southeast (p132); and on a tour out of Deloraine operated by Jahadi Indigenous Experiences (p225).

A Short History of Tasmania (1997), Michael Roe's updated edition of the classic Lloyd Robson book, offers a comprehensive and accessible history lesson of the state up until the late 1990s.

Early History

The land mass now called Tasmania was settled by Aborigines at least 35,000 years ago, when they probably migrated across the land bridge that joined Tasmania to the rest of Australia. The sea level was much lower then and the Tasmanian climate much drier and colder. Aborigines settled the western side of Tasmania, where extensive grasslands supported the animals they hunted, particularly wallabies. The eastern half of the state was probably too barren for settlement.

When the last ice age ended between 18,000 and 12,000 years ago, the glaciers retreated, sea levels rose and Tasmania detached from mainland Australia. From then on, the culture of the Tasmanian Aborigines diverged from that of their mainland counterparts. While people on the mainland developed more specialised tools for hunting, such as boomerangs, woomeras and pronged spears, the Tasmanian people continued to use simpler tools, such as ordinary spears, wooden war clubs *(waddies)* and stones. Tasmanian Aborigines did, however, produce boats of a design more sophisticated than those created on the mainland and used them to hunt seals and mutton birds on and around the offshore islands.

As the climate changed after the ice age, tall forests became established in the western half of the island, while in the east, rainfall increased and extensive grasslands developed. Most of the Aborigines abandoned their caves and shelters and followed the animals they hunted to the more open, eastern tracts of land. Those who remained in the west lived primarily on the coast.

Tasmanian Aborigines fed themselves by hunting, fishing and gathering, and sheltered in bark lean-tos. They protected themselves from the island's cold weather by rubbing a mixture of ochre, charcoal and fat on their skin. It's estimated there were between 5000 and 10,000 Aborigines in Tasmania when Europeans arrived. They were organised into 'bands' of around 50 people, with each band claiming rights over a specific area of land and being part of one of the nine main language groups.

TIMELINE

60,000–35,000 BC
Aborigines settled in Australia sometime during this period

12,000–8000 BC
Tasmania's Aborigines are separated from the mainland when sea levels rise

European Invasion

The first recorded European landing was in 1642 at Bruny Island's Fluted Cape by the Dutch navigator Abel Tasman; European settlers came to the island 161 years later. They established a base at Risdon after first killing an unknown number of peaceable Aboriginal people, and subsequently usurped traditional hunting grounds, fencing the fertile ground into farms. In 1816, Governor Thomas Davey produced his idealistic 'Proclamation to the Aborigines', which represented settlers and Aborigines living together amicably, in direct contrast to the realities of a brutal colonial society.

The 1820s saw a period known as the Black War, when Tasmanian Aborigines responded to the Europeans' treatment of them as subhuman by attacking settlers. The Europeans then stepped up their atrocities by abducting Aboriginal children to use as forced labour, raping and torturing Aboriginal women, giving poisoned flour to friendly tribes and laying steel traps in the bush.

The Black Line

In 1828, martial law was proclaimed by Lieutenant-Governor Arthur in Tasmania's central districts, giving soldiers the right to arrest or shoot on sight any Aboriginal person found in an area of European settlement. In 1830, in an attempt to flush out all Aborigines and corner them on the Tasman Peninsula, a human chain of about 2200 men, known as the Black Line, was formed by settlers and soldiers. This line moved for three weeks through the settled areas of the state. Three weeks later, the farcical manoeuvre had succeeded in capturing only an old man and a boy, and confirmed settlers' fears that they couldn't defeat the Aborigines by force of arms.

Some Tasmanian Aborigines use the word Palawa (First Man) as a collective noun for their people.

Lieutenant-Governor Arthur then consented to missionary George Augustus Robinson's plan to 'conciliate' the remaining Aborigines. During the next three years, Robinson travelled throughout most of the state and persuaded (through a mixture of encouragement and force) virtually all of the Aborigines in mainland Tasmania to lay down their arms and accompany him to new settlements.

There is strong historical evidence that the Aborigines were enticed to follow Robinson to a succession of settlements in the Furneaux Islands with promises of sanctuary and land. Instead, they were subjected to European attempts to 'civilise' and 'Christianise' them and made to work for the government. After enduring a number of moves to places such as Sarah Island on the west coast, they were finally settled at Wybalenna (Black Man's Houses) on Flinders Island, where one by one they began dying from a potent mixture of despair, homesickness, poor food and respiratory disease.

Oyster Cove Community

In 1847, the surviving residents petitioned Queen Victoria, complaining of their treatment and referring to the 'agreement' they thought Robinson had made with Lieutenant-Governor Arthur on their behalf. Wybalenna was eventually abandoned and the survivors transferred to mainland Tasmania. Of the 135 who had been sent to Flinders Island, only 47

1642
Abel Tasman discovers Tasmania and names it Van Diemen's Land after a Dutch governor

1788
The First Fleet arrives at Sydney with its cargo of convicts

survived to make the journey to Oyster Cove, south of Hobart. Their new accommodation proved to be substandard and the Aborigines once again experienced the criminal neglect of the European authorities, and growing demoralisation. Within a decade, half of them were dead. Truganini, the last of the Oyster Cove community, died in 1876 (see below).

Furneaux Islands Community

European sealers had been working in Bass Strait since 1798 and they raided tribes along the coast, kidnapping Aboriginal women as workers and sex slaves. The sealers were uninterested in Aboriginal land and eventually formed a reciprocal trade relationship with the Aborigines, whereby the sealers traded dogs and other items for accompaniment back to their islands by Aboriginal women, and occasionally men. A disapproving Tasmanian establishment contemptuously termed the descendants of sealers and Aboriginal women 'half-castes', and even though Cape Barren was designated an Aboriginal reserve in the 1880s, there was continual pressure on the Islanders to adopt European farming ways and assimilate with mainlanders.

Today

In 1997 the Tasmanian parliament became the first in Australia to formally apologise to the Aboriginal community for past actions connected with the 'stolen generation'.

Tasmanian Aborigines continue to claim rights to land and compensation for past injustices. Acknowledgement of the treatment meted out to Aborigines by Europeans has resulted in the recognition of native titles to land. In 1995, the state government returned 12 sites to the Tasmanian Aboriginal community, including Oyster Cove, Kutikina Cave and Steep Island. Wybalenna was added to this list in 1999, and there is state legislation in the pipeline to transfer Crown land on Cape Barren Island to the Aboriginal community.

It's interesting to note that the subject of Tasmania's early treatment of Aborigines is still a very contentious one. Keith Windschuttle released a controversial book in 2002 entitled *The Fabrication of Aboriginal History, Volume One: Van Diemen's Land 1803–1847,* which argues that the violence committed against the Tasmanian Aborigines has been vastly overstated. *Whitewash: On Keith Windschuttle's Fabrication of Aboriginal*

TRUGANINI

Truganini's name is often mentioned in historical accounts of the European invasion and its consequences for Tasmanian Aborigines. She was born on Bruny Island in 1812, a daughter of Mangana, the chief of the Nuennone Tribe. Along with her husband, Woureddy, she left her island home to travel with George Robinson on his island-wide expeditions to win the confidence of the remaining Aboriginal people. Twice during this three-year period she saved his life. Truganini then lived with fellow Tasmanian Aborigines in the derelict environment of Wybalenna on Flinders Island and afterwards at Oyster Cove.

After living out her final years in Hobart, Truganini died on 8 May 1876. For many years, her skeleton was displayed as a public curio in the Tasmanian capital. One hundred years after her death, her wishes were granted when her ashes were finally scattered in the channel beside her beloved Bruny Island. Travellers can visit a memorial to Truganini at The Neck on Bruny Island (p128).

1804
Tasmania's first permanent European settlements are established, at Sullivan's Cove (Hobart) and George Town

1822–53
Convicts are imprisoned at various penal colonies around the state, including at Sarah Island and Port Arthur

History (edited by Robert Manne) was released in reply and is a collection of arguments from noted historians refuting Windschuttle's claims.

EUROPEAN DISCOVERY

Known history records that the first European to see Tasmania was the Dutch navigator Abel Tasman, who arrived in 1642 and promptly called it Van Diemen's Land, after the governor of the Dutch East Indies. Between 1770 and 1790, Tasmania was sighted and visited by a series of other European sailors, including captains Tobias Furneaux, James Cook and William Bligh. They all visited Adventure Bay on Bruny Island and believed it to be part of the Australian mainland rather than an island off Van Diemen's Land (visit the Bligh Museum of Pacific Exploration at Adventure Bay, p127, for more information). In 1792, Admiral Bruni d'Entrecasteaux explored the southeastern coastline more thoroughly, mapping and naming many of its features. Most major landmarks still bear names bequeathed by this expedition.

European contact with the Tasmanian coast became more frequent after the soldiers and convicts of the First Fleet settled at Sydney Cove in 1788, mainly because ships heading to the colony of New South Wales (NSW) from the west had to sail around the island.

In 1798, Lieutenant Matthew Flinders circumnavigated Van Diemen's Land and proved that it was an island. He named the rough stretch of sea between the island and the mainland Bass Strait, after George Bass, the ship's surgeon. The European discovery of Bass Strait shortened the journey to Sydney from India or Africa's Cape of Good Hope by a week.

FOUNDING OF HOBART

In the late 1790s, Governor King of NSW decided to establish a second settlement in Australia, south of Sydney Cove. Port Phillip Bay in Victoria was initially considered, but the site was rejected due to a lack of water on the Mornington Peninsula and, in 1803, Tasmania's Risdon Cove was chosen. A year later, the settlement was moved 10km away to the present site of Hobart. The threat of other nations settling on the island prompted expansion, and in 1804 the first settlement on the Tamar River was established at George Town.

CONVICTS

Although convicts were shipped out with the first settlers, penal colonies weren't built until later when free settlers demanded social demarcation. Meeting the criteria that it had to be inhospitable and as far away as possible, Macquarie Harbour on the harsh west coast hosted the first penal colony in 1822. The actual site was on small Sarah Island and the prisoners sent there were those who had committed further crimes after arriving in Australia. Their severe punishment was the manual labour of cutting down Huon pines in the rainforest. It's believed conditions were so dreadful here that some prisoners committed murder in order to be sent for trial and execution in Hobart. Today, visitors can tour Sarah Island and hear more about convict life here on cruises out of Strahan (p274).

The number of prisoners sent to Van Diemen's Land increased in 1825, the year the island was recognised as a colony independent of NSW, when

Trying to find a convict in your family tree (or possibly erase one from it)? To help with genealogy searches, check the website of the Tasmanian Family History Society (www.tasfhs.org).

1830
The Black Line, a human chain of 2200, tries and fails to flush out Tasmania's Aborigines

1856
The state changes its name from Van Diemen's Land to Tasmania to remove the stigma of convict transports

another penal settlement was established, this one on the east coast of Maria Island, where prisoners were treated more humanely. In 1830, a third penal colony was established at Port Arthur on the Tasman Peninsula. Shortly after its construction, the other two penal colonies closed – Maria Island in 1832 and Macquarie Harbour in 1833.

Robert Hughes' compelling bestseller, *The Fatal Shore* (1987), offers a colourful and exhaustive historical account of convict transportation from Britain to Australia.

Punishments meted out to convicts at Port Arthur, which like its predecessors was considered escape-proof, included weeks of solitary confinement, sometimes in total darkness and silence. The worst prisoners were sent to work in the coal mines of nearby Saltwater River, where they were housed in miserably damp underground cells. A visit to Port Arthur (p117) evokes the terrible conditions suffered by prisoners during this era.

In 1840, convict transportation to NSW ceased, resulting in an increase in the number of people being sent to Van Diemen's Land; there was a peak of 5329 new arrivals in 1842. In 1844, control of the Norfolk Island penal settlement was transferred from NSW to Van Diemen's Land, and by 1848 the colony was the only place in the British Empire to which convicts were still being transported.

Vociferous opposition to the continued transportation of convicts came from free settlers, who in 1850 formed the Anti-Transportation League to successfully lobby for change. The last convicts transported to the colony arrived in 1853.

Port Arthur (www.portarthur.org.au) is often described as the most powerful historic site in Australia, and this website gives a good indication why.

Van Diemen's Land had been the most feared destination for British prisoners for more than three decades. During those years a total of 74,000 convicts had been transported to the island. The majority of these people had served out their sentences and settled in the colony, yet so terrible was its reputation that in 1856 – the year it achieved responsible self-government – it changed its name to Tasmania in an attempt to free its image once and for all from the shackles of its past.

EXPLORATION & EXPANSION

The establishment of Hobart Town and George Town in 1804 attracted new settlers, resulting in a demand for more land. Settlers initially spread along the southern coast towards Port Arthur, along the east coast and around the Launceston area. By 1807 an overland route from Hobart to Launceston had been forged. The earliest buildings were rough timber huts, but, as towns developed, settlers with stone masonry skills arrived. Stone was readily available for construction work and many early stone buildings have survived; some of the best examples of these buildings can be found in Richmond (p108) and the small towns along the Midland (Heritage) Highway (p144).

London-born Marcus Clarke visited Tasmania in the 1870s and wrote *For the Term of His Natural Life* (1874), an epic novel about convict life. Today it's still considered a ripping yarn.

To the Europeans, Tasmania's big unknown was its rugged hinterland, where difficult, mountainous country barred the way. The first Europeans to cross the island were escapees from Macquarie Harbour; many escaped, but only a few survived the journey across to Hobart Town. A significant though highly controversial early explorer was George Robinson, who set out in the 1830s to entice and cajole the Tasmanian Aborigines into leaving their traditional lands (see p21) and so became the first European to walk across much of the state.

In 1828 George Frankland was appointed Tasmania's surveyor-general. Determined to map the entire state, he sent many surveyors on

1870s
Gold and tin are discovered in the state's north, signalling the beginning of mining interests in Tasmania

1932
The Lyell Hwy is opened, linking Tasmania's west coast with Hobart

NATIONAL TRUST

The National Trust is an organisation dedicated to preserving historic buildings and important natural features throughout Australia. It owns and manages many properties, opening most of them to the public, and it also 'classifies' sites to ensure their preservation. Tasmanian National Trust properties open to the public include Clarendon near Evandale (p219), Franklin House in Launceston (p198) and Runnymede in Hobart (p73).

Membership to the National Trust entitles you to free entry to most of the properties it manages (in Australia, New Zealand and also the UK). Annual membership costs $55/35/84 adult/concession/family, and includes a monthly or quarterly newsletter put out by the state organisation that you join; there's also a first-year joining fee of $38.50. The **state head office** (☎ 6344 6233; www.tased.edu.au/tasonline/nattrust; 413 Hobart Rd, Launceston) is in Franklin House, while the organisation's **southern regional office** (☎ 6223 5200; cnr Brisbane & Campbell Sts, Hobart) is at the Penitentiary Chapel Historic Site (p72).

long, arduous journeys during the 1830s, often accompanying them. By 1845, when Frankland died, most of the state was roughly mapped and catalogued.

Building roads across the mountainous west was difficult, and many were surveyed across all sorts of difficult landscapes before being abandoned. But in 1932, the Lyell Hwy from Hobart to Queenstown was finally opened for business, linking the west coast to Hobart.

MINING

In the 1870s, gold was discovered near the Tamar River and tin in the northeast. These discoveries prompted a deluge of international prospectors. In the northeast a number of Chinese miners arrived, bringing their culture with them. Tourism authorities have plans for a themed 'Trail of the Tin Dragon' through the northeast to highlight this aspect of the state's history (see p182).

Mining was a tough way of life and most people didn't make their fortunes. Individual prospectors grabbed the rich, easily found surface deposits, but once these were gone the miners had to form larger groups and companies to mine deeper deposits, until eventually these either ran out or became unprofitable to work. Remains of the mine workings at Derby (p189) and Beaconsfield (p210) can be visited today.

Once it was realised that there was mineral wealth to be found, prospectors randomly explored most of the state. On the west coast, discoveries of large deposits of silver and lead resulted in a boom in the 1880s and an associated rush at Zeehan. In fact, so rich in minerals was the area that it ultimately supported mines significant enough to create the towns of Rosebery, Tullah and Queenstown. Geological exploitation went unchecked, however, and by the 1920s, copper mining at Queenstown had gashed holes in the surrounding hills, while logging, pollution, fires and heavy rain stripped the terrain of its vegetation and topsoil. The environment has only begun repairing itself over the past few decades.

The rich belt of land from Queenstown to the northern coast is still being mined in several places, but this is now being done with a little more environmental consideration and fewer visible effects than in the

1972
Lake Pedder is flooded as part of hydro-industrialisation

1982–83
The Franklin River Blockade is staged to oppose construction of a dam in the area, and is ultimately successful

past. New finds will undoubtedly occur in this mineral-rich belt, and may well see industry pitted against conservation interests yet again.

20TH CENTURY & BEYOND

Tasmania officially became a state when Australia's Federation took place in 1901. For Tasmanians, as for mainlanders in the new Commonwealth of Australia, the first half of the 20th century was dominated by war, beginning with the dispatch of a contingent of 80 Tasmanian soldiers to South Africa and the Boer War, through the Great War and WWII, with the Depression of the late 1920s thrown in for bad measure.

The Parks & Wildlife Service's website (www.parks.tas.gov.au/histher.html) has a section dedicated to exploring the past, with information on historic sites, plus whaling, sealing and shipwrecks off the state's coast.

The state's post-WWII economy was reassuringly buoyant, with industrial success embodied by Bell Bay's aluminium refinery and the ongoing developments of the powerful Hydro-Electric Commission. However, by the 1980s it had suffered a worrisome decline. Subsequent years saw economic unease reflected in climbing 'emigration' levels to the mainland (especially amongst the under-30s) and falling birth rates.

In the late 1990s and start of the 21st century this trend seems to have begun a slow reversal, with a revival of Tasmania's economy heralding a visible new era of optimism. A much-improved unemployment rate, record levels of investment, increased exports, a statewide real estate boom, a small but significant growth in the population, and a surge in tourist numbers have seen Tasmania finally shrugging off the undeserved tag of Australia's backwater. The man credited with much of the resurgence is Jim Bacon, a popular politician who presided over the state as premier from 1998 until early 2004, when he quit politics to fight lung cancer (a battle he ultimately lost, in June 2004).

It's not all good news in present-day Tassie, however – the long-running debate between pro-logging groups and conservationists continues (with some new bad guys, in the form of property developers, being added to the mix). Environmental issues are never far from the headlines – see p34 for more information.

1996

The Port Arthur massacre stuns the nation, and eventually results in stricter gun-control laws in Australia

2004

The issue of logging in Tasmania's old-growth forests becomes a political hot potato during the federal election

The Culture

REGIONAL IDENTITY

If you've ever entertained the notion that Australia is remote and isolated from the rest of the world, spare a thought for the Tasmanians, living on an island off an island at the bottom of the globe. It's a land with a dark history (Aboriginal decimation, convict incarceration, environmental damage, anti-gay laws), a spectacular but often dangerous wilderness, and a recent record of passionate divisions (forestry, mining and hydro-electric interests going head to head with conservationists with saddening regularity). How many times has this little island state been left off maps of Australia? How many times has it been dismissed as the country's cultural backwater, and been the butt of cruel jokes about two-headed inbreds? Given all this, it would be no great surprise to find the much-maligned Tasmanians harbouring decent-sized inferiority complexes and bloody big chips on their shoulders. The greatest surprise is that these days they don't appear to have much of either – Tasmanians (old-timers and newcomers) are some of the friendliest, most laid-back people you'll encounter. On your travels you're likely to become aware of their strong sense of Tasmanian identity and community, new-found pride in the state, and vibrant arts and sciences scene (perhaps to compensate for all those visiting artists and musicians who leave Tasmania off their touring schedules). Now that Tasmania's fortunes seem finally to be on the up, confidence in the state and its economic future is growing, and plenty of people are realising what a great place Tasmania is to visit (and possibly to live) – a remarkable turnaround from the days when Tasmanians left the state as soon as they were old enough, heading for greener pastures on the mainland.

'If you've ever entertained the notion that Australia is isolated, spare a thought for Tasmanians'

Australia's national identity is rooted in its past, and this is particularly true in Tasmania's case. The seminal times of the colony were characterised by extreme hardship, resentment at being sent so far with so little, and an incalculable sense of loss of loved ones and homes left behind. To cope with this struggle against nature and tyranny, Australians forged a culture based on the principles of a 'fair go' and back-slaps for challenges to authority, and told stories of the Aussie 'battler' that were passed down through generations.

Immigration has had a huge effect on Australian culture, as migrants have brought their own stories, cultures and myths to meld with those of the colonial 'battler'. Many migrants have come with a huge sense of hope and expectancy, to start life afresh. Colonial history has been revisited through art, literature and cinema, and as a result, the iconic 'battler' has become less relevant. And there's a long-overdue acknowledgment that the original inhabitants of this country are fundamental to a true definition of Australian culture today.

The immense prosperity the landscape has given has forged the title 'lucky country', the land of opportunity, and for most Australians this rings true. Australians enjoy a sophisticated, modern society with immense variety, a global focus, although not a regional one, and a sense of optimism sometimes tempered by world events.

Although there is some truth in the worn stereotypes that Australians are open-minded, down-to-earth, big-hearted, laconic, egalitarian, honest larrikins, these definitions are largely one-dimensional and derived from colonial times. Australian culture is much richer for its indigenous heritage and its multicultural mix. This exciting time of redefinition for Australia will throw unexpected people and experiences into your path. It's a young culture melding with the oldest culture in the world; and the incredibly rich opportunities are only starting to be realised.

LIFESTYLE

Australians have been sold to the world as outdoorsy, sporty, big-drinking, croc-wrestling country folk, but despite the stereotypes, you could count the number of Australians that wrestle crocodiles on one hand, many Australians can barely swim a lap, and loads wouldn't be seen dead in an Akubra hat.

'Despite the long-held reputation that Australians are boozers, recent figures show they drink less than the British'

The 'Australian Dream' has long been to own an overgrown house on a quarter-acre block, so sprawling suburbia is endemic in Australian towns and cities. Inside the average middle-class suburban home, you'll probably find a married heterosexual couple, though it is becoming increasingly likely they will be de facto, or in their second marriages.

Our 'Dad and Mum' couple will have an average of 1.4 children, probably called Joshua and Chloe, Australia's names of the moment. The average gross wage of either parent is probably around $A900 per week (compared to the UK's average of A$1160).

Our typical family, like most Australians, probably loves the sun. Australians have the highest rate of skin cancer in the world, with one in two people affected. Our family drags a caravan off to the beach every holiday, or a tent to a national park, and on weekends they probably watch sport, go to the movies or head to the shops. And our couple like a few quiet ones up the pub, though despite the long-held reputation that Australians are boozers, recent figures show they drink less than Brits and are way behind the world's leaders, Luxembourgers. Today, wine is the number one drink of choice.

POPULATION

The most recent census (2001) counted some 18,970,000 people in Australia, and Tasmania was home to only about 2.5% of the population. The state's 2001 populace was 472,931; this figure revealed a decrease in the state's population, continuing a pattern of decline as many locals headed to the mainland for work opportunities. Since the census, however, it is estimated that Australia's population has topped 20 million, and Tasmania's recent reversal of economic fortune has seen small but significant population growth (of around 1.1%) to reach a new population record of 481,658 in mid-2004.

Tasmania's population density is around seven people per square kilometre (although no-one's within cooee in the southwest); most people live in and around Hobart and Launceston, and along the north coast. The greater Hobart area has a population of around 200,000, while about 100,000 people live in greater Launceston.

Around 15,000 people of Aboriginal descent live in Tasmania. The state has a low percentage of overseas-born residents (around 10.5% of the state's population, compared with 23% for Australia overall). Of the overseas-born residents, about half are from the UK, and most Tasmanians have a British ancestry.

SPORT

If you're an armchair sports fan, Tasmania has much to offer. The football season has passions running high from about March to September, and when it ends, it's simply time for the cricket season to begin.

Tasmanians avidly follow the national Australian Football League (AFL), and York Park in Launceston hosts a handful of well-attended AFL matches each year – both St Kilda and Hawthorn (Melbourne-based teams) have committed to playing two home and away games in Launceston annually. The **AFL in Tasmania** (☎ 6234 2199; www.aflintasmania.com) website lists scheduled games and ticketing information.

Tasmania has two football leagues of its own: the **Northern Tasmania Football League** (NTFL; www.ntfl.com.au) and the **Southern Football League** (SFL; www.southernfootball.com.au). Squads from either end of the state occasionally play an intrastate match.

Cricket is played during the other (non-football) half of the year, and the state has produced two outstanding Australian test-side batsmen in recent times: David Boon and current team captain Ricky Ponting. Tasmania occasionally hosts one-day matches at Bellerive Oval, east of the Derwent River in Hobart, and also an occasional international test game. Tasmania takes part in the interstate Pura Milk Cup (formerly the Sheffield Shield) competition and also has district cricket matches. Contact the **Tasmanian Cricket Association** (☎ 6211 4000; www.tascricket.com.au) for tickets and match fixtures.

Hobart's harbour comes alive with spectators and party-goers for the finish of the famous **Sydney to Hobart Yacht Race** (http://rolexsydneyhobart.com), and the lesser-known Melbourne to Hobart race, at New Year.

ARTS

Cinema

Most people need little introduction to Australia's vibrant movie industry, one of the first established in the world and playground for screen greats Errol Flynn (a Hobart lad, see below), 'our' Nicole (Kidman) and come-hither-eyed Russell Crowe (born in New Zealand, but who's trifling over details?). Very few Australian movies are set or shot in Tasmania, however.

The expression 'in like Flynn' means a dead certainty, often in the sexual sense of a sure thing; many believe that the ease with which Errol Flynn charmed and bedded women gave rise to the phrase.

The Sound of One Hand Clapping, based on Richard Flanagan's harrowing book (and written and directed by the book's author), was released in 1998 and shot in Tasmania. It traces the impact on successive generations of war, displacement and abandonment through the story of a single family of European migrants from the time their grief finally becomes unendurable in a remote construction camp in the Tasmanian highlands.

Another Tasmanian film for which the highlands provide a grim setting is *The Tale of Ruby Rose* (1987), written and directed by Roger Scholes.

THE TASSIE SWASHBUCKLER

Errol Flynn was born in Hobart in 1909, but, as his father's work as a marine biologist and zoologist often took the family away for extended periods, Errol attended numerous schools in Hobart, Sydney and in England. After many jobs (as sailor, gold-hunter, slave-trader and journalist, if you believe all the publicity), Errol drifted into acting with his first role as Fletcher Christian in *In the Wake of the Bounty*, filmed in Sydney in 1933. By 1935 he had moved to Hollywood and became a celebrated star when he featured in *Captain Blood*. He starred in over 60 films, gaining screen-idol status playing such legends as Robin Hood and Don Juan. Flynn died of a heart attack in 1959; from his three marriages he fathered a son and three daughters (but who knows how many outside the vows of matrimony!). Despite a somewhat tarnished movie-star image, created by a private life of divorces, alcohol abuse and sex scandals (recounted in his autobiography, *My Wicked, Wicked Ways*), he is affectionately remembered as the devilishly handsome leading man and quintessential Hollywood swashbuckler.

It tells the story of a woman brought up in harsh isolation who has to come to terms with her marriage to a reclusive trapper.

Craft & Design

A strong crafts movement has existed in Tasmania since the turn of the century. Studio potters Maude Poynter and Mylie Peppin were active in the 1940s, and furniture-making has been particularly important, with cedar pieces from colonial times highly prized today. Contemporary furniture designers such as Patrick Hall, John Smith and Peter Costello are nationally recognised for their highly refined and often sculptural use of Tasmania's superb native timbers, such as Huon pine and sassafras.

http://amol.org.au/foundmade is an interesting site with good info on diverse subjects, taking in Aboriginal shell-necklace making, maritime craft, and wood design.

The Design Centre of Tasmania (p198) in Launceston displays and sells work by Tasmanian artisans. The galleries, shops and craft market at Hobart's Salamanca Place also show and sell crafts, while regional craftspeople advertise their creative efforts throughout the state.

Literature

Tasmania's unique culture and landscape and its unpalatable historical treatment of Tasmanian Aborigines and convicts have inspired and burdened writers of both fiction and nonfiction – the moody settings and often-gloomy subject matter of many books leading to the coining of a new term: 'Tasmanian Gothic'.

Marcus Clarke, a prolific writer who was born in London but spent most of his life in Australia, visited Tasmania in the 1870s and wrote *For the Term of His Natural Life*, an epic novel about convict life.

Queensland-born poet Gwen Harwood lived in Tasmania from 1945 until her death in 1996, and much of her work, such as *The Lion's Bride* (1981) and *Bone Scan* (1988), explores the island's natural beauty and the history of its Aboriginal population.

Literary buffs should get hold of the latest copy of Tasmania's quarterly literary journal, *Island* (www.islandmag.com), which publishes local writers' short stories, poetry, reviews, extracts from forthcoming novels, and a variety of articles and essays.

Robert Drewe's novel *The Savage Crows* (1976) also explores the oppression of Tasmanian Aborigines by the Europeans, while Hal Porter's *The Tilted Cross* (1961) is a novel set in old Hobart Town.

Christopher Koch is a Hobart-born author. His novels include *The Boys in the Island* (1958), an account of growing up in Tasmania; *The Year of Living Dangerously* (1978), which was made into a high-profile film; and *Out of Ireland* (1999), worked around the journal of a revolutionary Irishman who finds himself exiled in Van Diemen's Land.

Carmel Bird, born in Launceston but now living in Melbourne, is known for the quirky black humour of her stories and novels, including *The Bluebird Cafe* (1990), set in a fictional Tasmanian mining ghost town, and *Red Shoes* (1998), short-listed for the prestigious Miles Franklin award. Her latest offering, *Cape Grimm* (2004), is set in northwest Tassie.

The seven novels of James McQueen, who died in 1998, include *Hook's Mountain* (1982), which has as a subplot the struggle to save Tasmania's forests.

Tasmanian Amanda Lohrey's novels include *Morality of Gentlemen* (1984), set against the backdrop of Tasmania's waterfront disputes, and *Camille's Bread* (1995).

Hobart author Richard Flanagan is the state's best-known (and biggest-selling) literary star. His award-winning novel *Death of a River Guide* (1995) weaves together Tasmanian history and myths in a story set on the Franklin River – it makes an excellent introduction to Tasmanian history and life. His next novel, *The Sound of One Hand Clapping* (1997), won a national literary award, while the film of the same name was also well received (see p29). More recently Flanagan wrote an enigmatic fictional account of Sarah Island in *Gould's Book of Fish* (2002).

In 1999 Tom Gilling published *The Sooterkin,* an idiosyncratic novel about a highly unusual child, set in Hobart Town in the early 1800s, while Julia Leigh came up with the compelling, clinical tale of a man pursuing a living thylacine in *The Hunter*.

Matthew Kneale was short-listed for a Booker Prize for the historical fiction *English Passengers* (1999), a witty stew of multiple narratives telling the interwoven stories of a mid-19th-century expedition to Van Diemen's Land and the trials of the Tasmanian Aborigines.

Tasmania has a thriving literary scene – the website of the Tasmanian Writer's Centre (www.tasmanianwriters.org) is a good source of information.

Danielle Wood, one-time journalist with Hobart's *Mercury* newspaper, won the 2002 *Australian*/Vogel Literary Award (the country's richest and most prestigious award for an unpublished manuscript) with her debut novel, *The Alphabet of Light and Dark.* The story is set mostly on Bruny Island and melds personal, family and colonial history; it was inspired by the adventures of Wood's lighthouse-keeper great-great-grandfather.

Another well-received debut novel by a rising Australian literary star is *A Child's Book of True Crime* (2002), by Chloe Hooper. Her story is set in a fictional town near Port Arthur and centres around a young school teacher engaged in an affair with the father of one of her pupils.

Martin Flanagan's *In Sunshine or Shadow* (2002) is an entertaining account of the author's childhood in Tasmania and his investigation into the history of his ancestors and of the indigenous Australians before him.

Tasmania has become the adopted home of a number of seasoned writers, including novelist and radio presenter Robert Dessaix, and his partner, Peter Timms (both former Melburnians), and British writer Nicholas Shakespeare (see p15 for information on Shakespeare's recent publication, *In Tasmania*).

Painting & Sculpture

Tasmania's art scene flourished from colonial times, particularly in the early 19th century under the governorship of Sir John Franklin and the patronage of his wife, Lady Jane Franklin. One of the first artists to successfully capture the Australian landscape's distinctive forms and colours was John Glover, an English artist who migrated to Tasmania in 1830. The English sculptor Benjamin Law also arrived in Tasmania in the 1830s and sculpted busts of two of the better-known Tasmanian Aborigines, Truganini and Woureddy.

The Salamanca Arts Centre (www.salarts.org.au) is a font of information on Hobart's diverse and vibrant arts scene.

Benjamin Duterrau is best known for his somewhat coarse paintings of Tasmanian Aborigines, including *The Conciliation,* which commemorated George Robinson's pursuit of the Aborigines. Successful convict artists included portraitists TG Wainewright (a convicted forger and reputed poisoner), Thomas Bock, and WB Gould, who executed charmingly naive still lifes.

Hobart-born William Piguenit has been called 'the first Australian-born professional painter'. He painted romantic Tasmanian landscapes, including Lake St Clair and Lake Pedder, in the 1870s, and his works were among the first exhibited by the Art Society of Tasmania, founded in 1884. Other early exhibitors were J Haughton Forrest, who painted 'chocolate-box' landscapes and maritime subjects, and Belgian-born modernist Lucien Dechaineux, who also founded the art department at Hobart Technical College.

Major mainland Australian artists who visited Tasmania for inspiration early in the 20th century included Tom Roberts, Arthur Streeton and Frederick McCubbin.

In 1938 the Tasmanian Group of Painters was founded to foster the work of local artists. Founding members included Joseph Connor, a Hobart-born landscape watercolourist who was one of the early Australian modernists. Other innovators of the time were the under-recognised women artists Edith Holmes and Dorothy Stoner.

Since the 1940s a strong landscape watercolour school has developed in Tasmania, with artists such as Max Angus and Patricia Giles among the best known.

Launceston-born artist and teacher Jack Carington Smith won Australia's coveted Archibald Prize for portraiture in 1963. Tasmanian sculptor Stephen Walker has produced many bronze works that adorn Hobart's public spaces – he was also responsible for a sculptural tribute to the Midlands at The Steppes (p152), near Great Lake. Renowned Australian

TRUCHANAS & DOMBROVSKIS

> What would be the odds of two men from Baltic states, each of them finishing up in Tasmania, being top wilderness photographers, each dying out there, each devoted one to the other?
>
> *Max Angus*

On calendars, postcards and greeting cards, in books and on posters throughout Tasmania you will no doubt see breathtaking images of the state's incredible wilderness. Many of the best photographs will bear the name of Peter Dombrovskis; his story, and that of his mentor, Olegas Truchanas, is an extraordinary one.

Olegas Truchanas (1923–72) was born in Lithuania and came to Tasmania as a refugee in 1945; Peter Dombrovskis (1945–96) was born in a refugee camp in Germany near WWII's end to Latvian parents, and arrived in Tasmania with his mother in 1950. Both men came to Australia from war-ravaged countries, an experience that possibly left their senses open to the pristine, peaceful beauty of their new country. Both took reverential photographs of remote wilderness areas, and these beautiful images came to inspire the establishment of conservation movements in Tasmania and on the mainland.

Truchanas photographed Lake Pedder and campaigned passionately to save it from being flooded as part of a hydroelectricity scheme (p296); he also acted as a father-figure and mentor to Dombrovskis. In turn, Dombrovskis' stunning photographic images of the remote and wild Franklin River were central to the ultimately successful 1980s campaign (p282) to save the river from meeting the same dreadful fate as Lake Pedder did. Dombrovskis' image of the Franklin's Rock Island Bend, in particular, became a national icon. The philosophy of both men was simple and effective: if people could see the beauty of these wild places, then they might be moved to protect them.

Sadly, both died alone in the wilderness of the southwest, in the pursuit of their art. When Truchanas drowned while photographing the Gordon River in 1972, the year Lake Pedder was flooded, it was Dombrovskis who found his body. Dombrovskis died of a heart attack while on a photographic expedition in the Western Arthur Range in 1996.

Both men have left an amazing legacy of images. These days it is a little difficult to find examples of Truchanas' work, although an extensive collection of his wilderness photographs was compiled by Max Angus in *The World of Olegas Truchanas*. Dombrovskis' images are more readily available.

If you like Dombrovskis' work, check out *On the Mountain*, a selection of images of Mt Wellington, which was Dombrovskis' home for the greater part of 50 years. This book also contains a personal reflection on the mountain and its significance by Richard Flanagan and an account of its natural history by academic Jamie Kirkpatrick. *Wild Rivers* by Bob Brown contains photographs of the Franklin taken by Dombrovskis and is accompanied by the author's account of his own experiences on that river.

landscape painter Lloyd Rees spent his final years living and working in Tasmania. During this time he was also involved in the Tasmanian conservation movement.

Notable contemporary artists include Bea Maddock, whose serialised images incorporate painting and photography, and Bob and Lorraine Jenyns, both sculptors and ceramicists. Since the early 1980s Tasmania's art culture has been revitalised and the new wave includes printmaker Ray Arnold, painter David Keeling, photographer David Stephenson and video-maker Leigh Hobbs.

LIVE Tasmania (www.livetasmania.com), the joint project of a number of performing arts groups, can help you find live theatre, puppet shows, dance or music performances during your Tassie visit.

The Tasmanian Museum & Art Gallery (p73) in Hobart has a good collection of Tasmanian colonial art, and exhibits relating to Tasmanian Aboriginal culture. Galleries and studios in Hobart's Salamanca precinct (p69) are full of locally produced treasures. Also worth visiting are the Inveresk site of the Queen Victoria Museum & Art Gallery (p195) in Launceston, Burnie's Regional Art Gallery (p247) and the Devonport Regional Centre (p237). On your travels around the island, you'll also find plenty of smaller contemporary galleries to enjoy.

Performing Arts

The **Tasmanian Symphony Orchestra** (www.tso.com.au) is highly regarded and tours nationally and internationally. It gives regular performances at Hobart's Federation Concert Hall (p95), its home venue, and in Launceston's Princess Theatre (p205).

Tasmania's professional contemporary dance company is **TasDance** (www.tassie.net.au/tasdance), which is based in Launceston and tours statewide and interstate. It performs dance and dance-theatre, and often collaborates with artists in other fields. Another innovative company is **IHOS Opera** (www.ihosopera.com) in Hobart, an experimental music and theatre troupe.

Terrapin Theatre (www.terrapin.org.au) is a leading Australian contemporary performing arts company that has created puppetry productions for audiences of all ages both locally and internationally. Its works combine a variety of puppetry styles, including object theatre, black theatre, shadow puppetry and mobile interactive performances.

Environment Tim Flannery

THE LAND

Tasmania is the smallest Australian state and the only one that is an island. It's 240km south of Victoria, across stormy Bass Strait. To its east is the Tasman Sea, which separates Australia and New Zealand, while to its west and south is the Southern Ocean, which keeps Australia from bumping into Antarctica. Tasmania is 296km from north to south and 315km from east to west. Including its lesser islands, it has an area of 68,332 sq km.

Tim Flannery's *The Future Eaters* is a 'big picture' overview of evolution in Australasia, covering the last 120 million years of history, with thoughts on how the environment has shaped Australasia's human cultures, and vice versa.

Although Tasmania's highest mountain, Mt Ossa, only stands at 1617m (5300ft), much of the island's interior is extremely rugged. One indication of the dearth of flat land is the proximity of the centres of its two largest cities, Hobart and Launceston, to extremely steep hills.

The state's coastline is beautiful, with a multitude of coves and beaches, shallow bays and broad estuaries, the result of river valleys being flooded by rising sea levels after the last ice age. By contrast, the Central Plateau, which was covered by a single ice sheet during the last ice age, is a bleak, harsh environment unsuitable for farming; Australia's deepest natural freshwater lake, Lake St Clair (about 167m deep), is up here.

Most of the island's western half is a maze of mountainous ranges and ridges bearing signs of recent glaciation. The climate here is inhospitable and the annual rainfall a discouraging 3m or more, and for much of the year, uncompromising seas batter the coast. Yet the cliffs, lakes, rainforests and wild rivers of this magnificent region are among Tasmania's greatest attractions, drawing walkers, adventurers and photographers.

ENVIRONMENTAL HISTORY

Despite a long history of bad, often atrocious, environmental management, Tasmania is famous for its pristine wilderness areas. Both the air and water in parts of the state are claimed to be the purest on the planet, while the Tasmanian Wilderness World Heritage Area, which covers approximately 20% of the island, is internationally renowned. Yet, ironically, the preservation of much of the environment that Tasmania is proud of has been achieved only by protracted campaigns on rivers and in forests, in the media, and in parliaments and courts.

Gold was discovered in Tasmania in the 1870s and prospectors started exploring most of the state in search of mineral wealth, finding tin, silver, copper and lead. The subsequent prolonged exploitation of natural resources inevitably clashed with environmental preservation. In the late 1960s and early 1970s, the efforts of bushwalkers and conservationists to stop Lake Pedder in the southwest from being flooded for the purposes of electricity production (see p296) resulted in the formation of what's believed to be the first Green political party in the world. Although that campaign was ultimately unsuccessful, the lessons learnt during the fight were crucial in enabling a new generation of activists to plan and execute a vastly more sophisticated campaign a decade later, one that saved the Franklin River – one of the finest wild rivers on the planet – from being flooded for similar purposes (see p282). The Franklin River campaign saw the conservation movement mature as a political force and gain acceptance as an influential player in the policy-making process.

A successful campaign in the late 1980s to prevent construction of a pulp mill in the northwest saw a Green independents' party form, led by

Bob Brown (see below). Subsequently, five of its members were elected to state parliament. The Greens held the balance of power in the Tasmanian parliament from 1989 to 1998. Changes to the number of state parliamentarians, however, resulted in three of the four sitting Tasmanian Greens members losing their seats in the 1998 state election and a significant muting of the Greens' voice in parliament. In the 2002 election, the Greens increased their representation in state parliament to four seats.

The balance in Tasmania between conservation interests and industry (especially logging and mining) is still uneasy. This was dramatically evident during the run-up to the 2004 federal election, when logging and the preservation of old-growth forests became a central campaign issue. 'Old growth' is a term generally used to describe forest which has had little human disturbance and is ecologically mature. Such forests provide the best habitat for the widest range of species and therefore, according to the Wilderness Society and many other groups, are the most important ecosystem for conserving biodiversity.

In a startling statistic provided by the Wilderness Society, less than 20% of Tasmania's original, pre-settlement old-growth forests remain today. More than half of what remains (including large parts of the Styx, the Tarkine and northeastern Tasmania) is currently unprotected and targeted for logging and wood chipping.

In December 2004, the latest blow in the battle between industry and conservationists was dealt. Gunns Limited, the Tasmanian timber and wood chip conglomerate, is suing 20 prominent environmentalists

SIMPLE STEPS FOR SAVING THE FORESTS *Senator Bob Brown*

Tasmania's wild and scenic beauty, along with a human history dating back 30,000 years, is a priceless heritage available to all of us. The waterfalls, wild rivers, lovely beaches, snow-capped mountains, turquoise seas, and wildlife are abundant and accessible for locals and visitors alike.

Because we are all creations of nature – the curl of our ears is fashioned to pick up the faintest sounds of the forest floor – we are all bonded to the wilds. No wonder that in this anxiety-ridden world there is such a thirst for remote, pristine, natural places. Yet around the world, wilderness is a fast-disappearing resource and Tasmania is no exception.

This year 150,000 truckloads of the island's native forests, including giant eucalypt species producing the tallest flowering plants on earth, will arrive at the wood-chip mills, en-route to Japan. After logging, the forests are firebombed and every wisp of fur, feather and flower is destroyed. These great forests, built of carbon, are one of the world's best hedges against global warming. They are carbon banks. Yet they are being looted, taken from our fellow creatures and all who come after us. The log trucks on Tasmania's highways are enriching banks of a different kind.

Over two decades ago, people power saved Tasmania's wild Franklin and Lower Gordon Rivers (p282) which nowadays attract hundreds of thousands of visitors to the west coast. Those visitors, in turn, bring jobs, investment and local prosperity. Saving the environment has been a boon for the economy and employment.

The rescue of Tasmania's forests relies on each of us, and there are plenty of ways we can help. We can help with letters or phonecalls to newspapers, radio stations, or politicians; with every cent donated to the forest campaigners; and in every well-directed vote. The tourist dollar speaks loudly in Tasmania, so even overseas travellers, who cannot vote, should take the opportunity to write letters to our newspapers and politicians. With each step we take, we move toward ending this destruction of Tasmania's wild and scenic heritage.

Senator Bob Brown was elected to the Tasmanian parliament in 1983 and first elected to the Senate in 1996. His books include The Valley of the Giants *(The Wilderness Society, with Vica Bayley, 2005). Read more about Bob Brown at www.bobbrown.org.au.*

(including Senator Bob Brown, and Peg Putt, leader of the Tasmanian Greens Party) and environmental groups (including the Wilderness Society, and an organisation called Doctors for Native Forests) for $6.4 million, for what it alleges are a series of wrongful acts. Gunns claims that the defendants engaged in a campaign against Gunns which constituted a conspiracy to injure Gunns by unlawful means, and that the defendants illegally interfered with their trade and business, thus causing economic loss. Many commentators have condemned the lawsuit, calling it an attempt to silence critics and an attack on the rights of free speech. Read more about this battle at www.gunns20.org.

WILDLIFE

Animals

Tasmania's Parks & Wildlife Service has a wonderfully comprehensive website at www.parks.tas.gov.au. Click on 'The Nature of Tasmania' for further links to fact sheets on the state's magical flora and fauna.

The distinctive mammals of mainland Australia, the marsupials and monotremes, are also found in Tasmania. Marsupials, including wallabies and pademelons, give birth to partially developed young that they then protect and suckle in a pouch. Monotremes (platypuses and echidnas) lay eggs but also suckle their young. Most are nocturnal and the best time to see them in the wild is around dusk. The smaller mammals can be difficult to find in the bush, but there are plenty of wildlife parks around the state where they can be seen.

Tasmania's fauna is not as varied as that of the rest of Australia and it has relatively few large mammals. Its best-known marsupial, the Tasmanian tiger, which resembled a large dog or wolf and had dark stripes and a stiff tail, has been extinct for nearly 70 years (see opposite). The island is jam-packed with wallabies, wombats and possums, principally because foxes, which have decimated marsupial populations on the mainland, were slow to reach the island state (the first fox was found in Tasmania only as recently as 2001; the current size of the fox population is a matter of sometimes heated debate).

BIRDS

Some extremely rare birds are found in Tasmania; one of the best known is the orange-bellied parrot, of which only a small number survive, on the buttongrass plains of the southwest. They winter on the mainland and make the treacherous crossing of Bass Strait to reach their breeding grounds in southwest Tasmania. More common, but also threatened with extinction, is the ground parrot. To see it you'll need to visit Melaleuca in the southwest (p300) and wait in the specially constructed bird-hide.

Extinct, or living alongside Elvis in the Tassie wilderness? *Thylacine: The Tragic Tale of the Tasmanian Tiger* by David Owen traces the history of this remarkable animal and examines the reasons for its decline, using excellent illustrations and anecdotes.

Many bird-watchers visit the eastern side of Tasmania to try to catch a glimpse of the very rare forty-spotted pardalote, mainly found on Bruny Island (p125) and in Mt William National Park (p188). This bird prefers dry sclerophyll forest as its residence.

There's a very wide variety of sea birds, parrots, cockatoos, honeyeaters and wrens. Birds of prey such as falcons and eagles are also readily seen.

Black Currawongs

The black currawong, found only in Tasmania, lives primarily on plant matter and insects, but will sometimes kill small mammals or infant birds. You'll often see this large, black, fearless bird around picnic areas.

Mutton Birds

The mutton bird (a name derived after a marine officer on Norfolk Island nicknamed a closely related bird 'flying sheep') is more correctly called the short-tailed shearwater. It lives in burrows in sand dunes and migrates annually to the northern hemisphere. These small birds provide spectacular displays when they fly back to their burrows in their thousands at dusk. They are still hunted by some Tasmanians and you'll occasionally see cooked mutton bird advertised for sale.

Graham Pizzey and Frank Knight's *Field Guide to Birds of Australia* is an indispensable guide for bird-watchers, and anyone else even peripherally interested in Australia's feathered tribes. Knight's illustrations are both beautiful and helpful in identification.

Penguins

The little (fairy) penguin is the smallest penguin in the world and lives in burrows in the sand dunes. There are plenty of penguin rookeries around Tasmania where you can see them waddle from the ocean to their nests just after sunset, including at Bruny Island (p128), Burnie (p249), Stanley (p255), Penguin (of course! p243), Low Head (p212) and King Island (p303).

KANGAROOS & WALLABIES

The kangaroo and wallaby species found in Tasmania are related to those found on the mainland, but are usually smaller. The largest marsupial is the Forester kangaroo, which at one stage looked like becoming extinct because it favoured farmland for grazing. The Narawntapu National Park (p214) and Mt William National Park (p188) have been set aside to preserve this kangaroo.

The Bennetts wallaby thrives in colder climes and this is the animal you're most likely to see begging for food at the Cradle Mountain–Lake St Clair National Park (p284). Don't feed them, though, because the animals are meant to be wild and must feed themselves – also, giving them processed foods like bread causes a fatal disease called 'lumpy jaw'.

A TIGER'S TALE

The story of the Tasmanian tiger (*Thylacinus cynocephalus* or thylacine), a striped carnivore once widespread in Tasmania, currently has two different endings.

Version one has it that thylacines were hunted to extinction by European settlers in the 19th and early 20th centuries, and that the last tiger died in miserable captivity in Hobart's Beaumaris Zoo in 1936. Those who put their faith in the thylacine's extinction point out that no living specimen has been conclusively discovered since then, regardless of hundreds of alleged 'sightings'.

Version two maintains that thylacines continue a furtive existence deep in the Tasmanian wilderness. Advocates of this theory prefer to believe that the more often unsubstantiated tiger encounters get reported, the greater the likelihood of a substantiated one.

The physical mystique of a large nocturnal hunter that carried its young in a pouch and had a large, powerful jaw, combined with the conveniently perpetuated enigma of its existence, has made the tiger prime corporate fodder. Oblivious to the irony of using a long-dead animal to promote the relevance of their products, companies have plastered the animal's picture on everything from beer bottles (Cascade) to TV network promos (Southern Cross Television).

In recent years, scientists at Sydney's Australia Museum began scripting another possible ending to the tiger saga. Kicking off version three, biologists managed to extract DNA from a thylacine pup preserved in alcohol since 1866. Their aim was to successfully replicate the DNA, with the long-term goal of cloning the species. Needless to say, there were many obstacles, and the project drew criticism from those who would rather have seen the money spent on helping current endangered species. In early 2005 the project was shelved due to the quality of the extracted DNA being too poor to work with, but science may well add a new twist to the tiger's tale sometime in the future.

For information on the Tassie tiger and the cloning project, visit www.austmus.gov.au/thylacine. Another good source of information is at www.parks.tas.gov.au/wildlife/mammals/thylacin.html. You can see interesting black-and-white footage of a tiger in captivity at the Tasmanian Museum & Art Gallery in Hobart (p73).

Bennetts wallabies stand just over 1m in height and seem very friendly, but be careful, as these and other native animals are not tame and can sometimes be aggressive.

If you spy any shorter, rounder wallabies hiding in the forest, then you'll have seen a pademelon (also known as a rufous wallaby). This smaller species is shyer than its larger relatives.

The Mammals of Australia, edited by Ron Strahan, is a complete survey of Australia's somewhat cryptic mammals. Every species is illustrated and almost everything known about them is covered in the individual species accounts, which have been written by the nation's experts.

PLATYPUSES & ECHIDNAS

The platypus and the echidna are the only living monotremes. Monotremes are often regarded as living fossils, and although they display some intriguing features of their reptile ancestors, such as laying eggs, they are now recognised as a distinct mammalian lineage rather than a primitive stage in mammalian evolution. Although they lay eggs, they suckle their young on milk secreted from mammary glands.

The platypus lives in water and has a duck-like bill, webbed feet and a beaver-like body. You're most likely to see one in a stream or lake, searching out food in the form of crustaceans, worms and tadpoles with its electro-sensitive bill.

Echidnas are totally different and look similar to porcupines, being covered in sharp spikes. They primarily eat ants and have powerful claws for unearthing their food and digging into the dirt to protect themselves when threatened. They are common in Tasmania but if you approach one, all you're likely to see up close is a brown, spiky ball. However, if you keep quiet and don't move, you might be lucky: they have poor eyesight and will sometimes walk right past your feet.

POSSUMS

There are several varieties of possum in the state, one of which is the sugar glider, which has developed webs between its legs, enabling it to glide from tree to tree. The most common and boldest is the brushtail possum. They live and sleep in trees, but will come down to the ground in search of food. Possums show little fear of humans and regularly do late-night food 'shopping' at camping grounds. A shyer relation is the smaller ringtail possum.

SNAKES & SPIDERS

There are only three types of snake found in Tasmania and they're all poisonous. The largest and most dangerous is the tiger snake, which will sometimes attack, particularly in late summer. The other snakes are the copperhead and the smaller white-lipped whip snake. Bites are very rare, as most snakes are generally shy and try to avoid humans. If you do get bitten, don't try to catch the snake, as there's a common antivenin for all three – instead, get to hospital for treatment.

The eight-legged critter with the longest reach (up to 18cm) on the island is the Tasmanian cave spider, which spins horizontal mesh-webs on the ceiling of a cave to catch insects like cave crickets.

TASMANIAN DEVILS

This scavenging marsupial's diet consists mainly of insects, small birds and mammals, and carrion, and it can often be seen at night feasting on roadkill (a habit that unfortunately leads to it becoming roadkill itself). It is about 75cm long and has a short, stocky body covered in black fur with a white stripe across its chest. You'll see devils in plenty of wildlife parks around the state, and you can often watch them being fed – their squabbling as they do so is fearsome.

TOP FIVE WILDLIFE PARKS

Tasmania's wildlife is surprisingly accessible for most visitors – you may encounter a pademelon or wallaby on a bushwalk at dusk, or get lucky and spot a platypus in a quiet stream (sadly, you'll no doubt also see a lot of roadkill on your travels). If you're after more meaningful interaction with the local wildlife (including devils), visit the following animal parks:

- Something Wild (p106) near Mt Field National Park
- Tasmanian Devil Park (p116) in Taranna on the Tasman Peninsula
- Trowunna Wildlife Park (p227) Two kilometres west of Chudleigh
- Bonorong Wildlife Park (p111) Near Richmond
- East Coast Natureworld (p174) Just north of Bicheno

Causing much concern in Tasmania is the recent spread of a devastating disease through the devil population. Devil facial tumour disease is the term used to describe a fatal condition characterised by the appearance of obvious facial cancers. Affected animals appear to die within three to five months of the lesions first appearing, from starvation and the breakdown of bodily functions. A major investigation of the disease and its impacts on wild populations is currently underway. Read more about this on the website of the **Department of Primary Industries, Water & Environment** (DPIWE; www.dpiwe.tas.gov.au – click on 'Quarantine, Pests & Diseases', then 'Animal Diseases').

WHALES

Southern right whales migrate annually from Antarctica to southern Australia to give birth to their calves in shallow waters. So named because they were the 'right' whales to kill, they were hunted to the point of extinction. These majestic creatures are sometimes seen off the Tasmanian coast and occasionally beach themselves.

Long-fin pilot whales are more commonly involved in beach strandings. In November 2004 there were two mass strandings of pilot whales within one day of each other (one on King Island, the other on Maria Island), reigniting the debate about what causes such tragic incidents (for now, the answer remains a mystery).

The thylacine is the only mammal to have (possibly) become extinct in Tasmania since European settlement (in stark contrast to the mainland). In fact, Tasmania acts as a refuge for many species that have recently become extinct on mainland Australia, including the eastern quoll, bettong and pademelon.

WOMBATS

These are very solid, powerfully built marsupials with broad heads and short stumpy legs. They often weigh around 40kg. They live in underground burrows that they excavate, and are usually very casual, slow-moving animals, partly because they don't have any natural predators to worry about.

ENDANGERED SPECIES

Since Europeans arrived, Tasmania has lost over 30 species of plants and animals; currently, over 600 types of flora and fauna are listed under the state's Threatened Species Protection Act.

Among Tasmania's threatened birds are the forty-spotted pardalote, orange-bellied parrot and wedge-tailed eagle. Tasmania is also home to the largest invertebrate in the world, the giant freshwater crayfish, whose numbers have been so depleted by recreational fishing and habitat destruction that it's now illegal to take any specimens from their natural habitat.

INTRODUCED SPECIES

In mid-2001, Tasmania received some of the worst environmental news imaginable for native animals: a fox had been spotted near Longford in the state's north. Fox predation puts nearly 80 of the island's indigenous land species at enormous risk because of their vulnerability to attack from an animal against which they have no defence. Just as horrifying as the original sighting and subsequent reports of the European red fox in other parts of the state is the revelation that the foxes were deliberately introduced to Tasmania, probably for the purposes of hunting. A full-time fox task force has been set up by the state government, though it may be too late to eradicate the threat to Tasmania's biodiversity that the animal poses. The public are urged to report fox sightings and other evidence to the **Fox Hotline** (☎ 1300 FOX OUT – ie 1300 369 688).

Worried by foxes and other vermin? Read about the threats posed to Tasmanian wildlife on the website of the Department of Primary Industries, Water & Environment (DPIWE; www.dpiwe.tas.gov.au – click on 'Quarantine, Pests & Diseases').

The second-biggest entrenched threat to native wildlife in Tasmania is the feral cat (unless the speed-obsessed car drivers who kill incalculable numbers of native animals count as introduced pests). The cat has established itself throughout the state, including in the southwest and central highlands.

While feral dogs, goats and pigs can be found in Tasmania, they are not nearly so widespread as on the mainland. Even rabbits, which are a problem in rural areas, have had trouble penetrating the state's natural forests; this is just as well, because it appears that one of science's most touted weapons against the animal – calicivirus – is not particularly effective in cool, wet areas.

Plants

Tasmania's diverse flora ranges from the dry forests of the east, through the alpine moorlands of the centre to the rainforests of the west. Many of the state's plants are unlike those found in the rest of Australia and have ties with species that grew millions of years ago, when the southern continents were joined as Gondwanaland; similar plants are found in South America and fossilised in Antarctica.

Many of Tasmania's trees are unique to the state, with its native pines being particularly distinctive. Perhaps the best known is the Huon pine, which can live for thousands of years (see opposite), but there are other slow-growing Tasmanian pines, including King Billy pines, celery-top pines and pencil pines, all of which are commonly found in the higher regions and live for about 500 years. Some pencil pines on the Central Plateau have grown to be 1000 years old, but they are especially vulnerable to fire – one-third of the plateau's pencil pine population has been burnt out in the past 200 years.

A large part of Tasmania's wilderness is included on the World Heritage register (a UN register of natural and cultural places of world significance). See www.parks.tas.gov.au/wha for more information.

The dominant tree of the wetter forests is myrtle beech, which is similar to the beeches of Europe.

One of Tasmania's many flowering trees is the leatherwood, which is nondescript most of the year but can be positively eye-catching in summer, when it's covered with a mass of white and pale pink flowers that yield a unique and fragrant honey prized by apiarists.

While many of Tasmania's eucalyptus trees also grow on the mainland, its own are often extremely tall. The swamp gum (*Eucalyptus regnans*, known as mountain ash on the mainland) can grow to 100m in height and is the tallest flowering plant in the world. It's readily seen in the forests of the southeast, where you'll also find the state's floral emblem, the Tasmanian blue gum *(Eucalyptus globulus)*.

In autumn you might see the deciduous beech, the only truly deciduous native plant in Australia. It usually grows as a fairly straggly bush with bright green leaves. In autumn, however, the leaves become golden and sometimes red, adding a splash of colour to the forests. The best places to look for this plant are the Cradle Mountain and Mt Field National Parks.

A notable component of the understorey in Tasmanian forests is the infamous horizontal scrub (see below), a plant that can make life hell for bushwalkers attempting to avoid established tracks. More familiar to bushwalkers, but also considerably more benign, is buttongrass. Growing in thick clumps up to 2m high, this unique Tasmanian grass prefers broad, swampy areas like the many flat-bottomed valleys pressed out by ice ages. Buttongrass plains are usually so muddy and unpleasant to walk over that in many places, the Parks & Wildlife Service has incorporated sections of elevated boardwalk into tracks crossing such areas, for both walker comfort and the protection of the environment.

Another interesting specimen is the cushion plant, which is found in alpine areas and at first sight resembles a green rock. In fact, it's an extremely tough, short plant that grows into thick mats ideally suited to helping it cope with its severe living conditions.

HORIZONTAL SCRUB

This slender plant *(Anodopetalum biglandulosum)* is a feature of the undergrowth in many parts of Tasmania's southwest. It grows by sending up thin, vigorous stems whenever an opening appears in the forest canopy. The old branches soon become heavy and fall, then put up shoots of their own. This continuous process of growth and collapse creates dense, tangled thickets that are a notorious obstacle to bushwalkers venturing off the beaten track. You can see some good examples of this tangled plant on nature walks in the southwest and in the Hartz Mountains (p138).

HUON PINE

This is perhaps the most famous of Tasmania's native flora. The water-repellent qualities of its oily yellow wood are responsible for its reputation as an exceptional boat-building timber, but it's also prized by furniture-makers and wood-turners. It grows very slowly and so barely survived the widespread logging undertaken in the colony's early years, when its timber was premium shipbuilding material. Some older trees remain, however, and one 2500-year-old specimen can be viewed during a cruise on the Gordon River (see p274).

TASMANIAN CONSERVATION ORGANISATIONS

The **Tasmanian Conservation Trust** (Map p70; TCT; ☎ 6234 3552; www.tct.org.au; 102 Bathurst St, Hobart) is the state's primary nongovernmental conservation organisation. In addition to managing its own campaigns, the TCT hosts the Tasmanian offices of two other Australian environmental organisations: the National Threatened Species Network, which undertakes public education programmes aimed at students, landholders and the wider community; and the Marine and Coastal Community Network, which has particular interests in the establishment of no-take marine reserves and the promotion of safe marine waste-management practices.

The **Wilderness Society** (Map p66; ☎ 6224 1550; www.wilderness.org.au; 130 Davey St, Hobart) works hard to ensure the preservation of several important areas, including the Styx Valley (p297), which contains the tallest hardwood eucalypt forests on earth; and the Tarkine Wilderness (p263), which occupies 3500 sq km between the Arthur and Pieman Rivers. Both areas are under threat from logging.

ENVIRONMENTAL CHALLENGES FACING AUSTRALIA *Tim Flannery*

The European colonisation of Australia, commencing in 1788, heralded a period of catastrophic environmental upheaval, with the result that Australians today are struggling with some of the most severe environmental problems to be found anywhere. It may seem strange that a population of just 20 million, living in a continent the size of the USA minus Alaska, could inflict such damage on its environment, but Australia's long isolation, its fragile soils and difficult climate have made it particularly vulnerable to human-induced change.

Damage to Australia's environment has been inflicted in several ways, the most important being the introduction of pest species, destruction of forests, overstocking rangelands, inappropriate agriculture and interference with water flows. Beginning with the escape of domestic cats into the Australian bush shortly after 1788, a plethora of vermin, from foxes to wild camels and cane toads, have run wild in Australia, causing extinctions in the native fauna. One out of every 10 native mammals living in Australia prior to European colonisation is now extinct, and many more are highly endangered. Extinctions have also affected native plants, birds and amphibians.

The destruction of forests has also had a profound effect on the environment. Most of Australia's rainforests have suffered clearing, while conservationists fight with loggers over the fate of the last unprotected stands of 'old growth' trees. Many Australian rangelands have been chronically overstocked for more than a century, the result being extreme vulnerability of both soils and rural economies to Australia's drought and flood cycle, as well as the endangerment and extinction of many native species. The development of agriculture has involved land clearance and the provision of irrigation, and here again the effect has been profound. Clearing of the diverse and spectacular plant communities of the Western Australian wheat belt began just a century ago, yet today up to one-third of that country is degraded by salination of the soils. Between 70kg and 120kg of salt lies below every square metre of the region, and clearing of native vegetation has allowed water to penetrate deep into the soil, dissolving the salt crystals and carrying brine towards the surface.

In terms of financial value, just 1.5% of Australia's land surface provides over 95% of agricultural yield, and much of this land lies in the irrigated regions of the Murray-Darling Basin. This is Australia's agricultural heartland, yet it too is under severe threat from salting of soils and rivers. Irrigation water penetrates into the sediments laid down in an ancient sea, carrying salt into the catchments and fields. If nothing is done, the lower Murray River will become too salty to drink in a decade or two, threatening the water supply of Adelaide, a city of over a million people.

Despite the scale of the biological crisis engulfing Australia, governments and the community have been slow to respond. In the 1980s, coordinated action began to take place, but not until the 1990s were major steps taken. The establishment of **Landcare** (www.landcareaustralia.com.au), an organisation enabling people to effectively address local environmental issues, and the expenditure of $2.5 billion through the National Heritage Trust Fund have been important national initiatives. Yet so difficult are some of the issues the nation faces that, as yet, little has been achieved in terms of halting the destructive processes. Individuals are also banding together to help. Groups like the **Australian Bush Heritage Fund** (www.bushheritage.asn.au) and the **Australian Wildlife Conservancy** (AWC; www.australianwildlife.org) allow people to donate funds and time to the conservation of native species. Some such groups have been spectacularly successful; the AWC, for example, already manages many endangered species over its 450,000 hectares of holdings.

So severe are Australia's problems that it will take a revolution before they can be overcome; sustainable practices need to be implemented in every arena of life – from farms to suburbs and city centres. Renewable energy, sustainable agriculture and water use lie at the heart of these changes, and Australians are only now developing the road-map to sustainability that they so desperately need if they are to have a long-term future on the continent.

Tim Flannery is a naturalist and explorer and a professor at the University of Adelaide. He has written a number of popular books, including The Future Eaters *(1994).*

KING'S LOMATIA

This endemic Tasmanian plant, which is a member of the *Proteaceae family* and has flowers similar to those of the grevillea, grows in the wild in only one small part of the Tasmanian Wilderness World Heritage Area. Studies of the plant's chromosomes have revealed that it's incapable of reproducing sexually, which is why it must rely on sending up shoots to create new plants. Further research has shown that there's absolutely no genetic diversity within the population, which means that every King's lomatia in existence is a clone. The plant is believed to be the oldest known clone in the world and is thought to have been around for at least 43,600 years.

The small town of Coles Bay, on the beautiful Freycinet Peninsula, was the first town in Australia to ban plastic bags.

NATIONAL PARKS

About one quarter of Tasmania comprises dedicated parks and reserves. For full details, see p51.

RESPONSIBLE TRAVEL

Tasmania's 'disease-free' status is one of the things that makes its produce attractive to buyers, and the state government has stringent rules in place to ensure the island maintains this agricultural advantage. To this end, plants, fruit and vegetables cannot be brought into the state without certification. Essentially, this means tourists must discard all such items before their arrival.

Live fish that can breed in Tasmanian waters cannot be brought into the state. Anglers must not bring live bait into Tasmania and, in order to prevent the introduction of disease into native and recreational fisheries and aquaculture industries, they should also wash, disinfect and dry their gear before packing it for their trip.

Phytophthora is a root rot that's spread in soil and is devastating flora in parts of the state. Always clean dirt off your shoes and equipment before and after you spend time in the bush. For more information about responsible bushwalking, see p45.

For information on responsible four-wheel-drive touring, read *Cruisin' Without Bruisin'*, a free brochure available at most visitors centres around the state or online from the **Parks & Wildlife Service** (www.parks.tas.gov.au/recreation/4wd/4wd.html). And whether you're travelling in a four-wheel drive on bush tracks or in a conventional vehicle on a highway, watch out for wildlife on the road and try to avoid driving at dusk, which is when many animals become more active and harder to see. It's not uncommon to see more dead animals on the road than live ones in the bush.

Finally, be sure never to disturb or remove items from sites significant to Tasmanian Aborigines.

Tasmania Outdoors

Although Tasmania provides plenty of excuses to sit back and do little more than run your eyes across some fine landscape, that same landscape lends itself to any number of outdoor pursuits, from bushwalking to white-water rafting. However much you might enjoy wandering through historic towns and lazing about in cafés, you haven't fully experienced Tasmania until you've ventured into the mountains and onto the rivers, oceans and cliffs that are this beautiful island's greatest attractions.

The website of Networking Tasmanian Adventures (www.tasmanianadventures.com.au) details the offerings of assorted Tasmanian outdoor-activity companies which are categorised as either 'wild' (eg scuba diving, white-water rafting, abseiling) or 'mild' (eg fishing, scenic flights, river cruises).

The bushwalks you can do here are among the best (and at times the most taxing and treacherous) in Australia: try tackling Federation Peak or the Western Arthurs if you really want to test your endurance. White-water rafting on the Franklin River has acquired a deserved reputation for environmental grandeur and excitement, while abseiling and rock climbing on the Tasman and Freycinet Peninsulas is also literally thrilling.

For those who want less physically demanding activities, there's boating on the Arthur and Pieman Rivers in the northwest, sea kayaking on the waters of the southeast, and walks through caves at Hastings in the south. If you have a yacht, or can afford to charter one, you can spend lazy days exploring the bays and inlets of the D'Entrecasteaux Channel, while if you're a trout fisher with a desire for seclusion, you'll find plenty of remote Central Plateau lakes, well stocked with fish.

The most comprehensive source of information is the website of **Tourism Tasmania** (www.discovertasmania.com) – click on 'things to do & see', then 'outdoor adventure'. Another recommended source is the section dedicated to outdoor recreation on the website of the **Parks & Wildlife Service** (www.parks.tas.gov.au/recreation/recreation.html).

BUSHWALKING

Lonely Planet's *Walking in Australia* describes Tasmanian walks of varying length and difficulty, including short jaunts through Mt Field National Park and around Maria Island, as well as the Overland Track and a seven-day excursion along the South Coast Track.

Tasmania's glorious trail-riddled environment attracts walkers from all over the world. Its most famous track is undoubtedly the superb Overland Track (p285) in Cradle Mountain-Lake St Clair National Park. In fact, most of the state's great walks are in national parks, which you can read more about in the National Parks chapter (p51) and other relevant chapters throughout this book. Bear in mind that entry fees apply to all Tasmanian national parks (see p52).

Books, Maps & Equipment

Loads of books have been written specifically for walkers in Tasmania. If you prefer shorter walks (one day or less), the books by Jan Hardy and Bert Elson are worth finding. Two of these cover the Hobart area, one covers Mt Wellington, another covers Launceston and the northeast, and a fifth covers the northwest; all books focus on walks for the family. Other

THE TASMANIAN TRAIL

The Tasmanian Trail is a 480km route from Devonport to Dover, intended for walkers, horse riders and mountain-bikers. Most of the trail is on forestry roads, fire trails or country roads; it passes towns, pastoral land and forests, and there are camping spots about every 30km. All the information you need to follow the trail is in the *Tasmanian Trail Guide Book,* which costs around $22 and is available in many bookshops, outdoor-equipment shops and visitors centres. See the website of the **Parks & Wildlife Service** (www.parks.tas.gov.au/recreation/tastrail.html) for more information.

writers also produce small books on specific areas, such as the Tasman Peninsula and the mines of the west coast.

One very popular book of shorter walks throughout the state is *A Visitor's Guide to Tasmania's National Parks* by Greg Buckman. Well worth getting is *120 Walks in Tasmania* by Tyrone Thomas, which covers a wide variety of short and multi-day walks, or *Day Walks Tasmania* by John Chapman and Monica Chapman. There are also many detailed guides to specific walks or areas, including *South West Tasmania* by John Chapman and *Cradle Mountain–Lake St Clair & Walls of Jerusalem National Parks* by John Chapman and John Siseman.

TASMAP produces an excellent series of maps available at visitors centres; **Service Tasmania** (Map p70; ☎ 1300 135 513; 134 Macquarie St, Hobart); the **Tasmanian Map Centre** (Map p70; ☎ 6231 9043; www.map-centre.com.au; 96 Elizabeth St, Hobart); outdoor-equipment shops; Wilderness Society shops; and some newsagencies throughout the state.

There are lots of Tasmanian shops specialising in bushwalking gear and outdoor equipment (see p97 for options in Hobart, p205 for Launceston, and p235 for Devonport); a number of shops, hostels and activity operators can organise rental of outdoor gear.

You may not be tackling the Overland Track but you can still experience Tassie's famed wilderness on foot – the excellent *Tasmania's Great Short Walks* brochure (freely available at visitors centres) lists 60 of the state's best short walks, with durations from 10 minutes to all day.

Code of Ethics & Safety Precautions

The **Parks & Wildlife Service** (PWS; Map p70; ☎ 6233 6191; www.parks.tas.gov.au) publishes a booklet called *Tasmania's Wilderness World Heritage Area: Essential Bushwalking Guide & Trip Planner,* which has sections on the basics of planning, minimal impact bushwalking, first aid and what gear you need to bring to cope with Tasmania's changeable weather (the booklet is available online at www.parks.tas.gov.au/recreation/mib.html). You can pick up PWS literature at **Service Tasmania** (Map p70; ☎ 1300 135 513; www.service.tas.gov.au; 134 Macquarie St, Hobart) at any national park visitors centre or ranger station, or download it from the PWS website.

The Tasmanian Wilderness World Heritage Area and Freycinet National Park are 'fuel stove only' areas. A brochure outlining regulations relating to these and other areas under this classification is available from the PWS.

In Tasmania (particularly in the west and southwest), a fine day can quickly become cold and stormy at any time of year, so it's essential that you *always* carry warm clothing, waterproof gear and a compass. In addition, you should always carry a tent, rather than relying on finding a bed in a hut, particularly on popular walks such as the Overland Track.

On all extended walks, you must carry extra food in case you have to sit out a few days of especially bad weather. This is a very important point, as the PWS routinely hears of walkers running out of food in such instances and relying on the goodwill of better-prepared people they meet along the way to supplement their supplies. In the worst of circumstances, such lack of preparation and disregard for others puts lives at risk: if the bad weather continues for long enough, everyone suffers.

Tasmanian walks are famous for their mud, so be prepared: waterproof your boots, wear gaiters and watch where you're putting your feet. Even on the Overland Track, long sections of which are covered by boardwalk, you can sometimes find yourself up to your hips in mud if you're not careful.

- Bushwalkers should stay on established trails, avoid cutting corners and taking short-cuts, and stay on hard ground where possible.
- Before tackling a long or remote walk, tell someone responsible about your plans and arrange to contact them when you return. Make sure you sign a PWS register at the start and finish of your walk.

- Keep bushwalking parties small.
- Where possible, visit popular areas at low-season times.
- When camping, always use designated camping grounds where provided. When bush camping, try to find a natural clearing to set up your tent.
- When driving, stay on existing tracks or roads.
- Don't harm native birds or animals; these are protected by law.
- Don't feed native animals.
- Carry all your rubbish out with you; don't burn or bury it.
- Avoid polluting lakes and streams; don't wash yourself or your dishes in them, and keep soap and detergent at least 50m away.
- Use toilets provided; otherwise bury human waste at least 100m from waterways.
- Boil all water for 10 minutes before drinking it, or use water-purifying tablets.
- Don't take pets into national parks.
- Don't light fires in the Tasmanian Wilderness World Heritage Area or Freycinet Peninsula National Park; use only fuel stoves for cooking. In other areas, don't light open fires unless absolutely necessary; if you do, keep the fires small, burn only dead fallen wood and use an existing fireplace. Make sure any fire that you light is completely extinguished before moving on.
- On days of total fire ban, don't light any fire whatsoever, including fuel stoves.

Guided Walks

There are plenty of companies offering guided walks that range from one-day excursions to multi-day trips involving accommodation in everything from tents to upmarket lodges, plus trips that blend foot power with time on a bike, in a bus or in a canoe.

Some well-established companies offering trips along the Overland Track to Walls of Jerusalem and other popular destinations include **Craclair Tours** (☎ 6424 7833; www.craclair.com.au) and **Tasmanian Expeditions** (☎ 1300 666 856, 6334 3477; www.tas-ex.com) – see p326 for more information on these companies. Also hitting trails in the Cradle Mountain area is **Tasman Bush Tours** (☎ 6423 2335; www.tasmanbushtours.com), which operates out of Tasman House Backpackers in Devonport (p237).

John Chapman is an experienced bushwalker who has written a number of books on walks in Tasmania. His website (www.john.chapman.name) is a font of information, and lists his range of books.

If you want your walks to involve a touch more luxury than a camp mat on the hard ground at the end of a long day, you can definitely have your wishes fulfilled. A number of companies are offering guided multi-day walks, with gourmet dinners, wine, hot showers and a real bed en route (for a premium, of course!):

Cradle Mountain Huts (☎ 6391 9339; www.cradlehuts.com.au) Six-day walk along the Overland Track, staying in private huts; see p290.

Bay of Fires (☎ 6391 9339; www.bayoffires.com.au) A four-day walk along this magnificent stretch of coast in the northeast; see p187.

Freycinet Experience (☎ 6223 7565, 1800 506 003; www.freycinet.com.au) A fully catered, lodge-based, four-day stroll down that famous peninsula; see p169.

Maria Island Walk (☎ 6227 8800; www.mariaislandwalk.com.au) Another four-day option, this time on lovely Maria Island (a national park off the east coast); see p161.

CANOEING, KAYAKING & RAFTING

Tasmania is famous for its white-water rafting on the wild Franklin River, but it also has many other rivers that are popular for both rafting and boating. The Arthur (p262) and Pieman (p264) Rivers in the northwest and the Ansons River (p187) in the northeast are great places for a long, lazy paddle through some picturesque scenery. You can rent canoes at Arthur River. Rivers popular with rafters and kayakers, and situated closer to population centres, are the Picton, Huon, Weld, Leven, Mersey and North Esk, most of which are served by rafting companies.

The most challenging river to raft is the Franklin; if you pluck up the courage, see p282 for details of the three operators working on the river. Note that companies tackling the Franklin usually offer trips on other rivers too.

Sea kayaking is a popular activity from Kettering (p125), on the Freycinet Peninsula (p170), and around the docks of Hobart (p78). Experienced kayakers can rent equipment from **Roaring 40s Ocean Kayaking** (☎ 6267 5000, 1800 653 712; www.roaring40skayaking.com.au) in Kettering; this company also offers a fabulous array of guided kayaking tours to suit all levels of experience, from half-day trips to multi-day explorations of the southwest wilderness.

The Franklin River section of the Parks & Wildlife Service website (www.parks.tas.gov.au/recreation/boating/frankl.html), is invaluable for anyone considering rafting anywhere in Tasmania.

CAVING

Tasmania's caves are regarded as being among the most impressive in Australia. The caves at Mole Creek (p227), Gunns Plains (p244) and Hastings (p141) are open to the public daily. Both Mole Creek and Hastings offer the chance to get down and dirty on wild cave tours – see those sections for details of operators.

For experienced cavers, caverneering clubs regularly undertake trips to the more demanding wild caves.

CYCLING

Cycling is a popular way to get around Tasmania, especially the east coast, and to get up close and personal with the lovely landscapes. If you intend to cycle between Hobart and Launceston via either coast, count on the trip taking between 10 and 14 days. For making a full circuit of the island on a bike, allow between 18 and 28 days. If you're planning a cycling trip, the website of Bicycle Tasmania (www.biketas.org.au) might be a good source of information. Click on 'rides by region' for details of two- and three-week circuits. See p335 for further tips for cyclists.

Short- and long-term bike rental is available in Hobart (p78) and in Launceston (p206). If you prefer a guided cycling tour, contact **Island Cycle Tours** (☎ 1300 880 334, 6234 4951; www.islandcycletours.com) or **Tasmanian Expeditions** (☎ 1300 666 856, 6334 3477; www.tas-ex.com); see p326 for more information on what these two companies offer. Note, too, that Island Cycle Tours offers a great two-hour descent of Mt Wellington on two wheels (p77).

THE GREAT TASMANIAN BIKE RIDE

The popular Great Tasmanian Bike Ride is staged in Tasmania in odd-numbered years over nine days in February, exploring different cycling routes in the state each time. It covers around 500km to 600km each ride, with a rest day, and draws a couple of thousand riders (supported by a great team of volunteers), with most participants camping along the way.

This well-organised event costs about $650 to participate in, including camp sites and meals (BYO tent and bike), and is organised by **Bicycle Victoria** (☎ 8636 8888, 1800 639 634; www.bv.com.au); full details are on the website.

FISHING

All you need to know to go fishing in Tasmania is available online at www.fishonline.tas.gov.au.

Brown trout were introduced into Tasmania's Plenty River in 1866 and into Lake Sorell between 1867 and 1870. Since then, innumerable lakes and rivers have been stocked, including many of the artificial lakes built by Hydro Tasmania for hydroelectricity production. Needless to say, the fish have thrived, and today, national and international anglers make the most of the state's abundant and often beautiful inland fisheries. The Tamar River is another great fishing area and has a series of 10 fishing and mooring pontoons (accessible by disabled fishers) established on it between Launceston and George Town. The area around George Town (p211) is particularly good for both freshwater and saltwater fishing.

A licence is required to fish in Tasmania's inland waters and there are bag, season and size limits on most fish. Licence costs vary from $17.10 for one day to $56 for the full season and are available from sports stores, Service Tasmania outlets, post offices, visitors centres and some country shops and petrol stations. In general, inland waters open for fishing on the Saturday closest to 1 August and close on the Sunday nearest 30 April; the best fishing is between October and April. Different dates apply to some places and these (plus other essential bits of information) are all detailed in the *Fishing Code* brochure you'll be given when you buy your licence.

The sparsely populated Lake Country (p151), on Tasmania's Central Plateau, is a region of glacial lakes, crystal-clear streams and world-class fishing, home to the state's best-known spots for both brown and rainbow trout: Arthurs Lake, Great Lake, Little Pine Lagoon (fly-fishing only), Western Lakes (including Lake St Clair), Lake Sorell and the Lake Pedder impoundment. On some parts of the Great Lake you're only allowed to use artificial lures. You are also not allowed to fish in any of the streams flowing into that lake.

One of the best books available on trout fishing in Tasmania is *Tasmanian Trout Waters* by Greg French. Also worth a look is the bimonthly publication *Tasmanian Fishing News* ($4); order online from www.fishing-books-australia.com. In Hobart, a good place to stock up on lures and information is **Spot On Fishing Tackle** (☎ 6234 4880; 89 Harrington St).

Tasmanian trout (brown and rainbow) can be difficult to catch as they're fickle about what they eat; the right lures are needed for the season. If you find you just can't hook them yourself, there are dozens of operators that can help you organise guides, lessons or fishing trips; visit the website of **Trout Guides and Lodges Tasmania** (TGALT; www.troutguidestasmania.com.au), an industry body that lists as its members 'the finest and most respected trout fishing guides and lodges in Tasmania'. The website has lots of great info, plus links to various guides.

Rod fishing in saltwater is allowed year-round without a permit, but size restrictions and bag limits apply. If you're diving for abalone, rock lobsters or scallops, or fishing with a net, recreational sea fishing licences are required. These are available from post offices, Service Tasmania or online at www.fishonline.tas.gov.au. There are on-the-spot fines for breaches of fishing regulations.

ROCK CLIMBING & ABSEILING

Although dry weather is desirable for rock climbing and Tasmania's weather is often wet, the sport is nonetheless regularly conducted around the state, as is abseiling. Some excellent cliffs have been identified for climbing, particularly along the east coast where the weather is usually best. The Organ Pipes on Mt Wellington (above Hobart; p76), the Hazards at Coles Bay (p170), the cliffs on Mt Killiecrankie on Flinders Island (p307) and Launceston's Cataract Gorge (p194) offer excellent climbing on firm rock. Many enthusiasts see images of the magnificent rock formations on the Tasman Peninsula (p112) and head straight for that region, but, while the coastal cliffs there are indeed spectacular, it may be impossible to climb them at certain times if the swell is too big.

If you want to climb or abseil with an experienced instructor, try one of these outfits:

Aardvark Adventures (☎ 0408-127 714; www.aardvarkadventures.com.au)
Freycinet Adventures (☎ 6257 0500; www.adventurestasmania.com)
Tasmanian Expeditions (☎ 6334 3477; www.tas-ex.com)

The sheer-faced Federation Peak in the southwest wilderness is graded by bushwalking groups as the hardest peak to climb in Australia (rated 10 out of 10 for difficulty).

SAILING

Tassie's many harbours are well utilised by keen local sailors and those floating in from more distant land masses. Fleets of white sails often dot the Derwent River in the sailing season, while many Hobart residents own yachts and consider the city's sailing opportunities among its greatest attractions. The D'Entrecasteaux Channel is wide, deep and exceptionally beautiful. Its waters are sheltered by Bruny Island, although conditions can be difficult south of Gordon.

There are many good anchorages in the channel where you can spend a night or two, but it's best not to anchor overnight in the Derwent River between North Bruny and the Tasman Bridge, except in Ralph's Bay; moor at one of the yacht clubs or the city docks instead. For casual berths (overnight or weekly), contact the **Royal Yacht Club of Tasmania** (☎ 6223 4599; www.ryct.org.au), in Sandy Bay, or the **Hobart Ports Corporation** (☎ 6235 1000; www.hpc.com.au), which manages berths in the heart of Hobart's waterfront. North of the bridge, you can anchor in Cornelian Bay or New Town Bay. There's a good marina at Kettering, in the Channel south of Hobart, but it's usually crowded so finding a mooring isn't always easy.

If you're a capable sailor, you can hire a Beneteau Oceanis 411 from **Yachting Holidays** (☎ 6224 3195; www.yachtingholidays.com.au) in Hobart. Charter costs $650 per day, with reduced rates for six or more days or for rental during the off-peak (May to November) period. If you don't possess a little cap, sea legs and a nautical-mile stare, skippered charter is also available.

SCUBA DIVING & SNORKELLING

National Geographic magazine has said that Tasmania offers the 'most accessible underwater wilderness in the world'. Visibility ranges from 12m in summer to more than 40m in winter. From Bass Strait to Port Arthur, the temperate waters offer unique biodiversity. There are some excellent scuba-diving opportunities on the east coast; around Rocky Cape on the north coast; and around the shipwrecks of King and Flinders Islands. In addition, at Tinderbox near Hobart and off Maria Island there are marked underwater trails perfect for snorkellers.

If you want to learn to dive, doing a diving course in Tasmania is a good idea – they're considerably cheaper here than on the mainland. **Dive Tasmania** (☎ 6265 2251; divetas@eaglehawkdive.com.au) is an industry organisation with an aim to promote Tasmania as a world-class diving destination. They can give you information on a number of affiliated diving businesses. Otherwise, contact the dive operators in Eaglehawk Neck (p113), Bicheno (p174), St Helens (p184), Wynyard (p251), King Island (p303) and Flinders Island (p308). Equipment can also be rented by licensed divers from dive shops in Hobart and Launceston.

TOP TEN BEACHES

Pack your swimsuit, brace yourself for the cold water, and go for it! In a state of gorgeous (and often empty) coastline, here's our list of favourite beaches:

- Wineglass Bay (p166) Recently voted one of the top beaches in the world – once you've seen it, you'll understand why. Well worth the trek in.
- Friendly Beaches (p168) Often overshadowed by its near neighbour (Wineglass Bay), but offering just-as-lovely, more-accessible white sand and pristine water.
- Boat Harbour Beach (p252) The drive down the steep access road offers magical views of this divine little bay.
- Binalong Bay (p184) Long, inviting stretch of sand to the north of St Helens.
- Adventure Bay (p129) A few early European explorers also considered this stretch a good place to spend some down time.
- Kingston Beach (p100) A great escape, only about 15km from the capital.
- Marrawah (p260) For its truly awesome surf.
- Fortescue Bay (p117) A little slice of heaven, complete with low-key camping ground.
- Stanley (p255) Long arc of sand with an impressive backdrop in the Nut.
- Trousers Point (p307) A kooky name indeed, but this magnificent beach makes the waters of Bass Strait look unfeasibly alluring.

SKIING

There are two small ski resorts in Tasmania: Ben Lomond (p220), 55km southeast of Launceston, and Mt Mawson (p106) in Mt Field National Park, 80km northwest of Hobart. Both offer cheaper, though much less-developed, ski facilities than the main resorts in Victoria and New South Wales; for example, rope tows are still used on some runs. Despite the state's southerly latitude, snowfalls tend to be light and unreliable.

SURFING

Despite the relatively cold water, Tasmania has fine surf beaches. Close to Hobart, the best spots are Clifton Beach and the surf beach en route to South Arm. The southern beaches of Bruny Island, particularly at Cloudy Bay (p125), can be good when a southerly swell is rolling, while Eaglehawk Neck (p115) on the Tasman Peninsula is also worth checking out. The east coast from Ironhouse Point south to Spring and Shelly Beaches near Orford (p157) has some fine surf. King Island (p302) also gets its share.

The greatest spot of all is Marrawah (p260) on the west coast, where the waves are often huge because the ocean here is uninterrupted all the way to South America. It's far removed from urban centres and there's no public transport there, but the isolation just adds to its appeal.

Good websites to check on surf reports and conditions are www.surftasmania.com and www.tassiesurf.com.

SWIMMING

The north and east coasts have plenty of sheltered white-sand beaches offering excellent swimming, although the water is (to understate it) rather cold. There are also pleasant beaches near Hobart, such as Bellerive and Sandy Bay, but these tend to receive some urban pollution, so it's better to head further south towards Kingston and Blackmans Bay, or east to Seven Mile Beach for safe swimming. On the west coast, the surf can be ferocious and the beaches are not patrolled.

National Parks

You may encounter the slogan 'Tasmania – Australia's natural state' in some tourist literature, and it's not a bad summary, as a greater percentage of land is national park or reserve in Tasmania than in any other Australian state. In total, the Tasmania Parks & Wildlife Service (PWS) manages 441 reserves (including 19 national parks) covering 2,477,314 hectares – that's over a third of the total area of the state. Add more than 2000km of walking tracks (including some of Australia's finest), unique flora and abundant fauna, and you have a Mecca for naturalists, bushwalkers, wildlife-watchers, campers, photographers and anyone else who likes to go bush. But you don't have to rough it to experience the wilderness down here – guided walks, scenic flights and river cruises open this world up to the soft-option-seeker, while fair-dinkum outdoorsy types can trek through inspiring natural beauty in the challenging southwest for as long as their supplies last, or escape civilisation for long days on the majestic Franklin River.

Parks for All People is a handy brochure outlining access for mobility-impaired visitors to Tasmania's national parks and reserves. This information is also available online at www.parks.tas.gov.au/recreation/disabled/disabled.html.

NATIONAL PARKS

Tasmania's finest feature is its 19 national parks, and they're well worth visiting to walk on their trails, trek to their peaks, lie on their beaches or just take in the awesome diversity of their environments – highland lakes, windswept beaches, complex caves, wild rivers, dramatic coastline, wildlife-rich islands, rugged mountain ranges and dense temperate rainforest. Most of the parks are easily accessed by vehicle; two (Savage River, in the heart of the Tarkine Wilderness, and the Kent Group, a group of islets in Bass Strait) are virtually inaccessible and one, the Walls of Jerusalem, has no road access direct to the park itself. There is a car park about a half-hour walk from the park's boundary.

Public access to the national parks is encouraged as long as the safety and conservation regulations are observed. In all parks you're asked to do nothing to damage or alter the natural environment – and please don't feed the wild animals. See p45 for information about responsible bushwalking, and for various activities available within national parks.

Most people visit the national parks during the summer months (December to February), when the days are long and the weather is usually warm – although it has been known to snow in December! There are advantages to visiting outside these months, though – the main one being the smaller crowds. Autumn can be lovely as the foliage changes colour, winter sees snow on the peaks, and spring brings out new growth and wildflowers. See p13 for more climate information.

Contacts

National parks are managed by the **Parks & Wildlife Service** (PWS; ☎ 1300 135 513; www.parks.tas.gov.au; head office 134 Macquarie St, GPO Box 44A, Hobart 7001).

Major local offices and visitors centres include the following:

Cradle Mountain–Lake St Clair National Park (Cradle Valley ☎ 6492 1110; Lake St Clair ☎ 6289 1172)

Franklin–Gordon Wild Rivers National Park (Queenstown ☎ 6471 2511; Strahan ☎ 6471 7122)

Freycinet National Park (☎ 6256 7000)

Mt Field National Park (☎ 6288 1149)

Southwest National Park (Mt Field ☎ 6288 1149; Huonville ☎ 6264 8460)

Park Fees

Visitors fees apply to all parks, even when there's no ranger's office. Funds from the park entry fees remain with the PWS and go towards making improvements to walking tracks, camp grounds, toilets, lookouts and picnic facilities; a trainee programme; and the popular summer ranger activities (p57).

There are two types of fees – per vehicle and per person:

Pass type	Duration	Cost
vehicle (incl up to eight passengers)	24hr	$20
	8 weeks	$50
	1 year	$84
individual (arriving by bus, bicycle, motorbike or boat)	24hr	$10
	8 weeks	$30
	1 year	n/a

The Parks & Wildlife Services website (www.parks.tas.gov.au) is an absolute goldmine of information. Download fact sheets on all parks, walks, plants and wildlife, campgrounds within parks, and loads more.

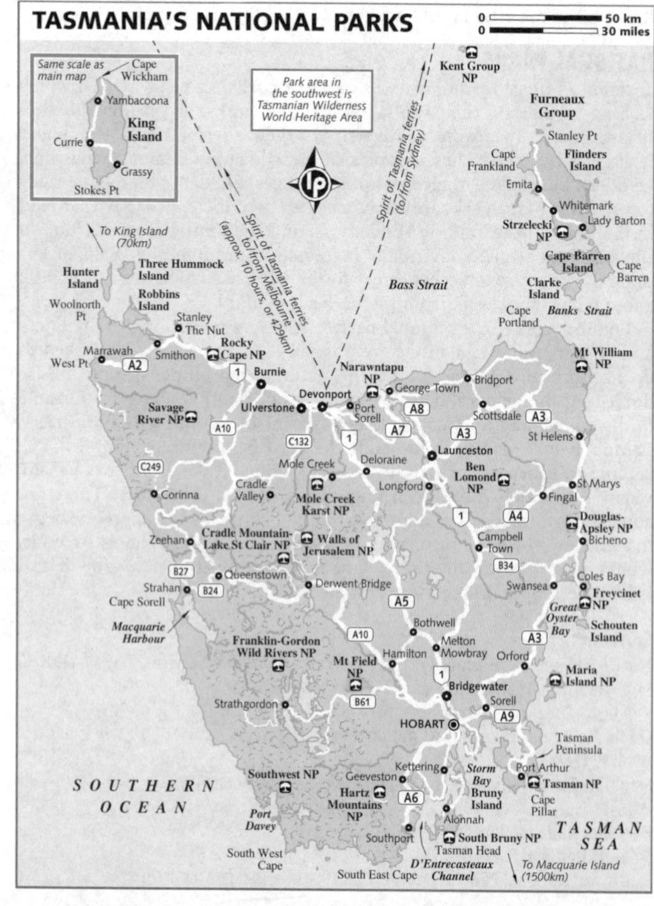

The longer-term passes are better if you're staying in Tasmania for a while or visiting more than a few parks. For most visitors, the holiday pass is the best value.

Passes are available at most park entrances, at many visitors centres, on board the *Spirit of Tasmania* ferries, and at the offices of **Service Tasmania** (Map p70; ☎ 1300 135 513; 134 Macquarie St, Hobart).

Some 9000 people now walk the Overland Track each year. To preserve and protect the area, changes – including a booking and quota system at peak times – are afoot. See p285 for more details.

Facilities

Staffed information centres are at both ends of the Cradle Mountain–Lake St Clair National Park, as well as Freycinet, Mt Field and Narawntapu National Parks. These are open daily and have helpful staff, useful walking information and educational displays on the history and ecology of their parks.

Of the 16 accessible parks (ie not the Savage River, Kent Group and Walls of Jerusalem National Parks), all have short walking tracks, toilets, shelters and picnic areas for day visitors to enjoy. Many also have barbecues. The entire World Heritage area and many national parks have been declared fuel-stove-only areas to protect the area's natural environment – this means no campfires, although some small areas have been designated as fire sites.

Camping sites are available in all accessible parks except for the Hartz Mountains, Mole Creek Karst and Rocky Cape National Parks. Some sites are free and others have a small charge per person ($2.20 to $10) in additional to park entry fees. Ben Lomond, Cradle Mountain–Lake St Clair, Freycinet, Maria Island and Mount Field also have accommodation options inside their boundaries, ranging from basic huts to five-star resorts. See the appropriate chapters for more information.

Short walks suitable for wheelchair users and some prams are at Cradle Mountain–Lake St Clair, Freycinet, Mount Field, Tasman and the Franklin–Gordon Wild Rivers National Parks (some wheelchair users may require assistance on these walks).

Note that dogs are not allowed in national parks.

The Tasmanian National Parks Association (TNPA; www.tnpa.asn.au) is a non-profit-making, nongovernment organisation committed to the protection of Tasmania's national parks and reserves, and to giving park-users a voice. See its website for good information.

WORLD HERITAGE AREAS

Covering 20% of Tasmania, the huge and internationally significant Tasmanian Wilderness World Heritage Area contains the state's four largest national parks – Southwest, Franklin–Gordon Wild Rivers, Cradle Mountain–Lake St Clair and Walls of Jerusalem – plus the Hartz Mountains National Park, the Central Plateau Conservation Area, the Adamsfield Conservation Area and a small part of Mole Creek Karst National Park.

The region was first accepted for listing as a World Heritage area in 1982, acknowledging that these parks make up one of the last great, temperate wilderness areas left in the world. An area nominated for World Heritage status must satisfy at least one of 10 criteria. The western Tasmania World Heritage Area satisfied a record seven categories. In 1989 the World Heritage area was enlarged to 13,800 sq km and renamed as the Tasmanian Wilderness World Heritage Area.

FROM 19 TO 22?

If Tasmanian conservation groups had their way, there would be at least three more national parks on this list – the Tarkine (see p263), the Styx Valley of the Giants (p297) and the Great Western Tiers (p225). Read more about the campaigns to protect these threatened areas on the Tasmania web pages of the **Wilderness Society** (www.wilderness.org.au/regions/tas).

TASMANIA'S NATIONAL PARKS

Park	Features	Activities	Best time to visit	Page
Ben Lomond National Park	wondrous alpine flora, the state's main ski field	walking, skiing, rock climbing	year-round	220
*Cradle Mountain–Lake St Clair National Park	moorlands and mountain peaks, the famed Overland Track, Australia's deepest freshwater lake	walking, scenic flights, wildlife spotting	year-round	284
Douglas-Apsley National Park	dry eucalypt forest, river gorges, waterfalls, wildlife, and a waterhole for swimming	walking, swimming	summer	177
*Franklin–Gordon Wild Rivers National Park	two grand wilderness watercourses, deep river gorges, rainforest, Frenchmans Cap, Aboriginal sites	rafting, cruises (from Strahan)	summer	282
Freycinet Peninsula National Park	stunning coastal scenery, Wineglass Bay, enormous granite hazards, great beaches, walks	walking, sea kayaking, abseiling, scenic flights, fishing	summer	166
*Hartz Mountains National Park	fantastic alpine heath, rainforest, glacial lakes, unforgettable views of the southwest wilderness	walking	spring–summer	138
Kent Group National Park	tiny Bass Strait islets (mostly inaccessible), fur seals, sea birds, historical significance	wildlife watching	year round	311
Maria Island National Park	traffic-free offshore island with convict history, peaceful bays, fossil-loaded cliffs	walking, cycling, swimming	summer	160
Mole Creek Karst National Park	more than 200 limestone caves and sinkholes, some open to the public	walking, caving	year-round	227
Mt Field National Park	abundant flora & fauna, alpine scenery, high-country walks, Russell Falls, ski field	walking, skiing, wildlife-spotting	year-round	106

The area is managed by the PWS, the same government agency that runs the national parks. Most of the area is managed as a publicly accessible wilderness, but, being so large, most of it is accessible only to bushwalkers who can carry at least one week's food. There are, however, a few slightly less demanding ways to visit. For information on guided walks, kayaking tours and scenic flights (including landings and walking time), see p299. Note also that there are scenic flights over the area

Park	Features	Activities	Best time to visit	Page
Mt William National Park	long, sandy beaches, the protected grey Forester kangaroo	walking, fishing, swimming	spring–summer	188
Narawntapu National Park	north-coast lagoons, wetlands, tea-tree mazes, native wildlife	swimming, walking, wildlife-spotting	summer	214
Rocky Cape National Park	bushland, rocky headlands, caves used by Aborigines, exceptional marine environment	swimming, fishing, walking	summer	253
Savage River National Park	cool temperate rainforest inside Tarkine Wilderness – utterly secluded, no road access	n/a	n/a	265
South Bruny National Park	wild southern cliffs, surf and swimming beaches, heathlands, wildlife	walking, swimming, surfing, wildlife-spotting, bird-watching, eco-cruises	spring–summer	128
*Southwest National Park	enormous multi-peaked wilderness, one of the world's most pristine natural wonders	walking, swimming, scenic flights, mountaineering, kayaking	summer	298
Strzelecki National Park	mountainous slice of islandscape, numerous rare flora and fauna	walking, rock-climbing, wildlife-spotting, swimming	summer	305
Tasman National Park	spectacular sea cliffs and rock formations, offshore islands, forests, bays and beaches	walking, sea kayaking, diving, surfing, eco-cruises, fishing	spring–summer	112
*Walls of Jerusalem National Park	a solitude-seeking bushwalker's favourite, spectacular alpine & mountain wilderness, no road access	walking	summer	228

* Part of the Tasmanian Wilderness World Heritage Area

out of Hobart (p81), Strahan (p275) and Cradle Mountain's Cradle Valley (p290).

In December 1997, the Macquarie Island World Heritage Area was proclaimed for its outstanding geological and faunal significance, but as a sub-Antarctic island located 1500km southeast of mainland Tasmania, Macquarie Island is difficult to visit. See p333 for details of one company offering cruises that visit the remote island.

TOP 10 WALKS

Walking is absolutely the best way to see Tasmania's wilderness in all its glory (and it's not a bad way to walk off all that great local food and wine, too). Pack comfy walking shoes and hit the tracks. Following are some of the most popular (and scenic) walks, ranging in length from 20 minutes to six days:

- Overland Track through Cradle Mountain–Lake St Clair National Park (p285)
- Wineglass Bay Lookout and Beach Walk, Freycinet Peninsula (p168)
- Cataract Gorge Walk, out of Launceston (p194)
- Tahune AirWalk, out of Geeveston (p138)
- Russell Falls Walk, Mt Field National Park (p106)
- Creepy Crawly Nature Trail, Southwest National Park (p298)
- Climbing the Nut in Stanley (p256)
- Tasman Coastal Trail, Tasman Peninsula (p115)
- Dove Lake Circuit, Cradle Mountain–Lake St Clair National Park (p289)
- South Coast Track, Southwest National Park (p299)

OTHER PROTECTED AREAS

Apart from the national parks, the PWS manages a further 422 reserves of land. These reserves are usually established around one significant, protected feature – often wildlife – but have fewer regulations than national parks and allow degrees of activities such as mining, farming, forestry and tourism development. Many of these places are very small and include caves, waterfalls, historic sites and some coastal regions. Usually there are no entry fees to these areas, except where the government has actively restored or developed the area.

Tasmania's National Parks, Forests & Waterways – A Visitor's Guide, freely available at visitors centres, is a glossy little brochure chock-full of useful information on key sites and activities.

Categories of reserves managed by PWS include state reserves such as Hastings Caves in the southeast (p141), and The Nut in Stanley (p255); conservation areas including the Arthur Pieman Conservation Area in the state's northwest (p263) and the Bay of Fires in the northeast (p187); nature reserves, which cover the marine reserves listed below; and historic sites including such high-profile spots as Port Arthur (p117) and the Richmond gaol (p108).

FOREST RESERVES

These are small areas that have been given some protection inside larger regions of state forests. They are on crown land and their primary purpose is for timber production. Many of the waterfalls and picnic areas on the state's scenic forest drives are in this type of reserve, which doesn't have real protection from future alterations. During weekdays some forestry roads are closed to private vehicles; if the roads are open, drive slowly and give way to logging trucks. There are no entry fees to the forests.

If you plan to do some serious national-park-hopping, you won't regret buying a copy of Greg Buckman's comprehensive book, *A Visitor's Guide to Tasmania's National Parks.*

MARINE RESERVES

Tasmania is becoming increasingly aware of the significance and vulnerability of its marine environment. Marine reserves aim to protect fragile ecosystems, so fishing or the collection of living or dead material within their boundaries is illegal. There are marine reserves at Tinderbox (p102) near Hobart, at Ninepin Point near Verona Sands south of Hobart, in the waters around the northern part of Maria Island, and around Governor Island off the coast at Bicheno. In 2004 two new marine reserves were

FREE SUMMER FUN

A fantastic programme of free, family-friendly, ranger-led activities, including guided walks, spotlight tours, slide shows, quiz nights and games, is held at popular parks during the peak season (usually from the week before Christmas until school goes back in early February).

Parks that stage these activities include Cradle Mountain–Lake St Clair, Freycinet, Maria Island, Tasman, Mt Field, Narawntapu and South Bruny. There are also nature-based events scheduled in Hobart and Launceston. Ask at visitors centres, or go online for the full rundown: www.parks.tas.gov.au/latest/summer_program/.

established – at Port Davey/Bathurst Harbour in the southwest, and around the Kent Group of islands in eastern Bass Strait (these islands are already a national park; see p311). Each new reserve will contain 'no take areas' to be known as sanctuary zones, and 'restricted take areas' to be known as habitat protection zones.

In 1999, the federal government established a 370-sq-km marine reserve 170km south of Hobart. The Tasmanian Seamounts Marine Reserve is a deep-sea reserve in which any activities that could threaten its population of rare animals and plants have been outlawed, including mining and trawling (though fishing can still occur down to 500m).

Tasmania has 19 national parks, comprising over 1.4 million hectares – or about 21% of the state's total land area.

Food & Drink

Born in convict poverty and raised on a diet heavily influenced by Great Britain, Tasmanian cuisine has come a long, long way. Today the so-called 'Apple Isle' is making good use of its surrounding seas, cool climate, fresh air, pure water and fertile soil, gaining a reputation for genuine culinary delights. The state is renowned for its superb range of seafood; other noted Tassie produce includes juicy berries and stone fruits, a fantastic range of dairy products and award-winning cheeses, well-produced beers and, of course, excellent cool-climate wines. Locals and travellers alike are reaping the rewards of a blossoming food and wine culture across the state.

A growing number of fine restaurants and cafés offer a wide variety of innovative food – and not just in the larger towns. Innumerable farms, orchards, vineyards and small enterprises are busy supplying fresh, local produce, and buyers (restaurants, markets, food stores and individuals) are snapping it up. Dishes on menus throughout Australia feature Tasmanian oysters, scallops and salmon, and King Island cream appears on dessert menus from Sydney to Perth.

Despite the relatively new-found fascination with tucker and Tasmania's reputation as a gourmet's paradise, at heart, Tasmanians are still mostly simple eaters, with the majority still novices in anything beyond meat and three veg. Foodies may find themselves despairing in some country towns, especially where the local pub is the only eatery. This is changing, however, as the influx of mainlanders and immigrants has seen locals trying (and liking) everything from lassi to laksa. This passionate minority has led to a rise in dining standards, better availability of produce and a frenetic buzz about food in general.

TOP 10 FOODIE EXPERIENCES

It's extremely tough to pick just 10, but here are some of our favourite culinary experiences in Tassie:

- Grazing on free samples of jams/fudges/whatever's going at the stalls of Salamanca Market (p69)
- Attending the Festivale (Launceston; p199) and Taste of Tasmania (Hobart; p82) festivals, where producers of fine food and wine converge to showcase their gastronomic prowess
- Eating fresh berries you picked yourself at Sorell Fruit Farm (p114)
- Sampling the rich, creamy cheeses produced on King Island (p302)
- Downing oysters fresh from the farm, particularly on Bruny Island (p125), the Freycinet Peninsula (p166) or Barilla Bay (p114)
- Vineyard-hopping for cool-climate wines in the Tamar Valley and nearby Pipers River region (p206)
- Munching on crisp apples bought from a roadside stall in the Huon Valley (p134)
- Ripping into fresh crayfish in a coastal town like St Helens (p182)
- Cooking up the trout you caught yourself in the highland lakes – fish never tasted so good (p152)
- Experiencing a fancy meal at one of the new breed of foodie temples, such as Peppermint Bay (p132), Franklin Manor (p278) or Stillwater (p203)

TOURING GOURMET TASMANIA

If you intend to expand your waistline while touring Tassie, two recommended publications are *Graeme Philip's Guide to the Wine & Food of Tasmania,* updated annually (around $15 from some visitors centres, newsagents and bookshops, or purchase it online at www.wine-guide-tasmania.com.au), and *Tasmania Wine & Food – Cellar Door & Farm Gate Guide,* a free brochure published by Tourism Tasmania and available at most visitors centres or from the Internet at www.discovertasmania.com. Click on 'things to do & see', then 'wine & food'. Both publications have details of the best restaurants, cafés, wineries and farm stores around the state, classified by region, plus details of wine and food annual events. The Tourism Tasmania brochure also has a helpful chart detailing when particular foods are in season.

If you'd like someone else to do the planning (and the driving, while you imbibe), consider taking a tour that focuses on the state's food and wine offerings. Two Sydney-based companies, **Gourmet Safaris** (☎ 02-9960 5675; www.gourmetsafaris.com.au) and **Convivial Times** (☎ 02-9380 8327; www.convivialtimes.com.au) organise such tours. Gourmet Safaris has an annual eight-day trip that includes visits to top restaurants and wineries, as well as cooking demonstrations from highly regarded chefs. The cost of $3250 includes seven nights' accommodation, transport in Tasmania, and most meals.

STAPLES & SPECIALITIES

Tasmania's best food comes from the sea. Nothing compares to this state's seafood, garnered from some of the purest waters you'll find anywhere, and usually cooked with care. Fish like trevalla (blue-eye) and striped trumpeter are delicious, as is the local Atlantic salmon. Rock lobster (usually called crayfish – fantastic tasting, and usually fantastically expensive), abalone, scallops, mussels and oysters are among the crustaceans and shellfish available.

Before We Eat: A Delicious Slice of Tasmania's Culinary Life, by Bernard Lloyd and Paul County, is a great, glossy book tracing the history of Tassie food and drink and spotlighting the people who shaped the state's gastronomic development.

Tasmania is well-known for high-quality beef, based on a natural, grass-fed production system (as opposed to grain-fed), and free from hormone growth promotants, antibiotics and chemical contaminants. Beef from King Island and Flinders Island is the pick of the crop. Flinders Island also farms prime lamb. These meats are available on many menus Tasmania-wide and in upmarket restaurants throughout Australia.

Don't be surprised to see game meats popping up on some restaurant menus – quail, wallaby and farmed venison are often available (and occasionally mutton bird). Wallaby meat is tender, lean and has a mild game flavour.

There's a brilliant cheese industry, somewhat hampered by the fact that all the milk must be pasteurised, unlike in Italy and France, the homes of the world's best cheeses. Despite that, the results can be great. Visit Pyengana Cheese Factory (p184), not far from St Helens, for sensational cheddar; Grandvewe Sheep Cheesery (p131), just south of Woodbridge, which produces organic cheese from sheep and cows milk; Ashgrove Farm Cheese (p225), near Deloraine, for traditional cheeses like Rubicon red, smoked cheddar and creamy Lancashire; Lactos Tasmania (p247) in Burnie for sundry speciality cheeses; and the big daddy of them all, King Island Dairy (p302), for superb brie and rich, thick cream, amongst other dairy delights. Alternatively, head for the cheese section of the supermarket, which will no doubt stock many of the state's finest cheeses.

'Trevalla' appears on the menu in countless Tassie eateries. This is *not* trevally. The more common name on the mainland for trevalla is blue eye (or blue-eyed cod), and it's the largest and possibly the best eating of all the fish caught in Tasmania.

Tasmania's cold climate means its berries and stone fruit are sublime, and picking your own (in season) is a great way to sample and enjoy them. Sorell Fruit Farm (p114) is a favourite – it gives visitors the opportunity to pick all sorts, including raspberries, cherries, apples and pears. Roadside stalls in the Huon and Tamar Valleys offer the chance to buy freshly-picked fruits. Other places worth a visit for their fantastic homemade fruity produce include Christmas Hills Raspberry Farm Café (p226) near Deloraine, Kate's Berry Farm (p166) outside Swansea, and Eureka Farm (p178) in Scamander.

The nickname 'Apple Isle' stemmed from the state's huge apple production, based largely in the Huon Valley. At its peak during the 1960s, there were over 2000 orchards exporting eight million boxes of apples, mainly to the UK.

Needless to say, the jams, sauces, fruit wines, ciders and juices made from Tasmanian fruits are excellent, and make great souvenirs of your stay. Lots of varieties are available at gourmet food stores and from stalls at Hobart's Salamanca Market (p69); otherwise, good places to head to include Doran's (p134), Australia's oldest jam company, outside Huonville, and Tasmanian Gourmet Sauce Co (p219), west of Evandale.

And that's not the half of it! Also produced in Tasmania is fantastic honey, chocolate and fudge, mushrooms, asparagus, olive oil, walnuts, and mustards and relishes. Locals are also getting creative and showing off their agricultural skill, growing or harvesting some wonderfully diverse products, including buckwheat, *wasabi*, *wakame* (edible seaweed) and saffron. Black truffles are even being harvested in Tasmania!

DRINKS

To go with all that fantastic local food, Tasmania produces some great beverages, including refreshing soft drinks (plenty of local stuff under the Cascade brand) and fruit juices – be sure to try the sparking apple juice.

Expect the best coffee in Hobart and Launceston, decent stuff in most other large towns, and a chance of good coffee in many rural areas (some of the better accommodation providers are getting in on the act too, with plunger coffee and tea leaves and teapots in guest rooms, instead of cheap instant coffee and teabags).

Tasmania excels in the beer and wine department, and even has a whisky distillery, in Hobart, but note that the maximum permissible blood-alcohol concentration level for drivers is 0.05%. If you blow a higher reading during one of the ubiquitous random breath tests or after being pulled over, you'll face a large fine and the loss of your licence.

When We Eat: A Seasonal Celebration of Fine Tasmanian Food and Drink, by Liz McLeod, Bernard Lloyd and Paul County, is the equally impressive companion guide to *Before We Eat* (p59). This title covers the availability of seasonal foods in the state, accompanied by great recipes and photographs.

Beer

Australian beer will be fairly familiar to North Americans and to lager enthusiasts from the UK. It may taste like lemonade to the European real-ale addict, but full-strength beer can still pack a punch. Standard beer generally contains around 5% alcohol, while low-alcohol (light) beer contains between 2% and 3.5%. It's invariably chilled before drinking, even in winter.

In terms of breweries, there's Cascade Brewery in the state's south and Boag's Brewery in the north, both with a core of loyal drinkers (usually divided along geographic lines). Cascade is based in Hobart and produces the very drinkable Cascade Premium Lager and Pale Ale. Visitors tend to ask for 'Cascade' expecting to get the bottle with the distinctive label bearing a Tasmanian tiger, but you're unlikely to get Premium unless you ask specifically for it – you'll probably get Cascade Draught. Boag's is located in Launceston and produces similar-style beers to the Cascade brews such as James Boag's Premium Lager and Boag's Draught. See p74 for details of tours of the Cascade Brewery, and p197 for information on touring Boag's Brewery.

Wine

Tasmania puts on a liquid smorgasbord of fine vintages for you to sample, either on your travels or back in the privacy of your own home. The local wine industry was started by a few pioneers in the mid-1950s and has gained international recognition for producing quality wines, characterised by their full, fruity flavour, along with the high acidity expected of cool, temperate wine regions. Tasmania's wines are expensive compared to similar mainland wines – you'll fork out more than $20 for an acceptable bottle of wine – but the best of them are simply superb. Today more than 140 vineyards across the state are producing award-winning pinot noirs, rieslings and chardonnays, and Tassie wineries are growing a large percentage of the grapes for many of the top Australian sparkling brands.

An informative overview of Tasmanian wines is given on the website of Wine Diva (www.winediva.com.au/regions/tasmania.asp), with excellent links to countless other useful wine sites.

Grapes are grown all over the state; the key wine-producing regions are the Tamar Valley and Pipers River in the north, and the Coal River Valley, Derwent Valley, Huon Valley and D'Entrecasteaux Channel in the south. Throughout these areas there are a growing number of larger operators with sophisticated cellar doors and restaurants (usually serving lunch only; see below for our pick of vineyard eateries), but there are also dozens of smaller, family-owned vineyards quietly going about the business of fine-wine-making, some open to the public by appointment only, others with restricted opening hours.

The Tamar Valley and Pipers River area is home to a number of well-established wineries, including Rosevears Estate (p208), Tamar Ridge Wines (p210) and Pipers Brook (p213). Wineries are dotted down the east coast from Bicheno to Dunalley, including the well-respected Freycinet Vineyard (p164). Further south, in the Huon Valley area, you'll find Hartzview Vineyard (p131), Panorama Vineyard (p133) and Home Hill (p134), among others. Major producers in the Derwent River Valley include Stefano Lubiana Wines and Moorilla Estate (p76); the latter was established in 1958, making it the oldest vineyard in southern Tasmania. The Coal River Valley, easily accessed from Richmond and Hobart, is home to an increasing number of wineries, among them Meadowbank Estate and the Coal Valley Vineyard (p112). To get an idea of the number of grape-wreathed properties around the island, pick up copies of the two *Tasmanian Wine Route* brochures (one each for the south and the north) from visitors centres or online at www.discovertasmania.com. Click on 'things to do & see', 'wine & food', then 'vineyards & wine routes'. Keep in mind, though, that these lists are nowhere near comprehensive.

The island's first winery was established in New Town, Hobart, in 1821.

The most enjoyable way to start educating your palate is to indulge in wine tastings right at the cellar door, where you can also pick up bottles of your preferred drops more cheaply than in retail outlets. Many wineries have such tastings; some of them are free but most charge a small fee (usually a few dollars), which is refundable if you purchase any wine. Bear in mind that the key word here is 'tasting', not 'guzzling' – you won't get

TOP FIVE VINEYARD RESTAURANTS

Wine often isn't the only thing on offer in the bigger wineries, many of which also have fine modern dining facilities with excellent upmarket menu choices. These are a few places worth heading to for a long leisurely lunch (bookings advised):

- Meadowbank Estate (p111), Cambridge
- Home Hill Winery Restaurant (p134), Ranelagh
- Moorilla Estate (p94), northern Hobart
- Strathlynn (p209), Rosevears
- Bay of Fires Wines (p213), Pipers River

endless glasses of the vineyard's finest, just enough in the bottom of a glass to whet your appetite.

If your visit to Tasmania is short but you'd still like to learn more about the state's wine industry (not to mention taste some drops, and purchase lots of bottles!), visit Benchmark Tasmania Wine Gallery (p205) in Launceston or the Tasmanian Wine Centre (p96) in Hobart. Both can arrange worldwide shipping of wine purchases.

CELEBRATIONS

Celebrating in the Australian manner often involves equal amounts of food and alcohol. A birthday could well be a barbecue (barbie) of steak (or seafood), washed down with a beverage or two. Weddings are usually a big slap-up dinner, though the food is often far from memorable.

If you get the chance, don't miss one of Tasmania's major food festivals: the week-long Taste of Tasmania is staged around the waterfront as part of the Hobart Summer Festival (p82), while Launceston celebrates the three-day Festivale in City Park in February (p199). Cradle Mountain also gets in on the act, warming up winter visitors with the three-day Tastings at the Top in mid-June (p285). Many other regions also celebrate their produce.

For many an event, especially in the warmer months, Australians fill the car with an Esky (an ice-chest, to keep everything cool), tables, chairs, a cricket set or a footy, and head off for a barbie by the lake/river/beach/mountains.

Christmas in Australia often finds the more traditional (in a European sense) baked dinner being replaced by a barbecue, in response to the warm weather.

WHERE TO EAT & DRINK

'Australians' taste for the unusual usually kicks in at dinner'

Australians' taste for the unusual usually kicks in at dinner only. Most people still eat cereal for breakfast, or perhaps eggs and bacon on weekends. They devour sandwiches for lunch, with most sandwich fillings in cafés now coming on grilled, fancy-pants Italian bread such as focaccia, on bagels, or on Turkish bread (also known as *pide*). They may also enjoy other café fare such as quiche, salad or pasta dishes – and then eat anything and everything in the evening.

A competitively priced place to eat is in a pub. Most serve two types of meals: bistro meals, which are usually in the $12 to $20 range and are served in the dining room or lounge bar; and bar (or counter) meals, which are filling, no-frills meals eaten in the public bar and costing around $6 to $12.

The quality of pub food varies enormously. Upmarket city pubs will change their menus as much as midrange restaurants do, while standard corner pubs will stick to the tried and true meals like schnitzels, roasts and basic seafood. The usual meal times are from noon to 2pm and 6pm to 8pm.

Solo diners find that cafés and noodle bars are welcoming, and good fine-dining restaurants often treat you like a star, but sadly, some midrange places may still make you feel a little ill at ease.

One of the most interesting features of the dining scene is the Bring Your Own (BYO), a restaurant that allows you to bring your own alcohol. If the restaurant also sells alcohol, the BYO bit is usually limited to bottled wine only (no beer, no casks of wine) and a corkage charge is added to your bill. The cost is either per person, or per bottle, and ranges from nothing to $15 per bottle in fancy places. Be warned, however, that BYO is a custom that is slowly dying out, and many if not most licensed restaurants don't like you bringing your own wine, so ask when you book.

Most restaurants open at noon for lunch and from 6pm or 7pm for dinner. Australians usually eat lunch shortly after noon, and dinner bookings are usually made for 7.30pm or 8pm.

Quick Eats

There's not a huge culture of street vending in Tasmania. Most quick eats traditionally come from a milk bar (small store selling basic provisions), which serves old-fashioned hamburgers (with bacon, egg, pineapple and beetroot if you want) and other takeaway foods. Every town has at least one busy fish and chip shop, particularly in the beachside areas, and it's an Aussie tradition to take your battered flake (shark – don't worry, it can be delicious) and chips down to the beach on a Friday night.

American-style fast food has taken over in recent times, though many Aussies still love a meat pie, often from a milk bar, but also from bakeries, kiosks and some cafés. Traditional pies are of the steak-and-gravy variety, but many bakeries offer more gourmet fare in their pastry casings. Be on the look out for a Tasmanian speciality, the scallop pie.

Pizza has become one of the most popular fast foods; most are of the American style (thick and with lots of toppings) rather than Italian style. That said, more and more wood-fired, thin, Neapolitan-style pizzas can be found in pizzerias and restaurants around the state.

Lots of information for foodies is available online at the website of Tourism Tasmania. Go to www.discovertasmania.com.au, click on 'things to do & see', then 'wine & food', and start salivating.

VEGETARIANS & VEGANS

Vegetarian eateries and vegetarian menu selections, including choices for vegans and coeliac-sufferers, are becoming common in large towns and are forging a stronger presence in areas visited by tourists, though small-town Tasmania mostly continues its stolid dedication to meat (in other words, vegetarians are usually well catered for in the parts of the state where the local pub isn't the only eatery). Cafés seem to always have vegetarian options, but take care with risotto and soups, as meat stock is often used. Vegans will find the going much tougher, but there are usually dishes that are vegan-adaptable at restaurants.

Vegetarians and vegans feeling neglected as they travel around the state should make a beeline for Sirens (p90) restaurant and Nourish (p89) café as soon as they reach Hobart. For coeliac-sufferers, a growing number of eateries are offering gluten-free options, and larger supermarkets usually stock gluten-free bread and pasta.

EATING WITH KIDS

Dining with children in Australia is relatively easy. Avoid the flashiest places and children are generally welcomed, particularly at Chinese, Greek or Italian restaurants. Kids are usually more than welcome at cafés, and you'll see families dining early in bistros and pub dining rooms. A number of fine-dining restaurants don't welcome small children (see p316).

Many that do welcome children don't have separate kids' menus, and those that do usually offer everything straight from the deep fryer – crumbed chicken and chips, and that kind of thing. Better to find something on the menu (say a pasta or salad) and ask to have the kitchen adapt it slightly to your children's needs.

The best news for travelling families, weather permitting, is that there are plenty of picnic spots, and sometimes free or coin-operated barbecues in parks.

BILLS & TIPPING

The total at the bottom of a restaurant bill is all you really need to pay. It should include GST (as should menu prices) and there is no 'optional' service charge added. Waiters are paid a reasonable salary, so they don't rely on tips to survive. Often, though, especially in urban Australia, people tip a few coins in a café, while the tip for excellent service can go as high as 15% in whiz-bang establishments. The incidence of add-ons (bread, water, surcharges on weekends etc) is rising.

HABITS & CUSTOMS

Australian table manners are fairly standard. Avoid talking with your mouth full, wait until everyone has been served before you eat, and don't use your fingers to pick up food unless it can't be tackled another way.

Smoking is illegal in Tasmania's indoor cafés, restaurants and pub dining areas. Drinkers can breathe easier too as a total smoking ban in all Tasmanian pubs and bars comes into effect from 1 January 2006.

If you're invited over for dinner at someone's house, always take a gift. You may offer to bring something for the meal, but even if the host downright refuses – insisting you just bring your scintillating conversation – still take a bottle of wine. Flowers or a box of chocolates are also acceptable.

'Shouting' is a revered custom where people in a bar or pub take turns to buy drinks for their group. Just don't leave before it's your turn to buy! At a toast, everyone should touch glasses.

Smoking is banned in most eateries in the nation, so sit outside if you love to puff. And never smoke in someone's house unless you ask first. Even then it's usual to smoke outside.

EAT YOUR WORDS

Australians love to shorten everything, including people's names, so expect many other words to be abbreviated. Here are some words you might hear:

barbie – a barbecue, where (traditionally) smoke and overcooked meat are matched with lashings of coleslaw, potato salad and beer

Esky – an insulated ice chest to hold your tinnies (see below), before you hold them in your tinny holder

pav – pavlova, the meringue dessert topped with cream, passion fruit, kiwi fruit or other fresh fruit

pot – a medium glass of beer (in Victoria and Tasmania)

sanger/sando – a sandwich

surf 'n' turf – a classic 1970s pub meal of steak topped with prawns, usually in a creamy sauce; also known as reef 'n' beef

The 'Food & Beverage' pages of the Brand Tasmania website (www.brandtasmania.com) is a font of information. Its A-Z of Food has a roll-call of Tassie delicacies, from abalone to *yolla* (the local Aboriginal term for mutton bird).

snags – sausages

Tim Tam – a commercially produced chocolate biscuit that lies close to the heart of most Australians

tinny – usually refers to a can of beer, but could also be the small boat you go fishing in (and you'd take a few tinnies in your tinny, in that case)

tinny holder – insulating material that protects your hand from your icy beer, and nothing to do with a boat

Vegemite – salty, dark-brown breakfast spread, popular on toast, adored by the Aussie masses, much maligned by visitors

Hobart

Straddling the Derwent River and backed by the towering bulk of Mt Wellington, Hobart has embellished its rich colonial heritage and splendid natural beauty with the youthful, lively atmosphere of numerous festivals and inner-city bars and restaurants. Its attractive Georgian buildings, busy Victoria Dock, relaxed populace and serene surrounding districts make it one of Australia's most stress-free and engaging cities, and visitors will no doubt be delighted to find all the urban delights (plush hotels, foodie temples of indulgence, a thriving arts scene), but with a lot less attitude and loads more charm than in many mainland destinations. Hobart is Australia's second-oldest city and the smallest state capital, making it a compact place to explore, so pack comfy shoes and get walking.

Regular visitors will notice Hobart's growing confidence. The stunning new Henry Jones Art Hotel (p88) is a prime example. But despite its new glossy new accoutrements, Hobart's essential attractions – the harbour, the architecture, the market, the mountain and the river – are unchanged. It's just that these days there are a whole lot more visitors heading south to enjoy them!

HIGHLIGHTS

- Stopping to smell the roses and admire the historic façades of cottages in charming **Battery Point** (p71)
- Eating, drinking and posing in waterfront restaurants and bars, especially the new **Henry Jones Art Hotel** (p88)
- Ransacking stalls for creative buys at the Salamanca Market in **Salamanca Place** (p69), followed by an alfresco brunch
- Taking in the views from the summit of **Mt Wellington** (p76) before careering down the mountain on two wheels
- Marvelling at Moorilla Estate's world-class **Moorilla Museum of Antiquities** (p73) – a real treasure in the 'burbs
- Joining the **dockside party** (p82) at Constitution Dock to celebrate the Sydney to Hobart Yacht Race
- Donning a ridiculous hairnet and discovering how your favourite sweet stuff is made at the **Cadbury Factory** (p74)

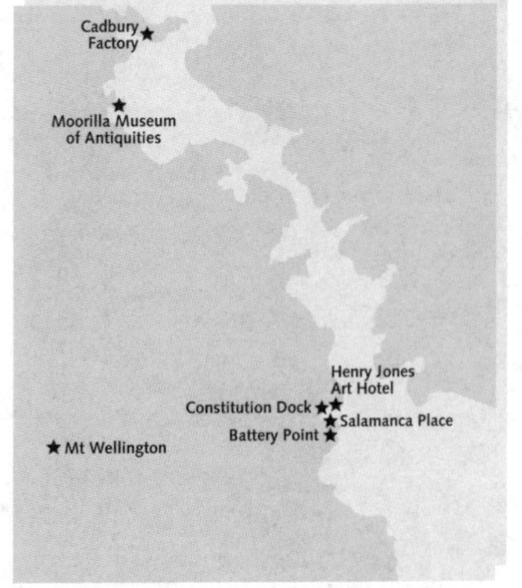

■ TELEPHONE CODE: 03	■ www.hobartcity.com.au	■ POPULATION: 128,600

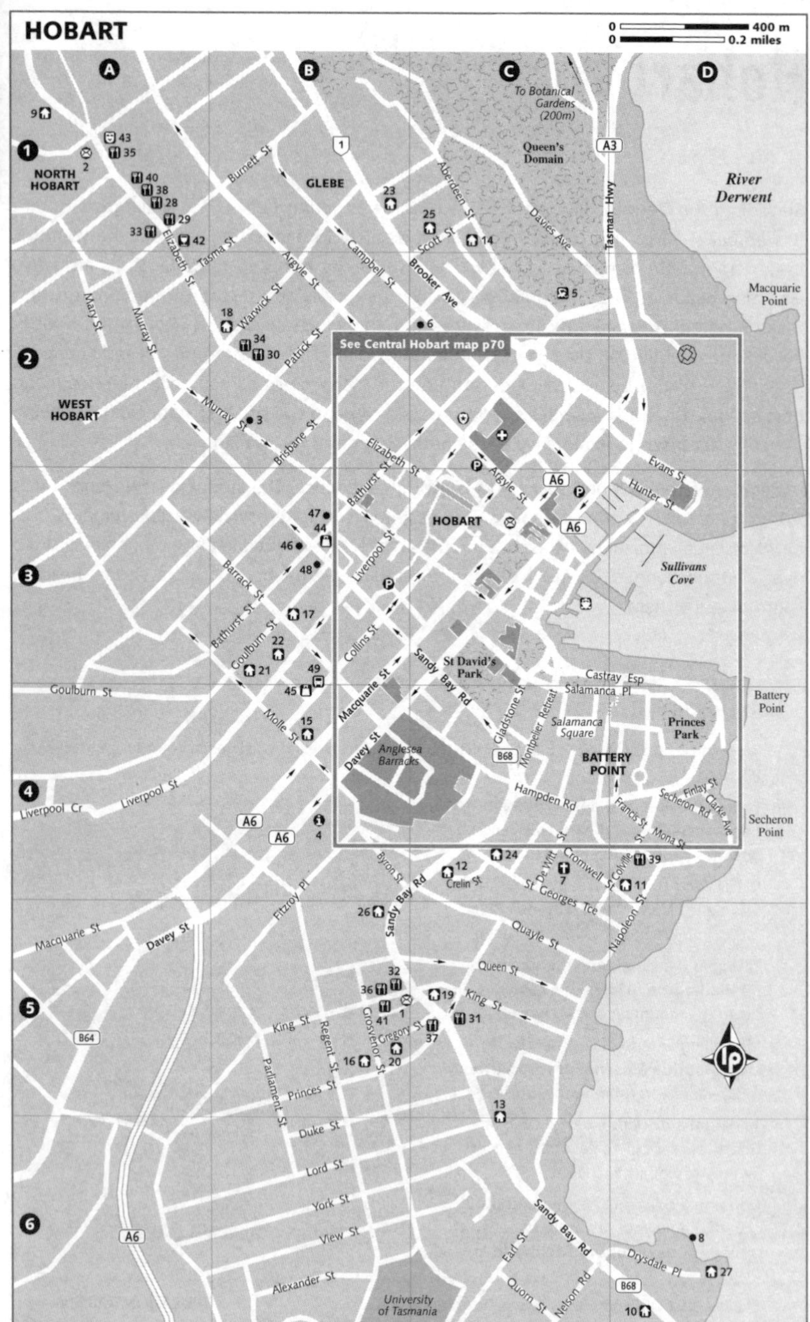
HOBART
0 400 m
0 0.2 miles
A
B
C
D
1
2
3
4
5
6
To Botanical Gardens (200m)
Queen's Domain
River Derwent
NORTH HOBART
GLEBE
WEST HOBART
HOBART
BATTERY POINT
Macquarie Point
Battery Point
Secheron Point
Sullivans Cove
St David's Park
Princes Park
Salamanca Square
Anglesea Barracks
University of Tasmania
See Central Hobart map p70
Tasman Hwy
Burnett St
Campbell St
Argyle St
Brooker Ave
Aberdeen St
Scott St
Davies Ave
Tasma St
Elizabeth St
Warwick St
Patrick St
Murray St
Mary St
Brisbane St
Bathurst St
Liverpool St
Barrack St
Goulburn St
Collins St
Macquarie St
Sandy Bay Rd
Molle St
Davey St
Evans St
Hunter St
Castray Esp
Salamanca Pl
Gladstone St
Montpelier Retreat
Hampden Rd
Francis St
Secheron Rd
Finlay St
Clarke Ave
Mona St
Liverpool Cr
Byron St
Crelin St
De Witt St
Cromwell St
Colville St
St Georges Tce
Napoleon St
Fitzroy Pl
Quayle St
Queen St
King St
Regent St
Grosvenor St
Gregory St
Parliament St
Princes St
Duke St
Lord St
York St
View St
Alexander St
Earl St
Quorn St
Nelson Rd
Drysdale Pl
A3
A6
B64
B68
1

HISTORY

The Tasmanian Aborigines who originally lived here were the Mouheneenner band of the South East Tribe, who called the area Nibberloonne. The first European colony in Tasmania was founded in 1803 at Risdon Cove – this is also where the first massacre of the land's traditional owners, the Tasmanian Aborigines, took place. Risdon Cove was one of a dozen sites returned to the Aboriginal community by the state government in 1995.

In 1804, Lieutenant-Colonel David Collins, governor of the new settlement in Van Diemen's Land, sailed down the Derwent River and decided that a cove 10km below Risdon and on the opposite shore was a better place to settle. The site of Tasmania's future capital city thus began as a village of tents and wattle-and-daub huts with a population of 262 Europeans (178 of whom were convicts).

Hobart Town, as it was known until 1881, was proclaimed a city in 1842. The deep-water harbour of the Derwent River estuary was important to its development, as many merchants made their fortunes from the whaling trade, shipbuilding and the export of products such as merino wool and corn.

ORIENTATION

Hobart is sandwiched between the steep hills of Mt Wellington and the wide Derwent River. Blessed with very little flat land, the city proper has spread along the riverbank and is now about 20km long, although it's very narrow. The urban development has climbed into the hills and you will find many western streets challengingly steep.

The city centre is fairly small and pretty easy to navigate, with its streets arranged in a simple grid pattern around the Elizabeth St Mall; the visitors centre and the main post office are located on Elizabeth St, and the main shopping area extends west from the mall. Hobart's major bus stations are also in this area. City authorities have tried to regulate traffic in their narrow streets by making them one-way: before you drive, it's a good idea to study a map.

Salamanca Place, the famous row of Georgian warehouses, is along the southern waterfront, while behind its historic façade is the café-lined expanse of Salamanca Sq. Just south of this is Battery Point, Hobart's delightful, well-preserved, early colonial district. If you follow the river south from Battery Point you'll come to Sandy Bay and its yacht clubs, the site of Hobart's university, and the circular tower of Wrest Point: a hotel/casino and one of Hobart's main landmarks.

The northern side of the city centre is bounded by the recreation area known as the Domain (short for Queen's Domain), which includes the Royal Tasmanian Botanical Gardens and the Derwent River. From here the Tasman Bridge crosses over the river to the eastern suburbs and the

INFORMATION
Post Office ... 1 B5
Post Office ... 2 A1
RACT ... 3 B2
Wilderness Society Office ... 4 B4

SIGHTS & ACTIVITIES
Ghost Tours ... (see 6)
Hobart Aquatic Centre ... 5 C2
Island Cycle Tours ... (see 22)
National Trust ... 6 C2
Penintentiary Chapel & Criminal Courts ... (see 6)
St George's Anglican Church ... 7 C4
Tasmanian Seaplanes ... 8 D6

SLEEPING
Allport's Hostel ... 9 A1
Amberley House ... 10 D6
Battery Point Manor ... 11 D4
Blue Hills Motel ... 12 C4
Clydesdale Manor ... 13 C5
Corinda's Cottages ... 14 C1
Edinburgh Gallery ... 15 B4
Grosvenor Court ... 16 B5
Hobart Hostel ... 17 B3
Lodge on Elizabeth ... 18 B2
Mayfair Plaza Motel ... 19 C5
Merre Be's ... 20 B5
Narrara Backpackers ... 21 B3
Pickled Frog ... 22 B3
Quest Trinity House ... 23 B1
St Ives Motel ... 24 C4
Transit Centre Backpackers ... (see 49)
Wellington Lodge ... 25 C1
Woolmers Inn ... 26 B5
Wrest Point Hotel ... 27 D6

EATING
Amulet ... 28 A1
Annapurna ... 29 A1
Casablanca ... 30 B2
Coles Supermarket ... 31 C5
Fish Bar ... 32 B5
Fresco Market ... 33 A1
Kaos Café ... 34 B2
Lickerish ... 35 A1
Metz ... (see 37)
Mitsuno ... 36 B5
Point Revolving Restaurant ... (see 27)
Satis ... 37 C5
Sen's Asian Sensation ... 38 A1
Shipwrights Arms Hotel ... 39 D4
Vanidol's ... 40 A1
Woolworths Supermarket ... 41 B5

DRINKING
Lizbon ... (see 30)
Republic Bar & Café ... 42 A1
Soak@Kaos ... (see 34)

ENTERTAINMENT
State Cinema ... 43 A1
Wrest Point Casino ... (see 27)

SHOPPING
Bathurst St Antique Centre ... 44 B3
Tasmanian Wine Centre ... 45 B4

TRANSPORT
AutoRent-Hertz ... 46 B3
Avis ... 47 B3
Europcar ... 48 B3
Redline Coaches ... 49 B3
Transit Centre ... (see 49)

airport (16km from the city centre, and connected by regular shuttle bus). North of the Domain, the suburbs continue alongside the Derwent River almost all the way to Bridgewater.

There are very few large local industries and the ones that exist are well out of the main city area, generally beside the Derwent a fair way upstream.

Maps

The visitors centre can supply basic maps. The best maps of Hobart are the *Hobart & Surrounds Street Directory* ($18) and the capital maps in the *UBD Tasmania Country Road Atlas* ($30). You can usually purchase these and other good maps at larger newsagents and bookshops.

Disabled travellers can get a copy of the useful *Hobart CBD Mobility Map* at the visitors centre; it's a guide to the relevant facilities and access.

Other Hobart sources for maps follow:

RACT (Map p66; ☎ 6232 6300, 13 27 22; www.ract.com.au; cnr Murray & Patrick Sts)

Service Tasmania (Map p70; ☎ 1300 135 513; www.service.tas.gov.au; 134 Macquarie St; 🕑 Mon-Fri)

Tasmanian Map Centre (Map p70; ☎ 6231 9043; www.map-centre.com.au; 100 Elizabeth St; 🕑 Mon-Sat) Also has a range of maps to guide bushwalking exploits.

Tourist Office (Map p70; ☎ 6230 8233; tasbookings@tasvisinfo.com.au; www.tasmaniasouth.com; cnr Davey & Elizabeth Sts; 🕑 8.30am-5.30pm Mon-Fri, 9am-5pm Sat & Sun & public holidays)

INFORMATION

Bookshops

Fullers (Map p70; ☎ 6224 2488; www.fullersbookshop.com.au; 140 Collins St) Great range of literature and travel guides, plus a good café upstairs.

Hobart Book Shop (Map p70; ☎ 6223 1803; 22 Salamanca Sq) Excellent range of Tasmania-specific titles and works of Tassie writers.

Tasmanian Map Centre (Map p70; ☎ 6231 9043; www.map-centre.com.au; 100 Elizabeth St) Specialises in maps and guidebooks.

Wilderness Society Shop (Map p70; ☎ 6234 9370; Shop 8, The Galleria, 33 Salamanca Pl) Has a range of environmental publications, wildlife posters, videos, maps and calendars.

Emergency

Emergency number ☎ 000 for police, fire and ambulance

Police (Map p70; ☎ 6230 2111; 37-43 Liverpool St)

Internet Access

You can log on at the following places:

Drifters Internet Café (Map p70; ☎ 6224 6286; Shop 9/33 Salamanca Pl; 🕑 10am-6pm Mon-Sat, 11am-6pm Sun; per 10min/hr $1/5) Printing, scanning and faxing available.

Mouse on Mars (Map p70; ☎ 6224 0513; www.mouseonmars.com.au; 27 Salamanca Pl; 🕑 10am-10pm; per hr $5) Has terminals at various outlets throughout the state (see website for list) – with one voucher you have access to them all. Mouse on Mars also offers cheap long-distance telephone calls, a tour-booking desk and good backpacker info.

HOBART IN...

Two Days

Start with a leisurely stroll in one of the city's oldest and prettiest neighbourhoods, **Battery Point** (p71). Morning tea at **Jackman & McRoss** (p92) will sustain you for exploration of the great stores, galleries and cafés of nearby **Salamanca Place** (opposite). Spend the afternoon brushing up on history at the **Tasmanian Museum & Art Gallery** (p73) before a walk around the docks, followed by a fresh seafood dinner.

On day two take in the fantastic views of Hobart from the top of **Mt Wellington** (p76), then come down to earth with dinner and drinks at one of the fine venues along the **North Hobart restaurant strip** (p92).

Four Days

Follow the two-day itinerary, then on the third day it's time to take this eating thing seriously! Venture north to the **Cadbury Factory** (p74), followed by lunch at **Moorilla Estate** (p94); these can be done as part of a river cruise. Walk off any over-indulging at the lovely **Royal Tasmanian Botanical Gardens** (p76). If you're feeling energetic, day four could see you hiring a bike and exploring Hobart's bike paths, or taking an easy day-trip to **Richmond** (p108) or **Mt Field National Park** (p106).

Pelican Loft (Map p70; ☎ 6234 2225; 35A Elizabeth St, upstairs; 8am-6pm Mon-Fri, 10am-4.30pm Sat; per 20 min $1)
Service Tasmania (Map p70; ☎ 1300 135 513; 134 Macquarie St; 8.15am-5.30pm Mon-Fri) Free 30-minute access.
State Library (Map p70; ☎ 6233 7529; 91 Murray St; 9.30am-6pm Mon-Thu, 9.30am-8pm Fri, 10am-2pm Sat) 30-minute sessions are free for Australians; the cost is $5.50 for international visitors. Worth booking – phone or drop in.

Medical Services

Chemist on Collins (Map p70; ☎ 6235 0257; 93 Collins St; 9am-5.30pm Mon-Thu, 9am-6pm Fri, 9.30am-5pm Sat)
City Doctors Surgery & Travel Clinic (Map p70; ☎ 6231 3003; 93 Collins St; 9am-5.30pm Mon-Fri, 10am-2pm Sat) Access through Chemist on Collins.
Dental Emergencies (☎ 6248 1546 for information)
Macquarie Pharmacy (Map p70; ☎ 6223 2339; 180 Macquarie St; 8am-10pm daily)
Royal Hobart Hospital (Map p70; ☎ 6222 8423; 48 Liverpool St; 24hr) Use Argyle St entry for Emergency department.

Money

All major banks have large branches on or near the Elizabeth St Mall, plus branches in many suburbs:
ANZ Bank (Map p70; 40 Elizabeth St)
Commonwealth Bank (Map p70; 81 Elizabeth St)
National Bank (Map p70; cnr Elizabeth & Liverpool Sts)
Westpac Bank (Map p70; 28 Elizabeth St)

Post

The following post offices are open during business hours, Monday to Friday:
Battery Point (Map p70; 61 Hampden Rd)
City (Map p70; cnr Elizabeth & Macquarie Sts)
North Hobart (Map p66; 412 Elizabeth St)
Sandy Bay (Map p66; cnr Sandy Bay Rd & King St)

Tourist Information

Hobart Travel & Information Centre (Map p70; ☎ 6230 8233; tasbookings@tasvisinfo.com.au; www.tasmaniasouth.com; cnr Davey & Elizabeth Sts; 8.30am-5.30pm Mon-Fri, 9am-5pm Sat & Sun & public holidays) is a visitors centre with loads of brochures, maps and information for travellers, plus a booking service covering the entire state (booking fee $3).

You can also get brochures and information from many accommodation and tourist establishments.

Useful Organisations

Parks & Wildlife Service (Map p70; ☎ 1300 135 513; www.parks.tas.gov.au; 134 Macquarie St) Information and factsheets for all national parks are inside the Service Tasmania office; bushwalking advisory staff here from December to March.
Tasmanian Environment Centre (Map p70; ☎ 6234 5566; www.tasmanianenvironmentcentre.org.au; 102 Bathurst St) Community resource centre containing a range of environmental publications in its library.
Wilderness Society (☎ 6224 1550; www.wilderness.org.au) office (Map p66; 130 Davey St) shop (Map p70; Shop 8, The Galleria, 33 Salamanca Pl) Has its head office on the outskirts of the city centre and its shop on Salamanca Pl.
YHA (Map p70; ☎ 6234 9617; yhatas@yhatas.org.au; 1st fl, 28 Criterion St) YHA's Tasmanian office.

SIGHTS

Most of Hobart's main sights are in or near the city centre and waterfront area, largely within walking distance of each other. On the outskirts of town are a few visit-worthy historic houses, plus wineries, a brewery, and the mountain that looms over it all, Mt Wellington.

Salamanca Place

The row of beautiful sandstone warehouses on the harbourfront at Salamanca Pl (Map p70) is a prime example of Australian colonial architecture. Dating back to the whaling days of the 1830s, these warehouses were

SALAMANCA MARKET

Every Saturday morning the open-air **Salamanca Market** (8.30am-3pm Sat) is held along Salamanca Pl, and browsing through the hundreds of stalls is a popular weekend ritual for many locals and a feature of any visit to Hobart. There are the generic goods you'll find at any large market, but there's also a fair proportion of quality items such as organic vegetables, jams and sauces, handmade accessories, creative woodwork and ceramics, and also the odd attention-getting curio or collectable. Many stalls have locally-produced items (perfect souvenirs of your trip). There's a buzzing atmosphere and excellent people-watching, plus good food available from market stalls or nearby cafés, and entertainment provided by buskers and other street performers. Don't miss it!

the centre of Hobart Town's trade and commerce. Only 35 years ago, many of these buildings were in a derelict state and under threat of demolition. Today, they have been tastefully developed to house restaurants, cafés, nightspots, and shops selling everything from vegetables to antiques. Visitors can enjoy the obvious tourist appeal of eating, drinking and browsing in such an attractive area, or go exploring behind the scenes to find the vibrant and creative arts community based here.

The **Salamanca Arts Centre** (SAC; ☎ 6234 8414; www.salarts.org.au; Salamanca Pl) is a non-profit-making arts centre to the east of Salamanca Sq, housed in seven sandstone warehouses.

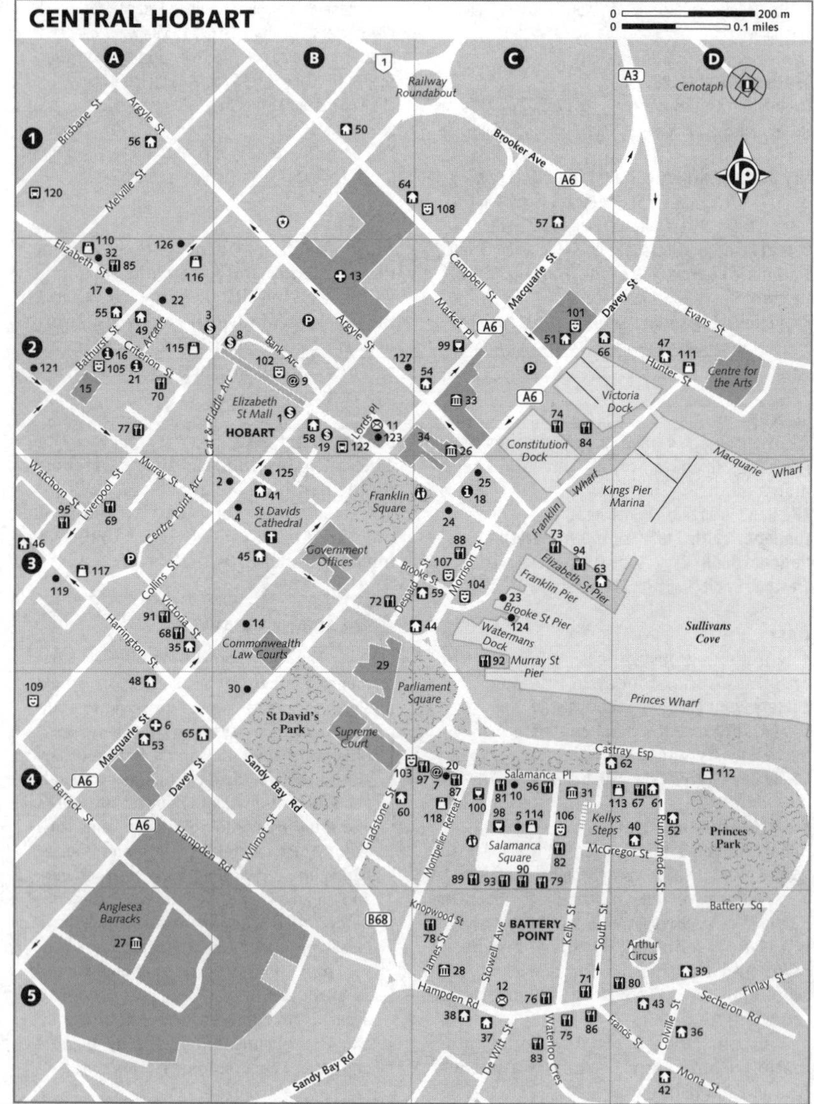

It is home to more than 75 arts-related organisations and individuals, including retail outlets, galleries, artists' studios, performing arts venues (including the Peacock Theatre) and public spaces. The website is a good source of information on what you might find here, and what events are going on.

The eastern side of Salamanca Pl has been the subject of some major developments in recent years, with four old silos being converted into slightly incongruous luxury apartment towers and a glut of upmarket accommodation being set up behind them.

The large building in the southwest corner of Salamanca Sq housed the Antarctic Adventure, which closed in late 2003; at the time of research the building had been bought by a developer but there was still speculation about what it would become (suggestions included a restaurant, shop or cinema).

To reach Battery Point from Salamanca Pl you can climb up **Kelly's Steps**, which are wedged between two warehouses about halfway along the main block of buildings.

Battery Point

Behind Princes Wharf and Salamanca Pl is the historic core of Hobart, the old port area known as Battery Point (Map p70). Its name comes from the gun battery that

INFORMATION

- ANZ Bank & ATM ... **1** B2
- Chemist on Collins ... **2** B3
- City Doctors Surgery & Travel Clinic ... (see 2)
- Commonwealth Bank & ATM ... **3** A2
- Drifters Internet Café ... (see 20)
- Fullers Bookshop ... **4** B3
- Hobart Book Shop ... **5** C4
- Macquarie Pharmacy ... **6** A4
- Mouse on Mars ... **7** C4
- National Bank & ATM ... **8** B2
- Parks & Wildlife Service Information ... (see 14)
- Pelican Loft ... **9** B2
- Port Arthur Region Travel Shop ... **10** C4
- Post Office ... **11** B2
- Post Office ... **12** C5
- Royal Hobart Hospital ... **13** B2
- Service Tasmania ... **14** B3
- State Library ... **15** A2
- Tasmanian Environment Centre ... **16** A2
- Tasmanian Map Centre ... **17** A2
- Visitors Centre ... **18** C3
- Westpac Bank & ATM ... **19** B2
- Wilderness Society Shop ... **20** C4
- YHA Tasmanian Office ... **21** A2

SIGHTS & ACTIVITIES

- Allport Library & Museum of Fine Arts ... (see 15)
- Bike Hire Tasmania (Appleby's Cycles) ... **22** A2
- Booking Offices for Boat Cruise Companies ... **23** C3
- Carnegie Gallery ... (see 26)
- City Council Offices (Waterways Tours) ... **24** C3
- Lark Distillery ... **25** C3
- Maritime Museum of Tasmania ... **26** C2
- Military Museum of Tasmania ... **27** A5
- Narryna Heritage Museum ... **28** C5
- Parliament House ... **29** B3
- Royal Tennis Court ... **30** B4
- Salamanca Arts Centre ... **31** C4
- Skigia & Surf ... **32** A2
- Tasmanian Museum & Art Gallery ... **33** C2
- Town Hall ... **34** C2

SLEEPING

- Astor Private Hotel ... **35** A3
- Avon Court Holiday Apartments ... **36** D5
- Barton Cottage ... **37** C5
- Battery Point B&B ... **38** C5
- Battery Point Boutique Accommodation ... **39** D5
- Battery Point Guest House ... **40** D4
- Central City Backpackers ... **41** B3
- Colville Cottage ... **42** D5
- Coopers Cottage ... **43** D5
- Customs House Hotel ... **44** C3
- Hadleys Hotel ... **45** B3
- Harrington's 102 ... **46** A3
- Henry Jones Art Hotel ... **47** D2
- Hobart Macquarie Motor Inn ... **48** A4
- Hobart Mid City Hotel ... **49** A2
- Hollydene Lodge ... **50** B1
- Hotel Grand Chancellor ... **51** C2
- Lenna of Hobart ... **52** D4
- Macquarie Manor ... **53** A4
- Montgomery's Private Hotel & YHA Backpackers ... **54** C2
- New Sydney Hotel ... **55** A2
- Ocean Child Hotel ... **56** A1
- Old Woolstore ... **57** C1
- Quest Savoy ... **58** B2
- Quest Waterfront ... **59** C3
- Salamanca Inn ... **60** B4
- Salamanca Terraces ... **61** D4
- Somerset on Salamanca ... **62** D4
- Somerset on the Pier ... **63** C3
- Theatre Royal Hotel ... **64** B1
- Welcome Stranger Hotel ... **65** A4
- Zero Davey ... **66** C2

EATING

- Atrium Lounge ... (see 51)
- Ball & Chain Grill ... **67** D4
- Blue Skies ... (see 92)
- Choux Shop ... **68** A3
- City Supermarket ... **69** A3
- Cove ... (see 51)
- Criterion St Café ... **70** A2
- Da Angelo Ristorante ... **71** C5
- Elbow Room ... **72** B3
- Fish Frenzy ... **73** C3
- Floating Takeaway Seafood Stalls ... **74** C2
- Francisco's on Hampden ... **75** C5
- Fresh Fruit Market ... (see 100)
- Jackman & McRoss ... **76** C5
- Jam Packed ... (see 47)
- Kafe Kara ... **77** A2
- Kelley's Seafood Restaurant ... **78** C5
- Machine Laundry Café ... **79** C4
- Magic Curries ... **80** D5
- Maldini ... **81** C4
- Meehan's Restaurant ... (see 51)
- Mezethes ... **82** C4
- Mummy's ... **83** C5
- Mures ... **84** C2
- Nourish ... **85** A2
- Orizuru Sushi Bar ... (see 84)
- Restaurant Gondwana ... **86** C5
- Retro Café ... **87** C4
- Rockerfellers ... **88** C3
- Salamanca Bakehouse ... **89** C4
- Say Cheese ... **90** C4
- Sirens ... **91** A3
- Sisco's ... **92** C3
- Steam Packet Restaurant ... (see 47)
- Sticky Fingers ... (see 92)
- Sugo ... **93** C4
- T-42° ... **94** C3
- Vanny's ... **95** A3
- Vietnamese Kitchen ... **96** C4
- Zum Café ... **97** C4

DRINKING

- Bar Celona ... **98** C4
- Hope & Anchor Tavern ... **99** C2
- IXL Long Bar at Henry Jones ... (see 47)
- Knopwood's Retreat ... **100** C4

ENTERTAINMENT

- Federation Concert Hall ... **101** C2
- Halo ... **102** B2
- Irish Murphy's ... **103** B4
- Isobar ... **104** C3
- Peacock Theatre ... (see 31)
- Playhouse Theatre ... **105** A2
- Round Midnight ... (see 100)
- Salamanca Arts Centre Courtyard ... **106** C4
- Syrup ... (see 100)
- Telegraph Hotel ... **107** C3
- Theatre Royal ... **108** C1
- Village Cinemas ... **109** A4

SHOPPING

- Antiques Market ... **110** A2
- Art Mob Gallery ... **111** D2
- Despard Gallery ... **112** D4
- Handmark Gallery ... **113** D4
- Kathmandu ... **114** C4
- Paddy Pallin ... **115** A2
- Recycled Recreation ... **116** A2
- Spot On Fishing Tackle ... **117** A3
- Wursthaus ... **118** C4

TRANSPORT

- Budget ... **119** A3
- Captain Fell's Historic Ferries ... (see 23)
- Hobart Bus Terminal ... **120** A1
- Lo-Cost Auto Rent ... **121** A2
- Metro City Bus Station ... **122** B2
- Metro Office ... **123** B2
- Port Arthur Cruises ... **124** C3
- Qantas ... **125** B3
- Rent-a-Bug ... (see 121)
- Selective Car Rentals ... **126** A2
- TassieLink Coaches ... (see 120)
- Thrifty ... **127** B2

stood on the promontory by the guardhouse. Built in 1818, the guardhouse is now the district's oldest building. The guns were never used in battle and the only damage they inflicted was on nearby windowpanes when fired during practice.

During colonial times, this area was a colourful maritime village, home to master mariners, shipwrights, sailors, fishers, coopers and merchants. The houses reflect the occupants' varying lifestyles, ranging from tiny one- and two-room houses, such as those around Arthur Circus, to mansions. While most houses are still occupied by locals, many are now guesthouses where you can stay and experience the area's unique village atmosphere. Battery Point's pubs, churches, conjoined houses and narrow winding streets have all been lovingly preserved and are a delight to wander around, especially when you get glimpses of the harbour between the buildings. Highlights of the area include **Arthur Circus**, a circle of quaint little cottages built around a village green, and **St George's Anglican Church** (Map p66; Cromwell St). To help with your exploration of the area, purchase the *Battery Point and Sullivan's Cove Trail of Discovery* pamphlet ($2) from the visitors centre.

The **Anglesea Barracks** were built in Battery Point in 1811. Still used by the army, this is the oldest military establishment in Australia. They house the volunteer-staffed **Military Museum of Tasmania** (Map p70; ☎ 6237 7160; Davey St; adult/child $5/1; 🕑 9am-1pm Tue, other times by appointment). Free 45-minute guided tours of the restored buildings and grounds leave from the front gates at 11am every Tuesday.

The Waterfront

Hobart's busy waterfront area (Map p70), centred on **Franklin Wharf**, is a great place for a stroll. At **Constitution Dock** are several floating takeaway seafood stalls (p90) – it's an obligatory holiday activity to sit in the sun munching fresh fish and chips while watching the busy harbour (the docks also have some fine restaurants if you prefer something more formal).

At the finish of the annual Sydney to Hobart Yacht Race around New Year, and during the Royal Hobart Regatta in February, Constitution Dock is swamped by boat crews and spectators.

Hunter St has a row of fine Georgian warehouses (including the old IXL jam factory) that have recently been restored and now house the super-swish **Henry Jones Art Hotel**, Hobart's new hotspot, plus affiliated restaurants and a couple of art galleries. While this development has remained true to the heritage of the area and retains much of its original façade, not all of the hotel's neighbours can make the same claim. It's no secret that the design of the large, modern hotel and apartment complex at the corner of Davey and Hunter Sts has few admirers; many Hobartians consider it totally inappropriate for the historic area (and you'd be forgiven for feeling the same way about the hotel and concert hall opposite, too).

The whole Hobart wharf area is actually reclaimed land. When the town was first settled, Davey St ran along the edge of the sea and the Hunter St area was an island used to safely store food and other goods. Subsequent projects filled in the shallow waters and provided land upon which the warehouses of Hunter St and Salamanca Pl were constructed. On Hunter St itself, there are markers indicating the position of the original causeway, which was built in 1820 to link Hunter Island with Sullivans Cove.

Historic Buildings

One of the things that makes Hobart exceptional among Australian cities is its wealth of remarkably well-preserved old buildings. There are more than 90 buildings classified by the National Trust and 60 of these, featuring some of Hobart's best Georgian architecture, are on Macquarie and Davey Sts. More information can be obtained from the local office of the **National Trust** (Map p66; ☎ 6223 5200; www.tased.edu.au/tasonline/nattrust/; cnr Brisbane & Campbell Sts; 🕑 9am-1pm Mon-Fri).

The court rooms, cells, tunnels and gallows of the **Penitentiary Chapel & Criminal Courts** (Map p66; ☎ 6231 0911; cnr Brisbane & Campbell Sts; adult/child/family tours $8/6/16; tours 🕑 10am, 11.30am, 1pm, 2.30pm) can be explored via the excellent National Trust-run tours. One-hour **ghost tours** (☎ 0417 361 392; adult/child $8.80/5.50; 🕑 after sunset – call for times) are also held here most nights; they're popular, so bookings are essential.

Close to the city centre is **Parliament House** (Map p70; Murray St), built in 1835 and originally used as a customs house; there is still a tunnel between it and the Customs House Hotel opposite, though the reason for the tunnel is unclear. Hobart's prestigious **Theatre Royal** (Map p70; 29 Campbell St) was designed by the architect of the Cascade brewery. Built in 1837 and originally called the Victoria Theatre, it's the oldest theatre in Australia.

The **royal tennis court** (Map p70; ☎ 6231 1781; 45 Davey St; 9am-4pm Mon-Sat) dates from 1875 and is one of only three such courts in the southern hemisphere. Royal (or 'real') tennis is an ancient form of the highly-strung game, played in a four-walled indoor court. Visitors are welcome, but there's no guarantee a game will be in progress.

Runnymede (Map p75; ☎ 6278 1269; 61 Bay Rd, New Town; adult/child/family $7.70/5.50/15.40; 10am-4.30pm Mon-Fri, noon-4.30pm Sat & Sun) is a gracious 1840 residence 5km north of the city centre, built for Robert Pitcairn, the first lawyer to qualify in Tasmania, and named by a later owner, Captain Charles Bayley, after his favourite ship. It's now managed by the National Trust. To get there take bus No 15 or 20.

There are free scheduled 20-minute tours behind the scenes of Hobart's **Town Hall** (Map p70; ☎ 6238 2711; Macquarie St; tours 2.45pm Tue, 10.45am Thu), built in the 1860s. The tours depart from the town hall's foyer; it's not essential to book – just turn up five minutes before the scheduled start time.

Museums & Galleries

The rewarding **Tasmanian Museum & Art Gallery** (Map p70; ☎ 6211 4177; www.tmag.tas.gov.au; 40 Macquarie St; admission free; 10am-5pm) complex is situated in the precinct where Hobart Town was established in 1804 and incorporates the city's oldest building, the 1808 Commissariat Store. The museum section features a display on the Tasmanian Aborigines and relics from the state's colonial heritage, while the gallery has a good collection of Tasmanian colonial art. It's worth taking a free 50-minute guided tour of the museum; these depart from the foyer at 2.30pm Wednesday to Sunday.

The **Maritime Museum of Tasmania** (Map p70; ☎ 6234 1427; www.maritimetas.org; 16 Argyle St; adult/child/family $6/4/16; 10am-5pm) is set up in the historic Carnegie Building, built by a philanthropic Scottish-American millionaire in the early 1900s to serve as Tasmania's first public library. The building is now home to an interesting, salt-encrusted collection of photos, paintings, models and relics that highlight Tasmania's strong shipping past. It can also organise a two-hour guided walk through the museum and docks area for interested parties ($12 per person; enquiries and bookings through the museum). Upstairs from the museum is the city-council-run **Carnegie Gallery** (admission free; 10am-5pm), which exhibits mainly contemporary Tasmanian art, craft, design and photography.

The **Allport Library & Museum of Fine Arts** (Map p70; ☎ 6233 7484; 91 Murray St; admission free; 9.30am-5pm Mon-Fri) is inside the State Library. It has a collection of rare books on Australasia and the Pacific region, as well as colonial paintings, antiques, and a collection of artworks that it displays several times a year.

Narryna Heritage Museum (Map p70; ☎ 6234 2791; 103 Hampden Rd; adult/child $6/3; 10.30am-5pm Tue-Fri, 2-5pm Sat & Sun, closed Jul) is a fine Georgian sandstone mansion built in 1836, set amid beautiful grounds in Battery Point and containing a colonial treasure-trove of domestic artefacts.

The most unexpected attraction at Moorilla Estate, a restaurant and vineyard 12km north of the town centre, is the world-class **Moorilla Museum of Antiquities** (Map p75; ☎ 6277 9999; www.moorilla.com.au; 655 Main Rd, Berriedale; admission free; 10am-4pm). The modernistic lines of the museum contrast with a wealth of antiquities brought together from private collections; on display are mosaics dating from the Roman Empire, sculptures and tribal art from Africa, gold jewellery and pre-Columbian figures from Central America, a collection of coins dating from ancient Greek and Roman civilisations, and an excellent Egyptian section, featuring a mummy case dating from around 600 BC. Catch bus No X1 from stop F on Elizabeth St.

Train rides are available on the first and third Sundays of each month at the **Tasmanian Transport Museum** (Map p75; ☎ 6272 7721; www.railtasmania.com/ttms; Anfield St, Glenorchy; adult/child $5/2.50; 1-4.30pm Sat & Sun). When the trains run, admission increases to $6/3 per adult/child. Take bus No X1 from stop F on Elizabeth St: the museum is a short walk from Glenorchy bus station.

For more railway amusement, head north to **Alpenrail** (Map p75; ☎ 6249 3748; www.alpenrail.com.au; 82 Abbotsfield Rd, Claremont; adult/family $12/26;

(⌚ 9.30am-4.30pm) to see its large (200 sq m), remarkably detailed, miniature recreation of the train-littered Swiss Alps. Take bus No 42 from stop E on Elizabeth St to the Abbotsfield stop.

Lady Franklin Gallery (Map p75; ☎ 6228 0076; Lenah Valley Rd; admission free; ⌚ 1.30-5pm Sat & Sun), in a colonnaded 1842 sandstone building called Ancanthe (Greek for 'Vale of Flowers'), displays work by Tasmanian artists. Take bus No 6, 7, 8, 9 or 10 to the Lenah Valley terminus from stop G on Elizabeth St.

The **Moonah Arts Centre** (Map p75; ☎ 6214 7633; 65 Hopkins St, Moonah; free admission to exhibitions; ⌚ 12.30-5pm Mon-Fri, 10am-2pm Sat) is a community arts centre involved in staging everything from indigenous arts exhibitions and concerts to workshops and special events. All buses departing stop E on Elizabeth St go to Moonah.

Fans of Boonie and Ricky Ponting might want to head out to Bellerive, east over the Derwent, for the **Tasmanian Cricket Museum** (Map p75; ☎ 6211 4000; cnr Church & Derwent Sts; adult/child $6/3; ⌚ 1-3pm major match days, plus 10am-3pm Tue-Thu, 10am-noon Fri) at the Bellerive Oval. You can also take a **tour** (adult/child $10/6, incl entry to the museum; ⌚ 10am Tue, not match days) of the oval itself, including the players' rooms. Bus Nos 285 and 287 service Bellerive Oval.

Tastes of Hobart

CADBURY FACTORY

This popular attraction is a must-see for sweet-tooths. The **Cadbury Factory** (Map p75; ☎ 6249 0333, 1800 627 367; www.cadbury.com.au; Cadbury Rd, Claremont; tours adult/child/family $12.50/6.50/31.50; bookings essential) offers guided tours Monday to Friday except public holidays, every half-hour from about 8am to 2.30pm (subject to demand). You are required to be wearing fully enclosed footwear. Participants get to enjoy samples along the way, and can buy low-priced products at the completion of the tour. The factory is some 15km north of the city centre; many companies offer day trips and river cruises that incorporate this tour (see p81), but you can also book directly with Cadbury and make your own way there. Take bus No 37, 38 or 39 to Claremont from stop E on Elizabeth St. See below for some historical background.

CASCADE BREWERY

Cascade (Map p75; ☎ 6224 1117; 140 Cascade Rd; tours adult/child/family $16/7/38; tour times ⌚ 9.30am, 10am, 1pm & 1.30pm Mon-Fri except public holidays; bookings essential), Australia's oldest brewery, began its frothy production in 1832 and continues to produce fine beer and soft drinks for nationwide consumption. It's an imposing, photogenic sight from the approach road, and its neighbouring gardens are good for a wander. Brewery tours last 1½ hours, involve plenty of stair climbing, and include free samples at the end. Visitors should wear flat, enclosed shoes and long trousers (no shorts or skirts); note that the tours are not suitable for children under five years.

SWEET DREAMS

Anyone who thinks making chocolate is just about sugary confection and not spiritual conviction has obviously never heard of George Cadbury. Born in 1839 the son of John Cadbury, founder of the all-things-sweet Cadbury empire, George became well versed in the Quaker ideology practised by his family. Quakers belong to the nonconformist Religious Society of Friends, which was established in the 17th century and preaches notions of equality and social change based on morality overriding individual differences.

George applied these reformist beliefs to Bournville, his factory near Birmingham in England, creating a 'garden city', with bucolic surrounds, recreational facilities and nice, affordable housing for workers. It was a place designed to reject the health - and spirit-sapping industrialisation of the time, while ensuring the highest productivity by having 'happier' workers and strict moral codes such as the segregation of males and females. The Cadbury Factory in Hobart was built in 1922 along the same lines, being outfitted as a mini-village that included sports facilities, with the Claremont site chosen because it was outside the city.

The Cadbury family's direct involvement in what has become a market-hungry multinational ended in the 1940s, but Quaker involvement in Tasmanian society continues through The Friends' School, a well-respected educational facility in North Hobart that began its teachings in 1887.

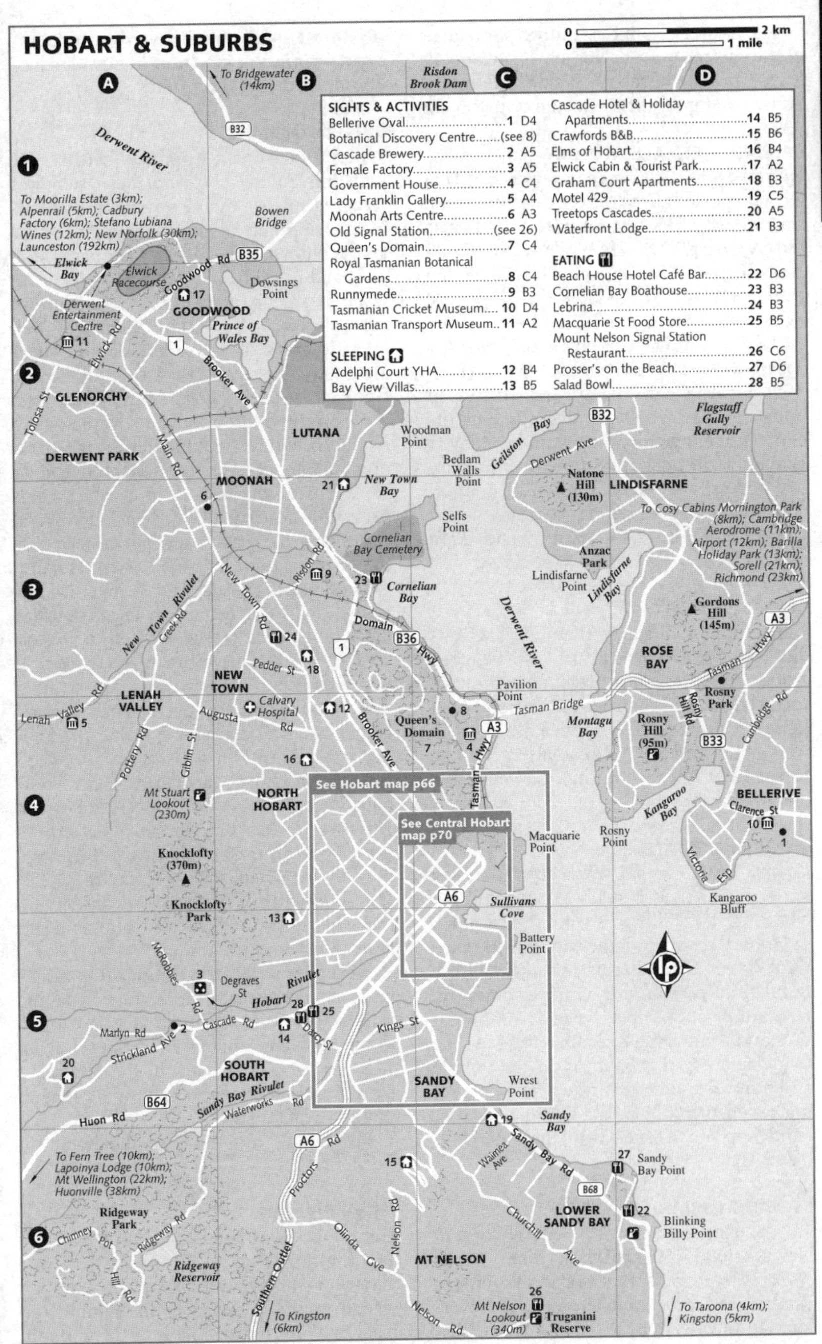

HOBART & SUBURBS
0 2 km
0 1 mile
A
B
C
D
1
2
3
4
5
6
SIGHTS & ACTIVITIES
Bellerive Oval 1 D4
Botanical Discovery Centre (see 8)
Cascade Brewery 2 A5
Female Factory 3 A5
Government House 4 C4
Lady Franklin Gallery 5 A4
Moonah Arts Centre 6 A3
Old Signal Station (see 26)
Queen's Domain 7 C4
Royal Tasmanian Botanical Gardens 8 C4
Runnymede 9 B3
Tasmanian Cricket Museum 10 D4
Tasmanian Transport Museum 11 A2
SLEEPING
Adelphi Court YHA 12 B4
Bay View Villas 13 B5
Cascade Hotel & Holiday Apartments 14 B5
Crawfords B&B 15 B6
Elms of Hobart 16 B4
Elwick Cabin & Tourist Park 17 A2
Graham Court Apartments 18 B3
Motel 429 19 C5
Treetops Cascades 20 A5
Waterfront Lodge 21 B3
EATING
Beach House Hotel Café Bar 22 D6
Cornelian Bay Boathouse 23 B3
Lebrina 24 B3
Macquarie St Food Store 25 B5
Mount Nelson Signal Station Restaurant 26 C6
Prosser's on the Beach 27 D6
Salad Bowl 28 B5
To Bridgewater (14km)
Risdon Brook Dam
B32
Derwent River
To Moorilla Estate (3km); Alpenrail (5km); Cadbury Factory (6km); Stefano Lubiana Wines (12km); New Norfolk (30km); Launceston (192km)
Bowen Bridge
Elwick Bay
Elwick Racecourse
Goodwood Rd
B35
Dowsings Point
Derwent Entertainment Centre
GOODWOOD
Prince of Wales Bay
Elwick Rd
Brooker Ave
GLENORCHY
Tolosa St
LUTANA
Main Rd
DERWENT PARK
MOONAH
Woodman Point
Bedlam Walls Point
Geilston Bay
Flagstaff Gully Reservoir
Derwent Ave
Natone Hill (130m)
LINDISFARNE
New Town Bay
Selfs Point
To Cosy Cabins Mornington Park (8km); Cambridge Aerodrome (11km); Airport (12km); Barilla Holiday Park (13km); Sorell (21km); Richmond (23km)
Cornelian Bay Cemetery
Anzac Park
Risdon Rd
Cornelian Bay
Lindisfarne Point
Lindisfarne Bay
Gordons Hill (145m)
A3
New Town Rivulet
Creek Rd
New Town Rd
Domain Hwy
B36
Derwent River
ROSE BAY
Tasman Hwy
Pedder St
NEW TOWN
Pavilion Point
Rosny Park
LENAH VALLEY
Lenah Valley Rd
Calvary Hospital
Augusta Rd
Tasman Bridge
Montagu Bay
Rosny Hill Rd
Rosny Hill (95m)
Cambridge Rd
Queen's Domain
B33
Pottery Rd
Giblin St
Tasman Hwy
BELLERIVE
Clarence St
Kangaroo Bay
Mt Stuart Lookout (230m)
NORTH HOBART
See Hobart map p66
See Central Hobart map p70
Macquarie Point
Rosny Point
Victoria Esp
Knocklofty (370m)
A6
Sullivans Cove
Kangaroo Bluff
Knocklofty Park
Battery Point
McRobbies Rd
Degraves St
Hobart Rivulet
Kings St
Marlyn Rd
Cascade Rd
Davey St
Strickland Ave
SOUTH HOBART
SANDY BAY
Wrest Point
B64
Sandy Bay Rivulet
Waterworks Rd
Huon Rd
Sandy Bay
A6
Sandy Bay Rd
Waimea Ave
To Fern Tree (10km); Lapoinya Lodge (10km); Mt Wellington (22km); Huonville (38km)
Proctors Rd
Sandy Bay Point
B68
Ridgeway Park
Ridgeway Rd
Nelson Rd
Churchill Ave
LOWER SANDY BAY
Blinking Billy Point
Chimney Pot Hill Rd
Olinda Gve
Ridgeway Reservoir
MT NELSON
Southern Outlet
Mt Nelson Lookout (340m)
Truganini Reserve
To Kingston (6km)
Nelson Rd
To Taroona (4km); Kingston (5km)

The brewery is on the southwestern edge of the city centre. Bus Nos 43, 44, 46 and 49 leave from the Elizabeth St side of Franklin Square and go right by it; alight at stop 18.

CASCADES FEMALE FACTORY

Not far from the Cascade brewery (p74), a few signposted turns off Cascade Rd, is the site of Australia's first purpose-built **Female Factory** (Map p75; ☎ 6223 1559; www.femalefactory.com.au; Degraves St), or prison, which operated from 1828 to 1877. Major archaeological work is now being conducted here, funded by the on-site **fudge factory** (shop ⏰ 9am-4pm Mon-Fri May-Nov, 9am-5pm Mon-Fri Dec-Apr).

You can take a 1¼-hour guided tour of both the historic site's diggings and the confectionery factory at 9.30am Monday to Friday (additional 2pm tour from December to April); the cost is $9/4.50/25 adult/child/family; bookings are essential.

Take bus Nos 43, 44, 46 or 49 and alight at stop 16.

LARK DISTILLERY

Continuing the boozy theme is the **Lark Distillery** (Map p70; ☎ 6231 9088; www.larkdistillery.com.au; 14 Davey St; ⏰ from 10am), near the visitors centre, which produces various fruit liqueurs (free tastings) and a single malt whisky (tasting $4); you can also get a bite to eat here. Of an evening, the venue becomes a lounge bar.

MOORILLA ESTATE

Moorilla Estate (Map p75; ☎ 6277 9900; www.moorilla.com.au; 655 Main Rd, Berriedale; ⏰ 10am-5pm) can be found in the suburbs some 12km north of Hobart's centre, on the banks of the Derwent River. It's a fascinating place with a number of reasons for visiting: vineyard, restaurant (p94), super-swish accommodation and a stunning museum (p87). At the estate's new tasting rooms you can sample and purchase some first-rate wines (including excellent pinot noir). Take bus No X1 from Stop F, or a cruise from the waterfront (see p81).

STEFANO LUBIANA WINES

About 20km northwest of Hobart (en route to New Norfolk) is **Stefano Lubiana Wines** (☎ 6263 7457; www.slw.com.au; 60 Rowbottoms Rd, Granton; ⏰ 11am-3pm Sun-Thu), a lovely vineyard overlooking the Derwent River. It's one of Tassie's most successful vineyards, producing award-winning pinot noir alongside chardonnay and sparkling wines.

Queen's Domain

When Hobart was originally settled, the high hill on the city's northern side was reserved for use by the governor, preventing development of any housing. Today the area is known as the Queen's Domain (Map p75) and is public parkland.

This large park contains reserves and grounds for cricket and athletics, as well as wide areas of native grasslands. There are good views across the river and the city from many parts of the Domain; the best are from the hilltop lookouts at the park's northern end. If walking across the park, don't try to descend the northern end to New Town, because deep road-cuttings prevent pedestrian access. There are several pedestrian overpasses on the western side that provide good access to North Hobart.

On the eastern side, near Tasman Bridge, is the small but beguiling **Royal Tasmanian Botanical Gardens** (admission free; ⏰ 8am-6.30pm Oct-Mar, 8am-5.30pm Apr & Sep, 8am-5pm May-Aug). It was established in 1818 and features more than 6000 exotic and native plant species, an outstanding conservatory and the Sub-Antarctic Plant House, with unique specimens from chilly Macquarie Island. Some paths are suitable for wheelchair-users. After wandering through the 14 hectares of flora, you can explore their world in more detail in the **Botanical Discovery Centre** (☎ 6234 6299; www.rtbg.tas.gov.au; admission free, donations welcome; ⏰ 9am-5pm), which also houses a gift shop, kiosk and restaurant.

Next door to the Botanical gardens is **Government House**, the residence of the state's governor. Although it is not open to the public and not visible from the road, you can get a good view of the building's turrets and towers from high up on the hill in Queen's Domain.

Bus No 17 runs daily to the Botanical Gardens.

Mt Wellington

Hobart is dominated by 1270m-high Mt Wellington (Map p77), which has fine views and many walking tracks. You can walk from the city centre to the summit and back in a day, but you need to be pretty fit.

The top is sometimes under cloud and in winter it often has a light cover of snow.

The mountain's summit is about 22km out of town. If you don't have your own set of wheels, you can catch bus No 48 or 49 to Fern Tree, a small suburb halfway up the mountain, with barbecues, picnic sites and forest walks on the mountain's lower slopes. From Fern Tree you can walk to the summit and back in about five to six hours via Fern Glade Track, Radfords Track, then the very steep Zig Zag Track. The Organ Pipes walk from the Chalet (en route to the summit) is an impressive flat walk below these outstanding cliffs. Buy a copy of the *Mt Wellington Walks* map ($4.40) for details of all tracks.

Many tour companies include Mt Wellington in their bus-tour itineraries (see p81); another option is the **Mt Wellington Shuttle Bus Service** (☎ 0417 341 804; tour per person $25), which does pick-ups from hotels or the visitors centre three times daily and drives to the summit and back, stopping en route at lookouts and for 40 minutes on the mountain top; bookings are required. The more adventurous should descend the mountain by bike: **Island Cycle Tours** (Map p66; ☎ 1300 880 334, 0418 234 181; www.islandcycletours.com; 281 Liverpool St), with its office inside the Pickled Frog backpackers, offers a van ride to the summit, followed by more than 20km of downhill riding (mostly on sealed roads, but with off-road options) back to sea level.

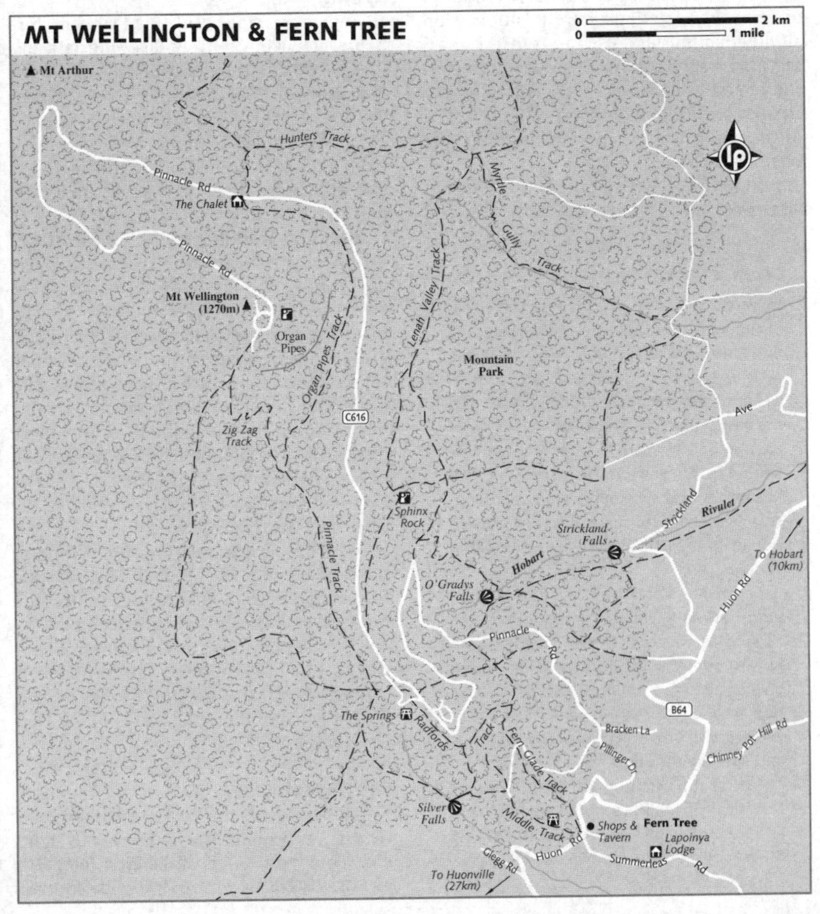

There are two trips a day (weather and minimum numbers permitting, at 9.30am and 1.30pm), plus the option of a night descent from December to March (7.30pm Friday to Sunday); the cost is $65 per adult, $55 for kids (with a minimum height restriction of 150cm) and includes hotel pick-up. There is also the option of combining a bike descent with kayaking trip – this five-hour 'pedal 'n' paddle' outing costs $110/95 for each adult/child, including a meal.

Mt Nelson

If Mt Wellington is under a cloud, the **Old Signal Station** atop Mt Nelson (Map p75), which is much lower, will still provide excellent views over the city. When Port Arthur was operating as a penal site, a series of semaphore stations were positioned on all the high hills and used to transmit messages across the colony. The one on Mt Nelson – first established in 1811, though the current building dates from 1910 – served as the major link between Hobart and the rest of the colony.

Beside the signal station is a restaurant (see p94), but there are also barbecues and picnic tables for visitors to utilise. The lookout can be reached by a steep, winding road from Sandy Bay, or via the turn off at the Southern Outlet (the main road from Hobart to Kingston) on top of the hill. You can also walk to it via the Truganini Track (90 minutes return) which starts at Cartwright Reserve, beside the Channel Hwy between Sandy Bay and Taroona. From the Macquarie St side of Franklin Square, catch bus No 57 or 58 to the lookout.

WHAT'S FREE

Hobart is so walker-friendly that just strolling around the docks, Salamanca precinct and Battery Point is probably the best free activity possible. The natural and cultural treats of the Botanical Gardens (p76) and the Tasmanian Museum & Art Gallery (p73) are also free. No park fees apply to Mt Wellington (p76), which is a fantastic place for bushwalks, and swimming is great at Kingston Beach or Blackmans Bay, just outside Hobart (see p101), if the weather is warm enough.

Salamanca Market (p69), held every Saturday morning along Salamanca Pl, is free as long as you can restrain yourself from buying something! Produce-sellers often give small, free samples; there are usually buskers about to keep you entertained; and you can also browse in the nearby galleries and speciality shops.

One of the best free activities in Hobart is listening to the live music staged every Friday evening in Salamanca Courtyard, just off Wooby's Lane – see p95 for details.

ACTIVITIES

See also p44 for information on activities such as sailing, skiing, scuba diving and rock climbing in the areas around Hobart.

Cycling

If you fancy a ride beside the Derwent, hire a bicycle from central **Bike Hire Tasmania** (Map p70; ☎ 6234 4166, 0400 256 588; www.bikehiretasmania.com.au; 109 Elizabeth St; 🕑 9am-6pm Mon-Fri, 9am-4pm Sat). They offer city or touring bikes by the hour, day or week, with city bikes from $7/20 per hour/day and touring bikes available from $252 per week, including rear panniers.

Island Cycle Tours (Map p66; ☎ 1300 880 334, 6234 4951; www.islandcycletours.com; 281 Liverpool St), operating out of the Pickled Frog backpackers, as well as hiring out bikes and gear (touring bikes from $30/140 a day/week) organises a great range of guided trips, some designed for outdoorsy types on a budget, others with a gourmet-food focus and upmarket accommodation for those looking for a little more luxury. Try the popular three-hour descent of Mt Wellington (p77), a one-day cycle to Mt Field ($120), or five days exploring the east coast (from $690).

A useful navigational tool for cycling in the capital is the *Hobart Bike Map* (around $4), available from the visitors centre and most bike shops. It contains details of the city's cycle paths and road cycling routes – there's a dedicated cycle path from Hobart through the northern suburbs to Berriedale, part of which follows the banks of the Derwent River.

Sea Kayaking

Kayaking around the docks in Hobart, particularly at twilight, is a lovely way to sightsee. Your best bet is **Island Cycle Tours** (Map p66; ☎ 1300 880 334, 6234 4951; www.islandcycletours

.com; 281 Liverpool St), which offers half-day 'pedal 'n' paddle' combo trips for $110/95 per adult/child (price includes a meal). Tours run daily from December to March (and at other times according to demand; minimum numbers apply) and involve a descent of Mt Wellington on two wheels, and a gentle two-hour paddle around the waterfront. You can do just the two-hour paddle trip for $50, including snack.

Swimming

There are pleasant beaches near Hobart, such as Bellerive and Sandy Bay, but these tend to receive some urban pollution, so it's better to head further south towards Kingston and Blackmans Bay, or east to Seven Mile Beach, for safe swimming. The best spots for surfing are Clifton Beach and the surf beach en route to South Arm.

The **Hobart Aquatic Centre** (Map p66; ☎ 6222 6999; Davis Ave; 🕓 6am-9pm Mon-Fri, 8am-6pm Sat & Sun) is a good place on a rainy day, with leisure pools and 'formal pools' (dressed in a tux?) for lap swimming etc. There's a spa, sauna and steamroom, aquaerobics, and aerobics and pump classes for land-lubbers. Entry for a swim is $4.85/3.70 per adult/child.

WALKING TOUR

Distance: approx 3km
Duration: 2½ to three hours

This walk starts at **Salamanca Place**, the main tourist precinct of Hobart. While waterside activity has moved away from this once-bustling area, restoration work has saved and preserved one of Hobart's best vistas. The sandstone Georgian warehouses were built from about 1835, replacing earlier wooden structures in what was called New Wharf. At street level, the majority of the warehouses are now speciality and craft shops, restaurants, cafés and bars.

Meandering east, a gap in the warehouses leads to **Kelly's Steps (1)**, built in 1839, which link the waterfront area with residential **Battery Point** (**2**; p71). These stone stairs were built on private land owned by Captain James Kelly, a larger-than-life character in early Hobart Town. You can take the steps to Kelly St, lined with small cottages from

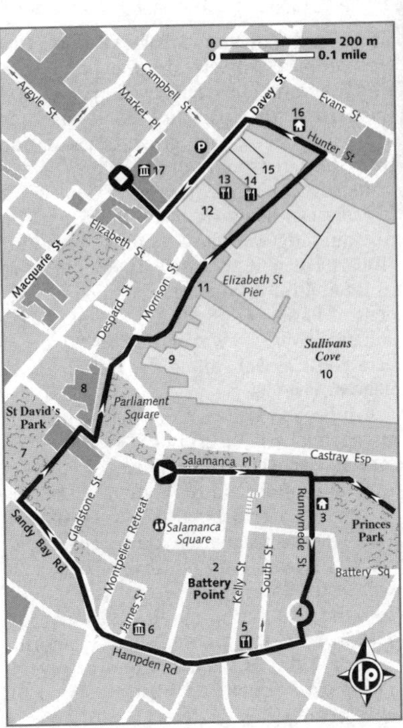

the 1850s; but continue your walk along Salamanca Pl past the old silo buildings, now converted into luxury apartments.

At Runnymede St, either continue straight ahead to pretty Princes Park or turn right and wander past the 1880 **Lenna of Hobart** (**3**; p88). Now a hotel, this splendid Italianate building was once a private residence. Continuing up Runnymede, you come to **Arthur Circus (4)**, a circle of quaint Georgian houses (some squeezed in by sacrificing plenty of living space) around a small village green.

Runnymede St ends at Hampden Rd, the main thoroughfare through Battery Point. Turn right for some window-shopping at the antique shops and peruse the restaurants to plan your evening meal. Pop into **Jackman & McRoss** (**5**; p92), a Hobart institution, for a cuppa and delectable pastry. Hampden Rd and surrounds has numerous interesting buildings for the period-architecture buff, but the highlight would have to be the 1836 **Narryna** (**6**; p73), now home to a heritage museum.

Just beyond Narryna, Hampden Rd meets busy Sandy Bay Rd; veer right and continue along Sandy Bay Rd to **St David's Park (7)**. This was Hobart Town's original cemetery, which became an overgrown eyesore and was turned into a park in 1926. It has some lovely old trees, and gravestones dating from the earliest days of the colony.

Across Salamanca Pl from St David's Park is **Parliament House** (**8**; p72). Built in 1835, this building was the Customs House for Hobart Town; it became Parliament House in 1856. Stroll through the manicured gardens of Parliament Square, in front of Parliament House, to **Watermans Dock (9)**. From here you can walk along the waterfront of **Sullivans Cove (10)**.

Just beyond Watermans Dock are the terminals for harbour cruises. The large **Elizabeth St Pier (11)** now houses upmarket accommodation and restaurants. Cross the drawbridge over the entrance to **Constitution Dock (12)**. This place really comes alive when yachties celebrate the finish of the famous Sydney to Hobart Yacht Race around New Year and also during the Royal Hobart Regatta in February. Moored along the northeastern side of the dock are several inexpensive **fish and chips barges** (**13**; p90), while behind them is **Mures** (**14**; p90), one of Hobart's gastronomic landmarks, and **Victoria Dock (15)**, home to much of Hobart's fishing fleet.

Walk up to Hunter St and pop into the stylish new **Henry Jones Art Hotel** (**16**; p88) for a look-see. It's housed in creatively converted warehouses that once held the IXL jam factory, headed by one Henry Jones. Entrepreneurial Mr Jones was once the largest private employer in Tasmania with interests in jam, fruit and timber as well as mining and shipping. There is a bar, restaurant and café here too, if you're feeling peckish.

From Hunter St it's a short walk back along the waterfront to Salamanca Pl or west to Elizabeth St and the mall, with the option of calling in at the nearby **Tasmanian Museum & Art Gallery** (**17**; p73).

HOBART FOR CHILDREN

There's no doubting Tasmania's status as a family-friendly holiday destination, but the historic buildings, museums and upmarket restaurants of the capital may not hold a little tacker's interest for too long. Attractions worth seeking out to satisfy your child (and inner child) are the Cadbury Factory (p74) and the Discovery Centre at the Botanical Gardens (p76).

The Friday-night free music in the Salamanca precinct (p95) is a fantastic family-friendly affair, and Salamanca Market (p69) has street performers to amuse all ages. The docks area is great for wandering and the floating fish and chip stalls provide a budget way to keep a family well fed.

Activities in and around the capital should also appeal to kids – take a boat cruise; do a nature walk and enjoy great views from Mt Wellington or Mt Nelson; rent a bike and explore the cycling paths. The minute you head out of town the child-friendly options increase, with an abundance of animal parks, beaches, caves, nature walks and mazes to explore.

TOURS

There's a plethora of tours on offer in Hobart, both around the sights of the city and further afield.

Guided Walks

A wealth of detailed literature on historic walks is available at the visitors centre to guide you around the docks and streets of the central business district (CBD) and Battery Point with ease. These include *Hobart's Historic Places* and the *Battery Point & Sullivan's Cove Trail of Discovery*.

Hobart Historic Tours (☎ 6278 3338; www.hobarthistorictours.com.au; tours adult/child $24.50/12) conducts a highly informative two-hour **Hobart Historic Walk** (🕑 10am Sep-May, winter on request), and also the fun two-hour **Hobart Historic Pub Tour** (🕑 5pm Sun-Thu, winter on request), taking in three watering holes with historic ambience or surrounds: the Hope & Anchor Tavern, Irish Murphy's and Knopwood's Retreat. Bookings and inquiries can be made at the visitors centre (see p69), which is also the departure point for the tours.

For a look at Hobart from the basement up, take a tour of the Hobart Rivulet, which runs beneath the CBD, with **Waterways Tours** (☎ 6238 2711; 16 Elizabeth St; adult/child/family $19/8/30; 🕑 4.45pm Tue & Thu Jan-Feb, 4.45pm Thu Mar-Dec). Tours are run by the city council, departing from its offices opposite the visitors centre, and explain the historical development of Hobart since the early 1800s. Bookings are essential.

GHOST TOURS

There are a couple of options for spooking yourself in Hobart. The National Trust offers nightly ghost tours of the Penitentiary Chapel (p72), and **Ghost Tours of Hobart** (☎ 6234 5068, 0419 122 609) has a walking tour filled with tall tales leaving Drifters Internet Café (p68) on Salamanca Pl nightly after sunset (weather and minimum numbers permitting). The cost is $25; bookings are essential.

Cruises

Several boat cruise companies operate from the Franklin Pier, Brooke St Pier and Watermans Dock area, offering a variety of cruises in and around the harbour. Note that timetables can be unreliable and schedules change regularly. Some cruises advertise running times but only operate if there are enough passengers; if you arrive to book just before it leaves, you may find that day's tour has already been cancelled.

One of the most popular cruises is the four-hour Cadbury Cruise (adult/child $45/20) run by **The Cruise Company** (☎ 6234 9294), leaving from Brooke St Pier at 10am Monday to Friday; the boat chugs to the factory, where you disembark and tour the premises before returning to the city.

Sailings offered by **Derwent River Cruises** (☎ 6223 1914) include a four-hour trip north to Moorilla Estate. The cruise alone costs $29.50, or you can opt for wine- and cheese-tasting at the estate ($39.50) or a two-course lunch at Moorilla's fine restaurant ($69.50). In summer Derwent River Cruises also offers a range of lunch and dinner cruises on the harbour.

Captain Fell's Historic Ferries (☎ 6223 6893) also offers good-value lunch (from $20 adult) and dinner ($32) cruises, and also has a rather complex array of sightseeing packages offering ferry, coach or double-decker bus trips (or a combination of these transport modes).

See also p132 for information on cruises to the excellent Peppermint Bay restaurant, and p119 for details of boat trips to Port Arthur's historic site.

Bus Tours

A wide range of day and half-day bus tours in and around Hobart are operated by **Tigerline Coaches** (☎ 6272 6611, 1300 653 633; www.tigerline.com.au; 64 Brisbane St), which has free pick-up from many city hotels and hostels. Its half-day trips include jaunts to Mt Wellington and various city sights (adult/child $46/28), the Cadbury Factory ($46/28) and Richmond ($52/32). Full-day destinations include Port Arthur ($77/46), Mt Field ($99/60) and the Tahune Forest AirWalk ($89/54). Tours originate from the terminal on Brisbane St but usually call at the visitors centre and harbourfront area too.

Gregory Omnibuses (☎ 6236 9116) offers sightseeing on an old London double-decker bus, including a full-day trip visiting the Cascade brewery and Cadbury Factory, as well as a river cruise, for $76/38 per adult/child. Alternatively, the City Hopper Explorer pass allows you an independent, hop-on-hop-off experience seeing the major sights (as far as the Cascade brewery, casino or Botanical Gardens). This service runs daily from December to May; the day pass costs $25/13 per adult/child.

The backpacker-oriented **Bottom Bits Bus** (☎ 1800 777 103, 6229 3540; www.bottombitsbus.com.au) caters to smaller groups and has a programme of day-trips out of Hobart – to Port Arthur; Freycinet Peninsula; Mt Field; or the Tahune AirWalk and Hastings Caves. All trips are good value at $89.

See also p128 for information on day trips to lovely Bruny Island.

Scenic Flights

Scenic flights are offered by **Par Avion** (☎ 6248 5390; www.paravion.com.au) and **Tasair** (☎ 6248 5088; www.tasair.com.au); Tasair flies from Hobart airport some 16km east of the city, while Par Avion flies from nearby Cambridge aerodrome. Thirty-minute flights over Hobart cost around $80, and there are also options for longer flights over the Tasman Peninsula, the east coast, and the southwest wilderness (see p299).

Rotor-Lift Helicopters (☎ 6248 4117; www.rotorlift.com.au) is also out by the airport, offering 20-minute helicopter flights over Hobart and Mt Wellington for $150, or one-hour sightseeing over Hobart and the Tasman Peninsula for $395.

Also offering a range of trips is **Tasmanian Seaplanes** (Map p66; ☎ 0418 509 699; www.tas-seaplane.com), based at a pontoon behind Wrest Point Casino. A 15-minute sightseeing flight over the capital costs $55.

HOBART'S ANTARCTIC LINKS

Hobart is a centre for the study of marine science, climate change, geology and Antarctic science. The Australian Antarctic Division has its headquarters on the outskirts of nearby Kingston, and has a display area open to the public (p101); the Commonwealth Scientific and Industrial Research Organisation (CSIRO) Division of Marine Research has its chief office and one of its three marine laboratories in Castray Esplanade, next to Princes Wharf; and a national cooperative research centre, the Antarctic CRC, is located on the campus of the University of Tasmania. The university itself is particularly strong in the fields of geology and Antarctic science and policy.

The Antarctic Division's research and resupply vessel the *Aurora Australis* and the CSIRO's research vessels the *Southern Surveyor* and the MV *Franklin* can often be seen docked at the wharves, as can a number of international research vessels.

The new, 10-day **Antarctic Midwinter Festival** (www.antarctic-tasmania.info), staged in June, warms up winter visitors with celebrations highlighting Tasmania's Antarctic connections.

FESTIVALS & EVENTS

Hobart plays host to a great number of festivals and events throughout the year.

December–January

Sydney to Hobart Yacht Race (http://rolexsydneyhobart.com) The arrival (from 29 December to 2 January) in Hobart of the many yachts that have competed in this annual race is celebrated with a lot of of noise and colour. Winning yachts arrive in time for New Year's Eve celebrations.

Melbourne to Hobart Yacht Race The competitors in this race (which travels down Tasmania's west coast) arrive on the same days as those competing in the Sydney to Hobart race.

Hobart Summer Festival (www.hobartsummerfestival.com.au) Hobart's premier festival is centred around the Hobart waterfront and starts around the time of the completion of the yacht races. It lasts for two weeks and incorporates numerous festivities along the way, including major New Year's Eve celebrations for revelling sailors, locals and visitors alike, and **The Taste of Tasmania**, a week-long celebration of Tassie's gastronomic prowess.

February

Royal Hobart Regatta Major aquatic carnival held over three days, with boat races and other activities.

Australian Wooden Boat Festival (www.australianwoodenboatfestival.com.au) Held every two years (the last in 2005) and timed to coincide with the Hobart Regatta. The festival showcases Tasmania's boat-building heritage and maritime traditions. Some 350 boats visit the harbour, plus there's music and entertainment.

March

Ten Days on the Island (www.tendaysontheisland.com) Biennial event (staged in odd-numbered years) which usually runs from late March until early April and is Tasmania's premier cultural festival, a statewide celebration of local and international 'island culture', with many excellent events in and around the capital.

June

Antarctic Midwinter Festival (www.antarctic-tasmania.info) Celebrate the winter solstice at this new, 10-day Hobart festival, designed to highlight and celebrate Tasmania's unique connection with the Antarctic.

October

Royal Hobart Show Large agricultural festival showcasing the state's primary industries, held annually in late October at Glenorchy showgrounds.

SLEEPING

Hobart has a variety of accommodation catering to all tastes and price brackets. The best areas to stay in are the docks, Salamanca Pl and neighbouring Battery Point, though prices here are high and vacancy rates low. Accommodation in the affluent neighbouring suburb of Sandy Bay is also generally expensive, except for the more dated motels. Sandy Bay Rd is long and winding, as is the suburb, so if you don't want to be too far from town, check distances from the city before making a booking.

The central business district and immediate surrounds is where you'll find most hostels and pubs offering rooms, plus a decent array of midrange hotels. There's not a great deal of atmosphere to the area at night, but from most places it's only a 10-minute walk to the waterfront area and Salamanca Pl.

Away from the water on the other side of the city centre, but still reasonably close to town, are the adjoining suburbs of North Hobart and New Town. Here you'll find a couple of hostels, good B&Bs and moderately priced motels within walking distance of a cluster of lively restaurants and cafés.

If you're planning to visit in January and are particular about accommodation, you should book well ahead.

Budget

HOSTELS

Hobart has a few very good hostels and a couple of budget hotels with backpacker accommodation.

City Centre

The Pickled Frog (Map p66; ☎ 6234 7977; www.thepickledfrog.com; 281 Liverpool St; dm $19-22, s/d $30/50; P 💻) Big, red, ramshackle hostel that's well placed for the city and has a young, social vibe. Prices include continental breakfast, and there's a bar and lounge for meeting fellow travellers. Extras include bike hire and good tour info.

Central City Backpackers (Map p70; ☎ 6224 2404; www.centralbackpackers.com.au; 138 Collins St; dm $18-22, s/d $36/48; 💻) In the heart of the central business district, this rambling hostel has loads of communal space, OK rooms, friendly staff and extras such as baggage storage and bike hire.

Narrara Backpackers (Map p66; ☎ 6231 3191; nigelruddock@hotmail.com; 88 Goulburn St; dm/s/d $19/24/40; P 💻) Central, well-maintained backpackers with the appealing atmosphere of a large, friendly group house and good facilities. It's run by an affable bloke with lots of regional knowledge and bushwalking advice. By the time you read this there should also be another hostel under the same management, **Hobart Hostel** (Map p66; ☎ 6234 6122; cnr Goulburn & Barrack Sts), in a former pub and with similar prices.

Hollydene Lodge (Map p70; ☎ 6234 6434; www.hollydene.com.au; 55 Campbell St; dm/d/f $22/48/87; P 💻) Huge, conveniently central hostel with lots of basic rooms and a roll-call of communal facilities, including barbecue area, games room, laundry, comfy lounge and large kitchen. Weekly rates available – this place hosts lots of overseas students.

Transit Centre Backpackers (Map p66; ☎ 6231 2400; www.salamanca.com.au/backpackers; 199 Collins St; dm/d $19/44; 💻) Functional hostel upstairs at the Redline bus station. It's small and the rooms are somewhat crowded, but it's a homely and relaxed option with helpful owners and decent facilities.

Montgomery's Private Hotel & YHA Backpackers (Map p70; ☎ 6231 2660; www.montgomerys.com.au; 9 Argyle St; dm $20-22, d without/with en suite $69/89; 💻) Another of the well-placed options, this bright, modern hotel includes decent hostel rooms but cramped communal facilities. The private rooms with shared bathroom are overpriced but the en suite rooms are reasonable value; family-sized rooms are also available. Next door there's a pub with cheap meals and karaoke (consider yourself warned!).

North

Allport's (Map p66; ☎ 6231 5464; 432 Elizabeth St; www.tassie.net.au/~allports; dm/d/tr/f $20/60/70/70; P 💻) Within walking distance of the restaurant strip of North Hobart is this bright and cheery hostel, in an impressive two-storey Italianate mansion. The atmosphere is relaxed and the facilities first-rate, including two kitchens, laundry and spacious common rooms. The friendly owner supplies veggies from the garden for guest use (in season) and quality bushwalking equipment for hire.

Adelphi Court YHA (Map p75; ☎ 6228 4829; adelphi@yhatas.org.au; 17 Stoke St, New Town; dm $20, d $60, d with en suite $65; P) Hobart's other YHA hostel is the friendly Adelphi, offering rooms in a spruced-up 1950s-style block built around a courtyard. It's out of the way – 2.5km from the city – but reasonably close to the North Hobart restaurant strip. Reception hours are limited – call ahead. Note that prices increase slightly (by around $6 per double) from Christmas to mid-February. Take bus No 15 or 16 from stop H in Elizabeth St to stop 8, or any bus leaving stop E to stop 13, which is close to Stoke St.

Waterfront Lodge (Map p75; ☎ 6228 4748; www.waterfrontnewtownbay.com; 153 Risdon Rd, New Town Bay; dm $25, motel d $75-98, extra person $15; P 🏊) This is a well-renovated waterside motel north of the centre, with spotless, modern motel units (all with kitchenette). It also has a separate pool-side lodge with great-value four-bunk dorms (each room with fridge and microwave). There's also a guest kitchen for motel and lodge guests.

PUBS

Cascade Hotel & Holiday Apartments (Map p75; ☎ 6223 6385; www.view.com.au/cascadehotel; 22 Cascade Rd, Sth Hobart; s/d $65/80, extra person $15; P) The

Cascade pub is en route to the Cascade brewery, in a very pleasant residential location 3km from town (on the continuation of Macquarie St). Behind the pub are a handful of comfy, self-contained brick units, with free guest laundry and rates that are a great bargain.

New Sydney Hotel (Map p70; ☎ 6234 4516; www.newsydneyhotel.com; 87 Bathurst St; dm $20; P 🖳) Fun, laid-back pub with kitchen facilities and small, basic dorms. They get a lot of live music and spirited patrons here, so don't expect a monastic retreat. Good pub grub too.

Ocean Child Hotel (Map p70; ☎ 6234 6730; 86 Argyle St; dm/d $20/40) This pub might look a bit shabby, but you could do a lot worse for budget accommodation. There are kitchen facilities available.

CAMPING & CABINS

None of the camping grounds listed here are within walking distance of the city centre. All prices listed are based on two people travelling.

Barilla Holiday Park (Map p75; ☎ 1800 465 453, 6248 5453; www.barilla.com.au; 75 Richmond Rd, Cambridge; unpowered/powered site $16.50/21.50, cabins $63-73; P 🖳) An excellent option for those with their own transport. It's more or less a midway point between Hobart (13km) and Richmond (14km) and close to the airport and excellent wineries. It has nice grounds and well-kept cabins, plus an on-site restaurant.

Elwick Cabin & Tourist Park (Map p75; ☎ 6272 7115; www.islandcabins.com.au; 19 Goodwood Rd, Glenorchy; unpowered/powered site $17/20, cabins $50-89; P) The nearest camping to town (about 8km north of the centre, next to the road leading across Bowen Bridge). Well equipped, with a range of cabins but with limited powered sites – book ahead for these.

Cosy Cabins Mornington Park (Map p75; ☎ 6244 7070; www.cosycabins.com/mornington; 346 Cambridge Rd, Mornington; cabins from $83; P ♿) Family-friendly cabin park out in the 'burbs (in the first suburb you reach approaching the city from the airport). No camping sites, but a good array of self-contained cabins (some with spa). Plus barbecues, playground and games room, and an indoor pool being built at time of research.

THE AUTHOR'S CHOICE

Edinburgh Gallery (Map p66; ☎ 6224 9229; www.artaccom.com.au; 211 Macquarie St; s $90, d $100-150; P 🖳) This funky, art-filled boutique hotel is owned by a writer and an artist who have put their individual stamp on a grand old Federation home in the western part of the city centre. The affordable rates include breakfast and rooms with quirky, eclectic décor (try for a veranda suite); some rooms have shared bathroom. There's also lots of modern art (some of it a little confronting!), and artists get discounted rates. Excellent winter reductions (May to September) see savings of up to 30%.

Midrange

GUESTHOUSES & B&BS

These are often housed in historic buildings, with facilities that vary widely but are usually of a high standard. Price is a decent guide to quality, except around Battery Point where you inevitably pay more. Guesthouse owners/managers usually live on-site, but there are plenty of exceptions, particularly in Battery Point. In many cases, an intercom phone is by the door for contacting the owners/managers upon arrival.

Battery Point

Battery Point Bed & Breakfast (Map p70; ☎ 6223 3124; www.batterypointbedandbreakfast.com; 74 Hampden Rd; r $100-165) Lovely heritage building with three accommodating rooms and cooked breakfasts on offer in the heart of B&B central.

Battery Point Manor (Map p66; ☎ 6224 0888; www.batterypointmanor.com.au; 13-15 Cromwell St; d $100-195; P) Take in the magic views from the outdoor terrace at this homely manor, built c 1834. There's a range of large in-house rooms available, some with king-size beds and views over the Derwent, plus a two-bedroom unit. Prices include buffet-style breakfast.

North

The two B&Bs listed here have furnishings, facilities and locations that could easily place them in the top-end price bracket, but instead offer value-for-money rates and are highly recommended. Book ahead.

Lodge on Elizabeth (Map p66; ☎ 6231 3830; www.thelodge.com.au; 249 Elizabeth St; s/d from $120/140;

P) In an elevated position in North Hobart, not far from the restaurant strip. Rooms in this grand Georgian manor are beautifully decorated with antiques, and extras include helpful owners, hearty breakfasts, and some spa rooms. In the courtyard there's also a popular self-contained spa cottage ($190, two-night minimum).

Wellington Lodge (Map p66; ☎ 6231 0614; www.wwt.com.au/wellingtonlodge; 7 Scott St; s $90, d $110-130; P) Next to Queen's Domain in the small northern suburb of Glebe (the easiest access is via Aberdeen St). The welcoming owners have four comfortable rooms in a restored Victorian townhouse set in magnificent gardens.

South

Merre Be's (Map p66; ☎ 6224 2900; www.merrebes.com.au; 17 Gregory St; r from $120; P) Close to the Sandy Bay shopping area is this colonial house in a quiet street, built in 1901 and transformed into a B&B, with lovely large rooms (some with spa).

Crawfords B&B (Map p75; ☎ 6225 3751; www.crawfordsbb.com; 178 Nelson Rd; s/d $100/120; P) Located on the chicane that winds up from Sandy Bay to Mt Nelson, Crawfords offers accommodation in a homely self-contained unit (breakfast provisions included). Great views too, plus private garden area.

Lapoinya Lodge (Map p77; ☎ 6239 1005; www.tassie.net.au/lapoinyalodge; 9 Lapoinya Rd, Fern Tree; s/d $100/120; P) This B&B has a great mountain location amid one hectare of gardens, yielding serene views of the city and the D'Entrecasteaux Channel. Its handful of in-house rooms come with a continental breakfast. To get to the lodge, drive towards Mt Wellington but go past the turn-off to the mountain and turn left at Fern Tree Tavern. It's wonderfully close to mountain walking trails.

HOTELS

City Centre

Harrington's 102 (Map p70; ☎ 6234 9277; www.harringtons102.com.au; 102 Harrington St; r $95-140) After the shock of the ultrabright colours in the reception area, you'll find the hotel rooms here are well equipped but small. Still, the price is good given that the continental breakfast is included and you're within walking distance of everywhere. Winter rates can drop to a bargain $70.

Astor Private Hotel (Map p70; ☎ 6234 6611; www.astorprivatehotel.com.au; 157 Macquarie St; s/d with shared bathroom $55/80, d with en suite $120-160) This large, central 1920s guesthouse has retained much of its character, full of stained-glass windows, great old furniture and family-run charm. There are old-style rooms with shared bathrooms (some suitable for families), plus brand new and very appealing en-suite rooms.

Welcome Stranger Hotel (Map p70; ☎ 6223 6655; welcomestranger@bigpond.com; cnr Harrington & Davey Sts; dm/s/d $18/75/99; P) Not much to look at from the outside, but this place is home to better-than-expected accommodation, in the form of en-suite rooms and a decent backpackers section. Thankfully the windows are double glazed, as it's on a busy, noisy street. Continental breakfast is included in the room rates (not for backpackers), and downstairs there is a public bar with pool tables, and a pizza bar. Limited parking.

Customs House Hotel (Map p70; ☎ 6234 6645; www.customshousehotel.com; 1 Murray St; d $105-120) Newly renovated, stylish rooms (all with en suite, some with harbour view) are on offer at this popular waterfront pub, but light sleepers should look elsewhere (especially later in the week, when the live entertainment downstairs might cause some tossing and turning).

Theatre Royal Hotel (Map p70; ☎ 6234 6925; 31 Campbell St; s/d with shared bathroom $70/80, s/d with en suite $90/100) Handily placed for theatre-goers (right next door to the Theatre Royal), this gracious hotel has high-standard rooms – en suites have recently been added to some. Downstairs there is a bright bar and dining room. Please also see Montgomery's Private Hotel, p83.

MOTELS

There are plenty of motels in Hobart, but the majority are typically a long way out and you'll need your own transport to reach them. See p83 for information about the excellent motel accommodation at Waterfront Lodge, north of town.

City Centre

Hobart Macquarie Motor Inn (Map p70; ☎ 6234 4422, 1800 060 954; www.leisureinns.com.au; 167 Macquarie St; r $89-115; P) This large, central motel won't win any architectural awards and offers uninspiring décor, but is well equipped (facilities include heated indoor pool and sauna) and offers reasonable value given the location.

Hobart Mid City Hotel (Map p70; ☎ 6234 6333, 1800 030 966; www.hobartmidcity.com.au; cnr Elizabeth & Bathurst Sts; r $115-145; P) The Mid City is another central, multistorey '70s motel block, offering a similar deal to that of the Hobart Macquarie.

South

Sandy Bay has some good options in this category, plus a considerably more appealing location than the motels that line the highways out of Hobart. See also p88 for information on Wrest Point offerings – its cheapest rooms fall into this price category.

St Ives Motel (Map p66; ☎ 6224 1044; www.stivesmotel.com.au; 86 Sandy Bay Rd; d $119-149, extra person $16; P) Within walking distance of Battery Point and the city is this reasonable option, where all rooms have kitchens. The large, two-bedroom family units can sleep up to five.

Blue Hills Motel (Map p66; ☎ 6223 1777, 1800 030 776; www.bestwestern.com.au/bluehills; 96a Sandy Bay Rd; d $130-140; P) Blue Hills is not far from St Ives and offers plain motel rooms and more spacious apartment-style dwellings (with kitchenettes), all featuring the best of '70s-style décor.

Woolmers Inn (Map p66; ☎ 6223 7355, 1800 030 780; www.woolmersinn.com; 123-127 Sandy Bay Rd; d from $130; P) A superior choice – we're pleased to report that this option has fresh, modern décor and is not too far from the action. It has spacious studio and two-bedroom units, all with kitchenette, cable TV and video. Some units have facilities for disabled guests.

Mayfair Plaza Motel (Map p66; ☎ 6220 9900; www.mayfairplaza.com.au; 236-244 Sandy Bay Rd; r $109-149; P 💻) Another good choice, with cavernous modern rooms opening onto an attractive indoor atrium. There are bonuses such as free cable TV and a complimentary guest laundry, plus an in-house business centre.

Motel 429 (Map p75; ☎ 6225 2511; www.motel429.com.au; 429 Sandy Bay Rd; d $105-155; P) Directly opposite the waters of Sandy Bay and not far from the casino is this motel, the recent recipient of a very smart makeover. Selling features include friendly staff, water views from the deluxe modern rooms, a small gym with spa and sauna, and even a glass-fronted elevator on the face of the building.

SELF-CONTAINED APARTMENTS

Hobart has a number of self-contained flats and units with fully equipped kitchens – perfect for longer stays and for families and small groups. Prices vary, as does what's on offer – in this price range the units are normally renovated flats in apartment blocks. The best self-contained bargains are out of the city.

Battery Point

Avon Court Holiday Apartments (Map p70; ☎ 6223 4837, 1800 807 257; www.view.com.au/avon; 4 Colville St; d $130-170, extra adult/child $30/16; P) If you overlook the dated furnishings, these spacious, self-contained apartments (behind a sandstone façade that's only 25 years young) represent excellent value for families and small groups. Larger apartments can sleep up to six, and have all the mod-cons you'll need for a comfy extended stay.

Coopers Cottage (Map p70; ☎ 6224 0355; www.cooperscottage.com.au; 44a Hampden Rd; d $135-150; P) Tucked in behind a shopfront is this cosy self-contained option, perfect for two and with extras such as video, CD player and washing machine. Reception is next door in the handy Village Store delicatessen and café.

Battery Point Boutique Accommodation (Map p70; ☎ 6224 2244; www.tasstays.com; 27-29 Hampden Rd; d $125-165, extra person $35; P) A well-positioned block of four salmon-coloured, modern, serviced apartments (sleeping three) in the heart of Battery Point; direct inquiries to unit No 1.

North

Graham Court Apartments (Map p75; ☎ 6278 1333, 1800 811 915; www.grahamcourt.com.au; 15 Pirie St, New Town; d $95-133, extra adult/child $23/17; P) In a quiet residential area in the northern suburbs is this large block of well-maintained apartments set in leafy gardens. Units range from one to three bedrooms and are perfect for families, with a large playground on the premises, cots and high chairs available and a babysitting service for when you need a break! Disabled access units available.

South

Grosvenor Court (Map p66; ☎ 6223 3422; www.grosvenorcourt.com.au; 42 Grosvenor St, Sandy Bay; d $100-140, q $150-220; P) Grosvenor Court features a large block of studio and two-bedroom units, all furnished with heritage-style décor and blackwood furniture. Helpful owners, DVD/CD players in each apartment, a barbecue area and guest laundry make this a good home away from home. There is also an enormous three-bedroom house (sleeping eight) available next door.

West

Bay View Villas (Map p75; ☎ 6234 7611, 1800 061 505; www.bayviewvillas.com; 34 Poets Rd, West Hobart; d $100-220, extra adult/child $25/20; P) Two kilometres from the city centre is this family-friendly option, with facilities including a games room, playground and indoor pool and spa. The well-equipped two- and three-bedroom units get booked out well in advance at peak times. The east-facing ones have bay views and are thus more expensive.

Top End

Compared with other Australian capital cities, the top-end accommodation in Hobart is cheap, generally starting at around $150 a double (and if your budget stretches to $200 you'll be able to afford something quite special). Outside the peak season and holidays, many of the plush hotels offer special weekend accommodation/dinner deals and walk-in rates, while luxury B&Bs may also reduce their prices.

COTTAGES

Corinda's Cottages (Map p66; ☎ 6234 1590; www.corindascottages.com.au; 17 Glebe St, Glebe; d $195-220, extra person $40) Wow – the gardens here are spectacular, and the same can be said for the accommodation, with wonderful attention to detail paid in the three sumptuously renovated outbuildings of a grand Victorian mansion. Located beside the greenery of Queen's Domain; a short walk from the city. Breakfast provisions included.

Treetops Cascades (Map p75; ☎ 6223 2839; rmawbey@aquenal.com.au; 165 Strickland Ave; d $150-160, extra person $35; P) Book ahead for this fantastic new three-bedroom house in an idyllic bush setting 2km west of the Cascade brewery. When word gets out about its excellent facilities and gorgeous rural location so close to town, everyone will want to stay here!

Moorilla Vineyard Suites & Chalets (Map p75; ☎ 6277 9900; www.moorilla.com.au; 655 Main Rd, Berriedale; d $290-310, extra person $40; P) For a taste of sheer luxury, rent one of the secluded chalets at Moorilla Estate, 12km north of the city centre and with a vineyard, museum and restaurant as neighbours. These modern self-contained apartments (one- and two-bedroom) are superbly equipped, and features include private balconies, wine cellars, water views, and even displays of antiquities from the museum's collection.

GUESTHOUSES & B&BS

The restoration work on many of Hobart's older mansions has resulted in some fine accommodation.

Battery Point

Colville Cottage (Map p70; ☎ 6223 6968; www.colvillecottage.com.au; 32 Mona St; s/d from $135/160) Our favourite B&B in Battery point is this option, where you can enjoy the lovely cottage gardens from the shady verandas. There's a welcoming, elegant interior, full of colonial heritage but without the clutter.

Battery Point Guest House (Mandalay; Map p70; ☎ 6224 2111; www.batterypointguesthouse.com.au; 7 McGregor St; s/d from $130/155; P) This lovely peaceful guesthouse, close to Salamanca Pl, was originally the coach house and stables for the nearby Lenna of Hobart. The fuss-free rooms come with cooked breakfast, and there are discounts for stays of more than three nights. Self-contained cottages are also available.

Barton Cottage (Map p70; ☎ 6224 1606, 0418 138 849; www.bartoncottage.com.au; 72 Hampden Rd; s/d from $120/166) In the midst of the well-heeled action of Battery Point is the double-storey Barton Cottage, a National Trust building dating from 1837. It has six well-appointed rooms and offers full cooked breakfasts.

North

Elms of Hobart (Map p75; ☎ 6231 3277; www.theelmsofhobart.com; 452 Elizabeth St, North Hobart; d $160-230; P) Close to the North Hobart action is this rather grand WWI-era mansion featuring lovely gardens, spacious, luxurious rooms and cooked breakfasts.

South

The following classy options are on Sandy Bay Rd, but both have double glazed windows to negate traffic noise.

Clydesdale Manor (Map p66; ☎ 6223 7289; www.clydesdale-accommodation.com.au; 292 Sandy Bay Rd, Sandy Bay; d $150-200; P) This quality guesthouse bills itself as the 'quintessential Hobart destination for discerning adults', so leave the ankle-biters behind and enjoy the warm hospitality, elegant furnishings, gourmet breakfasts and fine attention to detail. Try for a spa suite, complete with private balcony.

Amberley House (Map p66; ☎ 6225 1005; www.empress.com.au; 391 Sandy Bay Rd; d $150-200; P) Another high-standard guesthouse with new, young owners. This place is an elegant, high-ceilinged Victorian mansion that has benefited greatly from a recent makeover, which has seen the introduction of lots of soothing neutral colours and choice pieces of furniture.

HOTELS & MOTELS

There are a number of luxury lofts in the city centre. See also p86 for upmarket hotel rooms available at Wrest Point.

Macquarie Manor (Map p70; ☎ 6224 4999, 1800 243 044; www.macmanor.com.au; 172 Macquarie St; r $180-250; P) Plush, high-ceilinged heritage rooms and cooked breakfast buffets are the order of the day at this central, well-groomed, Regency-style guesthouse.

Hadleys Hotel (Map p70; ☎ 6223 4355, 1800 131 689; www.dohertyhotels.com.au; 34 Murray St; d from $175; P 💻) This is a sumptuous place that has clocked up more than 150 years of hospitality in the heart of the CBD, making it ideal for meeting-plagued businesspeople. It's gained plenty of modern embellishments since its colonial beginnings, including a restaurant and lobby bar.

Hotel Grand Chancellor (Map p70; ☎ 6235 4535, 1800 753 379; www.hgchobart.com.au; 1 Davey St; r $285-315, ste $410; P 💻 🏊) You can't miss this waterfront monolith, offering international-standard indulgence. The lobby has shops and restaurants; there's also a gym and indoor pool. The well-equipped rooms have good views; you'll pay more for a harbour outlook. There are packages that bring the high rack-rates down considerably; see the website.

Quest Savoy (Map p70; ☎ 6220 2300; www.questapartments.com.au; 38 Elizabeth St; r $168-220; P) The Savoy has superb modern studio suites – all with kitchenette and living/dining area – in the heart of downtown. If you're feeling travel-weary, in the same building is the Savoy therapeutic baths and spa services.

Lenna of Hobart (Map p70; ☎ 6232 3900, 1800 030 633; www.lenna.com.au; 20 Runnymede St; r & ste $179-249; P) This grand Italianate mansion is set in lovely grounds and is home to a fine-dining restaurant. The newer concrete wing of the property is where you'll find the accommodation; the rooms are large and the facilities first-class, but the décor is starting to look a little dated.

Wrest Point (Map p66; ☎ 6225 0112, 1800 030 611; www.wrestpoint.com.au; 410 Sandy Bay Rd; motel d $139-190, hotel d $189-270; P 💻 🏊) Three kilometres south of the city centre is this large, conspicuous waterfront complex, centred around a flashy, well-established casino and loaded with distractions, including restaurants, bars and health club. There are a couple of motel-style options (the pricier rooms with water views). Package deals regularly give attractive discounts for these and the more expensive hotel rooms and suites in the hotel's luxury-stuffed tower – see the website.

SELF-CONTAINED APARTMENTS

Somerset on the Pier (Map p70; ☎ 6220 6600, 1800 766 377; www.the-ascott.com; Elizabeth St Pier; apt from $250; P) In a quintessentially Hobart location on Elizabeth Pier, and with great restaurants as its neighbours, this stylish

THE AUTHOR'S CHOICE

The Henry Jones Art Hotel (Map p70; ☎ 62 107700, 1300 665 581; www.thehenryjones.com; 25 Hunter St; r $240-270, ste $310-850; P) Super-stylish HJs has been wowing guests since it first opened in mid-2004. This harbourside hotel-cum-gallery is housed in wonderfully restored warehouses and oozes sophistication – but it's not too cool for school (this is Hobart after all, not Sydney). Service, décor (including modern art on many spare walls), facilities and downstairs distractions (bar, restaurant, café) are all first-rate, and if you're feeling flush, you can blow the budget on a luxuriously appointed suite. See the website for pics and details.

complex offers luxurious apartments and great harbour views. All units are self-contained and have fresh modern décor; you'll pay more for a spa and/or balcony.

Somerset on Salamanca (Map p70; ☎ 6220 6600, 1800 766 377; www.the-ascott.com; 8 Salamanca Pl; apt from $220; P) This option has a similar up-market pedigree to its pier-bound sister establishment, with modern, well-equipped apartments close to the fun of Salamanca. It's managed by Somerset on the Pier: everything from inquiries to check-in should be directed there.

Quest Waterfront (Map p70; ☎ 6224 8630, 1800 334 033; www.questapartments.com.au; 3 Brooke St; hotel d $147, apt for up to 4 $168-205; P) This Quest complex has quality suites and apartments (with kitchenettes), plus motel-style rooms that are reasonable value considering the central harbourside location. All rooms come with spas.

The Old Woolstore (Map p70; ☎ 6235 5355, 1800 814 676; www.oldwoolstore.com.au; 1 Macquarie St; r $185, apt d $195-225; P) This is a large, lavishly equipped hotel and apartment complex – it's worth spending a little extra to get a spacious, family-friendly apartment (with up to three bedrooms), all with kitchen, laundry facilities, stereo and video.

Salamanca Terraces (Map p70; ☎ 6232 3900, 1800 030 633; www.salamancaterraces.com.au; 93 Salamanca Pl; apt $179-309; P) As well as its hotel rooms, Lenna of Hobart (opposite) also offers this nearby gathering of very comfy, modern, serviced studios and apartments overlooking Salamanca Pl.

Also recommended:

Salamanca Inn (Map p70; ☎ 6223 3300, 1800 030 944; www.salamancainn.com.au; 10 Gladstone St; d $198-260; P 💻 🏊) This inn has modern, well-equipped one- and two-bedroom apartments just behind Salamanca Pl.

Quest Trinity House (Map p66; ☎ 6236 9656, 1800 334 033; www.questapartments.com.au; 149 Brooker Ave, Glebe; d $158-199, q $199-242; P) Large complex of modern, townhouse-style serviced apartments (from studios to four bedrooms), north of the centre in Glebe.

Zero Davey (Map p70; ☎ 6270 1444, 1300 733 422; www.escapesresorts.com.au; 15 Hunter St; apt $220-280; P) Brand-new, ultramodern complex of studio apartments.

EATING

Hobart's central business district has some good spots for brunch and lunch, but evening options are generally better closer to the water or historic precincts. The waterfront streets, docks and piers are the collective epicentre of the city's restaurant scene, and quality seafood is on offer everywhere you look. Salamanca Pl is an excellent choice for cafés and restaurants, especially brunch-time during the Saturday market. For the most diverse selection of eateries, head to Elizabeth St in North Hobart, a cosmopolitan strip of pubs, cafés and restaurants.

Pubs serve up dependable, if somewhat predictable, meals that usually represent good value. Pub lunch hours are usually from noon to 2pm and 6pm to 8pm daily, though a few places have declared that Sunday night and/or Monday are cookery-free zones.

City Centre — Map p70

Criterion St Café (☎ 6234 5858; 10 Criterion St; lunch $6-12; 🕒 7.30am-5pm Mon-Fri, 9am-3pm Sat) Coffee-lovers, vegetarians and fans of creative café fare will be impressed by this light, bright and popular eatery.

Kafe Kara (☎ 6231 2332; 119 Liverpool St; lunch $8-18; 🕒 8am-4.30pm Mon-Fri, 9am-3pm Sat) Like the Criterion St Café, this local favourite offers early breakfasts and great all-day eating in its stylish interior. Its speciality is tasty Italian-style fare (*panini*, pasta, risotto).

Nourish (☎ 6234 5674; 129 Elizabeth St; meals $7.50-11; 🕒 7.30am-4pm Mon-Wed, 7.30am-8pm Thu-Fri, 11am-3pm Sat) A godsend for people with food allergies and intolerances. The menu at this café features tasty, well-prepared dishes (curries, salads, stir-fries, risotto, burgers) that are all gluten-free and largely dairy-free too. Vegetarians and vegans also catered for.

Choux Shop (☎ 6231 0601; 4 Victoria St; snacks & meals $5-10; 🕒 8am-5.30pm Mon-Fri) Fantastic, newly-opened bakery-café. The new lunch hotspot thanks to its superb array of pastries, sandwiches, savoury tarts and quality coffee and tea.

New Sydney Hotel (☎ 6234 4516; 87 Bathurst St; mains $9-19; 🕒 lunch Mon-Sat, dinner nightly) Cosy watering hole, popular for cheap, filling counter meals and – more than just the usual pub-grub offerings of steak, schnitzel and fish and chips – pasta with chicken and avocado and chicken caesar salad.

Rockerfellers (☎ 6234 3490; 11 Morrison St; lunch $12-19.50, dinner mains $18-25; 🕒 lunch & dinner) Set in the flamboyantly renovated confines of the old city mill is this fun, relaxed eatery, serving up loads of cocktails to accompany its something-for-everyone menus (just try to resist the desserts). Jazz is on the menu from 6.30pm Sunday.

The Elbow Room (☎ 6224 4254; 9-11 Murray St; mains $28.50; ⏲ lunch Tue-Fri, dinner Tue-Sat) Intimate, highly regarded restaurant in an old stone basement. The wine list is impressive, and the house specialities include local game and seafood.

Hotel Grand Chancellor (☎ 6235 4535; 1 Davey St) A true monolith that's home to some good eating options. Its **Atrium Lounge** does a traditional high tea ($20 per person) on Friday, Saturday and Sunday afternoons from 3pm – bookings are essential. **The Cove** (buffets $36-48; ⏲ lunch Sun, dinner nightly) offers buffet dining every night – Monday is European, Tuesday Asian, Wednesday offers 'great Aussie barbecue and carvery', Thursday is Mediterranean, Friday and Saturday feature seafood, and Sunday is all about the roast. Upstairs, fine-dining **Meehan's Restaurant** (mains $28-30; ⏲ dinner Tue-Sat) offers well-prepared meals highlighting fresh seasonal produce.

Vanny's (☎ 6234 1457; 181 Liverpool St; meals $5-9; ⏲ lunch Mon-Fri, dinner Mon-Sat) Super-modest café-takeaway serving up cheap Cambodian-style curries and satays, including vegetarian options.

THE AUTHOR'S CHOICE

Sirens (☎ 6234 2634; 6 Victoria St; lunch $8-13, dinner mains $16-23; ⏲ lunch Mon-Fri, dinner Tue-Sat) Sirens is a gem, serving up creative vegetarian and vegan food in a warm, welcoming space, accompanied by excellent service and impeccable ethics – tips and credit card surcharges are donated to charity; local and organic produce is used wherever possible; and all green waste is composted. But don't be misled – it's not all long-haired earnest types producing lentil stews; there's some sophisticated cooking going on in the kitchen. How about beetroot and orange soup with sour cream and hazelnuts, followed by braised baby fennel risotto made with raspberry and *talleggio*, or Moroccan-style barbecued eggplant on fruited couscous?

The most central option for self-caterers is **City Supermarket** (148 Liverpool St; ⏲ 8am-7pm Mon-Fri, 9am-6pm Sat, 9am-5pm Sun).

Waterfront Area Map p70

The waterfront is an understandably popular spot for diners, and restaurant menus here are heavy on piscatorial ingredients. You can feast on inexpensive or splurge-worthy seafood, knowing it's fresh.

Constitution Dock has a number of permanently moored barges that serve as **floating takeaway seafood stalls** (you can't miss them), which are a good option for an impromptu dockside picnic.

Mures (☎ 6231 2121; www.mures.com.au; Victoria Dock) A Hobart institution. On the ground level you'll find a fishmonger and an inexpensive, family-friendly bistro, the **Lower Deck** (meals $7-13; ⏲ 11m-9pm), serving meals for the masses: fish and chips, salmon burgers, crumbed scallops and so on. The **Upper Deck** (mains $20-28; ⏲ lunch & dinner daily) is a fancier restaurant with great harbour views and well-prepared seafood dishes, like grilled salmon, trevalla (blue eye) and crayfish. Also part of the Mures complex is the much-praised **Orizuru Sushi Bar** (☎ 6231 1790; sushi $7-10, mains $18-28; ⏲ lunch & dinner Mon-Sat), using fresh seafood to great effect in delicate sushi creations and other popular Japanese dishes.

Steam Packet Restaurant (☎ 6210 7706; Hunter St; lunch $8-16, dinner mains $23-34; ⏲ breakfast, lunch & dinner daily) A new addition to the waterfront scene, inside the glam Henry Jones hotel. Breakfast dishes can get pricey (up to $22) – lunch is better value and options include salads, local oysters and fish and chips. Dinnertime sees prices climb again, but the produce is of a high quality.

Jam Packed (☎ 6231 3454; Hunter St; snacks & meals $5-15; ⏲ 8am-6pm Mon-Fri, 8am-7pm Sat & Sun) Inside Henry Jones' airy glass atrium is this casual new café, serving up brekky and classic lunchtime fare.

Fish Frenzy (☎ 6231 2134; Elizabeth St Pier; meals $8.50-18.50; ⏲ lunch & dinner) Munch waterside on fish and chips (of course), spicy calamari salad or a fish burger, making your choice from a simple menu of fresh seafood and ordering at the counter. This is a casual, affordable and always-busy eatery; note that no bookings are taken.

T-42° (☎ 6224 7742; Elizabeth St Pier; mains $15-25; ⏲ 7.30am-late Mon-Fri, 8.30am-late Sat & Sun) A favourite among Hobart's fashionable crowd, especially late in the week, is this cool waterfront bistro/wine bar. There are innovative menu selections, good service, an extensive wine list, and lounges for a bit of reclining after dining. Dinner bookings recommended.

Sisco's (☎ 6223 2059; Murray St Pier; mains $20-29; lunch & dinner Mon-Sat) Mediterranean influences (predominantly Spanish) can be found on the menu at this striking first-level restaurant. Enjoy great views alongside paella, a seafood platter or oven-roasted ocean trout, followed by a dessert of Catalan cream custard or caramel soufflé.

Blue Skies (☎ 6224 3747; Murray St Pier; light meals $10-15, mains $17-27; from 11am-late) Earthbound beneath Sisco's is an enormous waterfront eatery with a no-surprises menu of pastas, burgers and light meals, or 'premium mains' (fillet steak, char-grilled lamb, seafood platter) for hungrier diners. Grab an outside table if you can.

Sticky Fingers (☎ 6223 1077; Murray St Pier; snacks $4-8; from 11.30am Mon-Fri, 10am Sat, 11am Sun) Fun, kid-friendly place for a pit stop, full of sweet treats like sundaes, smoothies, cakes, crepes and loads of flavoured ice cream and gelati.

Salamanca Map p70

This historic area has something to please everyone: bright cafés for people-watching over coffee, upmarket restaurants, cosy pubs and pit stops for a quick snack.

Salamanca Bakehouse (☎ 6224 6300; 5 Salamanca Sq; 24hr) The place for late-night munchies, with its ovens disgorging pies, pastries and rolls around the clock.

Maldini (☎ 6223 4460; 47 Salamanca Pl; mains $16-30; 8am-late) Classy Italian restaurant with the essential pasta and risotto dishes; mains such as Sicilian fish stew, osso bucco, and baked calamari; and tiramisu and grappa to wrap up the evening.

Ball & Chain Grill (☎ 6223 2655; 87 Salamanca Pl; mains $18-25; lunch Mon-Fri, dinner nightly) One for the carnivores (and for vegetarians to steer well clear of), this place serves up some of the best steak in town, cooked on a charcoal grill. The menu's not limited to steak – you can also have grilled game, chicken or seafood.

Retro Café (☎ 6223 3073; 31 Salamanca Pl; mains $8-12; 8am-6pm;) Top spot for Saturday brunch among the market stalls. There are huge breakfasts on offer, plus excellent coffee, and blackboard specials of bagels, salads, burgers and assorted lunchtime faves, served to a diverse and interesting clientele.

Zum Café (☎ 6223 7511; 27 Salamanca Pl; meals $7-15; 7am-6pm) Lots of heart-starting brekky options at this popular café-bakery, including pancakes and eggs Benedict or Florentine; also plenty of risottos, pastas and pastries to plug further holes in your stomach later in the day.

Sugo (☎ 6224 5690; 9 Salamanca Sq; mains $8.50-15; 9am-5pm) Tomato-red walls, good coffee and a menu heavy with Italian influences (pasta, pizza, risotto, *panini*) make this a *perfetto* café choice.

Mezethes (☎ 6224 4601; Salamanca Sq; mains $8.50-26; breakfast, lunch & dinner) Authentic Greek dishes are on offer here, including all the favourites (moussaka, souvlaki, lamb, fish) and, in true Hellenic style, a dazzling array of starters. The entrée platter ($18 for two) is a winner.

Machine Laundry Café (☎ 6224 9922; 12 Salamanca Sq; mains $8-15; 8am-6pm) Bright, retro-style café where you can wash your dirty clothes while discreetly adding fresh juice, soup or coffee stains to your clean ones (there's an on-site laundry).

Vietnamese Kitchen (☎ 6223 2188; 61 Salamanca Pl; mains $7.50-12; 11am-9.30pm) Cheap and cheerful eatery where you can happily overlook the daggy décor because the food and prices are just right. Two main courses from the *bain-marie* plus rice or noodles costs all of $7.50. Also cooked-to-order prawn and tofu dishes, and assorted noodle soups.

Say Cheese (☎ 6224 2888; 7 Salamanca Sq; mains $10.50-16.50; 9am-6pm) A friendly deli-café serving hearty breakfasts and great platters of cheese (of course), dips or antipasto – and even a kids' platter. Lots of wine options too. Leave some room for the lemon cheesecake.

Self-caterers looking for picnic supplies should head to Wursthaus (p96) for superb deli produce, or to the **fresh fruit market** (41 Salamanca Pl; 7am-7pm), which also stocks groceries.

Battery Point Map p70

With a few exceptions, options in Battery Point are along Hampden Rd.

Shipwrights Arms Hotel (Map p66; ☎ 6223 5551; 29 Trumpeter St; mains $15-24; ⏰ lunch & dinner Mon-Sat) Known locally as Shippies, this is a landmark 1834 yachties' pub, laid-back and popular with locals for its generously-portioned seafood meals and beer garden perfect for lazy summer afternoons.

Kelley's Seafood Restaurant (☎ 6224 7225; cnr James & Knopwood Sts; lunch $12.50-28, dinner mains $23-38; ⏰ lunch Mon-Fri, dinner nightly) An institution in Hobart, and well hidden in an 1849 sailmaker's cottage in the back streets of Battery Point. Offers lots of creatures fresh from the sea – the accidental occy (tenderised and grilled octopus) is a trademark dish. Bookings advised.

Da Angelo Ristorante (☎ 6223 7011; 47 Hampden Rd; mains $12.50-22.50; ⏰ dinner) Authentic *ristorante* specialising in Italian cuisine's best offerings. Choose from an impressively long menu of various homemade pastas, veal and chicken dishes, pizza with 20 different toppings, and calzone. Also offers takeaway.

Magic Curries (☎ 6223 4500; 41 Hampden Rd; mains $12-16; ⏰ dinner) The Indian cricket team have been known to dine here on occasion, so the food gets a good stamp of approval. Settle in with a Kingfisher beer and choose from the menu of Indian favourites, including fine vegetarian options. Takeaway available.

Restaurant Gondwana (☎ 6224 9900; cnr Hampden Rd & Francis St; dinner mains $25-33; ⏰ lunch Tue-Fri, dinner Mon-Sat) This place gets lots of recommendations from discerning Hobartians and has a menu of contemporary mod-Oz fare, utilising locally-sourced produce for dishes like macadamia-crusted trevalla, twice-roasted duck and poached wild scallops. Lunch is a little easier on the wallet. Bookings recommended.

Mummy's (☎ 6224 0124; 38 Waterloo Cres; mains $6-15; ⏰ Tue-Sun) Groovy licensed café, despite the somewhat worrying name. Enjoy all-day breakfast or classic café meals in the colourful interior or small courtyard. Often open for dinner in summer.

Francisco's on Hampden (☎ 6224 7124; 60 Hampden Rd; tapas plates $7-10, mains $21-25; ⏰ lunch Tue-Sun, dinner Tue-Sat) Upbeat, spacious tapas bar and restaurant, with strong Spanish leanings. There's a selection of snacky stuff to wash down with vino, plus larger meals (paella, seafood or meat platter) if you want a plate all to yourself.

Jackman & McRoss (☎ 6223 3186; 57-59 Hampden Rd; ⏰ 7.30am-6pm Mon-Fri, 7.30am-5pm Sat & Sun) This elegant bakery-café is deservedly popular – just check out that display cabinet full of fresh pies, tarts, baguettes and pastries, both sweet and savoury. Call in for an early-morning croissant and coffee, quiche or soup for lunch, and a pastry for afternoon tea.

North Hobart Map p66

Elizabeth St in North Hobart (between Burnett St and Federal Rd in particular, but with a few worthy options three blocks south) is a great hunting ground for restaurants, with a reputation for good-value cuisine reflecting a range of nationalities. There's no shortage of Asian and pizza joints, and plenty more besides.

Lickerish (☎ 6231 9186; 373 Elizabeth St; mains $24-28; ⏰ dinner Tue-Sat) One of our favourite Tassie meals was enjoyed at this gorgeous restaurant. The chef takes great local produce and gives it a winning new twist with primarily Asian and Middle-Eastern touches (such as Sichuan eggplant and organic tofu, curry of duck with flavours of tamarind, lemongrass and kaffir lime), and the results – together with the excellent service – are impressive. Bookings advised.

Amulet (☎ 6234 8113; 333 Elizabeth St; lunch $10-16, dinner mains $22-26; ⏰ lunch & dinner daily, also brunch Sat & Sun) The stylishly understated Amulet serves innovative, well-priced food – for lunch, how about asparagus ravioli with lemon crème fraîche, or roast-capsicum soup with pickled eggplant? Dinner choices are just as appealing, and desserts are worth leaving room for.

Annapurna (☎ 6236 9500; 305 Elizabeth St; mains $10-15; ⏰ lunch Mon-Fri, dinner daily) It seems like half of Hobart lists Annapurna as their favourite eatery – hence it's well worth booking. There's a delicious variety of northern and southern Indian cuisine, and the *masala dosa* (south Indian style of crepe filled with curried potato) is a crowd favourite (note that dosas are not available Friday or Saturday). Takeaway available.

Vanidol's (☎ 6234 9307; 353 Elizabeth St; mains $13-17; ⏰ dinner Tue-Sun) Busy BYO place offering a handful of Indian and Indonesian dishes, but predominantly Thai curries and stir-fries. There's seafood and plenty of vegetarian options; takeaway is available.

Sen's Asian Sensation (☎ 6236 9345; 345 Elizabeth St; mains $9-25; ⏲ lunch & dinner) Decent, cheap takeaways are available from the *bain-marie* at the front, but head to the informal restaurant section for great *yum cha*, noodles and excellent Chinese dishes.

Republic Bar & Café (☎ 6234 6954; 299 Elizabeth St; mains $13-20; ⏲ lunch Wed-Sun, dinner daily) Great pub with friendly atmosphere, an interesting mixed crowd, regular live music (see p95) and a kitchen producing what was recently voted the best pub food in Tasmania.

Kaos Café (☎ 6231 5699; 237 Elizabeth St; meals $12-19; ⏲ midday-midnight) A few blocks south of the restaurants listed above, this laid-back, gay-friendly café busies itself with a fine assortment of dishes, including great burgers, salads and risotto, serving until late (around 11.30pm most nights).

Casablanca (☎ 6234 9900; 213 Elizabeth St; mains $11-22; ⏲ dinner Mon-Sat) Loads of Italian choices at this friendly, bustling BYO restaurant a little south of Kaos Café. Needless to say, if you're after pizza, pasta, risotto and *scallopine* or *cotoletta*, you've come to the right place. Takeaway available.

A few blocks east of Elizabeth St is a **Woolworths supermarket** (189 Campbell St; ⏲ 7am-10pm), but self-caterers should also find most of what they need at **Fresco Market** (346 Elizabeth St; ⏲ 8.30am-8pm).

Sandy Bay — Map p66

Fish Bar (☎ 6234 5691; 50 King St; eat-in mains $6.50-16.50; ⏲ 8am-8pm) Cheerful, low-key café-takeaway, popular with locals for fresh (uncooked) seafood for sale, plus a variety of fish and chips combos (from $6.50), and other seafood treats (Thai fish cakes, seafood curry, Cajun-style trevally).

Metz (☎ 6224 4444; 217 Sandy Bay Rd; dinner mains $14.50-25; ⏲ from 10.30am Mon-Tue, from 8.30am Wed-Sun) Popular all-day café with large outdoor deck; transforms nightly into a bar (with DJs on Wednesday nights and Sunday afternoons). No surprises on the menu, which features salads, pastas and wood-fired pizza options, and some more upmarket mains at dinner time.

Satis (☎ 6224 0551; 231 Sandy Bay Rd; snacks & meals $5.50-11.50; ⏲ 8am-6pm Tue-Sat) This house is set back from the road, next door to Metz, and has been converted into smart modern tea rooms (no doilies or florals in sight). Order from the 75 varieties of tea on the menu, snack on yummy toasted *pides* or pastries, and enjoy the garden views from the front veranda.

Mitsuno (☎ 6223 3600; 50C King St; mains $20-25; ⏲ lunch Fri, dinner Tue-Sat) Wowing Hobartians with a delectable array of (in the owners' words) 'traditional and creative Japanese cuisine'. Visitors will love what the chefs do with fresh local produce, including Tassie salmon, seafood, steak and Bruny Island oysters. Bookings recommended.

Prosser's on the Beach (Map p75; ☎ 6225 2276; Beach Rd; mains $27-30; ⏲ lunch Wed-Fri, dinner Mon-Sat) Recent recipient of 'best seafood restaurant in Tasmania' award. Prosser's serves great (and surprisingly affordable) seafood dishes in relaxed, unpretentious premises overlooking the water at Sandy Bay Point (a taxi ride from town but worth the trip). Bookings recommended.

The Point Revolving Restaurant (☎ 6221 1701; 410 Sandy Bay Rd; mains $31-39; ⏲ lunch Fri, dinner nightly) A special-occasion choice, on the 17th floor of Wrest Point and boasting magnificent views. Some modern dishes such as crispy-skinned salmon on crab ravioli as well as daggy old favourites like steak Diane, flambé prawns and bombe Alaska, but at these prices you know they'll be excellent. Ask about the $57 set menu too. Bookings recommended.

Beach House Hotel Café Bar (Map p75; ☎ 6225 4644; 646 Sandy Bay Rd; mains $12-25; ⏲ from 9am daily) The Long Beach area is 2km south of Wrest Point, well off the tourist track and worth a visit for the lovely setting. Go for a wander before retiring to this welcoming café-bar with beachy décor and creative seafood and pasta.

Self-caterers should head to **Coles supermarket** (246 Sandy Bay Rd; ⏲ 7am-midnight) and nearby **Woolworths** (57 King St; ⏲ 7am-midnight).

South Hobart — Map p75

There's not a huge number of eateries out this way, but if you're visiting Cascade brewery or the Female Factory and feeling peckish, these are worth knowing about.

Macquarie St Food Store (☎ 6224 6862; 356 Macquarie St; snacks & meals $7-14; ⏲ 7.30am-6pm Mon-Fri, 8.30am-6pm Sat & Sun) One of Hobart's favourite cafés, and usually packed with locals. About 2km from the brewery, it's a perfect spot for reading the paper over breakfast (served until 3pm) and good coffee. There are a couple of outdoor tables with views of moody Mt Wellington.

Salad Bowl (☎ 6223 7728; 362 Macquarie St; from 7am daily) Great picnic fodder available at this store, as well as fresh fruit and veg, groceries, deli items and ready-cooked meals.

Other Locations

The following all offer a special experience (food and/or views, or a combination of the two) and are worth making the drive.

Lebrina (Map p75; ☎ 6228 7775; 155 New Town Rd, New Town; mains $30-35; dinner Tue-Sat) Food-lovers positively gush about this restaurant. Found in Hobart's northern reaches, it looks small and unremarkable from the outside, but inside it's all about your sheer dining pleasure, from the décor to the service to the wine list – and, of course, the food. Bookings essential.

Cornelian Bay Boathouse (Map p75; ☎ 6228 9289; Queen's Walk; lunch mains $12-23.50, dinner mains $19-25; lunch daily, dinner Mon-Sat) Popular, stylish restaurant-bar in a magic location on Cornelian Bay, just north of Queen's Domain. It serves contemporary cuisine starring lots of quality local produce, with great service too.

Mount Nelson Signal Station Restaurant (Map p75; ☎ 6223 3407; 700 Nelson Rd; light meals $5.50-14, mains $15-25; 9.30am-4.30pm daily, plus dinner Wed-Sat) Try to bag a table by the window at this elegant restaurant with a panoramic view, set in Mt Nelson's historic chief signalman's house. It serves morning and afternoon teas and light or more substantial lunches, plus dinner later in the week (dinner bookings essential in winter).

Moorilla Estate (Map p75; ☎ 6277 9900; 655 Main Rd, Berriedale; mains $19-27; lunch) Enjoy lunch overlooking the grapevines before a browse through the excellent museum here (p73). Menu options might include baked ocean trout or slow-cooked duck; the vineyard platter is a good choice, and you can complement your meal with a generous sample of five house wines for only $9.

DRINKING

Knopwood's Retreat (Map p70; ☎ 6223 5808; 39 Salamanca Pl; 10am-late) Follow the 'when in Rome…' advice and head for Knopwood's, a perennial Hobart favourite. It's usually hidden behind a solid mass of Friday-night drinkers loitering on the pavement section (well, it's been 'a Friday night institution since 1829', if you believe its publicity).

Irish Murphy's (Map p70; ☎ 6223 1119; 21 Salamanca Pl; noon-late Mon-Thu, 11am-late Fri & Sun, 9am-late Sat) Just as you'd expect from an Irish-themed pub anywhere in the world, this one is often crowded, lively, friendly and well stocked with Guinness. There's live music from Wednesday to Sunday, and it serves meals too.

Hope & Anchor Tavern (Map p70; ☎ 6236 9982; 65 Macquarie St; dinner) Make the time to call into this atmospheric old pub, dating from 1807. The downstairs bar (open from 3pm daily) has great lounges and a range of cheap bar snacks; upstairs is a gorgeous, museum-like bar and dining room.

Other commendable city pubs (see opposite for details) include the New Sydney Hotel, Customs House Hotel and Telegraph Hotel, all doing as good pubs should – serving food and alcohol-flavoured beverages, as well as putting on regular live music. In the north, don't miss everybody's favourite local, the Republic Bar & Café. In Battery Point, join the yachties and locals amongst the yachting paraphernalia at the Shipwrights Arms Hotel (Map p66; ☎ 6223 5551; 29 Trumpeter St), known affectionately as Shippies (see also p92).

Bar Celona (Map p70; ☎ 6224 7557; 24 Salamanca Sq; 10am-midnight) By day Bar Celona is a café-style spot with decent lunch menu; of an evening it's a popular wine bar with open fire (no meals). On Friday and Saturday nights, the upstairs loft-style lounge (called Elevation) is a cruisy little space with DJ.

T-42° (Map p70; ☎ 6224 7742; Elizabeth St Pier; until late) This waterfront place still draws a mass of barflies to its minimalist interior after dinner with plenty of booze and funky background music.

IXL Long Bar at Henry Jones (Map p70; ☎ 6210 7700; 25 Hunter St) Prop yourself at the bar of this fab new hotel and check out Hobart's fashionable folk over cocktails. If there are no spare stools at the not-so-long bar, or you just want to take a load off, flop onto the leather couches in the nearby lobby area.

Lizbon (Map p66; ☎ 6234 933; 217 Elizabeth St; 6pm-midnight Mon, 4pm-midnight Tue, 4pm-3am Wed-Sat) In the movie *Casablanca*, everyone wanted to leave the namesake town to have some fun in Lisbon. And now the owner of Casablanca Italian restaurant in North Hobart (p93) has cleverly worked the idea into his cool new wine bar, which boasts excellent wines by the glass, antipasto platters, smooth tunes and cosy nooks and crannies.

Soak@Kaos (Map p66; ☎ 6231 5699; 237 Elizabeth St; ⏰ midday-late) A great choice for an intoxicating late afternoon or evening. Gay-friendly Soak is an intimate little lounge bar attached to Kaos Café (p93), where you can eat burgers or cake from the café alongside pretty cocktails, while listening to the resident DJ on Friday and Saturday nights until 3am. And did anyone notice that Soak is Kaos spelt backwards?

Halo (Map p70; ☎ 6234 6669; upstairs, 37a Elizabeth St; ⏰ 4pm-late Thu-Sun) Locals drop into this shiny new bar for after-work or after-dinner drinks, or before hitting the town. There are often DJs spinning loungey tracks, and at least once a month the place gets pumping with dance events (including gay nights called Lalaland) – check the local press for details of these.

ENTERTAINMENT

Nightclubs

It's got to be said – few people come to Hobart for its nightlife! Still, there is action if you know where to find it. Anyone looking to tap into the (admittedly small and low-key) gay scene should contact the numbers listed in the Gay & Lesbian Travellers section of the Directory chapter (p320), or just head along to Kaos Café (p93) and make enquiries. See also the listing for Halo, above.

Round Midnight & Syrup (Map p70; ☎ 6224 8249; 39 Salamanca Pl; ⏰ Thu-Sat night) A great place for late-night drinks and a mixture of live music and techno/house DJs, above Knopwood's Retreat. Sharing the premises is Syrup, the best bar-club in town.

Isobar (Map p70; ☎ 6231 6600; 11 Franklin Wharf; ⏰ 10pm-5am Wed, Fri & Sat) Downstairs at Isobar is a popular bar, while 'Isobar the club' is a first-floor venue that generally plays commercial music, and blows hot and cold with the locals.

Live Music

Republic Bar & Café (Map p66; ☎ 6234 6954; www.republicbar.com; 299 Elizabeth St, Nth Hobart) The Republic is a fine, raucous bar hosting live music every night (usually, but not always, free entry). It's the No 1 live-music pub in town, with an always-interesting line-up and an understandably loyal following.

New Sydney Hotel (Map p70; ☎ 6234 4516; www.newsydneyhotel.com; 87 Bathurst St) Low-key Irish folk, jazz and blues from Tuesday to Saturday, mostly free. The occasional pub-rock outfit and the end-of-week crowd adds a few decibels. It has 10 beers on tap and is a sociable place for a drink or three.

Irish Murphy's (Map p70; ☎ 6223 1119; 21 Salamanca Pl; ⏰ noon-late Mon-Thu, 11am-late Fri & Sun, 9am-late Sat) This place has fake, prehistoric-looking earthenware walls that might have been built by a Guinness-soused Fred Flintstone, but it's nonetheless a popular pub that puts on free live music from Wednesday to Sunday. Trad sessions from 3pm Sunday.

Other bar/pub gig options (all free) include those at the **Telegraph Hotel** (Map p70; ☎ 6234 6254; 19 Morrison St) and the nearby **Customs House Hotel** (Map p70; ☎ 6234 6645; 1 Murray St), where live music usually plays Wednesday to Sunday nights.

CLASSICAL MUSIC

Federation Concert Hall (Map p70; ☎ 6235 3633, 1800 001 190; www.tso.com.au; 1 Davey St; box office ⏰ 9.30am-4.30pm Mon-Fri) Trapped inside the large, graceless metal cylinder welded to the Hotel Grand Chancellor is this concert hall, which is home to the Tasmanian Symphony

START THE WEEKEND RIGHT

The best live music in Hobart plays every Friday year-round from 5.30pm to 7.30pm at Salamanca Arts Centre courtyard (off Wooby's Lane) – and it's free (donations welcome). This community event started about five years ago and has come to be known as Rektango – but that's a bit of a misnomer, as Rektango is the name of a band that occasionally plays here. The bands vary from month to month, and could play anything from African beats to rockabilly to folk or gypsy-latino. This is a fantastic family-friendly event with lots of atmosphere. Drinks are available (including sangria in summer, mulled wine in winter); dancing is optional…

FINGER ON THE PULSE

The *Mercury* newspaper lists most of Hobart's entertainment options in its Thursday insert, 'Pulse'. Also check out the online gig guide at www.nakeddwarf.com.au.

LIVE Tasmania (www.livetasmania.com), a joint project from several performing arts groups, can help you to find live theatre, puppetry, dance or music performances during your time in Hobart.

Orchestra. It's also used to stage other classical performances. The box office is open before all performances.

Cinemas

State Cinema (Map p66; ☎ 6234 6318; www.statecinema.com.au; 375 Elizabeth St, Nth Hobart) Screens mainly independent local and international flicks.

Village Cinemas (Map p70; ☎ 6234 7288; 181 Collins St) Large inner-city complex showing mainstream releases.

Theatre

Live theatre can be enjoyed at a number of venues around town, including the venerable **Theatre Royal** (Map p70; box office ☎ 6233 2299, 1800 650 277; www.theatreroyal.webcentral.com.au; 29 Campbell St), which staged its first performance in 1837. At the back of the Royal, down Sackville St, is the smaller Backspace Theatre, staging innovative, more artistically alternative productions. There's also the **Playhouse Theatre** (Map p70; ☎ 6234 1536; www.playhouse.org.au; 106 Bathurst St), home of the Hobart Repertory Theatre Society.

The intimate **Peacock Theatre** (Map p70; ☎ 62 34 8414; www.salarts.org.au) is inside the Salamanca Arts Centre, along with a handful of other small performance spaces.

Casino

There is a maze of late-night, often lurid bars and lounges to be found at **Wrest Point** (Map p66; ☎ 6225 0112; www.wrestpoint.com.au; 410 Sandy Bay Rd), the oldest casino in Australia. Its centrepiece is the main **casino** (🕑 from 2pm), which is augmented by several early-bird **gaming lounges** (🕑 from 9am). Bus Nos 54 and 55 run to Wrest Point.

SHOPPING

Most of Hobart's speciality shops and services are in the city centre. The main shopping area extends west from the mall on Elizabeth St and shopping arcades dot the inner-city blocks. There are also shopping centres to the south at Sandy Bay, to the north at Glenorchy and on the eastern side of the river at Bellerive – these are fairly generic consumer rallying points, but they have been known to yield the odd interesting shop. The best shopping for fine Tasmanian arts and crafts is in the numerous shops and galleries on Salamanca Pl (and at the market held here every Saturday).

Antiques

Antique stores exist all over the state, some selling wares that qualify as little more than browse-worthy bric-a-brac and others specialising in well-aged articles of jewellery, artworks, furniture and other domestic artefacts. The wealth of colonial antiquities is a result of the large number of settlers who migrated here from Europe in the 19th century and brought their furniture with them.

There are a few good antique stores in the city centre, and around the junction of Hampden Rd and Sandy Bay Rd, in Battery Point. Pick up the *Antique Shops of Hobart* brochure (available at the visitors centre), which details a few options. These include:

Antiques Market (Map p70; ☎ 6234 4425; www.theantiquesmarket.com.au; 125 Elizabeth St; 🕑 daily)

Bathurst St Antique Centre (Map p66; ☎ 6236 9422; 128 Bathurst St; 🕑 Mon-Sat)

Food & Wine

Fine Tasmanian produce is available everywhere – just head to the nearest supermarket for great cheeses, sauces and other assorted digestibles. And be sure to check out Salamanca Market, where you can walk away with more oil, jams and fudge than you might have planned (trust us, we know!).

Other essential stops include these:

Tasmanian Wine Centre (Map p66; ☎ 6234 9995; www.tasmanian-wine.com.au; 201 Collins St; 🕑 Mon-Sat) Stocks a huge range of the state's wines; also organises shipping, winery tours and tutored wine tastings for groups.

Wursthaus (Map p70; ☎ 6224 0644; www.wursthaus.com.au; 1 Montpelier Retreat; 🕑 daily) Fine-food showcase just off Salamanca Pl. Hobart's best, selling speciality small goods, cheeses, breads, wines, pre-prepared meals and much more.

Galleries

Pick up a copy of the *Gallery Guide* brochure from the visitors centre to point you around the town's art hot spots. These include the following:

Art Mob (Map p70; ☎ 6236 9200; www.artmob.com.au; 29 Hunter St) By the Henry Jones Art Hotel, displaying and selling Aboriginal fine art.

Despard Gallery (Map p70; ☎ 6223 8266; www.despard-gallery.com.au; 15 Castray Esplanade) Exhibits and sells top-quality contemporary Tasmanian artworks.

Handmark Gallery (Map p70; ☎ 6223 7895; www.handmarkgallery.com; 77 Salamanca Pl) Interesting ceramics, glass, wood and textiles, as well as paintings and sculpture.

Outdoor Clothing & Equipment

There's a plethora of stores on Elizabeth St, between Melville and Bathurst Sts, catering to outdoorsy types in a state overflowing with national parks and wilderness. See p68 for information on where to purchase topographic maps.

Kathmandu (Map p70; ☎ 6224 3027; 16 Salamanca Sq)

Paddy Pallin (Map p70; ☎ 6231 0777; 119 Elizabeth St)

Recycled Recreation (Map p70; ☎ 6234 3575; 54 Bathurst St) At The Climbing Edge indoor rock-climbing centre – sells second-hand outdoor gear.

Spot On Fishing Tackle (Map p70; ☎ 6234 4880; 89 Harrington St) For fishing supplies.

GETTING THERE & AWAY

Air

For information on domestic flights to and from Hobart, see p332. **Qantas** (Map p70; ☎ 13 13 13; 130 Collins St) has an office in the centre of town.

Bus

See p335 for general information on intrastate bus services.

There are two main bus companies (and their terminals) operating to/from Hobart:

Redline Coaches (Map p66; ☎ 6336 1446, 1300 360 000; www.tasredline.com.au) Operates from the Transit Centre at 199 Collins St.

TassieLink (Map p70; ☎ 6271 7320, 1300 300 520; www.tassielink.com.au) Operates from the Hobart Bus Terminal at 64 Brisbane St.

Also based in the capital is **Hobart Coaches** (☎ 6233 4232, 13 22 01; www.hobartcoaches.com.au), with useful services running to Richmond, New Norfolk, Kingston and Blackmans Bay, and south along the D'Entrecasteaux Channel (Margate, Snug, Kettering, Woodbridge) and to Cygnet. See those towns for more specific information on services and prices to/from Hobart. For assistance visit the Metro bus information desk inside the main post office, on the corner of Elizabeth and Macquarie Sts.

GETTING AROUND

To/From the Airport

The airport is 16km east of the centre. The **Airporter shuttle bus** (☎ 0419 382 240) travels between the city (via various places to stay) and the airport for $9.70/4.80 per adult/child. Bookings for the city pick-ups are essential.

A taxi between the airport and city centre should cost $32 (6am to 8pm weekdays) or $37 (all other times).

Bicycle

See p78 for details of bike-rental places in Hobart.

Boat

There are plenty of cruises (p81), but little by way of commuter boats.

Captain Fell's Historic Ferries (Map p70; ☎ 6223 5893; Franklin Wharf) has a weekday service between Hobart and Bellerive, run primarily to transport residents to and from work. The boat departs Hobart's Franklin Wharf at 7.50am and 5.25pm; return boats are at 8.15am and 5.40pm. A one-way/return ticket is $3.50/7.

Bus

Metro (☎ 13 22 01; www.metrotas.com.au) operates the local bus network, and there's an information desk dispensing timetables inside the main post office at the corner of Elizabeth and Macquarie Sts. Most buses leave from this area of Elizabeth St, which is known as the Metro city bus station, or from around the edges of nearby Franklin Square.

One-way fares vary according to distance travelled (from $1.50 to $3.40). For $3.90 ($11 per family), you can get an unlimited-travel Day Rover ticket that can be used after 9am Monday to Friday, and all day Saturday, Sunday and public holidays. If you're staying in Hobart for a while, you should consider a Day Rover pass for $31.20, which is valid for any 10 days (not necessarily consecutive) and has the same restrictions on peak-hour travel. An alternative is to buy a book of 10 discounted tickets that can be used at any time of day.

Car

There are a large number of car-rental firms in Hobart; most have representation at the airport. The large multinationals have desks inside the terminal; smaller local companies have representation in the car park area. City offices are primarily found along Harrington St, including the following:

AutoRent-Hertz (Map p66; ☎ 6237 1111; www.autorent.com.au; cnr Bathurst & Harrington Sts)
Avis (Map p66; ☎ 6234 4222; www.avis.com.au; 125 Bathurst St)
Budget (Map p70; ☎ 6234 5222, 13 27 27; www.budget.com.au; 96 Harrington St)
Europcar (Map p66; ☎ 6231 1077, 1800 030 118; www.europcar.com.au; 112 Harrington St)
Thrifty (Map p70; ☎ 6234 1341, 1800 030 730; www.tasvacations.com.au; 11-17 Argyle St)

Some of the cheaper local firms, with daily rental rates starting around $30, follow:

Lo-Cost Auto Rent (Map p70; ☎ 6231 0550, 1800 647 060; www.rentforless.com.au; 105 Murray St)
Rent-a-Bug (Map p70; ☎ 6231 0300, 1800 647 060; www.rentforless.com.au; 105 Murray St)
Selective Car Rentals (Map p70; ☎ 6234 3311, 1800 300 102; www.selectivecarrentals.com.au; 47 Bathurst St)

See p337 for more details.

Taxi

For a taxi, try the following companies:

City Cabs (☎ 13 10 08)
Maxi-Taxi Services (☎ 6234 3573) Can provide vehicles that accommodate disabled people.
Taxi Combined Services (☎ 13 22 27)

Around Hobart

Hobart is hardly overrun with people, but when you've had your fill of cosmopolitan treats in the 'big smoke', you won't have to travel too far to swap the cityscape for great natural scenery, clean sandy beaches, and some popular historic sites. The lush countryside and water views between the capital and its satellite suburbs and towns are attractions in themselves. The historic penal settlement of Port Arthur and the stunning cliffs of the Tasman Peninsula make for a good side-trip, or you can immerse yourself in convict history in Richmond, with its fascinating old gaol and convict-built bridge. Alternatively, head to a beach and unwind (good options can be found south of Hobart at Kingston, or on the Tasman Peninsula), or to Mt Field National Park for waterfalls, wildlife and fantastic short walks.

There's no shortage of walking opportunities in Hobart's surrounds, but if you're looking to get your heart racing you'll also be well served: from winter skiing in Mt Field to jet-boating the Derwent River out of New Norfolk or scuba diving off the Tasman Peninsula. Those after something a little more sedate should also find activities to suit their taste(buds), including touring the vineyards of the Coal River Valley or picking fresh fruit in Sorell.

All the options in this chapter are within 100km of Hobart and can be done as a day trip from the capital (either independently or on a tour). To really get a feel for a place, however, you can't beat an overnight stay.

HIGHLIGHTS

- Sinking a few beers in the courtyard of the **Kingston Hotel** (p100) after a hard day doing very little on the nearby **beach**
- Tracing your fingers over old stonework at **Port Arthur** (p117) and getting spooked out of your wits on a **ghost tour**
- Getting your hands dirty picking fresh berries and cherries at **Sorell Fruit Farm** (p114)
- Feeling the spray of Russell Falls at **Mt Field National Park** (p106), then heading off for a longer walk
- Stopping for Devonshire tea or a glass of locally produced wine while exploring the history of **Richmond** (p108)
- Spotting a platypus while snacking alfresco at the idyllic **Possum Shed café** (p106) at Westerway
- Squealing through the turns of a **jet-boat ride** (p104) on the scenic Derwent River out of New Norfolk
- Escaping reality and pitching a tent at beautiful **Fortescue Bay** (p117)

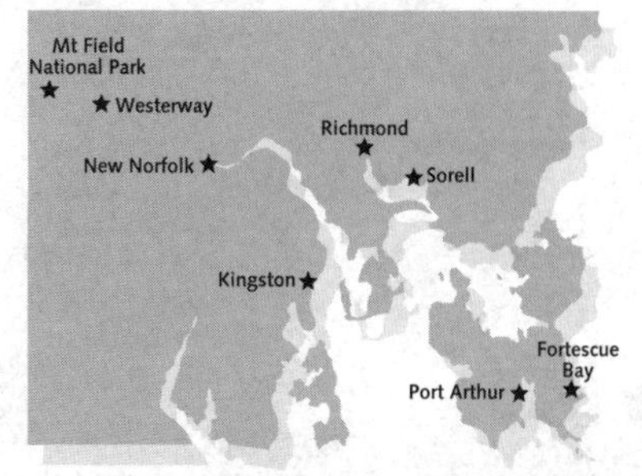

SOUTH OF HOBART

The Channel Hwy is the continuation of Sandy Bay Rd and hugs the coastline as it heads south. It became a pleasant tourist drive after the construction of the Southern Outlet (Hwy A6) from Hobart to Kingston and beyond removed most of the traffic. This winding road is benched into the lower slopes of Mt Nelson, so drive slowly and let your passengers check out the views, hilltop houses and fine gardens en route south.

TAROONA

☎ 03

Ten kilometres from Hobart is the town of Taroona, its name derived from an Aboriginal word meaning 'seashell'. Taroona's main claim to fame is as the hometown of Mary Donaldson, now Crown Princess Mary of Denmark (see opposite).

Just south of Taroona is the landmark **Shot Tower** (☎ 6227 8885; adult/child $5.50/2.50; 9am6pm daily). Completed in 1870, the 48m-high tower is made from sandstone, with every block curved and tapered. From the top are fine views over the Derwent River estuary. Lead shot for use in guns was once produced in high towers like this by dropping molten lead from the top, which formed a perfect sphere on its way down.

The tower is surrounded by leafy grounds and has a souvenir shop and a cosy **tearoom** (light meals $3-8); if it's sunny, devour a Devonshire tea on the stone rampart outside.

Hillgrove (☎ 6227 9043; 269 Channel Hwy; d $120, extra adult $25), directly opposite the Shot Tower, is a 19th-century Georgian cottage set in a lovely garden. Guests get the run of the two-bedroom, self-contained ground floor (sleeps three), plus a large veranda from which to enjoy the leafy surrounds and Shot Tower views.

To get to the Shot Tower, take bus No 56, 60 or 61 from Hobart's Franklin Square to stop 45.

KINGSTON

☎ 03 / pop 12,910

Kingston, 12km south of Hobart and basically a sprawling outer suburb of the city,

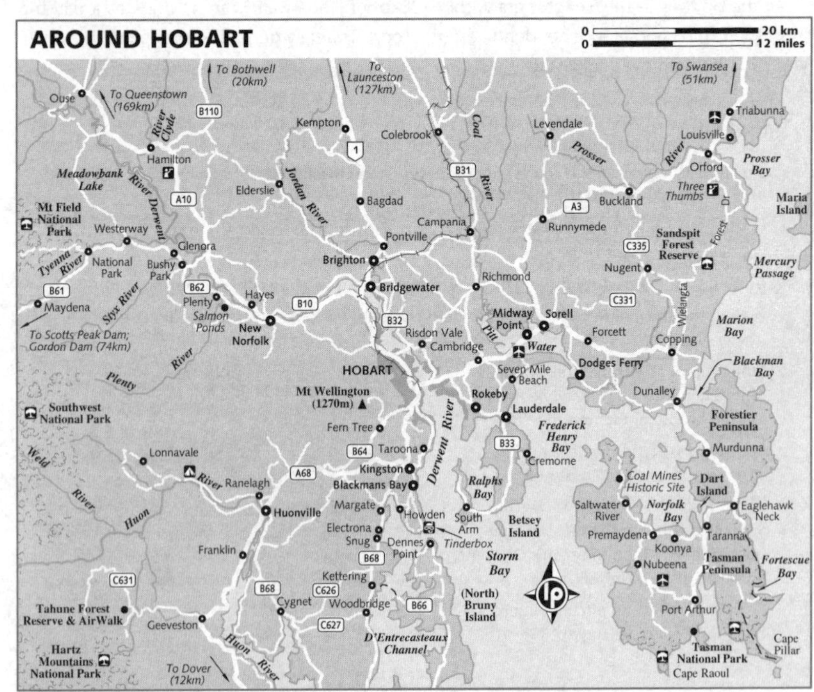

expanded rapidly once the Southern Outlet roadway provided fast access to the town, allowing commuters to move on in.

The beach here is a superb spot to laze away a sunny afternoon and reflect on how a long, clean, sandy beach so close to an Australian capital city has remained so low-key and uncommercial (there are no high-rise apartment blocks here – touch wood!).

Sights & Activities

KINGSTON BEACH

As you branch off from the Southern Outlet and approach Kingston, continue straight ahead at the first set of lights instead of turning right onto the Channel Hwy; this road takes you all the way to the beach. If coming down the Channel Hwy from Taroona, follow the arrow to Blackmans Bay.

Kingston Beach is a popular swimming and sailing spot, with attractive wooded cliffs hemming in a long arc of white sand. There's a good picnic area at the northern end, accessed by a pedestrian bridge over the reputedly pollution-prone, non-swimmable (and therefore aptly named) Browns River.

Located behind the sailing clubhouse at the southern end is the start of a track to a beautiful secluded beach called **Boronia**, which has a deep rock pool. Note, though, that sections of this walk are heavily eroded. **Blackmans Bay**, about 3km from Kingston Beach, has another good beach and a blowhole (down Blowhole Rd). The water at these beaches is usually quite cold, and there's rarely any surf.

ANTARCTIC DIVISION

Beside the Channel Hwy south of Kingston is the headquarters of the **Australian Antarctic Division** (☎ 6232 3209; www.aad.gov.au; 203 Channel Hwy; admission free; ⌚ 9am-5pm Mon-Fri), the department administering Australia's 42% portion of the frozen continent. Australia has had a long history of exploration and scientific study of Antarctica and is one of the original 12 nations that set up the Antarctic Treaty in 1961. Visitors are welcome to check out the fine displays here, which feature authentic equipment like clothing and vehicles used by scientists, plus ecology information and some stunning photographs (especially in the Frank Hurley Theatre). The centre's cafeteria is open to the public and sells souvenirs.

Sleeping

Kingston Beach Motel (☎ 6229 8969; 31 Osborne Esplanade; d $110, additional person $20) Old-style motel exterior but revamped rooms (with kitchenettes) directly opposite Kingston

THE CROWN PRINCESS OF DENMARK (AKA MARY DONALDSON OF TAROONA)

A few Tasmanians have found themselves in the spotlight in recent years, but no-one has captured more international attention than Mary Donaldson, the girl from Taroona now living the modern-day fairy tale in Europe. Mary was born in Hobart in 1972 to Scots who had emigrated to Australia a decade earlier. The youngest of four children, she attended Taroona High School before obtaining a degree in commerce and law from the University of Tasmania in 1993. After completing her education Mary moved to Melbourne and worked in advertising, then took off to travel in Europe and the US before eventually returning to Australia and settling in Sydney.

Mary met Denmark's Crown Prince Frederik in a Sydney pub during the 2000 Olympic Games; the prince was in Australia with the Danish sailing team. The pair began a relationship that set the gossip mags into a frenzy of speculation until Mary and Fred announced their engagement in October 2003. They married in a lavish ceremony in Copenhagen in May 2004 with a sea of well-wishers lining the streets, waving Danish and Australian flags. By all accounts, interest in Tasmania as a holiday destination for the Danes has escalated, and much Tassie produce has found a new export market due to the intense curiosity surrounding Mary and her background.

At the time of research, 'Our Mary' (sorry, HRH Crown Princess Mary) is never too far from the covers of Danish and Australian gossip mags as writers poke and probe into every aspect of her life: is she looking too thin? Does she own too many shoes (yes, really)? Was that a gallstone she had removed, or is she pregnant? At the time of writing, royal-watchers and magazine editors were delighted with the announcement that the photogenic couple were expecting a baby in late October 2005.

DETOUR

Make time to drive through Blackmans Bay and another 10km on to **Tinderbox**. The views along the way are lovely and at Tinderbox itself is a small beach bordering a marine reserve – here you can snorkel along an underwater trail that runs alongside a sandstone reef and is marked with submerged information plates explaining the rich ecosystems of the area (see www.parks.tas.gov.au/marine/tindbox). Bruny Island is just across the water and locals often launch their outboards here to skim over to Dennes Point.

From Tinderbox, you can continue around the peninsula to Howden and return to Kingston along the Channel Hwy.

Beach, and harbouring plans for expansion (including the addition of a café out front). There are cheaper rates in the off-season or for longer stays.

Tranquilla (☎ 6229 6282; 30 Osborne Esplanade; d $110, additional person $20) Next door to the motel, this tranquil establishment has a self-contained unit that can sleep up to four, set in lovely gardens and with breakfast provisions included.

On the Beach (☎ 6229 3096; wilksey@bigpond.com; 38 Osborne Esplanade; d $100) Not quite on the beach, but directly across the road and with one self-contained unit attached to the rear of the owners' home. There's also a large two-bedroom unit upstairs here that's ideal for two couples (no children).

Eating

Citrus Moon Cafe (☎ 6229 2388; 23 Beach Rd; mains $8-14; 🕑 9am-5pm Tue-Thu, 9am-9pm Fri, 10am-5pm Sat-Mon) Bright, retro-style café with a predominantly vegetarian menu. You can devour brekky until noon, then choose from burgers, bagels or salads for lunch, or stop in simply for coffee and cake (vegan, flourless or regular options available).

Beachside Hotel (☎ 6229 6185; 2 Beach Rd; mains $14-22; 🕑 lunch & dinner) Good-quality pub fare on offer, plus an outdoor dining area perfect during warm weather. There are also cheap bar snacks, and occasional live music in summer to draw the crowds.

The Beach (☎ 6229 7600; Ocean Esplanade, Blackmans Bay; snacks & mains $7-27; 🕑 10am-late) On a sunny day, there's no better spot than the outdoor terrace of this stylish, multipurpose café-restaurant-bar, south of Kingston, opposite the beach in Blackmans Bay.

Getting There & Away

Hobart Coaches (☎ 13 22 01; www.hobartcoaches.com.au) runs regular services (bus Nos 70 and 80) from Hobart to Kingston Beach and Blackmans Bay throughout the day; the fare to both destinations is $2.50 one way.

DERWENT & TYENNA VALLEYS

NEW NORFOLK

☎ 03 / pop 9000

Set in the lush, rolling countryside of the Derwent Valley is New Norfolk. The area was first visited by Europeans in 1793 and began taking on the hallmarks of a town in 1808, when an Irish convict built the first house. By the 1860s the valley had become an important hop-growing centre, which is why the area is dotted with old oast houses (used for drying the plant). Hops, which give beer its characteristic bitterness, are sensitive to wind and so trees were planted as a natural barrier. Today, distinctive rows of tall poplars mark the boundaries of former hop fields.

Originally called Elizabeth Town, New Norfolk was renamed after the arrival of settlers (from 1808 onwards) from the abandoned Pacific Ocean colony on Norfolk Island. Today the town is a mixture of colonial remnants and more contemporary sights and activities, and has a wide range of accommodation and good facilities, including banks (with ATMs), along High St.

The town **visitors centre** (☎ 6261 3700; Circle St; 🕑 10am-4pm) is behind the courthouse. There is good information about New Norfolk and surrounds at www.riversrun.net.au.

For Internet access, head to **Willow Court Budget Accommodation** (☎ 6261 8780; entry on George St; per 30/60 min $3/5).

Sights & Activities

HISTORIC BUILDINGS

The eye-catching **Oast House** (☎ 6261 4123; 🕑 9am-6pm), on the perimeter of Tynwald

Park, off the highway on the Hobart side of town, was built in the 1820s and served as a piggery before devoting itself to hops from 1867 to 1969. The timber building's kilns were used to dry and package hops for delivery to breweries. You can go on a self-guided tour of its **museum** (adult/child $5/3; ⌚ 10am-6pm), following the story of how hops were processed. Also here are an extensive craft gallery and restaurant.

St Matthew's Church (Bathurst St), built in 1823, is Tasmania's oldest Anglican church. It's been extensively altered since it first rose from the ground and its best features today are the excellent stained-glass windows. In the adjacent St Matthew's Close is a **craft shop** (⌚ 9am-5pm) that raises money for the church's ongoing restoration – on one wall is a large clockface from the clocktower (long demolished) of the Royal Derwent Hospital, the asylum around which the town was based in the 1850s.

The old asylum, **Willow Court** (George St), dates from the 1820s and housed invalid convicts before it began to provide services to the wider community. In 1968 it housed about 1000 patients as part of the state's mental health program. In the 1980s asylums began to be phased out in favour of community-based treatment and housing, and in 2000 the asylum was closed. The complex has since been sold to developers with grand plans for a number of facilities in varying stages, including gardens, restaurants,

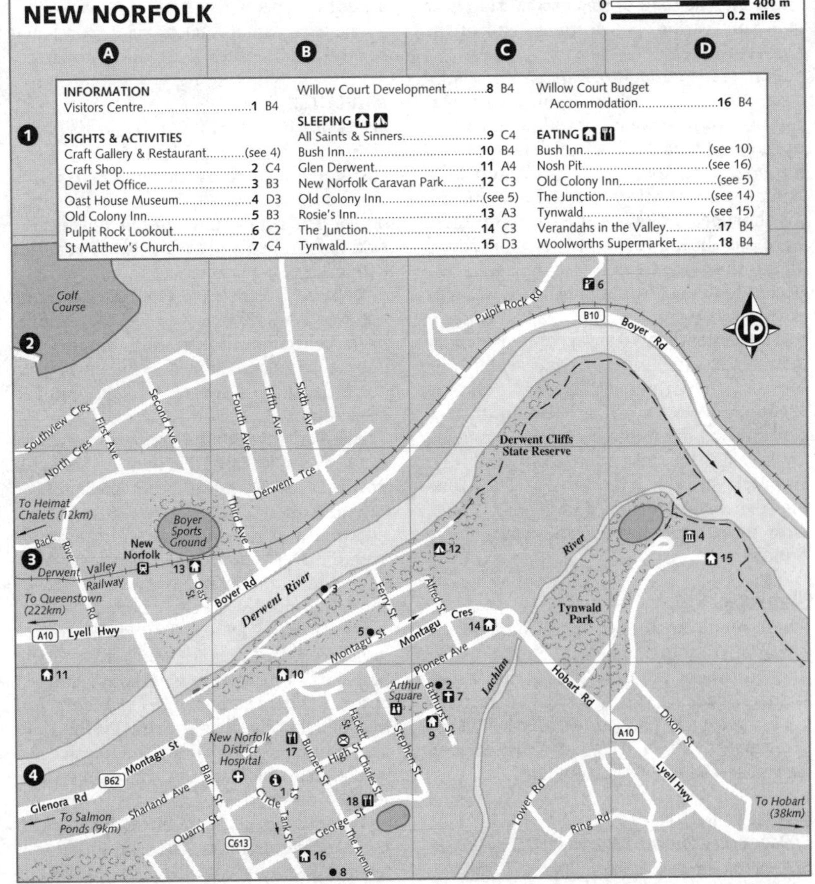

residential units and a five-star boutique hotel. At the time of research a hostel and family restaurant had opened and attention had turned to finishing a steakhouse-bar. Read more at www.willowcourt.com.au.

Old Colony Inn (☎ 6261 2731; 21 Montagu St; adult/child $2/50c; 🕑 10am-5pm) is a distinctive, black-and-white museum of colonial furnishings and artefacts, built in 1815 as a hop shed. It's on a one-way street, so prepare to make a tight U-turn at the top end of the road division on Montagu St if you're approaching from Hobart.

OTHER ATTRACTIONS

Get a fine view over New Norfolk by following the road along the northern side of the river eastward for 1km, then up a steep, unsealed side road to **Pulpit Rock**. From here you can overlook a sweeping bend of the Derwent River.

Devil Jet (☎ 6261 3460; www.deviljet.com.au; Esplanade; 🕑 9am-4pm) offers 30-minute jet-boat rides on the Derwent, whisking you 10km upriver and back. The 'jets' take off on the hour, and cost $50/25 per adult/child; bookings are recommended. Look out too for short **boat cruises** on the Derwent; these were only in the very early planning stages at the time of research but they were expected to depart from opposite the caravan park.

The **Derwent Valley Railway** (☎ 6261 1946; www.railtasmania.com/dvr) runs a train from New Norfolk to Mt Field National Park via Plenty and Westerway, at 10am on the second and fourth Sundays of each month, costing $30/20 per adult/child one-way. A much shorter rail journey is the one between New Norfolk and Plenty ($7/5), with trains operating on this route every Sunday.

Sleeping

There seems an inordinate amount of accommodation in and around New Norfolk, and outside of the peak times (Christmas, January, Easter), you shouldn't struggle to find a room. If you do, the **Derwent Valley Accommodation Line** (DEVAL; ☎ 6261 5566; www.derwentvalley.net.au; 🕑 24hr) can help.

BUDGET

Willow Court Budget Accommodation (☎ 6261 8780; entry on George St; dm $18-22, s/tw/d/f $24/48/55/85; 💻) Part of the Willow Court redevelopment is this new hostel, offering affordable accommodation in bright, simple rooms. Modern facilities include an Internet café, kitchens, common rooms and laundry.

Bush Inn (☎ 6261 2256; www.thebushinn.com.au; 49 Montagu St; s/d $50/70) Established in 1815, the Bush Inn claims to be the oldest continuously licensed hotel in Australia. It offers comfortable rooms with shared facilities and guest lounge; rates include cooked breakfast.

New Norfolk Caravan Park (☎ 6261 1268; Esplanade; unpowered/powered site $12/17, on-site vans $40, cabins $55) Shady ground on the Derwent's south bank. There are only two cabins, which have toilets. The only showers (coin-operated) are in the amenities block. Prices are for two people.

See also Heimat Chalets, below, for details of motor-home sites 12km out of town.

MIDRANGE

Old Colony Inn (☎ 6261 2731; 21 Montagu St; s/d $70/80) Set in pretty gardens, this inn has a cosy cottage for romantic types, plus a spacious suite (sleeps three) inside the main house. The good-value rates include breakfast; dinner, bed and breakfast packages for two are a very reasonable $120.

All Saints & Sinners (☎ 6261 1877; www.allsaintsandsinners.com.au; 93 High St; s/d $100/110) Named for its central location among churches and pubs, this renovated mid-19th-century inn has a handful of attractive, well-equipped B&B rooms.

Glen Derwent (☎ 6261 3244; www.glenderwent.com.au; 44 Hamilton Rd; d $125-180; 🚭) This luxurious, c 1820 mansion is hidden behind a hawthorn hedge in extensive grounds beside the Lyell Hwy, just west of the bridge over the Derwent River. It has several in-house B&B rooms and two self-contained cottages (one sleeping up to five people).

Heimat Chalets (☎ 6261 2843; www.heimatchalets.com; 430 Black Hills Rd, Black Hills; motorhome sites $25-30, chalets d $125-140, extra person $35) About 12km out of town (signposted off the Lyell Hwy, just west of the bridge over the river) is this popular option, offering family-friendly accommodation in a picturesque rural setting. There are two powered, en-suite sites for motorhomes and two self-contained chalets, with extras including children's playground, an all-weather barbecue hut, breakfast provisions

GARETH MCCORMACK

Victoria Dock, Hobart (p65)

Arthur Circus (p72) at Battery Point, Hobart

RICHARD I'ANSON

GRANT DIXON

Sign for Mures fishmonger and seafood restaurant (p90) on Hobart's waterfront

View of Hobart and the Derwent River from Mt Wellington (p76)

RICHARD I'ANSON

JOHN BANAGAN

Historic buildings, Richmond (p108)

GRAHAM TWEEN

Jet-boat ride (p104) on the Derwent River, New Norfolk

The granary, Richmond (p108)

GLENN BEANLAND

Port Arthur (p117)

CHRIS M

in the chalets, and evening meals by arrangement. Book ahead.

Other options include the following:

The Junction (☎ 6261 4029; 50 Pioneer Ave; s/d from $75/85) Recently refurbished motel complex.

Rosie's Inn (☎ 6261 1171; www.rosiesinn.com.au; 5 Oast St; d $95-150) Quiet, hospitable B&B.

TOP END

Tynwald (☎ 6261 2667; www.tynwaldtasmania.com; Tynwald St; d $145-180;) Tynwald is a striking three-storey 1830s mansion overlooking the river. It has six antique-furnished rooms, a heated swimming pool, extensive gardens and cooked breakfasts. There is also a self-contained cottage on the grounds. Tynwald is run by two chefs, so naturally its restaurant is first-rate (see below).

Eating

The Junction (☎ 6261 4029; 50 Pioneer Ave; mains $10-22; dinner Thu-Tue) The dining room at this newly renovated motel complex has an outdoor deck and an appealing menu. Choose between dishes such as Angus beef from just down the road, chilli-cured ocean trout, grilled tiger prawns or barbecued duck.

Bush Inn (☎ 6261 2256; 49 Montagu St; mains $11-19; lunch & dinner) This old pub has a classic menu of seafood- and meat-heavy pub favourites, including surf 'n' turf (steak topped with prawns), steak, roast of the day and schnitzel. There's a kids' menu too, plus an outdoor deck with views of the river.

Verandahs in the Valley (☎ 6261 4461; 21 Burnett St; mains $10-22; lunch & dinner Tue-Sat, lunch Sun) Verandahs is a café-restaurant with a pretty exterior and a crowd-pleasing menu of salads, pasta, noodles and heartier fare.

Tynwald (☎ 6261 2667; Tynwald St; mains $25-27; dinner) In addition to its accommodation (above), Tynwald has an excellent, regularly changing menu, featuring French influences and such great local produce as trevalla (blue eye), venison and seafood. Bookings advised.

Old Colony Inn (☎ 6261 2731; mains $14-18; 21 Montagu St; lunch & dinner) As well as its museum and accommodation, this jack-of-all-trades inn has a tearoom and a large garden for light lunches and Devonshire teas. Of an evening, there's a small menu of simple, home-style meals.

Nosh Pit (☎ 6261 8783; 15 George St; mains $6.50-15, buffet $12.50; breakfast, lunch & dinner) Adjacent to the new budget accommodation at Willow Court is this bright and breezy eatery with great-value lunch and dinner buffets ($12.50), plus a handful of à la carte meals.

There is a **Woolworths supermarket** (cnr Charles & George Sts; 8am-8pm) for self-caterers.

Getting There & Away

Hobart Coaches (☎ 13 22 01; www.hobartcoaches.com.au) is the main operator between Hobart and New Norfolk (bus Nos 30 and 134), and provides five services a day in both directions on weekdays, and three on Saturday ($5.60 one-way, 50 minutes). In New Norfolk, the buses leave from Burnett St; in Hobart they depart from stop F on Elizabeth St.

NEW NORFOLK TO MT FIELD

As you head west from New Norfolk towards Mt Field, you leave the Derwent River and follow the narrow valley of the Tyenna River.

In 1864, rainbow and brown trout were bred for the first time in the southern hemisphere at **Salmon Ponds Heritage Hatchery and Gardens** (☎ 6261 5663; Salmon Ponds Rd, Plenty; adult/child $6/4; 9am-5pm), 9km west of New Norfolk at Plenty. You can feed the fish in the display ponds, visit the hatchery and investigate an angling museum. You can also eat in the on-site restaurant, **Pancakes by the Ponds** (meals $11-14) – as the name suggests, it specialises in sweet and savoury crepes.

About 5km further west is **Kinvarra Estate Wines** (☎ 6286 1333; 1211 Glenora Rd, Plenty; 10.30am-4.30pm), with wine tastings and sales, plus light meals, in a lovely 1827 homestead. Try their wine with a ploughman's lunch or opt for a Devonshire tea.

Further west, in the three historic rural communities of **Bushy Park**, **Glenora** and **Westerway** you can see old barns, a water wheel and extensive hop fields. The many shingled buildings exemplify the way in which 19th-century farms were built. Hop-growing has vanished from much of Tasmania but it is still pursued commercially by the company Bushy Park Estates, and Bushy Park is the largest hops-producing town in the southern hemisphere. In late summer and autumn you can see the hops growing up the thin leader strings.

THE AUTHOR'S CHOICE

Platypus Playground (☎ 6288 1020; www.riverside-cottage.com; Gordon River Rd; d $110) You can't miss this cute red riverside cottage, brand new and offering eco-friendly accommodation. Winning features include an outdoor deck over the river and the chance to spot local platypuses, plus the Possum Shed as its neighbour. The affable owners of the cottage have a background in park ranging and have made it a priority to minimise guests' environmental impact: there's no stove as they'd prefer you didn't cook with oils and fats (but there is a toaster, kettle and microwave, and continental breakfast provisions are included); eco-friendly toiletries and detergents are supplied; and the *pièce de résistance* is an outdoor, gas-operated toilet!

Westerway is a substantial town with a general store and petrol station. Well worth a stop is the cheerful **Possum Shed** (☎ 6288 1477; Gordon River Rd; meals $7-13.50; 🕑 10am-5pm Sep-Jun, 10am-4pm Jul-Aug), a lovely little riverside café with a craft shop, outdoor seating, a resident platypus (sightings not guaranteed!) and excellent lunches and snacks.

About 5km west of Westerway (en route to Mt Field) is **Something Wild** (☎ 6288 1013; www.somethingwild.com.au; adult/child $10/5; 🕑 10am-5pm), an excellent wildlife sanctuary rehabilitating orphaned and injured wildlife, and providing habitats for animals who can't be released. You can visit the animal nursery, see native wildlife, and probably spot a platypus residing in the sanctuary's grounds.

MT FIELD NATIONAL PARK

☎ 03 / pop 170 (National Park township)

Mt Field, 80km northwest of Hobart (and 7km beyond Westerway), is a favourite of both locals and visitors for its spectacular mountain scenery, alpine moorlands and lakes, rainforest and waterfalls.

The area around Russell Falls was made a reserve in 1885 and by 1916 had become one of Australia's first national parks. To many locals it's simply known as National Park, a moniker given to the small town at its entrance. The abundance of wildlife that can be viewed at dusk makes this a great place to stay overnight with kids.

Visitors should note that Mt Field is *not* home to the Tahune AirWalk (see p138). It seems that some visitors confuse the AirWalk with Mt Field's Tall Trees Circuit, which definitely *isn't* a steel structure above the treetops!

Information

The park's **visitors centre** (☎ 6288 1149; Lake Dobson Rd; 🕑 8.30am-4.30pm Mon-Fri, 8.30am-5pm Sat & Sun, closing 30 min earlier May-Oct) has reams of information on the area's walks, and on the free, child-occupying, ranger-led activities usually held from late December until early February. Also inside are a café and displays on the origins of the park.

There are excellent day-use facilities in the park, including barbecues, shelters and a children's playground.

WINTER ROAD WARNING

If you're staying in the Lake Dobson huts, skiing on Mt Mawson or taking the Pandani Grove Nature Walk or any of the high-country walks, you'll have to drive along the 16km Lake Dobson Rd. To safely navigate this unsealed road in winter, you'll need chains and antifreeze (and so will your car). It's best to hire them in Hobart before setting off; this can be done through **Skigia & Surf** (Map p70; ☎ 6234 6688; 123 Elizabeth St, Hobart).

Walks

The park's most promoted attraction is the magnificent 40m-high **Russell Falls**, which is

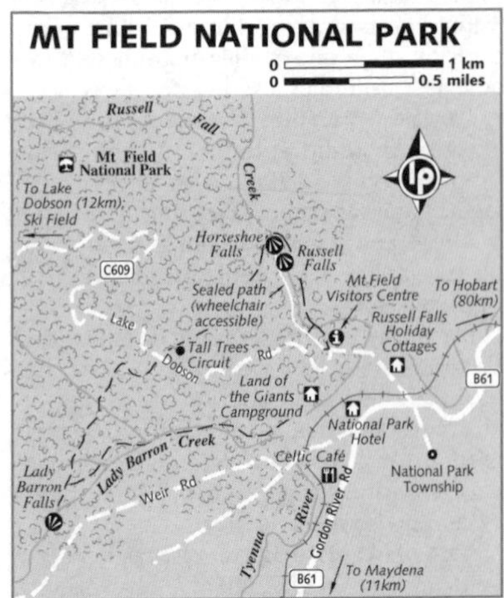

in the valley close to the park entrance. It's an easy 20-minute circuit walk from the car park along a wheelchair-suitable path. From Russell Falls, you can continue past **Horseshoe Falls** and **Tall Trees Circuit** to **Lady Barron Falls**, a walk of two hours return past swamp gums (the world's tallest flowering plants).

The 15-minute **Lyrebird Nature Walk** starts 7km up Lake Dobson Rd. It's an excellent introduction to the park's flora and fauna, particularly for children, with numbers along the track that correspond to information provided in a brochure available at the visitors centre.

For young children who don't mind a longer walk, there's the **Pandani Grove Nature Walk**, which follows the edge of Lake Dobson and passes through some magical stands of pandani (heaths resembling pandanus palms that grow up to 12m high before toppling over). This walk takes 40 minutes; park at the Lake Dobson car park, 16km from the park entrance.

HIGH-COUNTRY WALKS

There are several magnificent walks at the top of the range, where glaciation has cut steep cliffs and deep valleys into what was once a continuous plateau. Attractive lakes litter the floors of these valleys, but perhaps even more beautiful are the many tarns adorning the ridge-tops.

If you intend to go walking here, take waterproof gear and warm clothing because the weather can be volatile year-round; also double-check with the visitors centre as to current track conditions. There's a four-wheel-drive gravel road from Lake Dobson to the ski fields, but this is open only to authorised vehicles.

TARN SHELF

From the Lake Dobson car park, take the Urquhart Track to its junction with the gravel road; both track and road are steep. Continue along the road to the ski fields, at the top of which is the start of the Tarn Shelf Track. At this point the track is fairly level and a boardwalk has been laid across large sections of ground to protect the delicate vegetation and keep walkers out of the mud. Either continue as far as you like along the track and then return by the same route, or take one of two routes that branch off at Lake Newdegate and circle back to the ski fields: if you travel east past Twisted Tarn, Twilight Tarn and Lake Webster, the walk takes five or six hours return from the car park, while the wonderful Rodway Range circuit to the west takes six or seven hours return from the car park.

The Tarn Shelf is an enjoyable walk at any time of year in clear weather. In summer the temperature is pleasant, in autumn the leaves of the deciduous beeches along the way are golden, in winter you may need skis or snowshoes, while in spring the sound of melting snow trickling beneath the boardwalk somehow seems to enhance the silence.

Skiing

Skiing was first attempted here in 1922 on **Mt Mawson**. A low-key resort of club huts and rope tows has developed and when nature sees fit to deposit some snow (an infrequent event in recent years) it makes a refreshing change from the highly commercial developments in the ski fields of mainland Australia. The ski field is open 10am to 4pm weekends and school holidays, weather permitting, and the cost for a day is $25/15 per adult/child. Up-to-date snow reports are available online at www.ski.com.au/reports/mawson, or via a **recorded message service** (☎ 6288 1166).

There is no ski equipment hire in the area; again, it's best to hire gear in Hobart before setting off. Visit **Skigia & Surf** (Map p70; ☎ 6234 6688; 123 Elizabeth St, Hobart) for ski and board hire.

Sleeping & Eating

Note that the run-down YHA hostel at Mt Field is no longer operating. There are also good accommodation options 12km east at Maydena (see p296).

Land of the Giants Campground (unpowered/powered sites $20/25) This is a privately run, self-registration camping ground with good facilities (toilets, showers, laundry, free barbecues) just inside the park. Bookings not required. Site fees are for two people, and are additional to national park entry fees.

Lake Dobson Cabins (☎ 6288 1149; s & d $22, extra adult/child $11/5.50) Get back to basics at these three simple six-bed cabins located some 15km inside the park. They are all equipped with mattresses, cold water, wood stove and firewood (there's no power), and have a communal toilet block; visitors must take their own gas lamp and portable cooker, plus all utensils. Book at the visitors centre.

National Park Hotel (☎ 6288 1103; Gordon River Rd; s/d $40/80) This laid-back pub was up for sale at the time of research, and rumours were circulating that the new owners would transform it into a resort. In the meantime, on offer here are reasonable pub rooms with shared facilities, plus dinner most nights.

Russell Falls Holiday Cottages (☎ 6288 1198; Lake Dobson Hwy; d $85, extra adult/child $15/10) In a great location next to the park's entrance, off the main road, these spotless cottages have very dated furnishings but are roomy and well equipped.

Celtic Café (☎ 6288 1058; Gordon River Rd; snacks & meals $3-8; Sun only Jun-Nov, Sat-Thu Dec-May) About 600m west of the national park turn-off is this striking little café. It's an octagonal shape with only a couple of tables (takeaway available). Also being built here at the time of research were a few cabins (doubles from $60), including one with disabled access.

Waterfalls Café (☎ 6288 1516; meals $7-15) Simple eatery inside the visitors centre serving up reasonable café fare.

Getting There & Away

Public transport connections to the park are not regular. From December through March **TassieLink** (☎ 1300 300 520; www.tassielink.com.au) runs one bus on Tuesday, Thursday and Saturday from Hobart to Mt Field ($26, 1¾ hours); bookings are essential. The associated **Tigerline Coaches** (☎ 1300 653 633; www.tigerline.com.au) operates a one-day tour of the area from Hobart on Monday, Wednesday and Friday year-round, costing $99/60 per adult/child. Many other Hobart-based tour operators offer a day in the area; most take in Something Wild wildlife sanctuary (p106) as well as the national park.

COAL RIVER VALLEY

RICHMOND

☎ 03 / pop 750

Richmond is just 27km from Hobart and, with more than 50 19th-century buildings, is arguably Tasmania's premier historic town. Straddling the Coal River and on the old route between Hobart and Port Arthur, Richmond was once a strategic military post and convict station. The Richmond Bridge is the town's historical centrepiece.

With the completion of the Sorell Causeway in 1872, traffic travelling to the Tasman Peninsula and the east coast bypassed Richmond. The town remained the focus of a farming community but ceased to grow – in fact, for more than a century it changed very little. It has since transformed into a tourist destination and is a delightful spot for a day trip. It's also quite close to the airport, so it's a good overnight option if you have an early flight to meet.

There's no visitors centre as such, but plenty of brochures are available from the kiosk in front of the model village (below). Information is available online at www.richmondvillage.com. There are no banks in town, but both supermarkets on the main street have ATMs.

Sights & Activities

Richmond Bridge (Wellington St) still funnels traffic across the Coal River. You can walk under and around it, and there are good views on both sides. Built by convicts in 1823, and hence the oldest road bridge in Australia, it formed a vital link for the young colony and encouraged construction of the many old buildings seen today.

The northern wing of the remarkably well-preserved **Richmond Gaol** (☎ 6260 2127; Bathurst St; adult/child/family $5.50/2.50/14; 9am-5pm) was built in 1825, five years before the penitentiary at Port Arthur. Its locks and cells for punishment and solitary confinement have not been modified. The various displays describe the old penal system.

Of historical interest are the 1836 **St John's Church** (off Wellington St), the first Catholic church in Australia; the 1834 **St Luke's Church of England** (Edwards St); the 1825 **courthouse** (Forth St); the **old post office** (Bridge St), built in 1826; and the 1888 **Richmond Arms Hotel** (Bridge St).

There's also an interesting **model village** (☎ 6260 2502; off Bridge St; adult/child/family $7.50/3.50/18.50; 9am-5pm) of Hobart Town in the 1820s, recreated from the city's original plans. The detail of the 60-plus miniature buildings and Hobart's shrunken population is excellent.

Herd the kids into the wooden-walled **Richmond Maze** (☎ 6260 2451; 13 Bridge St; adult/

child/family $5.50/3.50/16; 9am-5pm). They'll be safe, as the resident Minotaur has taken long-service leave. There are also very good tea rooms here, serving breakfast, light lunches and the obligatory Devonshire tea. There's more family fun at the wildlife parks found outside Richmond (see p111).

Oak Lodge (☎ 6260 2761; Bridge St; entry by gold-coin donation; 11am-3.30pm Oct-Apr, noon-3.30pm May-Sep), opposite the maze, is worth a look. It's one of Richmond's oldest homes (c 1831), now owned by the National Trust and operated by the Coal River Historic Society. It contains a museum and gallery and sells collectables.

Tours of Richmond (☎ 0409 935 139; www.toursofrichmond.com; daytime tours 11am, 1pm, 3pm) offers a good-value, 1½-hour daytime walking tour of the town ($10), or a ghost tour after dark ($25). Tours leave from the courtyard of the bakery (off Edward St); bookings for the ghost tour are essential.

Sleeping

There's precious little budget lodging in Richmond. The majority of accommodation is in self-contained historic cottages (breakfast provisions supplied).

BUDGET

Richmond Cabin & Tourist Park (☎ 6260 2192; www.richmondcabins.com; Middle Tea Tree Rd; unpowered/powered sites $16/24, on-site vans $42, cabins $55-85;) A friendly park, a little out of town. This place offers the cheapest accommodation in Richmond in its neat, no-frills cabins, while kids will be happy with the indoor pool and games room. Prices are for two people.

MIDRANGE

Richmond Arms Hotel (☎ 6260 2109; 42 Bridge St; d from $99) The pub has four good-quality motel-style units in the adjacent, snug former stables, plus plans for development of more accommodation.

Richmond Antiques B&B (☎ 6260 2601; 2 Edward St; d $95) One of the cheapest places in town, with unremarkable but clean and spacious rooms above an antique shop. Rates include continental breakfast.

Mrs Currie's House (☎ 6260 2766; www.mrscurrieshouse.com; 4 Franklin St; d $128) At the time of our

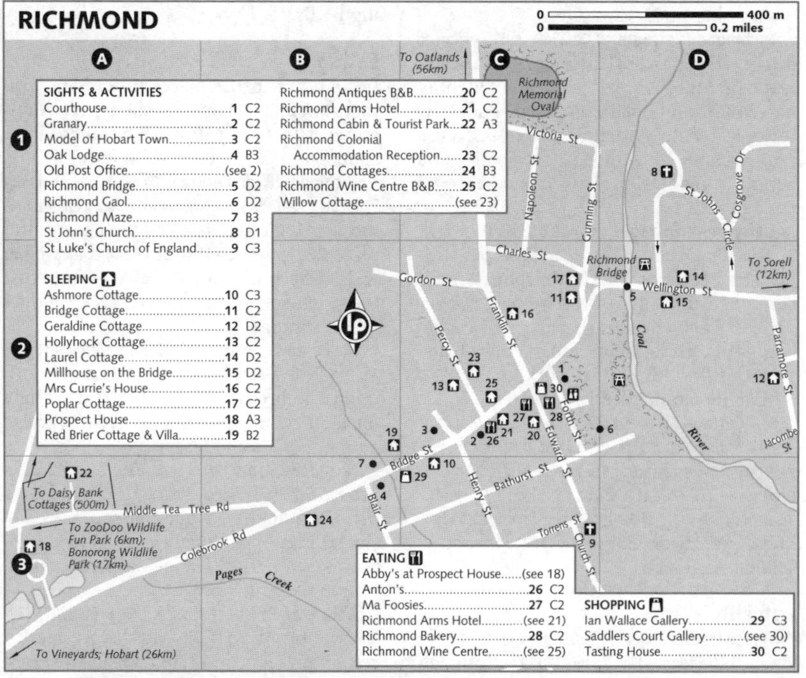

research, this pretty, double-storey 1860s Georgian guesthouse had just found new owners – presumably they will keep the place running to the previous owners' high standards. On offer are four nicely furnished rooms, cooked breakfasts, a guest lounge with open fire, and extensive gardens.

Hollyhock Cottages (☎ 6260 1079; www.hollyhockcottage.com.au; 3 Percy St; d $135-150, extra person $15-30) Hollyhock is a charming National Trust–listed brick-and-timber cottage modernised with a double spa. The owners also have a larger two-bedroom Georgian abode, **Geraldine Cottage** (12 Parramore St), for rent at the same rates. Personalised tours of the area (or further afield) can be arranged.

Richmond Colonial Accommodation (☎ 6260 2570; www.richmondcolonial.com; reception at 4 Percy St; d $130-150, extra adult/child $25/15) This company manages a number of well-equipped, family-friendly historic cottages in town, namely **Ashmore** (32 Bridge St), **Bridge** (47 Bridge St), **Poplar** (49 Bridge St) and **Willow** (4 Percy St, behind reception). All cottages are self-contained and have a roll call of colonial touches, with fantastic attention to detail by the owners making them very livable – including videos and log fires.

Richmond Cottages (☎ 6260 2561; richmondcottages@ozemail.com.au; 12 Bridge St; d $140, $25/30 extra adult/child) More historic cottages! On offer here are two fully self-contained abodes: **Ivy Cottage**, a family-friendly, three-bedroom home (complete with claw-foot bath), and behind it **The Stables**, a rustic one-bedroom cottage with spa.

Daisy Bank Cottages (☎ 6260 2390; Daisy Bank; d $140-150) Off Middle Tea Tree Rd, this place is a real treat, with two spotless, self-contained units (one with spa) in a converted 1840s sandstone barn. There are loft bedrooms, rural views and plenty of distractions for kids on this working farm.

Also recommendedthe following.

Laurel Cottage (☎ 6260 2397; jmwilt@southcom.com.au; 9 Wellington St; d $125, extra adult/child $25/18) Two-bedroom historic cottage beside the bridge.

Richmond Wine Centre B&B (☎ 6260 2619; www.richmondwinecentre.com.au; 27 Bridge St; d $125-150) Spacious, well-equipped B&B suite in cottage adjacent to restaurant (see right).

TOP END

Prospect House (☎ 6260 2207; www.prospect-house.com.au; 1384 Richmond Rd; d $160-190; 💻) Immediately west of Richmond on the Hobart road is this Georgian mansion offering heritage-style guest rooms in converted outbuildings. There are large grounds and a tennis court; the mansion itself is home to a quality restaurant (see below). A dinner, bed and breakfast package costs $249 for two.

Red Brier Cottage & Villa (☎ 6260 2349; www.redbriercottage.com.au; 15 Bridge St; d $140-200) There are two accommodation styles on offer here, behind the blue cottage that sells kitchenware and gourmet produce. The first is a cosy, fully equipped cedar cottage with heritage décor; the second option is a luxurious modern villa with king-size beds, two en suites, spa, flat-screen TVs, sound system and fantastic private garden with barbecue. Both options can sleep four.

Millhouse on the Bridge (☎ 6260 2428; www.millhouse.com.au; 2 Wellington St; d $160-220) The 1850s mill by the historic bridge has been masterfully restored and transformed into a luxury guesthouse. The addition of a self-contained cottage in the grounds, combined with features like helpful owners, large breakfast spread and extensive gardens, have helped to make this one of the state's most appealing B&Bs.

Eating

In addition to the places listed here, visitors should also consider the vineyard restaurants that are within 10 minutes' drive, south from Richmond (see opposite).

Richmond Wine Centre (☎ 6260 2619; 27 Bridge St; mains $10.50-22.50; 🕑 breakfast & lunch daily, dinner Wed-Sat) Don't be misled by the name – this place dedicates itself to fine food as well as wine. Select an outdoor table then peruse the extensive menu, where Tassie produce reigns supreme.

Ma Foosies (☎ 6260 2412; 46 Bridge St; dishes $4.50-15; 🕑 10.30am-5pm Thu-Tue) Cosy tearoom offering late breakfasts and an array of light meals, including ploughman's lunch, grilled *panini*, quiche and lasagne.

Richmond Arms Hotel (☎ 6260 2109; 42 Bridge St; mains $12-29; 🕑 lunch & dinner) This laid-back historic pub has a good menu selection (including a kids' menu) and better-than-average pub grub. There's also a decent selection of local wines.

Abby's at Prospect House (☎ 6260 2207; 1384 Richmond Rd; mains $24-26; 🕑 dinner) Upmarket restaurant set in an 1830s mansion just west of town. The menu includes staples such as duck breast, saddle of venison and eye fillet of beef; there's also an impressive wine list featuring local drops.

Anton's (☎ 6260 1017; 42a Bridge St; meals $7-14; lunch Tue-Sun, dinner Fri-Sun) Next to the pub is this small shop, producing first-class pizzas and pasta dishes, plus antipasto, salads, desserts and gelati. It's perfect picnic fodder (head down to the river), or there are a couple of tables here.

Richmond Bakery (☎ 6260 2628; Edward St; snacks $3-5.50; 7.30am-6pm) Choose between pies, pastries, sandwiches, muffins and cakes, then take away or sit in the large courtyard.

Shopping

There are several arts and crafts places located around the town selling paintings, woodcraft, books and furniture, much of it locally made. Prices aren't particularly cheap; many items are of good quality. **Saddlers Court Gallery** (☎ 6260 2132; 48 Bridge St) has some exceptional items for sale. **Ian Wallace Gallery** (☎ 6260 2200; 30 Bridge Rd) is worth a look for its excellent, affordable photographs of the state's wilderness. **Tasting House** (☎ 6260 2050; Shop 4, 50 Bridge St) sells only Tassie produce, including wine, whisky, oils, sauces and jams. There's a small wine-tasting fee (refundable on purchase) and, in addition, Coal River Valley wine tours can be organised here.

Getting There & Away

If you have your own transport, you'll find that Richmond is an easy day trip from Hobart. If not, you can take a half-day coach tour from Hobart with **Tigerline** (☎ 1300 653 633; www.tigerline.com.au). One tour visits Richmond and Sorell Fruit Farm (p114), the other Richmond and Bonorong Wildlife Park (right). Tours cost between $50 and $60 per adult.

The **Richmond Tourist Bus** (☎ 0408 341 804) runs a twice-daily service from Hobart ($25 return, 9.15am and 12.15pm, minimum two people) that gives you three hours to explore Richmond before returning. A far cheaper option is to catch a scheduled bus: **Hobart Coaches** (☎ 13 22 01; www.hobartcoaches.com.au) runs three buses a day to and from Richmond on weekdays only (one way/return $5.40/8.70, 20 to 30 minutes).

AROUND RICHMOND

Wildlife Parks

ZooDoo Wildlife Fun Park (☎ 6260 2444; www.zoodoo.com.au; 620 Middle Tea Tree Rd; adult/child $12/10; 9am-5pm), 6km west of Richmond on the road to Brighton, has steam train rides, playgrounds, picnic areas and enough captive wildlife – from miniature horses to Tassie devils, white wallabies to a nursery farm – to keep the kids absorbed.

Bonorong Wildlife Park (☎ 6268 1184; Briggs Rd; adult/child $12.50/6.50; 9am-5pm) is about 17km west of Richmond (or alternatively, signposted off Hwy 1 at Brighton). 'Bonorong' comes from an Aboriginal word that means 'native companion' and there are plenty of native companions here that receive regular feeding (scheduled at 11.30am and 2pm), like devils, koalas, wombats, echidnas and quolls. Besides its well-inhabited out-door spaces, including barbecues and picnic tables, the park also has a café.

Vineyards

Richmond is at the centre of Tasmania's fastest-growing wine region (known as the Coal River Valley), and there are wineries in all directions. Some are sophisticated affairs open daily with attached restaurants, while some are small vineyards quietly going about the business of fine-winemaking with cellar doors open by appointment only for tastings and sales. Get hold of the *Southern Tasmanian Wine Regions* brochure (also available online – go to www.discovertasmania.com, click on 'things to do & see', 'wine & food', then 'vineyards & wine routes') for details of vineyards and their opening hours.

The road heading west out of Richmond then south to Cambridge offers some great stop-offs. First is **Palmara Vineyard** (☎ 6260 2462; 1314 Richmond Rd, Richmond; noon-6pm mid-Sep–mid-May), one of Tasmania's smallest vineyards, offering free tastings of their boutique wines. In contrast to this small operator is the well-known **Meadowbank Estate** (☎ 6248 4484; www.meadowbankwines.com.au; 699 Richmond Rd, Cambridge; 10am-5pm), 9km from Richmond and a lovely setting for an acclaimed restaurant, art gallery, children's play area, and a large area for tastings and sales. Lunch is served daily from noon to 3pm (mains $21–27), with coffee and snacks served throughout the day. The estate often plays host to cultural events and musical performances (check the website).

Opposite Meadowbank is **Craigow Vineyard** (☎ 6248 4210; 528 Richmond Rd, Cambridge; 🕑 11am-5pm daily Dec-Apr, 11am-5pm Sat & Sun May-Nov), offering tastings in a colonial cottage, and not too far south is **Coal Valley Vineyard** (☎ 6248 5367; 257 Richmond Rd, Cambridge; 🕑 10am-5pm), also home to an excellent restaurant in a lovely setting (lunch served daily, mains $21 to $27).

TASMAN PENINSULA

The Arthur Hwy runs more than 100km from Hobart through Sorell to the southern reaches of the Tasman Peninsula, one of the state's most popular tourist regions. Sited here is Port Arthur, the infamous and allegedly 'escape-proof' prison of the mid-19th century. Yet the region is also famous for its 300m-high cliffs, which, along with its delightful beaches and beautiful bays, make this a fantastic place for bushwalking, diving, sea kayaking and rock climbing.

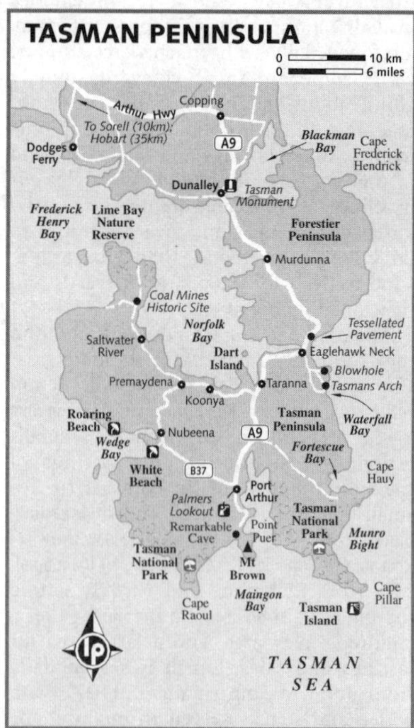

Much of the best bushwalking on the Tasman Peninsula is in **Tasman National Park**, a coastal enclave of spectacularly high cliffs and other towering rock formations, chunky offshore islands, magical underwater kelp forests, and heaths containing rare plants. The cliffs are favoured by numerous seabirds and wedge-tailed eagles nest there, while the waters far below are occupied by seals, dolphins and whales. The usual national park entry fees apply.

Figures show that the downturn in tourism to the peninsula following the 1996 Port Arthur massacre has been reversed in recent years, and a number of tourism developments (new resort-style hotels or expansions of existing hotels) are on the drawing board.

There are visitors centres at Sorell (opposite) and inside the entrance building of the Port Arthur historic site (p118). There is also a useful information office in central Hobart: the **Port Arthur Region Travel Shop** (Map p70; ☎ 6224 5333; 49a Salamanca Pl). The *Convict Trail* booklet ($2.50), available from the Port Arthur visitors centre, covers the peninsula's key historic sites.

Getting There & Around

Take care if driving down the peninsula to Port Arthur. Plenty of bad accidents have occurred on the Arthur Hwy due to its winding nature, road exits being hidden behind hills and around corners, and idiots with lead feet.

Public transport connections to the Port Arthur area are surprisingly poor. **TassieLink** (☎ 1300 300 520; www.tassielink.com.au) connects Hobart and the Tasman Peninsula, but the timetable is geared more to school students than to travellers. There's a weekday bus service between Hobart and Port Arthur ($21.20, 2¼ hours) during school terms, and a 4pm service from Hobart three times a week (Monday, Wednesday and Friday) in school holidays. Buses stop at all the main towns on the peninsula.

Redline Coaches (☎ 1300 360 000; www.tasredline.com.au) also operates some weekday services from Hobart to Sorell and Dunalley, but no further south.

TOURS

Those without their own transport might prefer to join a coach tour out of Hobart.

Many operators run trips to Port Arthur; **Tigerline Coaches** (☎ 1300 653 633; www.tigerline.com.au) has a full-day tour costing $77/46 per adult/child, which includes entry to the historic site.

Bottom Bits Bus (☎ 1800 777 103, 6229 3540; www.bottombitsbus.com.au) has a worthwhile small-group day-trip to the area twice a week. The price ($89) includes transport to and from Hobart, entry to the Port Arthur historic site plus the evening ghost tour. The tour also visits many of the natural attractions of the peninsula, such as Tessellated Pavement and Tasmans Arch.

Once or twice a week, **Port Arthur Cruises** (Map p70; ☎ 1300 134 561; www.portarthurcruises.com.au; Brooke St Pier, Hobart) has a morning ferry service from Hobart to Port Arthur. The price ($120/85 for an adult/child) includes transport (coach from Port Arthur back to Hobart) and entrance to the historic site. You can also take a one-way trip to Port Arthur for $85/55.

SORELL

☎ 03 / pop 1730

This is one of Tasmania's oldest towns, settled in 1808 primarily to supply locally processed wheat and flour to the rest of the colony, but its aura of history has diminished somewhat over time. Visitors information is available at the new **visitors centre** (☎ 6265 6438; 16 Main Rd; 9am-5pm).

A few 19th-century buildings have survived near the centre of town and are worth a look. The 1841 **Scots Uniting Church** is behind the high school. Also near the school are the **barracks** and the **Blue Bell Inn** (c 1829),

PENINSULA ACTIVITIES

Most tourists associate the Tasman Peninsula only with the Port Arthur historic site, but there are loads more attractions (natural and otherwise) down here – enough to warrant a stay of at least a couple of days. Bushwalkers should get hold of a copy of *Peninsula Tracks* by Peter and Shirley Storey, available from bookshops in Hobart and larger visitors centres, which contains track notes to 35 (mostly half- or full-day) walks in the area.

The following operators offer activities on the peninsula:

Eaglehawk Dive Centre (☎ 6250 3566; www.eaglehawkdive.com.au; 178 Pirates Bay Drive, Eaglehawk Neck) Regular dive sites include sea caves, giant kelp forests, a sea lion colony and shipwrecks. Boat dives, diving courses and equipment rental available. The cost per dive ranges from $39 to $55; full equipment hire for a day is $75. A range of PADI courses is available. A one-day introduction to scuba diving is $199.

Hire it with Denis (☎ 6250 3103; hirewithdenis@hotmail.com; 6 Andersons Rd, Port Arthur) About 5km north of the historic site. Denis offers reasonably priced rental of canoes, kayaks, aluminium dinghies, bikes, tents and more. Free delivery to Port Arthur and Taranna; minimal charge to other areas.

Personalised Sea Charters (☎ 6250 3370; seachart@southcom.com.au; 322 Blowhole Rd, Eaglehawk Neck) Takes small groups on game, deep sea, reef or bay fishing and sightseeing charter trips starting at around $100/500 per group per hour/day.

Sealife Experience (☎ 0428 300 303; www.sealife.com.au; departs from Pirates Bay, Eaglehawk Neck) Three-hour cruises take in the peninsula's dramatic eastern coastline, from Eaglehawk Neck to Cape Hauy. Two or three cruises daily; tickets are $85/45 per adult/child.

Seaview Riding Ranch (☎ 6250 3110; 60 Firetower Rd, Koonya) Horse riding for all ages and skill levels, from beginners to advanced, and also riding for the disabled. Scenic rides led by long-time locals; $30/55 for one/two hours. Signposted off the main road from Taranna.

Tasmanian Nature Guiding (☎ 6250 3268; www.tasnatureguiding.com.au; 70 Old Jetty Rd, Eaglehawk Neck) Ruth runs knowledgeable, customised flora- and ornithology-focused excursions on the peninsula for small groups. Prices vary with tours; a half/full-day excursion costs from $66/99.

Tasmanian Sea Charters (☎ 1300 554 049; www.tasmanseacharters.com; depart from Eaglehawk Jetty) Offering a similar product to Sealife Experience's – three-hour cruises (with commentary) along the peninsula's east coast, wildlife spotting from Eaglehawk Neck to Cape Hauy. Two cruises daily; tickets are $90/50 per adult/child.

Tasmanian Seaplanes (☎ 6250 1077; www.tas-seaplane.com; Port Arthur) Offers scenic flights along the spectacular local coastline, departing from the Port Arthur historic site. Prices range from $65/30 per adult/child for a 20-minute flight, to $130/68 for 40 minutes of air time.

on the corner of Somerville and Walker Sts. In the main street is **St George's Anglican Church** (1884) and next door is an interesting **graveyard** with headstones marking early settlers' plots.

Fruit Farm

At the friendly **Sorell Fruit Farm** (☎ 6265 2744; www.sorellfruitfarm.com; 174 Pawleena Rd; 8.30am-5pm late-Oct-May), on the road to Pawleena, you can pick your own fruit from a huge variety grown on the property: favourites such as strawberries, raspberries, cherries, apricots, peaches and apples, but also more exotic varieties such as loganberries, tayberries and silvanberries. December and January are the best months for variety but the fruits are in season at different times – check the website for a helpful chart. The cost is according to the weight of your pickings.

You can also enjoy a bite in the **tearooms** (lights meals & snacks $4.50-7), buy great berry-flavoured ice cream, or taste and/or purchase a wide range of fruity jams, chutneys, sauces, wines and liqueurs. To find the farm, head east through Sorell following the signs for Port Arthur, and not long after exiting the town you'll find Pawleena signposted on your left.

Sleeping & Eating

Given its proximity to the airport, Sorell makes a handy overnight stop if you have an early flight.

Blue Bell Inn (☎ 6265 2804; www.rcat.asn.au/bluebell; 26 Somerville St; s/d from $100/110) A welcoming, two-storey sandstone place offering fine rooms and a choice of cooked breakfasts in its elegant, plum-washed interior. The **dining room** (dinner mains $20-27; breakfast & dinner Thu-Tue) serves well-prepared meals (some with a Polish bent) to both guests and visitors, and will cater to vegans and coeliacs with prior notice; book ahead.

Cherry Park Estate (☎ 6265 2271; www.cherryparkestate.com.au; 114 Pawleena Rd; s/d $100/120) Close to Sorell Fruit Farm, this property has attractive rooms, lots of surrounding open spaces, homegrown apricots and creative flourishes like a wild-west themed bar, and an old phone booth in the front yard. The friendly owners supply cooked breakfast.

There's a handful of takeaways and cafés along the main street, and pubs serving meals.

Barilla Bay (☎ 6248 5454; www.barillabay.com.au; 1388 Tasman Hwy, Cambridge; mains $21-40; lunch & dinner daily, breakfast Wed-Sun) Some 7km west of Sorell (1.5km from the airport roundabout) is this well-known oyster and seafood sales outlet. They can package your purchase for flights – perfect given their location. They also sell quality Tasmanian produce (wines etc), and upstairs is a smart, expensive new restaurant, where the emphasis is, of course, on fresh seafood. There are also 45-minute **tours** (adult/child $8.50/3.85; 9am, noon & 4pm Wed-Sun) of the oyster farm; bookings advised.

Getting There & Away

The **TassieLink** (☎ 1300 300 520; www.tassielink.com.au) service down the Tasman Peninsula from Hobart stops at Sorell ($5.60, 40 minutes).

DUNALLEY

☎ 03 / pop 290

The well-timbered Forestier Peninsula is connected to Tasmanian soil by an isthmus known as Dunalley. A canal complete with a raisable bridge cuts across the isthmus, providing a short cut for small boats. Its attractions are top-notch sleeping and eating options.

At Dunalley's northern end is the welcoming, family-run **Potters Croft** (☎ 6253 5469; www.potterscroft.com.au; Arthur Hwy; s/d from $100/146), a craft gallery and wine outlet and provider of cosy, exceedingly well-catered accommodation. There are four en-suite rooms sharing a large kitchen and lounge area. Guided eco-expeditions can also be arranged (fishing, boat trips, walking, cycling, painting, photography – see the website).

Don't miss the fabulous **Waterfront Cafe** (☎ 6253 5122; Imlay St; dishes $9-20; 10am-4pm), a hybrid antique and collectibles store and elegant café with a large outdoor deck and views over the water. The menu lists interesting options, from gourmet sandwiches to flathead fillets and a sweet potato, spinach and cashew-nut burger.

Traditionalists might prefer the **Dunalley Hotel** (☎ 6253 5101; Arthur Hwy; mains $11-25; lunch & dinner), a friendly country pub serving up lots of local seafood.

Getting There & Away

The **TassieLink** (☎ 1300 300 520; www.tassielink.com.au) Tasman Peninsula service will take you to Dunalley from Hobart ($15, one hour).

EAGLEHAWK NECK

☎ 03 / pop 90

Eaglehawk Neck is another isthmus, this one connecting the Tasman Peninsula to the Forestier Peninsula. In the days of convict occupation, the 100m-wide neck had a row of unsociable dogs chained across it to prevent escape. Dog platforms were also placed in narrow Eaglehawk Bay to the west to prevent convicts from wading around the barrier. Rumours were circulated that the waters were shark-infested (not true) to discourage swimming. Remarkably, despite the authorities' precautions, a few convicts did escape.

There's an ATM and a handful of brochures at the Officers Mess (see p116).

Sights

As you drive down from the north, turn east onto Pirates Bay Dr to the **lookout** – there's a wonderful view of Pirates Bay and the rugged coastline beyond.

The only remaining structure from the convict days is the 1832 **Officers Quarters**, the oldest wooden military building in Australia. Sitting diagonally opposite the Officers Mess general store, its interior is fitted out with information boards on the history of the building and Eaglehawk Neck.

At the northern end of Pirates Bay is **Tessellated Pavement**, a rocky terrace that has eroded into what looks like tiled paving. At low tide you can walk along the foreshore to **Clydes Island**, where there are fine views of the coastline and several graves. You can see as far south as Cape Hauy.

Follow the signposted side roads to **The Blowhole** and **Tasmans Arch** for some close-up views of spectacular coastal cliffs. Take care around The Blowhole, and keep behind the fences at the other features, as the cliff edges are prone to crumbling. The Eaglehawk Neck jetty is opposite the car park for The Blowhole.

On the road to The Blowhole is the signposted turn-off to the 4km gravel road leading to **Waterfall Bay**, which has more great views (see right). For something a bit more gentle, drive further towards The Blowhole to catch a glimpse of the self-titled **Doo Town**, whose inhabitants have all given their homes quaint doo-goody names like Doo-Little, Wee-Doo, Thistle-Doo-Me and Love-Me-Doo.

Bushwalking

WATERFALL BLUFF

From the car park at Waterfall Bay, take the 1½-hour return walk to Waterfall Bluff. While much of the walk is through a forest of tall, slender trees that somewhat obscure the view, the track stays close to the bay and there are plenty of places to stop and admire the magnificent scenery from the clifftops, which are unfenced except at the car park. Make sure you continue to the bluff itself before returning to the part of the walk that takes you down past the falls, as the vista from here is breathtaking.

TASMAN COASTAL TRAIL

Waterfall Bay is also the start of the Tasman Trail, which climbs over Tatnells Hill then follows the coast to Fortescue Bay, out to Cape Hauy and on to Cape Pillar. Walkers should allow three to five days to complete the trip one way; see the website of the **Parks & Wildlife Service** (www.parks.tas.gov.au/recreation/tracknotes/tasman.html) for information.

If you'd prefer just a full day's walk, try from Waterfall Bay to Bivouac Bay (six hours) or to Fortescue Bay (eight hours), with camping available at both bays. If you need to return to your car, walk only as far as Tatnells Hill, where you can enjoy a wonderful view all the way from Eaglehawk Neck to the stunning rock formations of Cape Hauy.

Sleeping

The advantages of staying at the Neck are that it's far more scenic than Port Arthur, it's relatively uncrowded and it's close to all the peninsula's major features.

Eaglehawk Neck Backpackers (☎ 6250 3248; 94 Old Jetty Rd; camp sites per person $7, dm $18) Simple, endearing hostel in a peaceful location to the west of the isthmus. Apart from bunks, it also has a tiny camping area and bike hire is available for guests ($5).

Eaglehawk Cafe (☎ 6250 3331; eaglehawkcafe@bigpond.com; Arthur Hwy; d $115) Not content just to offer good food in fine surrounds, this classy eatery (see p116) now has two inviting B&B rooms above the café's dining area – try for the front room with lovely water views.

Lufra Hotel (☎ 6250 3262; www.lufrahotel.com; Pirates Bay Drive; s $65-75, d $80-120) There are great views from the water-facing rooms at this modernised hotel, perched above Tessellated Pavement. The rooms are pretty standard but comfortable; some have undergone refurbishment. Downstairs are good eating options (see below).

Osprey Lodge (☎ 6250 3629; www.view.com.au/osprey; 14 Osprey Rd, Eaglehawk Neck; d $160-200) Spoil yourself here in luxurious surrounds, not far from the beach. You can choose from a suite or self-contained unit, but you may find yourself spending a lot of time in the guest lounge, with its idyllic views. The price includes full breakfast and pre-dinner wine and cheese.

Eating

Eaglehawk Cafe (☎ 6250 3331; Arthur Hwy; mains $7-15; 9am-6pm) One of the peninsula's nicest dining options is this stylish café just south of Eaglehawk Neck. There's attractive décor, art on the walls (by local artists), and a fine menu of breakfast, lunch, wines by the glass, or just coffee and cake.

Lufra Hotel (☎ 6250 3262; Pirates Bay Drive) This large hotel aims to please all comers with its three dining options: a daytime café serving breakfasts, lunches, cakes etc; a **restaurant** (mains $15-27; dinner) featuring fine local produce such as seafood, quail and wallaby; and a public bar area with pool table where you can get traditional pub grub for around $15.

Officers Mess (☎ 6250 3635; off Arthur Hwy; mains $10-22; 8am-8pm Sun-Thu, 8am-9pm Fri & Sat) A pretty basic general store and café. There's not a lot to recommend it, but it does serve hot food and takeaways (including pizzas), and is opposite the historic Officers Quarters (see p115).

Getting There & Away

TassieLink (☎ 1300 300 520; www.tassielink.com.au) can bus you from Hobart to Eaglehawk Neck in 1½ hours; the one-way fare is $17.70.

TARANNA

☎ 03 / pop 160

Taranna is a small town stretched along the shores of Norfolk Bay about 10km north of Port Arthur, its name coming from an Aboriginal word meaning 'hunting ground'. It is a historically important village as it was the terminus for Australia's first **tramway**, which ran from Long Bay near Port Arthur to here. This public transport was powered by convicts, who pushed the carriages uphill, then jumped on for the ride down. In those days Taranna was called Old Norfolk.

Dart Island was used as a semaphore station to relay messages from Port Arthur to Hobart. Today, the waters near the island are used for oyster farming.

Taranna's main attraction is the **Tasmanian Devil Park** (☎ 6250 3230; adult/child/family $20/10/49.50; 9am-5pm), which displays the little devils (feedings 10am, 11am and 1.30pm year-round, plus 5pm from October to May) and a sea eagle (shows 11.15am and 3.30pm daily). It plays a key role in local wildlife rescue and conservation, and is a breeding centre for endangered birds of prey. It's considerably more expensive than other wildlife parks around the state, so be sure to visit at feeding time and for the bird show to get your money's worth. The park is also offers **Devils in the Dark** (adult/child/family $25/15/65; dusk Oct-Easter, Tue, Wed, Fri, Sat Easter-Sep), a much-hyped 'night-time prowl', but really it's just a walk through the park of an evening. There's also a decent café here.

The **Federation Chocolate Factory** (☎ 6250 3435; Arthur Hwy; 9am-5pm Mon-Sat) is a new addition to Taranna. Pop in to see chocolate being hand made, and sample (and purchase) some of the company's intriguing flavours (from favourites such as honeycomb or caramel nougat to the surprisingly good apple flavour, or perhaps brandied apricot, or licorice). Inside the factory is a museum of blacksmithing and saw-milling equipment.

Sleeping & Eating

Mason's Cottages (☎ 6250 3323; 5741 Arthur Hwy; d $85-100, extra person $17) On the northern edge of town, this place has a huddle of modern, brick-lined units available for your self-contained pleasure.

Teraki Cottages (☎ 6250 3436; 996 Arthur Hwy; s $60-70, d $70-80, extra adult $20) Some of the best-value accommodation on the peninsula, at the southern end of town. These three spotless, self-contained cottages have loads of rustic charm, including a quiet bush setting and open fires. Breakfast provisions (free-range eggs, home-made jams) are an extra $5 per person. No credit cards accepted.

Norfolk Bayview (☎ 6250 3855; norfolkbayviewbb@bigpond.com; 111 Nubeena Rd; s $55-60, d $80-88) Modern

B&B in a rural setting just west of Taranna (past Teraki Cottages), with rates including a cooked breakfast and far-reaching views from the elevated verandas over Norfolk Bay.

Norfolk Bay Convict Station (☎ 6250 3487; www.convictstation.com; 5862 Arthur Hwy; d $140) Built in 1838 and once the tramway's port station, now a very good waterfront B&B where the eclectic rooms come with a cooked breakfast.

The Mussel Boys (☎ 6250 3088; 5927 Arthur Hwy; mains $16-23; brunch, lunch & dinner) Open from 10am daily is this bright, fresh café-restaurant, with a menu worth stopping for. Try beetroot and goat-cheese ravioli, then macadamia-crusted trevalla or beer-battered fresh fish fillets.

Getting There & Away

The **TassieLink** (☎ 1300 300 520; www.tassielink.com.au) Tasman Peninsula service calls in at Taranna ($18.30 one-way, 1¾ hours) en route from Hobart to Port Arthur.

FORTESCUE BAY

Hidden 12km down a gravel road from the highway is this remote and captivating bay, with a sweeping sandy beach backed by thick forests. Apart from swimming and lazing on the beach, the main activity here is walking. Excellent tracks lead to some of the best coastal scenery in the state, with the cliffs taller and more impressive than those around Eaglehawk Neck. For those with their own boats, this is an excellent base for fishing; it has a boat ramp and calm waters.

The sheltered bay was one of the semaphore station sites used during the convict period to relay messages to Eaglehawk Neck. Early last century a timber mill was in operation and the boilers and jetty ruins are still visible near Mill Creek, as are the remains of some of the timber tramways used to collect the timber. The mill closed in 1952. Fortescue Bay is part of the Tasman National Park; the usual park entry fees apply.

The bay's **camping ground** (☎ 6250 2433; sites for 2-6 people $11) lacks powered sites, but firewood is available and there are fireplaces, gas barbecues, toilets and cold showers. Bookings are advised during major holiday periods and rates don't include the national park entry fee. There are no shops here so bring in all your own food.

Bushwalking

Several walking tracks start from the bay. The best walk is east to **Cape Hauy** (four to five hours return) – a well-used path leads out to sea cliffs with sensational views of sea stacks like **The Candlestick** and **Totem Pole**. To see rainforest, follow the same track towards Cape Hauy and then walk the steep side track to **Mt Fortescue**, which takes six to seven hours return. The tracks extend all the way to **Cape Pillar**, where the sea cliffs are 300m high; this requires two to three days to visit. For track notes, see Lonely Planet's *Walking in Australia*.

To the north, a good track follows the shoreline to **Canoe Bay** (two hours return) and **Bivouac Bay** (four hours return).

PORT ARTHUR

☎ 03 / pop 170

Port Arthur is the name of the small settlement in which the Port Arthur Historic Site is situated. In 1830, Governor Arthur chose the Tasman Peninsula as the place where prisoners who had committed further crimes in the colony would be confined. He called the peninsula a 'natural penitentiary' because it was connected to the mainland only by a strip of land less than 100m wide: Eaglehawk Neck.

Between 1830 and 1877, about 12,500 convicts served sentences at Port Arthur and for many it was a living hell, though convicts who behaved well often lived in better conditions than those they'd experienced back home. The soldiers who guarded them lived in similar conditions and they too were often imprisoned for what would be regarded today as minor offences.

The penal establishment of Port Arthur became the centre of a network of penal stations on the peninsula, but transcended its role as a prison town. It had fine buildings and thriving industries, including timber milling, shipbuilding, coal mining, shoemaking and brick and nail production.

A semaphore telegraph system allowed instant communication between Port Arthur, the penal outstations and Hobart. Convict farms provided fresh vegetables, a boys prison was built at Point Puer, and a church was erected.

Port Arthur was reintroduced to tragedy in April 1996 when a gunman opened fire on visitors and staff at the site, killing 35 people, either there or close by, and injuring several others. The gunman was finally captured after burning down a local guesthouse and was subsequently imprisoned.

Historic Site

Port Arthur's well-preserved **historic site** (☎ 6251 2310, 1800 659 101; www.portarthur.org.au; 🕑 grounds open 8.30am-dusk) is one of Tasmania's prime tourist attractions. Allow at least four hours for exploration. The restored buildings are open for visitors and tours at various times from 9am to 5pm.

INFORMATION

The large visitor and interpretation centre includes a **regional information counter** (☎ 6251 2371; www.portarthur-region.com.au). Some of the centre's other facilities (toilets, ticket counter, Felons Restaurant) are accessible until the last ghost tour finishes for the evening. There is no fee for accessing the visitors centre.

Buggy transport around the site can be arranged for people with restricted mobility; ask at the information counter. The ferry plying the harbour is wheelchair-accessible.

PRICES

For a fee of $24/11/52 per adult/child/family you can visit all of the site's 30-plus restored buildings and ruins, including the Asylum (now the Port Arthur Museum) and the Separate (or Model) Prison. The ticket, valid for the day of purchase and the following day, also entitles you to a guided tour of the settlement and a short harbour cruise (cruise not available during August). Tickets can be converted into two-year passes for an extra $3/6 per adult/family.

PENAL SETTLEMENT

To learn about the history of the site and its buildings, take the informative free guided tour and check out the visitor centre's bookshop for a range of publications on the subject. The **Port Arthur Museum**, containing numerous displays and a café, was origi-

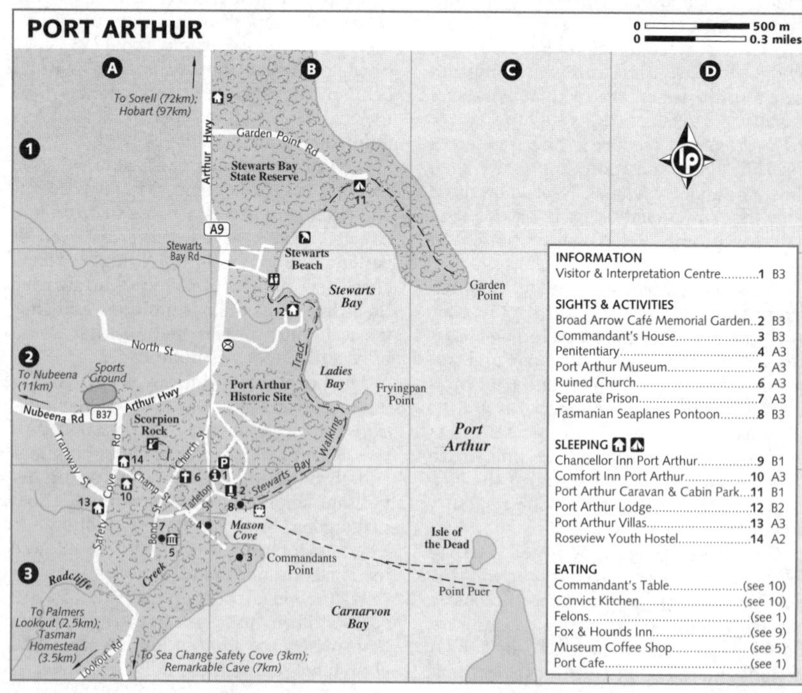

nally the Asylum, housing patients from throughout the colony. The **Separate Prison** was built as a place of punishment for difficult prisoners, following a decision to 'reform' prisoners by isolation and sensory deprivation rather than by flogging. The **church** was built in 1836 but was destroyed by fire in 1884, while the **Penitentiary**, converted from a granary in 1857, was also damaged by fire in 1897.

BROAD ARROW CAFÉ

The Broad Arrow Café, scene of many of the 1996 shootings, was gutted following the massacre. Today, the shell of the building has been preserved and a Memorial Garden established around it.

TOURS

Forty-minute **guided walking tours** of the historic site are included in the price of admission and leave regularly from the visitors centre. They're an excellent introduction to the site. Also included in the price of your ticket is a 20-minute **harbour cruise**, with commentary. When you purchase your ticket you'll be told the times of the next tour and cruise.

There are a number of additional ways to spend money here! The **Isle of the Dead Cemetery Tour** (adult/child/family $10/6.50/29) is a guided tour of Port Arthur's old burial ground on an island in the harbour. The **Point Puer Boys' Prison Tour** (adult/child/family $10/6.50/29) visits the first reformatory in the British Empire built for juvenile male convicts (aged nine to 18). Both of these tours should be booked well in advance.

Ghostly apparitions, poltergeists and unexplained happenings have apparently been recorded at Port Arthur since the 1870s, as explained during the hugely popular lantern-lit, 90-minute **Ghost Tours** (adult/child/family $15.50/9.50/40), which depart from the visitors centre nightly at dusk.

Sleeping

Given the iconic status of Port Arthur to Tasmania's tourism, it's surprising to find few quality accommodation or dining offerings down here – bland, dated motel units are the norm, with a few notable exceptions.

Port Arthur Caravan & Cabin Park (☎ 6250 2340, 1800 620 708; www.portarthurcaravan-cabinpark.com.au; Garden Point Rd; unpowered/powered sites $17/19, dm $15, cabins $85-95) Spacious, attractive and well-equipped park about 2km north of Port Arthur, not far from a sheltered beach. Pay your entry fees to the Port Arthur site at reception and follow a track around the shoreline from here to the historic site. Prices are for two people.

Roseview Youth Hostel (☎ 6250 2311; Champ St; dm/d $19/44; 💻) With a great location at the edge of the historic site, this YHA hostel has OK facilities and crowded dorms but a rough-around-the-edges charm. To get here, continue 500m past the Port Arthur turn-off and turn left into Safety Cove Rd at the sign for the hostel. You can buy your historic-site entry ticket here.

Comfort Inn Port Arthur (☎ 6250 2101, 1800 030 747; www.portarthur-inn.com.au; 29 Safety Cove Rd; d $120-168) Motel with flash views over the historic site and unremarkable accommodation (some rooms recently refurbished, some with spa). There are also good dining options (see p120). Ask about packages including accommodation, dinner, breakfast and a ghost tour of Port Arthur (from $218 for two).

Port Arthur Villas (☎ 6250 2239, 1800 815 775; www.portarthurvillas.com.au; 52 Safety Cove Rd; d $112-140) Not far from the Comfort Inn, this place has affordable, older-style self-contained units sleeping up to four. There's a lovely garden and outdoor barbecue area.

Tasman Homestead (☎ 62250 2239; www.tasmanhomestead.com; off Safety Cove Rd; d $220, extra adult/child $20/15) Enjoy fine views from the verandah of this large, modern homestead, perfect for families and groups (sleeps up to nine). It's 3.5km off Safety Cove Rd (past Palmers Lookout), fully self-contained (breakfast provisions included), and very private. Booking is through Port Arthur Villas – be sure to specify that it's the homestead you're after.

Port Arthur Lodge (☎ 6250 2262; www.portarthurlodge.com; Arthur Hwy; d from $149) This 'lodge' is a collection of well-equipped, self-contained log cabins; one of them is wheelchair-accessible. Cabins vary in size from one- to three-bedroom (sleeping up to seven), and all boast outdoor decks with views of bush land and the swimming beach below.

Chancellor Inn Port Arthur (☎ 6250 2217; www.grandhotelsinternational.com; Arthur Hwy; d $150-175) Incongruous mock-Tudor complex, formerly known as the Fox & Hounds Inn, with a choice of nondescript motel rooms or self-contained units, plus a restaurant that retains the old name (see right), and grand plans for redevelopment. See the website for packages and discounts on the high-season rack rates listed here.

Sea Change Safety Cove (☎ 6250 2719; www.safetycove.com; 425 Safety Cove Rd; d $140-166) Whichever way you look from this recommended guesthouse there are fantastic views – of peninsula cliffs, the neighbouring beach or of bush land. It's 5km south of Port Arthur, just off the sandy sweep of Safety Cove Beach. There are a couple of B&B rooms, plus a large, homey self-contained unit that can sleep five.

WINDGROVE

Windgrove, near Nubeena, is a large, isolated coastal property owned by Peter Adams, environmental campaigner and sculptor (creator of beautiful Huon-pine and myrtle benches, among other things). Peter bought the stunning property in the early 1990s and decided to treat it as a blank canvas, setting out to enrich it with sculptures and gardens that express a link between art, ecology and spiritualism. Peter has developed an eight-hectare Peace Garden here, which incorporates a 2km clifftop walk, lined with benches for rest and meditation; a contemporary communal 'midden'; an eternal flame for peace and reconciliation; and a number of large, reflective sculptures that include a 6m-high spiral-carved blue-gum log and a split 6-tonne piece of dolerite. His latest project is the development of the Windgrove Centre, a combination sanctuary, retreat, art studio and multi-purpose hall for writers, artists, dancers, musicians, meditators, ecologists and compatible souls.

You can find **Windgrove** (☎ 6250 1001; www.windgrove.com) on the Internet or in 3D reality by following the road to Roaring Beach from Nubeena for 5km, then heading left at the 'Windgrove' signage. Although this is not a tourist attraction per se, it is open to people who are interested in visiting. If you would like to visit Peter's property and learn more about his work, it's best to call ahead.

Eating

At the historic site there are a couple of daytime food options, including the **Museum Coffee Shop** in the Old Asylum and bustling **Port Cafe**, inside the visitors centre, serving café food and the usual takeaway suspects.

Felons (☎ 6251 2310; mains $15-26; ⏰ dinner) Also in the visitors centre and with the catchy slogan 'dine with conviction', Felons is a good choice before you head off on a ghost tour. It's an upmarket dinner spot serving creative options with a seafood emphasis, including Cajun-style fish of the day. Reservations advised.

Comfort Inn Port Arthur (☎ 6250 2101; Safety Cove Rd) There are two dining options inside the pub at this motel complex, both enjoying great views over the historic site. The **Convict Kitchen** (meals $12-18; ⏰ lunch & dinner) serves up standard pub fare like schnitzel, roast, fish and chips and steak, and has a kids' menu, while the **Commandant's Table** (mains $17-28, ⏰ dinner) offers more formal dining, and menu options to match such as seared salmon fillet and oven-roasted lamb.

Fox & Hounds Inn (☎ 6250 2217; mains $16.50-24.50; ⏰ lunch & dinner) This restaurant at the Chancellor Inn does reputable meals in its dated, ye-olde-themed dining room, mostly from the pub menu roll-call of favourites. It also has a children's menu.

Getting There & Away

See p112 for information on public transport and tours to Port Arthur.

REMARKABLE CAVE

South of Port Arthur is Remarkable Cave, a series of arches eroded into shape by the sea. A boardwalk and stairs provides access to a metal viewing platform, a few minutes' walk from the car park. From the car park you can also follow the coast east to **Maingon Blowhole** (one hour return) or further on to **Mt Brown** (four hours return), where there are excellent views.

On the way back it's worth deviating to **Palmers Lookout**, which also provides good views of the entire Port Arthur and Safety Cove area.

NUBEENA

☎ 03 / pop 230

Charmless Nubeena is the largest town on the peninsula, fanned out along the shore, yet it's much quieter than Port Arthur. It's really just a holiday destination for locals, and there's not a lot to recommend it. However, if all the other accommodation on the peninsula is already full, it's worth knowing that you may be able to find a bed here.

The surrounding natural areas are much more appealling than the town itself. The main activities here are swimming and relaxing on **White Beach**, or fishing from the jetty or foreshore. Down a side road 3km south of town is some energetic walking to **Tunnel Bay** (five hours return), **Raoul Bay Lookout** (two hours return) and **Cape Raoul** (five hours return). To the north is **Roaring Beach**, which gets good surf but isn't safe for swimming.

Sleeping & Eating

White Beach Caravan & Cabin Park (☎ 6250 2142; www.whitebeachcp.com.au; 128 White Beach Rd; unpowered/powered site $22/24, cabin $78-88) Beachfront park in quiet, ghost gum-dotted surrounds south of Nubeena. Good facilities, including laundry, store, playground and barbecue areas.

White Beach Holiday Villas (☎ 6250 2152; www.whitebeachholidayvillas.com.au; 309 White Beach Rd; d $100, extra person $15) At the other end of the beach, this holiday village has self-contained villas (one with spa) set in spacious grounds; the units furthest up the hill are newer.

There are a couple of takeaways in town, plus **Nubeena Tavern** (☎ 6250 2250; Main Rd; mains $12-25; lunch & dinner daily), with few surprises on its meat- and seafood-based menu.

Getting There & Away

The Tasman Peninsula service operated by **TassieLink** (☎ 1300 300 520; www.tassielink.com.au) will take you to Nubeena from Hobart in two hours and costs $20.40 one way.

KOONYA

☎ 03

There's little for visitors at this tiny settlement apart from some good accommodation choices.

Seaview Lodge (☎ 6250 2766; Nubeena Back Rd; dm/d $18/40) This is a rambling backpacker-style establishment with basic accommodation, kitchen and lounge, fantastic views and a peaceful location. School groups often visit in winter, so it's best to call. BYO linen, or pay extra to hire.

Cascades (☎ 6250 3873; www.cascadescolonial.com.au; 533 Main Rd; d $140-200) Originally an outstation of Port Arthur, with around 400 convicts working here at one time. Some of the buildings have now been restored in impressive period style to become cosy, self-contained cottages (including one luxury option with spa). Full breakfast provisions and entry to a private museum included in the rates.

Getting There & Away

TassieLink (☎ 1300 300 520; www.tassielink.com.au) will take you from Hobart to Koonya in 1¾ hours; the one-way fare is $19.20.

DETOUR

At Premaydena, take the signposted turning (road C431) 13km northwest for Saltwater River and the restored ruins at the **Coal Mines Historic Site** (24hrs), powerful reminders of the colonial past. Dug in 1833, the coal mines were used to punish the worst of the convicts, who worked in terrible conditions. The poorly managed mining operation was not economically viable. In 1848 it was sold to private enterprise and in 10 years it was abandoned. Some buildings were demolished, while fire and weather took a toll on the rest.

The old mines site is interesting to wander around (interpretive panels enable a self-guided tour) and provides a dramatic contrast to Port Arthur. Don't enter any mine shafts, because they haven't been stabilised and could be dangerous. You can, however, enter some well-preserved solitary confinement cells, which are torturously small and dark.

Apart from the mines, the area's attractions are rare birds and butterflies, and easy walks across gentle coastal country. From Lime Bay, the 2½-hour return journey to Lagoon Beach is the most popular walk.

Lime Bay Nature Reserve is a beautiful area where free bush camping is allowed north along a sandy track. Camping is very basic, with pit toilets and fireplaces. Drinking water must be taken in, and fuel stoves are recommended.

The Southeast

This slice of the state has much to offer, particularly if you have your own transport and enjoy driving through idyllic countryside and browsing roadside produce stores. Water views from the peninsula's mountain passes and the serenity of Bruny Island add to the region's laid-back character. The more energetic can also find fulfilment at Hartz Peak, Hastings Caves, and the South Coast Track at magnificent Recherche Bay.

The wide Huon River dominates the region. Synonymous with it is the famous Huon pine; sadly, only a few young specimens remain. The area is also known for its rainbows, which are probably due to a combination of southern latitude and abundant waterways. In the right conditions, you might also get lucky and catch a show of the aurora australis, the southern hemisphere's equivalent of the aurora borealis or northern lights.

In the 1960s, Huon Valley apple-growing put Tasmania on the international export map. At one stage there were over 2000 orchards. Farmers have since diversified into other fruit crops, and have also turned their attention to Atlantic salmon, wine and tourism, plus production of foodstuffs such as jams and sauces, cheese, mushrooms and even saffron.

HIGHLIGHTS

- Enjoying lazy drives with picture-perfect views alongside the mesmerising **D'Entrecasteaux Channel** or **Huon River** (p133)
- Taking time out at remote **Cockle Creek** or **Recherche Bay** (p142)
- Dining on sensational local produce in a million-dollar location at **Peppermint Bay** (p132) restaurant in Woodbridge
- Tiptoeing through **Tahune's tree-tops** (p138), then gliding like a bird above them
- Devouring **local fruits and jams** from roadside stalls and farms and at quirky cafés
- Taking a boat trip from unspoiled **Bruny Island** (p129) to view the incredible coastline and diverse wildlife
- Donning a hardhat and going underground on a caving expedition at **Hastings Caves** (p142)
- Watching dolphins frolicking in the picturesque bay at **Dover** (p139)

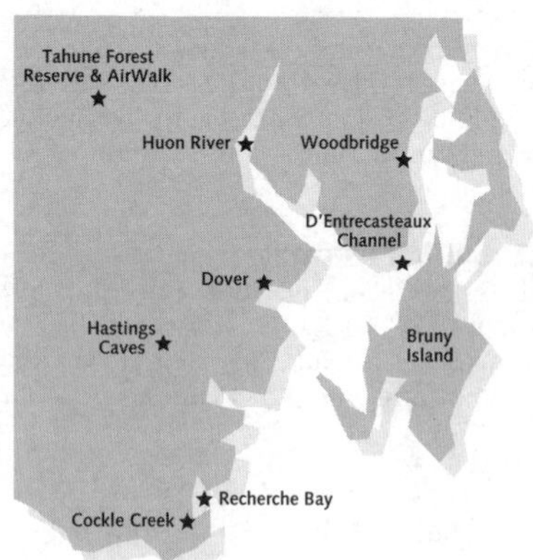

- www.huontrail.org.au
- www.farsouth.com.au

Getting There & Around

BUS

Hobart Coaches (☎ 132201; www.hobartcoaches.com.au) runs several buses each weekday from Hobart south through Margate, Snug and Kettering to Woodbridge. A bus also runs once each weekday from Hobart to Snug and inland across to Cygnet. There are no weekend services.

TassieLink (☎ 1300 300 520; www.tassielink.com.au) runs buses along the Huon Hwy from Hobart through Huonville, Frankin and Geeveston to Dover; there are up to seven services a day from Monday to Friday (five of these terminate in Geeveston), and one each on Saturday and Sunday (both terminating in Geeveston).

At 9am on Monday, Wednesday and Friday from December through March, a TassieLink bus departs Hobart and continues south all the way to the end of the road at Cockle Creek (bookings essential).

CAR

The views from the highway between Hobart and Woodbridge are especially lovely, particularly on sunny days during seasons of decent rainfall. At such times, the contrast between the lush green pastures and the deep-blue channel waters can be dazzling. If you then take the road from Woodbridge to Gardners Bay on the way to Cygnet, you'll be rewarded with stunning water views on both sides of the ridge. Another road across

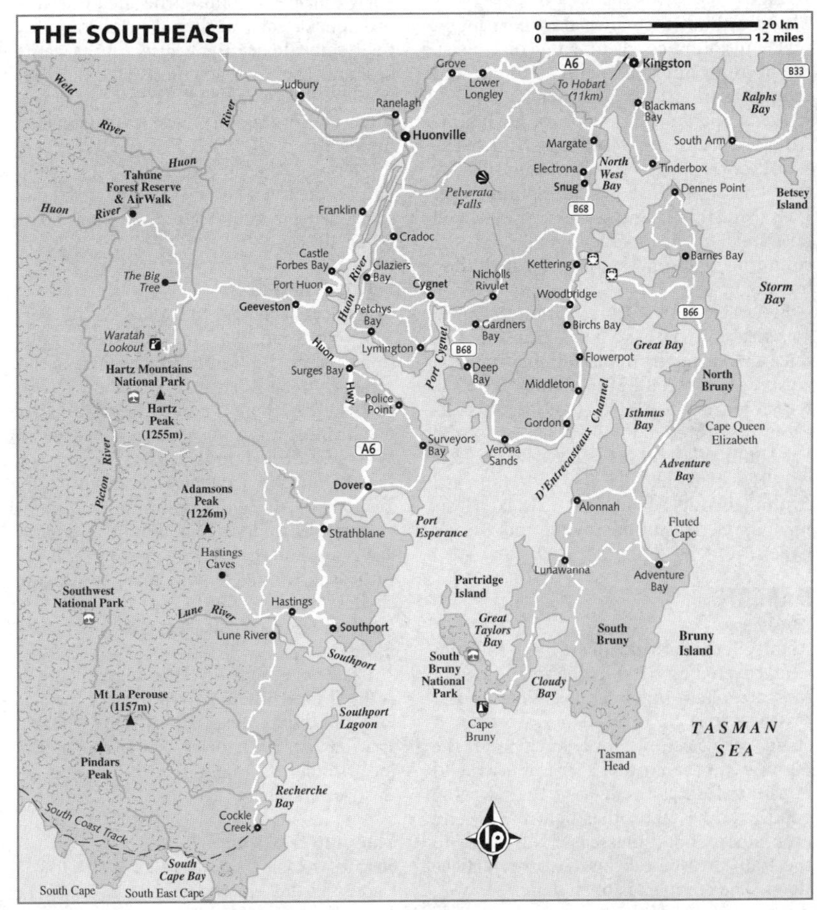

the peninsula to Cygnet leaves the highway just north of Kettering, but is less scenic. You can also follow the coast around from Woodbridge through Verona Sands to Cygnet on a road that occasionally passes very close to the channel, making it an impressive detour.

Further south, some sections of the side route from Surges Bay through Police Point and on to Dover are gravel, but the road is in good condition and the views are great. The 19km road from Lune River to Cockle Creek has been surfaced with very coarse gravel, which roughens the ride in an older vehicle. Check your tyres before you start out and make sure your spare is in good condition.

TOURS

Those without their own transport might prefer to join a coach tour out of Hobart. See p128 for information on getting to and around Bruny Island on a tour.

Many operators run trips to the Tahune AirWalk, including **Tigerline Coaches** (☎ 1300 653 633; www.tigerline.com.au), which has a full-day tour costing $89/54 per adult/child. **Tiger Trails** (☎ 6234 3931; www.tigertrails.green.net.au) will take small groups to the airwalk and surrounding wilderness for $99, including lunch.

Bottom Bits Bus (☎ 1800 777 103, 6229 3540; www.bottombitsbus.com.au) has a good-value day-trip once a week, taking in the Tahune AirWalk, Hastings Caves, and Mt Wellington on the return journey to Hobart ($89). It also offers a busy three-day tour ($345), based at Far South Wilderness Lodge & Backpacker (p140) which takes in the far south, including Bruny Island, the airwalk, Hastings Caves, adventure caving and Cockle Creek.

MARGATE

☎ 03 / pop 745

About 23km south of Hobart (beyond Kingston, covered on p100) is the small town of Margate. Train buffs can examine the last **passenger train** to be used in Tasmania. It stands on a piece of railway track beside the highway on the northern side of town and houses **craft shops**, a **café** (meals $6-16) serving good pancakes and other light meals, and even a barber and masseuse! Next door to the train are some browse-worthy **antique stores**. The complex is open daily.

Behind the train is **Inverawe Native Gardens** (☎ 6267 2020; www.inverawe.com.au; 1565 Channel Hwy; adult/child $6/3; 9.30am-5pm Tue-Sun Sep-May), a private, 9.5-hectare property with landscaped gardens, nature trails, good views and visiting bird-life.

The town itself has a few decent eateries along the main street.

Hobart Coaches (☎ 13 22 01; www.hobartcoaches.com.au) offers several bus runs from Hobart through Kingston to Margate ($5.50 one-way, 20 to 30 minutes), including two services on Saturday that do not continue further south.

SNUG

☎ 03 / pop 770

Early European explorers decided this area provided a safe, sheltered anchorage for their ships, hence the heartwarming name of Snug. The town was devastated in bushfires in 1967, when 80 houses burnt down. A temporary caravan village was established beside the oval, which eventually became the present-day caravan park. After being rebuilt, the town became a popular holiday spot due to its calm waters and good boating facilities.

Sights & Activities

Oyster Cove, accessed via Manuka Rd 5km south of Snug, was an important traditional camp for indigenous people (who called it Mena Loongana or Mannina), but in 1847 it became the next destination for the Tasmanian Aborigines who survived Wybalenna on Flinders Island (see p21). In 1995, Oyster Cove was returned to the Tasmanian Aboriginal community.

Snug Falls are located 3.5km off the highway (signposted). An easy 45-minute return walk, complete with seats and picnic shelters, leads to the foot of the falls. Just south of Snug at **Coningham** is a good swimming beach.

Beside the highway 1km south of town is the **Channel Historical & Folk Museum** (☎ 6267 9169; 2361 Channel Hwy; adult/child $4/0.50; 10am-4pm Wed-Sun), a historical showcase of the local timber, fishing and ship-building industries and the destructive 1967 fires.

Sleeping & Eating

Snug Beach Cabin & Caravan Park (☎ 6267 9138; 35 Beach Rd; powered/unpowered site $20/16, on-site van $40, cabin $65-90) This well-maintained park has grass-sprung, tree-sheltered sites beside the beach, and adjacent to the park are man-made distractions like a tennis court and playground. Prices are for two people.

Aside from the decent-value pub fare served up at **Snug Tavern** (☎ 6267 9238; 2236 Channel Hwy; mains $15-19; lunch & dinner Wed-Sun), there are slim pickings in Snug come mealtime. It might be worth a trip north to Margate to broaden your options.

Getting There & Away

Hobart Coaches (☎ 13 22 01; www.hobartcoaches.com.au) runs several weekday buses from Hobart through Margate to Snug ($6.20 one-way, 30 minutes).

KETTERING

☎ 03 / pop 300

The small, picturesque port of Kettering lies at the head of scenic Little Oyster Cove. This bay shelters a popular marina for fishing boats and yachts, as well as the Bruny Island car ferry terminal. It's a reasonable place to base yourself for regional explorations, and an essential stop for any kayakers keen to get on the water.

The **Bruny D'Entrecasteaux visitors centre** (☎ 6267 4494; www.tasmaniaholiday.com; 81 Ferry Rd; 9am-5pm) is located at the ferry terminal and provides loads of information on Bruny Island and the surrounding district.

At the marina is **Roaring 40s Ocean Kayaking** (☎ 6267 5000, 1800 653 712; www.roaring40skayaking.com.au; Ferry Rd), Tassie's leading kayaking tour operator. Among the company's offerings are classes in the basics of sea kayaking ($75) and gear rental to experienced kayakers (single/double kayak $15/20 per hour and $55/75 per day). They also organise a smorgasbord of day and overnight trips to suit all levels of experience: a half-day tour exploring Oyster Cove ($80) or full day on D'Entrecasteaux Channel ($150, including barbecue lunch), or overnight trips at Lake St Clair, the Lake Pedder impoundment or the Freycinet Peninsula, amongst other destinations. See p299 for details of their more challenging exploration of the southwest wilderness.

Sleeping & Eating

Oyster Cove Inn (☎ 6267 4446; oyster.cove@tassie.net.au; Ferry Rd; s/d $45/80) In a great setting with views over the boat-cluttered harbour, this large pub offers a mixture of budget singles and bigger rooms (all with shared bathroom, and a help-yourself breakfast). Also here is a good **restaurant** (mains $16-26) with an extensive menu and local wine selections, and a more casual bar (also offering meals, plus takeaway pizza). Eat or drink on the outside deck and check out some of the wooden sculptures decorating the landscape.

Herons Rise Vineyard (☎ 6267 4339; www.heronsrise.com.au; Saddle Rd; d $130-150, extra person $30) Just north of town, this vineyard has two upmarket, self-contained cottages set in delightful gardens. One cottage has two bedrooms and can sleep four. Each bright, spacious unit has a log fire, and breakfast provisions are supplied (and dinner by prior arrangement).

The Old Kettering Inn (☎ 6267 4426; ebaldwin@rezitech.com.au; 58 Ferry Rd; d $115) On the road to the ferry terminal, this 1894 property is set in flower-filled gardens and offers one comfortable, spacious suite – bedroom, bathroom, lounge and outdoor deck – with a private entrance. A cooked breakfast is included.

Tulendena (☎ 6267 4348; www.tulendena.com.au; 29 Bloomsbury Lane; d $130, extra person $30) Located just north of Kettering, signposted off the highway, is this quality self-contained abode, able to sleep four in modern comfort. The house is set in spacious gardens, and you can enjoy the views from the private terrace. Two-night minimum, and some deals for longer stays.

Mermaid Cafe (☎ 6267 4494; 81 Ferry Rd; snacks & meals $3-16; 9am-5pm daily, plus dinner Fri & Sat) Inside the waterfront visitors centre is this informal licensed café, offering everything from a quick coffee and toasted sandwich to a more leisurely meal.

Getting There & Away

Hobart Coaches (☎ 13 22 01; www.hobartcoaches.com.au) runs three or four buses each weekday from Hobart to Kettering ($7.10 one-way, 45 minutes).

BRUNY ISLAND

☎ 03 / pop 520

Beautiful, sparsely populated Bruny Island is two lumps of land joined by a sandy isthmus less than 100m wide; locals refer to the

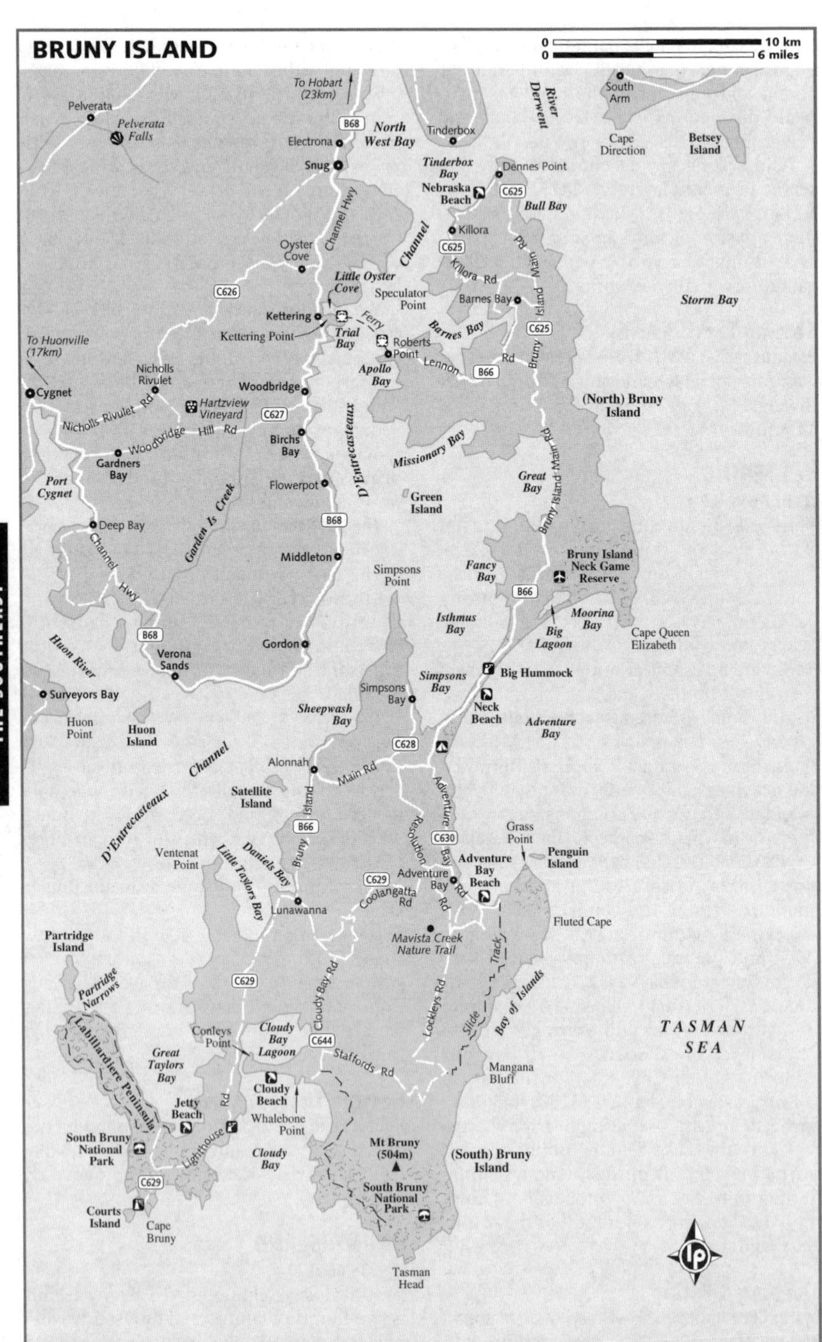
BRUNY ISLAND
0 10 km
0 6 miles
To Hobart (23km)
Pelverata
Pelverata Falls
North West Bay
Electrona
Snug
Tinderbox
River Derwent
South Arm
Cape Direction
Betsey Island
Tinderbox Bay
Dennes Point
Nebraska Beach
Bull Bay
Channel Hwy
Channel
Killora
Killora Rd
Main Rd
Oyster Cove
Little Oyster Cove
Speculator Point
Barnes Bay
Storm Bay
Kettering
Kettering Point
Ferry
Trial Bay
Roberts Point
Lennon Rd
Apollo Bay
Bruny Island Main Rd
To Huonville (17km)
Nicholls Rivulet
Cygnet
Woodbridge
Hartzview Vineyard
Nicholls Rivulet Rd
Woodbridge Hill Rd
(North) Bruny Island
Gardners Bay
Birchs Bay
D'Entrecasteaux
Missionary Bay
Port Cygnet
Flowerpot
Green Island
Great Bay
Deep Bay
Garden Is Creek
Middleton
Simpsons Point
Fancy Bay
Bruny Island Neck Game Reserve
Hwy
Isthmus Bay
Moorina Bay
Huon River
Gordon
Big Lagoon
Cape Queen Elizabeth
Verona Sands
Big Hummock
Simpsons Bay
Surveyors Bay
Sheepwash Bay
Neck Beach
Huon Point
Huon Island
Adventure Bay
Alonnah
Main Rd
D'Entrecasteaux Channel
Satellite Island
Bruny Island
Adventure Bay Rd
Resolution
Grass Point
Penguin Island
Ventenat Point
Daniels Bay
Little Taylors Bay
Adventure Bay Beach
Coolangatta Rd
Lunawanna
Fluted Cape
Partridge Island
Mavista Creek Nature Trail
Track
Cloudy Bay Rd
Lockleys Rd
Partridge Narrows
Slide
Bay of Islands
Labillardiere Peninsula
Conleys Point
Cloudy Bay Lagoon
TASMAN SEA
Great Taylors Bay
Staffords Rd
Mangana Bluff
Cloudy Beach
Jetty Beach
Whalebone Point
South Bruny National Park
Lighthouse Rd
Cloudy Bay
Mt Bruny (504m)
(South) Bruny Island
South Bruny National Park
Courts Island
Cape Bruny
Tasman Head
B68
C625
C626
C627
B66
C628
C630
C629
C644
THE SOUTHEAST

two different sections as North and South Bruny. North Bruny has rolling hills that are extensively farmed, while South Bruny is more scenic, with steeper, forested hills and the varied wildlife of South Bruny National Park. In between is the narrow 5km isthmus, home to penguins, mutton birds and other waterfowl.

The island's coastal scenery is superb and there are plenty of fine swimming and surf beaches, plus good sea and freshwater fishing. There are also several signposted walking tracks within the national park and reserves, especially on the southern Labillardiere Peninsula and at Fluted Cape.

The island was sighted by Abel Tasman in 1642 and later visited by Furneaux, Cook, Bligh and Cox between 1770 and 1790. It was eventually named after Rear-Admiral Bruni d'Entrecasteaux, who explored and surveyed the area in 1792. Strangely, confusion reigned about the spelling and in 1918 it was changed from Bruni to Bruny.

Tasmanian Aborigines belonging to the Nuennone band originally called the island Lunawanna-Alonnah, a name given contemporary recognition by being broken up and used to identify two of the island's settlements. Among their numbers was Truganini, daughter of Mangana, chief of the Nuennone band. Truganini left Bruny Island in the 1830s to accompany George Robinson on his infamous statewide journey to win the trust of all the Tasmanian Aborigines (see the boxed text, p22). Many of Bruny Island's landmarks, including Mt Mangana, are named after indigenous individuals.

The island has experienced several commercial ventures. Sandstone was mined from a rocky point and used in prominent buildings such as the post office and Houses of Parliament in Melbourne, and coal was also locally mined. But these industries gradually declined due to high transportation costs. Only farming and forestry had long-term viability.

Tourism is becoming increasingly important to the island's economy but remains fairly low-key. There are (as yet) no homogenised resorts, just plenty of interesting cottages and houses, most self-contained. Too many visitors try unsuccessfully to cram their experience of Bruny into a day or less. If you can, stay for a few days and really begin exploring the island's striking coastal environment and at least some of the walking tracks within its stunning national park.

Information

The **Bruny D'Entrecasteaux visitors centre** (☎ 62 67 4494; www.tasmaniaholiday.com; 81 Ferry Rd; 9am-5pm), at the ferry terminal in Kettering, can help you out with accommodation bookings, souvenirs, books and tourist information. It's a good idea to pick up the free handouts on island walks and camping, and the self-drive tour.

The best online source of information is the website www.brunyisland.net.

South Bruny has three **general stores**, all open seven days, all with eftpos facilities, and all selling petrol, takeaway hot food and provisions (though not everything your stomach desires will be found on their shelves). The largest is at **Adventure Bay** (Main Rd) and has a multicard ATM. The store at **Alonnah** (Main Rd) acts as post office. The third store is at **Lunawanna** (Cloudy Bay Rd). At the time of research there was no general store in North Bruny, although this may change by the time you read this – ask around.

Internet access in Adventure Bay is available at the **Penguin Café** (☎ 6293 1352; www.penguincafe.com.au; 10am-5pm daily, plus dinner Sat;), or at the **Online Access Centre** (☎ 6293 2036; closed Sun & Mon), at the local school in Alonnah (signposted) and with a rather complex schedule of opening hours (it's wise to phone first).

It's best to purchase national park passes at the visitors centre in Kettering.

Sights & Activities

MUSEUMS

The **Bligh Museum of Pacific Exploration** (☎ 6293 1117; 876 Main Rd, Adventure Bay; adult/child $4/2; 10am-3pm) details the Adventure Bay landings and Pacific exploits of early European explorers like Bligh, Cook and Furneaux. This small, interesting collection includes maps, charts and manuscripts – many of them originals or first editions – as well as globes and information on early Antarctic explorations.

At the council offices in Alonnah is a small, volunteer-run **History Room** (☎ 6260 6366; Main Rd, Alonnah; admission free; 10am-3pm Apr-Nov, 10am-4pm Dec-Mar), with numerous newspaper clippings, photos and records of the island community's past, plus information on walks and attractions on the island.

LIGHTHOUSE

South Bruny's lighthouse was built in 1836, making it the second-oldest such structure in Australia. Made from local stone, it's located at the stormy southern end of the island and is worth a visit just to see the rugged coastline. Public access is restricted to the surrounding **reserve** (🕑 10am-4pm).

NATIONAL PARK & RESERVE

Popular **Fluted Cape**, one of the scattered extremities of **South Bruny National Park**, is east of the small township of Adventure Bay. The easy trail leading here from the main beach passes **Grass Point** (1½ hours return), a great breakfast spot on a sunny morning. From here you can walk along the shore to **Penguin Island**, accessible at low tide, or complete a more difficult circuit and climb the cape for some glorious views (2½ hours return).

The park's southwestern portion comprises the large **Labillardiere Peninsula**, which features rugged coastal scenery and a lighthouse. Walks range from leisurely beach explorations to a seven-hour circuit of the entire peninsula (starts from and finishes at the Jetty Beach camping ground).

For descriptions of walks through the national park, as well as other walks around the island, like the easy **Mavista Creek nature trail** (20 minutes return) southwest of Adventure Bay, consult the booklet *Bruny Island: A Guide for Walkers* ($8.50), which is available from the Bruny D'Entrecasteaux visitors centre. Bear in mind, however, that the booklet was last published in 1998 and many changes have since taken place. The centre can also supply a free leaflet on local trails.

The **Bruny Island Neck Game Reserve**, in the centre of the island, makes a home for the mutton birds and little (fairy) penguins that nest in the sand dunes. The best time and place to see these birds is at dusk in the warmer months at **Highest Hummock Lookout**. Park at the Bruny Island Neck Game Reserve sign and climb the 273 timber steps to the **Truganini Memorial** and sweeping views of both parts of the island. A timber walkway also crosses the Neck to the other beach. Make sure you keep to the boardwalk in this area, as the mutton birds dig deep holes into the sand – the holes can be hard to see and you can break an ankle in them.

Bird-watchers visit the island to catch glimpses of species such as the endangered forty-spotted pardalote. During summer there are numerous ranger-led activities; for details, call the local **Parks & Wildlife Service** (☎ 6293 1419; www.parks.tas.gov.au/natparks/sthbruny).

MORELLA & HIBA

These two unique properties are found opposite each other on the main road about 6km north of Adventure Bay. As well as its quality accommodation and dining options, Morella Island Retreats is surrounded by stunning **gardens** (adults/family $4/7; 🕑 10am-5pm) with sizeable rhododendrons (best enjoyed in August and September) and incredible views over the island's isthmus.

Hiba (☎ 6293 1456; www.hiba.com.au; 53 Adventure Bay Rd; 🕑 10am-4pm Mon-Thu) is a strikingly modern chateau, complete with turrets, that houses the Original Tasmanian Fudge Company. Tastings and sales are available. The extensive **gardens** (admission $4) are also open to the public for exploration. Hours can vary, and the property is sometimes open Friday to Sunday – it's worth calling ahead.

Tours

FROM HOBART

From October to April, **Bruny Island Charters** (☎ 6293 1465; www.brunycharters.com.au) conducts highly recommended three-hour tours of the island's stunning southeast coastline, taking in rookeries, seal colonies, bays, caves and towering sea cliffs. Trips leave the Adventure Bay jetty at 11am daily and cost $85/45 per adult/child; for $145/100 the company offers a full-day tour from Hobart including transfers, the cruise, morning tea and lunch. Bookings are essential.

Travellers without their own transport might like to take advantage of the **Bruny Island Bus Service** provided by Bruny Island Charters. For $48, passengers get a return bus trip from Hobart to Adventure Bay, morning tea, admission to the Bligh Museum of Pacific Exploration, and four hours to explore (enough time to complete the

Fluted Cape Walk, if you're feeling energetic; or you can just laze on the beach).

Bruny Island Ventures (☎ 6229 7465, 1300 653 633) conducts small-group day tours of the island that cost $130/90 per adult/child. Tours depart from and return to Hobart four times a week and take in the island's prime features, including the Neck Game Reserve, Adventure Bay and Cape Bruny Lighthouse, with meals included.

ON THE ISLAND

See above for details on the excellent cruise out of Adventure Bay operated by Bruny Island Charters.

Other options include fishing charters, with all equipment provided, with **Ol' Kid** (☎ 6293 1128; www.capcookolkid.com.au), operating from the Captain James Cook Memorial Caravan Park in Adventure Bay (see right). Half-day charters cost from $75 per person (minimum two people).

Inala Nature Tours (☎ 6293 1217; www.inalabruny.com.au; Cloudy Bay Rd) runs highly regarded, personalised walking and four-wheel-drive tours of the island, with a focus on flora and fauna. The tour leader, Dr Tonia Cochran, is a botanist, zoologist and conservationist; her 250-hectare property is home to almost 90 bird species (and a three-bedroom cottage for rent). Tour prices vary; a walking tour of the Inala property costs around $130 for two people.

Sleeping

Bruny Island is a popular Tasmanian holiday destination, as evidenced by the multitude of self-contained cottages for hire, most suitable for medium-sized groups and offering economic rates for one-week rentals. Bookings are essential, as owners/managers and their keys are not always easily located – the visitors centre at Kettering is a good place to start.

The township of Adventure Bay on South Bruny's east coast is the main accommodation area (and the most attractive township in the southern part), but there are plenty of other places around the island. Alonnah is the other main settlement on South Bruny, and Dennes Point and Barnes Bay on North Bruny both have places to stay.

Note that there are no hostels on Bruny. Your best budget option is an on-site van or cabin.

BUDGET

National Park & Reserve

If you have a vehicle and a tent, the cheapest accommodation is at one of the free designated **bush camp sites**. Free camping on Bruny is restricted to these places to prevent the island's foreshores being damaged by indiscriminate tent placement. The sites have pit toilets and fireplaces; BYO firewood and water.

There are sites within South Bruny National Park (national park passes required) at **Jetty Beach**, a beautiful sheltered cove 3km north of the lighthouse, and also at **Cloudy Bay**. There is also a camping site outside the national park at **Neck Beach**, at the southern end of The Neck.

Adventure Bay

Captain James Cook Memorial Caravan Park (☎ 6293 1128; www.capcookolkid.com.au Main Rd; unpowered/powered site $12/15, on-site vans $32-40, cabins $80-90) Great beachside location with a mountainous backdrop, plus welcoming owners and good facilities (including new cabins with disabled access). Fishing charters are also available here (see left). Prices listed are for two people.

Adventure Bay Holiday Village (☎ 6293 1270; www.adventurebayholidayvillage.com.au; Main Rd; unpowered/powered site $14/16, on-site vans $32, cabins $50-95) Beside the beach at the end of Adventure Bay Rd (3km past the general store), with cabins to suit all budgets and pretty grounds filled with wildlife, especially at dusk when the white wallabies visit. There's a strict no-noise policy after 11pm, so party-goers should head elsewhere. Prices listed are for two people.

Alonnah

Bruny Island Hotel (☎ 6293 1148; Alonnah; s/d $45/80) There are two squat roadside units on offer at the pub – this doesn't sound too enticing, but they pass muster if all you're after is a clean room and comfy bed for the night.

MIDRANGE

Note that the prices listed in this section are for one-night stays, but that rates usually drop for stays of two or more nights.

South Bruny

Explorers' Cottages (☎ 6293 1271; www.brunyisland.com; Lighthouse Rd, Lunawanna; d $120, extra person $25)

In a secluded location south of Lunawanna on the way to the lighthouse, these six cottages offer excellent self-contained accommodation. Each two-bedroom unit can sleep six and has lounge and kitchen, log fire and outdoor deck.

Lumeah (☎ 6293 1265; www.lumeah-island.com.au; Main Rd, Adventure Bay; d $140, extra person $20) Lumeah, an Adventure Bay sawmiller's cottage built 115 years ago, offers accommodation perfect for two couples or two families, with two double rooms, two bathrooms and a bunk room sleeping six (maximum 10 guests). It's fully self-contained, across from the beach, and also has an outdoor barbecue area and spa.

Resolution House (☎ 6293 1168; www.resolutionhouse-islandaccommodation.com.au; 696 Adventure Bay Rd, Adventure Bay; d $130-145) Adventure Bay's only hosted B&B, with two rooms in an eye-catching A-frame house directly across the road from the beach and a few doors away from the Penguin Café. Try for the upstairs room, which enjoys a better view.

North Bruny

The north is indeed lovely – Nebraska Beach is a beautiful stretch of white sand and clear water – but it's worth stocking up on groceries and other requirements prior to arriving here, as at the time of research there was no store or petrol outlet. The south has more dining options and attractions.

Wainui B&B (☎ 6260 6260; www.wainuibandb.com; 87 Main Rd, Dennes Point; d $130) The two large attractive rooms and the great views from the outdoor deck are features of this modern B&B. Prices include continental breakfast, and to overcome the dearth of restaurants in the area, you can purchase barbecue packs ($35, including meat, salad and home-baked bread for two) from the host that you then cook for yourself on the barbie.

Bruny Beach House (☎ 5243 8486; www.brunybeachhouse.com; 91 Nebraska Rd, Dennes Point; d $120, extra person $10) On stunning Nebraska Beach is this large, good-value beach house that can sleep four. It's full of light and all the facilities you'll need, plus a great deck from which to enjoy the views. There's a two-night minimum stay.

Swanhaven B&B (☎ 6260 6428; www.swanonbruny.com.au; 150 Power Rd, Barnes Bay; d $130) Modern bushland retreat offering two upstairs B&B rooms and cooked breakfasts; three-course dinners can be arranged from $25 per person. You'll most likely need directions from the hosts to find this place, given its secluded setting west of Barnes Bay.

TOP END

South Bruny

Morella Island Retreats (☎ 6293 1131; www.morella-island.com.au; 46 Adventure Bay Rd; d $160-260) For something really special, book one of the unique secluded cottages at this fabulous complex about 6km north of Adventure Bay (they also have beachfront cottages down by The Neck). Cottages range from luxury retreats for couples, complete with garden bath and hammock for two, to family-sized holiday homes. All are self-contained, and the facilities, design and décor are superb. Prices drop by up to $60 for stays of longer than one night.

St Clairs (☎ 6293 1300; www.stclairs.com; Lighthouse Rd; d $190) On the road to the lighthouse (just past the Explorers' Cottages) is this plush getaway cottage just for two, surrounded by bushland. Renting it nets you a spa and cooked breakfast provisions; dinner by arrangement.

The Tree House (☎ 0405 192 892; www.thetreehouse.com.au; Alonnah; d $165, extra person $15) This is an attractive, open-plan timber place overlooking the unattractively named Sheep Wash Bay. It has two bedrooms, all the mod cons and superb views. The price drops to $145 for stays of two nights or more.

Eating

Provisions and takeaways are available at the island's **general stores** (see p127).

Penguin Café (☎ 6293 1352; www.penguincafe.com.au; Adventure Bay; meals $6.50-17; 10am-5pm daily, plus dinner Sat;) One of the island's few eateries, found beside the Adventure Bay store and serving toasted focaccias, interesting hot lunches (curried wallaby, anyone?), Devonshire tea and cakes. It also caters to holiday-makers with hampers available for picnics or dinner. Bookings essential for hampers or Saturday dinners.

Bruny Island Hotel (☎ 6293 1148; Alonnah; mains $12.50-18.50; lunch & dinner) Friendly, unpretentious pub in Alonnah. Outdoor seating with water views helps you unwind, plus a fine, well-priced menu heavy on local seafood. There's also a kids' menu, and a decent bar area.

Hothouse Cafe (☎ 6293 1131; 46 Adventure Bay Rd; snacks & meals $7-20; 🕑 from 10am daily) The best eatery on the island is this novel café at Morella Island Retreats (see opposite). It's in a converted hothouse enjoying magnificent views over the isthmus, with plenty of birds to keep you company and a menu of interesting snacks and meals. Closing hours vary from 4pm to 6pm; dinner is usually an option here in January.

Bay Café (☎ 6293 1588; Main Rd, Adventure Bay; snacks & meals $7-20; 🕑 11am-7pm daily) There's a cheery feel to this cute café, with its colourful décor and fresh flowers on the tables, and a family of ducks outside the windows. It's at the Adventure Bay Holiday Village and offers café fare by day (soup, baguettes, lots of sweet treats), then dinner between 6pm and 7pm (bookings essential).

Getting There & Away

Access to the island is via a **car ferry** (☎ 6272 3277) that motors from Kettering to Roberts Point on North Bruny in 20 minutes. There are at least 10 services daily; the first ferry to Bruny departs Kettering at 6.50am (7.45am on Sunday), while the last ferry to Kettering departs Roberts Point at 7pm (7.50pm on Friday). The timetable may vary, however, so double-check departure times.

The following fares are for return trips: a car costs $25 ($30 on public holidays and public holiday weekends); motorcycles $11 ($15 on public holidays and public holiday weekends); bicycles $3. There's no charge for passengers.

At least two weekday-only buses from Hobart to Kettering, run by **Hobart Coaches** (☎ 13 22 01; www.hobartcoaches.com.au), will stop, on request, at the Kettering ferry terminal. The Roberts Point terminal on Bruny is a long way from anywhere. Those without their own wheels should see p128 to see how to get to Bruny Island on a tour.

Getting Around

You'll need a vehicle to get around, as there are no buses; a bicycle is an option, but be prepared for long rides between destinations. Bruny Island has some narrow, winding gravel roads – the slippery, logging truck-infested road over Mt Mangana being the prime case in point – so drive carefully and, if possible, schedule at least a few days for a full exploration of the island.

WOODBRIDGE

☎ 03 / pop 250

Established in 1874 and originally called Peppermint Bay due to the area's peppermint gums, Woodbridge was eventually renamed by a landowner nostalgic for his old home in England. It's a quiet town with a tranquil waterfront setting, now on the tourist map due thanks to the sleek Peppermint Bay restaurant, bar and providore, which opened in late 2003 (see p132).

About 3km south of Peppermint Bay is another stop for food-lovers: **Grandvewe Sheep Cheesery** (☎ 6267 4099; www.grandview.au.com; 59 Devlyns Rd, Birchs Bay; 🕑 10am-5pm daily Sep-Jun, 10am-4pm Wed-Mon Jul-Aug), a farm producing organic cheese from both sheep and cows' milk. Stop in to sample some tasty produce, snack on a cheese platter, or sample some wine from the owners' nearby Grandview vineyard.

Hartzview Vineyard (☎ 6295 1623; www.hartzview.com.au; 70 Dillons Rd; 🕑 9am-5pm) is 7km from Woodbridge, off the road to Gardners Bay. It has a fine range of fortified wines and fruit liqueurs and also sells drops from a handful of other Tasmanian vineyards.

Sleeping & Eating

Old Woodbridge Rectory (☎ 6267 4742; www.rectory.alltasmanian.com; 15 Woodbridge Hill Rd; d $120-130) At the start of the Gardners Bay road is this friendly place with flower-filled gardens and two large en-suite rooms in a 100-year-old rectory.

Coach House (☎ 6229 7837; www.coachhousepeppermintbay.com.au; 3439 Channel Hwy; d $130-150, extra person $35) You're right next door to Peppermint Bay restaurant at this large three-bedroom house (c 1890) ideal for one to three couples (no children accepted). It's self-contained and offers billiard room, log fires and a roll-call of mod cons ideal for a longer stay (two-night minimum mid-December to February).

Hartzview Vineyard (☎ 6295 1623; www.hartzview.com.au; 70 Dillons Rd; d $160-200, additional adult/child $30/20) This secluded vineyard offers a well-equipped three-bedroom house endowed with antiques, log fire, breakfast provisions and fine views over Gardners Bay. Dinners by arrangement.

There are a couple of accommodation options on Pullens Rd, which intersects with the Channel Hwy on the northern

THE AUTHOR'S CHOICE

Peppermint Bay (☎ 6267 4088; www.peppermintbay.com.au; 3435 Channel Hwy) Right on D'Entrecasteaux Channel and enjoying wonderful views is this striking new development, housing a gourmet food store; the upmarket, à-la-carte **Dining Room** (mains $25-30, ⏲ lunch daily, dinner Sat); and the more casual **Local Bar & Terrace** (meals $10-17, ⏲ lunch daily, dinner Tue-Sat, closed Mon winter). The emphasis is on using local produce, so you'll find seafood, fish, fruit, meats, cheeses and other foodstuffs from just down the road, used to fantastic effect – and with good wine selections to accompany your choices. Bookings are advised for the Dining Room. The Local Bar is a good option for an informal meal or drink throughout the day, with an outdoor terrace to enjoy in fine weather.

One of the more interesting ways of getting to Peppermint Bay is by boat from Hobart; see below.

outskirts of Woodbridge, including **Telopea** (☎ 6267 4565; www.telopea-accommodation.com.au; 144 Pullens Rd; s/d $88/99, extra adult/child $22/11), a rural property with two wheelchair-accessible, self-contained brick units on offer.

Getting There & Away

Hobart Coaches (☎ 13 22 01; www.hobartcoaches.com.au) has four weekday services; the trip from Hobart takes one hour ($7.30 one-way).

Another option out of Hobart is **Peppermint Bay Cruises** (Map p70; ☎ 1300 137 919; www.hobartcruises.com.au; Brooke St Pier, Hobart; cruises ⏲ noon daily Oct-Apr, Wed, Fri, Sat, Sun May-Sep), which takes passengers on a half-day cruise to Peppermint Bay, to enjoy excellent scenery, wildlife, the use of underwater cameras and a visit to a salmon farm en route. The price (from $75/45 per adult/child) includes the option of lunch at the Dining Room of the restaurant (two courses from a limited menu), or lunch, prepared at the restaurant, eaten on board the boat while enjoying an extended cruise of D'Entrecasteaux Channel.

CYGNET

☎ 03 / pop 930

This small township was originally named Port de Cygne Noir (Port of the Black Swan) by Rear-Admiral D'Entrecasteaux because of the many swans seen on the bay. Youthfully reincarnated as Cygnet (a young swan), the town and surrounding area now have many apple and other fruit orchards, an eclectic mix of attractions, and activities such as fishing, bushwalking, flat-water canoeing and some fine beaches, particularly further south at Randalls Bay and Verona Sands.

Sights & Activities

The popular, three-day **Cygnet Folk Festival** (www.cygnetfolkfestival.org) is held annually in early January and attracts thousands to the town. Check out the family-friendly program and ticket details on the website.

The natural beauty surrounding Cygnet has drawn many artists to the area to live and work, and an alternative-lifestyle community has sprung up. Check out the town's galleries along the main street, and keep your eyes open for summer art and photography shows staged at the **Cygnet Town Hall** (14 Mary St) by the Huon Art Exhibitions Group.

To learn about the history of the town and its inhabitants, visit the small, photo-filled **Cygnet Living History Museum** (☎ 6295 1602; Mary St; admission by donation; ⏲ 12.30-3pm Fri-Sun, also Thu in summer), next to the church on the main street. An interesting new addition is the **Living History Museum of Aboriginal Cultural Heritage** (☎ 6295 0004; Cross Roads, Nicholls Rivulet; adult/child $4.50/2; ⏲ 10.30am-2.30pm), out of town at Nicholls Rivulet (5km from the turn-off south of Cygnet). The small museum contains general information, displays of Aboriginal arts and crafts, and a garden filled with plants used by Aborigines for bush tucker.

Not far from the Aboriginal museum is **The Deepings Woodturner** (☎ 6295 1398; www.deepingsdolls.com; 1118 Nicholls Rivulet Rd, Nicholls Rivulet; ⏲ 9am-5pm Mon-Sat, noon-5pm Sun), a gallery of hand-turned and hand-painted wooden dolls as well as other fine timber products.

Sleeping

Balfes Hill (Huon Valley) Backpackers (☎ 6295 1551; www.balfeshill.alltasmanian.com; 4 Sandhill Rd, Cradoc; dm/d/f $20/50/75; 💻) Off the Channel Hwy 4.5km north of town, this hostel has decent rooms, good facilities, extensive grounds and a great view from the large communal area. It's especially busy from November to May, when the friendly host helps backpackers find fruit-picking work. Offers courtesy bus to/from Cygnet bus stop.

Cygnet Holiday Park (☎ 6295 1267; 3 Mary St; unpowered/powered site $9/14) Basic and cheap camping ground accessed via the side road next to the Cygnet RSL. Enquiries and check-in is at Cygnet Hotel, opposite the park.

Deep Bay School House B&B (☎ 6297 8231; www.deepbayschoolhouse.com.au; Abels Bay Rd, Deep Bay; s/d $85/100, extra person $35) Easily our top pick for accommodation in the area is this fantastic-value B&B, 8km south of Cygnet in a tranquil location with stunning views. There's one suite here (two bedrooms sleeping up to five, plus bathroom and private lounge). Rates include cooked breakfast.

Leumeah Lodge (☎ 6295 0980; www.cygnetbay.com.au; Lot 22, Crooked Tree Point; d $110-150) Bayside B&B lodge in a very pretty spot 3km south of town, offering a handful of pleasant upstairs rooms (cooked breakfast included), plus a self-contained two-bedroom suite. All enjoy water views.

Wilfred Lodge (☎ 6295 1552; wilfredlodge@trump.net.au; 7393 Channel Hwy; s/d $85/97) Just south of the town centre is this old cottage (c 1915), set in pretty gardens and with two en-suite B&B rooms available.

Eating

The Red Velvet Lounge (☎ 6295 0466; 87 Mary St; meals $8-14; 10am-6pm; 💻) Eclectic wholefood café serving deliciously healthy light meals to a diverse clientele. Opt for the asparagus, olive and goats' cheese tart, the organic beef rendang curry or the mushroom, garlic and mozzarella pizza. In the back is an organic/health food shop where you can stock up on the likes of pecan halves, organic buckwheat flour and herbal teas.

School House Coffee Shop (☎ 6295 0237; Mary St; meals $4-10; 9am-5pm) Cute coffee shop serving hearty home-made pies and soups, Turkish bread sandwiches, and tempting cakes.

Commercial Hotel (☎ 6295 1296; 2 Mary St; snacks & meals $6-22) This pub has turned its dining room into an all-day café, serving up a good range of light meals (focaccia, salads, pasta), plus some hearty meals for the pub-goers too (steak, roast, mixed grill and so on).

Howard's Cygnet Central Hotel (☎ 6295 1244; mains $10-16; lunch & dinner Tue-Sun) A popular spot among locals, with affordable, predictable pub grub (lots of seafood and grilled meats) and little joy for vegetarians.

Getting There & Away

Hobart Coaches (☎ 13 22 01; www.hobartcoaches.com.au) travel to Cygnet via Snug only once each weekday (with extra services on Thursdays); the trip takes one hour and costs $8.80.

DETOUR

If you're in the area, don't miss driving the very scenic coastal road (the C639) between Cradoc and Cygnet. The direct route along the Channel Hwy (the B68) between these two towns is about 7km. The Cygnet Coast Rd makes the journey considerably longer – 27km, past Petcheys Bay and Glaziers Bay – but is well worthwhile.

To take the C639 from Cygnet, follow the sign on the main street pointing south to Lymington. In January and February, you may be able to pick your own fruit at one of the **blueberry farms** along the way, but these farms are also worth seeing in autumn, when the bushes turn a spectacular shade of red.

Much further around the coast (about 6.5km from the northern end) is **The Scented Rose** (☎ 6295 1816; 1338 Cygnet Coast Rd, Glaziers Bay; adult/child $7.50/3; 10am-5pm Sat & Sun Nov-Mar), a beautiful display garden and nursery nurturing specialist David Austin roses.

One kilometre from the Cradoc junction is **Panorama Vineyard** (☎ 6266 3409; www.panoramavineyard.com.au; Cygnet Coast Rd, Cradoc; 10am-5pm Wed-Mon), where you can sample several wine types (tastings free), including a highly acclaimed pinot noir, in impressive surroundings.

There are a couple of houses for rent along the Cygnet Coast Rd – ideal venues for recharging your batteries. Close to the Scented Rose, **Arundel Cottage** (☎ 6295 1577; 643 Silver Hill Rd, Glaziers Bay; d $75, extra person $10) is a simple, self-contained cottage that sleeps four; at the other end of the price scale, luxurious **Riverside** (☎ 6295 1952; 35 Graces Rd, Glaziers Bay; d $160, extra adult/child $50/35) is a modern abode (sleeps six) with all mod cons and fantastic views from the wide verandas.

HUONVILLE & AROUND

☎ 03 / pop 1530

Huonville straddles the banks of the Huon River and is only a short drive from some lovely vineyards, interesting small towns and other attractions. The town was originally sited beside the river's first rapid and served as an important crossing point; a modern bridge now spans the water, enabling access to the south.

The Huon and Kermandie Rivers were named after Huon d'Kermandec, second-in-command to the explorer d'Entrecasteaux. Prior to that, the area was known by Tasmanian Aborigines as Tahune-Linah. The region was originally covered in tall forests and so timber milling quickly became a major industry; the commercially coveted softwood Huon pine was first discovered here. The initial plundering of Huon pine groves nearly wiped the tree out because it is extremely slow-growing. Today, only immature trees survive along the river. Once the forest was levelled, apple trees were planted and thus began the orchard industry, still the region's primary agricultural activity.

Huonville is the region's commercial centre and has all the services you'll need lining its main street (banks and ATMs, supermarkets etc). The town isn't a typical overnight stop for visitors, but it does have some good accommodation options in its surrounds.

Information

The **Huon visitors centre** (☎ 6264 1838; Esplanade; 🕑 9am-5pm) is by the river, in the Huon River Jet Boats office (on the road south to Cygnet). The **Parks & Wildlife Service** (☎ 6264 8460; 24 Main Rd; 🕑 9am-4.30pm Mon-Fri) has an office on the main street, dispensing information about national parks in the south.

The **Huon Valley Environment Centre** (☎ 6264 1286; 3/17 Wilmot St; 🕑 9.30am-4.30pm Tue-Fri) is an excellent resource for anyone interested in the environmental issues the valley (and Tasmania) face.

Sights & Activities

Take a frenetic, 35-minute jet-boat ride through the local rapids with **Huon River Jet Boats** (☎ 6264 1838; www.huonjet.com; Esplanade; adult/child $55/35; 🕑 9am-5pm); bookings are recommended at peak times. Those seeking a less-aggressive water sport can opt for pedal boat hire, or book a two-hour **river cruise** (adult/child $35/20; 🕑 10am Mon-Fri Sep-May) on the MV *Southern Contessa;* the price includes morning tea and entry to the Wooden Boat Centre in Franklin (opposite).

The nearby township of Ranelagh (3km west of Huonville and well signposted) is home to the beautiful vine-surrounded environs of **Home Hill** (☎ 6264 1200; www.homehillwines.com.au; 38 Nairn St; 🕑 10am-5pm), producers of award-winning pinot noir, chardonnay and dessert wines. Tastings are free; there is also an excellent restaurant right here (see opposite).

About 13km from Huonville is Judbury, home to **Huon Valley Horsetrekking** (☎ 6266 0343; www.southcom.com.au/~horsehaven; 179 Judds Creek Rd). The company operates out of the owner's small farm in an idyllic setting, and can arrange horse treks from two hours to two weeks; a half-day ride is $89 and includes lunch. There is also a lovely cottage for rent here ($110 for a double).

If you find hooking fish problematic, visit the **Snowy Range Trout Fishery** (☎ 6266 0243; www.snowyrangetrout.com.au; adult/child $4/2; 🕑 9am-5pm) for a guaranteed catch (equipment available for rent). It's 28km west of Huonville, past Judbury (signposted). Besides the admission fee, you also pay by weight for any salmon or rainbow or brown trout you catch.

Grove, a small settlement 6km north of Huonville, has become the tourist centre of the region's apple industry. Located beside the highway in an old packing shed is the **Huon Apple & Heritage Museum** (☎ 6266 4345; 2064 Main Rd; adult/child $5/2.50; 🕑 9am-5pm Sep-May, 10am-4pm Jun-Aug), filled with restored machines, plus displays about 500 different types of apple and 19th-century apple-picking life.

Also in Grove is Australia's oldest jam company, **Doran's** (☎ 6266 4377; Pages Rd; 🕑 10am-4pm). Here, you can see jams and juices being readied for distribution, and sample some (don't miss the spiced apple butter).

Sleeping

Grand Hotel (☎ 6264 1004; 2 Main St; s/d $28/40) The only accommodation in Huonville itself is in this friendly old pub beside the bridge, with plenty of basic budget rooms (shared facilities).

Matilda's of Ranelagh (☎ 6264 3493; www.matildasofranelagh.com.au; 44 Louisa St, Ranelagh; d $150-200) One of Tasmania's finest heritage B&Bs, Matilda's offers luxurious, adults-only accommodation 2km northwest of Huonville. Guests enjoy beautifully decorated rooms, delightful gardens, cooked breakfasts and the attentions of the 'goldie gang' (a meet-and-greet team of five golden retrievers).

Huon Bush Retreats (☎ 6264 2233; www.huonbushretreats.com; 300 Browns Rd, Ranelagh; cabins $195, tent & campervan sites $20) Gay-friendly, disabled-friendly, wildlife-friendly nature retreat, set in an extensive habitat reserve on the sadly named Mt Misery. There are three modern, self-contained cabins, a larger cabin with disabled access, three tent sites, two campervan sites, and walking tracks, plus a large barbecue and picnic shelter, or meals can be arranged for cabin-dwellers. It's worth checking the website for more details, especially directions – the retreat is 10km from Huonville and not well signposted, plus the 3km stretch on Browns Rd is rough and steep (no caravans allowed).

Eating

Home Hill (☎ 6264 1200; 38 Nairn St; mains $17.50-26.50; ⌚ lunch daily, dinner Fri & Sat) Home Hill vineyard (see opposite) is home to a highly regarded restaurant set in a modern, rammed-earth building with lush green views. The excellent seasonal menu relies on Tassie produce like Bothwell goats' cheese, Huon Valley mushrooms and Spring Bay scallops, and King Island cream accompanies most delectable desserts. Morning and afternoon tea is served outside meal times.

For simpler fare, grab picnic fodder from **Banjo's Bakehouse** (☎ 6264 8755; 8 Main Rd; ⌚ 6am-6pm) and head to riverside tables, or choose good-quality pub meals from the **Grand Hotel** (☎ 6264 1004; 2 Main St; mains $12-20; ⌚ lunch daily, dinner Mon-Sat).

Huon Manor Bistro (☎ 6264 1311; Short St; dinner mains $19-25; ⌚ lunch Sun-Fri, dinner Mon-Sat) Opposite the Grand Hotel, in a lovely old home and with garden seating. The menu showcases local produce, with an emphasis on seafood. As well as the full menu, there are also cheaper lunchtime and café-style options.

JJ Cafe (☎ 6266 4377; Pages Rd, Grove; meals $3-10; ⌚ 10am-4pm) Café inside Doran's (see opposite), naturally offering all manner of dishes that go well with their delicious jams (scones, pancakes etc) as well as savoury snacks.

Getting There & Away

TassieLink (☎ 1300 300 520; www.tassielink.com.au) buses arrive at and depart from outside Banjo's Bakehouse on the main street; the trip from Hobart takes one hour and costs $8.70.

FRANKLIN & AROUND

☎ 03 / pop 465

The highway follows the Huon River south for a long way, passing through the settlements of Franklin, Castle Forbes Bay and Port Huon. These were once important shipping ports for apples but nowadays the wharves and packing sheds are rarely used.

Pretty Franklin is the oldest town in the Huon area and the wide, peaceful river it sits beside acts as one of Australia's best rowing courses. The town is fairly large considering its small population and there has been little change to many of its buildings in the last century, particularly the main street's Federation architecture. An excellent example is the **Palais Theatre**, begun in 1911 and ultimately an amalgamation of Federation and Art Deco styles, now with a superbly renovated interior thanks to dedicated members of the local community. Local events are held here, with proceeds going to the theatre's continued revitalisation.

The town's much-trumpeted attraction is the **Wooden Boat Centre** (☎ 6266 3586; www.woodenboatcentre.com; Main Rd; adult/child $5.50/4.50; ⌚ 9.30am-5pm), part of the School of Wooden Boatbuilding. This unique school runs accredited 18-month courses in traditional boat-building using some of Tasmania's sturdiest timbers, including Huon and King Billy pine. At the centre you can learn about boat-building and often watch a boat under construction.

Franklin has good information online at www.franklintasmania.com.

Sleeping & Eating

Franklin and its surrounds has quality accommodation at very reasonable prices.

FRANKLIN

Franklin Lodge (☎ 6266 3506; www.franklinlodge.com.au; Huon Hwy; d from $135) A two-storey building begun in the 1850s and eventually extended into the current grand Federation structure. It has four en-suite rooms, one with spa; a cooked breakfast is provided.

Huon Franklin Cottage (☎ 6266 3040; www.huonfranklincottage.com.au; 3554 Huon Hwy; d $100-120) Lovely home set high up off the road to enjoy river views. Offers two well-equipped B&B rooms, plus outdoor spa and exercise equipment, all at a very affordable rate. Dinner by arrangement.

Kay Creek Cottage (☎ 6266 3524; www.kaycreekcottage.com; 17 Kay St; d $100-120) This timber-lined, cosy cottage is self-contained and fully equipped and exhibits great attention to detail. It features stereo and a CD collection, games, wood fire, and bucolic setting with great views. Breakfast supplies at additional cost.

Franklin Woodfired Pizza (☎ 6266 3522; Huon Hwy; pizzas $11-18; dinner) Also called Smoke on the Water, this tiny spot produces fantastic takeaway pizzas (gourmet and traditional) inside its unique corrugated-iron oven.

Aqua Grill (☎ 0407 322 976; Huon Hwy; meals $6.50-8; 11.30am-7.30pm) Mighty fine takeaway fish and chips and other seafood snacks.

Franklin Tavern (☎ 6266 3205; Main Rd; snack & meals $5-18; lunch & dinner Wed-Sun) As well as beer and history, this characterful pub (built in 1853 and uniquely renovated since by an abalone diver) offers simple bar meals and all-day snacks, including toasted sandwiches and Devonshire tea. Stop in on Sunday for a bargain $10 roast.

Petty Sessions (☎ 6266 3488; 3445 Huon Hwy; mains $10.50-23.50; 10am-5pm daily, dinner Wed-Sun) A blue picket fence and pretty gardens surround this likeable café, housed in the town's former courthouse. Sit outside on the deck and choose from classic café fare, including salads, BLT, tandoori chicken burger and seafood fettucine, or try the house speciality – abalone soup.

CASTLE FORBES BAY

There's not much to this small settlement except for orchards, apple sheds and some very good accommodation (all signposted off the highway).

Castle Forbes Bay House (☎ 6297 1995; swilliams@southcom.com.au; Meredith Rd; B&B s/d $60/80, house d from $100) This former schoolhouse has apple orchards as neighbours, two B&B rooms (private bathrooms down the hall), guest lounge, friendly owners, lush gardens and cooked breakfasts. Next door is a family-sized house available for self-caterers, with a huge backyard to enjoy.

Camellia Cottage (☎ 6297 1528; www.vision.net.au/~maplehill; 119 Crowthers Rd; d $95, extra person $35) Charming farm cottage with open fire, set in magnificent gardens. The cottage sleeps three and doesn't have a full kitchen, but does have some cooking facilities and breakfast provisions are included. You'll probably want to take advantage of the barbecue and outdoor area too.

Donalea B&B (☎ 6297 1021; www.donalea.com.au; 9 Crowthers Rd; s/d $90/110) Another good-value B&B with welcoming hosts, relaxing views and lovely garden. Donalea has two bright, well-equipped rooms (one with spa) and a large guest lounge with log fire and video.

PORT HUON

Kermandie Lodge (☎ 6297 1110; www.kermandielodge.com.au; Huon Hwy; motel s/d $80/88, unit s/d $90/106, extra adult/child $25/15) Complex offering plain but comfortable and well-equipped two-bedroom units (with kitchen and washing machine), plus cheaper motel rooms.

Kermandie Hotel (☎ 6297 1052; Huon Hwy; s/d/tr $50/75/100) Next to Kermandie Lodge is this large pub, with refurbished rooms (all with en suite), plus an outdoor deck with water views – the perfect spot to enjoy lunch or dinner, served daily (mains $11-19).

Getting There & Away

TassieLink (☎ 1300 300 520; www.tassielink.com.au) services do the one-hour trip from Hobart to Franklin for $10.20 and to Castle Forbes Bay for $11.60; they arrive at and depart from Arthur's Takeaway on the main street of Franklin.

GEEVESTON

☎ 03 / pop 830

Geeveston, 31km south of Huonville, is the administrative centre for Australia's most southerly municipality and the gateway to the popular Tahune AirWalk and Hartz Mountains National Park. While most towns declined as apple sales dropped, this town reversed the trend and grew. It is an important timber industry base, with an economy encouraged by forestry operations and the tourists who come to see both the

GARETH MCCORMACK

Road sign, Bruny Island (p125)

Hastings Caves (p141), Hastings

CHRIS MELLOR

Neck Beach at sunset, Bruny Island (p125)

GARETH MCCORMACK

PETER HE

Freycinet National Park (p166)

RICHARD I'ANSON

The Hazards, Coles Bay (p166)

The Commissariat Store (p161) and cement works, Maria Island

GRANT D

forests and nearby wilderness. That said, the town has limited accommodation, so travellers might find that Dover or the Franklin area make a better overnight base.

Geeveston was founded in the mid-19th century by the Geeves family, whose descendants are still active in local affairs. In the 1980s the town was the epicentre of an intense battle over the future of the forests of Farmhouse Creek. At the height of the controversy, some conservationists spent weeks living in the tops of 80m-tall eucalypts to prevent them from being cut down. The conservation movement ultimately won – Farmhouse Creek is now protected from logging.

See Sights below for information on the town's visitors centre. There is a multicard ATM inside the **Geeveston One-Stop Shop** (Arve Rd), on the road out to the airwalk.

Sights

In the centre of town is the **Forest & Heritage Centre** (☎ 6297 1836; www.forestandheritagecentre.com.au; Church St; 9am-5pm;). Its **Forest Room** has comprehensive displays on all aspects of forestry, such as logging practices and land management, and regularly hosts wood-turners who displays their craft. Upstairs is the **Hartz Gallery**, which showcases the artistic abilities of a number of the craftspeople.

The complex also includes a **visitors centre** where you can go online, pick up national park passes, maps and descriptions of walks in the Hartz Mountains, and buy tickets for the Tahune Forest AirWalk ($11/7/30 per adult/child/family). You can also buy tickets at the airwalk itself, but it's worth stopping in here to pick up a map detailing the short walks you can do along the way (see right).

Another good place to browse for craft and locally-made timber furniture is the **Southern Forest Furniture Market** (☎ 6297 0039; 6a School Rd; 10am-5pm).

Sleeping & Eating

Bob's Bunkhouse (☎ 6297 1069; www.bobsbunkhouse geevestonbackpackers.com.au; cnr Huon Hwy & School Rd; dm/tw $20/50;) You won't miss this backpackers on the highway, painted bright blue and housing clean, comfy rooms and good facilities (wood heater, laundry, free tea and coffee).

Bears B&B (☎ 6297 0110; www.bearsoverthemountain.com; 2 Church St; d $90-125) The most central accommodation is this excellent B&B, attached to an antique and collectibles store and decorated with a whimsical bear theme. Expert friendly hosts, cooked breakfasts and well-equipped rooms.

Cambridge House (☎ 6297 1561; Huon Hwy; s/d shared facilities $70/90, d en suite $110) An attractive B&B offering upstairs accommodation in three bedrooms with shared facilities (ideal for families), or a downstairs en-suite room.

Kyari (☎ 6297 1601; Church St; meals $8-20; breakfast & lunch Wed-Mon, dinner Fri & Sat) This is a streamlined modern café with a friendly vibe, all-day breakfasts, enticing café fare, kids' menu and outdoor deck. If you're heading out to the airwalk or national park, consider picking up one of their picnic hampers ($8-18).

Ma Pippins (☎ 6297 0099; Church St; lunch $5-15, dinner mains $16-25; lunch & dinner Tue-Sun) A rustic café, Ma Pippins offers light lunches and afternoon teas during the day, then steak, salmon and seafood dishes plus blackboard specials of an evening. Depending on the weather, eat by the log fire or in the garden out the back.

Getting There & Away

TassieLink (☎ 1300 300 520; www.tassielink.com.au) buses arrive at and depart from the car park behind the visitors centre. The 1½-hour trip from Hobart costs $12.80.

ARVE ROAD

The Arve Rd, constructed to extract timber from the extensive forests, and now sealed thanks to the Tahune AirWalk, heads west from Geeveston through rugged, timbered country to the Hartz Mountains, the Tahune Forest Reserve and Tahune AirWalk (29km from Geeveston).

Stop in at the Geeveston Forest & Heritage Centre (left) to purchase your tickets to the airwalk, view the displays on the area's history and industry, and pick up a map detailing the walks and lookouts along Arve Rd. At times the stretch feels like one long PR exercise for Forestry Tasmania – ignore the hype and enjoy the scenery and easy short walks, including the following:

Arve River Picnic Area Has picnic tables and a short forest walk (10 minutes' round trip); 12km from Geeveston.

Turn-off to Hartz Mountains Situated 12km from Geeveston; the stretch from the turn-off to the national park is another 8km.
Keogh's Creek Walk A 15-minute streamside circuit, 14km from Geeveston.
Big Tree Lookout A brief walk leads to a timber platform beside a giant 87m-high swamp gum; turn-off is 14km from Geeveston.
West Creek Lookout Provides views from a bridge extending out onto the top of an old tree stump; 21km from Geeveston.

TAHUNE FOREST RESERVE

The name of this reserve is derived from Tahune-Linah, which was the Aboriginal name for the area around the Huon and Kermandie Rivers. The reason most people come here is to stroll along **Tahune Forest AirWalk** (☎ 6297 0068; www.forestrytas.com.au; adult/child/family $11/7/30; 9am-5pm), nearly 600m of horizontal steelwork suspended at an average height of 20m above the forest floor. The floor of the catwalk is see-through metal mesh, allowing views right past your feet to the ground. There's also a 24m cantilevered section designed to have a disconcerting sway and bounce to it, caused by vibrations from approaching footsteps. The airwalk has great views from its walkways, especially from the cantilever towards Mt Picton.

The visitors centre sells souvenirs and has a **café** (meals $6-12) serving the usual lunchtime fare. Getting to the beginning of the airwalk from the visitors centre involves a short trot across a bridge over the Huon River and a climb up a significant number of steps embedded in the hillside. Transportation to the start of the steelwork for disabled visitors can be arranged; just ask at reception.

There are also a couple of signposted walks at ground level; the most popular is a 20-minute riverside stroll through young stands of Huon pine. There are also picnic grounds in the area, and free camping for tents and campervans (minimal facilities); inquire at the visitors centre.

You'll need your own transport to visit the airwalk; alternatively, take a day-trip from Hobart – most tour operators include a visit to the airwalk on their itineraries; see p124 for details.

Activities

A new and novel way to see the forest is to fly above it, an opportunity provided by **Eagle Gliding** (☎ 6297 0068; adult/child $33/22). The experience is a fun, safe, all-ages ride in which passengers are strapped in to a hang-glider on a 220m static cable that passes 30m above the Huon River and forest. It's rather like a fancy flying fox ride, and you get two crossings for the price. Eagle Gliding's base is about 400m from the airwalk car park – look for the signs.

Other adventure activities possible in the Tahune Forest Reserve include rafting (subject to water levels and minimum numbers, from $100) and abseiling from the airwalk frame itself (from $25). Both these activities are offered by Hobart-based **Aardvark Adventures** (☎ 6273 7722, 0408 127 714; www.aardvarkadventures.com.au) and need to be arranged in advance.

HARTZ MOUNTAINS NATIONAL PARK

If you prefer your wilderness a little less prepackaged than that of the Tahune Forest Reserve, head to Hartz Mountains. A century ago, the Hartz plateau was receiving the attention of loggers, and local stocks of small varnished gums were being harvested for eucalyptus oil, which ended up being distilled in Hobart for medicinal applications. But eventually an area of nearly 65 sq km was declared a national park and in 1989 this area was made a part of the Tasmanian Wilderness World Heritage Area.

Hartz Mountains National Park is regularly visited by weekend walkers and day-trippers as it's only 84km from Hobart. The park is renowned for rugged mountains, glacial lakes, gorges and dense rainforest, not to mention wonderful alpine moorlands where fragile cushion-plant communities grow in cold, misty climes. Being on the edge of the Southwest National Park, the region is subject to rapid changes in weather, so take waterproof gear and warm clothing even on a day walk. The usual park entry fee applies.

There are some excellent isolated viewpoints and walks in Hartz Mountains National Park. **Waratah Lookout** is only 24km from Geeveston and is an easy five-minute walk from the road; look for the jagged peaks of the Snowy Range and the Devils Backbone. Other shortish walks on well-surfaced tracks include **Arve Falls** (20 minutes return) and **Lake Osborne** (40 minutes return). The walk to **Lake Esperance** (two hours return, moderate grade) takes you through some truly magnificent high country. You'll need to be fairly fit and experienced, however, to tackle the steep, rougher track that leads to **Hartz Peak** (five hours return), which is poorly marked beyond **Hartz Pass** (3½ hours return).

There are no camping facilities in the park, but basic day-visitor facilities exist (toilets, shelter, picnic tables, barbecue).

DOVER

☎ 03 / pop 570

This picturesque fishing port, 21km south of Geeveston, is a good spot to stay while you're exploring the far south. Dover was originally called Port Esperance after one of the ships in Rear-Admiral d'Entrecasteaux' fleet, but that name is now only applied to the bay. The bay's three small islands are known as Faith, Hope and Charity.

In the late 19th century, the processing and exporting of timber was Dover's major industry. Timber was milled and shipped from here and also the nearby towns of Strathblane and Raminea. While much of it was Huon pine, hardwoods were also harvested and sent to countries like China, India and Germany for use as railway sleepers. Today the major industries are fruit-growing, fishing and aquaculture. Fish factories near the town employ local workers to harvest Atlantic salmon, which is exported throughout Asia.

The town has reasonable services, including supermarkets and bank agents. There's not much by way of attractions in Dover itself, but lots of activities in the beautiful surrounding wilderness (ask around about fishing charters – at the time of research these were in a state of flux). If you're heading further south, buy petrol and food supplies here. The **Online Access Centre** (☎ 6298 1552; Old School, Main Rd; ⏰ Mon-Sat) is near the woodfired pizza restaurant; Internet access costs $3/5 for 30/60 minutes.

DETOUR

The main road (the A6) from Geeveston to Dover heads inland at Surges Bay and makes for an uninteresting but quick route (21km). The more scenic alternative is to leave the highway at Surges Bay and follow the Esperance Coast Rd through Police Point and Surveyors Bay. Some of this road is unsealed but has a firm gravel surface. The road allows fine views over the wide Huon River and passes many scenic places like Desolation Bay and Roaring Bay. Along the way you'll get close-ups of the waterlogged pens of commercial salmon farms.

Huon Charm Waterfront Cottage (☎ 62 976314; www.huoncharm.com; 525 Esperance Coast Rd; d $95-105, extra person $25) is actually two rustic, self-contained cottages (one studio-style sleeping two, the other with two bedrooms) right on the water's edge at Desolation Bay (ignore the name, it's actually a delightful, secluded little bay). There's quirky décor, breakfast provisions on the first night, a large bush trail area inland from the properties and, above all, a stunning location.

Sleeping

DOVER

Dover is the region's main tourist base, with accommodation for all budgets.

Dover Beachside Tourist Park (☎ 6298 1301; www.dovercaravanpark.com.au; Kent Beach Rd; unpowered/powered sites $16/20, on-site vans/cabins from $38/75) Well-maintained park opposite a sandy beach, plus has selling points such as helpful owners, plenty of greenery, barbecue area and good, clean facilities. Prices are for two people.

Dover Hotel (☎ 6298 1210; doverhotel@bigpond.com; Main Rd; pub s/d $40/60, motel d $90) Large pub with a range of accommodation, including budget rooms above the bar and dining area (a bit noisy when bands are playing), motel units at the hotel's rear, and a large adjacent house with two self-contained units, each sleeping up to seven ($150 for four adults).

Anne's Old Rectory (☎ 6298 1222; www.annesoldrectory.com.au; Huon Hwy; s $70-90, d $90-100) On the way into town (from the north), offering two pretty B&B rooms, each with private bathroom down the hall, in a late-19th-century building surrounded by colourful gardens. Includes cooked breakfast; evening meals by arrangement.

Smuggler's Rest (☎ 6298 1396; www.smugglersrest.info; Station Rd; d $75-95, extra person $15) This place has an external marquee look reminiscent of an old nightclub, and houses well-equipped, self-contained studio and

THE AUTHOR'S CHOICE

Far South Wilderness Lodge & Backpacker (☎ 6298 1922; www.farsouthwilderness.com.au; Narrows Rd, Strathblane; dm/d $22/60; 💻) Far South offers some of the finest budget accommodation in Tasmania, with a superb waterfront bush setting, quality accommodation, and a strong environmental focus. Activities on offer to help you enjoy the great outdoors include mountain-bikes and sea-kayaks for rent, bushwalks, and the chance to arrange caving or boating excursions. And to make visiting even easier, the TassieLink bus stops daily at the door.

two-bedroom units. The friendly owners offer bikes, fishing rods and old golf clubs for guest use.

Driftwood Holiday Cottages (☎ 6298 1441, 1800 353 983; www.farsouth.com.au/driftwood; Bayview Rd; d $150-200, f $210-300) Choose between modern, self-contained studio units or three large family-friendly houses that accommodate four to eight guests. Each option boasts all mod cons and has a veranda or outdoor area from which to enjoy the great bay views.

Also recommended:

Esperance Guest House (☎ 6298 1106; Cemetery Rd; d $110-130) B&B in beautiful setting south of town.

Dover Bayside Lodge(☎ 6298 1788; doverbaysidelodge@bigpond.com; Bayview Rd; d $85-110) Central guesthouse with bay views.

STRATHBLANE

The turn-off to these options is 5km south of Dover.

Riseley Cottage (☎ 6298 1630; www.riseleycottage.com; 170 Narrows Rd, Strathblane; s $85, d $105-120) Not far from Far South Backpackers is this lovely, gay-friendly guesthouse, with hospitable owners and a great garden setting, overlooking the water and bushland reserve. Cooked breakfast is included in the price and three-course dinners (by prior arrangement) are well-priced at $38 per person.

Eating

Dover Woodfired Pizza & Eatery (☎ 6298 1905; Main Rd; mains $10-19; 🕑 from 4pm Tue-Sun) Cosy pizza-pasta restaurant, offering traditional and gourmet woodfired pizzas as well as baked spuds and pasta. Eat in or take away.

Dover Hotel (☎ 6298 1210; Main Rd; mains $14-19; 🕑 lunch & dinner) Decent menu selections in this pub's bistro include catch of the day, local scallops, roast, steak and various blackboard specials. There's also a kids' menu and tempting desserts (when was the last time you had fruit pav?). This is also a popular watering hole, with occasional live music.

Gingerbreadhouse Bakery (☎ 6298 1502; Main Rd; meals $5-11; 🕑 8.30am-5pm) On the main bend as you enter town, this small bakery dishes out cooked breakfasts, stuffed croissants, home-made pies and tasty cakes.

Dover Grocery & Newsagency (☎ 6298 1201; Main Rd; 🕑 6.30am-7pm Mon-Sat, 6.30am-6pm Sun) A well-stocked store with excellent deli produce, and fresh fruit and veg. Stock up before heading further south.

Getting There & Away

TassieLink (☎ 1300 300 520; www.tassielink.com.au) buses arrive at and depart from the Dover Store on the main street; the trip from Hobart takes 1¾ hours and costs $17. There are two services each weekday from Hobart, except from December through to March when an extra service runs every Monday, Wednesday and Friday (en route further south to Cockle Creek).

SOUTHPORT

☎ 03 / pop 300

Originally, Southport was called Baie des Moules (Bay of Mussels) and it has been known by several other names during its history. Its current name is fairly descriptive as it's located at the southern end of the sealed highway. Many travellers don't visit the town, as there's a major road junction 2km to the north, but it's worth a detour to stay in some of the B&Bs now making good use of the appealing local landscape. No public transport makes its way here.

The bluff south of town is called **Burying Ground Point** because it was a convict cemetery; it's now a public reserve. There's also a memorial to an early shipwreck in which 35 people perished.

Sleeping & Eating

Southport Tavern (☎ 6298 3144; Main Rd; unpowered/powered site $10/15, on-site van $30) Small-town pub, general store and caravan park. The weary can stop for the night in the caravan paddock, while the hungry can fill up in the

dining room (lunch Sun, dinner Wed-Sat), or with takeaways from the **store** (8am-6pm).

The Jetty House (6298 3139; rosandcarl@bigpond.com; Main Rd; s $65-80, d $95-120, extra child $20) This rustic place down near the wharf is a lovely, gardened abode built in 1875 and tailor-made for relaxation. Rates at this friendly, family-run guesthouse include full cooked breakfast and afternoon tea. The cheaper rates apply to stays longer than one night.

Southern Forest B&B (6298 3306; souforest2@bigpond.com; Jager Rd; s/d $70/100, tr $130-140) Up the hill opposite Southport Tavern, this B&B is equally lovely and hospitable. It's a warm, wooden-floored hideaway set in native forest. Accommodation is in a suite sleeping six (three bedrooms, two bathrooms and lounge), so is ideal for families and groups.

HASTINGS

03

The excellent **Hastings Caves & Thermal Springs** (6298 3209; adult/child/family $19.50/9.75/48.50; 9am-5pm Mar, Apr & Sep-Dec, 9am-6pm Jan & Feb, 10am-4pm May-Aug) facility attracts visitors to the vicinity of this once-thriving logging and wharf town, 21km south of Dover. The admission price includes a 45-minute tour of the main cave, plus entry to the thermal pool; also here is a visitors centre and good **café**, plus barbecues and picnic areas (the café sells barbecue and picnic hampers in addition to light meals).

Though the main cave is called Hastings, this name is informally derived from the surrounding **Hastings Caves State Reserve**, which is riddled with karst formations. The official name of the cave is actually Newdegate. A computer-controlled, low-wattage lighting system gives visitors a crisper, more focused view of the formations.

The cave is 10km inland from Hastings and 5km beyond the visitors centre. To get there from the town centre, allow for a 10-minute drive, then a five-minute walk through rainforest to the cave entrance. Cave tours leave on the hour, the first an hour after the visitors centre opens and the last an hour before it closes.

THE UNSPOILED SOUTH NO MORE...?

It seems that the pristine far south of Tasmania may not remain this way for much longer: in late 2004, the Tasmanian government gave private owners permission to log the forests of the northeast peninsula of Recherche Bay. It was a decision that has stirred up much controversy – not only in Tasmania, but as far away as France.

In 1792 two French ships, *La Recherche* and *L'Espérance,* anchored in a harbour near Tasmania's southernmost point and called it Recherche Bay. More than a decade before British settlers arrived in Tasmania, French explorers were carrying out the first significant scientific studies in the nation. There are two recently discovered heritage sites at Recherche Bay, already given protected status (relics of the French observatory and garden, not accessible to the public), but the explorer' journals record them venturing far into the bush. Historians, scientists and conservationists are concerned that the area earmarked for clearfelling is potentially home to more sites of historic, scientific and cultural interest to both Australia and France. Logging the site will obliterate any history, and those opposed to such destruction have petitioned for the area to be given full heritage protection, at least until substantial archaeological surveys are undertaken to ensure that key sites are identified. Needless to say, tensions are high between the anti- and pro-logging groups – if logging trucks do start rolling into the area, it would not be surprising to see this place put well and truly under the conservation spotlight, and anti-loggers attempting to gain the sort of publicity generated when the Franklin River was under threat. Read more at www.recherchebay.org.

In other developments down south, Melbourne property developer David Marriner has plans to build a $15-million tourist complex at Cockle Creek East (an area which, interestingly, is inside the Southwest National Park, but not part of the wilderness World Heritage area). Marriner's company has been negotiating approval for the development for a number of years. The controversial complex is intended to be eco-friendly and will house a main lodge, 60 cabins, boatsheds and a jetty; construction is expected to begin in late 2005, with completion of the complex some way off.

Next to the visitors centre is a **thermal swimming pool** (adult/child/family $4.90/2.45/12), filled daily with warm water from a thermal spring. The wheelchair-accessible **Hot Springs Trail** does a big loop from the pool area, taking 20 minutes to navigate (note that the pool is also wheelchair-accessible).

Information on the attraction is available online at www.parks.tas.gov.au/reserves/hastings.

Tours

The **Hastings Caves & Thermal Springs visitors centre** (☎ 6298 3209) organises two additional guided cave tours. The first is to the lesser-known **King George V Cave**, a dolomite marvel reached via a forest walk. Three-hour tours cost $95 per person and six-hour tours (including a BBQ and entry to the pool) cost $185. Tours need to be booked at least a day in advance and a minimum of two people is required on weekdays, four on weekends. No caving experience is necessary and all equipment is provided.

The **Entrance Glowworm Experience** offers participants the chance to visit a cave with a significant glow-worm population. It starts with a half-hour rainforest walk, followed by about 90 minutes exploring a limestone cave. No experience is required, but you should be reasonably fit. The tour runs at noon every Friday, the cost is $69, and equipment is provided; the price also includes entry to the thermal swimming pool.

Southern Wilderness Eco Adventure Tours (☎ 62 97 6368, 0427 976 368; www.tasglow-wormadventure.com.au) runs more frequent tours to the same glow-worm cave and works together with Bottom Bits Bus (p124) and Far South Wilderness Lodge (p140). The highly rated tours last 3½ hours, include all equipment, and run daily at 1pm and 6pm (weather and minimum numbers permitting).

LUNE RIVER

☎ 03

A few kilometres southwest of Hastings is the tiny enclave of Lune River. In previous years visitors have been able to take a scenic 6km, 1½-hour ride on the **Ida Bay Railway**, a narrow-gauge affair that worked its way through scrub and light bush to the beach at Deep Hole Bay. However, at the time of research the railway was not operating and was up for sale; ask around at Dover to find out if it's operating when you visit.

COCKLE CREEK

The most southerly drive you can make in Australia is along the secondary gravel road from Lune River to Cockle Creek and beautiful **Recherche Bay**. This is an area of spectacular mountain peaks and endless beaches, ideal for camping and bushwalking. It's also the start (or end) of the challenging **South Coast Track**, which, with the right preparation and a week or so to spare, will take you all the way to Port Davey and beyond in the southwest. See Lonely Planet's *Walking in Australia* for detailed track notes.

Cockle Creek, which clings to the edge of the enormous **Southwest National Park**, provides a naturally scenic base for several walks. You can follow the shoreline northeast to the lighthouse at **Fishers Point** (two hours return), passing a sculpture of a southern right whale along the way. The South Coast Track can also be followed to **South Cape Bay** (four hours return), a popular short hike. National park entry fees apply to these walks; self-register at Cockle Creek.

There are several great free places to **camp** at Recherche Bay, including at Gilhams Beach, just before Catamaran. You can also camp for free at Cockle Creek itself, but national park fees apply as soon as you cross the bridge. Bring all your own provisions, including firewood (fuel or gas stoves are recommended). There are pit toilets (no showers) and some tank water (boil before drinking), but it's recommended you bring your own supplies.

Information on the area is available online at www.parks.tas.gov.au/natparks/southwest/.

Getting There & Away

TassieLink (☎ 1300 300 520; www.tassielink.com.au) buses arrive at and depart from the Cockle Creek rangers station. The service runs three times a week (Monday, Wednesday and Friday) from December through March; the 3½-hour trip from Hobart costs $57.

Midlands & Lake Country

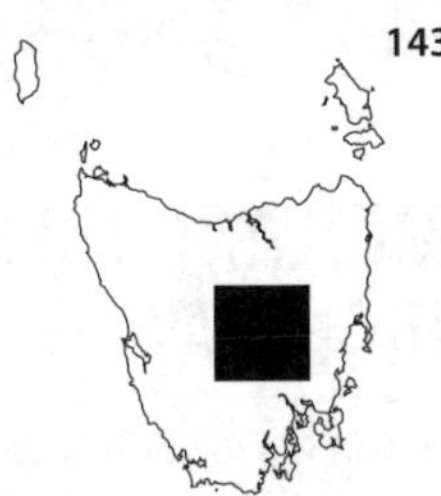

Parts of Tasmania's inland region have a definite pseudo-English atmosphere, due to the efforts of early settlers who planted English trees and hedgerows. Coach stations, garrison towns, stone villages and pastoral properties soon raised themselves up from the dirt.

These days it's well worth making a few detours to see the quiet old towns off the Midland Hwy. They're full of wonderfully preserved Georgian architecture and pretty, rose-filled gardens, plus plenty of antiques and other old wares. This route is now marketed as the Heritage Hwy and you can pick up a free tourist map at visitors centres around the state.

The sparsely populated Central Plateau is decidedly off the well-worn tourist track, but is worth a visit for its breathtaking scenery and trout-filled lakes. The fertile Derwent Valley is a verdant area home to vineyards, hop fields, orchards and eye-catching old oast houses.

The diamond-shaped region of this chapter extends from the Midland Hwy in the east to the Derwent River in the southwest, and north to the edge of Launceston. At its centre is the elevated, sparsely populated region known as the Lake Country. The region's three major highways are the Lyell , between Hobart and Queenstown; the Lake Hwy, which climbs onto the high Central Plateau; and the Midland Hwy, connecting Hobart to Launceston.

HIGHLIGHTS

- Fossicking for a bargain in the **antiques and collectables stores** (p144) along the Heritage Hwy
- Watching the mist descend on **Great Lake** (p152) in winter
- **Hooking a trout** (p152) – or just attempting to! – in the Lake Country
- Questioning your direction at the crossroads in pretty **Ross** (p147)
- Playing history detective along the Heritage Hwy in a game of **Skulduggery** (p145)
- Warming up over a **Devonshire tea** (p146) at cosy Blossom's Georgian Tea Rooms in Oatlands
- Hiring a houseboat for a relaxed few days on **Meadowbank Lake** (p154)
- Admiring art in the middle of nowhere when you stop to appreciate the quiet beauty of the **Steppes Sculptures** (p152)

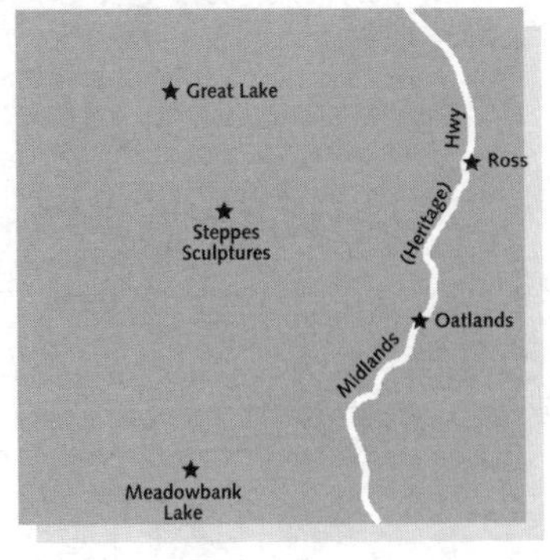

- www.tasmaniacentral.tas.gov.au

MIDLAND (HERITAGE) HIGHWAY

Hobart was founded in 1804 and Launceston in 1805. By 1807, the need for a land link between the two prompted surveyor Charles Grimes to map out an appropriate route. The road was constructed by convict gangs, and by 1821 was suitable for horses and carriages. Two years later a mail cart operated between the two towns and this became the first coach service, as it sometimes carried passengers. The main towns along this road were all established in the 1820s as garrisons for prisoners and guards.

Getting There & Around

Redline Coaches (☎ 1300 360 000; www.tasredline.com.au) buses run along the Midland Hwy several times a day; you can disembark at any of the main towns – Brighton, Kempton, Oatlands, Ross, Campbell Town and Perth – provided you're not on an express service. It's best to book your pick-ups and drop-offs in these towns. The fare from Hobart to Launceston is $28; the journey takes about 2½ hours.

KEMPTON

☎ 03 / pop 340

Tiny Kempton, about 50km north of Hobart, was founded in 1838, making it one of the state's earliest settlements. It was

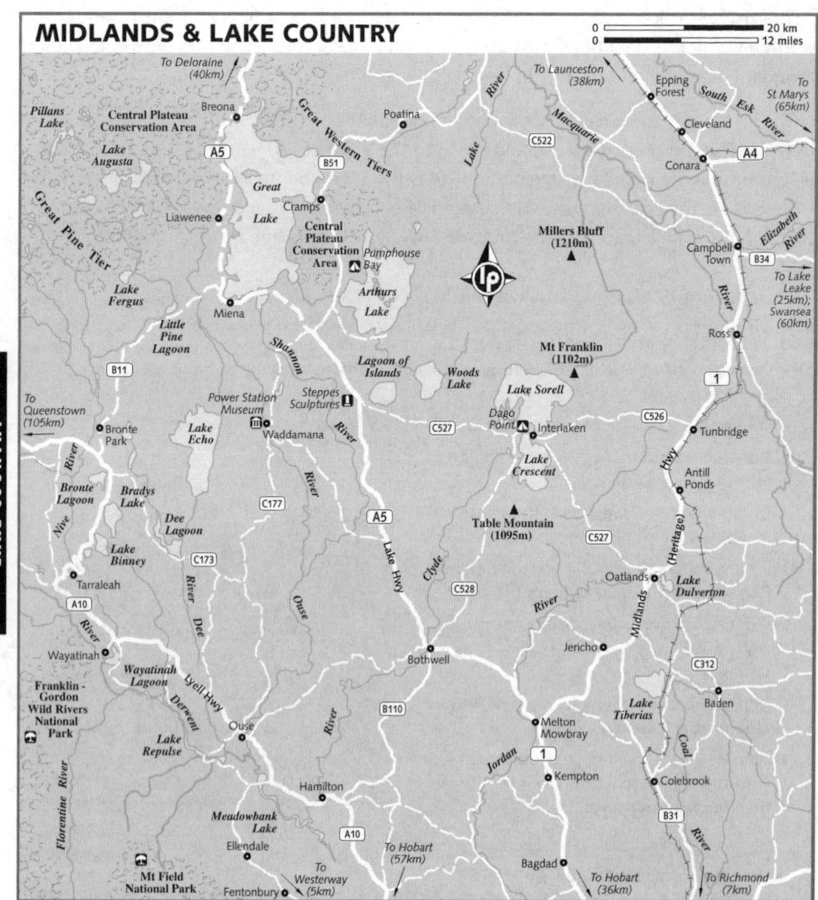

once known as Green Ponds, and is notable for its antiques stores and fine bucolic surrounds.

Hospitable **Wilmot Arms Inn** (☎ 6259 1272; wilmotarms@trump.net.au; Main Rd; s/d from $85/105) is a former coaching inn with pretty B&B rooms and a flower-filled garden. Across the road is **Huntington Tavern** (☎ 6259 1292; Main St; mains $13-19; lunch daily, dinner Wed-Sat), serving classic pub fare.

OATLANDS

☎ 03 / pop 550

Oatlands is home to Australia's largest collection of Georgian architecture and thus has an attractive, interesting streetscape. Many historic properties are now being spruced up and contain galleries and craft stores. On the main street alone, there are 87 historic buildings, the oldest being the 1829 convict-built courthouse. Much of the sandstone for these early buildings came from the shores of adjacent **Lake Dulverton**, a designated reserve that sustains nearly 80 types of birds.

The town's site was chosen in 1821 as one of four military posts on the road from Hobart to George Town, but was slow to develop. In 1832 a proper survey of the town was made and, in a spurt of optimism, the surveyor marked out 50 miles (80km) of streets on the assumption it would become the Midlands capital. Many people certainly made it their new home in the 1830s, erecting numerous solid buildings with the help of former convicts and soldiers who were skilled carpenters and stonemasons. But alas, the town never grew into the hoped-for capital.

Information

The helpful and efficient **Heritage Highway Centre** (☎ 6254 1212; oatlands@tasvisinfo.com.au; 85 High St; 9am-5pm) has lots of information, plus Internet access. The post office and a couple of banks are on the main street (High St), but the banks have restricted opening hours – better to use the multi-card ATM inside the **BP service station** (52 High St).

Sights & Activities

At the Heritage Highway Centre, check out the **history room** (admission free; 9am-5pm) and pick up the free handouts – *Welcome to Historic Oatlands* includes directions for a self-guided tour of town, while the *Lake Dulverton Walkway Guide* has tips for lakeside exploration.

Peter Fielding's Oatlands Tours (☎ 6254 1135; departs from 7 Gay St) offers a one-hour town tour ($5) departing on demand from 9am to 5pm daily. It also offers a popular 90-minute ghost tour ($8), starting at 8pm from May to September, and at 9pm from October to April. This is a candle-lit excursion that takes in the old gaol, courthouse

SKULDUGGERY

The course of the Midland Hwy has wavered slightly from its original route and many of the historic towns along it are now bypassed – this has been good news for motorists who want to travel between Hobart and Launceston as speedily as possible, but has isolated some of the smaller towns from the through-traffic that was their contemporary lifeblood.

As more tourists visit Tasmania, many of the state's smaller, less-publicised regions are devising novel ways to ensure that they get a fair share of the action (and a share of the tourist dollar), by enticing visitors away from the big-ticket tourist attractions and giving them reasons to linger longer in lesser-known areas. The state's northeast will try this with its 'Tin Dragon' touring route (see p182), while the Midlands hopes to get more travellers off the highway and into towns with Skulduggery, a game that gives participants the chance to solve crimes (resurrected from archives) that actually happened in the area some 170 years ago. There are three versions of the game (set in Longford, Oatlands and Ross), all created by Dr Hamish Maxwell-Stewart from the History department of the University of Tasmania. Visitors purchase an illustrated booklet ($20 from visitors centres and participating businesses), follow the story, find the clues and solve a mystery, all while interacting with the community and local businesses. The creators figure that this is a more interactive and appealing way of learning about the history of a town than by merely reading a plaque or information board.

More information can be found online at www.heritagehighway.com.au/skulduggery.

and other spirited convict sites. Telephone for bookings.

Callington Mill (☎ 6254 0039; Mill Lane; admission free; ⏲ 9am-4pm), off High St, was built in 1837 and used until 1891. Restoration work was begun after a century of neglect, but for the past few years the project has moved in fits and starts. There's not really a lot to do except for a vigorous climb of the fantail-capped, 15m-high mill tower, and a browse of **Dolls at the Mill** (admission $2), a collection of over 2000 dolls from around the world.

Sleeping

The town's two pubs, the **Kentish Hotel** (☎ 62 54 1119; 60 High St; s/d $55/80) and **Midlands Hotel** (☎ 6254 1103; 91 High St; s/d $45/55), offer OK rooms. The Kentish gets a better recommendation for its en-suite facilities and fresh coat of paint (inside and out), although its rooms are rather bare.

Free **camping** is permitted for up to three nights in the picnic area beside Lake Dulverton, at the northern end of the Esplanade. There are toilets and barbecues here.

Much of Oatlands' accommodation is of the colonial type, where 'convict-built' is regarded as a mark of historical excellence.

Oatlands Lodge (☎ 6254 1444; 92 High St; s/d $90/110) The pick of the town's accommodation is this guesthouse, run by very welcoming mainlanders. It's gay-friendly, warm and inviting, with a huge breakfast spread included in the rates and dinners by arrangement.

Thimble Cottage (☎ 6254 1212; 101 High St; s/d $70/90, extra person $20) This pretty sandstone cottage sleeps up to six people in attic and ground-floor rooms. It's self-contained, central, and is booked through the Heritage Highway Centre (see p145).

Waverley Cottages (☎ 6254 1264, 0409 125 049; waverleycottages@bigpond.com; s/d $130/150, extra person $25) These are fully equipped, thoroughly colonial cottages: **Amelia Cottage** (104 High St), opposite the Midlands Hotel; **Forget-me-not Cottage** (17 Dulverton St), directly behind Amelia; and **Waverley Cottage** and **Waverley Croft**, both 7km west of town. The stand-by rates are often significantly reduced.

Eating

Blossom's Georgian Tea Rooms (☎ 6254 1516; 116 High St; light meals $3-11; ⏲ 10am-4pm Thu-Mon) At the northern end of the main street, Blossom's exudes old-fashioned warmth and is a good place for a cuppa and light meal.

Mishka Dining Room at Kentish Hotel (☎ 0427 003 658; 60 High St; mains $7-21; ⏲ lunch daily, dinner Wed-Sun) This is the pick for evening dining in Oatlands, despite the daggy décor, and it offers a fine lunch as well. The menu presents well-prepared favourites such as steak and fish and chips, but there are also seafood crepes, smoked salmon salad, daily specials, and quite possibly Tassie's best sticky date pudding. Dinner bookings advised.

The Stables (☎ 6254 0013; 85 High St; lunch $5-10, dinner mains $15-18; ⏲ 9am-5pm Mon-Fri, dinner Fri & Sat) Next door to the visitors centre is this low-key café, with lacklustre décor but reasonably priced, hearty country cooking.

Opposite the Heritage Highway Centre are two browse-worthy galleries that both serve good coffee. **Oatlands Coach House** (☎ 62 54 1087; 88 High St) is a beautifully restored property selling art, rugs and assorted collectables, and the **Red Back Gallery** (☎ 6254 1510; 84 High St) features handcrafted glassworks and furniture.

Getting There & Away

Redline Coaches (☎ 1300 360 000; www.tasredline.com.au) services Oatlands, with buses arriving at and departing from Oatlands Roadhouse at 47 High St, 500m from the visitors centre. From Oatlands, the 1¼-hour trip to Launceston costs $20, and the one-hour trip to Hobart costs $16.

ROSS

☎ 03 / pop 280

This tiny ex-garrison town, 120km north of Hobart, is steeped in colonial history, with most of its buildings constructed from sandstone between 1820 and 1870. Ross has now added a peaceful charm to its résumé – there are strict rules on development, thankfully restraining the possibility of overcommercialisation. Soak up this ambience by exploring the town on foot – admire the architecture, check out the craft and antiques stores, and stop for Devonshire tea at one of the cafés.

History

Ross was established in 1812 as a protective shelter for highway travellers and was the fording point for the Macquarie River. In 1821 a low-level bridge was made with logs laid on stone buttresses. In 1836 this rough structure was replaced with the current stone bridge.

In the days of horse and carriage, Ross became important as a staging post. It consolidated its position at the centre of the wool industry, but ceased to grow in size. The historic value of Ross' buildings was eventually realised and development along the main street was rejected, further preserving its 'village' feel.

Information

The visitors centre is in the **Tasmanian Wool Centre** (☎ 6381 5466; Church St; 9am-5.30pm Mon-Fri, 9am-5pm Sat & Sun Apr–mid-Oct, 9am-6pm daily mid-Oct–Mar); pick up a brochure here (purchased by donation) detailing the town's historical buildings. The visitors centre offers Internet access. Note that there are no ATMs or banking facilities in town.

There's online information at www.rosstasmania.com.

Sights

ROSS BRIDGE

The famous, much-photographed, convict-built Ross Bridge is one of the oldest and most beautiful bridges in Australia, boasting unique, decorative carvings. Its graceful proportions were designed by John Archer and it was built by two convict stonemasons, Colbeck and Herbert, who were granted freedom for their work. Herbert has also been credited with the intricate work on the 186 panels that decorate the arches. Each panel is different, with Celtic symbols, animals and the faces of notable people all carved into the sandstone. At night the bridge is lit up and the carvings really stand out.

HISTORIC BUILDINGS

In the heart of town is a crossroads that can lead you in one of four directions – temptation (represented by the Man O'Ross Hotel), salvation (the Catholic church), recreation (the town hall) and damnation (the old gaol).

Other interesting old buildings include the 1832 **Scotch Thistle Inn** (Church St), now a private residence; the **Barracks** (Bridge St), restored by the National Trust and also a private residence; the 1885 **Uniting Church** (Church St); **St John's Anglican Church** (cnr Church & Badajos Sts), built in 1868; and the still gainfully employed, 1896 **post office** (26 Church St). The town's churches are floodlit at night.

WOOL CENTRE

The **Tasmanian Wool Centre** (☎ 6381 5466; www.taswoolcentre.com.au; Church St; 9am-5.30pm Mon-Fri, 9am-5pm Sat & Sun Apr–mid-Oct, 9am-6pm daily

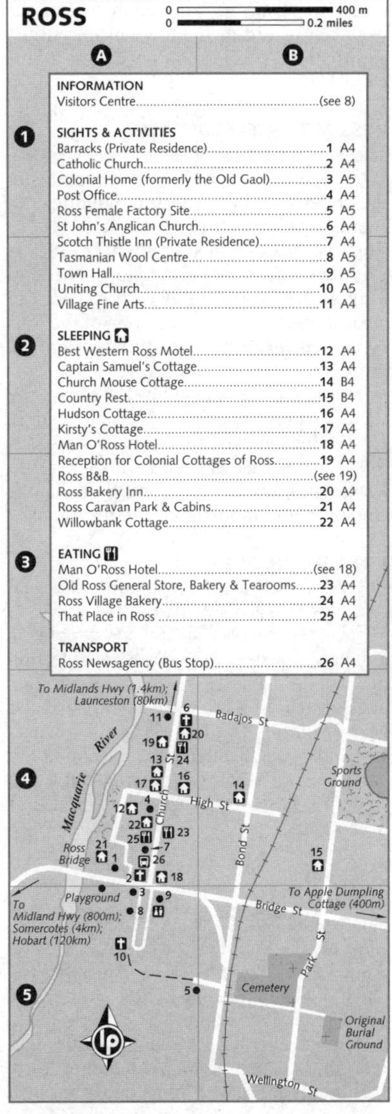

mid-Oct–Mar) is home to a craft shop, wool exhibition and **museum** (admission by donation). The museum has displays on the convict era, including mouldings of some Ross Bridge carvings, and on the Australian wool industry – there are bales of wool you can touch and an audiovisual display on the fibre.

The centre also runs guided tours for groups (minimum eight people; booking essential). Tours can be conducted of the wool centre and/or the town proper (tours adult/child $4/2.50, combined tour adult/child $7/4).

ROSS FEMALE FACTORY SITE

The **Ross Female Factory** (admission free; 9am-5pm) was one of only two female prisons in the convict period, with one building still standing. Although there's little to see inside, the husk of this weathered edifice is evocative and a few descriptive signs and a model of the prison give you an idea of what it was like. Pick up a copy of the *Ross Female Factory* brochure, available from the visitors centre.

To walk to the site, follow the sign at the top of Church St, near the Uniting Church. Up the hill on the other side of the site is Ross' original **burial ground** with its carved headstones; these were done by the same stonemasons who worked on the bridge.

VILLAGE FINE ARTS

Lovers of Australian art should pay a visit to **Village Fine Arts** (☎ 6381 5251; 6 Church St; admission $2; 10am-4pm Thu-Sun, or by arrangement), a gallery housing an impressive collection of original art from big-name Australian artists (including Pro Hart, David Boyd and Max Mannix). The knowledgeable owners will walk you through the collection, and can give your credit card a work-out if you so desire. The entry price goes to local children's activities.

Sleeping

BUDGET

Ross Caravan Park & Cabins (☎ 6381 5224; http://caravanpark.rosstasmania.com; Bridge St; unpowered/powered sites $13/16, cabins $40-65) An appealing patch of green adjacent to Ross Bridge. The simple conjoined cabins here each sleep two to four people, have cooking facilities and offer the cheapest accommodation in town. Bathrooms are shared; you'll need your own sheets and towels, or you can hire them. Reception is at the neighbouring Best Western Ross Motel. Prices are for two people.

MIDRANGE

Man O'Ross Hotel (☎ 6381 5445; www.manoross.com.au; cnr Church & Bridge Sts; s/d $70/85) Accommodation prices at this lovely old pub are a bit steep given that bathroom facilities are shared, but the rooms are bright and modernised, there's a guest lounge, and continental breakfast is included.

Ross Bakery Inn (☎ 6381 5246; www.rossbakery.com.au; 15 Church St; s/d $90/120) You can wake up to brekky fresh from a 100-year-old wood-fired oven if you stay in this pleasant 1830s coaching house, adjacent to the Ross Village Bakery (see opposite). The small, cosy rooms are well equipped, and there's a guest lounge with open fire and complimentary bakery treats. The owners can also arrange accommodation at Kirsty's Cottage, a two-bedroom self-contained cottage on the main street.

Colonial Cottages of Ross (☎ 6381 5354; www.rossaccommodation.com.au; reception at 12 Church St; d $135-150, extra person $25-33) This organisation manages four carefully restored, self-contained abodes: **Apple Dumpling Cottage** (Bridge St); **Captain Samuel's Cottage** (Church St); **Hudson Cottage** (High St); and **Church Mouse Cottage** (cnr High & Bond Sts). Sizes vary from one to three bedrooms (sleeping up to six people); continental breakfast provisions are provided. Apple Dumpling Cottage is more remote than the other three options (about 900m from the main street).

Willowbank Cottage (☎ 6381 5219; 28 Church St; d $100-120, extra person $20) There's plenty of self-contained room to move at this two-bedroom, two-bathroom, two-TV unit perfect for families. Reception is at the adjacent Ross Craft & Antiques store.

Other accommodation options include the following:

Ross B&B (☎ 6381 5354; www.rossaccommodation.com.au; 12 Church St; d $110-125) B&B rooms from the same company that has Colonial Cottages of Ross.

Country Rest (☎ 6381 5118; 22 Park St; B&B s/d $65/95) Plain, modern self-contained unit in town's east.

TOP END

Best Western Ross Motel (☎ 6381 5224; http://rossmotel.bestwestern.com.au; 2 High St; d $150, extra person $25) Finishing touches were going on when we visited this brand-new motel offering spic-and-span Georgian-style cottage units, each with microwave, fridge, TV and DVD (prices include breakfast provisions). There are also family units sleeping four. It's worth asking about stand-by rates, which may drop to between $120 and $130.

Somercotes (☎ 6381 5231; www.somercotes.com; off Mona Vale Rd; d $150, extra person $20) Off the Midland Hwy about 4km south of Ross is this splendid estate with a Georgian homestead and B&B in four restored cottages. Each cottage is self-contained (full breakfast provisions provided) and can sleep two or four people. Guided tours of the estate's historic buildings (including homestead) are available by appointment.

Eating

Ross Village Bakery (☎ 6381 5246; 15 Church St; snacks & meals $3-13; 9am-5pm) Overdose on the carbs in the produce fresh from this café-bakery's 100-year-old wood-fired oven. Choose from soup, salads, baked potatoes and all manner of pies, but leave room for something sweet.

Old Ross General Store, Bakery & Tearooms (☎ 6381 5422; Church St; snacks & meals $4-9.50; 8am-5pm) The tearoom at this jack-of-all-trades store has an old-fashioned feel, a warming open fire, and a fuss-free menu of breakfast until 11am, then pies, soup, quiche and sandwiches, plus the essential Devonshire tea.

That Place in Ross (☎ 6381 5413; 34 Church St; meals $6-13; 9am-5pm) That Place serves up good-quality tummy-fillers, including all-day breakfast, pancakes, burgers, salads and sandwiches (most menu items are available gluten-free). In high season it may be open until 8pm for dinner – pop by to check.

Man O'Ross Hotel (☎ 6381 5445; cnr Church & Bridge Sts; lunch $6.50-14, dinner mains $11-22; lunch & dinner) Evening dining options in Ross are slim pickings, so you may well find yourself here. Not that that's a bad thing – the dinner menu includes traditional pub fare like bangers and mash or chicken parmigiana, but also river trout and assorted daily specials. There's a children's menu, plus a leafy courtyard to enjoy in fine weather.

Getting There & Away

Redline Coaches (☎ 1300 360 000; www.tasredline.com.au) services Ross, with buses arriving at and departing from Ross Newsagency on Church St. The 1½-hour trip to Hobart costs $21; the one-hour journey to Launceston costs $14.

CAMPBELL TOWN

☎ 03 / pop 880

Campbell Town, 12km north of Ross, is another former garrison settlement on the Midland Hwy. Unlike Oatlands and Ross, however, the highway passes right through town, making it a popular loo-and-snack stop between Launceston and Hobart (or between Cradle Mountain and the east coast). The town has reasonable services, with a couple of hotels, a supermarket, a pharmacy and general stores lining the highway (known as High St in the middle of town).

Today Campbell Town is the commercial centre of a cattle and sheep farming area. The showgrounds, behind the high school, host the annual **Campbell Town Show** (also called the Midlands Agricultural Show) in late May/early June. Held every year since 1839, this is the oldest continuous show in Australia.

Information

The **visitors centre** (☎ 6381 1353; 103 High St; 10am-3pm Mon-Fri, occasional weekends) is beside the post office in the old courthouse, a 1905 building still used several times a year for judicial proceedings. The courthouse building is also home to the Heritage Highway Museum (below). There's a useful free brochure here detailing a self-guided tour of the town; the opening hours listed here are a general guide only – the centre is staffed by volunteers so hours can vary. If you're looking for town information outside of opening hours, pop into the takeaway store two doors down, next to the police station – it usually stocks a few useful brochures.

There is a multi-card ATM inside the **Festival IGA supermarket** (High St), and Internet access inside the takeaway section of Zeps restaurant (see p151).

Sights & Activities

The interesting **Heritage Highway Museum** (☎ 6381 1353; 103 High St; admission free; 10am-3pm Mon-Fri, occasional weekends) has potted histories of figures like John Batman and Martin Cash (a local bushranger), and artefacts like a 1930s film projector and old toys, coins and books. The museum, like the visitors centre, is volunteer-run and hence has varying hours.

Be sure to look down as you wander the main street. Along the western side of High St are **commemorative bricks** laid into the footpath detailing the names of convicts, their crimes and punishments and sometimes other notes of interest.

The town has many buildings which are more than 100 years old; they're scattered and display a variety of architectural styles. Most historic buildings can be seen by travelling along High St and returning along Bridge St. They include **The Grange** (High St), built in 1847; **St Luke's Church of England** (High St), constructed in 1835; the 1840 **Campbell Town Inn** (100 High St); the 1834 **Fox Hunters Return** (132 High St); and the 1878 **old school** (Hamilton St), in the current school's grounds.

The main bridge across the Elizabeth River was completed in 1838, making it almost as old as Ross Bridge. The '**Red Bridge**', so called because it was convict-built from more than 1.5 million bricks made on-site, is the subject of a comprehensive booklet available from the visitors centre.

Sleeping & Eating

Campbell Town Hotel (☎ 6381 1158; campbelltownhotel@goodstone.com.au; 118 High St; s/d $50/60) It seems unlikely from the outside, but part of this building predates all the other hotels in town. This pub offers down-at-heel but clean motel units out the back, and reasonably priced meals (traditional pub fare) at lunch- and dinner-time.

The Grange (☎ 6381 1686; www.thegrangecampbelltown.com.au; Midland Hwy; s/d $100/135) This Tudor Gothic manor is an imposing sight, set behind the town park and floodlit at night. Access is down the laneway beside the Caltex service station. This grand old place (built 1847) offers three B&B guestrooms, plus lovely communal areas and gardens.

Fox Hunters Return (☎ 6381 1602; www.foxhunters.com.au; 132 High St; s/d from $125/140) On the left as you enter town from Hobart is this fine establishment, built with convict labour in the 1830s as a coaching inn and now offering spacious rooms, each with private bathroom and sitting area. New owners were set to take over at the time of research, with plans for a restaurant in the cellars under the main house (once used to house convicts during the construction of the neighbouring Red Bridge).

The Gables (☎ 6381 1347; www.the-gables.com.au; 35 High St; house s/d $100/120, cottage s/d $120/140) The Gables, beside the highway on the northern side of town, has a large garden and offers two styles of accommodation: in-house B&B rooms (shared bathroom), or spacious, self-contained cottages.

St Andrews Inn (☎/fax 6391 5525; Midland Hwy, Cleveland; s/d $90/120) Built in 1845, this charming, National Trust–classified coaching inn

DETOUR

There is a secondary road from Campbell Town heading through the excellent fishing and bushwalking area around Lake Leake (33km from Campbell Town) to Swansea (69km) on the east coast. Redline buses travel this route once a day from Monday to Friday and can drop you at the Lake Leake turn-off, 4km from the lake.

Lake Leake itself is surrounded by holiday shacks and for passers-by there's a **camping area** (powered/unpowered sites $8/5) and a laid-back pub, the **Lake Leake Chalet** (☎ 6381 1329; www.lakeleakechalet.com.au; 340 Lake Leake Rd; s/d $40/70), offering meals and basic accommodation, plus boat hire and fishing trips.

After checking out the lake, those with their own transport should head further east to the Meetus Falls and Lost Falls Forest Reserves. **Meetus Falls** is the pick of the two – it's 10km from the signposted turn-off and has a sheltered picnic area, barbecues and toilets.

If you love fishing and/or seclusion, **Currawong Lakes** (☎ 6381 1148; www.troutfishtasmania.com.au; 1204 Long Marsh Rd, Lake Leake; d $120) is the perfect place. It's a trout fishery signposted west of the Lake Leake turn-off – after driving 12km (unsealed roads) you'll come across the property, home to trout-filled lakes, a handful of good-quality self-contained cabins, a deer farm and an abundance of peace and quiet. It also welcomes anglers for a half-day/day ($40/50) of fishing.

has three large, well-outfitted B&B rooms. The inn is 16km north of Campbell Town at Cleveland. Prices include cooked breakfast, and there's an on-site **café**.

Zeps (☎ 6381 1344; 92 High St; meals $7-22; breakfast, lunch & dinner;) Easily the best choice in town to refuel is bustling Zeps, serving brekky, *panini*, pasta and other café fare throughout the day, with pizzas and additional blackboard specials of an evening. In addition, takeaway pasta and pizza are available.

Getting There & Away

Redline Coaches (☎ 1300 360 000; www.tasredline.com.au) runs buses to Campbell Town, arriving at and departing from outside the milk bar at 107 High St, next to the police station. The 1¾-hour trip to Hobart costs $24 and the 45-minute journey to Launceston costs $12.

LAKE COUNTRY

The sparsely populated Lake Country of Tasmania's Central Plateau is home to steep mountains, glacial lakes, waterfalls, various wildlife and remarkable flora like the ancient pencil pine. The plateau's northwestern portion, roughly one-third of its total area, has been incorporated into the Tasmanian Wilderness World Heritage Area. It's also known for its fine trout fishing and for its controversially ambitious hydroelectric schemes, which have seen the damming of rivers, the creation of artificial lakes, the building of power stations (both above and below ground) and the construction of massive pipelines over rough terrain.

Tasmania has the largest hydroelectric power system in Australia. The first dam was constructed on Great Lake in 1911 and subsequently the Derwent, Mersey, South Esk, Forth, Gordon, King, Anthony and Pieman Rivers were also dammed. If you want to see the developments first-hand, go to the active Tungatinah, Tarraleah and Liapootah power stations on the extensive Derwent scheme between Queenstown and Hobart.

On the western edge of the Central Plateau is Walls of Jerusalem National Park (see p228), a favourite of mountaineers, bushwalkers and cross-country skiers. Well-equipped hikers can walk across the plateau into this national park and also into Cradle Mountain–Lake St Clair National Park.

BOTHWELL

☎ 03 / pop 400

Bothwell is a peaceful historic town in the beautiful Clyde River valley, with over 50 National Trust–acknowledged buildings. Standouts include an old **boot maker's shop** (☎ 6259 5649; High St), open by appointment; the 1820s **Thorpe Mill** (Dennistoun Rd); the lovely 1831 **St Luke's Church** (Dennistoun Rd); and the **Castle Hotel** (Patrick St), first licensed in 1821.

The **visitors centre** (☎ 6259 4033; Market Place; 10am-4pm Sep-May, 11am-3pm Jun-Aug) is inside the Australasian Golf Museum (see below). The leaflet *Let's Browse in Bothwell* has a map marked with the locations of all the historic buildings.

Although Bothwell is best known for its proximity to great trout-fishing spots, it also has **Australia's oldest golf course**, created by the Scottish settlers who established the town in the 1820s. The course is still in use today and is open to members of any golf club ($10 green fees; clubs can be hired from the visitors centre). Maintaining the golfing theme is the **Australasian Golf Museum** (☎ 6259 4033; www.ausgolfmuseum.com; Market Place; adult/child $3/1; 10am-4pm Sep-May, 11am-3pm Jun-Aug), set up in Bothwell's **old School House** (1887). You can hire golf clubs from here.

Bothwell is also home to **Thorpe Farm** (☎ 6259 5678), which produces fabulous goat cheese under the label Tasmanian Highland Cheeses (usually available in Bothwell at the visitors centre and at the Fat Doe Bakery, and also available at good cheese stores in Hobart). In addition, the farm produces *wasabi* and stoneground flour. Visits to the farm can be arranged by appointment; call ahead.

Sleeping & Eating

Bothwell Caravan Park (☎ 6259 5503; Market Place; unpowered/powered sites $10/15) This isn't exactly a park, more a small patch of dirt behind the visitors centre. Check in at the **council chambers** (Alexander St) or after hours at the Bothwell Garage on Patrick St. Site prices are for two people.

On Alexander St there are two well-equipped, self-contained houses for rent.

Park House (☎ 6259 5676; 25 Alexander St; d $65, extra person $20) sleeps up to six people; inquire at 28 Elizabeth St. Next door is the more visually appealing but considerably more expensive **Batt's Cottage** (☎ 6265 9481; 23 Alexander St; d $115, extra person $20), a National Trust–registered cottage dating from around 1840.

Bothwell Grange (☎ 6259 5556; Alexander St; d $125) At the time of research new managers had just moved into the Grange and reopened it to the public. Built as a hotel in 1836, the establishment has a charming Georgian atmosphere and comfortable B&B accommodation. Prices include booked breakfast, with evening meals available by prior arrangement.

Castle Hotel (☎ 6259 5502; Patrick St; mains $9-16; lunch daily, dinner Fri & Sat) The friendly and laid-back Castle has been continually licensed since 1829 and today offers better-than-average meals featuring lots of meat and assorted local produce. By the time you read this there should also be a couple of en-suite rooms here, with doubles expected to go for around $70.

Fat Doe Bakery (☎ 6259 5551; Patrick St; snacks $3-5; 7am-5pm) Make this a quick pit stop for a sandwich or one of the great range of pies on offer.

Getting There & Away

Hobart's **Metro** (☎ 13 22 01; www.metrotas.com.au) has a bus (No 140) departing stop F on Elizabeth St at 4pm each weekday for Bothwell ($13 one way, 1½-hours).

BOTHWELL TO GREAT LAKE

At Waddamana, on the dirt road that loops off the Lake Hwy between Bothwell and Great Lake, is the **Waddamana Power Station Museum** (☎ 6259 6158; admission free; 10am-4pm), a hydroelectric station constructed between 1910 and 1916. Although originally a private venture, financial difficulties resulted in the government taking over and creating a Hydro-Electric Department, which today is Hydro Tasmania. The power station has a display on the state's early hydro history and operational turbines; the machinery's scale is particularly impressive.

Signposted off the highway 35km north of Bothwell (about 25km south of Miena) and well worth a stop are the **Steppes Sculptures**, a ring of 12 stones with affixed iron representations of Midlands life – there's assorted wildlife, cattle drovers and Tasmanian Aborigines. They are the work of sculptor Stephen Walker, who created them in 1992 as a Midlands tribute. Enjoy the peaceful setting, or take the 900m track leading north from the stones to the remnants of a **historic homestead** that was the preserve of the locally notable Wilson family for 112 years from 1863.

THE LAKES

Located 1050m above sea level on the Central Plateau, **Great Lake** is the largest natural freshwater lake in Australia. The first European to visit the lake was John Beaumont in 1817; his servant circumnavigated it in three days. In 1870 brown trout were released into the lake and it soon became famous for its fishing. Rainbow trout were added in 1910 and they also thrived. Attempts were subsequently made to introduce salmon, but this time the fish simply refused to multiply. Trout have now penetrated most of the streams across the plateau, with some of the best fishing in the smaller streams and lakes west of Great Lake.

In the early days of the hydroelectric schemes, a small dam was constructed on Great Lake to raise the water level near Miena. The lake is linked to nearby Arthurs Lake by canals and a pumping station, and supplies water to the Poatina Power Station located on its northeastern shore.

For information on the area and the activities possible within it, try the **Parks & Wildlife Service visitors centre** (☎ 6259 8148) at Liawenee, 10km north of Miena on the western side of Great Lake.

The **general store** (Swan Bay), next door to the Great Lake Hotel, sells petrol, supplies and takeaway food.

There is no public transport servicing this area.

Fishing

There's excellent fishing all over the Central Plateau, with good access to most of the larger lakes. Great Lake, Lake Sorell, Arthurs Lake and Little Pine Lagoon are all popular spots. The plateau itself actually contains thousands of lakes; many are tiny but most still contain trout. You'll have to walk to many of the smaller lakes, which means getting some lightweight camping gear, as the region is prone to snowfalls.

HOOKED ON TROUT

It should be easy to catch a trout in Tasmania, as most of the state's rivers and lakes have been well stocked with the brown and rainbow varieties. But you still need to organise your fishing gear and be in the right place at the right time. There are also restrictions on the types of tackle that can be used in various areas at different times of the year.

The use of live bait is one tried-and-true fishing technique, requiring a grasshopper, grub or worm to be attached to the hook. However, this form of fishing is banned in most inland waters.

Artificial lures, which come in many different shapes, sizes, weights and colours, are a more acceptable way to fish. You cast the lure from a riverbank or boat and (hopefully) reel your catch in. Depending on the season, you might find that a 'Cobra' wobbler or Devon-type 'spinner' works well in lakes, while one of the most effective accessories in streams is the 'Celta'-type lure.

One of the most challenging forms of this activity is fly-fishing. Many keen anglers make their own artificial flies, but you can purchase a large variety. There are many areas in Tasmania specifically reserved for fly-fishing, which most often involves wading shallow rivers and lake shores in the early morning.

When fishing in the Lake Country, remember to always come prepared for Tasmania's notoriously changeable weather with warm and waterproof clothing, even in the middle of summer.

A wide variety of regulations apply to fishing in this area, aimed at ensuring fish continue to breed and their stocks aren't depleted. On some parts of Great Lake, for instance, you can use only artificial lures, and you're not allowed to fish in any streams flowing into the lake. On the Central Plateau, some waters are reserved for fly-fishing, and bag, size and seasonal limits apply to all areas. See p48 for more information, including details of how to find professional guided-fishing outfits who can tell you the difference between claret dabblers, brown bead head buggers and yum-yum emergers (all local trout flies). The website www.fishonline.tas.gov.au is an excellent source of information.

Sleeping & Eating

Campers can try the basic camping ground at **Dago Point** (camping per adult/child $3.30/1.65), beside Lake Sorell. A better bet for a family is the camping ground on Arthurs Lake at **Pumphouse Bay** (camping per adult/child $3.30/1.65), which has better facilities including hot showers. Campers self-register at both sites and fee payments rely on an honour system. Bring all your supplies; it's recommended that you boil tap water.

Central Highlands Lodge (☎ 6259 8179; www.centralhighlandslodge.com.au; Haddens Bay; s $95-105, d $120-130) On the southern outskirts of Miena, this lodge offers its clean and comfortable cabins from September to April, and can arrange fishing guides. The lodge restaurant is usually open to the public, but bookings are required.

Great Lake Hotel (☎ 6259 8163; Swan Bay; d $90-120) From Miena, take the turn-off to Bronte Park and you'll soon come across this small-town pub, offering a range of accommodation (from very basic anglers' cabins with shared facilities from $35, to self-contained motel-style units). There are also meals ($13-18, lunch and dinner) and a meat-based menu that would reduce a vegetarian to tears!

DERWENT VALLEY

Lake St Clair is the source of the Derwent River, which flows southeast towards Hobart; along its banks is the rich and fertile Derwent Valley. New Norfolk, the largest town in the area, is covered in the Around Hobart chapter (see p102). The Lyell Hwy largely follows the course of the Derwent River to the Central Plateau, past Derwent Bridge then west to Queenstown.

HAMILTON

☎ 03 / pop 150

This National Trust–classified town was originally laid out on a grand scale to be a major centre, but never developed beyond a small, sleepy village. Hamilton's historic buildings are spread out and surrounded by farms, and there are excellent views of mountain ranges and peaks further west.

It seems as if half the houses in town are cottages for rent.

The area was settled in 1808 when New Norfolk was established, and by 1835 had a population of 800, served by 11 hotels and two breweries. Many streets were surveyed, but the rich yet dry soils near town defeated many farmers, the town stagnated, and a number of buildings were eventually removed. The remaining structures are a reminder of what was a boom town during the mid–19th century.

The town's history is documented in the **Hamilton Heritage Centre** (Tarleton St; admission by donation), set up in the 1840 Warders Cottage; keys are available from the adjacent council chambers or Glen Clyde House (see right).

Sleeping & Eating

Hamilton Inn (☎ 6286 3204; Tarleton St; d from $85) New owners recently bought this once-crumbling historic pub and after huge restoration works have converted it into quality accommodation and dining. Rooms all have en suite and rates include continental breakfast. Lunch and dinner are served here daily.

THE AUTHOR'S CHOICE

Over the Back (☎ 6286 3332; www.overtheback.com.au; d $145, extra person $25) You feel a long way from anywhere at Over the Back, but that's a big part of its appeal. This fully self-contained cottage sleeps five and offers a secluded slice of rural life on a 300-hectare sheep farm, off the highway 3km west of Hamilton. The cottage is a further 3km from the farm's main house. It's beside Meadowbank Lake (good for fishing and swimming), and the views of the lake and gum trees from the deck are quintessentially Australian.

The friendly, helpful owners of Over the Back also offer the unique opportunity to hire a houseboat and cruise a 15km stretch of Meadowbank Lake. They offer two self-contained boats (one can sleep three, the other eight) and full instruction is given. It's best to call or email for prices as these vary depending on the number of people and length of rental (eg the eight-berth boat costs from $32 per person per night for seven nights).

Cherry Villa (☎ 6286 3418; www.cherryvilla.com.au; Arthur St; d $120-150) Cherry Villa, set in lovely gardens and offering two attractive rooms, is Hamilton's only traditional, hosted B&B (all other offerings are self-contained). And the bonus is that the hosts are warm and welcoming, and dinners can be arranged.

McCauley's Cottage (☎ 6286 3258; www.jacksonsemporium.biz; Main Rd; d $185, extra person $25) McCauley's is a large, historic sandstone-and-blackwood cottage owned and managed by nearby Jackson's Emporium. The meticulously renovated, olde-worlde interior comes at a premium; the house can sleep six.

Emma's, **George's**, **Victoria's** and **Edward's** (☎ 6286 3270) are old sandstone cottages with authentic furnishings, strung out beside the main road in the town centre and nestled in pretty gardens. They sleep between two and five people and are managed from **Uralla House** (☎ 6286 3270; cnr Main Rd & Clyde St; d $120, extra adult/child $35/25).

Old School House (☎ 6286 3292; www.schoolhouse.southcom.com.au; Main Rd; d $140, extra adult/child $45/35) This imposing place was built in 1856 and served as the school until 1935. The owners have two comfortable self-contained cottages that can accommodate up to five. Full breakfast provisions supplied.

Glen Clyde House (☎ 6286 3276; Lyell Hwy; dishes $9-14; 9.30am-5pm) On a sharp bend at the town's northern end is this popular pit-stop, part licensed tearoom (Devonshire teas to smoked trout pâté) and part craft gallery. The outdoor deck is a lovely spot for a snack.

Aside from the pub, there are few options for evening meals in Hamilton. Many accommodation providers can supply dinner by prior arrangement, or you can pop in to **Jackson's Emporium** (☎ 6286 3258; Main Rd;), which cleverly caters to visitors with a range of chef-prepared frozen meals and desserts (and wine) for sale. **Platter Pie** (Main Rd) is a new café open until 8pm most nights, with a short menu of takeaway favourites (burgers etc) or items such as BLTs or Caesar salad.

Getting There & Away

TassieLink (☎ 1300 300 520; www.tassielink.com.au) runs buses once daily (except Monday and Wednesday) between Hobart and Queenstown via Hamilton, Ouse and Lake St Clair.

The 1¼-hour trip from Hobart to Hamilton costs $12; buses arrive at and depart from Hamilton newsagency.

ELLENDALE

☎ 03 / pop 470

This small village is on a quiet, narrow, but sealed link road joining the Lyell Hwy with Westerway. It's a convenient shortcut to Mt Field National Park. The route isn't serviced by bus. Shortly after turning on to the signposted Ellendale Rd, which leaves the Lyell Hwy about midway between Hamilton and Ouse, you cross **Meadowbank Lake**, part of the Derwent River hydroelectric power scheme.

Ellendale was once a hop-growing area, though few remnants of the industry remain. There's little in town apart from a picnic shelter beside the creek, a general store and some accommodation, making it a quiet base for day trips to the nearby national park.

Sleeping

Hopfield Country Cottages (☎ 6288 1223; 990 Ellendale Rd; d $130, extra person $25) Hopfield offers two self-contained abodes under the one conjoined roof, including full breakfast provisions and lots of quaint touches.

Hamlet Downs (☎ 6288 1212; www.users.bigpond.com/hamletdowns; 50 Gully Rd; d $120-150) Some 6km south of Ellendale at Fentonbury is Hamlet Downs, offering the choice of B&B rooms or a self-contained unit (sleeps six) in a century-old house on a permaculture farm. You can unwind on long relaxing walks around the well-gardened property.

Platypus Cottage (☎ 6288 1280; nigeltomlin@bigpond.com; 38 The Avenue; d $120) This farm cottage comes fully equipped with kitchen, washing machine, TV, video and other conveniences, plus bright, modern décor and a relaxing rural setting.

OUSE

☎ 03 / pop 160

This area was settled early in the saga of colonialism, but for a long time there was no town and Ouse (pronounced ooz) was little more than a river crossing; most of its ordinary weatherboard buildings were erected in the last 100 years. Ouse is a popular highway food-stop, with a pub, roadhouse serving takeaway food (renowned for its great pies) and supermarket; the riverside picnic ground is great for al fresco dining.

The **Lachlan Hotel** (☎ 6287 1215; Lyell Hwy; s/d $45/65) offers rooms with continental breakfast and shared facilities, plus pub lunches and dinners (mains $12–19).

Rosecot (☎ 6287 1222; Victoria Valley Rd; s/d $80/110, extra adult/child $28/22), signposted off the main road north of town, is a good choice – it's a very pretty self-contained cottage that sleeps six. Another self-contained option is the suburban-looking **Sassa-del-Gallo** (☎ 6287 1289; d $85, extra person $25), opposite the Lachlan Hotel and also with room for six.

TARRALEAH

☎ 03

Tarraleah Highland Village (☎ 6289 1199; www.tarraleahvillage.com.au), halfway between Hobart and Queenstown, is a novel place. It was built as a residential village for staff of the nearby hydroelectric power stations and dams, and in its peak it had a population in the thousands, complete with services such as police station, town hall, shops, church, golf course and about 100 houses. Once the Hydro work dried up, the village went into decline and the population dropped. Hydro sold off the majority of the houses for removal in the 1990s, and then put the remainder of the village up for sale.

In 2002 Tarraleah was purchased by a family from the mainland (the 'family that bought a town', as the tabloids tagged them) and since then they have been restoring the village and hosting travellers. It still feels a little like a ghost town if you visit outside of the peak season, but there is a full range of facilities here, including **camp sites** (unpowered/powered sites $10/20), **rooms** (dm/s/d $30/60/80) with breakfast and shared facilities in an Art Deco lodge, and **self-contained houses** (d $140, extra person $20) with one to three bedrooms. Rates are $10 to $20 cheaper from May to September.

There is also a café, and a restaurant in the lodge open for unadventurous but reasonably priced meals of an evening.

There is no public transport service to Tarraleah.

East Coast

Tasmania's scenic east coast, known as the 'sun coast' because of its mild climate and above-average exposure (by Tasmanian standards) to the great yellow orb, devotes itself to long sandy beaches, fine fishing and that special sort of tranquillity that occurs only by the ocean. The light-hued granite peaks and glorious bays of Freycinet Peninsula are among the state's most attractive features, but even from the highway the water views are often magnificent. And if you have a yen for seaside towns, this is the place to fulfil it.

Settlement of the region proceeded after Hobart was established in 1803. Fishing, whaling, tin mining and timber cutting became particularly important. Many former convicts helped establish the fishing, wool, beef and grain industries that are still prominent today.

The major towns along the coast are Orford, Triabunna, Swansea and Bicheno. There are also three national parks: Maria Island National Park has been reserved as much for its interesting history as its natural beauty; the large, dramatic peninsula of Freycinet National Park is an excellent walking venue; and Douglas-Apsley National Park has waterfalls, rainforest and remnants of the dry eucalypt forests that once blanketed the region.

There's plenty of accommodation, for which you'll pay 50% more over summer and public holidays. As this coast is a first-choice holiday destination for many Tasmanians, it crowds out at Easter, and during the last week of December and most of January. If you plan to cruise the coast at these times, book well ahead.

HIGHLIGHTS

- Getting white sand in your shorts at any of the east coast's lovely, semideserted **beaches**
- Taking a dip in the divine **Wineglass Bay** (p168) after you've worked up a sweat getting here
- Getting back to basics on unhurried **Maria Island** (p160) by walking, biking and snorkelling
- Knocking on some east-coast **cellar doors** (p164) en route from Swansea to Bicheno
- Escaping all your stresses with a stay at the simple, welcoming **St Marys Seaview Farm** (p178)
- Exploring the river gorges and wildlife of **Douglas Aspley National Park** (p177) before cooling down in the waterhole
- Detouring to devour heavenly fruit-flavoured ice cream at **Eureka Farm** (p178), near Scamander
- Soaking up the awesome beauty of the **Freycinet Peninsula** (p170) from a kayak

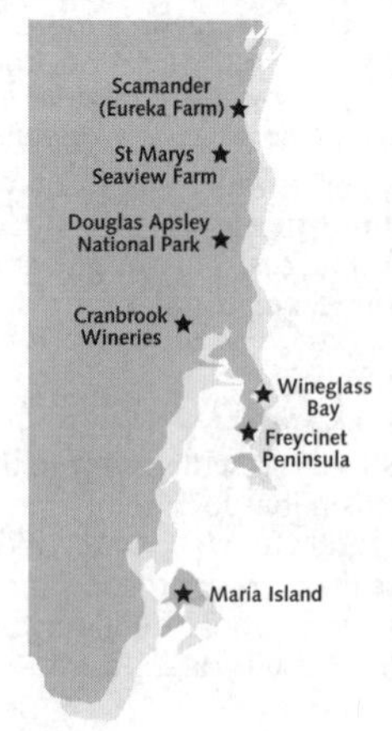

Getting There & Around

BICYCLE

Arguably the most popular cycle route in Tasmania; a wonderfully varied ride. Traffic in the area is usually light and the hills are not too steep, particularly if you follow the coastal highway from Chain of Lagoons to Falmouth.

For those cycling between Swansea and Coles Bay, there's an informal **boat service** (☎ 6257 0239) that costs $15 per person (including bikes) from Point Bagot to Swanwick, 6km north of Coles Bay, which will save you 65km of cycling. The approximate cycling time from Swansea to Point Bagot is one hour. The service operates October to late April, weather permitting; call first.

BUS

The main bus companies serving the east coast are **Redline Coaches** (☎ 6336 1446, 1300 360 000; www.tasredline.com.au) and **TassieLink** (☎ 6271 7320, 1300 300 520; www.tassielink.com.au).

Redline runs one service each weekday from Launceston to Swansea, the Coles Bay turn-off, and Bicheno (and return), via the Midland Hwy and the inland B34 linking road. Services from Hobart connect with these services – you change buses at Campbell Town, where you'll have to wait from five minutes to three hours depending on your particular service. Redline also runs daily services (except Saturday) from Launceston to St Helens (and vice versa) along the A4 via Fingal, St Marys and Scamander. Again, Hobart buses connect with this service, at Conara on the Midland Hwy.

TassieLink runs three times a week between Hobart and Bicheno via Buckland, Orford, Triabunna, Swansea and the Coles Bay turn-off; on Friday and Sunday this service presses on further north to Scamander and St Helens. TassieLink also runs one bus each weekday (three times a week during school holiday periods) from Hobart to Swansea via Richmond, Orford and Triabunna. TassieLink also has a twice-weekly service between Launceston and Bicheno via the A4, calling at Fingal and St Marys.

Neither Redline nor TassieLink services the Freycinet Peninsula. You must rely on **Bicheno Coach Service** (☎ 6257 0293), which runs from Bicheno to Coles Bay (see p172), connecting with Redline and TassieLink services at the Coles Bay turn-off.

Note that all the bus services are limited at weekends.

ORFORD

☎ 03 / pop 500

The highway approaches this township from the west by following the Prosser River through the rock-lined, emphatically named

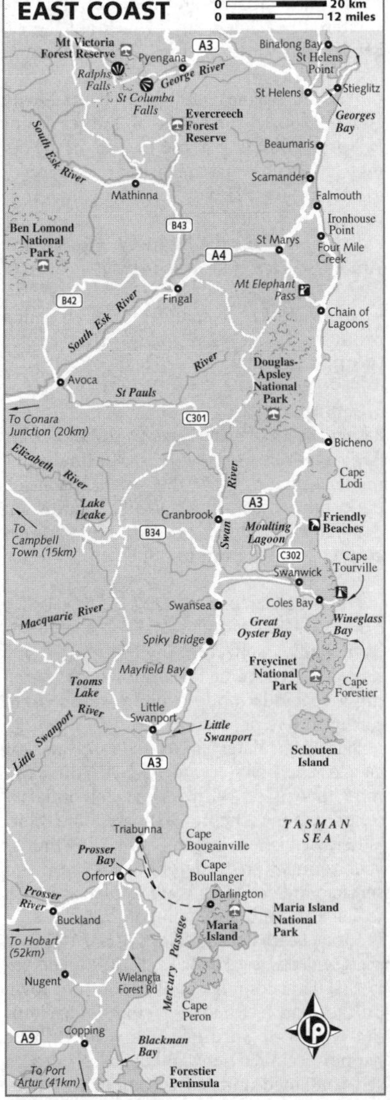

Paradise Gorge. Within the gorge, close to town on the northern side of the river, are the remains of an incomplete **convict-built road**, now a pleasant riverside walk.

Orford was once an important sea port which served whalers and the local Maria Island garrison. Local **Prosser River** received its name after an escaped prisoner was captured on its banks. The area has excellent fishing and diving, and swimming at the sheltered beaches near town. Idyllic **Spring Beach**, 4km south of town, is a good surfing location.

A 2km **walking track** leads from Shelly Beach around the cliffs of Luther Point to Spring Beach, passing the site of an old quarry which was the primary source of sandstone for many of the older buildings in Melbourne and Hobart.

Signposted off the highway opposite the Ampol service station is **Darlington Vineyard** (☎ 6257 1630; Holkham Court; ⌚ 10am-5pm daily Jan-Feb, Fri-Mon Mar-Nov), a small family affair which produces lovely, reasonably priced wines (tastings free).

Sleeping

Raspin's Beach Camping Park (☎ 6257 3575; Tasman Hwy; unpowered/powered site $12/14) Minimal man-made aesthetics grace this small, beachside park, but it has a great sandy location on the water, just north of town. Hot showers cost $1 for five minutes. Site prices are for two people.

Prosser Holiday Units (☎ 6257 1427; cnr Tasman Hwy & Charles St; d $85, extra adult/child $20/10) These family-friendly, self-contained highway-side units are great value for money, each featuring a spacious modern interior and room for up to five people.

Blue Waters Motor Inn (☎ 6257 1102; www.islandcabins.com.au; Tasman Hwy; d $75-110) You can't miss this place, with its eye-catching exterior colour scheme of purple and blue. When we visited, however, the large motel-style rooms were undergoing a revamp and service and facilities were haphazard. Ask to see a room before you commit.

Spring Beach Holiday Villas (☎ 6257 1440; www.springbeachvillas.com; Rheban Rd; d $110-140, extra person $30) This complex is 4km south of town on the road to Rheban, facing the beckoning waters of Spring Beach. Kids will be happily occupied here, and the two-bedroom self-contained units each come with wood-fired stove, private outdoor area with barbecue, and views of Maria Island.

Sanda House (☎ 6257 1527; www.orfordsandahouse.com.au; 33 Walpole St; d $90-130) Readers speak highly of this B&B, housed in Orford's oldest house (a stone cottage dating from 1840). It's in a quiet spot on the south side of the river, with attributes such as a pretty garden, helpful hosts and charming rustic décor.

Eastcoaster Resort (☎ 6257 1172; www.eastcoaster.com.au; Louisville Point Rd; unpowered/powered site $19/29, motel d $99-121, cabin d $130-145; ♿) New owners recently took over this sprawling resort 3km north of Orford, and at the time of research it was in the early stages of a much-needed spruce-up. Camp sites, one- to three-bedroom cabins and large motel-style rooms with kitchenettes are on offer (heavy on '70s mission-brown décor), plus diversions including indoor and outdoor pool, spa, tennis court, games rooms, tavern and restaurant. A ferry to Maria Island leaves from the wharf opposite the resort (see p162).

Orford Riverside Cottages (☎ 6257 1655; www.riversidecottages.com.au; Old Convict Rd; d $140-175, extra adult/child $30/20) If your budget extends this far, opt for one of these four luxurious cottages beside the Prosser River. As well as the mod-con-studded accommodation, guests enjoy continental breakfast provisions, private spa, free dinghy use and a video and DVD library to ransack. There are plans for an on-site restaurant too.

Eating

East Coast Seafood & Just Hooked Restaurant (☎ 6257 1549; Tasman Hwy; lunch mains $11-17, dinner $15-23; ⌚ takeaway daily, restaurant lunch Wed-Sun, dinner Wed-Sat) Just Hooked is a small restaurant serving local seafood (not much joy on the menu for non-fish-lovers, however). It also has an adjacent takeaway section, East Coast Seafood, offering burgers and fresh fish and chips – perfect for a beachside picnic.

Blue Waters Motor Inn (☎ 6257 1102; Tasman Hwy; mains $15.50-22; ⌚ lunch & dinner) The pleasant dining room of this motel has big windows looking out on the river, and serves a menu of traditional pub fare: steak, roast, chicken kiev, fisherman's basket etc.

Scorchers on the River (☎ 6257 1033; 1 Esplanade; meals $7-18; ⌚ 10am-9pm daily) The best eating in town can be done at this cheerful café-restaurant on the south side of the river. There are lots of focaccia options, local wines (many by the glass), wood-fired pizza (served all day) and pasta dishes (after 5pm). In summer, ask here about canoes for rent for river exploration.

Getting There & Away

TassieLink (☎ 1300 300 520; www.tassielink.com.au) coaches stop at the Orford Roadhouse (south of the river) en route from Hobart to Swansea and Bicheno (and vice versa); the 1½-hour trip from Hobart costs $15.

TRIABUNNA

☎ 03 / pop 930

Eight kilometres north of Orford is the larger community of Triabunna; its name is derived from an Aboriginal word for a species of native hen. Located at the head of the sheltered inlet of Spring Bay, it was originally a whaling station, then a military base during the area's penal era, and is now the region's commercial centre. Triabunna handles woodchip processing and is the port of call for scallop and cray-fishing boats. Except for the great backpackers here, it doesn't make a particularly appealing overnight stop – Orford is a better, more picturesque option.

Down at the Triabunna docks is the **Tasmanian Seafarers' Memorial**, a modest fish-shaped monument that is dedicated to Tasmanians who have died at sea, and to those who have died in the state's waters. One of the more recent plaques commemorates the six sailors who died during the storm-tossed 1998 Sydney to Hobart yacht race.

Next to the memorial, the well-stocked **visitors centre** (☎ 6257 4772; triabunna@tasvisinfo.com.au; cnr Esplanade & Charles St; 10am-4pm) can provide information on chartering boats for fishing, plus walks and activities in the area, and is the best source of information if you plan to visit Maria Island.

East Coast Eco Tours (☎ 6257 3453; http://springbay.net/ecotours/) conducts customised tours of the local coastline from the wharf near the visitors centre, including trips out to a seal colony and Maria Island.

Sleeping & Eating

Triabunna Cabin & Caravan Park (☎ 6257 3575; www.mariagateway.com; 6 Vicary St; unpowered/powered site $14/16, on-site van $33-44, cabin $66-77) This is a friendly, low-key compound with good-value accommodation and facilities.

The Udda Backpackers (☎ 6257 3439; udda@southcom.com.au; 12 Spencer St; dm/s/d $18/25/40) This fantastic, laid-back YHA hostel gives you a warm rural welcome and has spotless rooms, inviting common areas, homegrown veggies for sale and a licence to sell alcohol to parched travellers. Call ahead to arrange pick-up from the Triabunna bus stop. The

DETOUR

For east-coast explorers, it's worth knowing that there's an interesting short cut from the Tasman Peninsula to Orford. The road leaves the Tasman Hwy at Copping and follows 35km of gravel north through **Wielangta Forest**, which is managed for timber harvesting. Significant portions of the forest have been reserved for recreational use and contain a couple of good walking tracks.

About halfway between Copping and Orford is **Sandspit Forest Reserve**, with a picnic shelter and a 20-minute walk through beautiful rainforest, beginning at an impressive bridge constructed of massive logs and passing rock formations once used as shelters by Tasmanian Aborigines. There's also a longer track (90 minutes return) called the **Wielangta Walk**, which follows the river valley. Just south of the reserve is a **viewing platform** revealing the reserve's wet and dry eucalypt forests.

Thumbs Lookout is only 6km from Orford. A rough side road leads to a picnic ground and lookout giving good views of Maria Island. The two-hour return walk to the open, rocky summit of the highest 'thumb' rewards you with even better panoramic views of the coast.

There are no bus services along this road. If you've driven from Orford, you'll reach a give-way sign at the southern end of the forest road – turn right and head past nearby Kellevie to reach the turn-off to either Buckland or Copping. Cyclists should think seriously about using the road – many consider it too steep and rough to contemplate. There's also the occasional logging truck and tour bus passing through.

Udda is in 'east' Triabunna; head over the bridge and keep left, following the signs.

Spring Bay Hotel (☎ 6257 3115; 1 Charles St; s/d $35/55) An old-style pub – rough and ready but full of character (and characters). The no-frills rooms have shared facilities and prices include continental breakfast. Basic pub grub is on offer nightly from Monday to Saturday.

Tandara Motor Inn (☎ 6257 3333; Tasman Hwy; s/d $66/77) A charmless place on the highway, with motel units and a restaurant. Best to push on until Orford!

Girraween Gardens & Tearooms (☎ 6257 3458; 4 Henry St; light meals $3-12; 9.30am-4pm daily, closed Sat Jun-Aug) Girraween has two acres of rigorously manicured private gardens, plus indoor and outdoor tearooms serving sandwiches, quiche and cake. Garden access costs $2/6 per person/family (free for tearoom diners).

Getting There & Away

TassieLink (☎ 1300 300 520; www.tassielink.com.au) coaches stop at the visitors centre; the 1½-hour trip from Hobart costs $16.

MARIA ISLAND NATIONAL PARK

This peaceful, car-free island (pronounced Ma-*rye*-ah Island) was declared a national park in 1972. It features some magnificent natural scenery: forests, fern gullies, fossil-studded sandstone and limestone cliffs, and beautiful white beaches. It has some invigorating walks for hikers, while mountain bikers have plenty of great trails to ride, bird-watchers have plenty to look at, and snorkellers and divers are in for a treat in the waters of the island's marine reserve.

On a day trip to Maria Island, you can see a lot of its restored buildings and wildlife. But it's well worth staying for longer for a true back-to-basics experience.

History

At various times, Maria Island has been a penal settlement, a factory site and a farming district. The island was originally occupied by the Oyster Bay Tribe of Tasmanian Aborigines, who called it Toarra Marra Monah. They lived primarily on shellfish and crossed to the mainland in canoes, resting on tiny Lachlan Island.

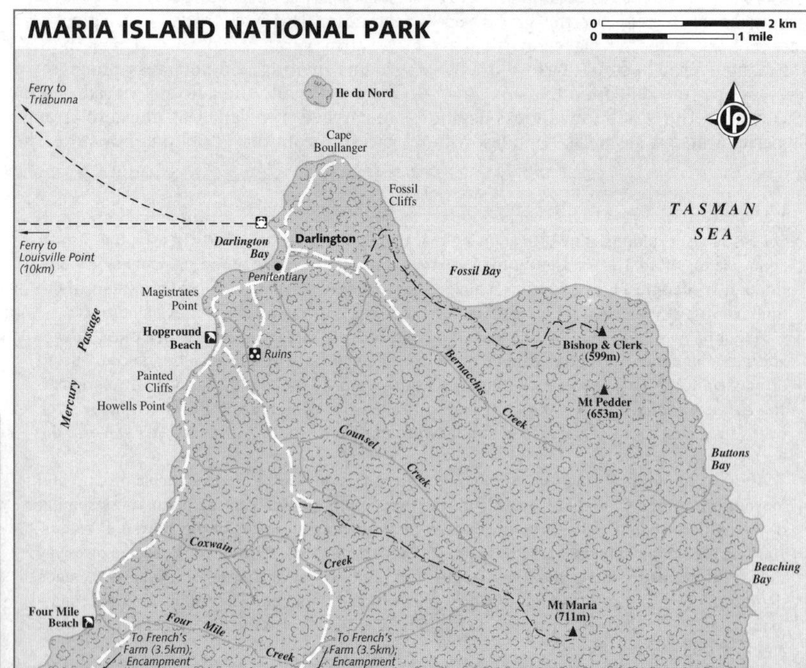

In 1642 Abel Tasman bumped into the island and gave it a European name in honour of Anthony Van Diemen's wife. The island was selected as Tasmania's second penal settlement in 1821; four years later the first convicts arrived and began work on the settlement of Darlington.

Over the next seven years many major buildings, such as the Commissariat Store (1825) and the Penitentiary (1830), were constructed using locally made bricks. A water race, mill pond and jetty were also built. However, in 1832 it was decided that the costs involved in running three penal settlements outside Hobart were too great, and the convicts were moved. For the next 10 years, whalers, farmers and smugglers used the island.

Darlington reopened in 1842 (after renovations) to be used as a probation station. In 1845 a second settlement was established at Long Point and by 1850 a road connected the two sites. The road allowed ready access to the island, and at one stage there were more than 600 convicts at Darlington. However, the flow of convicts to Tasmania slowed and in 1850 Darlington closed. Long Point followed suit the next year and the island was leased for grazing.

In 1884 an enterprising businessman, Diego Bernacchi, leased the island to develop silk and wine-making industries. Darlington's buildings were again renovated and structures like the coffee palace added (1888), and the town of 260 was renamed San Diego. Over the next 40 years there were various other industries here, the most notable being the cement plant established in 1922. The plant soon closed due to the Great Depression, however, and the island reverted to a farming district.

In the 1960s the government gradually bought the properties on the island. Since European occupation, none of the larger animals or birds had survived on the island, so in the late 1960s, Forester kangaroos, Bennett's wallabies, Cape Barren geese and emus were reintroduced; the kangaroos and geese have since thrived. In 1971 the island was declared a wildlife sanctuary and a year later became a national park.

Information

The visitors centre in Triabunna (p159) can help with pre-trip information. Get information online at www.parks.tas.gov.au/natparks/maria.

On the island, various brochures are available from the **visitors reception area** in the old Commissariat Store (close to where the ferry docks), including information on the Bishop & Clerk peaks walk, the Fossil Cliffs and tips for enjoying the island by bike. There's a public telephone close to the centre of Darlington.

Sights & Activities

The old township of **Darlington** is worth wandering around. The best short walk (two hours return) is to **Painted Cliffs** at the southern end of Hopground Beach. The sandstone, stained with iron oxide, forms intricate, colourful patterns.

There's a good circuit walk of 1½ hours, which takes in **Cape Boullanger**, the **Fossil Cliffs** and the old brickworks. If the air is clear, you'll be rewarded with great views by climbing **Bishop & Clerk**; a good track leads to the summit and takes about four hours return from Darlington. A walk of six or seven hours return takes you to **Mt Maria** (711m), the island's highest point.

The coastline from Return Point to Bishop & Clerk is a marine reserve, which means no fishing is allowed, including in the Darlington area. The reserve, together with the giant kelp forests and caves around **Fossil Bay**, has some fantastic scuba diving and snorkelling. Two of the best underwater spots are at the ferry pier and further south at Painted Cliffs. The water is chilly and wetsuits are essential.

Feather fanciers can see 11 of the state's native bird species here, including the endangered forty-spotted pardalote.

Tours

If you'd like to see Maria Island in some degree of comfort, consider taking a walking tour: from October to May, **Maria Island Walk** (☎ 6227 8800; www.mariaislandwalk.com.au) offers four days of fairly gentle, fully guided exploration (an average of 10km to 12km walking per day) combined with quality meals. The first two nights are spent at private, established beach camps, and the final night is in the restored former home of Diego Bernacchi. The tour's cost of $1549 includes return transport from Hobart to the island, and all meals and accommodation.

Sleeping & Eating

Penitentiary Accommodation Units (☎ 6257 1420; dm/6-bed room $8.80/22) The island's old penitentiary has been converted into basic, unpowered bunkhouses, each equipped with bunks with mattresses only, plus table and wood-fired heater. Shared toilet and washing-up facilities are nearby. Bedding is not supplied and there are no cooking facilities; visitors must take their own gas lamp and portable cooker, plus all utensils. The units are very popular (with school groups as well as travellers) and it's essential to book ahead.

Camping (sites per adult/child/family $4.40/2.20/11) is possible by the creek to the east of Darlington (bookings not required). Fires are allowed only in designated fireplaces and during summer these are often banned; portable stoves are therefore recommended. Hot showers are available behind the barbecue shelter.

For those keen to walk or cycle, the free camp sites at **French's Farm** and **Encampment Cove** are three to four hours away. Both have limited rainwater supplies; French's Farm is a fire-free area where you'll need a portable stove, but fireplaces and wood are provided at Encampment Cove.

You'll need to bring *all* your supplies, as the island has no shops. You'll also need clothing suitable for cool, wet weather, but remember the hat and sunscreen too. A current national park pass is also required.

Getting There & Away

At the time of research there were two boats operating passenger services to Maria Island: one from Triabunna, the other from the Eastcoaster Resort between Orford and Triabunna. However it's unlikely visitor numbers to the island can sustain two services. If you're planning a visit, the best idea is to call the Triabunna visitors centre (p159) beforehand to confirm boat departure points and times.

The **Triabunna service** (☎ 0427 100 104) operates from the marina near the visitors centre, departing 9.30am and 1.30pm daily (returning from Maria Island at 12.30pm and 4.30pm). The journey takes about 50 minutes and a return ticket per adult/child costs $25/12; to transport a bike costs $2.

The **Eastcoaster Express** (☎ 6257 1589) is again operating from the wharf next to the Eastcoaster Resort on Louisville Point Rd, a few kilometres north of Orford (services from here were suspended for some time while repairs were done to the wharf). The Eastcoaster Express offers faster (25 minutes) and more regular crossings: boats depart Louisville Point at 9.30am, 1.30pm and 3.15pm, and return from Darlington at 10am, 2pm and 4pm. The return fare per adult/child is $25/12; bikes, kayaks and dive tanks incur an extra $2 charge.

It is also possible to land on the airstrip near Darlington by light plane. These can be chartered from Triabunna, Hobart or Launceston.

SWANSEA

☎ 03 / pop 550

The appealing holiday town of Swansea lies on the western shore of Great Oyster Bay and is popular with visitors for the local camping, boating, fishing and surfing, not to mention the superb views across to Freycinet Peninsula. Originally known as Great Swanport, the town also has some interesting historic buildings.

European settlers arrived in the 1820s and the town eventually became the administrative centre for Glamorgan. It's Australia's oldest rural municipality. In 1993 it merged with Spring Bay and the administration moved to Triabunna.

Because it's a holiday-maker magnet, food and accommodation prices are generally higher here than in most other coastal towns. Another consequence of its popularity is that several modern accommodation blocks now dominate part of the old waterfront. Regardless, Swansea has retained a laid-back friendliness and still ranks as one of the nicest towns on the east coast, with an abundance of high-quality accommodation.

Information

Online Access Centre (☎ 6257 8806; Franklin St; 🕑 10am-3pm Mon & Fri, 10am-5pm Tue-Thu, 10am-1pm Sat) Adjacent to the town's primary school.

Swansea Corner Store (cnr Victoria & Franklin Sts; 🕑 7am-7pm) Has a multicard ATM.

Visitors centre (☎ 6257 8383; 96 Tasman Hwy; 🕑 9am-5pm) Inside the Swansea Bark Mill (opposite), north of town.

Note that at the time of research, boiling tap water before drinking it was recommended.

Sights & Activities

HISTORIC BUILDINGS

Conduct a self-guided tour of the town's prime buildings using the *Swansea Heritage Walk* booklet ($2.50), available from the visitors centre. Many of these buildings are along Franklin and Noyes Sts, including the 1838 **Morris' General Store** (13 Franklin St), still trading, with a small roomful of artefacts and visitor information, and the 1860 **council chambers** (Noyes St), housing a history room.

Most of Swansea's historic buildings are privately owned but the Glamorgan Community Centre, dating from the 1860s, houses a **museum of local history** (☎ 6257 8215; Franklin St; adult/child $3/1; 🕑 9am-5pm Mon-Sat). The major feature here is an impressive oversized billiard table, bought from Hadleys Hotel in Hobart. It's possible to play on the table after 5pm for a small fee ($2 per person per game) if you book. The museum also contains Aboriginal artefacts and early settlers' possessions. There's also a war memorial and an interesting display of old local photographs.

SWANSEA BARK MILL & EAST COAST MUSEUM

In the front section of this **museum** (☎ 6257 8382; 96 Tasman Hwy; adult/child/family $6/3.80/14.50; 🕑 9am-5pm), the processing of black-wattle bark is demonstrated on restored machinery. This bark produces tannic acid, a basic ingredient used in the tanning of heavy

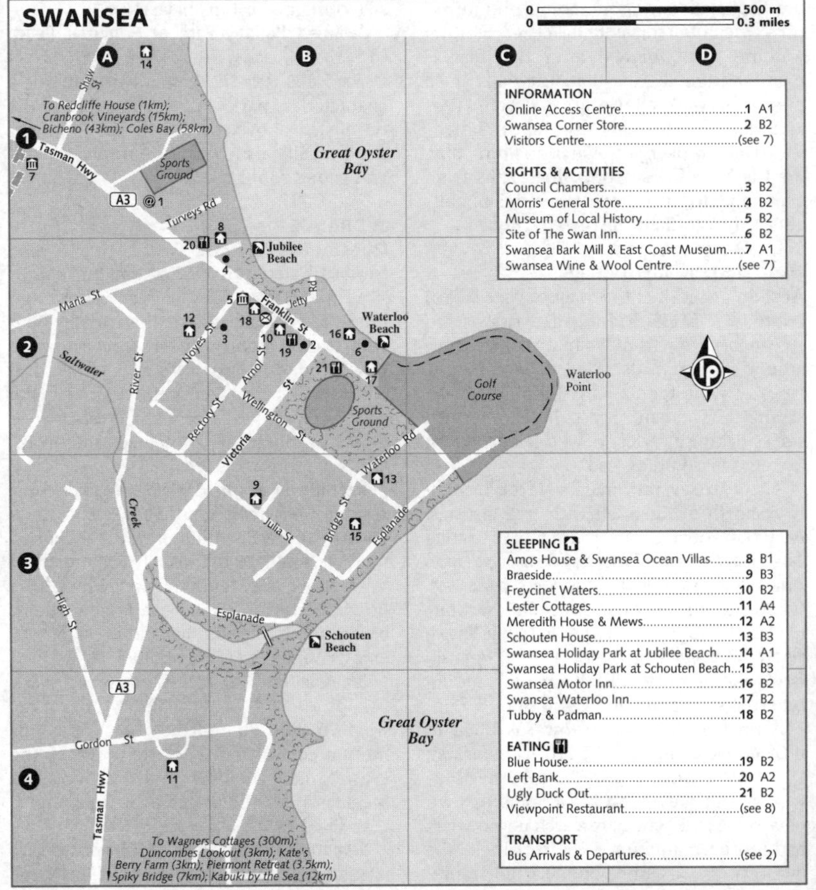

leathers. The mill was made from scavenged materials and what you see today is how it actually operated. The bark mill was one of the few local industries that remained in operation throughout the Great Depression and it helped keep Swansea alive. The adjoining museum features displays of Swansea's early history.

OTHER ATTRACTIONS

Duncombes Lookout, 3km south of town, provides panoramic views of Oyster Bay and Freycinet Peninsula. A further 4km south is **Spiky Bridge**, which was convict-built in 1843 using thousands of local fieldstones but no mortar. The nearby beach and headland are popular for picnics and rock fishing.

Running between Waterloo Beach and the Esplanade is the 40- to 60-minute return **Loon.tite.ter.mair.re.le.hoin.er.** coastal walking track, named after the Tasmanian Aboriginal tribe that originally lived here. The walk allows great ocean views and passes through the short-tailed-shearwater rookery on Waterloo Point; during the breeding season, which runs from September to April, you can see the inhabitants return to their burrows at dusk.

WINE TASTING & WINERIES

At the Bark Mill is the **Swansea Wine & Wool Centre** (☎ 6257 8382; 96 Tasman Hwy; admission free; 🕑 9am-5pm). It sells Tasmanian wines from around 50 vineyards; you can sample four types of wine for $2 and shipping can be arranged. The centre also has a sheepish side, stocking a variety of woollen products; there's a tearoom as well.

There are several wineries off the Tasman Hwy north of town, all with free tastings. At Cranbrook, about 15km north, **Spring Vale Vineyards** (☎ 6257 8208; www.springvalewines.com; 130 Spring Vale Rd; 🕑 10am-5pm Sep-May, until 4pm Jun-Aug) produces some great chardonnay and pinot noir. Nearby is **Craigie Knowe Vineyard** (☎ 6257 8252; 80 Glen Gala Rd; 🕑 generally 9am-5pm, best to call first), producing outstanding cabernet sauvignon and pinot noir.

A further 10km or so towards Bicheno is **Coombend Estate** (☎ 6257 8881; off Tasman Hwy; 🕑 9am-5pm), which produces cabernet sauvignon and sauvignon blanc, plus its own olive oil. At the time of research new owners had just been announced (surprisingly, the new owners are Gunns Limited, the Tasmanian timber and woodchip conglomerate, see p35), so there may be changes regarding access to visitors. Never fear – just down the road from Coombend is the highly regarded **Freycinet Vineyard** (☎ 6257 8574; off Tasman Hwy; 🕑 9am-5pm), producing acclaimed pinot noir and chardonnay.

Sleeping

BUDGET

The prices listed below are for two people.

Swansea Holiday Park at Jubilee Beach (☎ 6257 8177; www.swansea-holiday.com.au; Shaw St; unpowered/powered site $16/18, cabin $80-140; 💻 🏊) This neat, spruced-up park has family-friendly facilities and a beachfront location on the way out of town, heading north. Prime camping sites are right on the beach; some self-contained cabins have a spa.

Swansea Holiday Park at Schouten Beach (☎ 6257 8148; unpowered/powered site $16/18, on-site van $40-50, cabin $70-90; 🏊) This flat, fairly characterless park isn't as appealing as the one listed above, though it has similarly good facilities such as a pool, playground and games room.

MIDRANGE

Guesthouses & B&Bs

Freycinet Waters (☎ 6257 8080; www.freycinetwaters.com.au; 16 Franklin St; s $100-130, d $120-150) Fresh and bright décor is a feature of this friendly B&B with seaside ambience. The three in-house rooms (one with spa) are well equipped and come with private deck for enjoying the water views (plus full cooked breakfast), or there's a modern self-contained unit (breakfast provisions included).

Redcliffe House (☎ 6257 8557; www.redcliffehouse.com.au; 13569 Tasman Hwy; s $110, d $126-160) This is a warm and welcoming option – a charmingly restored farmhouse 1.5km north of town beside the Meredith River. You'll have no choice but to relax, with large gardens, barbecues, DVDs and cooked breakfasts to enjoy. Winter rates are about $20 less.

Braeside (☎ 6257 8008; www.tassie.net.au/braeside; 21 Julia St; s $85-110, d $95-132) Braeside, which means 'Side of the Hill', is a good-humoured Scottish enclave south of the centre, where you'll be spoiled with cooked breakfasts, lots of places to lounge, and a rose-filled garden.

Schouten House (☎ 6257 8564; www.schoutenhouse.com.au; 1 Waterloo Rd; d $110-130) This large

Georgian house with an earthenware façade contains six elegant B&B rooms decorated in heritage style, with antiques aplenty in the cosy guest areas.

Motels

Swansea Motor Inn (☎ 6257 8102; www.swanseamotorinn.com; 1 Franklin St; d $68-106) This salmon-coloured motel has a range of comfortable rooms, from good-value budget rooms fronting the car park to standard and water-view options.

Swansea Waterloo Inn (☎ 6257 8577; 1a Franklin St; d $77-145) The higher prices you pay for the bay-facing rooms at this large, red-brick inn are explained by the water views afforded from their balconies, but there's no explanation for why the inn's several dozen rooms begin at number 729. Décor is uninspiring.

Self-Contained Apartments & Cottages

Lester Cottages (☎ 6257 8105; www.lestercottages.com.au; 42 Gordon St; d $126-138, extra adult/child $25/10) The friendly owners of this complex have a clutch of appealing, colonial-style cottages, with one- and two-bedroom options available (sleeping up to six). Full breakfast provisions are included. Low season sees good reductions.

Wagners Cottages (☎ 6257 8494; www.wagnerscottages.com.au; d $120-178) Wagners has four very stylishly restored cottages set in pretty gardens beside the highway a couple of kilometres south of town. Each cottage has a private outdoor area, attractive furnishings, open fire, spa and cooked breakfast provisions.

Amos House & Swansea Ocean Villas (☎ 6257 8656; www.swanseaoceanvillas.com.au; 3 Maria St; villa d $100-135, q $140-180) Amos House offers motel-style accommodation above the complex's busy restaurant, but a far better option here is the attractive, two-storey villas (one- and two-bedroom) close to the beachfront. Each villa has full kitchen, wood-fired stove and washing machine.

THE AUTHOR'S CHOICE

Tubby & Padman (☎ 6257 8901; www.tubbyandpadman.com.au; 20 Franklin St; cottage ste d $150-160, units d $130-140, extra person $30) Swansea has an excess of quality accommodation, but this friendly place with the kooky moniker (it's named for the original owners) gets our vote thanks to its fabulous décor and fine attention to detail. Inside the richly renovated 1840s cottage are heritage suites built for romance (each with bedroom, living room and bathroom, some with spa) – but if you're travelling with family or in a group with no time for such shenanigans, opt for one of the two modern, two-bedroom, self-contained units behind the cottage in a garden setting. Full breakfast provisions are supplied in both options.

TOP END

Meredith House & Mews (☎ 6257 8119; www.meredith-house.com.au; 15 Noyes St; d $170-200) A short walk uphill from the main street is the National Trust classified Meredith House, a renovated 1853 home offering pretty B&B suites and full cooked breakfasts. Adjacent to the house is a row of luxurious studio apartments, each equipped with a spa and back veranda overlooking the huge, flower-filled gardens. Hearty home-cooked dinners can be arranged.

Piermont Retreat (☎ 6257 8131; www.piermont.com.au; Tasman Hwy; d $210-310) For a special occasion or serious splurge, head here. Some 3.5km south of town is this collection of six luxurious stone-walled, self-contained cottages overlooking a quiet beach. Beautiful, understated décor, open fires and spas inside, and a solar-heated pool, bikes and a tennis court for when you're feeling suitably recharged. Dinners can be arranged.

Kabuki by the Sea (☎ 6257 8588; www.kabukibythesea.com.au; Tasman Hwy; d $180-220) Now here's something you don't expect to find in eastern Tasmania! Some 12km south of Swansea is this unique complex, enjoying stupendous ocean views from its cliff-top location and offering self-contained units ('with a touch of Japan') plus a restaurant (see p166). The prices quoted here include dinner, bed and breakfast.

Eating

In late 2004 Swansea suffered a blow when the town's only pub, the Swan Inn, burned down; at the time of research there were differing opinions as to whether it would be rebuilt. Residents expressed concern about the limited number of restaurants in town and whether they could cope with the summertime influx of visitors (in other words, make dinner reservations!). Keep an eye on the old Swan Inn site (next to the Swansea Motor Inn) – it shouldn't take long for someone to spy the business potential of this waterfront property and build something new.

The Left Bank (☎ 6257 8896; cnr Main & Maria Sts; light meals $5-16; ⌚ 9am-5pm Wed-Mon Sep-Apr, Thu-Mon May-Jul, closed Aug) Behind the bright red door here is one of the east coast's best stops for great coffee and winning café fare. Choose from breakfast dishes, toasted *panini*, pasta and salads, plus a lemon tart worth travelling miles for!

Kate's Berry Farm (☎ 6257 8428; Addison St; cakes $6-8; ⌚ 9am-6pm) About 3km south of Swansea is another treat – a fruit farm that's home to a store selling jams, wines, sauces and divine ice cream, and a café serving perfect afternoon-tea fodder including superb Devonshire teas (a choice of seven different jams) and berry-filled desserts.

Blue House (☎ 6257 8446; 10 Franklin St; daytime meals & snacks $8-20, dinner mains $20-27; ⌚ lunch Fri-Mon, dinner nightly) This sleek new restaurant is wowing patrons with a menu of creative, well-prepared meals, heavy on local seafood (but not exclusively so). The fancy fish and chips (grilled trevalla with salad and hand-cut potato chips) is one of the best meals we've eaten in Tassie. Bookings advised.

Viewpoint Restaurant (☎ 6257 8656; 3 Maria St; lunch $3.50-20, dinner mains $16-32; ⌚ lunch & dinner) Ocean View often has all of its 40 seats occupied by diners enjoying the seafood selections, so book ahead. Lunch options run from soup to T-bone steak – a good bet is the crayfish sandwich ($9).

The Ugly Duck Out (☎ 6257 8850; 2 Franklin St; meals $6-18; ⌚ 11am-9pm) For a casual meal or picnic takeaway, drop into this bizarrely named diner. There's a good range of edibles to choose from, including fish and chips, pasta, flat-bread roll ups, gourmet burgers and curries.

Kabuki by the Sea (☎ 6257 8588; Tasman Hwy; mains $22-26; ⌚ lunch daily, dinner Tue-Sat Dec-Apr, Fri & Sat May-Nov) Take a seat by the window at this restaurant 12km south of Swansea; enjoy the views, then order from a menu of simple, well-prepared Japanese or local dishes, or an interesting combination of the two such as wallaby *yakiniku* – thinly sliced wallaby pan-fried with veggies). Aussie-style morning and afternoon tea is also available.

Getting There & Away

Buses arrive at and depart from the Swansea Corner Store, on the corner of Franklin and Victoria Sts. The fare for the 2¼-hour **TassieLink** (☎ 1300 300 520; www.tassielink.com.au) bus journey to/from Hobart is $22.60; the **Redline Coaches** (☎ 1300 360 000; www.tasredline.com.au) fare from Hobart/Launceston is $28/25.40. See p157 for more about bus routes.

COLES BAY & FREYCINET NATIONAL PARK

☎ 03 / pop 120

The small township of Coles Bay is both dominated and sheltered by the spectacular 300m-high pink granite outcrops known as The Hazards. This formation marks the northern boundary of the beautiful Freycinet National Park, noted for its magnificent scenery, stunning beaches, coastal heaths and orchids and other wildflowers. Local fauna includes black cockatoos, yellow wattlebirds, yellow-throated honeyeaters and Bennett's wallabies.

History

The Oyster Bay Tribe of Tasmanian Aborigines inhabited the Freycinet area, living off the abundant shellfish – there are some large shell middens along Richardsons Beach.

The first European to visit this area was Abel Tasman in 1642, who identified and named Schouten Island, but also mistook Freycinet for another island. In 1802, Baudin's French expedition discovered that Freycinet was actually a peninsula and named it and many other nearby features. When other expeditions noted the high numbers of seals, sealers arrived from Sydney and quickly wiped most of their number out.

In 1824 a whaling station was established at Parsons Cove, but by the 1840s the whales had been slaughtered and the station had closed. Coles Bay was named after Silas Cole, who arrived in the 1830s and burnt some of the midden shells to produce lime. Mortar made from this lime was used in the construction of many of Swansea's older buildings.

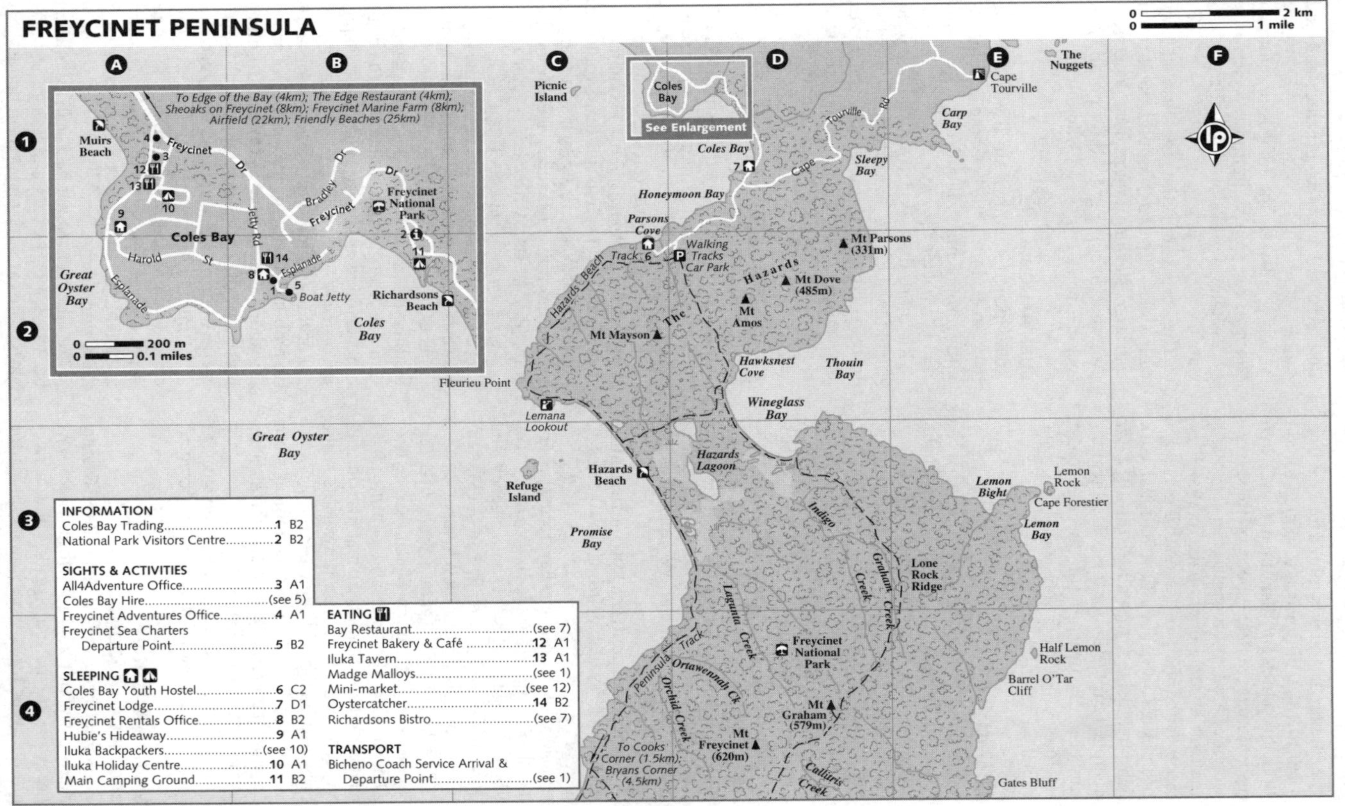
FREYCINET PENINSULA
0 2 km
0 1 mile
A
B
C
D
E
F
1
2
3
4
To Edge of the Bay (4km); The Edge Restaurant (4km); Sheoaks on Freycinet (8km); Freycinet Marine Farm (8km); Airfield (22km); Friendly Beaches (25km)
Muirs Beach
Freycinet Dr
Bradley Dr
Freycinet National Park
Jetty Rd
Coles Bay
Harold St
Esplanade
Boat Jetty
Richardsons Beach
Coles Bay
Great Oyster Bay
0 200 m
0 0.1 miles
Picnic Island
Coles Bay
See Enlargement
Coles Bay
Honeymoon Bay
Parsons Cove
Track
Walking Tracks Car Park
Hazards Beach Track
The Hazards
Mt Parsons (331m)
Mt Dove (485m)
Mt Amos
Mt Mayson
Cape Tourville
The Nuggets
Tourville Rd
Cape
Carp Bay
Sleepy Bay
Fleurieu Point
Lemana Lookout
Hawksnest Cove
Thouin Bay
Wineglass Bay
Great Oyster Bay
Refuge Island
Hazards Beach
Hazards Lagoon
Promise Bay
Indigo
Graham Creek
Creek
Lone Rock Ridge
Lemon Bight
Lemon Rock
Cape Forestier
Lemon Bay
Lagunta Creek
Freycinet National Park
Half Lemon Rock
Barrel O'Tar Cliff
Peninsula Track
Ortawennah Ck
Orchid Creek
Mt Graham (579m)
Mt Freycinet (620m)
To Cooks Corner (1.5km); Bryans Corner (4.5km)
Callitris Creek
Gates Bluff
INFORMATION
Coles Bay Trading....1 B2
National Park Visitors Centre....2 B2
SIGHTS & ACTIVITIES
All4Adventure Office....3 A1
Coles Bay Hire....(see 5)
Freycinet Adventures Office....4 A1
Freycinet Sea Charters Departure Point....5 B2
SLEEPING
Coles Bay Youth Hostel....6 C2
Freycinet Lodge....7 D1
Freycinet Rentals Office....8 B2
Hubie's Hideaway....9 A1
Iluka Backpackers....(see 10)
Iluka Holiday Centre....10 A1
Main Camping Ground....11 B2
EATING
Bay Restaurant....(see 7)
Freycinet Bakery & Café....12 A1
Iluka Tavern....13 A1
Madge Malloys....(see 1)
Mini-market....(see 12)
Oystercatcher....14 B2
Richardsons Bistro....(see 7)
TRANSPORT
Bicheno Coach Service Arrival & Departure Point....(see 1)

EAST COAST

Schouten Island was mined for coal from 1840 to 1880, and was also mined for tin. Both Freycinet and Schouten Island were also farmed. In 1906, both of those areas were declared to be game reserves to stop the over-hunting of animals. In 1916 Freycinet shared the honours with Mt Field in becoming Tasmania's first national park; Schouten Island was added in 1977. To complete protection of the coastal regions, the Friendly Beaches (on the east coast, north of Coles Bay) were added to the national park in 1992.

Information

Coles Bay is 31km down a sealed side road from the Tasman Hwy and has reasonable amenities. It's the man-made gateway to the glorious beaches, coves and cliffs of the Freycinet Peninsula.

Park information is available from the helpful **national park visitors centre** (☎ 6256 7000; freycinet@parks.tas.gov.au; 🕑 8am-5pm May-Oct, 8am-6pm Nov-Apr) at the park entrance. From late December to February, inquire here about free ranger-led activities such as walks, talks and slide shows. Park information is also online at www.parks.tas.gov.au/natparks/freycinet.

Town maps and general tourist information are available from most stores in Coles Bay.

Jack-of-all-trades **Coles Bay Trading** (☎ 6257 0109; 1 Garnet Ave; 🕑 8am-6pm Mar-Nov, 7am-7pm Dec-Feb) is the general store, newsagency and post office. It has a café and ATM, sells petrol, and also offers bicycle hire.

The **Iluka Holiday Centre** (☎ 6257 0115; Coles Bay Esplanade), off Muir's Beach, has a takeaway food outlet, pub and petrol, plus a **mini-market** (🕑 8am-6.30pm) that also houses an ATM. Internet access is available at the Freycinet Bakery & Café (see p172).

You can hire camping equipment from **Freycinet Adventures** (☎ 6257 0500; www.adventurestasmania.com; 2 Freycinet Dr).

An excellent online guide to the area can be found at www.freycinetcolesbay.com.

Sights & Activities

BEACHES & LAGOONS

The signposted turn-off towards the **Friendly Beaches** is about 26km north of Coles Bay. From the car park at Isaacs Point, a five-minute walk leads to a vantage point for uninterrupted views of pristine sand and water.

You've all seen the images of stunning **Wineglass Bay** – but a dip in the waters here necessitates a walk of about three hours return.

The road connecting the Tasman Hwy with Coles Bay skirts around the edge of the large **Moulting Lagoon Game Reserve**, a protected breeding ground for birdlife that includes black swans and wild ducks.

BUSHWALKING

Roads penetrate only a small way into the park, so exploring the lie of the land means hitting some much-plodded tracks – this area is a walker's paradise.

It's more than 5km from Coles Bay to the national park's walking tracks car park. Instead of driving this distance, from Coles Bay you can follow the shoreline on foot via Honeymoon Bay (1½ hours one way).

One of the most popular walks in Tasmania is to the famously beautiful **Wineglass Bay** (2½ to three hours return). From here you can continue along the Isthmus Track to Hazards Beach and return via the coast (about four hours return). Alternatively, walk along the same track only as far as **Wineglass Bay Lookout** (one to 1½ hours return), with its inspired, postcard-captured view. Another superb walk, if you're fit, is the trek to the spectacular views from the summit of **Mt Amos** (three hours return).

The **Freycinet Peninsula Circuit** is a two-day, 31km trek around the peninsula, from Hazards Beach south to Cooks and Bryans Beaches, then across the peninsula over a heathland plateau before descending to the water at Wineglass Bay. Details of the walk can be found in Lonely Planet's *Walking in Australia*.

For those with less time, inclination and/or mobility, there are also plenty of worthy shorter walks, like **Sleepy Bay** (10 minutes), just off the Cape Tourville Rd, and the easy boardwalk track at **Cape Tourville**, a 20-minute circuit that affords great coastal panoramas (including a less-strenuous glimpse of Wineglass Bay) and is suitable for some wheelchair-users and folks with prams.

For all long national park walks, remember to get a parks pass and to sign in (and out) at the car park registration booth.

GUIDED WALKS

A couple of companies offer guided, small-group, multi-day walks in the park, for those after a 'softer' outdoor experience:

All4Adventure (☎ 6257 0018; www.all4adventure.com.au; Coles Bay Esplanade) In conjunction with Freycinet Lodge, this company offers the 'Beyond Wineglass' three-night package; $1295 gets you a cruise along the coastline, one night of camping at Cooks Beach and a full day walking (11km) back to Freycinet Lodge, with two nights' accommodation here, meals, and a massage to help with any residual aches and pains!

Freycinet Adventures (☎ 6257 0500; www.adventurestasmania.com; 2 Freycinet Dr) Offers a good-value two-day 'Hazards Escape' walk from October to April ($499, including meals and camp accommodation), plus trips that combine walking with sea-kayaking for the chance to see the peninsula from different perspectives. See p170 for information on these.

Freycinet Experience (☎ 6223 7565, 1800 506 003; www.freycinet.com.au) Between October and April, this company guides a four-day peninsula walk, with accommodation at permanent camp sites and at the beautiful Friendly Beaches Lodge. Accommodation, food, wine, boat trips and transport from Hobart are provided for $1975 per person.

CAPE TOURVILLE LIGHTHOUSE

The best short drive is to follow the 6.4km road out to Cape Tourville lighthouse. The road enters the park (so national park fees apply). The cape has a boardwalk (500m circuit) – accessible to some wheelchair-users and prams – and extensive coastal views.

FISHING

There's excellent fishing around the bay; charter a boat or hire a dinghy and go catch your own dinner. From March to May, Coles Bay is a fantastic base for big-game fishing, especially when the giant bluefin

WINEGLASS BAY

The hype surrounding Wineglass Bay is quite remarkable. You've no doubt seen the iconic images of this perfect arc with its stunning clear waters and pure white sand used heavily in Tourism Tasmania's brochures, as is the line that it's been voted one of the top 10 beaches in the world (by US-based magazine *Outside*). The images of Wineglass Bay are definitely reaching the public, and travellers no doubt visit Tasmania's east coast planning to see this magnificent beach for themselves – and yet somehow the reality of how the beach is accessed is not quite reaching the same audience!

It's interesting to hear how many people turn up to the national park's visitors centre wanting to know directions to the bay, and are surprised to learn that you can't drive to it. Lonely Planet has received letters along the same lines, including one from disappointed parents stating 'We were both very keen to see Wineglass Bay yet missed out because the tracks were not accessible with our pram, despite it being designed for off road'!

So it bears repeating here: the return walk to the Wineglass Bay lookout takes one to 1½ hours and involves climbing about 600 rough bush steps each way. To frolic on the sand and/or paddle in the bay's pristine waters involves walking for 2½ to three hours return, with the initial part of the walk following the same path as to the lookout. It's mildly strenuous in parts, but if you carry lots of water and take your time, you'll inevitably find the rewards are worth the pain!

But don't despair if that sort of physical exertion is beyond you – other options for seeing the bay do exist. You can catch a glimpse of it from the easy, flat Cape Tourville walk, take a scenic flight over it, or – even better – take a boat trip to it.

Interestingly, Freycinet National Park is now the second-most popular national park in Tasmania (after the Cradle Mountain–Lake St Clair National Park, p284). The number of visitors to Freycinet has been growing by about 7% annually in recent years, and most recent figures estimate that the park receives somewhere between 200,000 and 250,000 visitors annually. This has put pressure on the parks infrastructure, and at the time of research plans were underway for a new walking track car park (doubling the current car park's capacity). The Parks & Wildlife Service are also investigating options for turning the walk to the lookout into a circuit walk (that is, clearing a new track for either the ascent or descent), thereby easing congestion on the sometimes-narrow path. Conservation issues are paramount, so the route of any new track must be carefully assessed. Stay tuned.

tuna run. **Freycinet Sea Charters** (☎ 6257 0355; www.freycinetseacharters.com) can take you to the best spots; **Coles Bay Hire** (☎ 6257 0355; The Jetty) has 12ft dinghies for rent ($30 per hour, then $15 each additional hour; fishing equipment also available for hire).

SEA KAYAKING

Coles Bay is at the head of the large, sheltered Great Oyster Bay; the sea kayaking in this area is superb. **Freycinet Adventures** (☎ 6257 0500; www.adventurestasmania.com; 2 Freycinet Dr) offers a great range of guided tours year-round, including a three-hour morning explorer ($85), two-hour twilight paddle ($55) and full-day trip ($150, including lunch). Multi-day tours of many of the fine walks in the area are also offered (from October to April); three/five-day trips cost $890/1190, including all meals, camping accommodation and equipment, and transfers from Hobart. Experienced sea kayakers can hire gear for self-guided exploration.

CRUISES

Freycinet Sea Charters (☎ 6257 0355; www.freycinetseacharters.com) offers peninsula cruises where you may see dolphins, seals, sea eagles, albatrosses, penguins (in flat conditions) and/or whales (in winter). A two-hour trip down the peninsula's west coast to Schouten Island leaves at 3pm daily (weather permitting) and costs $55 per person, while a four-hour chug taking in Wineglass Bay departs at 10am and costs $88 per person.

The company also offers a pick-up and drop-off service for campers and walkers.

ABSEILING & ROCK CLIMBING

Freycinet Peninsula is regarded as one of the best abseiling and rock-climbing spots in Australia. The tempting granite peaks of The Hazards and other cliffs in the area attract both experienced climbers and novices. **Freycinet Adventures** (☎ 6257 0500; www.freycinetadventures.com; 2 Freycinet Dr) runs half/full-day abseiling trips for $95/150 per person.

FOUR-WHEEL-DRIVE TOURS, QUAD-BIKING & MOUNTAIN BIKING

Two local companies offer the chance to get off the beaten track and explore the local terrain, with the option of mountain-bike, quad-bike (a four-wheeled motorbike) and four-wheel-drive tours available.

All4Adventure (☎ 6257 0018; www.all4adventure.com.au; Coles Bay Esplanade) Has quad bike tours that vary in length: one-hour sunset trips are $60, two hours is $90, and half a day costs $160. These are suitable for beginners, but a car driving licence is essential. Four-wheel-drive tours are also available.

Freycinet Adventures (☎ 6257 0500; www.adventuretasmania.com; 2 Freycinet Dr) Rents mountain bikes ($20/30 for a half/full day) and takes guided bike tours (two hours from $55). Also offers four-wheel-drive trips: $85 for three hours, $150 for seven hours (including lunch).

SCENIC FLIGHTS

Thirty-minute scenic flights over the area are available for $82 per person (minimum two people) from **Freycinet Air** (☎ 6375 1694; www.freycinetair.com.au); longer flights are also available. The airfield is close to Friendly Beaches, signposted off the main road.

MARINE FARM

Off the road to Coles Bay is **Freycinet Marine Farm** (☎ 6257 0140; 88 Flacks Rd), which conducts guided tours of its oyster-cultivating operation, usually including a barge trip to the cages and oyster tastings. The tours must be prebooked, take place at 10am daily and cost $30 to $40 per person (depending on whether the trip stays 'on-shore' or heads off on the barge). You can also buy your fill of top-quality oysters here. The turn-off to the farm is 8km north of Coles Bay.

Sleeping

Accommodation is at a premium at Christmas, January and Easter; book well ahead for these periods. Owing to the popularity of the area, you'll also find prices higher here than in other parts of the state.

BUDGET

Small camp sites worth walking to for their scenery include **Wineglass Bay** (around 1½ hours from the walks car park), **Hazards Beach** (two to three hours), **Cooks Beach** (4½ hours) and **Bryans Beach** (5½ hours). Further north, at **Friendly Beaches**, are two basic camp sites with pit toilets. While there are no camping fees at the aforementioned sites, national park entry fees apply. Note that the park is a fuel-stove-only area, and campfires are not permitted.

Bush camping can be done for free outside the national park at the **River & Rocks site** at Moulting Lagoon; drive 8km north of

Coles Bay, turn left onto the unsealed River & Rocks Rd, then turn left at the T-junction. Note there's no permanent drinking water at any of the free camp sites. There's a water tank at Cooks Beach, but this can run dry (ask about its current status at the visitors centre). It's better to carry your own water.

Richardsons Beach at the national park entrance is the main **camping ground** (☎ 6256 7000; fax 6256 7090; freycinet@parks.tas.gov.au; unpowered site per adult/child/family $5.50/2.75/13.75, powered site $6.60/3.30/16.50). Note that site prices are additional to national park entry passes. Facilities include powered sites, toilets, and water, but there are no showers or laundry facilities. Camping here is extremely popular, and sites for the busy period from mid-December to just after Easter are determined by a ballot drawn on 1 October (applications must be made by post, fax or email before 30 September). Some dates may remain unfilled after the ballot, so if you're travelling during this period, it's still worth inquiring after vacancies (just don't expect to find any over Christmas–New Year, or Easter!). All is not lost, however; during the peak period there is limited, first-come-first-served tent space available in the designated backpacker camping area (no vehicle access, hence no campervans or caravans; no bookings taken), but this fills quickly. Outside of the ballot period, advance bookings are taken.

Iluka Holiday Centre (☎ 6257 0115, 1800 786 512; www.ilukaholidaycentre.com.au; Coles Bay Esplanade; unpowered/powered site $20/25, on-site van $55-65, cabins & units $80-130, additional adult/child $15/10) This large, busy park is well maintained and has good amenities, plus a shop, pub and bakery next door. There are decent self-contained cabin options, but it's wise to book well ahead for these. All prices are based on two people travelling. Also here is the popular **Iluka Backpackers** (dm/d $20/52), a YHA hostel that's light on for character but very clean and with a large kitchen.

Coles Bay Youth Hostel (dm $10, r $45-50) Another YHA facility, this one at scenic Parsons Cove in the national park. It comprises two basic five-person cabins, equipped with a fridge and stove but pit toilets and no running hot water. Bunks are $10 per person (minimum two people per booking) and entire cabins can be rented for $45 to $50 via a ballot system from mid-December to mid-February and at Easter (call before mid-September to register for the summer ballot, by mid-January for the Easter ballot). Bookings are essential and must be made through Tasmania's **YHA head office** (Map p70; ☎ 6234 9617; yhatas@yhatas.org.au; 1st fl, 28 Criterion St, Hobart); keys are obtained from the Iluka Holiday Centre.

MIDRANGE

Freycinet Rentals (☎ 6257 0320; www.freycinetrentals.com; 5 Garnet Ave, Coles Bay) If you're looking for holiday accommodation in Coles Bay, this is the best place to start. The managers have 14 houses/units on their books, of varying sizes (sleeping up to six). All include linen, and feature kitchen, laundry, lounge, TV and video, and barbecue. Many boast great views of the Hazards. Summer prices range from $130 to $180 for two people (extra adult costs $15 to $25, extra child $5 to $15); a minimum stay applies for long weekends and Christmas holidays. Prices are lower in the off season (from May to August) and for longer stays. Check out the website for more detailed information and pictures of each property.

See also the Budget section, for details of self-contained cabins at Iluka Holiday Centre (left). Other options include:

Coles Bay Retreat (☎ 0418 132 538; 29 Jetty Rd; www.colesbayretreat.com; house d $200, unit d $120) Well-equipped, strikingly modern three-bedroom house; also one-bedroom unit.

Freycinet on the Bay (☎ 6257 0109; 1 Garnet Ave; d $135-180, extra person $20) Large four-bedroom house (sleeps eight).

Hubie's Hideaway (☎ 0419 255 604; 33 Coles Bay Esplanade; d $110-140, extra adult/child $20/10) Family-friendly two-bedroom unit close to tavern and shops.

Sheoaks on Freycinet (☎ 6257 0049; www.sheoaks.com; 47 Oyster Bay Crt; d $140-150, extra person $20-30) This quality B&B (see below) also manages two nearby houses (sleeping four to six people).

TOP END

Sheoaks on Freycinet (☎ 6257 0049; www.sheoaks.com; 47 Oyster Bay Crt; s/d $135/165) Readers have been reporting great things about this new B&B. It's a stylish, modern house enjoying fantastic views of Great Oyster Bay. Friendly, knowledgeable hosts, well-equipped rooms and first-class breakfasts complete the package. Packed lunches (for walkers) and evening meals can be arranged. Not suitable for kids. To get here, take Hazards View Rd (about 6km north of Coles Bay), then turn left at Oyster Bay Court.

Freycinet Lodge (☎ 6257 0101; www.freycinetlodge.com.au; cabin s or d $260-395, extra person $54) Situated within the national park at the southern end of Richardsons Beach, this pricey lodge has 60 plush, private cabins with balconies set in bushland, some with self-catering facilities and/or spas and several with disabled access. Activities and guided walks are organised for guests, and there are good on-site eating choices (see right); a continental breakfast is included in the price. From Christmas until the end of March, a minimum stay of two nights applies.

Edge of the Bay (☎ 6257 0102; www.edgeofthebay.com.au; 2308 Main Rd; suite d $212-240, cottage d $180-208, q $228-256) About 4km north of Coles Bay, this resort has snazzy modern suites with private deck and secluded, family-friendly cottages that sleep five; there's a minimum two-night stay. It offers free use of bikes and dinghies for guests, and there are tennis courts and a restaurant here too.

Eating

Dining options in Coles Bay are somewhat limited; dinner bookings are advised for the restaurants.

Freycinet Bakery & Café (☎ 6257 0272; Shop 2, Coles Bay Esplanade; meals $3-10, pizzas $9-24; 8am-7.30pm;) Fuel your walking with this bakery's all-day brekky options, or choose from pies and pastries, focaccias, and cakes galore. Pizzas are served after 5pm.

The Oystercatcher (☎ 6257 0033; 6 Garnet Ave; meals $5-15; lunch & dinner Nov-Apr) Keeps itself busy serving up an assortment of takeaway meals, including fish and chips, salads and sandwiches.

Iluka Tavern (☎ 6257 0429; Coles Bay Esplanade; mains $10-24; lunch & dinner) A sociable and family-friendly place, serving good-value pub lunches and dinners daily (porterhouse and *parmigiana,* of course, but also chicken curry, ocean trout and kangaroo shanks). It's home to a popular bar and bottleshop, as well, and occasional live music in summer.

Madge Malloys (☎ 6257 0399; 7 Garnet Ave, Coles Bay; mains $24-30; dinner Tue-Sat) Madge's informal eatery has a huge wine list (lots of local drops) and a great reputation for fresh seafood.

The Edge (☎ 6257 0102; 2308 Main Rd; mains $23-27; dinner) Edge of the Bay's view-blessed restaurant serves contemporary dishes showcasing the excellent local produce – you can't go wrong choosing the chef's signature seafood pie. The restaurant is usually also open for lunch in the high season.

Richardsons Bistro (☎ 6257 0101; mains $7-20; from 10am daily, dinner Nov-Apr only) This casual option is at Freycinet Lodge; here the punters can select from a menu of café-style fare and uncomplicated dinner dishes. Nab a table on the deck for alfresco dining and glorious views.

The Bay (☎ 6257 0101; mains $19-28.50; dinner) The Bay is Freycinet Lodge's more formal offering, and bookings are essential. As you'd expect, service and views are top-notch, as are the menu selections such as grilled west-coast salmon on baba ghanoush; seafood and saffron risotto; and Flinders Island lamb. Leave room for dessert.

Getting There & Away

Bicheno Coach Service (☎ 6257 0293, 0419 570 293) runs buses between Bicheno, Coles Bay and the national park (the walking tracks car park, to be precise), connecting with east-coast Redline Coaches and TassieLink services at the Coles Bay turn-off. If you're coming from Hobart, take TassieLink; the fare to the turn-off is $26.90. From Launceston, opt for Redline Coaches; its fare to the turn-off is $31.10.

From May to November there are usually three Bicheno–Coles Bay services on weekdays and at least one on Saturday and Sunday. Extra services are scheduled on demand from December to April. Many services run only if bookings exist, so book at least the night before. The one-way fare from Bicheno to Coles Bay is $9.30 ($10.80 from Bicheno to the walking tracks car park; $7.70 from the highway turn-off to Coles Bay; $9.30 from the turn-off to the walking tracks).

The bus picks up from accommodation if requested. Buses depart Bicheno from the **Freycinet Bakery & Café** (cnr Burgess and Morrison Sts) and in Coles Bay from **Coles Bay Trading store** (1 Garnet Ave).

Getting Around

It's more than 5km from the town to the national park walking tracks car park. **Bicheno**

Coach Service (☎ 6257 0293, 0419 570 293) does the trip three times each weekday and once on Saturday and Sunday; bookings are essential. The one-way/return cost from Coles Bay township to the car park is $4.50/8. Park entry fees apply.

Cycling is also a good way to get around the area. You can hire a bike from **Coles Bay Trading** (☎ 6257 0109; 1 Garnet Ave) for $11/17 per half/full day, or choose a mountain bike from **Freycinet Adventures** (☎ 6257 0500; 2 Freycinet Dr) for $20/30 per half/full day.

BICHENO

☎ 03 / pop 700

Bicheno has all the attributes of a successful holiday resort, including soporific water views, a mild climate and abundant sunshine. Fishing is the community's mainstay and the local fleet shelters in a tiny, picturesque harbour called The Gulch. With reasonable prices for food and accommodation, plus good sandy beaches, it's a good place to stay for a few days, but you'd be mad to turn up over the Christmas–New Year period without a reservation.

History

The town began as a sealers' port and was called Waubs Bay Harbour after an Aboriginal woman, Waubadebar, who was enslaved by sealers in the early 19th century. A strong swimmer, she became famous for rescuing two sealers when their boat

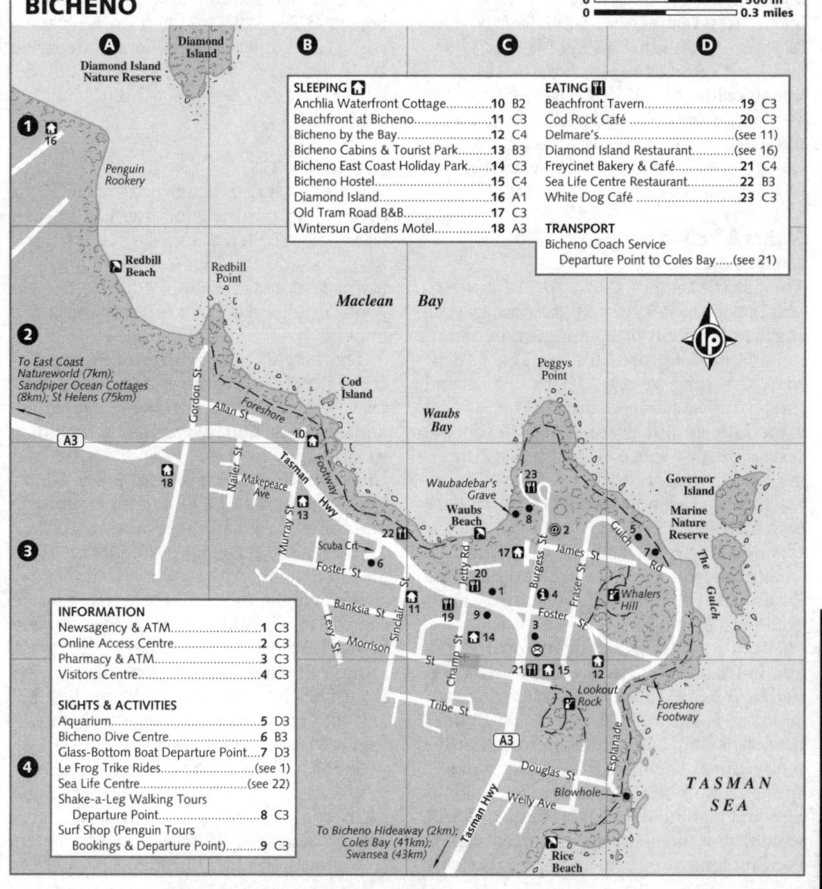

was wrecked 1km offshore. Years after her death, the town honoured her by constructing a grave off the main beach. Bicheno was renamed after James Ebenezer Bicheno, colonial secretary of Van Diemen's Land in the 1840s.

In 1854 the town became a coal-mining port, but a year later most of the miners left and joined the Victorian gold rush. The town shrank drastically, which is why so few historic buildings remain. Around the 1940s, the town's fortunes changed as it started developing into the holiday destination it is today.

Information

ATMs There are multicard ATMs outside the pharmacy on Burgess St (close to the post office), and inside the newsagency on the town's main strip.

Online Access Centre (☎ 6375 1892; The Oval, Burgess St; 9am-2pm Mon & Wed, 9am-5pm Tue, Thu & Fri, 1-6pm Sat) Behind the public loos at the oval.

Visitors centre (☎ 6375 1500; 69 Burgess St; 10am-4pm Mon-Fri, 1-4pm Sat & Sun) The volunteer staff at this new centre can help with information on what to do in the area. At the time of research, opening hours in the high season were expected to be increased.

Sights & Activities

WILDLIFE CENTRES

The **Sea Life Centre** (☎ 6375 1121; 1 Tasman Hwy; adult/child/family $6.50/4/20; 9am-5pm) has a small, rather dimly lit aquarium and a scramble around a restored trading ketch (two-masted sailing vessel). There are several interesting species on display, but it's all a bit forlorn and overpriced. The on-site restaurant, also specialising in sea creatures, is a better deal (see p176).

There's a second **aquarium** (☎ 0418 300 620; Gulch Rd; adult/child $3/2; 10am-4pm) in town – this one is cheaper and can be found in a small waterside shed. At both you can see local marine life including seahorses, giant crabs and crayfish.

Seven kilometres north of town is the family-friendly, 52-hectare **East Coast Natureworld** (☎ 6375 1311; www.natureworld.com.au; adult/child/family $12.90/6.60/34.80; 9am-5pm), under new ownership and with plans for extensive renovations. There are free-roaming native species; a walk-through aviary; scenic lookout; and a population of Tasmanian devils, wombats, wallabies, roos and tiger snakes. Feeding times are 10am and 4pm; also a big hit with kids are the battery-operated self-drive cars for hire ($8.80 per hour). There are tea rooms serving excellent clotted-cream Devonshire teas, and novel evening meals (see p176).

WALKS

The 3km **Foreshore Footway** extends from Redbill Point to the Blowhole; the best stretch is from the Sea Life Centre east past **Peggys Point**, through The Gulch and along to the **Blowhole**, where there's a large, sea-rocked granite boulder. You return along footpaths with panoramic views over town. In whaling days, passing whales were spotted from **Whalers Hill**.

If you're interested in learning about the history, flora and fauna of the area, you can join a guided walking tour run by **Shake-a-Leg** (☎ 6375 1478, 0425 745 360). Two-hour tours cost $12.50/5 per adult/child and depart at 10am and 1pm from close to Waubadebar's Grave (off Burgess St); bookings are essential.

WATER SPORTS

Waubs Beach and Rice Beach are fairly safe ocean beaches for swimming. For warmer water, the sheltered and shallow Denison River, beside the highway 8km north of town, is popular. Redbill Point often has good surfing breaks and water skiing is also popular.

The helpful new owners of **Bicheno Dive Centre** (☎ 6375 1138; www.bichenodive.com.au; 2 Scuba Court; 9am-5pm) hire out diving equipment and organise underwater trips, including to dive sites in the Governor Island Marine Reserve, just offshore from The Gulch. One-day charters including all equipment and one/two boat dives cost $105/145. There is also budget accommodation available to divers.

If you prefer to stay above water, you can see the local sealife on a 45-minute **glass-bottom boat tour** (☎ 6375 1294; $15/free adult/child) around the local marine park. Tours leave from The Gulch at 10am and 2pm, weather and minimum numbers permitting (bookings advised).

Go Fish (☎ 0419 750 757), as the name suggests, can help you get out on the water and catch something fishy. Tailor-made tours can be arranged, or take a two-hour trip (equipment provided) from $75 per person.

Tours

There's a **fairy penguin rookery** (☎ 6375 1333; adult/child $18/9) at the northern end of Redbill Beach. The best way to learn about the birds and avoid overly disturbing them is to take the one-hour tour that leaves nightly at dusk from the surf shop on the main road in the centre of town; bookings are essential. Penguin numbers vary with the season – September to November see the highest numbers. Don't use torches or flash photography around the penguins.

For something a little different, **Le Frog Trike Rides** (☎ 6375 1777) offers passenger rides for all ages on a three-wheeled trike (a cross between a motorbike and convertible car) in and around town (with a French driver – hence the name). Prices start at $12 for a 10-minute 'sampler' cruise around Bicheno, then move upwards in duration and cost. Inquiries can be made at the souvenir shop in the centre of town.

Sleeping

Bicheno has a good range of affordable options, but lags behind Swansea in upmarket, stylish B&Bs and self-contained cottages.

BUDGET

Bicheno Hostel (☎ 6375 1651; www.users.bigpond.com/bichenobackpackers; 11 Morrison St; dm $19-21, d $53-60; 💻) With its young, enthusiastic owners, good facilities and friendly, laid-back atmosphere, this hostel is the best choice for budget accommodation. One lodge houses dorms (with well-designed bunks) and the other has double rooms – try for the front room with large balcony and sea views.

Bicheno East Coast Holiday Park (☎ 6375 1999; bichenoecholidaypark@bigpond.com; 4 Champ St; unpowered/powered site $18/18, on-site van $35-45, cabins & units $55-105) This neat, well-maintained park has a central location, friendly managers, all the requisite amenities and a range of old and new cabins for rent.

MIDRANGE & TOP END

Cabins

Bicheno Cabins & Tourist Park (☎ 6375 1117, 1800 789 075; www.bichenocabins.com; 30 Tasman Hwy; d $70-139, extra person $9-18) This place eschews the greenery of a standard 'park' for concrete and gravel, but its range of cabins are new and mod-con-filled, and can sleep up to six. Note that there are no camping sites here.

Guesthouses & B&Bs

Old Tram Road B&B (☎ 6375 1298; ronmer@intas.net; 3 Old Tram Rd; d $135-145) The town's best B&B, with its convivial hosts offering two large, comfy rooms. Only 100m from a beach accessed via a private track from the lovely back garden. The B&B's gourmet cooked breakfasts will get you started.

Motels

Beachfront at Bicheno (☎ 6375 1111; beachfront_bicheno@bigpond.com; Tasman Hwy; d $105-125; ♿) Comfortable but generic motel units are available at this large, central complex opposite the beach. There are good on-site facilities, including a swimming pool, barbecue areas, a playground, a pub and a bistro.

Wintersun Gardens Motel (☎ 6375 1225; wintersun.motel@tassie.net.au; 35 Gordon St; d $88-106; ♿) More motel units are on offer here, but with a more personal touch and a more appealing rose-filled setting, with pool and barbecue area. The spic-and-span units are modest but well equipped – opt for the newer Room 11 if it's available.

Self-Contained Apartments & Cottages

Sandpiper Ocean Cottages (☎ 6375 1122; www.sandpiper.au.com; Tasman Hwy; d $133-143, extra person $33) A top choice for comfort and seclusion. These three cottages are 8km north of Bicheno on Denison Beach. Each modern two-bedroom cottage sleeps five and features full kitchen and laundry, plus large balconies from which to enjoy the peaceful surrounds.

Diamond Island (☎ 6375 1161; www.diamondisland.com.au; 69 Tasman Hwy; d $135-165, extra person $20; ♿) About 2km north of Bicheno is this beachside complex of well-appointed units, all enjoying great coastal views. The units are newly renovated with stylish furnishings and extras such as bread-makers and cable TV. There's the added bonus of an excellent restaurant on the premises, too (see p176).

Bicheno Hideaway (☎ 6375 1312; www.bichenohideaway.com; 179 Harveys Farm Rd; s/d $75/120) This impressive option is 3km south of town. It's in a tranquil bushland setting, home to a handful of striking arc-shaped units (with quirky décor) enjoying ocean views.

Bicheno by the Bay (☎ 6375 1171; www.bichenobythebay.com.au; cnr Foster & Fraser Sts; 1-bedroom unit

$110-150, 2-bedroom $140-180;) New owners are breathing new life into this resort, home to several one- to four-bedroom units spread out in private bushland. Also planted in the undergrowth are a tennis court, pool, small lake and restaurant. The larger units sleep up to eight people; the western-most units with ocean views are recommended.

Anchlia Waterfront Cottage (6375 1225; wintersun.motel@tassie.net.au; 2 Murray St; d $120-180, extra person $20) The owners of the Wintersun Gardens Motel (see above) also offer two self-contained waterfront options set in lovely gardens. Cod Rock Terrace is a two-storey, two-bedroom home; Penguin Nook is a spacious one-bedroom unit.

Eating

If you're visiting outside the peak summer season (December to Easter), your evening dining options are restricted, with many places closing or considerably reducing their opening hours. Ask at your accommodation for recommendations.

Freycinet Bakery & Café (6375 1972; cnr Burgess & Morrison Sts; meals $3-10, pizzas $9-19; 8am-5pm Sun-Thu, 8am-8pm Fri & Sat) The sister operation of the bakery in Coles Bay (p172), this place has a similarly tasty, carb-loaded menu of cooked breakfasts, pies, pastries and focaccias. Pizzas are served after 5pm Friday and Saturday.

Cod Rock Café (6375 1340; 45 Foster St; meals $5-10; 9am-8.30pm) Pumps out lots of local seafood in various takeaway guises, with fish and chips cooked to order, and fresh crayfish in season. Also burgers, souvlaki and pies for those suffering seafood-overdose.

Sea Life Centre Restaurant (6375 1121; 1 Tasman Hwy; lunch $12-17, dinner mains $19-25; lunch & dinner) This casual restaurant offers a variety of sea morsels (choose your crayfish natural, char-grilled, mornay or thermidor) and other meaty options, plus fine bay views. Lunches are lighter on both stomach and wallet. Meals are served less frequently over winter.

Beachfront at Bicheno (6375 1111; Tasman Hwy) This crowd-pleasing complex has two eateries: **Delmare's** (mains $12-25; dinner Oct-Apr), offering Mediterranean fare such as pizza, pasta, seafood and salads; and the laid-back **Beachfront Tavern** (mains $14-22; lunch & dinner), which serves standard pub fare – lots of grilled meats, plus fish of the day, schnitzels and so on.

Diamond Island Restaurant (6375 1161; 69 Tasman Hwy; mains $22-28; dinner) It's well worth a trip to this spruced-up resort, now home to an impressive restaurant serving up the best of Tassie produce, including plenty of (you guessed it!) fresh seafood: local oysters or abalone, seafood chowder or risotto, herb-crusted trevalla (blue eye) etc. Bookings advised.

East Coast Natureworld (6375 1311; Tasman Hwy; dinner nightly except Mon & Fri) Bicheno's favourite local chef has moved to an unlikely location – the animal park 8km north of town! Here he's working with the park's owners to create a themed 'bush tucker banquet and eco-tour' experience ($38) each Sunday, Tuesday and Thursday (Saturday is seafood night, and Wednesday is roast night). At the time of research the final planning was underway. The bush tucker banquet is expected to include a three-course meal (mains including game pie, sausages, fish, venison and wallaby), followed by a tour of the park and then singing around a campfire. It's best to call and confirm further details with the park, and bookings will be essential. If successful there will be a reduced schedule over winter.

THE AUTHOR'S CHOICE

White Dog Café (6375 1266; Burgess St; light meals $5-9.50; 7.30am-4pm) At the rear of the Silver Sands Resort is this light-filled, laid-back place serving classic café fare at extremely reasonable prices. The deck here boasts fabulous water views and is the perfect spot for breakfast (served all day) in the sun, or you can interrupt your beach-bumming or exploration for a serve of great coffee and cake.

Getting There & Away

Redline Coaches (1300 360 000; www.tasredline.com.au) and **TassieLink** (1300 300 520; www.tassielink.com.au) serve the town. TassieLink's 2½- to three-hour trip from Launceston/Hobart costs $26/27.70. The Redline fare from Launceston is $31.70.

Bicheno Coach Service (6257 0293, 0419 570 293) runs between Bicheno to Coles Bay, departing from the Freycinet Bakery & Café (cnr Burgess and Morrison Sts). The fare is $9.30/17.50 one way/return to Coles Bay, and $10.80/20 to the national park walking tracks car park.

DOUGLAS-APSLEY NATIONAL PARK

This is a large area of undisturbed dry eucalypt forest, typical of much of the original east-coast land cover. It was declared a national park in 1989 after public concern was expressed over local wood chipping and the large-scale clearing of old-growth forests. The park's significant features include rocky peaks, river gorges, beautiful waterfalls and abundant bird and animal life.

Access to the park is by gravel roads. To reach the southern end, turn west off the highway 4km north of Bicheno and follow the signposted road for 7km to the car park. A basic camping ground with a pit toilet is provided and you can throw yourself into the **Apsley Waterhole** for refreshment. To access the northern end, at **Thompsons Marshes**, turn west off the highway 24km north of Bicheno onto the rough 'E' Rd. This is a private road, so obey any signs as you follow it to the car park and boom gate at the park border (four-wheel drive recommended for the final section). You won't find suitable places to camp near this car park.

National park entry fees apply. Open fires are not permitted here from October to April, when cooking is only allowed on fuel stoves.

Bushwalking

At the Apsley Waterhole is a 10-minute, wheelchair-standard track leading towards a lookout with a great view over the river. A three- to four-hour return walk leads to **Apsley Gorge**.

At the park's northern end is the walk to **Heritage and Leeaberra Falls**, which takes five to seven hours return. There's camping near the falls.

For experienced walkers, the major walk in the park is along the **Leeaberra Track**, which takes three days one-way, to the Apsley Waterhole. The walk should be done from north to south to prevent the spread of a plant disease present in the south.

SCAMANDER & BEAUMARIS

☎ 03 / pop 990 (combined)

The low-key townships of Scamander and Beaumaris stretch along white-sand beaches in a coastal reserve. You can take long walks along the beach, fish for bream from the old bridge over the Scamander River, or try catching trout further upstream.

The wide ocean beaches are great for swimming, while water-skiers head for the lagoons north of Beaumaris. There are good surfing spots as far south as Four Mile Creek; local surfers congregate just north of there.

For a fine view of the area, a 5km drive along gravel forestry roads takes you to the start of a steep five-minute walk to **Skyline Tier Scenic Lookout**; take Skyline Rd, signposted by the Surfside Motor Inn in Beaumaris.

Sleeping & Eating

Kookaburra Caravan Park (☎ 6372 5121; Scamander Ave; unpowered/powered sites $14/16, on-site vans $40,

DETOUR

The road following the coast from Chain of Lagoons to Falmouth, then Scamander, passes through some excellent coastal scenery and avoids the slow climb over two passes to St Marys. Much of the coastline is rocky and the best place to stop along it is at **Ironhouse Point** and **Four Mile Creek**, where the beaches begin.

This area feels off the beaten path, and if you like the unhurried atmosphere, there are a couple of options for accommodation here. Family-focused **White Sands Resort** (☎ 6372 2228; www.white-sands.com.au; 21554 Tasman Hwy, Four Mile Creek; d $80-120;) has a number of two- and three-bedroom cabins sprawled around tennis courts, a pool, a nine-hole golf course and a restaurant. It's worth paying extra for the renovated cabins – the old ones are quite dated.

Two kilometres north of White Sands is the signposted turn-off to **Ivory Fields** (☎ 6372 2759; www.ivoryfieldsretreat.com.au; 56 Davis Gully Rd, Four Mile Creek; r $185-235), a herb farm and spa retreat in an undeniably relaxing setting. Unwind in the outdoor spa or sauna, be pampered with a massage or treatment, and then tuck in to a gourmet evening meal (dinner $55 per person).

cabins $60) Shady hillside sites and helpful managers are the selling points of this simple park close to the beach in Scamander.

Carmens Inn (☎ 6372 5160; 4 Pringle St; s/d from $55/66, extra adult/child $22/11) Carmens in Scamander has good-value older-style self-contained units a short roll from the sand.

Pelican Sands (☎ 6372 5231; www.pelicansandsscamander.com.au; 157 Scamander Ave; dm $21, unit d/f $105/150;) Immediately north of the bridge in Scamander, this friendly motel offers simple, well-equipped motel units with cooking facilities; hostel-style rooms with good bunks; and a pool and playground. It's absolutely beachfront, and there are kayaks for rent too.

Surfside Motor Inn (☎ 6372 5177; Tasman Hwy; s/d $68/90) This welcoming, well-managed motel on the northern outskirts of Beaumaris offers clean and comfy motel rooms with cooked breakfast. The **restaurant** (mains $16-24; lunch & dinner) here has ultra-fresh seafood and other good meals. The bar is a social place for a drink too.

Chancellor Inn Scamander Beach (☎ 6372 5255; www.ghihotels.com; Tasman Hwy; d $110;) You can't miss this large hotel, which does little for the aesthetics of the Scamander foreshore. The rooms are decent and facilities (including pool and playground) good, but better-value accommodation can be found elsewhere in town. Meals are available at the on-site **Swells Restaurant** (mains $16-23; lunch & dinner).

Seafarers Rest Guest House (☎ 6372 5568; www.seafarers-rest.com.au; 16 Belair Cres; d $185-200) If the other options in the area look a tad too pedestrian and you're after something upmarket, consider staying at this lovely B&B in Beaumaris (close to the Surfside Motor Inn). The higher rate snares a spa suite; all guests enjoy a full cooked breakfast.

Eureka Farm (☎ 6372 5500; Upper Scamander Rd; light meals $5-11; 8am-5pm Oct-Jun) About 2km south of Scamander is a sign for this fruit-lover's paradise, well worth a detour for succulent fresh fruit, light lunches and wonderful desserts like summer pudding, choc-raspberry pavlova and some of the fruitiest ice cream you'll ever taste.

ST MARYS

☎ 03 / pop 590

St Marys is a serene little town near the Mt Nicholas range, 10km inland of the Tasman Sea. A visit here entails peaceful country-side wanderings that take in waterfalls, state forest and hilly heights.

The rocky hills around town have good views and are worth climbing. The top of **South Sister** (832m), towering over German Town Rd, 6km north of town, is a 10-minute walk from the car park. Just east of town, turn south down Irish Town Rd to get to **St Patricks Head** (683m), where you'll be confronted by a long, steep 90-minute climb (one-way) complete with some cables and a ladder; the top has some of the best views around.

Call into **e.ScApe Tasmanian Wilderness Café & Gallery** (☎ 6372 2444; Main Rd) for town information.

Sleeping & Eating

St Marys Hotel (☎ 6372 2181; Main Rd; s/d $30/45) This classic country pub has a friendly atmosphere and offers low-key accommodation. Inexpensive counter meals ($10 to $18) are also available.

Addlestone House (☎ 6372 2783; addlestone@bigpond.com; 19 Gray Rd; s/d $75/$95) On the road to Bicheno, Addlestone House has two charming en-suite rooms, and nourishes guests with a full English breakfast. The immaculate rooms are well-equipped and good value for the price.

THE AUTHOR'S CHOICE

St Marys Seaview Farm (☎ 6372 2341; www.seaviewfarm.com.au; German Town Rd; dm without/with linen $20/25, units $60) Don't book just one night here – this is the kind of place you intend to visit for a night but end up staying in for a week. Seaview Farm is in a peaceful, remote setting, surrounded by state forest and enjoying blissful views of the coastline and mountains. The friendly owners are committed to providing quality accommodation, and indeed the rooms are far nicer than their bargain prices would indicate! The cosy backpackers cottage has a kitchen and lounge for all guests, and there are also great-value en-suite units. You'll find Seaview Farm at the end of a dirt track 8km from St Marys – take Franks St opposite St Marys Hotel, which becomes German Town Rd. Bring your own supplies from town; note that the farm doesn't allow kids under 12.

e.ScApe Tasmanian Wilderness Café & Gallery (☎ 6372 2444; Main Rd; dinner mains $14.50-23.50; ⌚ breakfast, lunch & dinner) This café opens from 7.30am and is kicking goals with its all-day breakfast, kids' meals, good daytime café nosh and real coffee. The appealing dinner menu features the likes of fettucine *marinara*, Thai-style green curry and scotch fillet steak.

Mt Elephant Pancake Barn (☎ 6372 2263; Mt Elephant Pass; savoury pancakes $12-17, sweet pancakes $8-10; ⌚ 8am-6pm) Crepe-fanciers have been known to go troppo over this place, 9km south of town off the highway to Bicheno. In the scenic mountain location, take your pick from a range of very tasty but overpriced pancakes. No credit cards.

Getting There & Away

By bus, St Marys is best accessed from Launceston, St Helens or Bicheno. **Redline Coaches** (☎ 1300 360 000; www.tasredline.com.au) runs a daily service (except Saturday) between Launceston and St Helens that calls at St Marys (buses from Hobart connect with this service at Conara on the Midlands Hwy). The fare for the 1¾-hour journey from Launceston is $20.20; from St Helens it costs $5.10 and takes 30 to 40 minutes.

TassieLink (☎ 1300 300 520; www.tassielink.com.au) has a twice-weekly Launceston–Bicheno service that runs via St Marys. From Launceston the fare is $18.70; from Bicheno (40 minutes away) it costs $8.30.

Broadby's (☎ 6376 3488) runs a weekday postal run that takes passengers between St Helens and St Marys, departing the Mobil service station in St Helens around 7.30am, and leaving St Marys post office around 8.45am; the fare is $5 each way.

WARNING

Cyclists riding Elephant Pass must be extremely careful. The road is steep, narrow and winding, and it's difficult for vehicles (particularly trucks) to negotiate their way around bicycles.

FINGAL

☎ 03 / pop 400

Sleepy, landlocked Fingal is 21km west of St Marys. Its main claim to fame is the annual Fingal Valley Festival, held in early March, which includes World Roof Bolting and World Coal Shovelling Championships.

The surrounding valley contains several abandoned mining-era towns. Mangana, Rossarden and Storys Creek display piles of tailings, mine machinery and deserted cottages. If you prefer something verdant, visit **Evercreech Forest Reserve**, 34km north of Fingal, near Mathinna. A 20-minute circuit walk through blackwood and myrtle takes you to the White Knights, a group of the world's tallest white gums *(Eucalyptus viminalis)*; the loftiest branches reach 91m.

Fingal Hotel (☎ 6374 2121; 4 Talbot St; s/d $30/45) has good, no-frills rooms (doubles with en suite) and serves meals daily. **Glenesk** (☎ 6374 2195; www.gleneskb-andb.com.au; 9 Talbot St; d $85, extra person $15), located behind the post office on the main road, is a lovely old-fashioned cottage, self-contained with two bedrooms and lots of personal touches.

The Northeast

Tasmania's northeast is a beautifully secluded, unspoilt part of the state. Many visitors overlook the area in favour of the east coast, but a leisurely week or so meandering through this region brings its own rewards. This is the sunniest corner of the state, and its landscapes include beaches, waterfalls, a wildlife-rich national park, and miles of scenic coastline (with great fishing opportunities and outstanding seafood on offer). The area is blessed with colours that look awesome in holiday snaps – from the dazzling blue water and white-sand beaches of Binalong Bay and the Bay of Fires, to the splendid purple lavender outside Scottsdale, with lush-green tones at places like St Columba Falls and the Weldborough Pass.

The area is bypassed by the main route from Launceston to the east coast but if you take the Tasman Hwy (A3) or the B81 from Launceston to Scottsdale, you can head in several directions: north to Bridport, with fine vineyards not far west and a great new golf course to the east; east to the old mining village of Derby, then northeast to Mt William National Park, Ansons Bay and the Bay of Fires; or southeast from Derby to the waterfalls around Ringarooma and Pyengana, with the pretty seaside town of St Helens just beyond.

HIGHLIGHTS

- Camping on the serene **Bay of Fires** (p187) and taking in the remote arcs of white sand and turquoise water
- A lazy day on the beach at **Binalong Bay** (p184), followed by a meal of fresh local seafood in **St Helens** (p186)
- Detouring to take in the diverse treats of **Pyengana** (p184) from cheddar cheese to a beer-drinking pig and picturesque waterfalls
- Engaging in some rafting rivalry in the **Derby River Derby** (p189)
- Dreaming of your own personal pilot to whisk you away while lingering over coffee and cake at Bridport's **Flying Teapot café** (p192)
- Being mesmerised by a sea of purple at the **lavender farm** (p190) near Nabowla during the summer flowering season
- Driving the scenic, snaking curves of the A3 highway from **St Helens** (p182) to **Scottsdale** (p190)
- Getting up close and personal with the abundant roos at **Mt William National Park** (p188)

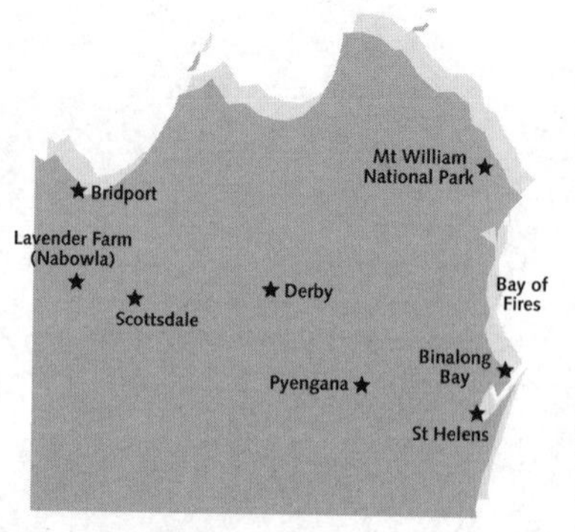

- www.netasmania.com.au

Getting There & Around

BICYCLE

The Tasman Hwy (the A3) is a winding, narrow road that crosses two major passes as it heads west through Weldborough and Scottsdale – it demands vigilance from cyclists. An alternative is to follow the secondary roads around the coast, where there's little traffic and fewer hills to climb. Pack a tent to take advantage of the camping areas at Mt William National Park and at Tomahawk en route from St Helens to Bridport; there's also accommodation at Gladstone.

BUS

The main bus company servicing Tasmania's northeast is **Redline Coaches** (☎ 6336 1446, 1300 360 000; www.tasredline.com.au), which runs daily, except Saturday, from Launceston to Conara Junction, then through Fingal ($17, 1½ hours) and St Marys ($20, 1¾ hours) to St Helens ($25, 2½ hours) – Redline services from Hobart connect with this service in Conara. Redline also runs coaches daily, except Saturday, from Launceston to Scottsdale ($14, 1¼ hours), Derby ($19, 2½ hours) and then Winnaleah ($22, 2¾ hours), where you can catch the Broadby's (Suncoast) bus to St Helens.

Broadby's (☎ 6376 3488), also operating as Suncoast, makes a weekday postal run (that takes passengers) between St Helens and St Marys, departing from the Mobil service station in St Helens around 7.30am, and

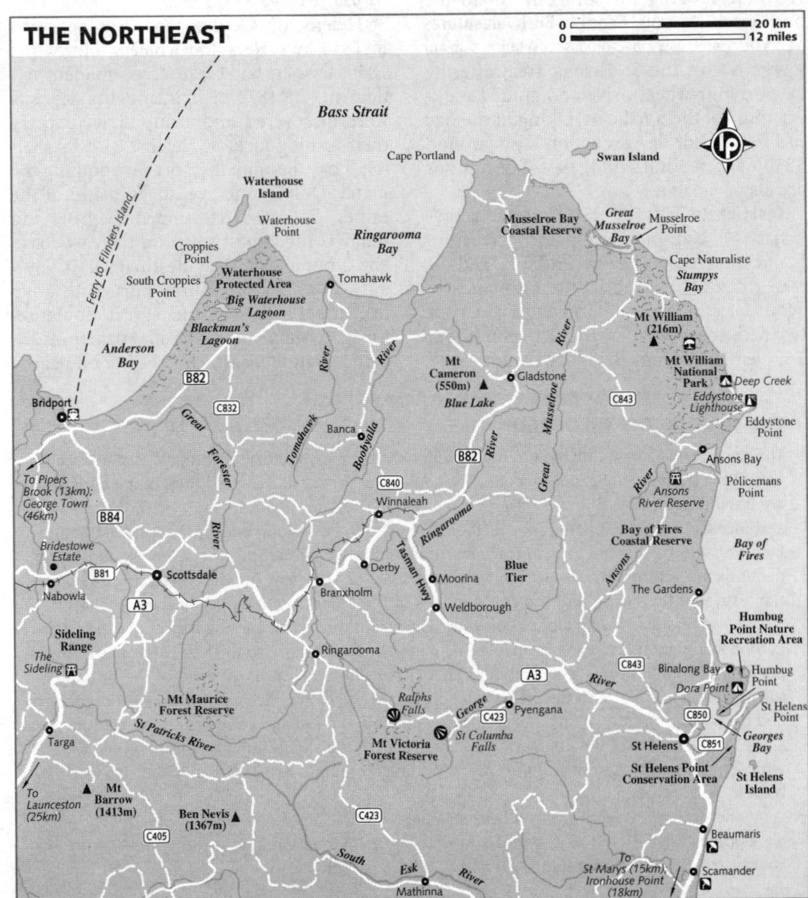

leaving St Marys post office around 8.45am; the fare is $5 each way. Broadby's also runs a bus from St Helens to Derby, on to Winnaleah, then direct to St Helens; this run connects with Redline's northeast service at Winnaleah. This bus departs St Helens post office weekdays at 10.15am, leaves Derby at 12.15pm and Winnaleah around 12.45pm; the fare is $7 one-way to/from either Derby or Winnaleah.

TassieLink (☎ 6271 7320, 1300 300 520; www.tassielink.com.au) has a service from Hobart to St Helens via the east coast on Friday and Sunday; the trip takes four hours and the fare is $40 one-way.

TOURS

If you're looking for someone to do the hard work for you, **Beach to Bush Adventures** (☎ 6372 5468; www.beachtobushadventures.com.au) works out of the St Helens area, offering catered four-wheel-drive and guided walking tours of the northeast, taking in the Bay of Fires. A full-day excursion costs around $210/66 per adult/child; half-day options are also available.

Cool Climate Tours (☎ 6354 6333; www.coolclimatetours.com.au) can pick up passengers from Launceston, Scottsdale or Bridport, and offers a day-trip taking in the farmlands of Scottsdale, the lavender farm and a winery or two in the nearby Pipers Brook region ($124/145 leaving from Bridport/Launceston). Other trips can focus on golf, wineries or gardens of the region, and there are also good two-day itineraries.

Pepper Bush Adventures (☎ 6352 2263; www.pepperbush.com.au) knowledgeably roams the topography of the northeast in four-wheel drives looking for natural splendour and local fauna, some of which (like kangaroo) is presented on a plate at mealtime. This is not roughing it – day tours cost in the vicinity of $260/130 per adult/child; prices depend on itinerary, size of group and catering options. There are also multi-day tours available. Pick-ups can be made in Launceston or elsewhere in the region.

ST HELENS

☎ 03 / pop 2000

St Helens, on Georges Bay, was occupied in 1830 by sealers and whalers, but by the 1850s farmers had created a permanent settlement. In 1874 rich inland tin deposits were discovered and many arrived to try their mining luck; St Helens, with its sheltered bay, became the port for shipping the metal. Despite the eventual closure of the mines, St Helens continued to grow and today is the largest town on the east coast, and a popular holiday destination. It's also Tasmania's largest fishing port, with a big fleet afloat in the bay and a great reputation for its oysters and crayfish. Attractions include boating, fishing and lazing on nearby

THE TRAIL OF THE TIN DRAGON

The northeast is a beautiful region but is overlooked by many visitors to Tasmania as they race to tick off the state's various tourist 'icons'. The council authorities and communities of the northeast are hoping to change all that in the next few years. They aim to attract more traffic to the area and increase tourist expenditure, and therefore drive the development of better infrastructure, by introducing a themed touring trail along the A3 highway. The 'Trail of the Tin Dragon' is the name of the venture, which will run from Scottsdale to St Helens (or vice versa) and celebrate the history of tin mining and the contributions of the Chinese community to the northeast.

Chinese tin-miners were among the early pioneers of the region and the largest group of non-European immigrants to early Tasmania. The miners started arriving in the late 1870s, and at their peak numbered approximately a thousand. The remaining physical evidence of the tin-mining towns, camps and shops in the area will be preserved and highlighted, while new visitors centres and displays, promotional material, interpretive panels and signage are proposed to capture the stories and histories of the Chinese here – there is even the suggestion of relocating the Chinese temple 'joss house', currently in the Queen Victoria Museum & Art Gallery in Launceston (p195), back to Weldborough.

At the time of research this trail was still largely in the planning stages – look out for more developments when you visit, and if you want more information, ask at the visitors centres in Launceston (p194), Scottsdale (p190) and St Helens (p184).

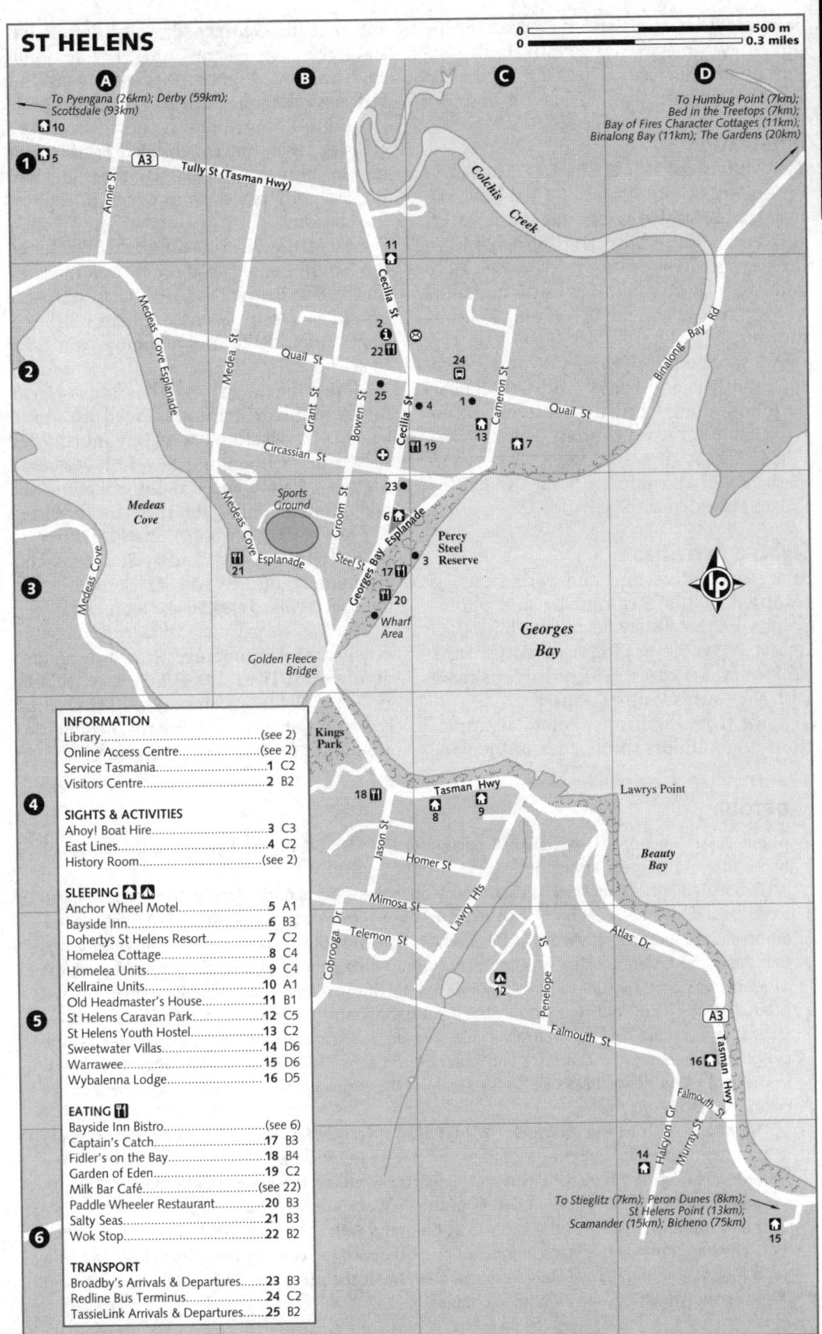

INFORMATION	
Library	(see 2)
Online Access Centre	(see 2)
Service Tasmania	1 C2
Visitors Centre	2 B2
SIGHTS & ACTIVITIES	
Ahoy! Boat Hire	3 C3
East Lines	4 C2
History Room	(see 2)
SLEEPING	
Anchor Wheel Motel	5 A1
Bayside Inn	6 B3
Dohertys St Helens Resort	7 C2
Homelea Cottage	8 C4
Homelea Units	9 C4
Kellraine Units	10 A1
Old Headmaster's House	11 B1
St Helens Caravan Park	12 C5
St Helens Youth Hostel	13 C2
Sweetwater Villas	14 D6
Warrawee	15 D6
Wybalenna Lodge	16 D5
EATING	
Bayside Inn Bistro	(see 6)
Captain's Catch	17 B3
Fidler's on the Bay	18 B4
Garden of Eden	19 C2
Milk Bar Café	(see 22)
Paddle Wheeler Restaurant	20 B3
Salty Seas	21 B3
Wok Stop	22 B2
TRANSPORT	
Broadby's Arrivals & Departures	23 B3
Redline Bus Terminus	24 C2
TassieLink Arrivals & Departures	25 B2

beaches. St Helens is also the venue for the three-day Suncoast Jazz Festival, an outstanding music festival held during the last weekend in June.

Information

The **visitors centre** (☎ 6376 1744; 61 Cecilia St; 9am-5pm Mon-Fri, 9am-noon Sat year-round, plus 10am-2pm Sun Sep-Apr) is on the main street, adjacent to the library and also home to the town's history room (see below). Here you can pick up a number of useful handouts on fishing, scenic drives and walks in the area.

All services, including the post office, supermarkets and banks (with ATMs) can be found along Cecilia St. Internet access is available at the **Online Access Centre** (☎ 6376 1116; 61 Cecilia St; 9am-5pm Mon-Fri, 10am-noon Sat & Sun) as well as inside the library and at the Garden of Eden café (see p187).

Sights & Activities

St Helens' interesting and varied past is recorded in the memorabilia and photographs in the **History Room** (☎ 6376 1744; 61 Cecilia St; 9am-5pm Mon-Fri, 9am-noon Sat year-round, plus 10am-2pm Sun Sep-Apr), which shares its space with the town's visitors centre.

Aside from the history room, all attractions are outdoors. Both sides of the wide entrance to Georges Bay are designated state recreation areas and provide some easy walking. A good track circles around **St Helens Point** (one hour return; take St Helens Point Rd out). On the north side, **Skeleton Bay** (10km north) and **Dora Point** (11km north), both accessed from Binalong Bay Rd, are good places from which to explore the coastline.

Ask at the visitors centre for details of the handful of walks and old tin mine sites on the **Blue Tier** plateau, northwest of town. For $2 you can purchase a map outlining four walks in the Tier, ranging from two to six hours.

While the town's beaches aren't great for swimming, there are excellent scenic beaches at **Binalong Bay** (11km north, accessed along Binalong Bay Rd), **Jeanneret Beach** and **Sloop Rock** (about 15km north; take Binalong Bay Rd then the turn-off to The Gardens for both), **Stieglitz** (7km east on St Helens Point), and at St Helens and Humbug Points. Also on St Helens Point are the spectacular **Peron Dunes** (8km east).

The flat, clear waters of Georges Bay are excellent for canoeing, windsurfing and diving. **East Lines** (☎ 6376 1720; 28 Cecilia St; 9am-5pm) hires equipment (snorkelling gear and wetsuits, body boards, fishing rods etc), and also has bikes for rent ($5/15/25

DETOUR

About 26km west of St Helens you'll encounter the turn-off to tiny **Pyengana** (pie-en-gana), home to a trio of great attractions.

The settlement of Pyengana sits reclusively up in the hills, its name derived from an Aboriginal word describing the meeting of two rivers in the valley in which it's situated. A century ago, European pioneers recognised that this beautiful green spot was ideal dairy country. Exporting milk from the isolated valley was impractical, but when converted into cheese and butter the produce was able to survive the slow journey to the markets. Today, cheddar cheese is still produced using the old methods at the **Pyengana Dairy Company** (☎ 6373 6157; St Columba Falls Rd; 9am-5pm Sep-May, 10am-4pm Jun-Aug), open daily for tastings and sales. Besides mature clothbound cheese, you can taste and purchase different flavoured cheddars, then take a seat in the **Holy Cow! Café** (meals $7-15) for some of the best cheese on toast, milkshakes and ice cream you're likely to taste.

The nearby **Pub in the Paddock** (☎ 6373 6121; St Columba Falls Rd; s/d $40/50) has been plying its trade as a hotel for well over a century and has good rooms with clean, shared facilities. The counter meals served here for lunch and dinner daily are on the larger side of big, and there's the added attraction of Priscilla, Princess of the Paddock – a beer-drinking pig.

The best-known feature of the valley is **St Columba Falls**, 8.5km past the pub. At around 90m high, they are among the state's highest falls. Although you can see them from the road, you get a much more impressive view from the platform at their base, an easy 20-minute walk from the car park (which has loos and picnic tables).

per one hour/four hours/day). For diving in the area, contact **Bay of Fires Dive** (☎ 6376 8335; paulsenent@dodo.com.au).

Visitors can charter boats for game fishing or take a lazy cruise. **Ahoy! Boat Hire** (☎ 0418 140 436; www.our.net.au/~chrinsy/ahoy.html; Oct-May) is on the waterfront, behind the Bayside Inn, and hires out kayaks, canoes, motor boats, sail boats and fishing tackle, plus a pontoon boat complete with barbecue for cruising in style ($80/120 for two/four hours, or $240 for a full day).

Charter boats and fishing trips can be arranged with the following operators. Most offer the option of sport, game, reef, deep-sea and bay fishing. All of them supply equipment; prices vary according to group numbers and the type of fishing.

Blue Water Sportsfishing Charters (☎ 0419 537 943; www.bluewatersports.com.au)

Professional Charters (☎ 6376 3083; www.gamefish.net.au)

Roban Coastal Charters (☎ 6376 3631; www.robancoastalcharters.com.au)

Tours

Bay of Fires Eco Tours (☎ 6376 8262; www.bayoffirescottages.com.au) Based at Bay of Fires Character Cottages (see p186), this tour is a two- to three-hour morning boat trip from Binalong Bay along the Bay of Fires coast for $55.

Johno's 'Quicky' 4WD Tas Tours (☎ 6376 3604, 0418 132 155; www.johnos4wdtours.com.au) Offers a 'quicky', 1½-hour tour of St Helens and immediate surrounds for $28. Alternatively, small-group half-day tours venture to Pyengana or the Bay of Fires ($55, lunch included), and a full-day tour takes in both these options ($110). Night spotlight tours in search of native wildlife are $30. Bookings are essential.

Sleeping

You can sleep very well in St Helens for a lot less than in other parts of the state – there's an impressive range of affordable accommodation here.

BUDGET

There are free camping sites in bushland north of St Helens at Humbug Point Nature Recreation Area. The turn-off is about 7km out of town, en route to Binalong Bay; the camping area is a further 5km through the reserve, at Dora Point.

Kellraine Units (☎ 6376 1169; 72 Tully St; d/tr/q $55/75/95) The best value in St Helens (possibly in northern Tassie) are these large, self-contained units. It is next to the highway about 800m northwest of the centre of town, and each roomy unit has full kitchen, laundry, video, and living and dining areas (one has wheelchair access).

St Helens Youth Hostel (☎ 6376 1661; 5 Cameron St; dm/d/f $18/40/55) The rooms at this simple, friendly YHA are nothing flash but the facilities (laundry, bike hire) are very good. The hostel, in a converted house, is in a quiet spot but only a block from the centre of town. Prices here are for YHA members; nonmembers pay $3.50 extra.

St Helens Caravan Park (☎ 6376 1290; sthelenscp@hotmail.com; Penelope St; unpowered/powered site $17/22, on-site vans $35-45, cabins $55-85) This park has a pleasant bushland setting to the south of town and good, family-friendly amenities (including games room and playground). Prices are for two people.

Anchor Wheel Motel (☎ 6376 1358; anchorwheel@vision.net.au; 59 Tully St; s/d $50/65) Opposite Kellraine is this cheap and cheerful option, with classic daggy motel décor and a raft of clean and comfy budget rooms.

MIDRANGE

Bayside Inn (☎ 6376 1466; www.baysideinn.com.au; 2 Cecilia St; r $68-118;) Opposite the wharf is this slightly creaky motel with a heated indoor pool, where rooms are priced from budget to poolside to 'ocean-view deluxe'. There's a bistro and bar on site – early-to-bed folk won't like the muted sounds of live bands on Friday night.

Old Headmaster's House (☎ 6376 1125; www.theoldheadmastershouse.com.au; 74 Cecilia St; r $85-115) This is a quaint 1900s B&B cottage set back from the main street, and without a blackboard in sight. Antiques, a rose garden, cooked breakfasts and helpful owners are selling points.

Sweetwater Villas (☎ 6376 1424; www.sweetwatervillas.com.au; 16 Halcyon Grove; d $50-100, extra adult/child $15/10) Formerly known as Halcyon Grove Holiday Units, this hillside place has a motel-style frontage and affordable self-contained units looking out to the distant water. The one-bedroom units have dated furnishings and aren't as nice as the two-storey, two-bedroom options with modernised living areas.

Homelea Accommodation (☎ 6376 1601; http://homelea.bookingtools.com; 16 & 22 Tasman Hwy; cottage d $110, units d $60-95, extra adult/child $15/10) On a hillside south of the town centre, Homelea has a self-contained, two-bedroom spa cottage on offer, plus a bright blue complex of older-style conjoined units, all self-contained, some with fun retro touches. The adjacent small park has a couple of playground swings.

TOP END

Bed in the Treetops B&B (☎ 6376 2238; www.bedinthetreetops.com.au; 701 Binalong Bay Rd; d $180-240) About 7km out of St Helens en route to Binalong Bay is the turn-off to this secluded, romantic retreat. It's a great set-up: large, modern suite with kitchenette, spa and outdoor deck, from which you can enjoy the great bush and sea views. The friendly owners provide a gourmet cooked breakfast (and dinner with advance notice).

Wybalenna Lodge (☎ 6376 1611; www.wybalennalodge.com; 56 Tasman Hwy; r $160-240) An elegant Edwardian guesthouse with luxurious rooms, a couple of cottages and fantastic bay views; it's very English, down to the surrounding garden. Sumptuous in-house dinners can be arranged with reasonable notice; it also serves local oysters and crayfish to the public between noon and 2pm daily (bookings advised).

Warrawee (☎ 6376 1987; www.vision.net.au/~warrawee; Kirwans Beach; r $140-210) Warrawee is a colonial homestead retreat in the south of town, with restful acreage looking down on the nearby water and a choice of cooked or continental breakfast. All the rooms are decorated in pretty English country style – ask for one opening onto the large veranda.

Doherty St Helens Resort (☎ 6376 1999, 1800 833 980; www.dohertyhotels.com.au; 1 Quail St; r $165-240;) The newest kid on the block in St Helens (and it is a huge, waterfront block) is this modern, well-appointed hotel, which opened in late 2003. More expensive rooms have water views and spa; all rooms have private balcony, plus there's the bonus of the resort swimming pool and two on-site restaurants.

THE AUTHOR'S CHOICE

Bay of Fires Character Cottages (☎ 6376 8262; www.bayoffirescottages.com.au; Binalong Bay Rd; d $130, extra adult/child $25/15) In a million-dollar location opposite a stunning beach, some 11km from St Helens, is this welcoming enclave of eight colourful, modern, one- to three-bedroom cottages. All have great facilities like full kitchen and laundry, plus barbecue and private balcony. The breezy hilltop vistas should be enjoyed from the veranda while clutching a glass of something appropriately refreshing. At the time of research, finishing touches were being applied to a neighbouring café and store so you won't have to travel too far for food and drink (but it's a good idea to stock up on groceries in St Helens en route). Boat tours along the coast can also be arranged here (see p185).

Eating

Wok Stop (☎ 6376 2665; 57a Cecilia St; meals $4-15; 10am-8pm, closed Jul) Drop in to this fresh, friendly eatery for your tomato or spinach *dhal*, satay chicken, lamb korma or one of the other delicious curries on offer. It's opposite the post office and you can eat in (there are outdoor tables) or take away.

Milk Bar Cafe (☎ 6376 2700; 57b Cecilia St; meals $4-12; 9am-4pm) Right next door to the Wok Stop, this bright place serves up café fare with flair. Choose from tasty brekky options, focaccias, burgers, salads, nachos and delish cakes.

Paddle Wheeler Restaurant (☎ 6376 1208; Wharf Area; mains $14-26; dinner Tue-Sun) This BYO-only restaurant, onboard the *Lady Annie Elizabeth*, moored at the wharf off Georges Bay Esplanade, dishes up fresh seafood most nights. Start with chowder or local oysters, then move to the catch of the day or assorted other fishy options; credit cards are not accepted.

Captain's Catch (☎ 6376 1170; Wharf Area; takeaway meals $9-14; lunch daily) Order superbly cooked fish and chips from this small kiosk and picnic off Georges Bay Esplanade, by the water (doing battle with the seagulls, of course). It also sells fresh, uncooked fish and seafood (including crays).

Fidler's on the Bay (☎ 6376 2444; cnr Tasman Hwy & Jason St; mains $19-26; dinner Mon-Sat May-Nov, lunch & dinner Mon-Sat Dec-Apr) Fidler's is a highly regarded restaurant that showcases the region's fine food from the sea – particularly in its famed starter, 'a trip around the bay', featuring morsels of scallops, calamari, oysters and salmon. The signature main dish is crown roast of hare, if you're feeling adventurous. Bookings advised.

Bayside Inn Bistro (☎ 6376 1466; 2 Cecilia St; mains $15-24; breakfast, lunch & dinner) A big, crowd-pleasing menu is on offer at this bistro, with lots of the expected meat and fish dishes (roast of the day, schnitzel, steak and fish and chips), but also crayfish at market prices and a few veg options.

Salty Seas (☎ 6376 1252; 16 Medeas Cove Esplanade; daily) Buy oysters, mussels, crayfish and fish fresh off the boat at this high-quality seafood-processing plant and retail outlet.

Garden of Eden (☎ 6376 2244; 12 Cecilia St; light meals $6-10; 9am-4pm Mon-Fri, 10am-2pm Sat;) Tired of seafood? This small, central café offers primarily vegetarian, organic meals (and a few vegan options), including veggie burgers, jacket potatoes, salads and cakes – and all meals 'can be shrunk for kids'. Internet access is available, plus second-hand books for sale.

Getting There & Away

Redline buses have a terminal on Quail St; TassieLink buses also stop on Quail St, opposite the RSL Club. Broadby's depart from the Mobil service station or from the post office, depending on the route. See p181 for details of Redline, TassieLink and Broadby's bus services.

BAY OF FIRES

A minor road (Binalong Bay Rd) heads northeast from St Helens to meet the coast at the start of the Bay of Fires, and then continues north, up to **The Gardens**. The bay's northern end is reached via C843, the road to the settlement of Ansons Bay and Mt William National Park.

This captivating bay, also a coastal reserve, is a series of sweeping beaches, rocky headlands, heathlands and lagoons. The ocean beaches provide some good surfing but some aren't safe for swimming due to the numerous offshore rips – instead, plunge into the calmer waters of a lagoon.

South of Ansons Bay, the road crosses the **Ansons River Reserve**. Just before the floodway, on the left as you drive towards Ansons Bay, is a tiny, overgrown picnic area with a lovely outlook upriver. Ansons River is good for a relaxed paddle and you can launch a boat at the picnic area. There are no petrol stations or shops at Ansons Bay, so fill up at either St Helens or Gladstone.

FIRE WALKING *Tony Wheeler*

Stretching south of Mt William National Park is the Bay of Fires, a long sweep of white sand named by early European explorers after the Aboriginal fires they spotted along the coastline. Middens (piles of discarded mollusc shells) are mute evidence of those age-old feasts.

From November to May, Launceston-based **Bay of Fires Walk** (☎ 6391 9339; www.bayoffires.com.au) conducts a four-day, three-night Bay of Fires experience, where a maximum of 10 people embark on an extremely well-catered journey of natural discovery, at a cost of $1495 per person.

Perched on a ridgetop high above the bay's blue waters is the stunning Bay of Fires Lodge. Architecturally it's good enough to grace the title page of *Australian Architecture Now,* a weighty coffee-table book featuring some of the 1990s' most noteworthy Australian buildings. But the resort is far more than simply a beautiful design. It's also built according to the very best ecological principles, right down to composting toilets, and showers for which water has to be hand-pumped up to a holding tank.

To ensure prospective guests really appreciate the environmentally sensitive luxury, the superb views and the fine food and wine, they have to pass a test before reaching the check-in desk: they have to walk for two days.

After a bus trip down from Launceston, the first day sees participants do a 9km walk to a permanent camp hidden in dunes behind the beach. The second day's exertions alternate between beachside and inland walks, and include fording Deep Creek, a lunch break near Eddystone lighthouse, and, finally, crossing a series of headlands and dramatic little coves before climbing up to the lodge.

The next morning, guests can do a spot of kayaking on Ansons River or simply laze around enjoying the views and working up an appetite for dinner. The final day comprises a short walk out to a waiting minibus, which whisks you back to Launceston.

There are some deliriously beautiful free camping spots along the bay, many of which come *au naturel* (without toilets or fresh water). There are good options immediately north of Binalong Bay, accessed by road from St Helens (take the turn-off to The Gardens). In the northern reaches, particularly recommended are the sheltered beachfront sites at **Policemans Point**, reached by a turn-off before Ansons Bay.

MT VICTORIA FOREST RESERVE

It's possible to drive a scenic, rugged loop (on gravel roads; caravans not recommended) from St Columba Falls into the wild Mt Victoria Forest Reserve to visit magnificent **Ralphs Falls** before continuing north to **Ringarooma**, thanks to the dedication of members of this small community. Construction of the road began during the Depression but wasn't finished until 1998, after years of laborious vegetation clearing and earth-moving by locals.

Ralphs Falls, a 20-minute return walk from the car park, is a spectacular sight, a thin pipe of water snaking its way down tall curving cliffs. From the same car park there's also a 50-minute return walk via scenic Cash's Gorge.

WELDBOROUGH

☎ 03 / pop 80

As the Tasman Hwy approaches the **Weldborough Pass**, an arabesque cutting which is famously popular with motorcyclists, it follows a high ridge with glimpses of surrounding mountains. As you ascend to the north, stop at the **Weldborough Pass Rainforest Walk** for a 15-minute interpretive-signed circuit through myrtle rainforest.

Weldborough went through a boom last century when tin was discovered nearby, but today its inhabitants are few in number. At one stage the town had 800 Chinese inhabitants, mostly miners, who brought many examples of their own culture, including an ornate joss house now on display in Launceston's Queen Victoria Museum & Art Gallery (p195). Other mining towns in the area also had a Chinese contingent – at **Moorina** to the north is a cemetery (off Amos Rd) with a memorial dedicated to the Chinese who lived and worked there.

With its tongue planted firmly in its cheek, the characterful **Weldborough Hotel** (☎ 6354 2223; Tasman Hwy; unpowered/powered sites $6/8 per person, d/tw $45/50) calls itself the 'worst pub in the world'. It offers camp sites in the small, sheltered grounds behind it and a handful of budget rooms, plus serves up good grub daily for lunch and dinner (except Sunday night).

GLADSTONE

☎ 03

About 25km north of Weldborough, off the Tasman Hwy between St Helens and Scottsdale, is the tiny town of Gladstone. It was one of the last tin-mining centres in northeastern Tasmania, up until the mine closed in 1982 and forced the inhabitants to look for new ways to eke out a living. The surrounding area also held a number of mining communities and a large Chinese population, though today many of the towns are deserted. There's a general store selling supplies, takeaway food and fuel, and the **Gladstone Hotel** (☎ 6357 2143; Chaffey St; s/d $30/60) provides meals as well as accommodation (shared facilities).

MT WILLIAM NATIONAL PARK

This marvellous park consists of long sandy beaches, low ridges and coastal heathlands. The highest point, Mt William, is only 216m high yet allows some fine views. The area was declared a national park in 1973, primarily to protect the endangered Forester kangaroo – an animal that prefers open grassy areas, the very lands also preferred by farmers. Thankfully, the kangaroos have flourished here and can now be seen throughout the park.

It's best to visit during spring and early summer, when the heathland wildflowers are at their colourful best. Mt William provides good views of the Furneaux Group of islands. When sea levels were lower, these formed part of a land bridge to what we now call the mainland. This bridge was used by Aborigines to migrate to Tasmania. Aboriginal habitation of the area is illustrated by the very large midden at **Musselroe Point**.

The main activities in the national park include bird- and animal-watching, fishing, swimming, surfing at Picnic Rocks, and diving around Stumpys Bay and Cape Naturaliste.

The easy climb to the rocky summit of **Mt William** takes around one hour return. The view extends from St Marys in the south to Flinders Island in the north. Further south at Eddystone Point is the impressive **Eddystone lighthouse**, assembled by the Galloway brothers in 1889 using granite blocks; if you follow the fence line at the car park down to the beach, you'll find the quarry from which the granite was cut, plus huge stone remnants of the quarrying process. There's a small picnic spot here overlooking a beach of red-granite outcrops. A short drive away is the idyllic, free camping ground of **Deep Creek**, beside a lovely tannin-stained creek and yet another magnificent arc of white sand and aqua water.

Free camping is allowed at four spots at Stumpys Bay, and also at Musselroe Top Camp and in the south at Deep Creek. Facilities are very basic, with only pit toilets, bore water for washing (at Stumpys Bay and Deep Creek) and fireplaces provided; there's no power and you'll need to bring your own water. Fires are allowed only in established fireplaces and it's advisable to bring your own wood (available from Gladstone) or, preferably, a portable stove. On days of total fire ban, only gas cookers are permitted. All rubbish needs to be taken back out as there's no refuse disposal here.

National park entry fees apply. If you're arriving via the northern access road, you can register your visit at the kiosk. If approaching from the south, you can buy a pass from the general store in Gladstone, or from the St Helens office of **Service Tasmania** (☎ 1300 135 513; 23 Quail St; 🕑 8.30am-4.30pm Mon-Fri).

Getting There & Around

You can enter the park, which is well off the main roads, from the north or the south. The northern end is 17km from Gladstone and the southern end is around 60km from St Helens. From Bridport, take the road towards Tomahawk and continue on to Gladstone. Don't forget to get petrol at Gladstone or St Helens, as there's no petrol station at Ansons Bay. And try to avoid driving here at night, as that's when animals are most active.

DERBY

☎ 03 / pop 175

In 1874 tin was discovered in Derby (pronounced *der*-bee, not *dar*-bee) and the little township flourished. Several mines soon operated in the area and these eventually amalgamated into one large mining company, which supported a town of 3000 people. Operations continued until 1929 when the local dam burst, flooding the town and drowning many residents. The mines closed for five years, reopened, then closed for good in 1940, causing an exodus. Derby has since utilised its hard-working past by creating a museum to attract the tourist dollar, and has tried to reinvigorate itself. It has undergone its first stages of rejuvenation and is home to an appealing strip of main-street cottages transformed into cafés and craft shops, but at the time of research was in a state of flux, as almost every store was up for sale or had just been sold.

Sights & Activities

Some of Derby's historic old mine buildings form part of the informative **Derby Tin Mine Centre** (☎ 6354 2262; Main St; adult/child/family $5/3/13; 🕑 9.30am-4.30pm). The museum, housed in the old schoolhouse, displays old photographs and mining implements. Outside is a modest re-creation of an old mining shanty town, with shops and cottages, and a re-creation of a 1938 radio station. The owner, a long-time local, is a good source of information.

Next door to the museum is the **Bankhouse Manor** (☎ 6354 2222; 51 Main St), a beautifully restored timber bank building dating from 1888. It's now owned by an artist who has transformed it into a very browse-worthy gallery, showcasing local art and craft as well as housing the Tin Dragon Parlour, a display of Chinese cultural artefacts to complement the Tin Dragon Trail initiative (see p182). B&B accommodation is planned for the manor.

Derby gets inundated by visitors in late October for its annual **Derby River Derby**. The derby sees around 500 competitors in all sorts of inflatable craft, including the distinctly home-made, racing down a 5km river course. The primary goal in this enthusiastically good-humoured contest is not so much to reach the finish line, but to sabotage your neighbours' vessels and be the last one floating. As a free-for-all spectacle, it's hard to beat.

If you're driving, as you cross the bridge into Derby from the north, check out the mutant rockfish stranded on the cliffs across the river.

Sleeping & Eating

There's not a great deal of accommodation in Derby. Free short-term camping (no powered sites) is permitted in the riverside picnic area at the western end of town.

Merlinkei Farm YHA (☎ 6354 2152; mervync@vision.net.au; 524 Racecourse Rd, Winnaleah; dm $18; 💻) This is an authentically rural, family-friendly hostel on a commercial dairy farm 10km from Derby. Besides letting you get up close and personal with the property's cows (overalls and gum boots provided), it also has terrific views of the Blue Tier plateau, and decent bunks and a pool table. To get here, drive 2km north of Derby on the Tasman Hwy and take the turn-off to the township of Winnaleah. Head out of Winnaleah towards Banca, turn right on Racecourse Rd and follow it for about 5km. Alternatively, ring from Winnaleah or Derby and the manager will pick you up.

Cobbler's (☎ 6354 2145; 63 Main St; d $120, extra person $20) Cobbler's is a centrally located, self-contained cottage (sleeping four managed by the nearby Federal Hotel. It's expensive for what you get: it doesn't look like much from the outside and the décor is dated, but it is roomy and comfortable.

There are a couple of gracious old pubs in the area offering budget accommodation and hefty counter meals: the **Dorset Hotel** (☎ 6354 2360; Main St) in Derby; the impressive, 1907 **Imperial Hotel** (☎ 6354; Stoke St), in the nearby town of Branxholm; and the **Winnaleah Hotel** (☎ 6354 2331; Main St) in Winnaleah, north of Derby.

Other eating options include the **Briseis View Eatery** (☎ 6354 2262; Main St; light meals $3-10) at the tin mine centre (named after the Briseis mine). On offer is homely fare including pancakes, soups, scones and cakes. Otherwise, you're bound to find a café along the main street.

Getting There & Away

See p181 for buses servicing Derby.

SCOTTSDALE

☎ 03 / pop 2000

Scottsdale, the largest town in the north-east, services some of Tasmania's richest agricultural and forestry country. The town was named after a surveyor called Scott, who opened the area for European settlement. The rich, fertile valleys were conducive to farming and Scottsdale grew into the region's business centre; its array of services may be useful for travellers, but attractions lie outside the town.

Information

Opened with great fanfare in 2002, the **Forest EcoCentre** (☎ 6352 6466; King St; admission free; 🕑 9am-5pm Mon-Fri, 9am-3pm Sat & Sun), run by Forestry Tasmania, is shaped like part of a giant shuttlecock and contains Scottsdale's **visitors centre** (☎ 6352 6520; scottsdale@tasvisinfo.com.au), which stocks loads of very good handouts on drives, walks and accommodation in the area.

There are various services and banks with ATMs located along King St, the main road through town.

Sights & Activities

Near Nabowla, 22km west of Scottsdale, is the turn-off to the **Bridestowe Estate Lavender Farm** (☎ 6352 8182; www.bridestoweestates.com.au; 296 Gillespies Rd; 🕑 9am-5pm daily Nov-Apr, 10am-4pm Mon-Fri May-Jul & Sep-Oct, by appointment Aug), the largest lavender-oil-producing farm in the southern hemisphere and the only source of perfumed lavender outside Europe. During the lavender's spectacular flowering season, from around mid-December to late January, admission is $4 per adult (children free), which covers a guided tour; at other times admission is free. You can purchase numerous lavender products in the farm shop, or sample lavender-flavoured muffins or ice cream at the café here.

The road from Scottsdale to Launceston crosses a pass called **The Sideling** (about 15km south of Scottsdale). Outfitted with toilets, picnic tables, a shelter and outstanding views stretching as far as Flinders Island on a clear day, it makes a great respite from the winding road.

Sleeping & Eating

The **North-East Park** (Tasman Hwy) squeezes free, unpowered camping spots between a small river-fronted wildlife sanctuary and the road to Derby.

Scottsdale Hotel-Motel (☎ 6352 2510; 18-24 George St; s/d $47/59) A handful of no-frills motel rooms are available out the back of this distinctive custard-and-clay-coloured place. The bistro here serves good basic meals for lunch and dinner daily (no lunches on Saturday).

Anabel's of Scottsdale (☎ 6352 3277; www.vision.net.au/~anabels; 46 King St; s/d $99/140, extra adult $20; mains $22-28; ⏲ dinner Tue-Sat) Anabel's is an endearing National Trust–classified abode supplemented by spacious modern motel-style units (some with cooking facilities) beside a beautiful overgrown garden. The salubrious restaurant indulges you with quality Tassie wine, seafood and game; bookings are essential (and note that lunch can be arranged).

Beulah (☎ 6352 3723; 9 King St; s $110, d $140-160) This elegant cottage, built in 1878, offers three rooms, full cooked breakfast, a wandering garden and a congenial atmosphere, due in large part to the congenial hosts. Those who have recently endured physical activity might choose to recover in the room equipped with a private spa and sauna.

Pop into the **Cottage Bakery** (☎ 6352 2273; 9 Victoria St; ⏲ 6am-5.30pm Mon-Fri) to pick up picnic fodder – the pies here are tops.

TOMAHAWK

☎ 03

The small holiday settlement of Tomahawk is out on an isolated bit of the north coast, 40km from Bridport on a sealed road. For most of the year its beaches are largely devoid of humanity, so it's a good place to get away from your travelling peers. It has excellent fishing for keen anglers; particularly good is the trout fishing at **Blackman's Lagoon** in the Waterhouse Protected Area, about 10km west of Tomahawk.

The sole place to stay is **Tomahawk Caravan Park** (☎ 6355 2268; Main Rd; unpowered/powered site $12/15, on-site vans & cabins $45-50). At the park entry are petrol bowsers, a café and a small shop, although the selection of food is limited. The vans and cabins use the main amenities block; you'll need to BYO linen.

BRIDPORT

☎ 03 / pop 1235

This well-entrenched holiday resort is on the shore of Anderson Bay. Just 85km from Launceston, it's popular with leisure-seeking Tasmanians and there are plenty of holiday houses lazing about town. This is also an ideal base from which to explore the winery-studded Pipers River region, some 30km west (p213).

Sights & Activities

The town has safe swimming beaches and its sheltered waters are also ideal for water skiing. Sea, lake and river fishing are also popular here. The area is renowned for its native orchids, which flower from September to December, and for its spectacular, abundant birdlife. Follow the road 2km past the caravan park entrance to reach walking tracks through the **Bridport Wildflower Reserve** (Richard St; admission free).

One new attraction in the area bound to bring a few visitors is **Barnbougle Dunes** (☎ 6356 0094; www.barnbougledunes.com), Tasmania's newest golf course, opened in December 2004. It's a stunning par-71 links course, set in sand dunes some 5km east of Bridport. Green fees for nine/18 holes are $50/80; golf set hire is from $30. The attractive clubhouse is home to a bar and restaurant; there is also on-site accommodation.

Sleeping & Eating

Bridport Caravan Park (☎ 6356 1227; Bentley St; unpowered/powered sites $14/17.50, on-site vans $50) Strung out along Bridport's sheltered beachfront, this laid-back place fills up quickly during summer's tourist high tide. Site prices are for up to four people.

Bridport Seaside Lodge Backpackers (☎ 6356 1585; www.bridportseasidelodge.com; 47 Main St; dm/tw/d $19/44/47) Enjoy the water views from the lounge and front deck of this high-quality hostel-cum-beachhouse sporting a chilled-out atmosphere, bikes and canoes for hire, comfy dorms and double rooms, and barbecue area.

Bridport Hotel (☎ 6356 1114; Main Rd; s/d $25/50) Pub with modest, no-frills rooms with shared bathroom. Meals from breakfast through dinner (mains $14 to $22) are available in the huge auditorium-like dining area, with the usual suspects in pub dining well represented (roast, steak, seafood etc).

Bridport Bay Inn (☎ 6356 1238; 105 Main St; s $72-77, d $82-87) A row of budget motel units (simple but comfy) are available behind this restaurant-bar, while inside are satisfying meat- and seafood-heavy meals (mains $14 to $21), exemplified by a surf-and-turf speciality (steak smothered with seafood in a creamy garlic sauce).

THE AUTHOR'S CHOICE

The Flying Teapot (☎ 6356 1918; 1800 Bridport Rd; light meals $7-15; ⏰ 10am-4pm Wed-Sun, closed winter) The nicest café in the area is this cheery, welcoming place about 3km south of the T-junction to Bridport. It's set in a pretty garden on a cattle farm and serves up tasty light meals such as salads, quiche, cheese platters and wraps. The novelty here is the setting: the café overlooks a private airstrip, so viewing pleasure is provided by small aircraft taking off or landing.

Platypus Park Country Retreat (☎ 6356 1873; www.platypuspark.com.au; Ada St; d $70-140) Just out of town beside the Brid River, this option has self-contained family-friendly units situated on a peaceful expanse of land. The appealing accommodation is enhanced by helpful owners (fifth-generation Tasmanians), sunny verandas and rustic views, and there are trout-stocked dams nearby.

Bridport Resort (☎ 6356 1789; www.bridport-resort.com.au; 35 Main St; 1/2/3-bedroom villa $150/180/210;) This well-situated resort has bred an architecturally cloned crop of 16 roomy, well-equipped timber villas, fully self-contained and sized from one to three bedrooms. Each villa has a laundry, spa and private outdoor area. Resort extras include games room, kids' play areas, heated indoor pool and tennis court. Off-peak prices (May to mid-December) are discounted by $25.

Joseph's (☎ 6356 1789; 35 Main St; mains $18-31; ⏰ dinner Tue-Sat) Joseph's, at Bridport Resort, is a licensed restaurant serving up Flinders Island lamb, wallaby shanks and eye fillet steak for discerning carnivores, and an array of well-cooked fish and seafood treats.

The Main St strip of shops is home to a bakery, takeaway outlet and coffee shop.

Getting There & Away

There is a **bus service** (☎ 6352 2413) that runs a couple of times on weekdays between Scottsdale and Bridport ($3 one-way).

See p310 for details of the weekly ferry service connecting Bridport to Flinders Island (which occasionally calls at Port Welshpool in Victoria too).

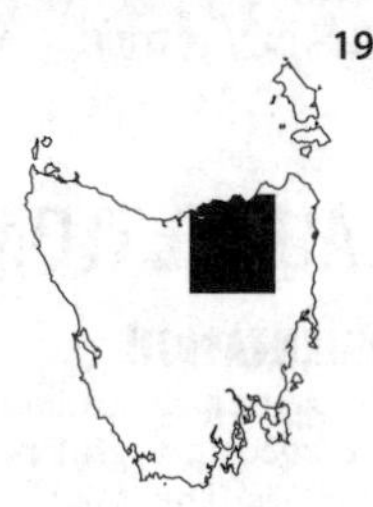

Launceston & Around

Launceston may be Tasmania's second-largest city but peak hour here lasts an unbearable 10 minutes! Life here moves at a relaxed big-country-town pace. The town's major attraction is Cataract Gorge and Launceston is dubbed the 'garden city' for its parklands.

Though a wander around town on a weeknight will reveal few signs of life, in recent years Launceston has shaken off her weary image with new sophisticated eateries (the food!) and culture, leisure and tourist development, as well as a burgeoning art scene.

Launceston is also the popular nucleus for the Tamar Valley wine route, which celebrates the notion of 'eat, drink and be merry'. Skip the highways and hug the quieter minor roads that weave through rural hamlets and small towns, pausing at a friendly B&B.

Scattered to the south of Launceston are impressive heritage homesteads such as Clarendon and Woolmers and quaint villages such as the authentic, still-working Brickendon.

Dominating the eastern skyline is Ben Lomond National Park and Legges Tor, a craggy plateau that has been drawing explorers, skiers, rock climbers and walkers for two centuries.

HIGHLIGHTS

- Hovering over Launceston's gorgeous **Cataract Gorge** (p194) on the longest single-span chairlift in the world
- Soaking up the marvellous heritage factor of **Franklin House** (p198)
- Sipping your way through the Tamar Valley's numerous **wineries** (p206)
- Wending your way up **Ben Lomond National Park** (p220), plastered to the cliff face of Jacob's Ladder
- Wandering through the quaint, heritage-listed buildings of **Evandale** (p218)
- Witnessing the bizarre mating rituals of unique marine creatures at Beauty Point's **Seahorse World** (p211)
- Meandering through the historic working farming village of **Brickendon** (p217)
- Sighing with contentment as you sink your teeth into some delicious bread cooked in a wood-fired oven at the **White House Bakery** (p216) in Westbury

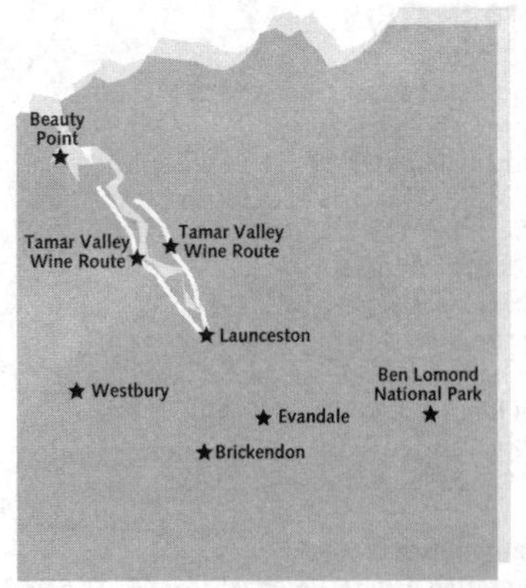

TELEPHONE CODE: 03	POPULATION: 68,450	www.discoverlaunceston.com

LAUNCESTON

ORIENTATION

The compact Launceston city centre is arranged in a grid pattern whose central point is The Mall, on Brisbane St, between Charles and St John Sts. The main shopping centre is based around this mall and the nearby Quadrant Mall, which is a semicircular side street. Two blocks north, on Cameron St, there's another pedestrian mall in the centre of a block called the Civic Sq, around which many of Launceston's public buildings can be found. Two blocks east of Civic Sq is the small Yorktown Sq, a charming not-really-square-shaped cluster of restored buildings that have been spruced up since the old days and converted into an array of shops and restaurants.

Flanking the old seaport, north of Royal Park, are the new redevelopments, comprising a string of contemporary riverfront eateries and a resort hotel.

Close to the city centre are the formal gardens of City Park, the wide sweeping lawns of Royal Park and the more intimate open spaces of Princes Sq and Brickfields Reserve. To the west of the city centre is Cataract Gorge, a magnificent, naturally rugged ravine formed thousands of years ago that is one of the city's major tourist drawcards.

INFORMATION

Bookshops

Angus & Robertson (Map p196; ☎ 6334 0811; 80-82 St John St) A popular bookery.

Birchalls (Map p196; ☎ 6331 3011; 118-120 Brisbane St) Considered Australia's oldest bookshop (c 1844).

Internet Access

Cyber King (Map p196; ☎ 0417 393 540; jwking@vision.net.au; 113 George St; per min 17¢; 9am-8pm Mon-Fri, 9am-6pm Sat, 10am-6pm Sun)

iCaf Internet Cafe (Map p196; ☎ 6334 6815; icaf@tassie.net.au; 22 Quadrant Mall; per 15min $2; 9am-5.30pm Mon-Fri, 10am-2pm Sat)

Medical Services

Launceston General Hospital (Map p195; ☎ 6348 7111; Charles St)

St Vincent's Hospital (Map p196; ☎ 6332 4999; 5 Frederick St)

Money

ATMs are installed at most banks in the city centre, which are mainly on St John St or Brisbane St near The Mall.

Post

Post office (Map p196; 107 Brisbane St; 9am-5.30pm Mon-Fri, 9.30am-1pm Sat) Near Quadrant Mall.

Tourist Information

Visitors centre (Map p196; ☎ 1800 651 827, 6336 3133; www.gatewaytas.com.au; cnr St John & Cimitiere Sts; 9am-5pm Mon-Fri, 9am-3pm Sat, 9am-noon Sun & public hols) A new resident of Cornwall Sq; houses racks of pamphlets, and handles statewide accommodation, tour and transport bookings.

SIGHTS

Cataract Gorge Map p195

A 10-minute walk west of the city centre is the magnificent **Cataract Gorge** (☎ 6331 5915; www.launcestoncataractgorge.com.au; 9am-dusk). Near-vertical cliffs crowd the banks of the South Esk River as it enters the Tamar and the area around the gorge is a wildlife reserve.

Two walking tracks, one on either side of the gorge, lead from Kings Bridge up to First Basin, where you'll find a **swimming pool** (admission free; Nov-Mar), picnic grounds, an à la carte restaurant with sociable peacocks loitering outside, and trails leading up to the vista-packed Cataract and Eagle Eyrie Lookouts. The gorge walk takes about 30 minutes; the northern trail is the easier, while the southern Zig Zag Track has some steep climbs as it passes along the cliff tops. The gorge is well worth visiting at night when it's floodlit.

You don't have to walk to First Basin, however. To drive to the main car park, follow the signs from York St to Hillside Crescent, Brougham St, then Basin Rd.

The world's longest single-span **chairlift** (adult/child one-way $7/5, return $8.50/6; 9am-dusk) makes the 10-minute crossing over the First Basin (you can board the chairlift at either end); upstream, also spanning the water, is the swingin' Alexandra Suspension Bridge. A good walking track (45 minutes one way) leads further up the gorge to Second Basin; further upstream from there is the site of the first municipal hydroelectric power station in Australia (established 1895) at Duck Reach.

Queen Victoria Museum & Art Gallery

The **Queen Victoria Museum & Art Gallery** (☎ 6323 3777; www.qvmag.tas.gov.au; adult/child/senior $10/free/9; 🕐 10am-5pm) has two branches, one at a site that was purpose-built for the museum in 1891 at **Royal Park** (Map p196; 2 Wellington St) and the other at the revamped **Inveresk railyards** (Map p195; 2 Invermay Rd). Both have cafés and wheelchair access. The one-off admission fee allows access to both sites.

The Royal Park branch includes exhibitions about the island's Aboriginal inhabitants and Tasmanian fauna, a splendid joss house donated by the descendants of Chinese settlers, and a **planetarium** (adult/child/family $5/3/12) with shows at 3pm Tuesday

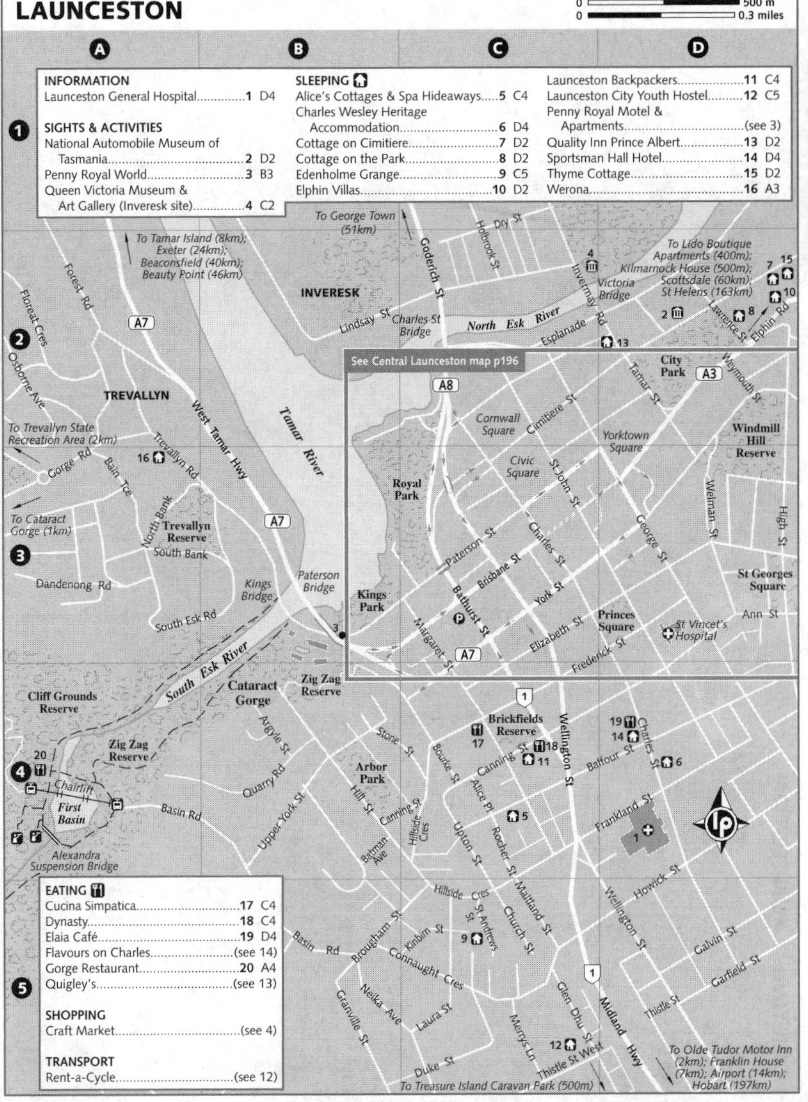

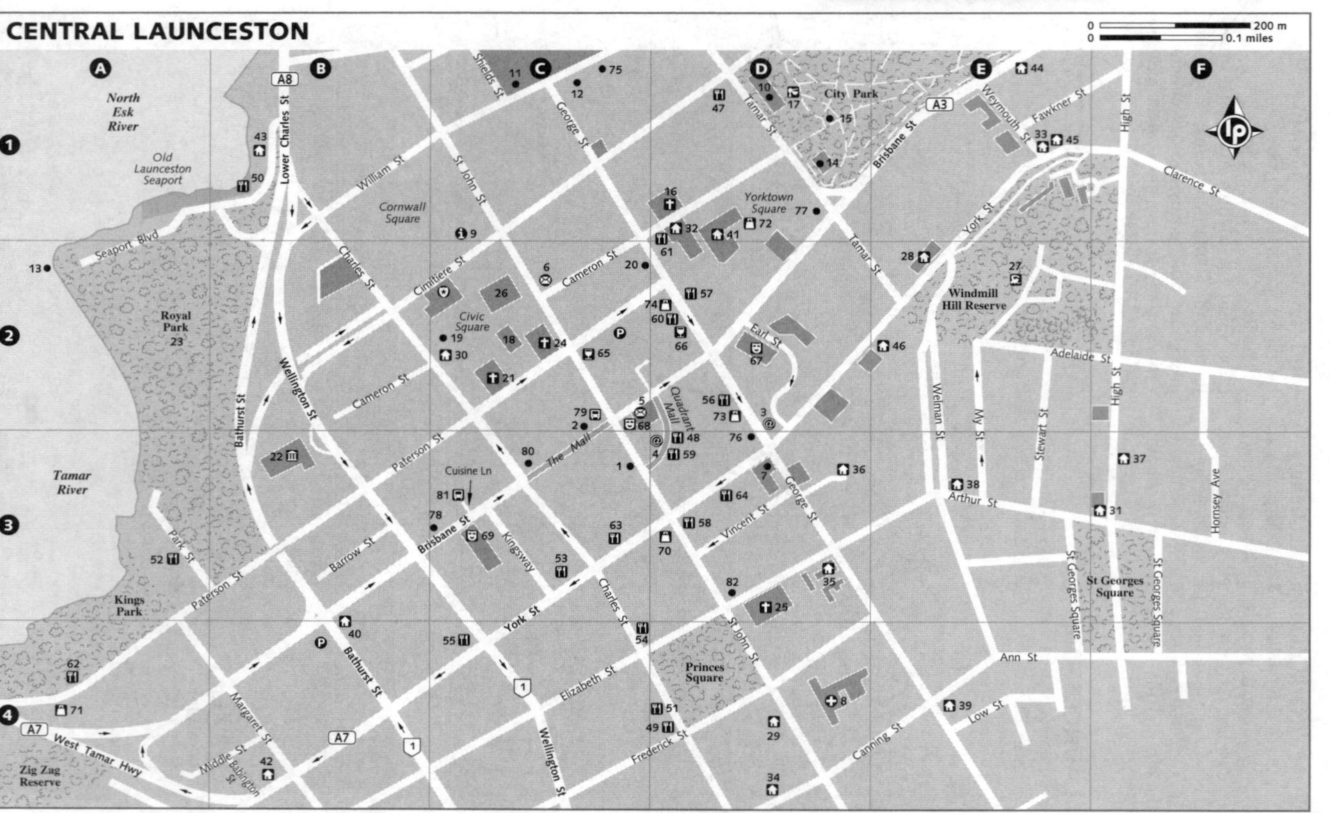
CENTRAL LAUNCESTON
200 m
0.1 miles
North Esk River
Old Launceston Seaport
Tamar River
Seaport Blvd
Royal Park
Kings Park
Zig Zag Reserve
West Tamar Hwy
Lower Charles St
Wellington St
Bathurst St
Paterson St
Park St
Margaret St
Middle St
Babington St
Cornwall Square
William St
Charles St
Cimitiere St
Cameron St
Civic Square
St John St
Shields St
George St
Brisbane St
Cuisine Ln
Kingsway
Barrow St
York St
Elizabeth St
Frederick St
The Mall
Quadrant Mall
Yorktown Square
Earl St
Tamar St
City Park
Vincent St
Princes Square
Canning St
Low St
Ann St
Arthur St
Welman St
My St
Windmill Hill Reserve
Stewart St
Adelaide St
High St
St Georges Square
Hornsey Ave
Clarence St
Weymouth St
Fawkner St

to Saturday. The museum has an interactive children's gallery, conducts astronomy shows and is where kids over five years are treated as detectives and given a bundle of clues to discover the mystery in the museum. No bookings are required and there's a 50% discount for admission to the planetarium if you've a general museum pass.

The Inveresk site houses an art gallery, which has a significant collection of colonial and contemporary Tasmania-related sculpture and painting. One of the biggest cultural statements is Robert Dowling's culturally white-washed *Aborigines of Australia* (1859). Also at Inveresk are displays of Aboriginal shell necklaces and Asian artworks, a display on the history of migration, and a railway-history exhibition including the Blacksmith Shop.

Boag's Brewery Map p196

The ubiquitous Boag's beer (the beer of choice for most northern Tasmanians – southerners are loyal to Cascade, brewed in Hobart) has been brewed in a monolithic building on William St since 1881, though other beers were produced here 50 years before that. If you want to see the kettles in action, take one of the 90-minute guided tours operated from the irresistibly-named **Boag's Centre for Beer Lovers** (Map p196; ☎ 6332 6300; www.boags.com.au; 39 William St; adult/child $16/12; tours ⏰ tours at 9am & 11am Mon-Fri, also 2pm Fri), opposite the brewery. Bookings are essential.

Penny Royal World Map p195

The **Penny Royal complex** (☎ 6331 3377; www.pennyroyalworld.com.au; 147 Paterson St; adult/child/family $20/9.50/45; ⏰ 9am-4.30pm) is a historical re-creation that includes working 19th-century wind-, corn and gunpowder mills, and a 10-gun sloop of war that bobs around a small lake. Barges float along a canal underground through the mills and foundry, or there's a restored city tram (No 16) that takes you past the windmill and corn mill. If you're interested in the traditional methods of making boiled lollies then check out **Gourlays Sweets** (☎ 6331 4730), a lolly shop–factory from the 1890s, housed in the corn mill. Parts of the complex are interesting, but overall it struggles to justify the full admission price – unless you're a mill enthusiast.

Historic Buildings

Launceston's architectural heritage is less significant than that of Hobart and other towns in Tasmania. The older buildings

INFORMATION
- Angus & Robertson 1 C3
- Birchalls 2 C2
- Cyber King 3 D2
- iCaf 4 D3
- Main Post Office 5 C2
- Old Post Office 6 C2
- Royal Automobile Club of Tasmania (RACT) 7 D3
- St Vincent's Hospital 8 D4
- Visitors Centre 9 C1

SIGHTS & ACTIVITIES
- Albert Hall 10 D1
- Boag's Brewery 11 C1
- Boag's Centre for Beer Lovers 12 C1
- Cataract Cruises 13 A2
- Design Centre of Tasmania 14 D1
- Glass Conservatory 15 D1
- Holy Trinity Anglican Church 16 D1
- Japanese Macaque Enclosure 17 D1
- Library 18 C2
- Macquarie House 19 C2
- Old Umbrella Shop 20 C2
- Pilgrim Uniting Church 21 C2
- Planetarium (see 22)
- Queen Victoria Museum & Art Gallery (Royal Park site) 22 B3
- Royal Oak Hotel (see 77)
- Royal Park 23 A2
- St Andrews Presbyterian Church 24 C2
- St Johns Anglican Church 25 D3
- Tamar River Cruises (see 13)
- Town Hall 26 C2
- Windmill Hill Swimming Centre 27 E2
- Wood Design Collection (see 14)

SLEEPING
- Adina Place 28 E2
- Airlie 29 D4
- Airlie on the Square 30 C2
- Ashton Gate 31 F3
- Batman Fawkner Inn 32 D1
- Best Western Coach House Motor Inn 33 E1
- Canning Cottage 34 D4
- Colonial on Elizabeth 35 D3
- Fiona's B&B 36 D3
- Hatherley House 37 F3
- Highfield House 38 E3
- Hillview House 39 E4
- Hotel Tasmania (see 54)
- Irish Murphy's 40 B4
- Launceston International Hotel 41 D1
- Old Bakery Inn 42 B4
- Peppers Seaport Hotel 43 B1
- Sandor's on the Park 44 E1
- Waratah on York 45 E1
- York Mansions 46 E2

EATING
- Caffé Fiore 47 D1
- Elaia Café 48 D3
- Fee & Me 49 D4
- Fish 'n' Chips 50 B1
- Fresh 51 D4
- Hallam's Waterfront 52 A3
- Hari's Curry 53 C3
- Hotel Tasmania 54 C4
- Jailhouse Grill 55 C4
- Konditorei Cafe Manfred 56 D2
- La Cantina 57 D2
- Metz 58 D3
- Pasta Resistance Too 59 D3
- Pierre's 60 D2
- Ric's Cafe Bar 61 D1
- Stillwater 62 A4
- Sushi Shack 63 C3
- Three Steps on George (see 35)
- Toro's on York 64 D3

DRINKING
- Lounge Bar 65 C2
- Royal on George 66 D2
- Saloon Bar (see 54)

ENTERTAINMENT
- Club 54 (see 32)
- Princess Theatre 67 D2
- Ursula's on Brisbane 68 C2
- Village Cinemas 69 C3

SHOPPING
- Allgoods 70 D3
- Benchmark Tasmania Wine Gallery 71 A4
- Craft Market 72 D1
- Paddy Pallin 73 D2
- Swiss Chocolatier 74 D2

TRANSPORT
- Cornwall Square Transit Centre (see 9)
- Economy Car Rentals 75 C1
- Europcar 76 D3
- Ghost Tours Departure 77 D1
- Lo-Cost Auto Rent 78 C3
- McDermotts Coaches 79 C2
- Qantas 80 C3
- Seaport Boat & Bike Hire (see 50)
- Tamar Valley Coaches 81 C3
- Thrifty 82 D3

that still stand, however, are more varied than those seen elsewhere because they date from several architectural periods.

In Civic Sq is **Macquarie House** (Map p196), built in 1830 as a warehouse but later used as a military barracks and office building, and the **Town Hall** (Map p196), an imposing building erected in 1864 in a Victorian Italianate style. Opposite the Town Hall is the **old post office** (Map p196; Cameron St) with its unique round clock tower.

One block away is the **Batman Fawkner Inn** (Map p196; 35 Cameron St), built in 1822 and known as the Cornwall Hotel until 20 years ago. It was on this site that John Batman and John Fawkner got together to plan what is now the city of Melbourne.

One corner of City Park contains **Albert Hall** (Map p196), erected in 1891 for a trade fair. The hall features the unusual Brindley water-powered organ.

The National Trust–classified **Old Umbrella Shop** (Map p196; ☎ 6331 9248; 60 George St; admission free; 9am-5pm Mon-Fri, 9am-noon Sat) was built from Tasmanian blackwood in the 1860s and still displays old brollies. Along with an assortment of gifts, this rare period treat is worth walking into if only to sample the friendly service of a bygone era.

Many of Launceston's churches were built between 1830 and 1860 (12 in all). The wide range of religions and denominations represented reflect the influence of the 1837 Church Act which acknowledged the existence of all religions and exempted places of worship from many taxes. On the Civic Sq block are the **Pilgrim Uniting** (Map p196) and the **St Andrews Presbyterian** (Map p196) churches, and opposite Princes Sq is **St Johns Anglican Church** (Map p196).

Some 8km south of town is the attractive Georgian **Franklin House** (☎ 6344 7824; 413 Hobart Rd, Breadalbane; adult/child $7.70/free; 9am-5pm Oct-Mar, 9am-4pm Apr-Sep). Built in 1838, it has been beautifully restored and furnished by the National Trust. An outstanding feature of its interior is the woodwork, which has been carved from New South Wales red cedar. To get here by bus, take Metro bus No 21 or 25 from St John St near The Mall and get off at stop No 28.

LAUNCESTON & AROUND FOR CHILDREN

- Squealing with delight at the **Japanese macaques** (right)
- Floating through the air on the **Cataract Gorge chairlift** (p194)
- Working the pioneer machinery and farm implements at the **Grubb Shaft Gold & Heritage Museum** (p210)
- Playing the detective and discovering the mystery at the **Planetarium** (p195)
- Viewing the tiny critters at **Seahorse World** (p211)

Parks & Gardens

The 13-hectare **City Park** (Map p196) is a fine example of a relaxing Victorian garden that features an elegant fountain, a bandstand, a giant outdoor chess set, a fabulous **Japanese macaque enclosure** (8am-4pm Apr-Sep, to 4.30pm Oct-Mar) and the 1832 John Hart **glass conservatory** (8.30am-4.30pm Mon-Fri Apr-Sep, 9am-5.30pm Oct-Mar).

Princes Sq (Map p196; btwn Charles & St John Sts) features a bronze fountain bought at the 1855 Paris Exhibition.

Other public parks and gardens include **Royal Park** (Map p196), which is near the junction of the North Esk and Tamar Rivers (and includes a river-edge boardwalk taking in the Cataract Gorge Reserve, Ritchies Mill, Home Point and the new Seaport development), and **Windmill Hill Reserve** (Map p196), to the city's east, where you can take a dip in the swimming pool.

A 10-minute drive north of the city is **Tamar Island** (☎ 6327 3964; West Tamar Hwy; adult/child/family $2/1/5; 9am-dusk), where you'll find a 2km wheelchair-friendly boardwalk through a significant wetlands reserve teeming with bird life (including brown falcons and white-bellied sea eagles).

Other Attractions

Design Centre of Tasmania (Map p196; ☎ 6331 5506; www.twdc.org.au; cnr Brisbane & Tamar Sts; 9.30am-5.30pm), on the edge of City Park, is a retail outlet displaying high-quality work by Tasmanian craftspeople. The **Wood Design Collection** (Map p196; ☎ 6334 6558; adult/child/family $2.20/1.10/5.50), also incorporated into the centre, showcases designs by locals.

The oxymoronic **National Automobile Museum of Tasmania** (Map p195; ☎ 6334 8888; 86 Cimitiere St; adult/child/family $8.50/4.50/21.50; 9am-5pm Sep-May, 10am-4pm Jun-Aug) will please motor enthusiasts as it's one of Australia's best presentations of classical and historical relics, with a ground floor devoted to four-wheelers (from old Bentleys to a 1969 Monaro) and a loft full of classic motorbikes, including a 1927 Harley Davidson.

Further upstream from Duck Reach is the **Trevallyn State Recreation Area** (8am-dusk), where Trevallyn Dam constricts the flow of Lake Trevallyn. Here you can view a 90m-long elver ladder, constructed to help young eels negotiate the dam wall during their annual 3500km-long migration. The reserve here comprises a lake popular for watersports and picnic facilities. To get to the reserve, follow Paterson St west (after crossing Kings Bridge it becomes Trevallyn Rd and then Gorge Rd), then turn right into Bald Hill Rd, left into Veulalee Ave and veer left into Reatta Rd to the reserve. Access is restricted when the river is in flood, and camping isn't allowed here.

ACTIVITIES

Hang-gliding

At the Trevallyn Dam quarry you can have a go at simulated **hang-gliding** (0419 311 198; Reatta Rd; www.cablehanggliding.com.au; adult/child $15/10, tandems $20; 10am-5pm Dec-Apr, 10am-4pm May-Nov & school hols), which involves swooping down a 200m-long cable – great fun until you hurtle over the lip of the quarry and your stomach tries to turn around and go back. Head west along Paterson St and from King's Bridge follow the signs.

Skydiving

For those who prefer free fall, **Tandemania** (Map p207; 0418 550 859; Hangar 14, Launceston airport; skydives $345) will strap you to an instructor and then throw you both out of a plane at 10,000 feet (it involves 15 minutes of flight time and around five minutes of plummeting). This activity is restricted to those over 14 years of age and weighing less than 95kg.

TOURS

Visit the visitors centre (p194) to get the lowdown on the many tours available within and beyond Launceston. Some old local favourites include a one-hour guided **historic walk** (6336 3133; adult/child/concession $15/free/11) taking in the city centre's architecture, departing at 9.45am Monday to Friday.

In the evening, get spooked on a 90-minute **ghost tour** (0421 819 373; adult/student/family $20/17/45) conducted by professional theatrical guides around the city's back alleys and lanes. Tours depart from the front of the **Royal Oak Hotel** (Map p196; 6331 5346; 14 Brisbane St) at dusk and bookings are essential.

Coach Tram Tours (6336 3133, 0419 004 802; coachtramtour@vision.net.au) operates tours that depart from the visitors centre, which also handles bookings. Among its programmes is a three-hour tour of the city's key attractions (adult/child/family $32/24/90), which leaves daily at 10am May to December (also at 2pm January to April). In addition, it runs excursions around the Tamar Valley and Beauty Point (adult/child $55/46).

Based at Home Point in Royal Park, **Tamar River Cruises** (Map p196; 6334 9900; www.tamarrivercruises.com.au; Home Point Pde; adult/child/concession/family $15/8/14/38) conducts excellent 50-minute cruises through the Cataract Gorge on the luxurious *Lady Launceston*. Other cruises are available; bookings are recommended. From the same departure point, **Cataract Cruises** (Map p196; 6334 9900) also operates good-value 50-minute cruises of the gorge (adult/child $15/6). Cruises operate every hour from 9.30am to 3.30pm.

FESTIVALS & EVENTS

Festivale (www.festivale.com.au) Three days in February feverishly devoted to celebrating eating, drinking, arts and entertainment, staged in City Park. The event involves over 70 Tasmanian food and wine stalls, dancing, theatre, and bands twanging through electric and acoustic gigs.

Launceston Cup Held in February; horses work up a sweat on the track.

Australian Three Peaks Race A four-day nonstop nautical rush in March to sail from Beauty Point (north of Launceston) to Hobart, pausing long enough for teams of runners to jump ashore and scale three mountains along the way.

Easter Pacing Cup Over Easter the trotting track gets pounded.

Royal Launceston Show October sees old hands showing off their herds.

SLEEPING

Budget

HOSTELS

Launceston Backpackers (Map p195; 6334 2327; www.launcestonbackpackers.com.au; 103 Canning St;

4-/6-bed dm $19/18, tw/tr $22/20, d with/without bathroom $65/55; ☐) Opposite Brickfields Reserve and buzzing with a friendly vibe, this well-managed renovated hostel is housed in an impressive Federation building. The staff is friendly, offering great advice on local attractions. The rooms are clean and spacious, and the common areas and facilities are well maintained.

Launceston City Youth Hostel (Map p195; ☎ 6344 9779; tasequiphire@email.com; 36 Thistle St; dm/s/f $15/22/40) This is a rambling private hostel 2km south of the city centre, set up in the former canteen of the nearby Coats Patons Woollen Mill. It's a sound choice – unless you're averse to the strict single-sex dorm policy. The hostel rents out bicycles (p206) and bushwalking gear.

HOTELS, MOTELS & PUBS

Sportsmans Hall Hotel (Map p195; ☎ 6331 3968; www.maskhospitality.com.au; cnr Charles & Balfour Sts; s/d from $44/55) This 1890 pub is located in a relatively peaceful part of town, and has been completely refurbished in recent times. All rooms have been upgraded, are incredibly clean and include a private bathroom. B&B rates are available.

Batman Fawkner Inn (Map p196; ☎ 6331 7222; fax 6331 7158; 35 Cameron St; dm $25, s/d from $40/65) The Batman Fawkner has a historic, eye-catching façade that fronts a rabbit warren of basic but comfortable budget rooms. The Batty downstairs sometimes attracts some vocal patrons on the weekend, and it's OK if you don't mind being lulled to sleep by the soothing scratches of the nightclub's local DJ.

Irish Murphy's (Map p196; ☎ 6331 4440; cnr Brisbane & Bathurst Sts; dm/d $17/35) This pub has good cheap bunks, an appealing common room and a balcony to pose on. It also has a downstairs bar that becomes particularly lively when bands are on.

Hotel Tasmania (Map p196; ☎ 6331 7355; hotel@saloon.com.au; 191 Charles St; s $60, d & tw $75) This place has decent and spacious en suite rooms that fortunately forgo the Wild West kitsch of the 'cantina' downstairs. Benefits include continental breakfast and tea- and coffee-making facilities.

CAMPING & CABINS

Site prices are for up to two people.

Treasure Island Caravan Park (Map p196; ☎ 6344 2600; treasureislandlaunceston@netspace.net.au; 94 Glen Dhu St; unpowered/powered sites $19/20, on-site vans $46 cabins $70-80) About 2.5km south of the city, this park has good facilities but is in a somewhat noisy location beside the highway.

Midrange

COTTAGES

Canning Cottage (Map p196; ☎ 6331 4876; 26-28 Canning St; B&B d $95) These two fully furnished two-bedroom self-contained cottages are conjoined buildings on the one lot. Both are very snug, with plenty of steep steps and narrow doorways.

Cottage on the Park (Map p195; ☎ 6334 2238; 29 Lawrence St; d $100-145) This is a two-bedroom abode sleeping five people, and off City Park, as is **Cottage on Cimitiere** (Map p195; ☎ 6334 2238; 33 Cimitiere St; s/d from $120/130). For both of the cottages, inquire at 27 Lawrence St; rates include breakfast.

Thyme Cottage (Map p195; ☎ 6331 1906; www.thymecottage.com.au; 31 Cimitiere St; d $110-155) A delightful 1880s cottage providing self-contained heritage accommodation. With cottage furniture and antiques, it exudes a warmth and charm. It includes modern facilities, provides full breakfast provisions and welcomes ankle biters.

GUESTHOUSES & B&BS

Kilmarnock House (Map p195; ☎ 6334 1514; www.kilmarnockhouse.com; 66 Elphin Rd; s $85, d $135-150 f $170) This National Trust–listed 1905 Edwardian mansion provides gracious accommodation. Turned blackwood staircase rails lead to antique-furnished, elegant, self-contained rooms. The rate includes a generous breakfast and kids are most welcome.

Hillview House (Map p196; ☎/fax 6331 7388, cnr George & Canning Sts; s $85, d $115-125) This impressive National Trust–classified house (c 1840) offers exceptional views over the city, river and valley. It was once a girls' boarding house for the Launceston Church & Grammar School. It exudes charm and comfort with well-furnished rooms that have TV, bar fridge and en suite. Guests can enjoy a full cooked or continental breakfast, served by the friendly hosts in a quaint colonial dining room.

Charles Wesley Heritage B&B (Map p195; ☎ 6331 3703; 261 Charles St; d $120) This interesting 1882 Gothic Victorian heritage building comprises two bedrooms and is suited to a maximum of four people. There are glorious views over the town and estuary, and the rate includes generous breakfast provisions for the morning.

Airlie (Map p196; ☎ 6334 2162; airlie.bed.b@bigpond.com.au; 138 St John St; s $85-90, d $125-135) Airlie provides very cosy B&B in a warm 1888 Victorian terrace house. The continental breakfast provisions include wonderful fresh fruit salads and a fabulous to-die-for marmalade. Airlie is next to a strikingly dishevelled, deconsecrated church in the city's south, just a skip from Princes Park.

Airlie on the Square (Map p196; ☎ 6334 0577, 0427 480 008; 77 Cameron St, Civic Sq; s $85, r $90-125; 💻) At the time of writing this B&B, run by the same people who run Airlie, had just opened in the heart of the city. This new accommodation is in a beautiful, heritage-listed Federation building and includes fridge, TV, electric blanket, heating and a gym for guest.

Fiona's B&B (Map p196; ☎ 6334 5965; res@fionas.com.au; 141a George St; s/d $90/124, ste $135-260) Fiona's is a hospitable B&B in a lush garden setting, with immaculate modern, comfortable rooms, some with panoramic views over Launceston. The rates include a full breakfast and many of the rooms have either a balcony or private courtyard.

Ashton Gate (Map p196; ☎ 6331 6180; www.ashtongate.com.au; 32 High St; s $90, d $120-150) This thoroughly welcoming and refreshing Victorian B&B exudes a sense of home; each en suite room is beautifully furnished with charming touches and there's also a self-contained apartment in the Old Servant's Quarters. Guests should note that this is a nonsmoking property.

HOTELS & MOTELS

Quality Inn Prince Albert (Map p195; ☎ 6331 7633; reservations@qualityinnprincealbert.com.au; cnr Tamar & William Sts; d $135-280) An Italianate façade betrays a widely extravagant affair. The en suite rooms are spacious and elegant, and every room boasts high-quality French-polished woodwork; the executive suite features an ornately carved Chinese four-poster bed. Home-cooked or continental brekky is available; Quigley's restaurant (p203) is also here.

Sandor's on the Park (Map p196; ☎ 1800 030 140, 6331 2055; 3 Brisbane St; d $85-105) Well positioned opposite City Park, Sandor's provides neat and tidy rooms, including family rooms. Facilities include TV, fridge, tea- and coffee-making facilities, and free in-house movies.

Best Western Coach House Motor Inn (Map p196; ☎ 1800 062 377, 6331 5311; www.bestwestern.com.au/coachhouse; 10 York St; d from $110) Conveniently located, this motel offers clean rooms with all the mod cons needed for a comfy stay. The executive suites have a spa and separate lounge room, and all rooms have queen-sized beds.

Old Bakery Inn (Map p196; ☎ 1800 641 264, 6331 7900; oldbakeryinn@bestwestern.com.au; cnr York & Margaret Sts; r from $125) Established for over 130 years and now run by the Best Western crew, this old bakery offers heritage accommodation in comfortable, stylish and charming rooms that include all the mod cons like minibars and electric blankets. There's also a self-contained suite in the Loft.

Penny Royal Motel & Apartments (Map p195; ☎ 1800 060 954, 6331 6699; www.leisureinns.com.au; 147 Paterson St; motel r from $134, 1-/2-bedroom apartments from $135/165) A short walk from Cataract Gorge, this place has motel rooms trying to take in the heritage, old-world look of dark-wood furniture and exposed ceiling timbers, plus a picturesque and comfortably row of modern apartments.

Colonial on Elizabeth (Map p196; ☎ 1800 060 955, 6331 6588; www.colonialinn.com.au; 31 Elizabeth St; d $125-250) Formerly the Launceston Church & Grammar School, today this 1847 building houses boutique colonial rooms with lovely décor, en suite and all the modern amenities. Attached to it is a formal restaurant and a café–wine bar, Three Steps on George (p203), also serving meals.

SELF-CONTAINED APARTMENTS

Olde Tudor Motor Inn (Map p195; ☎ 1800 802 090, 6344 5044; fax 6344 1774; Westbury Rd; s/d $80/90, self-contained units $130; 🏊) Some 4km south of town, this place has well-furbished rooms, an indoor heated pool and a kids' playground. The old Tudors must have had a gambling problem – this is a place with the words 'Gaming' and 'Family' on the same sign.

Adina Place (Map p196; ☎ 1800 030 181, 6331 6866; adinacityview@bigpond.com; 50 York St; s/d from $105/135) Located near Windmill Hill Reserve, Adina Place offers smart and tidy studio apartments, two-bedroom units and spa suites; continental brekky is provided.

Top End

COTTAGES

Alice's Cottages & Spa Hideaways (Map p195; ☎ 63 34 2231; alices.cottages@bigpond.com; 129 Balfour St; r from $230) Alice's manages several sumptuous, romantic B&B cottages, including 'Camelot', 'Aphrodites' and 'French Boudoir' – just the ticket for those who want to indulge in 'lurve'. Most are located in the Balfour/Margaret St area.

GUESTHOUSES & B&BS

Hatherley House (Map p196; ☎ 6334 7727; www.hatherleyhouse.com.au; 43 High St; junior deluxe ste from $160, deluxe ste from $200) This place is simply adored by those who crave sophisticated accommodation. One of the best B&B options in town, this 1830s mansion is decked out with out-of-context cultural exotica and includes ultramodern fittings, underfloor heating, king-sized beds in most suites and a nicely sculpted garden. Leave the kiddies at home.

Waratah on York (Map p196; ☎ 6331 2081; info@waratahonyork.com.au; 12 York St; d $175-260) The Waratah is set in an 1862 Victorian Italianate mansion and is an opulent and unashamedly old-fashioned B&B (and gay friendly, to boot). Its luxurious heritage rooms are fully equipped and the executive spa suites all have panoramic views. Grab yourself a port and relax in the spacious guest lounge.

Werona (Map p195; ☎ 6334 2272; www.werona.com; 33 Trevallyn Rd; ste s $130-190, d $160-230) This opulent B&B is a Queen Anne Federation home comprising three storeys with unsurpassed views over the river, city and surrounding hills. Spacious and decorated with restored antiques and *objets d'art,* all rooms include an en suite, and some have spas. I say, anyone for a game of billiards?

Edenholme Grange (Map p195; ☎ 6334 6666; www.edenholme.com; 14 St Andrews St; s/d from $130/180) True to its National Trust–classified Victorian heritage, this place presents guests with lavish, antique-furnished 'romantic theme' rooms, complete with double spas. Other stately accoutrements include complimentary evening port and truffles, and gourmet cooked breakfasts.

Highfield House (Map p196; ☎ 6334 3485; www.highfieldhouse.com.au; 23 Welman St; s/d from $115/150) Classical music heralds your arrival here at this quiet Victorian boutique place. Its five rooms have queen-sized beds and en suite facilities. The cheery manager will fuel you up every morning with a fully cooked breakfast.

HOTELS & MOTELS

Peppers Seaport Hotel (Map p196; ☎ 6345 3333; www.seaport.com.au; 28 Seaport Blvd; d with breakfast $310-510, without breakfast $250-450) Built in the shape of a ship on the site of an old dry dock, this new glam hotel epitomises the recent dockside developments. The hotel's contemporary design extends to the deluxe rooms (accentuated by natural timbers and muted tones). The rooms and suites are very spacious and include all the mod cons, and most have balconies with spectacular views.

Launceston International Hotel (Map p196; ☎ 18 00 555 811, 6334 3434; res.launceston@dohertyhotels.com.au; 29 Cameron St; r from $165) This hotel dominates the eastern end of Cameron St, with all the luxury you'd expect from a place with a fountain in its foyer. North-facing rooms have a view to the attractive Holy Trinity Anglican Church.

SELF-CONTAINED APARTMENTS

York Mansions (Map p196; ☎ 6334 2933; www.yorkmansions.com.au; 9-11 York St; apt $190-230) Yearning to spend a night as the Duke or Duchess of York? Stay in one of the five opulent, historically themed apartments in the 1840 Georgian, National Trust–classified York Mansions. Besides the old-era luxury (the apartments are serviced daily), rates include provisions for a fully cooked, hearty breakfast.

Lido Boutique Apartments (Map p195; ☎ 6334 5988; www.thelido.com.au; 47-49 Elphin Rd; apt $190-420) The Lido offers designer boutique apartments that have 1930s flair and elegance. Its deluxe quarters have queen-sized bed, full-sized bath and separate lounge and dining area with balcony. However the exotic three-bedroom 'Japanese Imperial' with full-sized spa and king-sized bed might be more you. All rooms have modern amenities, include breakfast and include the all-important well-stocked minibar.

Elphin Villas (Map p195; ☎ 6334 2233; www.elphinvillas.com.au; 29a Elphin Rd; villas $130-185, apt $190-230) Offering a touch of 'Tuscany' in the heart of Launceston with spacious two- and three-bedroom villas (some spa-equipped), or less-spacious motel rooms for the agoraphobic. It also manages comfortable one- or two-bedroom studio apartments with separate lounge and dining areas. The ground floor apartments open on to a serene garden courtyard.

EATING

Restaurants

Hallam's Waterfront (Map p196; ☎/fax 6334 0554; 13 Park St; mains $23.50-28.50 ⏰ lunch & dinner) Adjacent to the Tamar Yacht Club and decked out with the requisite nautical theme, this place has friendly service and specialises in exquisite rock-lobster dishes. The scallop trio ($15.50) gets a big thumbs-up; moreover the meals are so fresh you'll need your own spear to pin the squid to your table. There's also a takeaway attached, catering to gourmet fish 'n' chippery lovers.

Cucina Simpatica (Map p195; ☎ 6334 3177; cnr Frederick & Margaret Sts; lunch meals $6-15, dinner mains $18-28; ⏰ lunch & dinner) This long-serving place has first-rate, modern cuisine that marches through the continents with flair. Fresh produce is the key ingredient here, with a dash of casual chic thrown in for good measure.

Fee & Me (Map p196; ☎ 6331 3195; cnr Charles & Frederick Sts; 3/4/5 courses per person $14/16/18; ⏰ dinner Mon-Sat) This restaurant does outstanding, innovative, upmarket cuisine, which has won awards year after year. Set in the National Trust–registered Morton House, this elegant restaurant specialises in fine dining and an interesting degustation menu structure – all dishes are entrée size and brackets of dishes move from light to rich; most diners choose between three and five courses, depending on appetite. Be sure to book.

Stillwater (Map p196; ☎ 6331 4153; Ritchies Mill, 2 Bridge Rd; dinner mains $20-30; ⏰ breakfast, lunch & dinner) Having scratched a few notches in its awards belt, this is where you come to impress and be impressed. Set in the stylishly renovated 1840s Ritchies flour mill beside the Tamar, culinary delights include all manner of seafood and meat dishes, vegetarian options and a comprehensive wine list. By day it's a relaxed café churning out breakfast (smoked-salmon bagels, homemade muesli) and lunch (roast-pumpkin pizza, Thai lamb salad). Of an evening the restaurant struts its stuff. Be sure to book as it's deservedly popular.

Three Steps on George (Map p196; ☎ 6334 2084; 158 George St; mains $16-22; ⏰ dinner) This sophisticated café–wine bar is part of the Colonial on Elizabeth complex (p201). Try the tender lamb shanks and follow the meal with a balanced *millefeuille* layered with orange curd, cream and seasonal berries. Sensational.

Quigley's (Map p195; ☎ 6331 6971; 22 Tamar St; mains $25-30; ⏰ breakfast, lunch & dinner) Quigley's has moved recently from its quaint 1860s terrace and is now incorporated into the Quality Inn Prince Albert hotel (p201). The generous à la carte meals include tasty game dishes, but if you want to impress, order the chateaubriand for two ($55), which is silver-served direct to your plate.

Hari's Curry (Map p196; ☎ 6331 6466; 150 York St; mains $10-15; ⏰ lunch Fri, dinner) Cooks an admirable selection of authentic north Indian and tandoori suspects; the prawn *masala* is superb. It also serves up top-notch vegetarian delights, such as *dahl* ($8), and the creamiest mango lassi ($3).

Toro's on York (Map p196; ☎ 6331 8676; 63-65 York St; mains $12; ⏰ lunch & dinner) With friendly staff serving sumptuous Spanish cuisine, this restaurant offers a great ambience, and best of all, paella good enough to stop short a cranky bull in its tracks.

Jailhouse Grill (Map p196; ☎ 6331 0466; cnr Wellington & York Sts; mains $15-20; ⏰ lunch Fri, dinner) A favourite of the meat-and-three-veg aficionados, this wood-fired grilling mecca takes your choice of steak (eye fillet, scotch, rump or porterhouse) and cooks it just the way you like it. It doesn't do a bad job with the chicken and seafood dishes either, and you can pig out on the all-you-can-eat salad bar with your mains. For the record, the building, which dates from the mid-1800s, was convict-made but was an inn, not a jail.

Sushi Shack (Map p196; ☎ 6331 4455; 134 York St; sushi dishes $3.50-15; ⏰ lunch & dinner Mon-Sat) This is *the* spot for fresh sushi, tempting you with classic Japanese mains such as *yakisoba*, crispy tempura and teriyaki. Your best bet is to be here on Wednesday or Thursday night for the all-you-can-eat sushi fest ($18).

La Cantina (Map p196; ☎ 6331 7835; 61-63 George St; mains $10-20; ⏰ lunch Mon-Sat, dinner) La Cantina is a huge favourite with locals. This gingham-infected, cavernous eatery serves all the Italian standards, including terrific

THE AUTHOR'S CHOICE

Pierre's (Map p196; ☎ 6331 6835; 88 George St; mains $15-26; breakfast, lunch & dinner Mon-Sat) Back in 1956 three magnificent coffee machines headed for Australia: the famed Melbourne icon Pellegrini's took one machine and Frenchman Pierre Lecomte set up the second, making Pierre's the nation's second-oldest café. Choices involve either light meals, such as bagels, focaccias, burgers or pasta, or more substantial and innovative mains, such as warm char-grilled quail salad or *chemoula* lamb loin (with a spiced, roasted ratatouille, grilled haloumi cheese and redcurrant glaze). Early risers can expect sumptuous croissants, house-made fruit loaf or any choice of brekky-style eggs. Finally, in the finest café tradition, the desserts are an experience and the coffee – pure class. (As for the third coffee-machine: it went to Sydney but the café has since closed.)

marinaras and homemade pesto – and the pizza! Wash it all down with a glass of Lambrusco or Chianti for a truly authentic experience.

Dynasty (Map p195; ☎ 6334 7000; 95 Canning St; mains $10-20; lunch & dinner Mon-Sat, dinner Sun) Attracting locals in their droves, Dynasty dishes up incredible Chinese cuisine to eat in or take away. The unpretentious service is a little bit too attentive, but the meals are worth it; try the Mongolian lamb – absolutely divine. Note that the elaborately stylised décor festooning the walls and ceiling is actually Taiwanese.

Pubs

Irish Murphy's (Map p196; ☎ 6331 4440; cnr Brisbane & Bathurst Sts; lunch & dinner) This popular pub offers a better-than-average take on the humble counter meal. The menu consists of delicious Irish fare – stew may be involved.

Hotel Tasmania (Map p196; ☎ 6331 7355; 191 Charles St; mains $6-12; lunch & dinner) If you don't mind eating under the watchful gaze of a stuffed moose or the odd deer then you'll be fine in this local institution. Popular with families, it serves a decent steak and excellent fresh seafood, and there's also a good Tasmanian wine selection – yes, cowboys do drink wine. The pub also hosts live music in its Saloon Bar (opposite).

Cafés & Quick Eats

Elaia Café Central Launceston (Map p195; ☎ 6331 3307; 238-240 Charles St; mains $16.50-24; breakfast, lunch & dinner); Quadrant Mall (Map p196; ☎ 6331 6766; 14 Quadrant Mall; 8.30am-5.30pm Mon-Sat) This Mediterranean-influenced café offers you friendly service and a seasonal menu involving delicious twists on salads, *pides*, pizzas and pastas. The coffee is intense to the correct degree, the gourmet desserts are yummy and you can down a glass or two from the sizeable wine list.

Caffé Fiore (Map p196; ☎ 6331 5146; 65-67 Cimitiere St; mains from $6.50; breakfast & lunch) This personable café has lifted a bit of Sydney and moved it into Launceston. It offers savoury, home-style Italian bagel melts and an asparagus-and-chicken pie creation that is almost ceremonial. It also provides organic and gluten- and wheat-free goodies. Fringing the corporate edge of town, it caters to business clientele while still retaining intimacy (ie no room for the group thang).

Ric's Cafe Bar (Map p196; 35-39 Cameron St; mains $13-25; breakfast, lunch & dinner) By day this sophisticated new venue dishes out an array of café fare; options include an extensive seafood menu, pizzas, or something special like a Yankee pot roast or a moussaka that's bound to line your tummy. It also provides late-night entertainment (see opposite).

Fish 'n' Chips (Map p196; ☎ 6331 1999; 30 Seaport Blvd; meals $10-15; lunch & dinner) Perched on the riverfront, this modern affair offers fresh fish 'n' chips (from around $6), seafood salads and antipasto platters. Kids are bound to get into a feathered fist fight with a seagull or two in its alfresco dining area.

Flavours on Charles (Map p195; ☎ 6331 3968; 252 Charles St; mains $18.50-25; breakfast, lunch & dinner) Part of the Sportsman Hall Hotel, this place has been completely renovated. Offering café-style ambience, with more formal dining of an evening, it serves mod-Oz cuisine, such as pasta, chicken and seafood.

Konditorei Cafe Manfred (Map p196; ☎ 6334 2490; 106 George St; mains $10-16; breakfast & lunch) This eatery allows you to gorge yourself on really tasty baked goods (gourmet breads, tarts, tortes) and plenty of creative vegetarian dishes either at a downstairs table or upstairs on the weather-proofed terrace.

Fresh (Map p196; 6331 4299; 178 Charles St; mains $8-16; breakfast & lunch) This all-welcoming retro-arty place, opposite attractive Princes Sq, offers tasty vegetarian snacks, including terrific pizza, bruschettas and a plug-your-stomach brekky 'with the works'.

Metz (Map p196; ☎ 6331 7277; 119 St John St; mains $8-20; breakfast, lunch & dinner) This casual café-bar has a comfortable, well-worn feel. The menu has Mediterranean flair, with filling, traditional breakfasts, gourmet wood-fired pizzas and vegetarian delights.

Pasta Resistance Too (Map p196; ☎ 6334 3081; 23 Quadrant Mall; lunch meals $4.50-6; breakfast & lunch) Attracting a mixed crowd, this popular, tiny eatery is famous for its wonderfully fresh pasta and sauces. You can bulk-buy pasta or sauces (*bolognaise, marinara,* mushroom) for around $12 per kg.

DRINKING & ENTERTAINMENT

Most of Launceston's entertainment options are advertised in the daily newspaper the *Examiner*.

Ursula's on Brisbane (Map p196; ☎ 6334 7033; 63 Brisbane St; 11am-11pm Tue-Sat) This cosmopolitan and stylish wine-and-tapas bar is great for grazing on morsels of sustenance while sipping through choice Tassie wines. Soak up the Euro ambience on comfy leather sofas; the savvy are onto this one.

Ric's Cafe Bar (Map p196; 35-39 Cameron St; 11pm-2am Fri & Sat) By night this eatery (opposite) dons a different cap and entertains the cool set with funky jazz bands, letting the crowd unwind with a drink without smoking them into live herrings.

Club 54 (Map p196; ☎ 6331 7222; rear of Batman Fawkner Inn, 35 Cameron St) In a town where nightclubs are as rare as hen's teeth, this newcomer has quickly earned a popular reputation for staging top live acts and DJ music on Friday and Saturday nights. Located just behind the Batty. Entry to the club is off the side lane.

Saloon Bar (Map p196; ☎ 6331 7355; 191 Charles St; noon-midnight Sun-Tue, noon-3am Wed-Sat) Part of the Hotel Tasmania complex, this bar has *Bonanza* décor that's a mixture of the good, the bad and the ugly, but it does have DJs and cover bands strutting their stuff Wednesday to Saturday nights.

Lounge Bar (Map p196; ☎ 6334 6622; 63 St John St; 4pm-late Sun-Tue, 3pm-late Wed & Thu, noon-late Fri, 2pm-late Sat) This late-night venue, inside an atmospheric 1907 former bank building, has a cool, loungey atmosphere, complete with hanging lampshades and lanterns. It host regular bands (usually Thursday to Saturday nights) upstairs or in the downstairs bar, which used to be the bank vault.

Irish Murphy's (Map p196; ☎ 6331 4440; cnr Brisbane & Bathurst Sts; admission free; noon-midnight Sun-Wed, noon-2am Thu-Sat) These 'drinking consultants' challenge the notion that it's a mere pub stuffed full of Emerald Isle paraphernalia – this excellent venue also has live music Thursday through Saturday nights and you can eavesdrop on the Sunday arvo jam sessions.

Princess Theatre (Map p196; ☎ 6323 3666; 57 Brisbane St) Built in 1911, and including the smaller Earl Arts Centre, this theatre stages an eclectic mix of drama, dance and comedy, drawing acts from across Tasmania and the mainland.

Village Cinemas (Map p196; ☎ 6331 5066; 163 Brisbane St; adult/child $12/8.50) Escape the everyday and take in a big-budget flick.

SHOPPING

Swiss Chocolatier (Map p196; ☎ 6334 3411; 83 George St) The no-frills shop displays a serious concentration on hand-making the most sumptuous, delectable chocolates this side of the Alps. Float over to the counter and try some gourmet pralines or liqueur-imbued morsels. Treats include gourmet shortbreads and Stollen bread.

Benchmark Tasmania Wine Gallery (Map p196; ☎ 6331 3977; www.benchmarkwinegallery.com; 135 Paterson St; 10am-6pm Mon-Thu, to 7pm Fri & Sat, 11am-7pm Sun) Just near Ritchies Mill, this gallery showcases an extensive range (over 250 types) of rare and premium local and imported wines and offers free tastings of selected Tassie wines.

Paddy Pallin (Map p196; ☎ 6331 4240; 110 George St) sells (and hires out) camping gear, maps and travel accessories, as does **Allgoods** (Map p196; ☎ 6331 3644; cnr York & St John Sts).

If you're in a market mood, there are craft markets held every weekend at **Inveresk** (Map p195; Railyards, off Forster St; 10am-4pm Sun) and **Yorktown Sq** (Map p196; 9am-2pm Sun).

GETTING THERE & AWAY

Air

There are regular flights between Launceston and both Melbourne and Sydney, with connections onward to other Australian capital cities. For flight details see p332. **Qantas** (Map p196; ☎ 13 13 13, 6332 9911; www.qantas.com.au; cnr Brisbane & Charles Sts) has an office in the centre of town.

For details of the daily flights from Launceston to Flinders Island see p335. Charter flights with the smaller airlines can also be arranged.

Bus

The main bus companies operating out of Launceston are **Redline Coaches** (☎ 1300 360 000; www.tasredline.com.au) and **TassieLink** (☎ 1300 300 520; www.tassielink.com.au); the depot for services is at **Cornwall Square Transit Centre** (Map p196; cnr St John & Cimitiere Sts), at the rear of the visitors centre.

Redline runs buses to Bicheno ($28, 2¾ hours), Burnie ($24, 2¾ hours), Deloraine ($10, 45 minutes), Devonport ($18, 1½ hours), George Town ($9.10, 45 minutes), Hobart ($25, 2½ hours), Stanley ($37, four hours), St Helens ($25, 2¾ hours) and Swansea ($22, two hours). It also runs weekday services along the eastern side of the Tamar River.

TassieLink has a regular city express service linking Launceston with Devonport ($18, 1¼ hours), tying in with the ferry schedules, and linking Launceston and Hobart ($24, 2½ hours). It services the north and west from Launceston, including Sheffield ($20, two hours), Gowrie Park ($24), Cradle Mountain ($50, three hours), Rosebery ($45, five hours), Zeehan ($50, 5½ hours), Queenstown ($60, six hours) and, after a break in Queenstown, to Strahan ($65, 8¾ hours). TassieLink also runs a twice-weekly service between Launceston and Bicheno ($26, 2½ hours) – service is increased to four times weekly in summer.

Tamar Valley Coaches (Map p196; ☎ 6334 0828; 4 Cuisine Lane), off Brisbane St, operates bus services along the West Tamar Valley, stopping at Legana ($3), Rosevears ($3.20), Beaconsfield ($6.40) and Beauty Point ($7.20, one hour).

Car

There are plenty of car-rental firms in Launceston. All the major firms have desks at the airport, and most also have an office in town. The bigger ones include **Europcar** (Map p196; ☎ 1800 030 118, 6331 8200; 112 George St) and **Thrifty** (Map p196; ☎ 6333 0911, 1800 030 730; 151 St John St). Cheaper operators include **Economy Car Rentals** (Map p196; ☎ 6334 3299; 27 William St), with prices starting at $31 per day (older cars, and rentals of at least seven days) and **Lo-Cost Auto Rent** (Map p196; ☎ 1800 647 060; www.rentforless.com.au; 174 Brisbane St), with a good selection of vehicles and starting rates from $30 to $45 daily for multi-day hire. See p338 for more information.

GETTING AROUND

To/From the Airport

Launceston airport is 15km south of the city. A **shuttle bus** (☎ 0500 512 009) runs a door-to-door airport service costing $10/5 per adult/child. A taxi to the city costs about $30.

Bicycle

Rent-a-Cycle (Map p195; ☎ 6344 9779; tasequiphire@email.com; 36 Thistle St), at the Launceston City Youth Hostel (p200), has a good range of touring/mountain bikes from $12/18 per day (ask for weekly or monthly rates), plus camping equipment for hire and lots of walking advice.

Seaport Boat & Bike Hire (Map p196; ☎ 6331 8999; hire@jmc.com.au; 26 Seaport Blvd) has bikes for rent (from $10/40 per hour/day), plus canoes ($10/50) and motorboats ($35/155) for river exploration. Touring bikes are also available for longer-term hire.

Bus

The local bus service is run by **Metro** (☎ 13 22 01; www.metrotas.com.au); the main departure points are on the two blocks of St John St between Paterson and York Sts. For $3.60 you can buy a daily pass that can be used after 9am Monday to Friday and all day Saturday, Sunday and public holidays. Most routes, however, don't operate in the evening and Sunday services are limited.

AROUND LAUNCESTON

TAMAR VALLEY

The Tamar Valley funnels the river of the same name north from Launceston to Bass Strait. Tidal for this 64km stretch, the Tamar River separates the east and west Tamar districts and links Launceston with its ocean port of Bell Bay near George Town. Crossing the river near Deviot is Batman Bridge, a unique single-tower structure that is the only bridge on the lower reaches of the Tamar.

The Tamar Valley and the nearby Pipers River are among Tasmania's main wine-producing areas, and the dry premium wines produced here have achieved international recognition.

Getting There & Around

BICYCLE

The ride north along the Tamar River is an absolute gem. On the west bank, it's possible to avoid most of the highway and follow quiet roads with few hills through the small settlements. On the eastern shore, follow the minor roads inland to Lilydale: there are plenty of hills but the varied landscape more than compensates for the work. The only way to cross the lower reaches of the Tamar River is either via Batman Bridge (p209) or by ferry (p208).

BUS

On weekdays (not weekends or public holidays) **Tamar Valley Coaches** (Map p196; ☎ 6334 0828; 4 Cuisine Lane) runs three to five buses a day from Launceston up and down the West Tamar Valley. Destinations from Launceston are Legana ($3), Rosevears ($3.20), Exeter ($4), Gravelly Beach ($4.70), Sidmouth ($5), Beaconsfield ($6.50) and Beauty Point ($7.20, one hour).

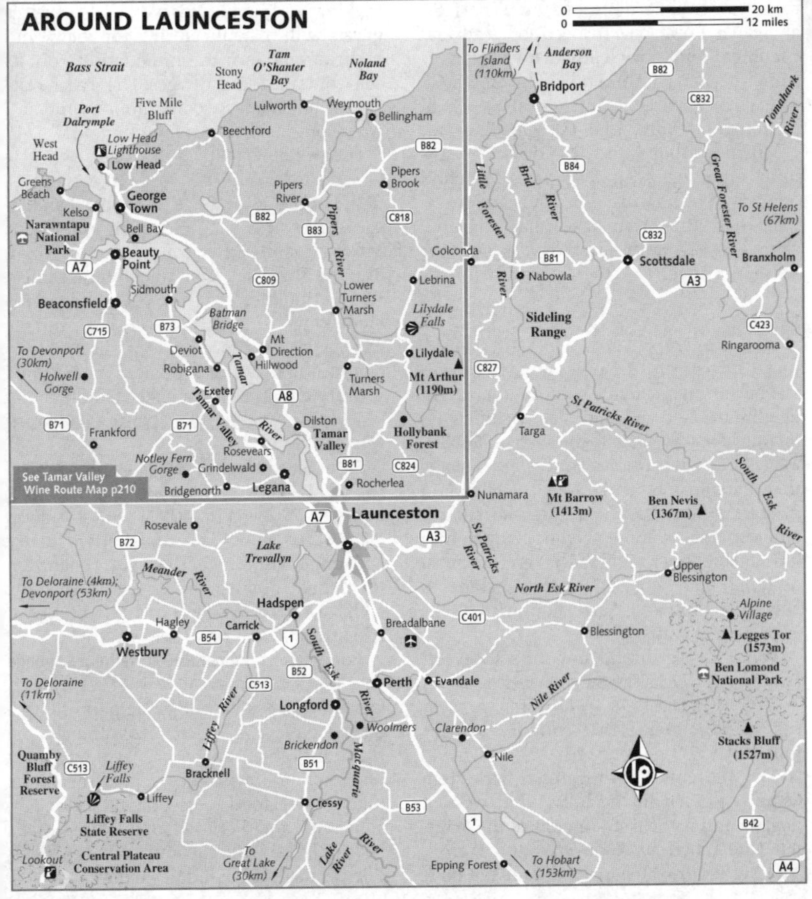

Redline Coaches (☎ 1300 360 000, 6336 1446; www.tasredline.com.au) runs three buses every weekday (no weekend services) along the eastern side of the Tamar from Launceston to Hillwood ($5.50), the Batman Bridge turn-off ($6.60) and George Town ($8.60, 45 minutes).

Four times each weekday, Redline runs between Launceston and Deloraine ($10, 45 minutes), via Carrick ($3.50) and Westbury ($5).

FERRY

There's now a **Shuttlefish ferry** (☎ 6383 4479, 0412 485 611; www.shuttlefishferry.com.au; Wed-Mon Oct-May) on-demand service making regular trips across the Tamar River between Beauty Point and George Town. The ferry runs from public pontoons on Wharf Rd at Beauty Point, via Inspection Head and Clarence Point. In George Town it leaves from the pier at the end of Elizabeth St. The ferry departs Beauty Point at 10am, 1.30pm and 3pm, and George Town at 10.40am, 2.10pm and 3.40pm. The 25-minute journey costs $9/5 per adult/child one way, $16/9 return. Bookings are essential. Cyclists in particular will appreciate the short-cut, saving the backtrack to get over Batman Bridge.

Legana

☎ 03 / pop 1990

Just 12km north of Launceston, Legana is fast becoming a satellite suburb of its larger neighbour. A conspicuous and somewhat incongruous feature of the area is **Grindelwald** (☎ 6330 0400; Waldhorn Dr), a Swiss 'village' that inexplicably emigrated to Tasmania to start a new life as a residential suburb and resort (even some neighbouring homes have taken on decidedly Swiss architectural designs). The shopping village includes a chocolate shop and a gift shop or two selling arts and crafts.

Wine lovers should not miss **Rosevears Estate** (☎ 6330 1800; www.rosevearsestate.com.au; 1A Waldhorn Dr; tastings $2; 10am-5pm), a prestigious wine-maker that conducts winery tours for $3.30 per person.

The authentically overgrown **Notley Fern Gorge** is hidden in the hills 14km west of Legana and is the last remnant of the original forest that once covered the region. The big hollow burnt-out tree in the park was reputedly the hiding place of Matthew Brady, a famous 19th-century bushranger. It's a nice cool place on a warm day and the circuit walk takes about 45 minutes.

SLEEPING & EATING

Launceston Holiday Park (☎ 6330 1714; launceston@islandcabins.com.au; 711 West Tamar Hwy; unpowered/powered sites $16/20, on-site vans from $40, cabins $65-85) Conveniently located, this park has a range of cabins (some with spa), from basic stuffy budget versions to deluxe spa units. There's a full-sized tennis court for the very active; site prices are for up to two people.

Rosevears Estate (☎ 6330 1800; www.rosevearsestate.com.au; 1A Waldhorn Dr; 1-/2-bedroom cottages $230/380; mains $16.50-28; lunch, dinner Wed-Sat) Not content with juggling viticulture, winemaking and food, Rosevears also serves guests with magnificent hill-top views and luxurious modern accommodation from its self-contained stilt cottages. The stylish restaurant offers a tasty contemporary menu – we recommend the seafood linguine.

Freshwater Point (☎ 6330 2200; www.freshwaterpoint.com; 56 Nobelius Dr; B&B d $180, cottages $190;) Tucked away on a sweeping bend of the Tamar, this 1824 Georgian homestead offers elegant B&B accommodation. There are also three self-contained cottages nestled within the grounds (all cottages include king-sized beds and one has a double shower). Surrounded by deep, shady verandas and stands of elms planted more than a century ago, there's a pocket-handkerchief vineyard, orchards, and a private riverfront to stroll along.

Chancellor Resort Tamar Valley Grindelwald (☎ 1800 817 595, 6330 0400; reception@chancellorresorttvg.com.au; 7 Waldhorn Dr; hotel ste d $170-240, chalets $185-270, apt $205-250) This resort offers luxury accommodation; whether you've chosen the deluxe, honeymoon or executive suite, all have a spa and complimentary brekky at Alpenrose Restaurant (below).

Food-wise, try **Alpenrose Restaurant & Lounge Bar** (☎ 6330 0550; Waldhorn Dr; mains $17-22; breakfast, lunch & dinner). Despite being part of Grindelwald village, it's fortunately dragged the menu into the 21st century, avoiding most references to 'Swiss cheese'. Try the exotic ragout of seafood (a medley of seafood in a banana and Pernod curry sauce that's been infused with coconut cream; $23). It doesn't neglect the kiddies either.

Rosevears

☎ 03 / pop 160

On the western side of the Tamar, it's worth leaving the highway and following the narrow sealed road along the river and through the pretty riverside settlement of Rosevears, an area great for wine buffs.

Along the scenic riverbank drive, you'll come across **Rosevears Waterfront Tavern** (☎ 63 94 4074; 215 Rosevears Dr; mains $15-20; lunch & dinner). First opened in 1831, it's still serving pub fare today, though the food is now a tad more upmarket with such delights as seafood vol-au-vents, or T-bone with tomato and pepper chutney.

Near the tavern is the not-for-profit **Waterbird Haven Trust** (☎ 6394 3744; Rosevears Dr; adult/child $5/3; 9am-dusk), a marine-bird sanctuary on tidal mud flats that harbour a huge variety of ducks, pheasants and teals, among others. Guided tours are by appointment only. Here, too, you'll meet the 91-year-old Norah Doray, who set up the trust some 25 years ago; she's a little hard of hearing but always has time for a cuppa and a chat.

Wine aficionados can guzzle some vino at **Strathlynn** (☎ 6330 2388; www.pbv.com.au; 95 Rosevears Dr; tastings $3; 10am-5pm), an outlet for the Pipers Brook Vineyard. Its highly polished **restaurant** (mains $18-28; noon-3pm) features Tassie produce. Nearby **St Matthias Vineyard** (☎ 6330 1700; www.moorilla.com.au; 113 Rosevears Dr; free tastings; 10am-5pm) carries the theme to the stunning church-like cellar door, where you can sample Moorilla favourites with cheese and antipasto. There's Sunday jazz and BBQs over summer.

Just north of St Matthias is the fully self-contained **Conmel Cottage** (☎ /fax 6330 1466; conmel.cottage@bigpond.com; 125 Rosevears Dr; s/d $120/130). Prices include a fully cooked breakfast, and there's a veggie garden and orchard for seasonal produce.

When you rejoin the highway, follow the signs to the nearby **Brady's Lookout State Reserve**. The well-known bushranger Brady used this rocky outcrop to spy on travellers on the road below. Nearby you'll find the outstandingly modern self-contained **Bradys Lookout B&B** (☎ 6394 4009, 0400 639 409; bradyslookout@bigpond.com; 1876 West Tamar Hwy; d $165), perched high up on the hillside with panoramic views across the valley. Guests receive a gourmet breakfast hamper and complimentary vino.

Exeter & Around

☎ 03 / pop 400

This is predominantly an orchard and mixed farming area. The local **Tamar visitors centre** (☎ 6394 4454; www.wtc.tas.gov.au; West Tamar Hwy; 10am-4pm May-Nov, 9am-5pm Dec-Apr), which sits on the main street, can arm travellers with regional information.

For budget accommodation, try the large, dirt-cheap rooms at the **Exeter Hotel** (☎ 6394 4216; Main Rd; s/d $15/30). Counter meals are served here from Wednesday to Saturday. Another food option is the **Exeter Bakery** (☎ 6394 4069; Main Rd; 7am-5pm Jun-Aug, 7am-6pm Sep-May). Its 103-year-old wood-fired oven produces all manner of pies; the seafood pie is a winner, and if you're lucky you might find speciality pies, such as wallaby, or lambs fry and bacon. It also serves up tasty veggie rolls and banbury slices.

South of Exeter, Gravelly Beach Rd will take you to **Kookla's** (☎ 6394 4013; 285 Gravelly Beach Rd; lunch & dinner Wed-Sat), a BYO café serving sensational Mediterranean cuisine, just the way mama always made it. The same road will take you to Robigana (derived from the Aboriginal word for 'swans'), the spot where the road crosses the Supply River. From here there's a marked walking track (one hour return) beside the Tamar River to **Paper Beach**. There's also a pleasant 400m walk along the river to the meagre ruins of Australia's first water-driven **flour mill**. Further along is the **Artisan Gallery** (☎ 6394 4595; www.artisangallery.com.au; 32 Deviot Rd, Robigana; 10am-5pm Sep-May, 10am-4pm Fri-Mon Jun-Aug), which showcases crafts of well-known artisans, including some stunning water-etched porcelain bowls and vases and intricately designed perfume bottles. It also has a strong collection of boutique Tasmanian wines.

Further upstream on the Supply River is **Norfolk Reach B&B** (☎ /fax 6394 7681; norfolkreachguesthouse@bigpond.com; 84 Motor Rd, Deviot; d from $90), a wonderfully isolated homestead surrounded by 72 acres of bird-stocked bushland. It's nearly 5km up Motor Rd. Ring ahead in case the managers aren't around.

BATMAN BRIDGE

An important link between the two banks of the Tamar River, and opened in 1968 as one of the world's first cable-stayed truss bridges, the Batman Bridge has an eye-catching design that resulted not so much from creative inspiration as from foundation problems. The east bank offered poor support for a large bridge, so it holds up just a minor part of the span. Most of the bridge is actually supported by the 100m-tall west tower that leans out over the river. Try the river's east bank for good views.

Passing underneath the bridge on the western bank is a gravel road leading to **Sidmouth** and the long-worshipped local institution of Auld Kirk ('old church'). Proceed north on the C724 to the Auburn Rd junction at Kayena. Turning left on Auburn road for about a kilometre leads you to another institution, **Tamar Ridge Wines** (☎ 6394 1114; Auburn Rd, Kayena; 🕑 10am-5pm), known for its trophy-winning riesling and Pinot Noir – a must for wine connoisseurs.

Beaconsfield & Around

☎ 03 / pop 1015

The once-thriving but now somewhat subdued gold-mining town of Beaconsfield is dominated by the **Grubb Shaft Gold & Heritage Museum** (☎ 6383 1473; museum@wtc.tas.gov.au; West St; adult/concession/family $8/6/20; 🕑 9.30am-4.30pm Oct-Apr, 10am-4pm May-Sep), once Tasmania's largest gold mine. The museum's hands-on interactive exhibits, including a noisy water wheel–powered battery, are popular with children.

Nine kilometres south of Beaconsfield is the small **Holwell Gorge** reserve, which con-

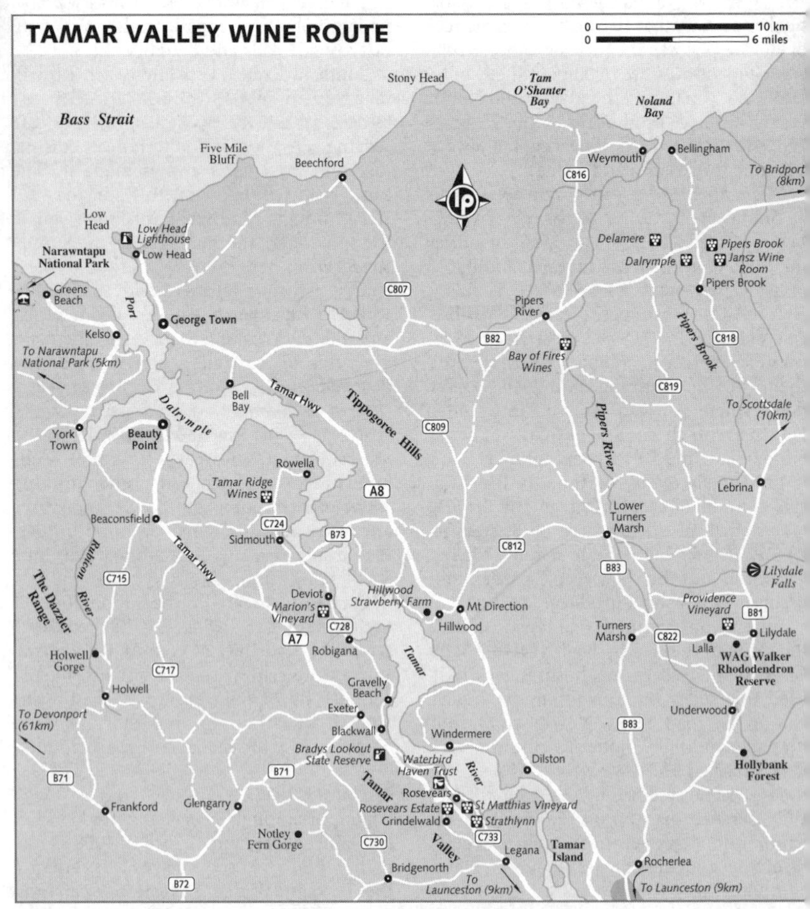

tains secluded sections of original forest, giant trees reaching 60m and three waterfalls. The walking track linking the southern and northern entrances of the gorge (4.5km apart by road) takes around two hours one way.

Beauty Point

☎ 03 / pop 1500

Though the surrounding landscape is certainly beautiful, with rolling hills and great river views, the town's name actually derives from a bullock called Beauty (no relation to Sandra).

Beauty Point's main attraction is **Seahorse World** (☎ 6383 4111; www.seahorseworld.com.au; Beauty Point Wharf; adult/child/concession/family $15/8/12/40; 9.30am-4.30pm), based around a sea-horse farm where the tiny critters are grown to supply aquariums worldwide and eventually, it's hoped, the Chinese-medicine market. There's an interesting one-hour tour where you get right up close to the fascinating *Hippocampus abdominalis* (pot-bellied sea horse) and watch the feeding frenzy too.

Next to Seahorse World, the new venture **Platypus House** (☎ 6383 4884; www.platypushouse.com.au; Inspection Head Wharf; adult/child/concession/family $15/8/12/40; 9am-4pm) seemed a little underdeveloped when we visited. The informative one-hour guided tour consisted of only two platypuses on show and no butterflies at all in the much-touted Butterfly House, and while it lived up to its promise on the creepy crawlies, such as scorpions and killer spiders, the entire operation didn't do enough to warrant the full entry fee.

SLEEPING & EATING

Redbill Caravan Park (☎ 6383 4536; www.redbillpark.com.au; Redbill Point; unpowered/powered sites $14/18, on-site vans $35, cabins $65-75) This park has some of its comfortable cabins overlooking the boat-littered waters behind the point. Site prices are for up to two people.

Tamar Cove (☎ 6383 4375; 4421 Main Rd; motel r $55-65; meals $12-21; lunch & dinner) These clean and tidy rooms are a decent option. The on-site restaurant attracts hungry crowds to its bright interior and alfresco terrace with designer-tastebud fare such as orange-marmalade-glazed quail, and scallops in a shiraz-and-cream sauce.

Beauty Point Cottages (☎ 6383 4556, 0428 768 790; 14 Flinders St; d $120-165) Offering stylish spa cottage accommodation or cosy homestead en suites. Guests can laze about under wide verandas or toast some snags on the BBQ in the lovely gazebo overlooking country gardens and river views.

Pomona B&B (☎ 6383 4073; www.pomonabandb.com.au; 77 Flinders St; homestead/cottage d from $140/160) In this Federation homestead at the southern end of town the rooms come with full cooked breakfasts and porch-front river views. Pomona also has two hideaway spa cottages providing cosy, romantic retreats.

Gallus@seahorseworld (☎ 6383 4964; Beauty Point Wharf; mains $10-18; breakfast & lunch) Upstairs at Seahorse World and proudly displaying outstanding views of the Tamar, this restaurant-café serves terrific snacks, such as Boag's beer-battered flathead plus fries and scrumptious Devonshire teas and muffins ($6). Is that a chocolate sea horse on my cappuccino froth? Adjacent to the restaurant there's a wine centre that tops up your glass for just $5.

The nearby holiday settlements of Kelso and Greens Beach also appeal. Site prices are for up to two people.

Greens Beach Caravan Park (☎ 6383 9222; Main Rd; unpowered/powered sites $11/14) Adjacent to a calm ocean beach.

Kelso Sands Caravan Park (☎ 1800 039 139, 6383 9130; kelsocaravanpark@tassie.net.au; 86 Paranaple Rd; unpowered/powered sites $15/18, on-site vans $45, cabins $80;) Offers cosy, well-equipped cabins just 100m from the water.

George Town

☎ 03 / pop 5600

George Town, on the eastern shore of the Tamar River, close to the heads, grew on the site occupied by Lt Colonel Paterson in 1804 to stave off a feared French occupation. Some of the older buildings in town date from the 1830s and 1840s, when it prospered as the port linking Tasmania with Victoria. George Town's main drawcard is its proximity to good beaches, penguin rookeries and the maritime history of the Low Head pilot station and lighthouse.

INFORMATION

Commonwealth Bank (Macquarie St) Has an ATM.

Post office (Macquarie St)

Visitors centre (☎ 6382 1700; Main Rd; 9am-5pm) On the main road as you enter from the south – if you're interested in a self-guided tour of the town and of nearby Low Head, pick up the *George Town Heritage Trail* brochure.

SIGHTS

The **Grove** (☎ 6382 1336; thegrove@intas.net.au; cnr Cimitiere & Elizabeth Sts; adult/child $7.50/3.50; 10am-5pm mid-Sep–mid-May, 10.30am-3pm Mon-Fri mid-May–mid-Sep) is an extensively restored Georgian bluestone residence (c 1830s), classified by the National Trust and well worth a look. To spend the night, see Nanna's Cottage, right).

Another historical stalwart is the 1843 **old watch-house** (Macquarie St). Its historical exhibits include an early George Town model village. On nearby **Mt George**, play spot-the-restored-semaphore-mast-and-flagstaff amid a litter of newer communication towers, or just enjoy the view. There's a wheelchair-accessible ramp from the car park to the mountain top.

TOURS

Seal & Sea Adventure Tours (☎/fax 6382 3452, 0419 357 028; www.sealandsea.com) offers three- to four-hour trips in a glass-bottom boat out to the seal colony at Tenth Island, with an enthusiastic and knowledgeable guide at the helm; trips cost $121 per person for two people and $94 per person for groups of three to six. Tamar River cruises, and fishing and dive charters can also be arranged.

North of town at the airport (follow the road to Low Head and turn right down North St for about 2km) you can take 30-minute ultralight-plane flights over the hills with **Freedom Flight** (☎ 6382 4700). These cost from $75 per person; book a couple of days in advance.

SLEEPING & EATING

For camping and caravan parks in the area see opposite.

George Town Heritage Hotel (George Town Hotel; ☎ 6382 2655; gt.hotel@bigpond.net.au; 75 Macquarie St; d $80; mains $12-22) Built in 1846, this historic pub offers spacious and comfortable accommodation with en suites, and includes a decent bistro serving excellent steaks and seafood. It also houses a gallery featuring 'Art in the Pub', where you can buy locally crafted posters, tapestries, watercolours or $300 acrylic-painted ostrich eggs.

Pier Hotel Motel (☎ 13 24 00, 6382 1300; info@pierhotel.com.au; 5 Elizabeth St; r with/without bathroom $110/55, villas from $150; mains $12-20; lunch & dinner) This hotel offers modern and refurbished riverside lodgings. Some rooms are bedecked in startling hues and florals, but all are good-sized and comfortable. The popular bistro satisfies meat-eaters with seafood and scotch fillets; vegetarians are not totally forgotten, they just have fewer options.

Nanna's Cottage (☎ 6382 1336; thegrove@intas.net.au; cnr Cimitiere & Elizabeth Sts; d $85-90) This delightful cottage at the Grove provides cosy B&B accommodation with all modern amenities included; BYO nanna. Light lunches and teas are also available at the Grove, served in the spirit of the past by staff in period costume.

Signature Cafe (☎ 6382 1748; 48 Macquarie St; mains $8-10; 8am-5pm Mon-Fri) This is a cheerful place with a good range of light meals such as focaccias and salads.

Red Dragon (☎ 6382 2833; 94-96 Macquarie St; mains $10-15; 5-10pm Mon, noon-10pm Tue-Sun) Red Dragon serves Chinese favourites from a pink penthouse at the eastern end of Macquarie St.

GETTING THERE & AWAY

The George Town agent for Redline is **Pino's Gift & Hardware** (21 Elizabeth St).

Low Head

☎ 03 / pop 465

Located on the eastern side of the Tamar River where it enters Bass Strait, this scattered settlement doesn't have a 'town centre' as such – most inhabitants rely on the shops and eateries of George Town, only 5km away.

The historic **pilot station** was established in 1805 (making it Australia's oldest continuously operating station), with the current buildings erected between 1835 and 1962. In fact, most of the buildings here pre-date Batman's voyage north to Melbourne. Here you'll find the recently upgraded **Pilot Station Maritime Museum** (☎ 6382 2826; Low Head Rd; adult/child/pensioner/family $5/3/4/20; 9am-6pm), which has rooms cluttered with an incredible number of maritime historical items, archives and displays, including an impressive communications exhibit. Bound to impress seafaring folk and landlubbers alike.

It's from here that those with sea legs can set sail on the brigantine **Windeward Bound** (☎ 1800 008 343; www.windbound.com; sailings ⏰ Wed-Sun Oct-Apr), tracing aspects of Matthew Flinders' first voyage into the Tamar River. Two- or three-hour sailings depart from the Low Head pilot station, or you can tour the docked tall ship. Bookings can also be made at Galley Café (right).

At the head itself, the grounds of the 1888 **lighthouse** (grounds ⏰ to 6pm) provide great views over the river mouth and surrounding area. There are also several navigational leading lights (mini-lighthouses) around town dating from 1881. If you keep an ear out you'll catch the bellow of the **foghorn** every Sunday at noon.

Penguins return to their burrows near the lighthouse at dusk and can be viewed via **Nocturnal Tours** (☎ 0418 361 860; www.penguin tours.com.au). Tours cost $14/8 per adult/child and take place nightly, departing from a signposted spot beside the main road just south of the lighthouse.

There's good surf at **East Beach** on Bass Strait and safe swimming at all beaches.

SLEEPING & EATING

Low Head Beachfront Holiday Village (☎ 6382 1000; fax 6382 1555; 192 Gunns Pde; sites per person $18, cabins $60-75) This holiday park has claimed a good location on East Beach for its multitude of bush sites and pine-drenched cabins.

Pilot Station (☎ 1800 008 343, ☎/fax 6382 1143; Low Head Rd; B&B d from $90) Low Head's historic precinct offers a range of pleasant, fully self-contained, waterfront colonial cottages for up to eight people, well suited to overnight or extended stays.

Mandalay (☎ 6382 2575, 0438 822 575; 155 Low Head Rd; d $80-125, per week $350-600) Secluded and private, this three-bedroom holiday cottage provides excellent accommodation for families, with good self-contained facilities, large, open plan living and its own beach frontage, including a hot outdoor shower for sandy beach feet.

Moana by the Sea (☎ 6382 1082; drlawrence@ bigpond.com; 201 Old Aerodrome Rd; d $140) This great-value boutique option offers very comfortable lodgings, with en suite, spa, all the mod cons and a Tuscan-style dining area opening onto a sundeck and gardens.

Belfont Cottages (☎ 6382 1399, 0418 300 036; 178 Low Head Rd; d $125) These cottages, built to house the caretakers of the leading light next door, offer B&B accommodation in well-equipped, period-style interiors.

Galley Café (Low Head Rd; Pilot Station; ⏰ 10am-5pm) This café, housed in the historic Coxswain's Cottage, serves up light snacks and refreshments, including hearty soups ($7.50). Staff can also take bookings for sailings on the tall ship *Windeward Bound* (left).

PIPERS RIVER REGION

This northerly rural region plays a pivotal role in the Tasmanian wine industry, producing nearly half of the state's wines. The countryside through which you drive to visit the vineyards is unremarkable, but some of the vineyards themselves are quite attractive.

The most famous local grape-squeezer, popular with weekend warriors and locals alike, is **Pipers Brook** (☎ 6382 7527; 1216 Pipers Brook Rd, Pipers Brook; tastings $3; ⏰ 10am-5pm), which was started in the wake of an academic exercise by Dr Andrew Pirie, who compared the famous wine regions of France with Australian regions. Here you can try Pipers Brook Vineyard and Ninth Island wines. The architecturally innovative main building includes the **Winery Café** (mains $20; ⏰ lunch), which serves a changing menu of light snacks, including quiche ($12.95), and a delectable platter of Tasmanian cheeses.

Also within the Pipers Brook estate about 700m along, you can visit the separately-run **Jansz Wine Room** (☎ 6382 7066; 1216B Pipers Brook Rd, Pipers Brook; ⏰ 10am-4.30pm) where you can taste a damn fine sparkly, and good Chardonnay/Pinot Noir blends. There are self-guided tours clarifying some of the '*méthode Tasmanoise*' wine production; there's a cheesery to complement the sparkly, and a garden terrace to enjoy your wine or coffee on.

Some 15km away and located south of Pipers River, **Bay of Fires Wines** (☎ 6382 7622; 40 Baxters Rd, Pipers River; tastings free; ⏰ 10am-5pm) includes a stylish **restaurant** (mains $12-35) serving good Tasmanian produce indoors or alfresco. Relax with a glass of the fine rose-gold-coloured Pinot Grigio 2003.

Other local vineyards worth a visit include the friendly **Delamere** (☎ 6382 7190; 4238 Bridport Rd, or B82 Hwy, Pipers Brook; ⏰ 10am-5pm), which offers superb unwooded Chardonnay and

Pinot Noir varieties, and **Dalrymple** (☎/fax 6382 7222; 1337 Pipers Brook Rd, Pipers Brook; 10am-5pm) for good French-style Pinot Noir and award-winning Sauvignon Blanc.

NARAWNTAPU NATIONAL PARK

Located 25km east of Devonport (12km off the B71), the Narawntapu (formerly the Asbestos Range) National Park's scenery isn't as rugged as in many other parks; its more gentle landscape allows visitors around dusk to see lots of Forester kangaroos, foraging wombats, wallabies and pademelons.

Park entry fees apply and permits are available from the **rangers** (☎ 6428 6277; 10am-4pm Mar-Nov, 10am-5pm Dec-Feb) at Narawntapu National Park's western end. Rangers also provide guided walks and activities over summer. Horse riding is allowed and the park has corrals and a 26km trail; bookings with the ranger are required, as facilities are limited. **Bakers Beach** is the safest swimming area and water-skiing is permitted here in summer.

There are some engaging walking trails in the park. You can round **Badger Head** in around six to eight hours (via Copper Cove), while the **Archers Knob** (114m) walk (around two hours return) has good views of Bakers Beach. The one-hour **Springlawn Nature Trail** includes a boardwalk over wetlands to a bird-hide. The beach from Griffiths Point to Bakers Point is good for beachcombing and sunset-watching; try the **West Head Lookout** for great views over Bass Strait.

The park has four **camp sites** (per person adult/child $4.40/2.20), each with bore water and some firewood provided; sites must be prebooked through the ranger. The old pit toilets have been upgraded (to the eco-friendly septic types) as has the local road network. Note there's no fresh reliable drinking water available.

The park can be reached from the Beaconsfield area or Greens Beach (via C721), or from Port Sorell (via C740).

LILYDALE

☎ 03 / pop 345

Tiny Lilydale is 25km north of Launceston and is popular with visitors for its walks, wineries and gardens. The town's landmark is the 1888 National Trust–listed **Bardenhagen's General Store** (Main Rd; 7am-7pm Mon-Fri, 7.30am-6pm Sat), stocking provisions including superb Bardenhagen bread. The wall paintings are replicas of the images painted on various telephone poles, a display reminiscent of Sheffield's murals (p232).

On the road to Lalla is the **WAG Walker Rhododendron Reserve** (admission per vehicle $2;

TALL POPPIES

Wine making is a well-known and lucrative Tasmanian industry, but less well known is the fact that this small island is also one of the world's most successful opium poppy entrepreneurs. Since the first commercial poppy-growing season began in 1970, after six years of intensive government-supervised agronomic trials, Tasmania has cornered 40% of the international poppy market – it's the only place in the southern hemisphere where this farming activity is legal, and the industry currently involves around 1200 growers who cultivate 200 sq km of the plant every year.

Tasmanian poppies are raised in the healthy soils along the state's north and east coasts, in the southeast and in the midlands. Using a method developed by Hungarian chemist Janos Kabay in the early 1930s, opiate alkaloids are extracted directly from the dry poppy straw, rather than from poppy juice (in the nonsanctioned opium businesses conducted elsewhere in the world, this juice is dried and condensed before being distributed as an illegal narcotic). The extracted alkaloids, primarily codeine, are then used in the production of painkillers and other medicines.

Predictably, the growing and harvesting of poppies in Tasmania is strictly controlled by the state government, which established the Poppy Advisory and Control Board to manage the licensing of the crops. However because poppies are grown in conjunction with a range of rotated farm crops, accidents can happen. A local horse trainer was surprised to learn that some of his steeds had ingested poppy seeds that had stowed away in horse feed – in the space of one week, three of his horses were disqualified from racing after testing positive for opium 'use'. If you can't resist clicking your camera at the fields, do so discreetly, and never try to enter a poppy field – the 'opium police' can get cranky.

☉ 9am-6pm Apr, May & Sep–mid-Dec, 9am-6pm Sat & Sun mid-Dec-Mar), a fine swathe of greenery that includes exotic trees, endless slopes and a distinct lack of noise; wonderful floral displays happen from September to December.

Nearby is the oldest working vineyard, **Providence Vineyard** (☎ 6395 1290; www.providence-vineyards.com.au; 236 Lalla Rd; tastings free; ☉ 10am-5pm), making available around 40 wines from across the state.

Lilydale Falls & Reserve, 3km north of town, has an easy 10-minute walk to two waterfalls. More energetic walkers may feel the urge to hike up **Mt Arthur** (five to seven hours return) which towers dramatically above Lilydale. To drive to the walk's starting point, follow Mountain Rd at the southern extremity of town.

Sleeping & Eating

Camping is possible for $6 (for up to two people) at Lilydale Falls Reserve. Head for the distinctive red building housing **Lilydale Takeaway** (☎ 6395 1156; Main Rd), where you'll pay a $20 deposit for a key to the amenities block; $14 is refunded on return of the key (two-night stay limit).

Cherry Top (☎ 6395 1167; 81 Lalla Rd; cherrytop@bigpond.com; cottage d $110) Take the C822 and you come across this highly recommended self-contained unit. Sprawling across 20 acres with superb views to Mt Arthur, accommodation includes well-equipped kitchen, heating and laundry. The charming owners are cultivating various orchards of olives and cherries, plus natives, and it's a relaxed environment where kids can play with the ducks, goats and hens, or clamber up an impressive treehouse.

Plovers Ridge Host Farm (☎/fax 6395 1102; 132 Lalla Rd; s/d from $95/130) Nestled behind an established hazelnut grove, Plover offers accommodation with full breakfast in two snug, timber-lined units with fantastic valley views. Each unit includes private bathroom. Other meals (both veggie and meaty) are also available (two courses from $25 per person).

HADSPEN & CARRICK

☎ 03

The popular residential suburb of Hadspen, 15km southwest of Launceston, has some attractive 19th-century Georgian buildings, notably the **Red Feather Inn** (42 Main St), built in 1844. Down the street, the bluestone Anglican **Church of the Good Shepherd**, built in 1868, is also worth a reverent gaze.

Two kilometres west of Hadspen, beyond the South Esk River, off Old Bass Hwy, is the heritage-listed **Entally House** (☎ 6393 6201; adult/child/family $7.70/5.50/15.40; ☉ 10am-4pm). Built in 1819 by shipping entrepreneur Thomas Haydock Reibey (his mother, Mary Reibey, is featured on the A$20 note), it offers a vivid period picture of rural affluence, from the coach house and stables through to the abundance of fine Regency furniture and silverware. At the time of writing there were plans to include Derby coaches that would tour the estate's grounds; the estate includes a cricket field dating from 1834 and the oldest conservatory in Australia (1847), housing wonderful old camellias, which were planted here in the belief that these 'exotics' could not tolerate the elements.

Just 4km along from Hadspen is Carrick, on the old highway to Deloraine. Carrick's most prominent feature is the 1846 four-storey, ivy-smothered **Carrick Mill** (67 Bass Hwy), now a magnificent pub (p216). Behind the mill is the dramatically crumbled 1860 ruin known as **Archers Folly** (Bishopsbourne Rd), twice burnt down. Next door, in a building seemingly assembled by an inebriated fisherman, is the **Tasmanian Copper & Metal Art Gallery** (☎ 6393 6440; www.tascoppermetalart.com; 1 Church St; ☉ 9.30am-5pm), where you'll find an Aladdin's Cave of acclaimed imaginative metalwork for sale. The gallery is a magnificent feature itself, and also includes sculptures, jewellery, gems and paintings.

Sleeping & Eating

Red Feather Inn (☎ 6393 6331; www.redfeatherinn.com.au; 42 Main St, Hadspen; mains from $19; bar ☉ from 4pm, restaurant ☉ dinner) This atmospheric old inn from 1844 includes a restaurant housed in cavernous, cellar-like rooms. Its à la carte menu features mod-Oz cuisine, including generous steak and seafood dishes, plus vegetarian options. The desserts are worth saving room for.

Hawthorn Villa (☎ 6393 6150, 0412 446 364; cnr Meander Valley Hwy & Church St, Carrick; B&B s/d from $90/120) Set among some gorgeous gardens on a picturesque hill overlooking Liffey River, Hawthorn Villa comprises four colonial 'stables', providing charming B&B accommodation in self-contained quarters, each on two levels. Guests are well catered for, with full breakfast provisions, wood fires and all the mod cons.

Carrick Mill (☎ 6393 6922; 67 Bass Hwy; mains $12; 11am-late;). This ivy-smothered restaurant provides hearty local specialities, and includes a fab beer garden (open year-round) – just the spot for a contemplative ale.

WESTBURY

☎ 03 / pop 1300

Historic Westbury, 32km west of Launceston, is best known for its **White House** (☎ 6393 1171; King St; adult/child/concession/family $7.70/5.50/3/15; 10am-4pm Tue-Sun), a property built by Thomas White in 1841–42 as a general store. Managed by the National Trust, it features collections of colonial furniture, vintage cars and 19th-century toys, including the wonderfully intricate, 1.8m-high, 20-room Pendle Hall doll's house. The onsite **White House Bakery** (right) is also worth visiting. Across the road is the **village green**, a narrow park that includes a maypole and war memorial.

Pearn's Steam World (☎ 6397 3313; 65 Bass Hwy; adult/child $5/2; 9am-4pm) comprises two huge sheds filled with the world's largest collection of antique steam engines and relics. This place will appeal most to old-machinery enthusiasts. If that's not enough to oil your engines then head on over to the **Vintage Tractor Shed Museum** (☎ 9363 1167; 5 Veterans Row; adult/child $3/free; 9am-4pm), home to a private collection of 80 vintage and classic tractors, and over 300 model versions.

Call into the **John Temple Gallery** (☎ 6393 1666; 103 Bass Hwy; admission free; 10am-5pm) to purchase or admire the work of this leading Tasmanian landscape photographer.

Wander through the **Westbury Maze** (☎ 63 93 1840; 10 Bass Hwy; adult/child/family $5.50/4.50/20; 10am-5pm Sep-Jul, to 6pm Jan), a 3000-bush walk-in puzzle. The tearoom serves Devonshire teas (with over 30 types of tea) and light snacks.

Sleeping

Gingerbread Cottages (☎ 6393 1140; 52 William St; s/d from $125/140) These award-winning fully self-contained cottages are delightful. Filled with a cosy ambience, memorabilia and quirky touches, antiques, mod cons and surrounded by fragrant gardens, you can choose between the Gingerbread cottage (c 1880) and the Old Bakehouse (c 1850). There's also a spa.

Fitzpatricks Inn (☎ 6393 1153; fitzpatricksinn@bigpond.com; 56 Bass Hwy; s/d $55/85) This large, white and grandly porticoed 1833 building has been extensively refurbished, retaining all of its period charm and grandeur. Offering four spacious rooms with en suite, tea- and coffee-making facilities, light breakfast and majestic garden views.

Olde Coaching Inn (☎ 6393 2100; fax 6393 2578; 54 William St; s/d $65/90) Dating from 1833, this place was the original inn of the village. This B&B option comprises comfortable and spacious quarters set in beautiful English garden surrounds.

Other recommendations:

Andy's (☎ 6393 1846; 45 Bass Hwy; 24hr) Offers free camping for caravans and motor-homes only, not tents, out the back of its diner, which sells great hot savouries, focaccias and bread.

Westbury Hotel (☎ 6393 1151; 107 Bass Hwy; s/d from $40/60) This pub has the usual basic hotel rooms with shared facilities. Rates include brekky. Its counter meals (mains $12 to $19) are hearty.

Eating

White House Bakery (☎ 6393 1066; King St; 9am-4pm Tue-Sun) Nestled into the side of the White House historic estate, Bernadette creates magic with dough using a wood-fired oven (dating from 1840) to give you the freshest and tastiest hot bread this side of the Bass Strait. She also bakes tarts and incredible biscuits.

Pioneer Homestead (☎ 6393 2828; 44 William St; mains $7-12.50; breakfast & lunch, dinner Fri & Sat) The recipes are for authentic home-style fare, all the way from good ol' US of A. Midwestern staples include great-value burger stacks, waffles, chillies and chowder – even veggie options. The generous portions are bound to hit the sides and line the tummy nicely. And of course, cups of coffee or tea are bottomless.

Hobnobs (☎ 6393 2007; 47 William St; mains from $35; lunch Wed-Sun, dinner Thu-Sat) Hobnobs is anything but a pretentious affair. Set in a National Trust–listed building (c 1860), this fully licensed restaurant-café is in fact rather friendly (as well as for those in wheelchairs), elegant and inviting, with a fabulous courtyard to enjoy alfresco dining in. It operates a changing à la carte menu for dinner, Devonshire teas and traditional Sunday roasts (two/three courses $24/28), complete with Yorkshire pudding. The desserts are divine and are worth sharing over a smooth coffee designed to pulsate, just the way it should.

LIFFEY VALLEY

This valley is in the Liffey Falls State Reserve (34km southwest of Carrick) at the foot of the Great Western Tiers (Kooperona Niara; 'Mountains of the Spirits'). It has served as the site of a holiday home belonging to Dr Bob Brown, the well-known conservationist turned politician – it's no coincidence that the Tasmanian Wilderness World Heritage Area starts at the back fence of that property.

The natural centrepiece of this beautiful rainforested valley is the Liffey Forest Reserve, in which lie the impressive **Liffey Falls**. There are two approaches to the falls, which are actually four separate cascades. From the upstream car park (reached by an often steep and winding road, and where there's a rather intimidating 50m-high browntop stringybark) it's a 45-minute return walk on a well-marked track. You can also follow the river upstream to the Gulf Rd picnic area; allow two to three hours return. The area has some fine fishing.

Hidden in the undergrowth 15km before the falls car park is **Liffey Tea Gardens & Retreat** (☎/fax 6397 3213; 40 Gulf Rd; d from $100). Here, among serene gardens, you'll find a handful of compact, self-contained chalets with mind-emptying views of Drys Bluff – at 1297m it's the highest peak of the Great Western Tiers. You can also grab muffins or quiche in the **tearooms** (9am-6pm).

LONGFORD

☎ 03 / pop 2830

Longford is 27km south of Launceston and is classified as a historic town due to its abundance of colonial buildings. The Europeans initially called the area Norfolk Plains because of land grants given in 1812 to settlers from the abandoned colony on Norfolk Island; it was one of the few towns in the state established by free settlers rather than convicts.

The village is proud of its gardens, hosting the **Longford Garden Festival** each November. Well known to brown-trout-fishing enthusiasts, Longford is also a popular base for fishing in the nearby rivers and streams and at Cressy, 13km south of Longford.

There's an **online access centre** (☎ 6391 2200; Wellington St; 10am-3.30pm Mon, to 9pm Tue, to 3pm Wed, to 7pm Thu & Fri, to 2pm Sun), just behind the library, costing around $5.50 per hour and you'll find a Commonwealth Bank ATM next to the BP service station on Marlborough St.

Sights & Activities

Spread out around **Memorial Park**, the town is best known for its Georgian architecture. Buildings worth seeing include the bluestone **Anglican Church** (Goderich St), the **Town Hall** (Smith St), the **library** (Wellington St) and the **Queens Arms Hotel** (Wellington St).

From the 1950s to the early 1960s, the streets of Longford regularly doubled as a racetrack for motor car races, including three Australian Grand Prix. The **Country Club Hotel** (19 Wellington St) is a veritable shrine to this period in the town's history, with numerous motor racing photos and other paraphernalia arranged around the bar. Nowadays the town's main event is the **Blessing of the Harvest Festival** in March, with a street parade and country-fare stalls.

Two historic estates established by William Thomas Archer are **Woolmers** (☎ 6391 2230; www.woolmers.com.au; Woolmers Lane; adult/child/senior/family from $15/3.50/12/32; 10am-4.30pm), a grandly furnished 1819 homestead with beautiful surrounds that include the flourishing walled-in **National Rose Garden** (over 4000 roses planted across two hectares), and **Brickendon** (☎ 6391 1383; www.brickendon.com.au; Woolmers Lane; adult/child/senior/family $9/3.50/8/27; 9.30am-5pm Tue-Sun), a combination of heritage gardens and a historical farming village with heaps of rural-type activities. Sites include a still-working pillar granary and a smithy – the blacksmith appears to have just downed tools and gone for lunch. There are guided tours of Woolmers at 11am, 12.30pm, 2pm and 3.30pm (plus self-guided tours of the rose garden, outbuildings and grounds); an additional guided tour leaves at 10am, November to March. The properties are south of Longford and both offer accommodation (p218); just follow the signs from Wellington St and note the glorious hawthorn *(Crataegus* *monogyna)* hedges lining Woolmers Lane (C520); these hedges (stretching approximately 30km around Brickendon) flower profusely throughout October.

Sleeping & Eating

Longford Riverside Caravan Park (☎/fax 6391 1470; Archer St; unpowered/powered sites $13/17, dm from $25, d $40, on-site vans with bathroom $55, cabins with/without bathroom d $50/40) This picturesque park meanders along the quiet banks of the Macquarie River, close to the town centre. It also has a couple of cheap bunks in two small cabins and allows dogs on the premises as long as they're kept on leads. It has a purpose-built amenities block for the disabled. Site prices include up to two people.

Country Club Hotel (☎ 6391 1155; 19 Wellington St; s/d $30/40, unit $60; bistro 🕑 breakfast, lunch & dinner) This is a welcoming, often busy pub offering good-value budget rooms, some with en suite and others without. The unit is self-contained and rates include continental brekky provisions. Downstairs, the Chequered Flag bistro dishes up hearty pub tucker.

Racecourse Inn (☎ 6391 2352; www.racecourseinn.com; 114 Marlborough St; d $140-185) Providing refined nondiscriminatory hospitality in a restored Georgian inn on the southern side of town, the Racecourse offers mere mortals the chance to stay in five antique-decorated estate and attic rooms (one with a spa), and provides fully cooked breakfasts. There's also à la carte dining in an elegant, licensed restaurant.

Brickendon (☎ 6391 1383; accommodation@brickendon.com.au; Woolmers Lane; B&B historic cottage d $160-180, farm cottage s $85, d $110-150) Brickendon has two well-equipped, early-19th-century cottages (one each for 'coachman' and 'gardener' wannabes), furnished with antiques and family collectables, plus three much newer self-contained cottages with old-style trimmings.

> **BURIED ARTY FACT**
>
> The famous artist Tom Roberts is buried in the grounds of Christ Church in Longford. One of his best known works includes the painting of the *Opening of the First Federal Parliament of the Commonwealth of Australia.*

Woolmers (☎ 6391 2230; fax 6391 2270; www.woolmers.com.au; Woolmers Lane; B&B d from $170) Woolmers offers self-contained colonial accommodation in its 1840s free-settlers' cottages; prices include breakfast provisions and a guided tour of the main house.

Servants Kitchen Restaurant (☎ 6391 1163; Woolmers Lane) This licensed restaurant is also run by Woolmers, and offers a delectable array of morning and afternoon teas, including salmon and crab pâté served with toasties and salad ($16), or lamb shanks with sweet-potato mash ($16). Soup of the day comes with homemade damper. You can choose to be served in front of its cosy log fire or arrange a two/three-course hamper ($30/35) for your cottage.

Longford Gallery Café (☎ 6391 2021; cnr Wellington & Marlborough Sts; mains $10; 🕑 9.30am-4pm Tue-Fri, 10.30am-late Sat, 10.30am-4pm Sun) Located in the Corner Shop (c 1830s; formerly the 'London', later the 'Plough Inn'), in what was once a chemist's dispensary and a watchmaker's, this informal arty café offers light snacks, salads, gourmet pizzas, lasagne and other filling favourites in a bright interior. The room at the rear exhibits contemporary art and sculpture.

JJ's Bakery & Old Mill Cafe (☎ 6391 2364; 52 Wellington St; mains $10-20; 🕑 7am-5.30pm Mon-Fri, 7am-5pm Sat & Sun) This option, in the restored Old Emerald flour mill, produces a wide variety of light snacks and delicious baked goods, and serves wood-fired pizzas and daily specials in its licensed café. There's live jazz most Sundays, mostly in summer, and alfresco dining upstairs.

EVANDALE

☎ 03 / pop 1035

One of Tasmania's most impressive National Trust–classified towns, Evandale is 22km south of Launceston in the South Esk Valley, near Launceston's airport. Many of its 19th-century buildings are in excellent condition.

Information

The volunteer-staffed **visitors centre** (☎ 6391 8128; 18 High St; 🕑 10am-3pm) has lots of written information about the region. Pick up the pamphlet *Evandale Heritage Walk* ($2.20), which will guide you around the town's historic features. The extensive history room here holds an informative display on the local painter and character John Glover. A bronze statue of Glover, all 18 stones of him (club feet and all), stands at Falls Park.

Sights & Activities

HISTORIC BUILDINGS

Places worth noting around town include the brick **water tower** (High St), which includes remains of a convict-built 24m-deep tunnel designed to supply water to Launceston, two photogenic **churches** (High St), opposite each other – both are St Andrews but one is a former Presbyterian church, now Uniting, and the other is Anglican – and historic houses such as **Solomon House** (High St), **Ingleside** (Russell St) and **Fallgrove** (Logan Rd).

A stuccoed 1842 Georgian building, **Brown's Village Store & Café** (☎ 6391 8048; 5 Russell St; 7.30am-6pm) is still operating as an old-fashioned country grocery store and features a magnificent cedar counter and old-style pine shelving. The store stocks deli items, cheeses, other local produce, souvenirs, giftware, confectionery and jams, and the small café sells light snacks and refreshments; the side entrance to the café also sports a lovely mural.

Ten kilometres south of Evandale, via Nile Rd, is the National Trust property **Clarendon** (☎ 6398 6220; 634 Station Rd; adult/concession/family $7.70/5.50/15.40; 10am-5pm Sep-May, 10am-4pm Jun-Aug), a grand 1838 French neoclassical building. In its heyday it was considered important enough to have its own railway – the only property in all of Australia to have this honour. There are also three cottages available for accommodation (right).

LOCAL PRODUCE

A sizeable **market** (Falls Park; 9am-1pm Sun) is held weekly in Evandale. Kiddies should still be able to get their fix of miniature railway rides here (second-last Sunday of each month). The wares range from general bric-a-brac to local produce, and it's worth a wander.

Foodies shouldn't miss the **Tasmanian Gourmet Sauce Co** (☎ 6391 8437; www.gourmetsauce.com.au; 174 Leighlands Rd; admission $3; 10am-5pm Oct-Apr, 10am-4pm Wed-Sun May-Sep, or by appointment), 3km west of Evandale, ideal for sampling fine gourmet relishes, chutneys, jams, mustards and dessert sauces, including the alluring strawberry chilli, and for wandering through the extensive topiary nursery.

Festivals & Events

Every February, Evandale dresses itself up in old-fashioned splendour for the **Evandale Village Fair & National Penny Farthing Championships** (www.evandalevillagefair.com; adult/child $7/free), where national and international competitors wrestle these asymmetrical two-wheelers around a mile-long town circuit.

To try this unwieldy device for yourself, **Penny Farthing Cycle Tours** (☎ 6391 9101) offers two half-day tours ($75 per person), one a circuit of Evandale and the other a ride out to historic Clarendon; alternatively you can take a town mini-tour for $49 per person (two hours) or simply learn to ride only ($25). Bookings are essential.

Sleeping

Stables Accommodation (☎ 6391 8048; www.vision.net.au/~thestables; 5 Russell St; B&B s/d $95/150) The Stables has three comfortable self-contained units (in the old stables) for you to flop in, and include central heating and laundry facilities. Inquire at Browns Village Store & Café (left).

Greg & Gill's Place (☎/fax 6391 8248; 35 Collins St; B&B s/d $50/85) This place is run by very friendly hosts who offer antique-furnished accommodation in three separate units that each sleep three. Its eclectic surrounds are real child-pleasers: kiddies and adults alike will find inspiration in the host family's camera displays, model plane and car collections, paintings and great garden.

Solomon Cottage (☎ 6391 8331; 1 High St; s/d $80/110) This cottage was originally built in 1838 as a bakery. Joseph Solomon most probably would never have envisaged his oven eventually being taken up by a queen-size bed (note the brick-vaulted ceiling!). The cottage, next to Solomon House (the old country store), has two bedrooms and the price includes a cooked breakfast.

Grandma's House (☎ 6391 8088, 0408 295 387; 10 Rodgers Lane; d $135) Situated on the historic Marlborough House property (c 1847), Grandma's boasts spacious, comfy rooms in a character-filled home. Guests can be entertained with cable TV, DVD or CD player; weekly rates are available.

Clarendon (☎ 6398 6220; 634 Station Rd; cottages $100) Nestled on the Clarendon estate, these self-contained cottages each include a fridge, TV, microwave and tea- and coffee-making facilities. The location is idyllic, made even more so by the fact that there's no phone available within the cottages – switch your mobile off and relax.

Other recommendations:

Clarendon Arms Hotel (☎ 6391 8181; 11 Russell St; s/d $40/65) This pub has decent budget rooms with shared facilities.

Prince of Wales Hotel (☎ 6391 8381; cnr High & Collins Sts; d $55-70, f $70-80) This is another pub offering budget accommodation.

Eating

Ingleside Bakery Café (☎ 6391 8682; 4 Russell St; mains $7-20; breakfast & lunch) Desperate for a great pie ($3), crusty sourdough or pesto and cheese cob ($4.20)? This café is set in the atmospheric former council chambers in an 1867 Victorian Classical Revival building. Its oven contains 25,000 bricks – enough to complete three cottages! It also displays for sale a selection of arts and antique items and other collectables.

Menzies @ Clarendon (☎ 6398 6190; 634 Station Rd; mains $12-19; breakfast & lunch) Part of the Clarendon estate, these conservatory tearooms offer delicious light lunches, such as great club sandwiches ($7.50) or hearty soups ($4.50). One of the Valhalla ice creams goes down a treat as you stroll the estate's grounds.

Clarendon Arms Hotel (☎ 6391 8181; 11 Russell St; mains $13-20; lunch & dinner) This pub serves meaty and substantial counter meals and has an outdoor beer garden.

BEN LOMOND NATIONAL PARK

This 165-sq-km park, 55km southeast of Launceston, includes the entire Ben Lomond Range and is best known for its skiing. The range does not have any dramatic peaks but rather is an elevated craggy alpine plateau, roughly 14km long by 6km wide. The plateau is around 1300m high, with its gentle hills stretching to 1500m. The highest point is Legges Tor (1573m), the second-highest peak in Tasmania and well worth climbing, in good weather, for its panoramic views, which stretch across to Ben Nevis. The park has an incredible landscape of dolerite columns (popular with rock climbers and abseilers) and scree slopes.

The scenery at Ben Lomond is magnificent year-round. The park is particularly noted for its alpine wildflowers, which run riot in spring and summer. For a winter prelude, check out the great snowcam at www.ski.com.au/snowcams/benlomond1.html.

Ben Lomond was named after its Scottish namesake by the founder of Launceston, Lt Colonel Paterson, in 1804. From 1805 to 1806 Colonel Legge explored the plateau and named most of the major features after explorers of the Nile River in Africa, and members of the fledgling Van Diemen's Land colony.

Sights & Activities

In summer, the plateau provides some easy walking. The most popular place to visit is the highest point, **Legges Tor**. It can be reached via a good walking track from Carr Villa, about halfway up the mountain, and takes about two hours each way. You can also climb to the top from the alpine village on the plateau, which takes about 30 minutes each way on marked tracks. (All walkers and cross-country skiers should register at the self-registration booth at the alpine village.)

You can walk across the plateau in almost any direction, but there are no marked tracks and navigation is difficult in mist. Unless you're well equipped, walking south of the ski village isn't advised.

There's accommodation year-round at Tasmania's highest pub, **Creek Inn** (☎ 6390 6199; dm s/d/f $40/75/115, B&B unit d $170). The unit rate includes a continental breakfast, en suite, heating and a lovely deck (one unit has cooking facilities). There's also a fully licensed **restaurant** (mains $20; 10am-4pm), which serves snacks all day, a wholesome buffet, and has à la carte dining.

There's also a good **camping** area, 1km along from the park entrance, which offers secluded, cleared, unpowered sites, flushing toilets, drinking water and a fantastic lookout.

Operating during the ski season (early July to late September) there's also a kiosk and ski shop. Ski lifts cost $40/23 per adult for a full/half day, and $17/11 per child. Ski rental package deals (skis, boots, poles, lift ticket and lesson) cost $85/71/61 per adult/child 13 to 17 years/child under 13. Skiing or snowboarding lessons cost $36 for a 90-minute group lesson or $70 for a one-hour private lesson. At the time of research there were six tows (three T-bars and three Poma lifts) available for skiers and a heated day-visitor shelter.

Getting There & Away

McDermotts Coaches (Map p196; ☎ 6394 3535; 40 St John St, Launceston; adult/concession/family return $26/20/85) runs a service to Ben Lomond (during the ski season) departing from the back entrance of the Launceston Sport & Surf store (the Birchills car park) at 8.30am daily, departing the mountain at 4pm. An additional shuttle service runs between the rangers station ($13/10 per adult/concession return) and the alpine village at frequent intervals throughout the day. You can also book your bus tickets through the store. Park entrance fees cost $3.50/10 per person/vehicle.

Outside the ski season, driving is your only transport option. It's 8km from the Ben Lomond Rd turn-off to the park boundary and 18km to the alpine village. Note that the track is unsealed and includes Jacob's Ladder, a very steep climb including six dramatic hairpin bends with no safety barriers; during the snow season chains are standard equipment.

Note: fill up with fuel before heading out to Ben Lomond. Your best bet is at Launceston (55km from the village); take snow chains with you (not available at the village) and don't forget the antifreeze for your engine!

The North

In this region of Tasmania travelling is touring; there's no such thing as just getting from A to B. Your views will take in the northern plains' rolling farmlands and hill country that extend from the Tamar Valley north of Launceston and west to the Great Western Tiers, which rise up to Tasmania's Central Plateau. Heading west from Launceston, the main highway skirts the foot of the sacred Tiers, running through picturesque Deloraine before heading north to Devonport, the state's third-largest city and the most common entry point for visitors with its terminal for the ferry services plying Bass Strait from both Melbourne and Sydney. Devonport is also the gateway to Cradle Mountain–Lake St Clair National Park.

Hidden in the hills between Devonport and Cradle Mountain are a series of small towns. Latrobe is a picturesque country town developing ecologically friendly tourist ventures, such as a platypus haven. Spelunkers cannot miss the Mole Creek Karst National Park, a subterranean wonderland, nor can anyone ignore the Kentish region's majestic Mt Roland, with its changing hues comparable with Uluru's. The mural artworks in Sheffield wear the history of this region on their painted sleeves; it's hard not to feel like you're part of the family here.

In a region renowned for its warmth and hospitality, the beachside towns in particular have a lifestyle that refuses to hurry. It's here that pristine waters lap at coastal areas framed by incredible floral roadside gardens.

HIGHLIGHTS

- Hiking the spectacular and remote **Walls of Jerusalem National Park** (p228)
- Sampling luscious honey ice-cream at Chudleigh's **Honey Factory** (p228)
- Exploring the magnificent subterranean wonderland of the **Mole Creek Karst National Park** (p227)
- Ship-spotting from Devonport's geological marvel, **Mersey Bluff** (p235)
- Shopping 'till you drop' at Deloraine's famous **craft fair** (p225), the nation's largest display of arts and crafts
- Treating the family to some fun and cracking a smile at **Lower Crackpot** (p230), a whimsical miniature village in Promised Land
- Bushwalking the rugged charm of the **Great Western Tiers** (p225)
- Catching a glimpse of the impressive alfresco art that is Sheffield's **murals** (p232)

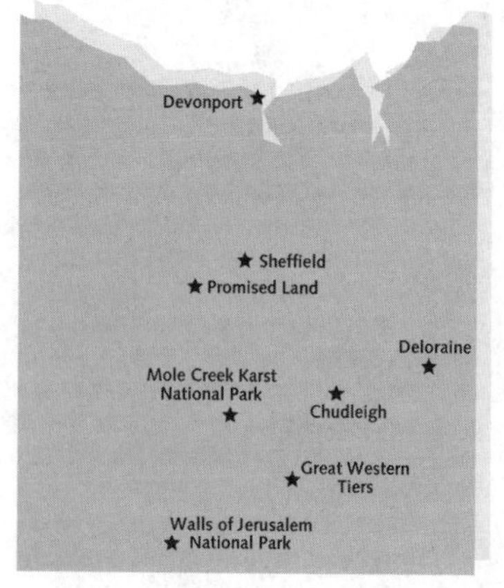

Getting There & Around

BICYCLE

The old highway between Launceston and Deloraine is a good cycling route, as most vehicles follow a newer thoroughfare. It's slower and climbs more hills than the more recent highway, but it's far more interesting, passing through all the small towns. From Deloraine, the rebuilt highway that heads directly to Devonport through Latrobe is best avoided by travelling through the more subdued towns of Railton or Sheffield.

BUS

The bus company **Redline Coaches** (☎ 1300 360 000, 6336 1446; www.tasredline.com.au) has several services daily from Launceston to Devonport ($19, 1¼ hours), Ulverstone ($23.10), Penguin ($23.80) and Burnie ($26.80, two to 2½ hours); bookings are required for all stops. Redline also runs services four times each weekday from Launceston to Deloraine ($10, 45 minutes) – one afternoon service each day continues to Mole Creek ($14.30, 1¼ hours).

TassieLink (☎ 1300 300 520, 6272 7300; www.tassielink.com.au) runs a daily express service that picks up passengers who have disembarked from Devonport's Bass Strait ferry terminal in the morning and then heads to Launceston ($18, 1¼ hours) and Hobart ($45, four hours); this service also runs daily in reverse from Hobart, reaching Devonport in time for the nightly ferry sailing.

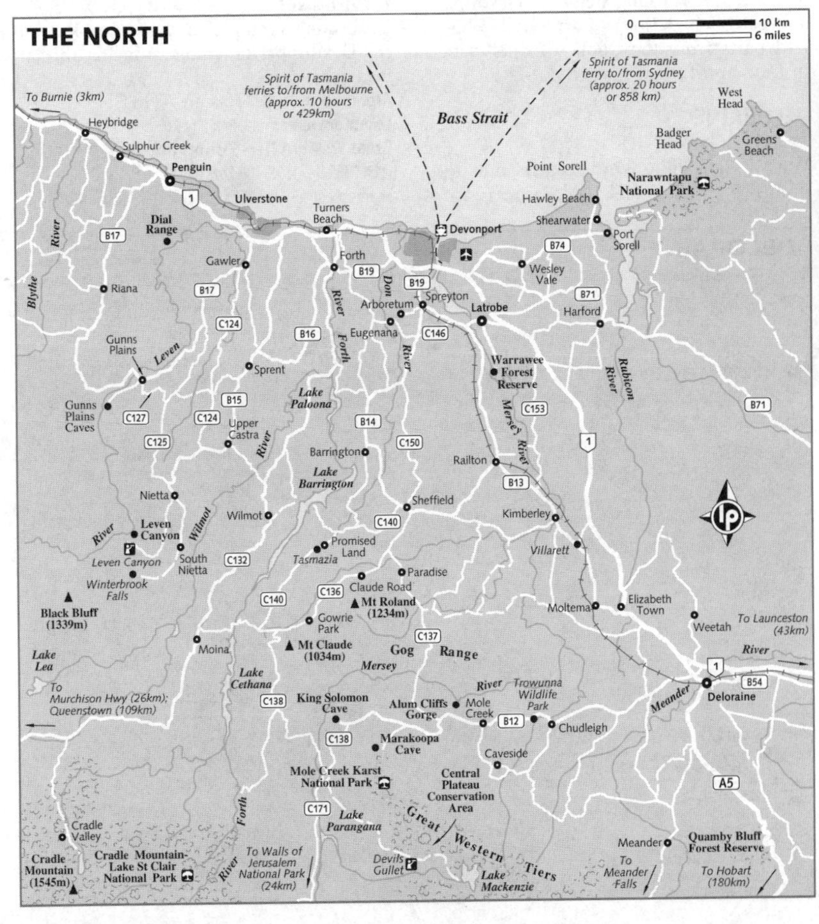

Also connecting with the morning ferry arrival in Devonport every Wednesday and Friday is a service that heads west to Burnie ($10, one hour), with onward connections to Tullah ($25.40, 2¼ hours), Rosebery ($27.30, 2½ hours), Zeehan ($34.40, three hours), Queenstown ($42.50, 3¾ hours) and Strahan ($50.50, 4¾ hours) – the route is also run in reverse on the same days. On Monday, Tuesday, Thursday and Saturday, TassieLink also has a service from Launceston to Strahan that passes through Devonport (no drop offs, pick-up only), Sheffield ($19.80, 2½ hours), Gowrie Park ($23.40) and Cradle Mountain ($46.60, 3½ hours).

There's a local shuttle service operated by **Merseylink** (☎ 1300 367 590) from Monday to Saturday, running between Devonport and Latrobe ($3.30) via Port Sorell ($3.50). It departs from the Rooke St interchange in Devonport.

DELORAINE

☎ 03 / pop 2170

With its charming rural centre and pronounced English feel, Deloraine is in a superb setting at the foot of the Great Western Tiers. It owes a great deal of its charm to its Georgian and Victorian buildings, many of which have been faithfully restored, but most people come to Deloraine to bushwalk and explore the nearby waterfalls or the caves of the Mole Creek Karst National Park. The other attraction is the large number of arts, antique and second-hand shops in town.

If you're travelling in this area during spring, it's worth noting that Deloraine's annual craft fair (opposite) draws tens of thousands of visitors in late October and/or early November, when accommodation can book out from Launceston to Devonport.

Information

Bushwalkers can pick up basic supplies, but try Devonport or Launceston for specialised gear.

ANZ (54 Emu Bay Rd) Has an ATM.

Commonwealth (24 Emu Bay Rd)

Great Western Tiers Visitors Information Centre (☎ 6362 3471; 98-100 Emu Bay Rd; ⏲ 9am-5pm) Shares premises with the Deloraine Folk Museum & Yarns:

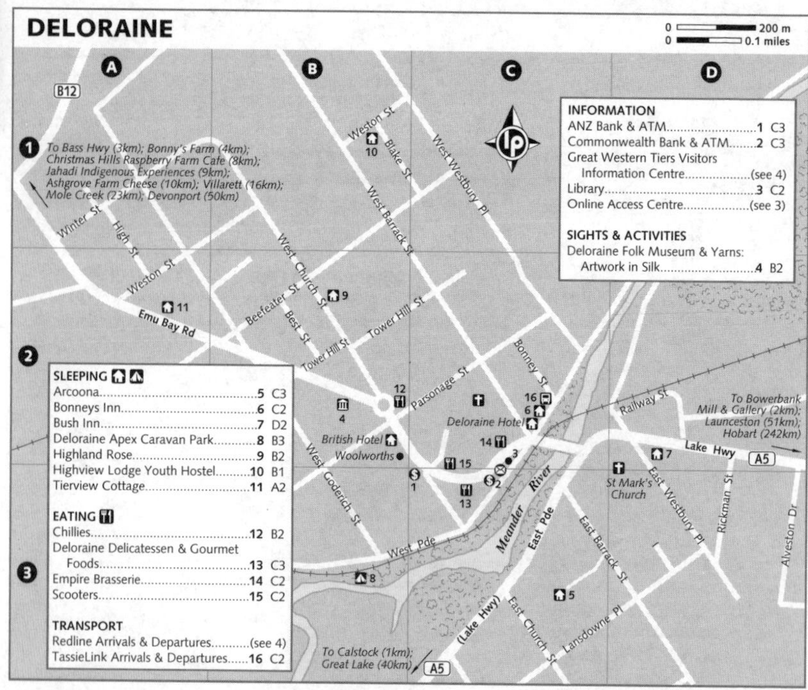

Artwork in Silk (below) and has information on antique, arts and crafts, and gallery outlets. Internet access also available ($2 per 15 minutes).

Main post office (West Pde)

Online access centre (☎ 6362 3537; West Pde; per 30min/hr $3/5) At the rear of the library.

Sights & Activities

MUSEUMS & GALLERIES

The **Deloraine Folk Museum & Yarns: Artwork in Silk** (☎ 6362 3471; 98 Emu Bay Rd; adult/concession/child/family $7/5/2/15; 9am-5pm), in the National Trust–listed Family & Commercial Inn (dating from the 1860s), has undergone extensive renovations and now displays interesting local-history exhibits. A purpose-built theatrette houses an exquisite four-panel, hand-dyed silk depiction of the Meander Valley through a year's worth of seasonal change. Tours every half-hour from 9.30am describe each of the four panels in glorious detail. The silkwork took over 300 local women a dedicated three years to complete and is an absolute masterpiece – a perfect blend of history and craft.

Two kilometres east of Deloraine, on the road to Launceston, is **Bowerbank Mill & Gallery** (☎ 6362 2628; 4455 Bass Hwy; admission free; 10am-5.30pm). This former corn mill, built in 1853 and classified by the National Trust, houses a leading art gallery and provides heritage accommodation (p226).

ASHGROVE FARM CHEESE

Ten kilometres north of Deloraine you'll find **Ashgrove Farm Cheese** (☎ 6368 1105; 6173 Bass Hwy; Elizabeth Town; 9am-5.30pm), a cheese factory specialising in award-winning traditional cheeses like Rubicon red, smoked cheddar and creamy Lancashire. You can watch the cheeses being made and then taste the fine results of a crumbly vintage or an adventurous *wasabi*-infused sample. It's also a great place to purchase deli fare for a picnic.

BUSHWALKING

Dominating the southern skyline are the Great Western Tiers (their Aboriginal name is Kooparoona Niara: 'Mountain of the Spirits'), which provide some excellent walking. They feature waterfalls, exceptional forest and some long climbs. The **Meander Forest Reserve** is the most popular starting point. From here **Split Rock Falls**, starting at the swing bridge over the Meander River, can be visited in three hours, or you can walk to **Meander Falls**, which are five to six hours return. Camping is allowed in the area.

Other good walks on the Great Western Tiers include those to **Projection Bluff** (two hours), **Quamby Bluff** (five hours) and **Mother Cummings Peak** (three hours). Note that several tracks on the tiers that require the crossing of private land have been closed due to public liability issues, including Montana Falls, Westmoreland Falls and the South Mole Creek Track.

Tours

Jahadi Indigenous Experiences (☎ 6363 6172; www.jahadi.com.au; 900 Mole Creek Rd; tours Tue & Sun) operates half-/full-day four-wheel-drive tours of Kooparoona Niara and Liffey Falls Reserve. The tours depart from Jahadi; the full-day tour includes a BBQ lunch and traditional Aboriginal bush tucker. There's also a two-hour indigenous-culture experience involving a smoke ceremony, arts and crafts, clap-stick making, spear throwing and billy tea and damper (adult/child/family $15/8.50/48). To get here travel about 9km from Deloraine on the Mole Creek Rd – you can't miss the large Aboriginal flag flying at the gate.

Festivals & Events

The impressive four-day-long **Tasmanian Craft Fair** is held in Deloraine in late October and/or early November (the event always ends on the first Monday in November).

DETOUR

Take the Railton side road that departs the B13 highway about 8km north of Elizabeth Town and you'll come to the beautiful four-hectare, sculpture-studded gardens at **Villarett** (☎/fax 6368 1214; Moltema; s/d $75/90; 9am-5pm Sat-Thu), which are worth visiting even if you don't intend to eat or sleep here. It provides B&B accommodation in the form of a spacious modern cottage where you can enjoy your complimentary breakfast overlooking lush, undulating countryside. The **teahouse** (mains from $15; breakfast & lunch Sat-Thu) serves tasty focaccias, hearty four-course meals and fabulous, rich desserts, plus Devonshire teas.

Up to 30,000 people visit 200 stalls at 10 venues around town, the main one being the Deloraine Community Complex.

Sleeping

BUDGET

Highview Lodge Youth Hostel (☎ 6362 2996; 8 Blake St; dm/d/f from $19/45/56) This welcoming hillside YHA hostel has warm, timber-floored confines and friendly staff. It's a relatively steep walk from town, but the compensation includes some incredible views of the Great Western Tiers, even from the toilets! There are also bikes for hire. Travellers not staying overnight are welcome to use the showers/kitchen plus shower facilities for $3/5 per person.

Bush Inn (☎ 6362 2365; fax 6362 2329; 7 Lake Hwy; r per person $20) Good-value, simple pub accommodation in very spacious rooms. The price includes a simple continental breakfast (a rather stingy affair – we were lucky to find milk).

Deloraine Apex Caravan Park (☎ 6362 2345; West Pde; unpowered/powered sites $14/17) This park has a picturesque location beside the Meander River, except guests become a tad nervous during winter when the river is prone to flooding. Inquiries should be made at the house directly opposite the park. Site prices are for up to two people.

MIDRANGE

Bonney's Farm (☎ 6362 2122; 76 Archer St; d from $80) Some 4km out of town, with three self-contained units (two or three bedrooms) and a guesthouse; breakfast is included in the guesthouse, but costs extra for the other units. To get there, head towards Devonport and take the turn-off to Weetah.

Bonney's Inn (☎ 6362 2974; www.bonneys-inn.com; 19 West Pde; s $120, d/tw with bathroom $132/148) This place claims historical kudos as Deloraine's first brick building (c 1830). Originally a coaching inn, it has comfortably upgraded colonial-style en suite rooms with full breakfasts, plus its own bar and dining room.

Tierview Cottage (☎ 6362 2377; 125 Emu Bay Rd; d $90) This cottage is a little out of the town centre but is still a pleasant place to stay. Inquire at the Shell service station opposite.

Highland Rose (☎ 6362 2634; highland rose.bb@bigpond.com; 47 West Church St; d $95-105) This is a very hospitable and friendly two-bedroom B&B in a garden setting at the quiet end of West Church St. The comfortable rooms come with a hearty cooked breakfast and a separate lounge features a cosy log fire. Weekly rates are available.

Bowerbank Mill (☎ 6362 2628; www.view.com.au/bowerbank; 4455 Bass Hwy; s/d $110/165) Some 2km east of the town centre, this place has a pair of comfortable, double-storey, self-contained stone-walled cottages, filled with colonial and heritage character. Three-course dinners are available from $40 per person and there are reduced accommodation rates for longer stays.

TOP END

Calstock (☎ 6362 2642; www.calstock.net; Lake Hwy; s & d $270-320, family unit $400) An 80-hectare property south of Deloraine, on which sits a marvellous mid-19th-century manor built by John Field, who bred highly successful racehorses including two Melbourne Cup winners, Malua (1884) and Sheet Anchor (1885). There are seven bedrooms (one with wheelchair accessible), grand lounges, hearty breakfast fare, and dinners by arrangement. We noted the property was up for sale when we visited.

Arcoona (☎ 6362 3443; arcoona@vision.net.au; East Barrack St; s $165, d $185-220) A grand old hilltop home, set amid enchanting gardens on the eastern side of the river. Originally the town doctor's residence and then the district hospital, its credentials as a luxury B&B now include king-size beds, a spa suite and a billiards room.

Eating

Christmas Hills Raspberry Farm Cafe (☎ 6362 2186; www.raspberryfarmcafe.com; Christmas Hills Rd, Elizabeth Town; meals $7-17; 🕑 7.30am-5pm) Eight kilometres north of town, off Bass Hwy, this place is wildly popular for its (surprise!) raspberries. It serves a variety of gourmet sandwiches, salads, burgers and other light meals, but most head here for the desserts menu, which runs across two pages – just try to choose between the raspberry crepe, sundae, cheesecake, tart, pavlova, ice cream, sorbet, waffles…

Chillies (☎ 6362 3669; 81 Emu Bay Rd; mains around $10; 🕑 breakfast & lunch Mon-Sat) This is a funky new place just up the road from the visitors centre. It provides lots of groove with your food, serving up Mexican treats, jacket potatoes, salads and wraps, and does great coffee and cake for just $5.

Empire Brasserie (☎ 6362 2075; 19 Emu Bay Rd; mains $10-20; ⏰ breakfast, lunch & dinner) The hotel's brasserie has an à la carte selection that offers mussels, duck and Atlantic salmon cutlets.

Scooters (☎ 6362 3882; 53-55 Emu Bay Rd; mains $15-18; ⏰ breakfast, lunch & dinner) The name sounds like a small-town US soda fountain, but in fact it's a well-managed, licensed restaurant with contemporary tastes, issuing excellent seasonal dishes that include venison sausages, char grills and mushroom risotto. It also has a kids' menu.

Deloraine Delicatessen & Gourmet Foods (☎ 63 62 2127; 36 Emu Bay Rd; mains $5-10; ⏰ breakfast & lunch Mon-Sat) A fine place for late-morning baguettes, bagels and focaccias, with a variety of tasty fillings. Its coffee is pungently superb, and it does dairy- and gluten-free meals, too.

Getting There & Away

See p223 for details of the Redline service from Launceston to Deloraine and then to Mole Creek. Redline Coaches arrive at and depart from outside the visitors centre.

Over summer, **TassieLink** (☎ 1300 300 520, 62 72 7300; www.tassielink.com.au) has special 'Wilderness' services departing 9.30am Monday, Wednesday and Saturday from Launceston and running to Lake St Clair via Deloraine ($15, 45 minutes); there's a connecting service to Hobart from Lake St Clair ($41). Bookings are essential for these services as minimum numbers of passengers are required.

CHUDLEIGH

☎ 03

Those who like sticky fingers will want to make a beeline (sorry…) for Chudleigh's **Honey Farm** (☎ 6363 6160; www.thehoneyfarm.com.au; admission free; 39 Sorell St; ⏰ 9am-5pm Sun-Fri), where there are literally dozens of free samples, including Leatherwood honey, honey ice cream and lots of other sweet merchandise, including medicinal products. There's also a small, glass-enclosed apiary containing thousands of bees.

Two kilometres west of Chudleigh is the **Trowunna Wildlife Park** (☎ 6363 6162; adult/child $14/7.50; ⏰ 9am-5pm Feb-Dec, 9am-8pm Jan, tours at 11am, 1pm & 3pm), which specialises in Tasmanian devils, wombats and koalas. The park operates an informative 75-minute tour where you get to pat, feed or even hold the critters; the park also features many birds, including rosellas, geese, white goshawks and two wedge-tailed eagles.

MOLE CREEK

☎ 03 / pop 260

About 25km west of Deloraine and just around the bend from Chudleigh is pretty Mole Creek, a handy access point for spelunking and bushwalking.

Sights & Activities

MOLE CREEK KARST NATIONAL PARK

The word 'karst' refers to the scenery characteristic of a limestone region, including caves and underground streams. The Mole Creek area contains over 300 known caves and sinkholes. The park itself is in a number of small segments and at the time of writing there were plans for wild cave tours to start in early 2005. For bookings contact **Mole Creek Caves** (☎ 6363 5182; fax 6363 5124; mccaves@parks.tas.gov.au).

Public Caves

There are two public caves: **Marakoopa** (its name derives from an Aboriginal word meaning 'handsome'), a wet cave 15km from Mole Creek featuring two underground streams and an incredible glow-worm display; and **King Solomon**, a dry cave with amazing light-reflecting calcite crystals. During peak seasons there are five guided interpretive tours daily of each cave. The earliest tour of Marakoopa is usually at 10am, while the first King Solomon tour usually departs at 10.30am (the last tour at both caves is 4pm). It's a 15-minute drive between the two caves, and tours of one cave cost $11/5.50/8.80/27.50 per adult/child/pensioner/family. Prices were due to increase from mid-2005.

Wild Caves

Cyclops, Wet, Honeycomb and the magnificent Baldocks are among the better-known caves in the Mole Creek area that are without steps or ladders. If you're an experienced caver who wants to take on some vertical rope work, you'll need to make arrangements with a caving club. Alternatively you can take one of the excursions offered by

Wild Cave Tours (☎ 6367 8142; 165 Fernlea Rd, Caveside), which provides tours for $85/170 per half/full day, including caving gear (not for children under 14 years). Book, and take spare clothing and a towel (you'll get wet).

R.STEPHENS LEATHERWOOD HONEY FACTORY

At this **factory** (☎ 6363 1170; 25 Pioneer Dr; admission free; 9am-4pm Mon-Fri Jan-Apr), you can watch the leatherwood honey (the leatherwood trees – *Eucryphia lucida* and *Eucryphia milligani* – are endemic to Tasmania) extraction and bottling plant in operation. There are also honey sales here and you might be able to arrange a guided tour of the factory.

MOLE CREEK BIRD PARK

The owner of this new **bird park** (☎ 6363 1490; 7 Caveside Rd; adult/senior/family $5/3/12.50; 9am-5pm Sep-Jun, 9am-5pm Thu-Tue Jul-Aug), opposite Memorial Hall, takes you on a personalised one-hour guided tour through a fantastic Australian (and exotic) parrot collection, with over 250 varieties.

DEVILS GULLET

Those with transport should head for the Western Tiers. The only road that actually reaches the top of the plateau is the one to Lake Mackenzie. Follow this road to **Devils Gullet**, where there's a 40-minute return walk leading to a platform bolted to the top of a dramatic gorge: looking over the edge isn't for the faint-hearted.

BUSHWALKING

There are a number of popular short walks in the area, including **Alum Cliffs Gorge** (one hour return), a short scenic walk along a sloping spur to an impressive lookout. Alum Cliffs (or Tulampanga as it's known to the tribal custodians, the Pallittorre people,) is a sacred celebration place; many tribes from ancient times met here for corroborees. Note: the South Mole Creek Track crosses private land and remains closed to walkers due to public liability issues. For information about walking in the Walls of Jerusalem National Park, see right.

Sleeping & Eating

Mole Creek Caravan Park (☎ 6363 1150; cnr Mole Creek & Union Bridge Rds; unpowered/powered sites $12/15) This is a thin sliver of a park about 4km west of town beside Sassafras Stream, at the turn-off to the caves and Cradle Mountain. Site prices are for up to two people.

Mole Creek Hotel (☎ 6363 1102; tigerbar69@hotmail.com; Main Rd; s $45, d with/without bathroom $65/75; mains $10-15; lunch & dinner) This pub has bright upstairs rooms, all except one, which has shared facilities; rates include continental breakfast. Downstairs in the Tiger Lair Cafe-Bar you can get roasts, burgers and flame-grilled chicken, or just sip on an ale in the large beer garden.

Mole Creek Guest House & Restaurant (☎ 6363 1399; fax 6363 1420; 100 Pioneer Dr; s from $100, d $120-140; cottage d $100; mains $16-22; breakfast, lunch & dinner Wed-Sun, breakfast & lunch Mon & Tue) This is a friendly, comfy place to stay, with nicely presented rooms. The more-expensive rooms are larger and have en suites; rates include cooked breakfast. It also rents out Engadine, a self-contained cottage, while its Laurelberry Restaurant serves good food, including chicken *amandine*, vegetarian stacks and a delicious chicken with laurel-berry sauce.

Blackwood Park Cottages (☎ 6363 1208; 445 Mersey Hill Rd; cottages $110-145) Off a side road between Mole Creek and Holiday Village, this place offers two lovely self-contained cottages set among well-maintained gardens in a rural setting with views to the surrounding mountains. It also includes excellent crafted furniture, heated floors, homemade bread and muffins, a scrumptious brekky and good facilities. Children are most welcome.

Mole Creek Cafe (☎ 6363 1200; 76 Pioneer Dr; mains $4-10; breakfast, lunch & dinner) This friendly café aims to serve fare that will hit the sides of a football field: pies, Southern fried chicken, fish and chips, steak sandwiches, and various burgers (including vegetarian). For the unfortunate souls that can't pig out, there's also a seasonal menu of light meals.

WALLS OF JERUSALEM NATIONAL PARK

This remote national park comprises a series of glacial valleys and lakes on top of the Central Plateau and is part of the Tasmanian Wilderness World Heritage Area. It has wild alpine flora and rugged dolerite peaks, and is famously appealing to bushwalkers who prefer an isolated and

CLIMBING THE WALLS

The most popular walk in the park is the full-day steep trek to the 'Walls' themselves. The quickest, easiest route is the trail from the car park off Mersey Forest Rd (near Lake Rowallan; the last 11km is on a gravel road) to Trappers Hut (two hours return), Solomon's Jewels (four hours return), through Herod's Gate to Lake Salome (six to eight hours return), then Damascus Gate (nine hours return), to Dixon's Kingdom Hut & Pine Forest (10 hours return), finally reaching the top of Mt Jerusalem (12 hours return). If you have the time and equipment, it's really worth camping in the park. The park is also exposed and subject to extremely harsh weather conditions, so you must be prepared for strong winds and snowfalls, even in summer. Walks across the park are described in *Cradle Mountain Lake St Clair and Walls of Jerusalem National Parks*, by John Chapman & John Siseman, and in Lonely Planet's *Walking in Australia*.

spectacular hiking challenge (see the boxed text, above, for details).

Tasmanian Expeditions (☎ 1800 030 230, 6334 3477; www.tas-ex.com) has multi-day guided walks combining trips to the Walls of Jerusalem and Cradle Mountain (p290).

Getting There & Away

BUS

For buses on demand contact **Maxwells** (☎/fax 6492 1431), which runs from Devonport to the Walls of Jerusalem (one to four passengers $180, five or more $45 per passenger) and from Launceston to Cradle Mountain via the Walls of Jerusalem ($240/60).

CAR

The quickest access to the Walls is from Sheffield or Mole Creek. From Mole Creek take the B12, then the C138 and finally the C171 (Mersey Forest Rd) to Lake Rowallan; remain on this road, following the C171 and/or Walls of Jerusalem signs to the start of the track.

MOLE CREEK TO SHEFFIELD

From Mole Creek you'll pass through the aptly entitled Paradise before arriving at a major T-intersection at which you must turn right to Sheffield or left to Gowrie Park and Cradle Mountain.

Gowrie Park

Situated at the foot of Mt Roland just 14km from Sheffield, this makes an excellent base for walks up the mountains or for a rural retreat. It's also the site of a huge 94m-long mural on a Hydro Tasmania maintenance shed (see the boxed text, p232). There are walks to the summits of Mts Roland (1234m), Vandyke (1084m) and Claude (1034m), including shorter walks in the cool, shady forests of the lower slopes, such as the pleasant meander through the bush at nearby O'Neills Creek Reserve. Bird lovers take note: there are 94 species in the Mt Roland area.

SIGHTS

At 1234m high, Mt Roland looks like it would be extremely difficult to climb but is, in fact, graded as medium; that said, don't climb it in winter.

There are two main access points. The first is from Claude Rd village, a short distance towards Gowrie Park from the T-junction at Paradise. To use this access, turn off at Kings Rd and head south for about 1.5km to the start of the Mt Roland Track, which is 6.5km long and takes 3½ hours return (this track is very steep and awkward in places, necessitating clambering up and over boulders). The other access point is at Gowrie Park itself, where you turn off the main road just near the sports ground and travel 2km to a gate, which is the start of a 10km track that takes approximately four hours return.

SLEEPING & EATING

Mt Roland Budget Backpackers (☎ 6491 1385; fax 6491 1848; 1447 Claude Rd; powered sites $5, dm $10) Well signposted off the main road, this village offers basic camping (site prices are for up to two people) and good-value hostel-style accommodation (amenities include piping hot water, woolly blankets and a well-equipped kitchen).

Gowrie Park Wilderness Cabins (☎ 6491 1385; fax 6491 1848; 1447 Claude Rd d from $66) Adjacent to the backpackers and run by the same people are these four self-contained cabins. The settlement here is also home to

> **THE AUTHOR'S CHOICE**
>
> **Weindorfers** (☎ 6491 1385; www.weindorfers.com; Claude Rd; mains $10-26.50; 🕑 10am-late Oct-May) Tucked into the foothills of Mts Roland, Vandyke and Claude, this nostalgic, rustic cabin-style restaurant serves top-notch hearty fare. Each dish is exquisite. Starting with a creamy soup, lace the flavours with a hot, crusty bread roll. Then sip a bouncy red, working your way through the tasty Swedish meatballs, coated with a rich yet balanced mushroom sauce and bedded with a ratatouille that's bound to have you pine with longing for years. If you've room, sample the ginger cake with a scoop of homemade greengage ice cream, polishing off with the trademark plunger coffee. Weindorfers caters to vegetarians and those with special diets (ring ahead to discuss your needs). Dinner reservations are essential.

the restaurant Weindorfers (see the boxed text, above).

Silver Ridge Wilderness Retreat (☎ 6491 1727; www.silverridgeretreat.com.au; 46 Rysavy Rd; apt $125-240; 🏊) This option, 3km north of Gowrie Park and less than 10 minutes from Sheffield off the C136, has wonderful Mt Roland views, a licensed restaurant and an indoor pool. It also has comfortable two-bedroom abodes, and one disabled unit with wheelchair access. Bushwalking, horse riding and birdwatching activities can be arranged.

C140 & Lake Barrington

Approximately 6km down the road from Gowrie Park to Cradle Mountain, turn off onto the C140, which will take you north back towards Sheffield. From the southern end of this road, there are incredible, picturesque views of Mt Roland, and 2km along you'll pass **Highland Trails Horse Riding** (☎ 6491 1533, 0417 145 497), offering one-/two- or four-hour day rides, and overnight rides.

A further 1km north is **Cradle Vista** (☎ 6491 1129; www.cradlevista.com.au; 978 Staverton Rd; r $130-150), a 50-acre farm property offering B&B in a couple of en suite rooms in the main house and a large, open-plan unit. Dinners can be arranged. Besides hospitable, bright lodgings, this place also has fantastic views of the surrounding mountains.

The **Granary** (☎ 6491 1689; www.granary.com.au; 575 Staverton Rd; s $77-99, d $99-$132; 💻) sits on a hill top within a marvellous garden. It has one- to four-bedroom, self-contained timber cottages featuring windows produced in an on-site **stained-glass workshop** (🕑 9am-5pm Wed-Fri, to noon Sat). Linen and electric blankets are supplied. Kids will stay well amused in the enormous treehouse, bouncing a ball on the basketball court, in the DVD/games centre, and by generally scampering around the property on bikes. There's also a spa, gym and sauna.

Down the road past Promised Land is the turn-off to Lake Barrington. Right beside the turn-off is **Tasmazia** (☎ 6491 1934; 500 Staverton Rd; adult/child $15/8; 🕑 10am-4pm Mar-Nov, 9am-5pm Dec-Feb), a complex of eight viburnum-hedge mazes that the owners claim is the largest of its kind in the world. The mazes are entertaining, as is an extensive and whimsical miniature village called **Lower Crackpot** (replete with its own post office and postcode – 7306!). Built by a self-professed 'stress doctor', the village is fully paved and has a network of English-style lamp posts; allow about an hour to explore (note last entry to the maze is 5pm during summer). There's also a lavender farm (harvested late January/February) and a large **pancake parlour** (pancakes $9-19; 🕑 to 4pm) serving breakfast toasts, scones, soup and a huge range of sweet and savoury pancakes – the biggest is called 'Wild Boar Loose in the Feedshed'.

The approach road from the turn-off near the maze leads to the section of **Lake Barrington** that has been marked out for international, national and state rowing championships. Other access roads lead to picnic areas and boat ramps; camping is also available.

Further along the C140 road, and flanked by a hedge the size of Texas, is **Carinya Farm Holiday Retreat** (☎ 6491 1593; fax 9491 1256; 63 Staverton Rd; s/d $89/99). Staying in pine-lined loft-bedroom chalets peacefully overlooking farm land and Mt Roland, guests receive homemade bread and freshly laid farm eggs, and breakfast and supper provisions can be arranged.

Wilmot

☎ 03

Wilmot, on the western side of Lake Barrington, is worth staying at if you're visiting Cradle Mountain and don't mind a drive (note the amusing trail of novelty letter boxes all along the C132). You can fill up on petrol and diesel here, and there's an ATM.

The township boasts the first **Coles store** (☎ 6492 1335; 7.30am-6pm) operated by GJ Coles. It's now a general store and worth a look around for a slice of corporate history (the Coles name is now part of one of Australia's largest supermarket chains).

Jaquie's (☎ 6492 1117; Cradle Mountain Rd; d $88), set in the 1893 Wilmot bakery, offers five nice rooms and a full cooked breakfast. It also has a **restaurant** (mains $15) with homemade Thai soups, chicken dishes and desserts such as sticky date pudding. Bookings are essential.

Five kilometres north of Wilmot is the turn-off to **Lake Tea Gardens** (☎ 6492 1394; Lake Barrington Rd; meals $6-9; noon-4pm Sat-Thu Oct-Apr), a further 3km down a gravel side road in a garden-studded location beside Lake Barrington. Indulge in homemade soup or milkshakes while sitting outside and gazing across at Mt Roland.

SHEFFIELD

☎ 03 / pop 1020

A couple of decades ago Sheffield was in a state of economic decline. With the return from traditional rural industry shrinking, clever folk came up with the idea of decorating the town with large, colourful murals, mainly depicting the history of the local pioneers. The first was so well received that over the years around 50 of these artworks have been daubed in town and a dozen in the surrounding district (see p232). These days the 'town of murals' attracts much tourism; it's a good base for bushwalking and there are some excellent trout-fishing spots in the rivers and lakes nearby.

Information

Newsagency (Main St) Acts as a Westpac agent; also has a multibank ATM.

Post office Agent for the Commonwealth Bank.

Slater's Country Store (☎ 6491 1121; 52 Main St; 8.30am-5.30pm Mon-Sat, 9am-5pm Sun) Has an ATM.

Visitors centre (☎ 6491 1036; 5 Pioneer Cres; 8.30am-5pm) Supplies information on the Kentish region, and provides Internet access ($2 per 15 minutes).

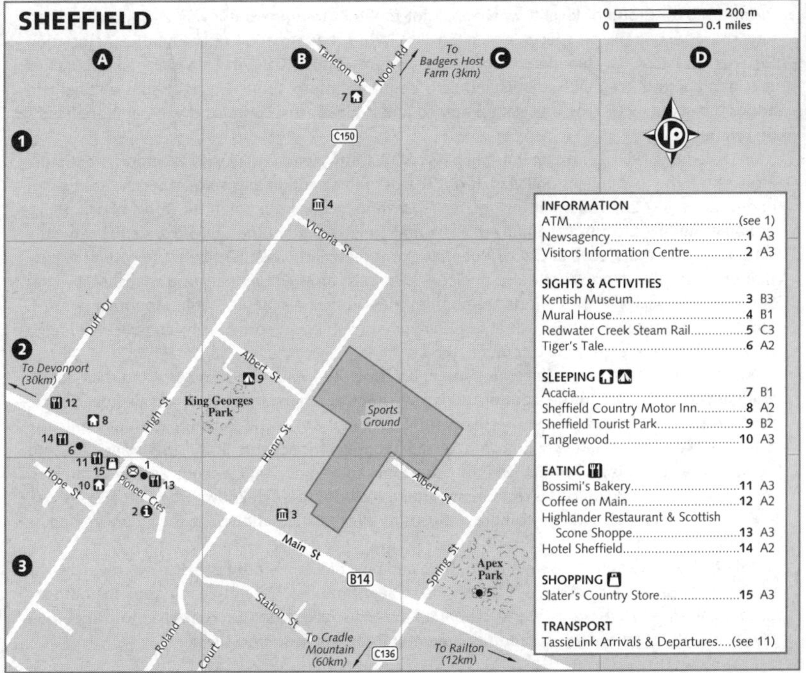

THE NORTH

Sights & Activities

KENTISH MUSEUM

This **museum** (☎ 6491 1861; 93 Main St; adult/child $4/2; 10am-noon & 1-4pm Mon & Wed, 1-3pm Tue, Thu & Fri, or by appointment) has interesting artefacts from the municipality's past, including a 1948 Rural Automatic (telephone) Exchange, old organs, typewriters, photos and military and sports paraphernalia. There's also a display on Gustav Weindorfer, the founder of Waldheim (p290) near Cradle Mountain, and one on the world's first petrol pump!

MURAL HOUSE

Interesting **Mural House** (☎ 6491 1784; 100 High St; adult/student $2/1; 1-5pm Tue, Thu, Sat & Sun) contains interpretations of native art of various cultures in the form of internal wall murals. Diego Rivera's spirit must be in the air.

TIGER'S TALE

A must-see attraction, one that will delight kids (and grown-ups), is the **Tiger's Tale** (☎ 6491 1075; www.tigerstale.com.au; 38a Main St; adult/child/family $5/3/13; 9am-5pm), a unique animatronics theatre and robot display of high-tech comedic drama. It's main feature is an amazing 10-minute performance in which the Tasmanian tiger comes to life through computer-controlled robotics. The script is a little primitive but the technical wizardry is exemplary.

REDWATER CREEK STEAM RAIL

At the eastern end of town, departing from the original Sheffield train station, the **Steam Rail** (☎ 6491 1613; cnr Main & Spring Sts; adult/child/concession $4/1/2) usually has locomotives running on a narrow-gauge track from 11am to 4pm over the first weekend of each month, for two weeks in early January and on special days.

Festivals & Events

On the annual Tasmanian Labor Day weekend (early March), Sheffield hosts a **Steamfest**, which includes displays of steam

ALFRESCO ART

In the 1980s, a group of local townspeople got together to figure out a way of improving Sheffield's dour economic prospects, a meeting that led to the formation of the Kentish Association for Tourism Inc (KAT). One member of KAT had heard about a Canadian town called Chemainus that had painted itself with murals and thus begun to attract tourists, and suggested Sheffield adopt the same tactic. The association agreed and it hired artist John Lendis to paint Sheffield's first mural.

In December 1986, Lendis' mural, 'Stillness and Warmth', featuring Gustav Weindorfer of Cradle Mountain fame (p290), was unveiled. It got the desired attention and so became the start of an endeavour by KAT to retell the history of the town through these colourful works of art.

Some murals, such as *The Smithy at Work* and *Early Trading at the Skin Shed,* depict the early settlers, while others, such as *Cradle Mountain Beauty* and *Forth Falls*, highlight the natural beauty that envelops the town. Murals also depict events, such as *Mountain Rescue,* a snapshot of (late) Snr Constable Harry Clark's efforts to organise a helicopter rescue at Cradle Mountain in 1971. Still others are more esoteric, such as *Masonic Lodge Symbols,* a geometrically complicated image that only furtive Freemasons can understand.

More than 10 artists have been involved in painting the local murals, some taking their handiwork outside Sheffield to the sides of sheds and shops at nearby locales such as Railton, Gowrie Park, Roland and Moina. The impressive 94m-long mural at Gowrie Park, for example, tells the history of when the village set up camp for the hydroelectric scheme in the 1960s and '70s, and depicts what Gowrie looked like when it was home to around 3000 workers and their families. Also at Gowrie, the Weindorfers restaurant gardens includes the well-known *Honeymooners* mural, a wonderful pictorial homage to Kate and Gustav Weindorfer, who spent their honeymoon at Mt Roland in 1906.

Sheffield has realised it's onto a good thing and now efficiently promotes itself as the 'Town of Murals' or 'Tasmania's Outdoor Art Gallery'. Each year from late March to early April, the outdoor gallery continues to grow with artists from all over Australia taking up residence to compete in Sheffield's Mural Fest, daubing another nine murals annually around town.

equipment, heritage games for children, and stalls. The town also conducts the **Mural Fest** late March to early April. Essentially it's a massive paint-off; a theme is set and artists from all over Australia descend upon the town to compete for a cash prize, and to add another nine murals to the town.

Sleeping

Sheffield Tourist Park (☎ 6491 2611; Albert St; unpowered/powered sites $11/16, on-site vans $35) This is a small, patchy park behind the old town hall. Its amenities are adequate and it makes a good budget option and base for exploring. Prices are for two people.

Sheffield Country Motor Inn (☎ 6491 1800; fax 6491 1966; 51-53 Main St; motel s/d $60/80, units s $70, d $90-100) This option has adequate, neat and tidy motel rooms with private bathroom and two self-contained units (one of them a large three-bedroom place).

Acacia (☎/fax 6491 2482; 113 High St; s from $50, d $70-100) North of the town centre, Acacia is a 1910 home with three comfortable bedrooms and cooked or light breakfasts, and dinner, to order. Tea- and coffee-making facilities are available to grab a cuppa and enjoy a homemade biscuit or two.

Tanglewood (☎/fax 6491 1854; fax 6491 2195; 25 High St; s from $90, d $95-110) Set in a beautifully restored Federation home, this B&B provides comfortable accommodation surrounded by lovely English-style gardens. The rate includes breakfast and dinner, and facilities include private bathroom, electric blankets and TV.

Badgers Host Farm (☎ 6491 1816; fax 6491 2488; 226 Nook Rd; s/d $80/125) This is a view-struck property nestled beneath the rambling Badgers Hills, offering a three-bedroom suite, private bathroom, tea- and coffee-making facilities, a fully cooked breakfast (dinner bookings required) and complementary farm animals. Follow High St northeast past Acacia for 3km and look for the gate on the right after Golf Course Rd.

Eating

Highlander Restaurant & Scottish Scone Shoppe (☎ 6491 1077; 60 Main St; mains $18-20; ⏰ breakfast & lunch, dinner Wed-Sun) No kilt required! This is a delightful place serving delicious pumpkin scones ($5) and hearty café fare by day, such as homemade pies and desserts, and an extensive full à la carte menu by night, including traditional roasts.

Coffee on Main (☎ 6491 1893; 43 Main St; mains $10-15; ⏰ breakfast, lunch & dinner) Refreshingly cosmopolitan, this art-filled gallery café serves light meals in a casual, friendly setting. The smoked salmon with camembert on pide ($7) is lush. It certainly lives up to its reputation: it makes one mean, creamy coffee.

Bossimi's Bakery (☎ 6491 1298; 44 Main St; ⏰ breakfast, lunch & dinner) This bakery does the industry justice with lots of speciality pastries, cakes and bread.

Hotel Sheffield (☎ 6491 1130; 38 Main St; mains; $10-16; ⏰ lunch & dinner) You could always try the pub, which offers good-value counter-meal options and a lively local atmosphere to boot.

Getting There & Away

TassieLink buses stop outside the bakery on the main street.

LATROBE

☎ 03 / pop 2770

Just 10km south of Devonport via the Bass Hwy, this historic town exudes the flavour of a bustling, rural centre. Once functioning as a busy shipping port community, it's slowly becoming subsumed by Devonport, but these days it's focussing attention on the antiques trade, and educating the masses in the joys of the platypus. The town has some lovely parks, and at the time of writing, the local wetlands were ging to be developed at the Pig Island–Mersey River precinct. Latrobe also holds the distinction of being the birthplace of the sport of wood-chopping.

Information

The Latrobe **visitors centre** (☎ 6421 4699; tourism@latrobe.tas.gov.au; 46 Gilbert St; ⏰ 8.30am-4.30pm Mon-Fri, 9am-4.30pm Sat & Sun) sits just in front of Kings Creek, adjacent to Lucas' Hotel (look out for the giant fibro platypus perched over the side entrance of the hotel).

Sights

Warrawee Forest Reserve (gates ⏰ 9am-dusk) is a fantastic Mersey-side 2.3-sq-km recreational area. Its walks include a 10-minute, wheelchair-accessible Pond Circuit, a 20-minute walk downstream to Farrell Park, and a one-hour return Forest Circuit. However the area's star attractions are the resident platypuses. **Platypus-spotting tours** are organised through the visitors centre; book ahead for these tours ($10; 1½ to two hours). Warrawee is 4.5km south of town down Hamilton St; turn off Gilbert St at the ANZ bank.

If you're into unlocking the secrets of monotremes then take a tour of the **platypus interpretation centre** (☎ 6421 4699; 46 Gilbert St; adult/concession/family $5/3.50/15; 8.30am-4.30pm Mon-Fri, 9am-4.30pm Sat & Sun), part of the Lucas' complex but accessed via the visitors centre. Its dioramas, videos and models include a small birds-of-prey exhibit.

The town's history is depicted through the 600 prints and original architectural drawings on display in the **Court House Museum** (Gilbert St; adult/child $2/1; 2-5pm Fri & Sun), next to the post office in the centre of town.

The **Australian Axeman's Hall of Fame** (☎ 6426 2099; davaxe@keypoint.com.au; adult/child/family $9/5/18; 1 Bells Pde; 9am-5pm Oct-Mar, 9am-5pm Mon-Sun Sep-Apr) is a shrine to legendary Australian woodchoppers, particularly wood-chopper extraordinaire David Foster. Held up with salvaged tree-trunks, the vast hall displays logging memorabilia and includes an impressive trophy room dedicated to Foster's lifetime of achievements. Every inch of its display cabinets and wall space is crammed or lined with trophy items – even the ceiling is dripping with ribbons. There's a fully licensed bar and café serving light snacks and refreshments.

Adjacent to Axeman's is **Sherwood Hall** (☎ 6426 2888; Bell's Pde; 10am-2pm Tue & Thu, 1-4pm Sat, Sun & public hols, or by appointment), a historic cottage of some significance, as it was built by the remarkable pioneer couple, ex-convict Thomas Johnson and his half-Aboriginal wife Dolly Dalrymple Briggs.

Festivals & Events

Henley-on-the-Mersey carnival Held on Australia Day at Bells Pde in Latrobe, site of the town's former docks.

Latrobe Wheel Race Annual bicycle race held on Boxing Day, attracting professional riders from around Australia.

Sleeping & Eating

Lucas' Hotel (☎ 6426 1101; fax 6426 2546; 46 Gilbert St; s with/without bathroom $75/60, d $85/70, s/d with spa $95/105; mains $11-20; breakfast, lunch & dinner) This award-winning restored pub at the western end of Gilbert St offers very comfortable and well-maintained rooms. The carpet's a little lairy but Lucas' does offer a generous continental/full cooked breakfast ($8/12.50 per person), and the brasserie-style café-bistro cooks up a decent batch of mod Oz–style fare.

Latrobe Motel (☎ 6426 2030; latrobemotel@southcom.com.au; 1 Palmers Rd; s/d $65/75) These standard (but fastidiously neat and roomy) ground-floor brick lodgings are a decent option for a night. The motel sits just off the Bass Hwy roundabout, opposite the hospital.

Lucinda (☎ 6426 2285; lucindabnb@ozemail.com.au; 17 Forth St; s/d from $85/120) Lucinda provides very nice colonial B&B accommodation (with private bathroom) in an 1891 National Trust–classified dwelling. A couple of its heritage rooms have spectacular plasterwork, such as grand ceiling roses, or pressed-metal ceilings, and one room has a spa. The rate includes a cooked breakfast.

Erica Cottage (☎ 6428 2678; 35 Gilbert St; d $110-130) This quaint 1869 self-contained cottage provides guests with all the modern amenities in a cosy, log-fire-in-the-lounge sort of way. The master bedroom has an en suite and the fully equipped kitchen includes a dishwasher.

Glo Glo's (☎ 6426 2120; 78 Gilbert St; mains $20-30; dinner Mon-Sat) It's so nice to be able to spend an evening fine-dining in a fine 1885 Georgian mansion. Menu choices include roast duck, marinated Lenah wallaby and various vegetarian selections, usually accompanied by wine suggestions.

PORT SORELL

☎ 03 / pop 1820

Just east of Devonport is the leisure conglomerate of Port Sorell, Shearwater and Hawley Beach, a triad of well-established holiday retreats and retirement villages on the shallow estuary of the Rubicon River.

The township is split into two sections by the flats of Poyston Creek, and there are several islands in the estuary that can be reached at low tide – the flats are pretty muddy, so it's best to return before the tide rises (beware the strong rips).

An alternative scenic walk follows the track along the shoreline 6km north to Point Sorell, which takes around two hours return.

Hawley Beach has sandy, sheltered swimming beaches, and is a very popular fishing spot. The region is an easy 20-minute drive to Narawntapu National Park (p214).

Sleeping & Eating

Port Sorell Lions Caravan Park (☎ 6428 7267; fax 6428 7269; 44 Meredith St, Port Sorell; unpowered/powered sites $10/15) A friendly camping ground with sites sprawled along the enticing waterfront. Site prices are for up to two people.

Sails on Port Sorell (☎ 6428 7580; www.sailsonportsorell.com.au; 54 Rice St, Port Sorell; motel d $95, studio apt $115, unit d $135) Only a short stroll to the beach, this friendly place includes modern comforts in its nautical-themed units, 'Dolphin', 'Oyster' or 'Lighthouse'. A child-friendly option, it also offers bike hire.

Shearwater Cottages (☎ 6428 6895; shearwatercottages@vision.net.au; 7-9 Shearwater Blvd, Shearwater; r $80-130) This place has a handful of self-contained suites that are eerily clean, and the gardens surrounding the cottages are also manicured to the quick. A breakfast basket or BBQ pack can be supplied on request.

Hawley House (☎ 6428 6221; www.hawleyhousetas.com; Hawley Esplanade, Hawley Beach; d $155-180) Hawley House is a nicely landscaped, welcoming, peacock-laden historic homestead with ocean views over a calm beach. It offers luxury accommodation at a white Gothic mansion (1878) in either the main house or stables/lofts (some with spa). You can sample delicate but hearty four-course gourmet dinners by arrangement.

Tranquilles (☎ 6428 7555; www.tranquilles.com; 9 Gumbowie Dr, Port Sorell; d $140-195) This luxury B&B offers good-value accommodation. Set in serene, bushy surrounds, the spacious rooms have garden views and complimentary bubbly and chocolates on arrival. The on-site gallery displays roving exhibitions of local and interstate artists and its licensed **teahouse** provides light meals, and morning and afternoon teas (Thursday to Sunday).

The area's other digestive options are restricted to the various takeaways around town and the busy bistro at the **Shearwater Country Club** (☎ 6428 6205; Shearwater Blvd, Shearwater; mains $10-18; lunch & dinner).

DEVONPORT

☎ 03 / pop 25,000

Devonport is Tassie's third-largest city. The dominant feature of the town is the lighthouse-topped Mersey Bluff, from where there are fine views of the coastline and ships. The compact lighthouse was built in 1889 to aid navigation for the expanding port, which is still important today, handling much of the produce from northern Tasmania's agricultural areas.

Information

Most banks have branches and ATMs in or near the Rooke St Mall.

Visitors centre (☎ 6424 4466; tourism@dcc.tas.gov.au; 92 Formby Rd; 7.30am-5pm or 9pm) Open to meet all ferry arrivals – the 9pm closure is for day crossings of the ferry, which arrive at 7pm.

Post office (88 Formby Rd)

Online access centre (☎ 6424 9413; 21 Oldaker St; per 30min/hr $3/5) In the library.

Backpacker's Barn (☎ 6424 3628; 10-12 Edward St; 9am-6pm Mon-Fri, to noon Sat) Excellent bushwalking shop with gear for sale or hire; also handles accommodation, tour, car rental and bus bookings.

Sights & Activities

TIAGARRA

The impressive Aboriginal culture centre and museum, **Tiagarra** (☎ 6424 8250; Bluff Rd; adult/child/family $3.60/2.50/10; 9am-5pm), which means 'keep', is on the road to the lighthouse. It has a rare collection of more than 250 indigenous rock engravings, thought to date around 10,000 years, some of which can be seen by following the marked geological trail on the bluff. The centre displays indigenous art and crafts, such as woodcarvings and fabrics. The excellent interpretive display complex depicts recordings of the first encounters with the Europeans, including mural dioramas, tools and artefacts, photographs, paintings and sculptures.

DEVONPORT MARITIME MUSEUM

This excellent **museum** (☎ 6424 7100; 6 Gloucester Ave; adult/child/family $3/1/6; 10am-4.30pm Tue-Sun Oct-Mar, to 4pm Tue-Sun Apr-Sep) is in the former harbourmaster's residence (c 1920) and pilot station near the foreshore. It has an extensive collection of flags and other maritime paraphernalia, including a superb set of models from the ages of sail through steam to the present seagoing passenger ferries.

HOME HILL

The National Trust–administered **Home Hill** (☎ 6424 3028; nat_trust@vision.net.au; 77 Middle Rd;

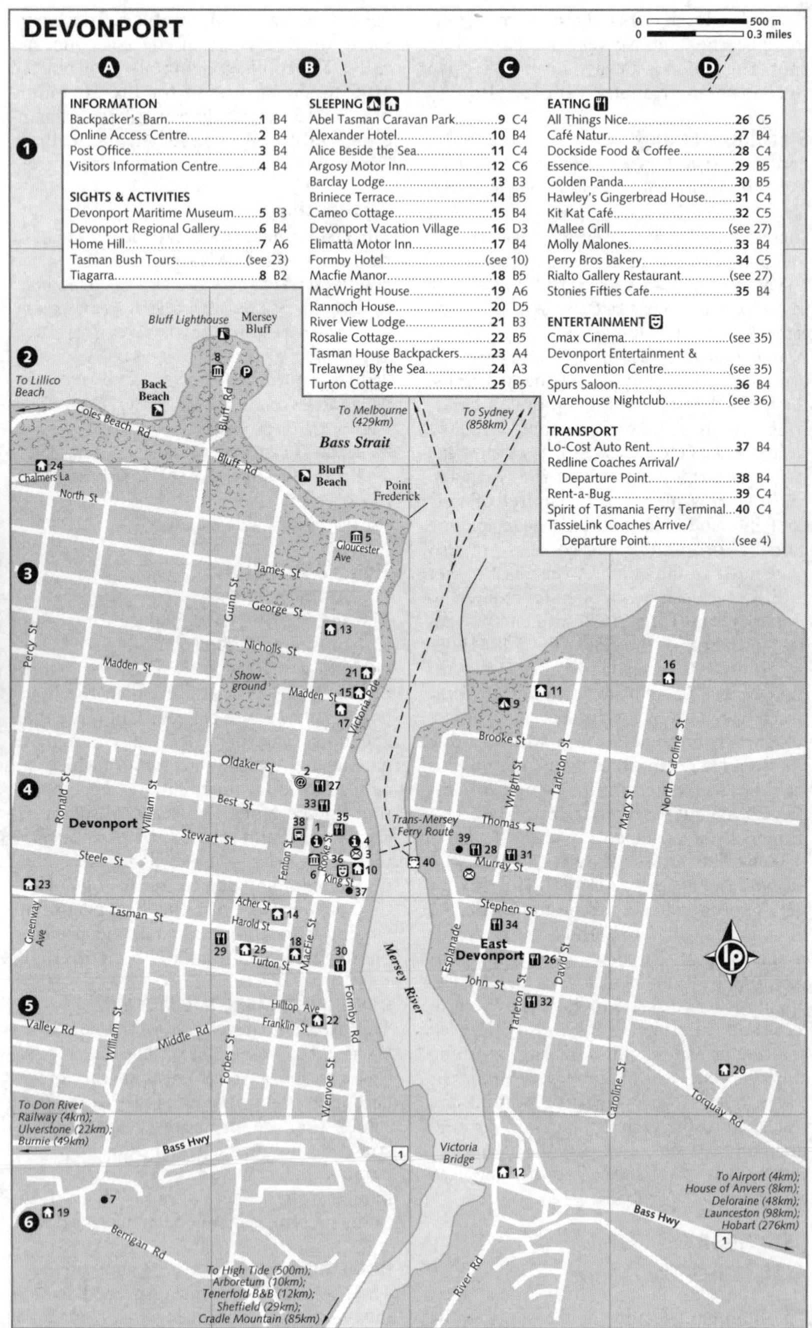
DEVONPORT
0 500 m
0 0.3 miles
A
B
C
D
1
2
3
4
5
6
INFORMATION
Backpacker's Barn 1 B4
Online Access Centre 2 B4
Post Office 3 B4
Visitors Information Centre 4 B4
SIGHTS & ACTIVITIES
Devonport Maritime Museum 5 B3
Devonport Regional Gallery 6 B4
Home Hill 7 A6
Tasman Bush Tours (see 23)
Tiagarra 8 B2
SLEEPING
Abel Tasman Caravan Park 9 C4
Alexander Hotel 10 B4
Alice Beside the Sea 11 C4
Argosy Motor Inn 12 C6
Barclay Lodge 13 B3
Briniece Terrace 14 B5
Cameo Cottage 15 B4
Devonport Vacation Village 16 D3
Elimatta Motor Inn 17 B4
Formby Hotel (see 10)
Macfie Manor 18 B5
MacWright House 19 A6
Rannoch House 20 D5
River View Lodge 21 B3
Rosalie Cottage 22 B5
Tasman House Backpackers 23 A4
Trelawney By the Sea 24 A3
Turton Cottage 25 B5
EATING
All Things Nice 26 C5
Café Natur 27 B4
Dockside Food & Coffee 28 C4
Essence 29 B5
Golden Panda 30 B5
Hawley's Gingerbread House 31 C4
Kit Kat Café 32 C5
Mallee Grill (see 27)
Molly Malones 33 B4
Perry Bros Bakery 34 C5
Rialto Gallery Restaurant (see 27)
Stonies Fifties Cafe 35 B4
ENTERTAINMENT
Cmax Cinema (see 35)
Devonport Entertainment & Convention Centre (see 35)
Spurs Saloon 36 B4
Warehouse Nightclub (see 36)
TRANSPORT
Lo-Cost Auto Rent 37 B4
Redline Coaches Arrival/ Departure Point 38 B4
Rent-a-Bug 39 C4
Spirit of Tasmania Ferry Terminal 40 C4
TassieLink Coaches Arrive/ Departure Point (see 4)
Bluff Lighthouse
Mersey Bluff
To Lillico Beach
Back Beach
Coles Beach Rd
Bluff Rd
To Melbourne (429km)
To Sydney (858km)
Bass Strait
Bluff Beach
Point Frederick
Chalmers La
North St
Gloucester Ave
James St
George St
Gunn St
Nicholls St
Percy St
Madden St
Show-ground
Victoria Pde
Oldaker St
Best St
Ronald St
Devonport
William St
Stewart St
Steele St
Fenton St
Rooke St
King St
Trans-Mersey Ferry Route
Brooke St
Wright St
Tarleton St
Thomas St
Murray St
Mary St
North Caroline St
Acher St
Harold St
Tasman St
Greenway Ave
Turton St
MacFie St
Stephen St
Esplanade
East Devonport
David St
John St
Mersey River
Hilltop Ave
Franklin St
Formby Rd
Valley Rd
Middle Rd
Forbes St
Wenvoe St
Caroline St
Torquay Rd
To Don River Railway (4km); Ulverstone (22km); Burnie (49km)
Bass Hwy
Victoria Bridge
To Airport (4km); House of Anvers (8km); Deloraine (48km); Launceston (98km); Hobart (276km)
Berrigan Rd
To High Tide (500m); Arboretum (10km); Tenerfold B&B (12km); Sheffield (29km); Cradle Mountain (85km)
River Rd

adult/child/family $7.50/5.50/15.40; 11am-4pm Tue-Thu, Sat & Sun, Jan-Apr, 2-4pm Tue-Thu, Sat & Sun May-Dec) was the former residence of Joseph and Dame Enid Lyons. Joseph Lyons (see p256) is the only Australian to have been both a state premier (1923–28) and a prime minister of Australia (1932–39), and Dame Enid Lyons was the first woman to be sworn in as a member of the House of Representatives (1943) and as a Federal cabinet minister (1949).

DON RIVER RAILWAY

This **railway** (6424 6335; www.donriverrailway.com.au; Forth Main Rd; adult/child/pensioner/family $10/6/8/25; 9am-5pm), 4km west of town off the Bass Hwy, has lots of brightly coloured engines and carriages for kids to clamber on. Diesel trains run Monday to Saturday and steam trains run on Sunday and public holidays – the trains leave on the hour between 10am and 4pm inclusive for 30-minute round trips alongside the Don River.

DEVONPORT REGIONAL GALLERY

This excellent **gallery** (6424 8296; 45-47 Stewart St; admission free; 10am-5pm Mon-Sat, 2-5pm Sun) houses predominantly 20th-century Tasmanian paintings, contemporary art by local and mainland artists, plus ceramics and glasswork.

HOUSE OF ANVERS

Southeast along the Bass Hwy (follow the signs for Launceston) about 8km out of Devonport you'll come upon the **House of Anvers** (6426 2958; anvers@bigpond.com.au; 9025 Bass Hwy, Latrobe; 7am-5pm), which produces velvety smooth Belgian-style chocolates and truffles. You can watch production (Monday to Saturday), sample and buy the results, and check out the chocolate museum. Its café supplies crispy croissants and *pain au chocolat* (of course), among other delights.

ARBORETUM

Ten kilometres south of the city, beside the Don River at Eugenana (via C146), is the **Arboretum** (6427 2690; 46 Old Tramway Rd; www.tasmanianarboretum.org.au; adult/family $2/4; 9am-dusk), featuring 58 hectares of various native and exotic trees and shrubs. It includes a limestone outcrop and an ornamental lake, so grab a picnic hamper and relax.

PENGUIN-WATCHING

Between October and March you can observe the comings and goings of a little penguin colony at dusk, from a special viewing area at Lillico Beach, just off the Bass Hwy on the western edge of town.

Tours

Tasman Bush Tours (6423 2335; www.tasmanbushtours.com; 114 Tasman St) Operating out of Tasman House Backpackers, Tasman Bush Tours offers guided walks along the Overland Track (p290).

Tasair (6427 9777; www.tasair.com.au) From Devonport, Tasair offers charter flights over Cradle Mountain and the surrounding areas for $285 per hour.

Sleeping

BUDGET

Hostels

Molly Malone's (6424 1898; mollymalones@vantagegroup.com.au; 34 Best St; dm $15, d with/without bathroom $50/30) There's nothing fancy about this central option, located above Molly Malone's Irish pub (p240), but it has clean, basic four-bed dorms and a comfy lounge. The crowds can get rowdy of a Fridee or Sa'dee night.

MacWright House (6424 5696; 115 Middle Rd; dm/s from $20/25) This YHA number offers simple, clean accommodation and a friendly vibe. It's 3km from the city centre, about a 40-minute walk or a five-minute bus ride (No 40).

Tasman House Backpackers (6423 2335; www.tasmanhouse.com; 114 Tasman St; dm/tw per person $13/15, d with/without bathroom $40/35) This sprawling army barrack–style independent hostel is actually the converted nurses' quarters of the old regional hospital. It's a 15-minute walk from town, or you can arrange transport when booking. Camping and hiking equipment is also available for hire.

Hotels

Alexander Hotel (6424 2252; 78 Formby Rd; s/d $30/40) A good central place. Rooms feature shared facilities plus continental breakfast (cooked breakfast $8).

Formby Hotel (6424 1601; fax 6424 8123; 82 Formby Rd; s/d $30/55) This pub has straightforward singles with shared facilities and doubles with en suites (continental breakfast $10).

Camping & Cabins

Site prices are for up to two people.

Mersey Bluff Caravan Park (☎ 6424 8655; fax 6424 8657; Bluff Rd; unpowered/powered sites $14/17, on-site vans $40, cabins from $60) This is a pleasant park with some good beaches nearby.

Abel Tasman Caravan Park (☎ 6427 8794; 6 Wright St; unpowered/powered sites $15/20, on-site vans/cabins $45/65) Offering very clean amenities, perfect for those with an aversion to mould, this park also has a good beachfront location in East Devonport, just five minutes from the ferry terminal.

Devonport Vacation Village (☎ 6427 8886; fax 6427 8388; 20-24 Nth Caroline St; unpowered/powered sites $14/18, cabins $50-75) This large village is another budget option and its location in East Devonport makes it a convenient place to stay if you need to hop on/hop off the ferry.

MIDRANGE

Cottages

Both **Rosalie Cottage** (66 Wenvoe St) and **Turton Cottage** (28 Turton St) are managed by **Devonport Historic Cottages** (☎ 1800 240 031; www.devonportcottages.com; d from $140). Both are very comfortable and are fitted out with all the mod cons, but are restored with period furniture and lots of memorabilia to keep the heritage atmosphere. There are ample breakfast provisions and log fires to doze in front of. Extra touches include an old gramophone in Rosalie and hand-stencilled walls in Turton.

Guesthouses & B&Bs

River View Lodge (☎ 6424 7357; www.riverviewlodge.com.au; 18 Victoria Pde; s with/without bathroom $65/50, d from $80/70) This foreshore lodge is a friendly, old-fashioned country-style place opposite a strip of picnic table–dotted greenery. The en suite rooms are good value and the rates include breakfast.

Macfie Manor (☎ 6424 1719; fax 6424 8766; 44 Macfie St; s $85, d $95-110) Offering B&B close to the city centre is this beautiful two-storey Federation building. Superbly furnished, guests have the option of staying in an en suite room or cosy terrace apartment.

Tenerfold B&B (☎ /fax 6427 3170; www.tenerfoldbandb.com.au; 84 Melrose Dr, Aberdeen; ste $125-135) Just a 10-minute drive from the CBD, this luxuriously appointed two-bedroom suite is good value, with rural views in a secluded and private setting. To get here take the Devonport Main Rd (B14) south continuing on Sheffield Rd, turning right at the C146.

Alice Beside the Sea (☎ /fax 6427 8605; alice@alicebesidethesea.com; 1 Wright St; d $110-150) Located close to the ferry terminals, this compact B&B is a decent option offering comfortable, two-bedroom, self-contained accommodation within cooee of the beach and supermarket. Its blend of modern and cottage décor is a refreshing change from the olde-worlde frilly style.

Trelawney by the Sea (☎ /fax 6424 3263; 6 Chalmers Lane; r around $130) Trelawney's spacious, two-bedroom, self-contained unit has an overdose of timber panelling, but also has great views beyond Coles Beach. Guests can use its outdoor spa and the rate includes a good breakfast. Dinners can be arranged.

Rannoch House (☎ 6427 9818; maala@dodo.com.au; 5 Cedar Ct; s/d from $100/120) This is a peaceful, faintly Irish historic Federation homestead set among relaxing landscaped grounds in East Devonport. All five rooms have en suite and rates include a fully cooked breakfast.

Cameo Cottage (☎ 6427 0991, 0439 658 503; www.devonportbedandbreakfast.com; 27 Victoria Pde; d $140) Close to the ferry terminals, shops and restaurants, Cameo Cottage (1914) provides neat and comfortable lodgings. The fully self-contained, two-bedroom cottage includes TV, CD/DVD players and a BBQ.

Briniece Terrace (☎ 6423 4441; lovey@hotkey.net.au; 3-5 Archer St; d from $140) Each boutique, one-bedroom, self-contained apartment (c 1891) in this grand, restored Victorian terrace has an open fire place, a two-person spa and lots of room to stretch out and take a breather in, including a balcony over the Strait. The kitchens are well equipped and the beds very comfy – overall, a good choice.

Motels

Elimatta Motor Inn (☎ 6424 6555; 15 Victoria Pde; s $65-75, d & tw $80-85) Elimatta isn't anything to write home about, with ordinary and basic motel-style rooms, but its staff is friendly, it's well managed and it's an easy walk from the city centre.

Argosy Motor Inn (☎ 1800 657 068, 6427 8872; Tarleton St; s $80-110, d $85-120) Argosy has a dowdy, brown-brick-on-steroids exterior, but the rooms are clean and tidy, ranging from standard to 'executive' suites with spa, and the views over the Mersey are lovely.

Barclay Lodge (☎ 1800 809 340, 6424 4722; 112 North Fenton St; s/d from $85/125) These lodgings appear to be an overgrown Lego set with a scattering of brick motel suites and apartments with odd-looking roofs. One unit is equipped for disabled travellers.

Eating

RESTAURANTS

Hawley's Gingerbread House (☎ 6427 0466; Murray St; mains $7-15, pancakes from $9; ⏰ breakfast, lunch & dinner) Located near the ferry terminals and on the roundabout, this clean, homely place is a terrific option if you want to line the tummy with some brekky fare or a tasty char-grilled rump steak ($15). Desserts include hearty pancakes and meringues and, of course, gingerbread men (from $2). This is also the cellar door for Hawley Vineyards.

Rialto Gallery Restaurant (☎ 6424 6793; 159 Rooke St; mains from $15; ⏰ lunch & dinner Tue-Sat) The Rialto is a decent Italian place specialising in prompt platefuls of pasta, lasagne and other standards. The staff is friendly and the food authentic, saucy and tasty.

High Tide (☎ 6424 6200; 17 Devonport Rd; mains $15-30; ⏰ lunch & dinner) High Tide (formerly The Cove), south of town off the road to Spreyton, is a modern waterfront restaurant with great, varied meals like sushi and sashimi plates, and thyme venison with Guinness compote. There's a glossary of terms on the dinner menu if you don't know your *wasabi* from your *tapanade*.

Golden Panda (☎ 6424 9066; 38-39 Formby Rd; mains $10-18; ⏰ lunch Tue-Fri, dinner) The Golden Panda has Chinese dishes such as chilli calamari, and braised broccoli with crab-meat sauce, along with more-conventional Asian dishes.

Mallee Grill (☎ 6424 4477; 161 Rooke St; mains $15-25; ⏰ lunch Mon-Fri, dinner) This den has some seafood and gourmet sausages, but steak claims most of the menu – the biggest feed is the mixed charcoal grill.

Essence (☎ 6424 6431; 28 Forbes St; mains $25-45; ⏰ lunch Tue-Fri, dinner Tue-Sat) A licensed restaurant and wine bar (from 5.30pm), with upmarket contemporary innovative cuisine and seasonal menus.

PUBS

Alexander Hotel (☎ 6424 2252; 78 Formby Rd; mains $10-18; ⏰ lunch & dinner) This local favourite churns out good counter meals with exotic panache, such as turkey filo, but there's always the reliable roast with three veg for those seeking real comfort food.

Molly Malone's (☎ 6424 1898; 34 Best St; mains $10-18) This authentically fake Irish den has a bistro, with plenty of fish, roasts, stews and grills. Wash it all down with a Guinness or two, or three.

CAFÉS & QUICK EATS

All Things Nice (☎ /fax 6427 0028; 175 Tarleton St ⏰ 24hr) This bakery and café is located near the ferry terminals. It offers all manner of bakery items: gourmet chunky pies (including Tassie's iconic scallop pie, $4), cakes and other sweets, and a good strong cuppa.

Dockside Food & Coffee (☎ 6427 9127; 25 Murray St; ⏰ breakfast & lunch) Just the thing as you stumble bleary-eyed off the ferry, this place offers an all-day, no-limits hot brekky ($9.50) – just what the doctor ordered – plus it does very tasty focaccias ($6) and filling pancakes ($7.50).

Kit Kat Cafe (☎ 6427 8437; 175 Tarleton St; ⏰ breakfast, lunch & dinner) This lovely place offers hearty breakfasts, such as bacon and eggs ($6) and great burgers (from $7). It also does hot fresh rolls or you can tuck into a fresh scallop pie for around $4.

Stonies Fifties Cafe (☎ 6424 2101; 77 Rooke St; ⏰ breakfast & lunch) Serving big brekky options and meals all day, this place is a gem if you're looking for some tucker after that long boat trip across the Bass Strait. It offers big 1950s-style burgers and enough coffee options to stun a tiger.

Café Natur (☎ 6424 1917; 10-12 Edward St; meals $6-10; ⏰ breakfast & lunch Mon-Sat) This café, at the front of the Backpacker's Barn (p235), does fresh, healthy burgers, salads, foccacias and soups, including vegan and gluten-free meals. There's also a selection of organic and biodynamic fruit, vegetables and grains.

Perry Bros Bakery (☎ /fax 6427 8706; 67 Wright St; ⏰ 6am-5pm Mon-Fri, 6.30am-2.30pm Sat) Specialises in excellent pies (around $2.70), great lunchtime menus and fabulous sandwiches, a great option if you're looking to fill up after a long ferry ride.

Entertainment

Check the *Advocate* newspaper for entertainment listings.

Warehouse Nightclub (☎ 6424 7851; 18 King St; admission $6-10; ⏰ 10pm-late Fri & Sat) This is one of very few clubbing hangouts, and where the town's youth congregates to listen to DJs strut their stuff and to check out a live act or two.

Spurs Saloon (☎ 6424 7851; 18 King St; 🕑 5pm-late Wed-Sat) This venue fronts the Warehouse and, judging by its name, hankers for another era on another continent, but it will still quench your thirst.

Molly Malone's (☎ 6424 1898; 34 Best St) An expansive, wood-panelled Irish den that gets big crowds guzzling its beer and watching live music on Friday and Saturday nights.

Cmax cinema (☎ 6420 2111; 5-7 Best St; adult/child $12/9) The Cmax hosts blockbusters and teen flicks.

Devonport Entertainment & Convention Centre (☎ 6420 2900; 145-151 Rooke St; box office 🕑 10am-4pm Mon-Fri) This venue stages everything from children's concerts to ABBA impersonators.

Getting There & Away

AIR

For information on domestic flights to/from Devonport, see p332 and p335. There are regular flights to/from Melbourne with Qantas and Regional Express (Rex), while Tasair flies between Devonport and King Island via Burnie/Wynyard.

BOAT

See p333 for details of the **Spirit of Tasmania ferry** (☎ 13 20 10; www.spiritoftasmania.com.au) between Melbourne or Sydney and Devonport. The ferry terminal is on the Esplanade in East Devonport.

BUS

See p223 for details of Redline services from Launceston to Devonport and on to Burnie (for details of a route further west from Burnie to Smithton, see p246). Also see this section for details of the TassieLink services that run disembarked ferry passengers to Launceston, Hobart and Burnie, and that deliver embarking passengers from Strahan/Queenstown and Hobart. TassieLink also runs from Launceston to Devonport (drop-off only) and then via Sheffield to Cradle Mountain (for details of a route further west from Cradle Mountain to Strahan, see p267).

Redline Coaches (☎ 1300 360 000, 6336 1446; 9 Edward St) has its terminal opposite the Backpacker's Barn and will also stop at the ferry terminal when the ferry is in, while TassieLink coaches pull up outside the Devonport visitors centre and the *Spirit of Tasmania* terminal.

If none of the scheduled services suit your particular bushwalking needs, charter a minibus from **Maxwells** (☎ 6492 1431, 0418 584 004) or through the Backpacker's Barn (p235). For example, if you hire a Maxwells bus from Devonport to Cradle Mountain, it will cost $160 for one to four people and $40 for each extra person.

CAR

Devonport has plenty of cheap car-rental firms, such as **Rent-a-Bug** (☎ 6427 9034; 5 Murray St) and **Lo-Cost Auto Rent** (☎ 1800 802 724, 6424 9922; 22 King St), where high-season rates for older cars start at $35.

Budget (☎ 13 27 27, 6427 0650) and **Thrifty** (☎ 1800 030 730, 6427 9119) have representatives at the airport and ferry terminal, and hire out everything from new cars to old petrol guzzlers.

Getting Around

The airport is 5km east of town. A **shuttle bus** (☎ 0400 035 995) runs between the airport/ferry terminals, the visitors centre and your accommodation for $10 per person. The shuttle can meet all arrivals into Devonport. Bookings for all departures are essential. Alternatively, a **taxi** (☎ 6424 1431) will cost $12 to $15.

A small ferry ($2 one way) departs from opposite the post office, docking on the eastern side of the river beside the ferry terminal. It runs on demand from around 9am to 5pm (8am to 6pm summer) Monday to Saturday.

DETOUR

To escape Devonport, make a detour for Forth, which is 10km west of Devonport. Turn off the Bass Hwy on to the B19 and head south for 3km and you come to the self-titled 'Village by the River'. Filled with rolling hills and sweeping views, the drive through this one-pub town is incredibly scenic and if you take a left up Mackillop Hill, there are grand views to the mouth of the Forth and across the ocean.

ULVERSTONE

☎ 03 / pop 9800

At the mouth of the River Leven, Ulverstone is a relaxed base from which to explore the surrounding area. The town's main features are spacious parklands and several war memorials, the most impressive being the clock-topped **Shrine of Remembrance**, built in 1953 and incorporating an older WWI memorial.

The Ulverstone **visitors centre** (☎ 6425 2839; 13 Alexandra Rd; 9am-5pm) is a treasure-trove of local knowledge. The Internet is available at the **online access centre** (☎ 6425 7579; 15 King Edward St; per 30min/hr $3/5), in the local library.

The **Ulverstone Local History Museum** (☎ 6425 3835; 50 Main St; admission $4; 1.30-4.30pm Tue, Thu, Sat & Sun) concentrates on the area's early farmers, displaying tools, manuscripts, an extensive photographic collection, and assorted artefacts behind a mock-pioneer façade.

See p247 for details of a **historic train** service running between Burnie, Penguin and Ulverstone.

Sleeping

BUDGET

Site prices are for up to two people.

Apex Caravan Park (☎ 6425 2935; Queen St; unpowered/powered sites $11/14) This friendly, well-managed park is right off Picnic Point Beach on the western side of the Leven River mouth.

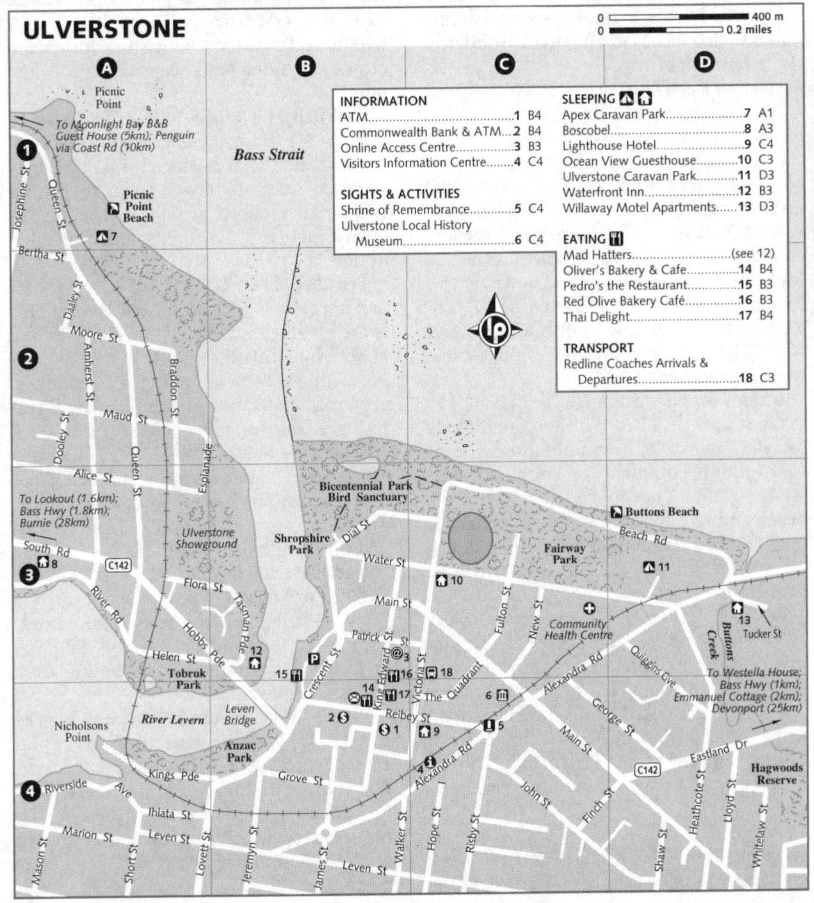

Ulverstone Caravan Park (☎ 6425 2624; fax 6425 4654; 57 Water St; unpowered/powered sites $17/20, on-site vans $45, 3-bunk cabins from $70-80, units from $70) Just a puddle from the water and a skip to the town centre, this caravan park also has a campers' kitchen, playgrounds and adjoining parkland, making it a decent option.

Emmanuel Cottage (☎ 6425 3155; 52 Eastland Dr; d $80) Built in 1918, this fully self-contained cottage is a comfortable three-bedroom weatherboard only a few minutes from the beach. It sleeps six people and welcomes kiddies; Pudda or Fido are welcome, too.

MIDRANGE

Waterfront Inn (☎ 6425 1599; Tasman Pde; s/d $70/95) Across the River Leven from the town centre, this motel has a crowd of economical waterfront rooms, including spa and family units. It also has Mad Hatters, a wonderful restaurant (right).

Willaway Motel Apartments (☎ 6425 2018; www.willaway.southcom.com.au; 2 Tucker St; s/d $80/100) You can't go wrong with this collection of generic, tidy self-contained modern units. They're opposite a nice stretch of lawn with BBQ facilities, and only a minute to the beach.

Westella House (☎ 6425 6222; westella@westella.com; 68 Westella Dr; s/d from $90/125) Close to the highway towards the east of town is this spacious, National Trust–listed B&B, a colonially furnished house with a distinctive roof. The very comfortable rooms come with cooked breakfast.

Ocean View Guesthouse (☎/fax 6425 5401; 1-3 Victoria St; s $75-130, d $100-150) If you're looking for heritage-style, well-appointed rooms (one suite is equipped for disabled travellers), try this guesthouse, 100m from the beach and an easy walk from the town centre. Choose a standard en suite room or pay a bit more for a spa suite. Prices include cooked breakfast.

Boscobel (☎/fax 6425 1727; www.boscobel.com.au; 27 South Rd; d $110-160; 🏊) Boscobel supplies luxurious guest-house accommodation in the formal surroundings of a 19th-century National Trust–listed home; the frills extend from the bedroom through to the alfresco dining tablecloths. Prices include cooked breakfast and use of a heated indoor pool.

TOP END

Moonlight Bay B&B Guest House (☎/fax 6425 1074; moonlightbay@austarnet.com.au; 141 Penguin Rd; d $140) With absolute beach frontage this luxury (and gay friendly) boutique B&B commands views over Bass Strait, the Three Sisters (opposite) and Goat Islands. Both suites include a lace canopy four-poster bed (one king-sized). The rate includes full English buffet-style brekky and the use of a spa. The guesthouse is unsuitable for children.

Lighthouse Hotel (☎ 6425 1197; lighthouse@goodstone.com.au; 33 Victoria St; d $100-210) The light and bright, well-run Lighthouse offers large and comfortable rooms with good facilities. There's a large atrium space downstairs giving the hotel an appealing atmosphere. This place also offers great meals (see below).

Eating

Oliver's Bakery & Cafe (☎ 6425 4118; 41 Reibey St; mains from $5; 🕑 6am-6pm) Oliver's has inventive focaccias, tasty savoury pies and crispy croissants, along with heaps of other baked fare.

Thai Delight (☎ 6425 3055; 25 King Edward St; mains from $10; 🕑 lunch Wed-Fri, dinner Tue-Sun) Serving authentic Thai cuisine, this BYO restaurant/takeaway offers wonderful soups and vegetarian versions of most of the menu's meaty mains. It's a highly recommended option.

Red Olive Gallery Café (☎ 6425 2625; 26 King Edward St; mains $10; 🕑 breakfast & lunch Mon-Sat) This is the place to chill out with a coffee in one hand while the other holds the Mediterranean menu. Browse among the paintings, artworks, crafts, gift lines and rustic furniture available for sale.

Lighthouse Hotel (☎ 6425 1197; 33 Victoria St; mains $18-22; 🕑 lunch, dinner Mon-Sat) This place dishes up lots of chicken, steak and seafood, including pasta and risotto creations that will fill even the emptiest tank.

Mad Hatters (☎ 6425 1599; Tasman Pde; mains $17.50-23.50; 🕑 lunch & dinner Mon-Sat) Located at the Waterfront Inn, this fully licensed restaurant and bar serves generous helpings of hearty restaurant fare, including fresh salads and pasta dishes.

Pedro's the Restaurant (☎ 6425 6663; Wharf Rd; mains $20-40; 🕑 lunch & dinner) Sitting on the port where Pedro's boats bring in the daily catch, this is an appealing restaurant specialising in upmarket seafood dishes (the paradise platter is top-notch and worth every penny at $75). There are meat and vegetarian meals, too.

Pedro's Takeaway (☎ 6425 5181; 🕒 11am-8pm) Next door to Pedro's Restaurant.

Getting There & Away

See p223. Redline Coaches arrive at and depart from outside Victoria St Collectibles, where you can also purchase tickets.

During the week, **Metro** (☎ 13 22 01, 6431 3822) has regular local buses from Burnie to Ulverstone ($3.40).

AROUND ULVERSTONE

Penguin

☎ 03 / pop 3050

This pretty little seaside town comes complete with a large, emphatic ferroconcrete penguin posing for countless photo ops on the foreshore, and smaller artificial penguins adorning rubbish bins along the main street. The town also attracts many visitors for its glorious roadside garden displays, as well as its fantastic beaches.

Penguin has a well-stocked **visitors centre** (☎ 6437 1421; 78 Main Rd; 🕒 9am-4pm Oct-Mar, 9.30am-3.30pm Apr-Sep, 9am-12.30pm Sat), with friendly staff offering lots of advice, including details on the Penguin-to-Cradle trail that starts at Dial Range (see p244).

The **online access centre** (☎ 6337 0771; 125 Ironcliffe Rd; 🕒 8am-3pm Mon, Wed & Fri, 8am-9pm Tue & Thu, 9am-noon Sat) is located on the grounds of the Penguin High School.

Real penguins still appear around dusk each day from September to March at **Penguin Point** and can be seen via a 1½-hour **tour** (☎ 6437 2590; adult/child $10/5) running Sunday to Friday (flash photography not permitted). **Hiscutt Park**, beside Penguin Creek, has good playground equipment and a scaled-down working **Dutch windmill**. In September, the tulip display surrounding the Wipmolen mill adds a touch of brightness.

On Johnson's Beach Rd, near the caravan park, is a **miniature railway** (rides $1; 🕒 1-4pm) that operates on the second and fourth Sunday of each month, when the popular, 150-stall **Penguin Old School Market** (admission free; 🕒 9am-3.30pm) takes place. For details of a life-size **historic train** that visits Penguin, see p247.

SLEEPING & EATING

Penguin Caravan Park (☎ 6432 2785; Johnson's Beach Rd; unpowered/powered sites $12/17, cabins $55) This well-managed caravan park has all the usual amenities. Site prices are for up to two people.

Madsen (☎ 6437 2588; 64 Main St; d $110-150; 💻) Offering superbly appointed rooms with comfort in mind, the Madsen has queen-sized luxury with breathtaking views of the Strait, electric blankets, en suite, tea- and coffee-making facilities and TV. There's also a friendly café where one can sip a caffeine brew or two.

Glenbrook House B&B (☎ /fax 6437 1469; glenbrookhouse@bigpond.com; 89-91 Browns Lane; d $85) Just 3km south of Penguin Beach, Glenbrook is nestled on 50 acres of beautiful, secluded valley views. It's run by two very charming owners, who provide lovely accommodation in a self-contained cottage, or B&B rooms with en suite. Breakfast provisions are included in the cottage, otherwise breakfast is served in the dining room of the house (either continental or full).

Groovy Penguin Café (☎ 6437 2101; 74 Main Rd; mains $8-13; 🕒 breakfast & lunch Wed-Sun) This lesbian- and gay-friendly retro-gallery café is a living artwork filled with kitsch paraphernalia and magnificent views of the ocean. Its supernice staff serve great food with a funky, casual ambience. There are more than a few items on the menu to whet the appetite, such as warm chicken salad ($12.50) or groovy lentil burgers ($12.50).

Monty's (☎ 6437 2080; Johnson's Beach Rd; mains $10-25; 🕒 breakfast & lunch, dinner by reservation) This licensed beachside restaurant serves everything from focaccias and bouillabaisse to Cajun ocean trout.

GETTING THERE & AWAY

See p223. During the week, **Metro** (☎ 13 22 01, 6431 3822) runs regular local buses from Burnie to Penguin ($3.40).

Gunns Plains Scenic Circuit (B17)

If you're staying in Ulverstone for a couple of days and have your own transport, consider spending a day doing this circuit, particularly if you have children with you. Begin by driving to Penguin (left) along the **Old Bass Hwy**, a narrow, winding road that follows the coast and offers attractive views of the shores around Penguin Point. The three small islands known as the **Three Sisters** are particularly scenic, and there are some pretty roadside gardens as you enter the town.

PENGUIN TO GUNNS PLAINS

From Penguin, follow the signs to Riana. In the **Dial Range**, behind the town, there are some good walking tracks, including the Penguin Cradle Trail, an 80km-long path (it takes about six or seven days to traverse) that passes through the eastern side of the range, taking in tall eucalypt forests and fern understorey along an old tramway. Contact Penguin's visitors centre (p243) for details, including the free *Penguin Cradle Trail Route Guide*.

GUNNS PLAINS

The drive down to the plains (follow the B17) is picturesque, with views over the lush valley and some extensive hop fields.

Wings Farm Park (☎ 6429 1151; www.wingsfarmpark.com.au; 137 Winduss St; adult/child $12.50/6; ⏲ 10am-4pm) has plenty of family rural attractions such as domesticated deer and ostriches, bushwalks, trout in the nearby Leven River, and an animal nursery. A reptile centre features some tortoises and snakes, pretend reptiles in the shapes of quolls, bandicoots and a confiscated axolotl. A **camping ground** (unpowered/powered sites $14/10; dm s/d $15/20, cabins $70-85) is also available, as are light meals at Nan's Tearooms.

Gunns Plains Caves (☎ 6429 1388; adult/child/concession $10/5/8; ⏲ 10am-4pm), 32km from Penguin and 25km from Ulverstone, are limestone caves that feature glow-worms, making for an entertaining guided exploration (six tours are held daily from 10am, the last at 3.30pm). Note: the cave contains a steep flight of 54 steps, a 10-rung ladder, low points requiring visitors to bend low, and uneven and clipped pathways.

From the caves, return to the turn-off on the main road. From here continue the circuit back to Ulverstone or take the C127 to the C125, which will lead you to Leven Canyon. On the C124 you'll find **Leven Valley Vineyard & Gallery** (☎ 6429 1186; www.levenvalleyvineyard.com.au; 321 Raymond Rd; ⏲ 10am-5pm Wed-Mon), a small, commendable vineyard producing Pinot Noir and a fruity Chardonnay, and displaying wood-turning, pottery and prints by local artists.

Leven Canyon

On the southern side of Gunns Plains, the River Leven emerges from a 250m-deep gorge. To view the gorge, follow roads through Nietta to the **Leven Canyon Lookout**, 41km from Ulverstone. A 15-minute track leads to the sensational gorge-top lookout, a sky platform peering over hundreds of metres below to the Leven River. Driving beyond the car park turn-off takes you to the canyon floor. You can walk through the gorge but this takes at least 10 hours and is recommended only for experienced walkers (but it's worth the effort as the scenery is spectacular). Nearby day walks lead to **Winterbrook Falls** (three to four hours return) or to **Black Bluff** (six hours return).

There are several smaller waterfalls around Upper Castra and Nietta, and Cradle Mountain is only a short drive away. Be warned that the road linking Upper Castra to Wilmot crosses a deep river gorge and is very steep – don't use it in very wet weather or with low-powered vehicles.

There's B&B accommodation in garden surrounds at **Kaydale Lodge** (☎ 6429 1293; 250 Loongana Rd, Nietta; s/d $60/100), with rooms upstairs in a modern, timber-lined home. Kaydale offers friendly farm-style service, with morning and afternoon teas plus good country food served daily.

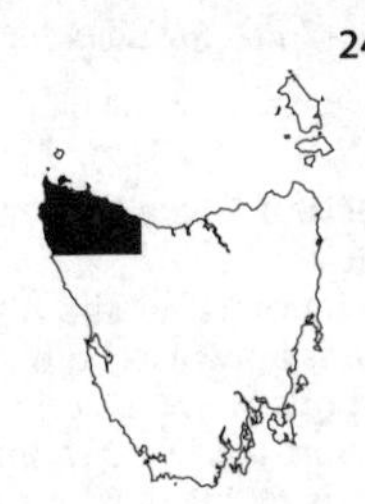

The Northwest

Swept clean by the winds of the Roaring 40s and washed annually by more than 2000mm of rain, the northwest coast sees coastal heaths, wetlands and dense rainforests of ancient Gondwana times. Its story stretches back 35,000 years to when giant kangaroos and wombats were not yet extinct, and Aboriginal tribes took shelter in the caves along the coast, where they left a remarkable legacy of rock engravings and middens.

Massive bluffs nudge out into the sea here, and while Table Cape rolls out a magic-carpet display of tulips, Rocky Cape is *au naturel,* with native orchards and abundant wildlife. The picturesque village of Stanley is idyllic, as it snuggles up against the 13-million-year-old monolithic Nut, surrounded by incredible beaches.

The enormous wild area between the Arthur and Pieman Rivers is known as the Tarkine Wilderness and it was here that conservationists fought a protracted and ultimately unsuccessful battle over a decade ago to prevent the upgrading of the track between Corinna and Balfour. The resulting road, the C249, now forms part of what was christened the Western Explorer, somewhat of a rattler route forming a real link between the depths of the west coast to the northwestern edge of Smithton.

This region has a feeling of true isolation, and apart from the rape of working forests there's a lot of virgin territory.

HIGHLIGHTS

- Peering for a glimpse of Argentina from the **Edge of the World** (p262) at Arthur River
- Climbing the 13-million-year-old **Nut** (p256) dominating the skyline at Stanley
- Surfing mega waves at remote and unspoilt **Marrawah** (p260)
- Strolling through exotic gardens and cool-temperate rainforest at **Allendale Gardens & Rainforest** (p258)
- Feeling in awe of the pristine beauty of the wild **Tarkine Wilderness** (p263)
- Clattering through the rugged terrain along the **Western Explorer Rd** (p263)
- Looking through a window to the past at Burnie's impressive **Pioneer Village Museum** (p247)
- Marvelling at the visual splendour of tulips in season on the flat-topped fertile outcrop of **Table Cape** (p251)

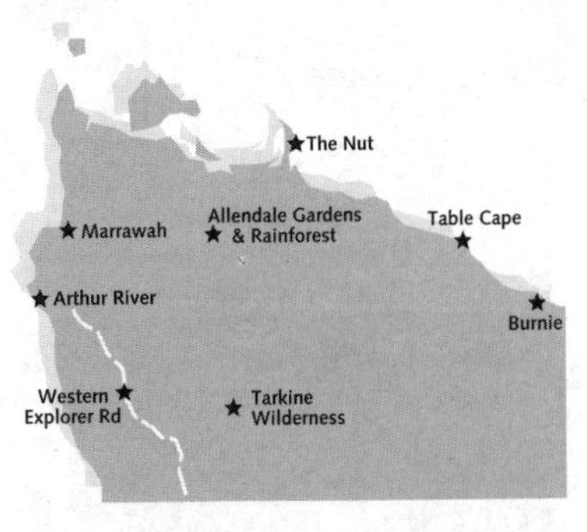

Getting There & Around

AIR

The airport for the region is in Wynyard, and is known as both Wynyard and Burnie airport (we refer to it as 'Burnie/Wynyard airport'). See p252 for details of airlines servicing the northwest.

BUS

Several **Redline Coaches** (☎ 1300 360 000, 6336 1446; www.tasredline.com.au) run daily from Hobart to Launceston ($27 one way, 2½ hours) – these usually connect with a service running from Launceston along the north coast to Devonport ($18, one to 1½ hours) and Burnie ($28, two to 2½ hours). From Burnie, Redline runs two times each weekday (three times on Friday) to Wynyard ($3.40, 20 minutes), the Boat Harbour turn-off ($6, 30 minutes), the Rocky Cape turn-off ($8, 40 minutes), Stanley ($16, one hour) and Smithton ($16, 1½ hours). It also services Deloraine ($10, 45 minutes).

TassieLink (☎ 1300 300 520, 6272 7300; www.tassielink.com.au; Wed, Fri) runs a bus service from Devonport's ferry terminal to Burnie ($10, one hour), with connections to Tullah ($25, 2¼ hours), Rosebery ($27, 2½ hours), Zeehan ($34, three hours), Queenstown ($43, 3¾ hours) and also over to Strahan ($51, 4¾ hours).

BURNIE

☎ 03 / pop 20,000

Burnie, Tasmania's fourth-largest city, sits on the shores of Emu Bay – cargo shipping is an important part of its economy. Assisted by various attractions and the odd nearby glade Burnie has developed a very appealing coastal atmosphere.

Information

North West Regional Hospital (☎ 6430 6666; Brickport Rd) A few minutes west of the city centre: take Brickport Rd off the Bass Hwy just east of Cooee.

Online access centre (☎ 6431 9469; 2 Spring St; per hr $5) Internet access is also available at the visitors information centre.

Visitors information centre (☎ 6434 6111; Little Alexander St; 9am-5pm Mon-Fri, 1.30-4.30pm Sat & Sun Mar-Nov, 9am-5pm Mon-Fri, 10.30am-4.30pm Sat,

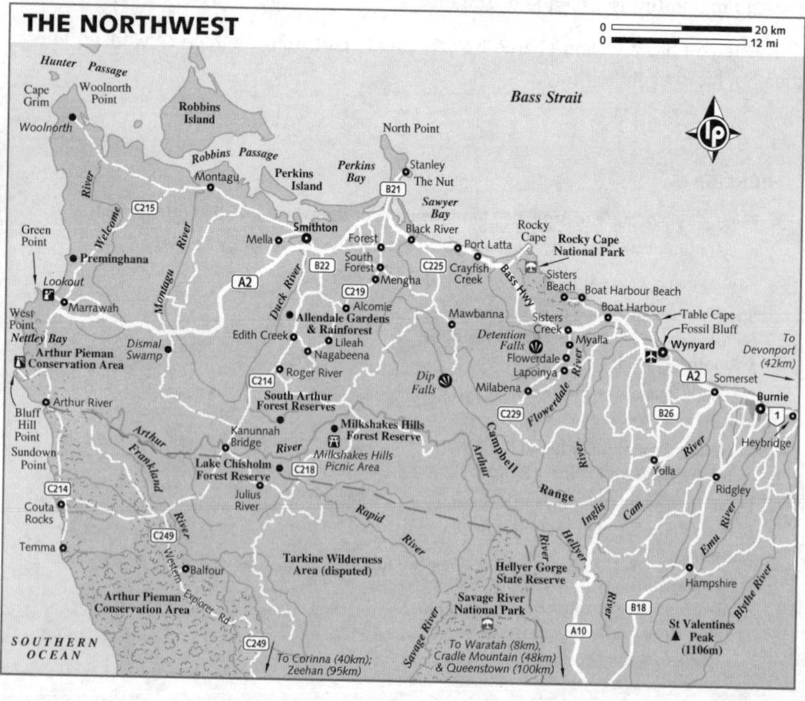

1.30-4.30pm Sun Dec-Feb) Located in the same building as the Pioneer Village Museum (opposite). Offers several interesting walking brochures, including a 17km-long circuit that will take you to public art, parks, creeks and beachside boardwalks, as well as details on local country and western events.

Sights & Activities

PIONEER VILLAGE MUSEUM

This absorbing **museum** (☎ 6430 5746; Little Alexander St; adult/child $6/2.50; 🕑 9am-5pm Mon-Fri, 9am-4pm Sat, Sun & public hols), is an authentic indoor re-creation of a village streetscape (c 1900). It includes a blacksmith, printer, wash house, stagecoach depot and boot-maker and has over 30,000 items on display.

BURNIE REGIONAL ART GALLERY

This **art gallery** (☎ 6431 5918; gallery@burnie.net; Civic Centre Precinct, Wilmot St; admission free; 🕑 9am-5pm Mon-Fri, 1.30-4.30pm Sat, Sun & public hols) has excellent exhibitions of contemporary Australian artworks, including photography, sculpture and painting.

PARKS & GARDENS

Burnie Park (🕑 car access sunrise-sunset) features an animal sanctuary and the oldest building in town, **Burnie Inn**. The National Trust–classified inn was built in 1847 and in 1973 moved from its original site on Marine Tce to the park. The oval on the park's northern side is the site of the annual Burnie Athletics Carnival, held on New Year's Day for more than 100 years.

The serene **Emu Valley Rhododendron Garden** (☎ 6433 0478; Breffny Rd; adult/child $5/3; 🕑 10am-5pm Aug-Feb), 8km south of Burnie (on the B18) via Mount St and then Cascade Rd, sprouts over 20,000 flowers on 13 colourful hectares (flowering peaks mid-September to mid-November).

About 9km south of Burnie (situated on the B18) are the rather English **Annsleigh Gardens & Tearooms** (☎ 6435 7229; 4 Metaira Rd; adult/child $4.50/free; 🕑 9am-5pm Sep-May), set on five acres of well-established gardens.

There are some waterfalls and viewpoints a few kilometres from the city centre, including **Round Hill Lookout** and **Fern Glade**, where you're sure to spot a platypus or two. Round Hill is accessed by a side road off Stowport Rd, which departs the Bass Hwy on the eastern fringe of suburban Burnie. Fern Glade is also east of the city centre – turn off the Bass Hwy into Old Surrey Rd, just past the old Australian Paper Mill, then take Fern Glade Rd to the left.

LACTOS TASMANIA

Down Old Surrey Rd, the first part of the route to Fern Glade, you'll find the cheese maker **Lactos Tasmania** (☎ 6433 9255; 145 Old Surrey Rd; 🕑 9am-5pm Mon-Fri, 10am-4pm Sat & Sun), where you can taste and purchase sundry speciality cheeses, such as Tasmanian Heritage, Mersey Valley and Heidi Farm. Tastings finish a half-hour before closing.

CREATIVE PAPER MILL

Just behind the Australian Paper Mill is **Creative Paper Mill** (☎ 6430 7717; Old Surrey Rd; adult/child/family $10/6/28 🕑 9am-4pm Oct-Apr, 10am-4pm Mon-Sat May-Sep), a studio where paper and paper mementos are handmade using the traditional mould-and-deckle technique. Here you can make your own paper, which you hang up to dry for the next lot of visitors to purchase, or buy some paper-thin souvenirs, including the work of local artists. Guided tours depart at 11am and 1pm (11am and 2.30pm winter) and cost $8/5 per adult/child. Bookings are essential.

BURNIE RAIL

The **Burnie Railway Station** (☎ 6432 3400, reservations 6434 6111), formerly the old Emu Bay Railway Station, is the departure point for the Market Train and a Saturday Shuttle, both utilising a restored locomotive. The station is off Marine Tce.

The Market Train, which coincides with the Penguin Old School Market, departs Burnie at 9am and noon to travel to Penguin, then Ulverstone, then back to Penguin and Burnie. Each individual town-to-town 'sector' involves a 25- to 35-minute ride and costs $6.50/5/15 per adult/child/family.

The Saturday Shuttle usually runs on the Saturday before each Market Train, and on other Saturdays when there's a tie-in with a local event. Services to Wynyard depart Burnie at 8.30am, 11.30am and 3pm, while services to Penguin and back depart Burnie at 10am, 1.30pm and 4.30pm. Sector prices are the same as those for the Market Train.

Bookings can be made at the railway station from 8am on the day of a train service; at all other times book through the visitors information centre.

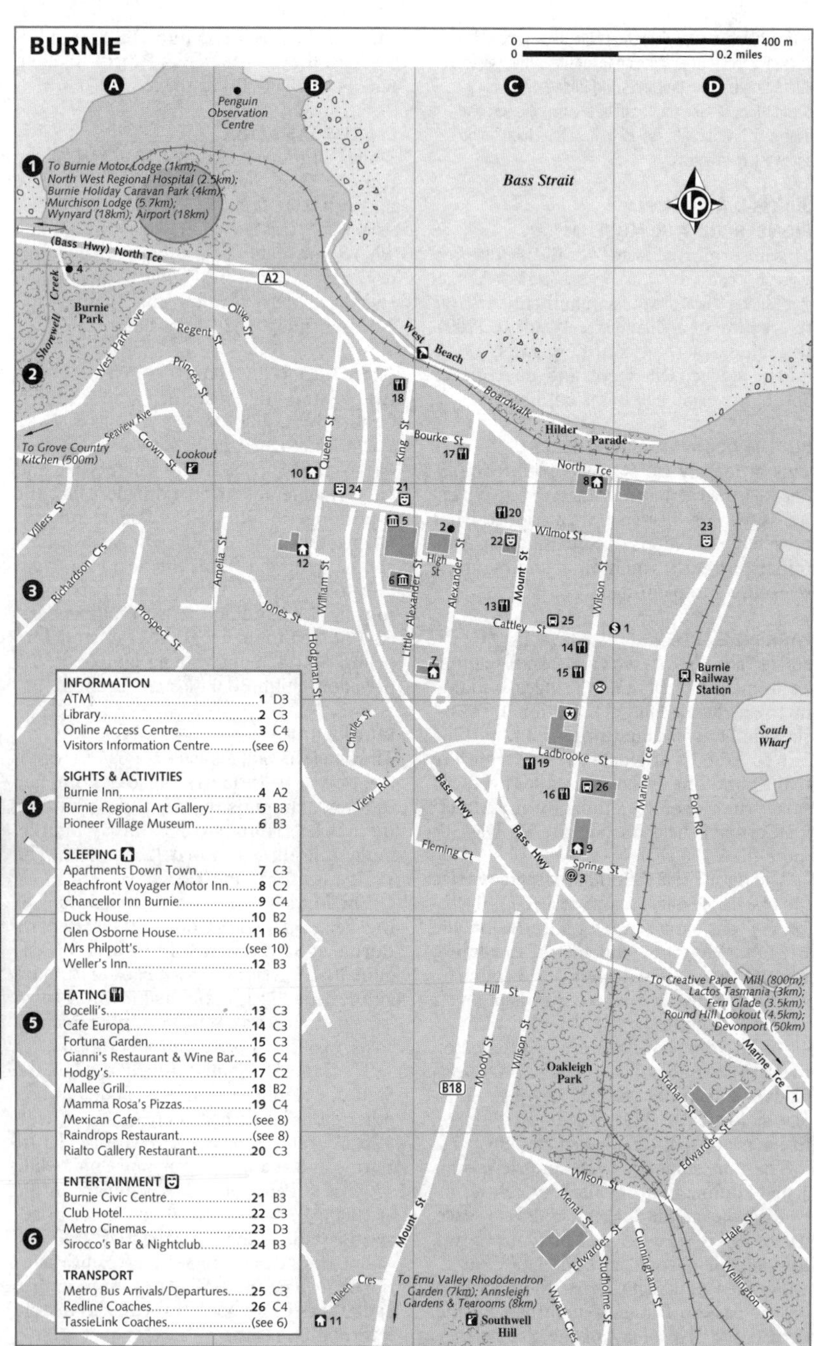
BURNIE
0 400 m
0 0.2 miles
Penguin Observation Centre
Bass Strait
To Burnie Motor Lodge (1km); North West Regional Hospital (2.5km); Burnie Holiday Caravan Park (4km); Murchison Lodge (5.7km); Wynyard (18km); Airport (18km)
(Bass Hwy) North Tce
A2
Shorewell Creek
Burnie Park
West Park Gve
Regent St
Olive St
Princes St
Seaview Ave
Crown St
Lookout
To Grove Country Kitchen (500m)
West Beach
Boardwalk
Hilder Parade
Queen St
King St
Bourke St
North Tce
Wilmot St
High St
Alexander St
Mount St
Wilson St
Villers St
Richardson Crs
Amelia St
William St
Little Alexander St
Jones St
Prospect St
Hodgman St
Cattley St
Burnie Railway Station
South Wharf
Charles St
Ladbrooke St
Marine Tce
View Rd
Bass Hwy
Port Rd
Fleming Ct
Spring St
Hill St
To Creative Paper Mill (800m); Lactos Tasmania (3km); Fern Glade (3.5km); Round Hill Lookout (4.5km); Devonport (50km)
Moody St
Oakleigh Park
B18
Strahan St
Edwardes St
Wilson St
Menai St
Hale St
Cunningham St
Studholme St
Wellington St
Wyatt Cres
Alleen Cres
To Emu Valley Rhododendron Garden (7km); Annsleigh Gardens & Tearooms (8km)
Southwell Hill
INFORMATION
ATM.....1 D3
Library.....2 C3
Online Access Centre.....3 C4
Visitors Information Centre.....(see 6)
SIGHTS & ACTIVITIES
Burnie Inn.....4 A2
Burnie Regional Art Gallery.....5 B3
Pioneer Village Museum.....6 B3
SLEEPING
Apartments Down Town.....7 C3
Beachfront Voyager Motor Inn.....8 C2
Chancellor Inn Burnie.....9 C4
Duck House.....10 B2
Glen Osborne House.....11 B6
Mrs Philpott's.....(see 10)
Weller's Inn.....12 B3
EATING
Bocelli's.....13 C3
Cafe Europa.....14 C3
Fortuna Garden.....15 C3
Gianni's Restaurant & Wine Bar.....16 C4
Hodgy's.....17 C2
Mallee Grill.....18 B2
Mamma Rosa's Pizzas.....19 C4
Mexican Cafe.....(see 8)
Raindrops Restaurant.....(see 8)
Rialto Gallery Restaurant.....20 C3
ENTERTAINMENT
Burnie Civic Centre.....21 B3
Club Hotel.....22 C3
Metro Cinemas.....23 D3
Sirocco's Bar & Nightclub.....24 B3
TRANSPORT
Metro Bus Arrivals/Departures.....25 C3
Redline Coaches.....26 C4
TassieLink Coaches.....(see 6)

WILDLIFE WATCHING

During summer, get down to nearby Fern Glade (p247) by 6.30pm on Monday, Wednesday or Friday, when trips to spot **platypus** in Emu Creek take place. The free guided excursions last up to 90 minutes.

A boardwalk on Burnie's foreshore leads from Hilder Pde to the western end of West Beach, where there's a **penguin observation centre**. Over summer you can observe for free the shy birds at dusk, if they choose to make an appearance. Wildlife guides are present to talk about the penguins and their animal habits.

Sleeping

BUDGET

Burnie Holiday Caravan Park (☎ 6431 1925; fax 6431 1753; 253 Bass Hwy, Cooee; unpowered/powered sites $15/20, dm $36, on-site vans $42, cabins $75-85) Four kilometres west of the city centre, this park has two budget lodge rooms (four to six bunks) equipped with fridge and stove, some decent camping sites at the property's rear, vans with kitchenettes and a range of cabins. It's a friendly, well-managed park. Site prices are for up to two people.

MIDRANGE

Weller's Inn (☎ 6431 1088; 36 Queen St; r from $100) It's an uphill battle to walk from the city centre to the large Weller's Inn. Room rates can be flexible depending on the occupancy rate. It also has an upper-level restaurant on-site that will plug the void in your tummy left from your workout just to get here.

Glen Osborne House (☎ 6431 9866; fax 6431 4354; 9 Aileen Cres; s/d from $80/110) It may be set in the suburban hills in Burnie's south (off the B18), but there's nothing suburban about this establishment. It provides high-standard hospitality in a lavish, National Trust–listed 1885 Victorian house with established gardens. The rate includes a home-style cooked breakfast.

Murchison Lodge (☎ 6435 1106; fax 6435 2778; 9 Murchison Hwy, Somerset; r/units $105/140) West of Burnie, in a peaceful spot opposite the Cam River picnic ground, this place has ordinary motel rooms and a single two-bedroom unit. The on-site restaurant offers hearty dinners Monday to Saturday.

Beachfront Voyager Motor Inn (☎ 1800 355 090, 6431 4866; fax 6431 3826; 9 North Tce; r $120-155) Opposite the surf lifesaving club on the main section of West Beach, this motel has large, very well-equipped rooms; those with a balcony overlooking the beach are recommended.

Apartments Down Town (☎ 6432 3219; www.apartmentsdowntown.com.au; 52 Alexander St; s/d from $99/110) This option lives in a bygone era, a classic Art Deco one to be precise. Its spacious and well-equipped two- or three-bedroom fully serviced apartments are full of the trimmings of the 1930s and make a pleasant change from the colonial time warp offered by other guesthouses.

Duck House (☎ 6431 1712; 26 Queen St; s/d $90/110) Fittingly, Bill Duck's name has been immortalised at this charming two-bedroom cottage where he lived with Winnie Duck for 30 years. Inquiries should be made at 24 Queen St.

Mrs Philpott's (☎ 6431 1712; 28 Queen St) Managed by the same people as Duck House, this equally charming place next door is enhanced by leadlight and an unusual keyhole-shaped entry. Inquiries should be made at 24 Queen St.

Burnie Motor Lodge (☎ 1800 252 025; burniemotorlodge@tassie.net.au; 12-16 Bass Hwy; d & tw from $90) Opposite the beach, this family operated motel offers neat and tidy motel rooms with all the usual room amenities, such as TV. There's also a restaurant on-site.

Chancellor Inn Burnie (☎ 6431 4455; ciburnie@southcom.com.au; 139 Wilson St; r $85-120) This place has received a significant upgrade since its former incarnation as Burnie Town House ended. The rooms and facilities are pretty good, and include private bathrooms, laundry and dry-cleaning, and the downstairs bar, Maginty's Irish Bar, is good for a drink.

Eating

RESTAURANTS

Bocelli's (☎ 6431 8441; 63 Mount St; mains around $20; ⏰ lunch Mon-Fri, dinner Mon-Sat) You'll be singing with joy after you've tasted Bocelli's full à la carte menu, which includes delicious lamb shanks, marinated chicken, smoked salmon salads and tasty veggie risottos.

Gianni's Restaurant & Wine Bar (☎ 6431 9393; 104 Wilson St; ⏰ dinner Tue-Sat) This long-term à la carte restaurant marches through the Italian menu with confidence and dishes up specialities such as pasta with Italian chic and panache. It also does a great trade in glasses of local vintages, served idyllically in its low-lit confines.

Rialto Gallery Restaurant (☎ 6431 7718; 46 Wilmot St; mains $11-18; ⌚ lunch Mon-Fri, dinner) This restaurant looks like it's always been there, pre-dating the town itself. Some mouth-watering smells waft from its doorway, emanating from the huge range of pasta, beef and veal specialities.

Hodgy's (☎ 6431 3947; 8 Alexander St; mains $18-22; ⌚ lunch Wed-Fri, dinner Tue-Sat) An à la carte establishment serving contemporary Oz food, including vegetarian options. Its wine bar is open from 4.30pm Wednesday to Friday.

Fortuna Garden (☎ 6431 9035; 66 Wilson St; mains $10-15; ⌚ lunch Mon-Sat, dinner) This is a licensed and friendly BYO Chinese restaurant-takeaway with plenty of braised prawns, fried squid and stir-fried vegetables to keep diners happy.

Raindrops Restaurant (☎ 6431 4866; 9 North Tce; mains $18-25; ⌚ lunch & dinner) Part of the Beachfront Voyager Motor Inn accommodation complex, this eatery serves up reasonable seafood and has a steak bar to hang your diet. Also at the Beachfront is the poncho-plagued **Mexican Cafe** (mains $10-20; ⌚ lunch & dinner), where you can pig out on rich Mexican standards.

CAFÉS & QUICK EATS

Cafe Europa (☎ 6431 1897; cnr Cattley & Wilson Sts; mains $6-15; ⌚ breakfast, lunch & dinner) For some carefree Spanish-style ambience, give Café Europa a try. Within its cruisey sky-blue walls, you can order liquids from coffee to wine and cocktails, and food such as croissants, toasted Turkish bread and tapas platters.

Grove Country Kitchen (☎ 6431 9779; 63 West Park Grove; mains $5-14; ⌚ breakfast & lunch) This is a great place for light meals, serving sweet chilli chicken and vegetarian grills in its pleasant interior or on the outdoor deck. It's at the West Park Nursery (drive up West Park Grove alongside Burnie Park) and you'll need your own transport to get there.

Mamma Rosa's Pizzas (☎ 6431 3194; 25 Ladbrooke St; medium pizzas $12-15; ⌚ dinner Tue-Sun) This no-frills pizzeria concocts very good edible frisbees. The marinara flying saucer is our favourite.

Mallee Grill (☎ 6431 1933; 26 North Tce; mains $12-18; ⌚ lunch Mon-Fri, dinner) In the Regent Hotel, Mallee Grill is a meat showcase, serving gourmet sausages and seafood, but with steaks as the kitchen's centrepiece. The biggest meal is 50g of rump ($25).

Entertainment

Metro Cinemas (☎ 6431 5000; www.metrocinemas.com.au; cnr Marine Tce & Wilmot St) This is a shiny cinema with shiny, mainly first-release Hollywood flicks, also serving up some marathon, all-night screenings of old classics.

Club Hotel (☎ 6431 2244; 22 Mount St) This place hosts DJs late on Thursday, Friday and Saturday night, and some nights include that good ol' equaliser, karaoke.

Burnie Civic Centre (☎ 6431 5033; Wilmot St) This multifunctional complex (enter via King St) sees everything from concert divas to comedy acts to readings.

Sirocco's Bar & Nightclub (☎ 6431 3133; 64 Wilmot St) This late-night venue entertains a mixed crowd with a regular line-up of DJs and live music pumping out the latest techno, dance, pop and rock.

Getting There & Away

AIR

The Burnie/Wynyard airport (known as either Burnie or Wynyard airport) is at Wynyard, 20km northwest of Burnie. See p252 for details of services.

BUS

See p246 for details of Redline and TassieLink services to/from Burnie.

From Monday to Friday, except on public holidays, **Metro** (☎ 13 22 01, 6431 3822; 28 Strahan St) has regular local buses to Penguin, Ulverstone and Wynyard ($3.40 each), departing from bus stops on Cattley St.

WYNYARD & AROUND

☎ 03 / pop 4510

Sheltered by the impressive Table Cape and Fossil Bluff, and surrounded by beautiful patchwork farmland, Wynyard sits both on the seafront and on the banks of the Inglis River. While Burnie down the road eventually nabbed the shipping trade, Wynyard remained the centre of a rich agricultural region, and today it still holds firm to its roots, exuding a strong, rambling rural atmosphere, popular with retirees for the beautiful beach at its doorstep.

Information

At the time of research there were plans to relocate the visitors centre to a new building, which would also house a veteran car collection.

Online access centre (☎ 6442 4499; 21 Saunders St; per hr $5) At the library, just behind the police station and ATMs on Goldie St.

Visitors centre (☎ 6442 4143; wynyard@tasvisinfo.com.au; Goldie St; 🕑 9.30am-4.30pm Mon-Sat, 12.30-4.30pm Sun) Offers the brochure *Scenic Walks of Wynyard and the Surrounding Districts*, with details on how to get to Fossil Bluff on foot, as well as of walks in the Oldina Forest Reserve.

Sights

FOSSIL BLUFF

Three kilometres from the town centre is Fossil Bluff, where the oldest marsupial fossil found in Australia was unearthed (estimated at 20 million years old). The soft sandstone here features numerous shell fossils deposited when the level of Bass Strait was much higher, some of which are on display in the Tasmanian Museum & Art Gallery in Hobart (p73). At low tide you can walk along the foot of the bluff and find the fossils yourself – pick up the *Looking for Fossils* brochure from the visitors centre. It's also worth walking east along the rocks to the mouth of the Inglis River, where there's a seagull rookery. If the tide is high, it's still worth climbing to the top of the bluff for the good views.

The Bluff is quite close to Wynyard on the northern side of the river, a pleasant two-hour return walk from town; by car, the route winds through several side streets, so keep your eyes peeled for the signs. It's a shame that a housing estate development extends all the way to the base of the bluff.

TABLE CAPE

Ignore the highway and follow the minor roads (C234) towards Table Cape, 4km north of Wynyard and one of the coast's more dominant natural landmarks. The narrow sealed roads lead to a car park and lookout on top of the cape, 177m above the ocean. It's often windy here but the view over Wynyard and the coast is excellent. You can also visit the nearby **lighthouse**, which began its seaside vigil in 1888. From the lookout to the lighthouse, there's a 30-minute return walk along formed paths over the cliffs.

The **Table Cape Tulip Farm** (☎ 6442 2012; 363 Lighthouse Rd; admission free; 🕑 10am-4.30pm late-Sep–mid-Oct) is worth visiting when in full flower. It's beside the road to the lighthouse, where its brightly coloured fields contrast with the rich chocolate-red soils of the cape. You can wander around the paddocks and also view the large display of tulips in the greenhouses.

FLOWERDALE LOBSTER HAVEN

Signposted west of Wynyard on the C229 is the **Flowerdale Lobster Haven** (☎ 6442 2800; 241 Robin Hill Rd, Flowerdale; 🕑 10am-4pm mid-Oct–May). There's a viewing room with a pond and waterfall where you can see these endangered creatures up close. You can stroll around another four ponds and a nursery stream amid landscaped natives. The large tearoom provides light snacks.

Activities

Hire scuba gear from the **Scuba Centre** (☎ 6442 2247; 62 Old Bass Hwy), diagonally opposite the Leisure Ville Holiday Centre (p252), for dives in Wynyard Bay, Boat Harbour or at Sisters Beach. The centre also runs occasional charters to Bicheno and Eaglehawk Neck.

See p247 for details of a **historic train ride** between Burnie and Wynyard.

South of Wynyard the hills of the Oldina State Forest Reserve feature the **Noel Jago Walk**, a short nature walk beside Blackfish Creek. Passing under man-ferns and eucalyptus trees, it takes 30 to 45 minutes to complete. There are reputed to be platypuses in the creek.

Scenic flights over Cradle Mountain ($110 per person, one hour) and the southwest ($220 per person, 2½ hours) can be arranged with **Western Aviation** (☎ 6442 1111), located next to the airport.

The best time to visit Wynyard would have to coincide with the **Wynyard Tulip Festival**, held in early October. It's smack bang in the middle of the season when the Van Diemen Bulb Farm's flowers burst into colour (there's a nominal admission fee).

Sleeping

Beach Retreat Tourist Park (☎ 6442 1998; 30 Old Bass Hwy; unpowered & powered sites $16, s/d/motel unit/cabin $20/35/65/70) Close to town right beside the beach, this park is on a mission to conquer dirt – all the enclosed accommodation, from the small, basic bunk rooms to the old-style vans to the bright motel rooms lining the park's road, have been scrubbed into submission. The backpackers' lounge is well equipped. Site prices are for up to two people.

Leisure Ville Holiday Centre (☎ 6442 2291; www.leisureville.com.au; 145a Old Bass Hwy; powered sites with/without toilet $28/22; on-site van s/d $40/56, cabin s/d $65/74, villa s/d $75/100;) This is a large, well-managed accommodation/recreation centre some distance from town. The huge range of facilities includes an indoor pool/spa, tennis court and a kids' playground. Site prices are for up to two people.

Waterfront (☎ 6442 2351; fax 6442 3749; 1 Goldie St; s/d from $80/100;) This riverside motel won't win any architectural or interior-design awards, but it does have clean, good-value rooms with a top waterfront location. Facilities include cable TV and the on-site restaurant Riverview (right).

Alexandria (☎ 6442 4411; alexandria@ozemail.com.au; 1 Table Cape Rd; s/d from $130/150;) On the northern side of town at the start of the road to Table Cape, beside the Inglis River, Alexandria is a high-quality B&B in a 1905 Federation home. It has several rooms in the main house, en suite rooms in the back garden near the pool and BBQ, and a relaxed atmosphere.

Skyescape (☎ 6442 1876; 282 Tollymore Rd, Table Cape; d $175-275) Only a few minutes' drive from Wynyard, this lavishly modern home, with its panoramic windows and private beach access, provides gourmet breakfasts and (by arrangement) equally gourmet lunches and dinners. There are excellent cape views from the very private, 'exclusively yours' wing.

Eating

Buckaneers for Seafood (☎ 6442 4104; 4 Inglis St; mains $11-23; lunch & dinner) This is a hugely popular seafood emporium – you won't ever be surrounded by more marine paraphernalia unless you're underwater. Diners sit around the clinker-built sailing boat in the middle of the dining room and chow down on fresh catches; steaks, pasta and takeaways are also available. Inglis St angles off Goldie St at the roundabout in the town centre. Bookings are advised.

Cafe Ricardo (☎ 6442 1755; 8 Inglis St; mains from $10; dinner) Even if you're not a fan of Italian, once you've tried Ricardo's baked pizzas and other Italian delights you'll be a convert for good. Finish off the generous course with some exquisite dessert – the homemade ice cream is blended with seasonal local fruits, and the chocolate is divine. You'll get a touch of love with every meal.

Riverview (☎ 6442 2351; 1 Goldie St; mains $15-25; dinner Mon-Sat) Part of the Waterfront motel, this friendly eatery overlooking the water has efficient service and a range of good-quality meals, such as duck sausage and sea-run trout.

Inglis River Hotel/Motel (☎ 6442 2344; 10 Goldie St; mains $12-17; dinner) Serves reef 'n' beef and other typical pub selections, including main-sized schnitzels, mixed grills and curried scallops, plus great burgers and lots of blackboard specials.

Gumnut Gallery Restaurant (☎ 6442 1177; 43 Jackson St; mains $10-25; lunch Mon-Fri, dinner Fri & Sat) This restaurant serves excellent lunchtime fare (sandwiches, Spanish omelettes, fried seafood), while dinner is chosen from a small à la carte menu.

Getting There & Away

AIR

The Burnie/Wynyard airport (often listed as Burnie airport) is just one block from Wynyard's main street. If you're looking to get a ride to/from Burnie, the **Burnie Airbus** (☎ 0439 322 466; adult $10) meets most flights and can pick up from pre-arranged points and from the visitors centre; bookings are advised.

Both **Qantas** (☎ 13 13 13; www.qantas.com.au) and **Rex** (☎ 13 17 13; www.regionalexpress.com.au) fly to Burnie/Wynyard from Melbourne for around $260.

Tasair (☎ 1800 062 900, 6248 5088; www.tasair.com.au) flies between Devonport and King Island via Burnie/Wynyard at least once a day (advance bookings essential). One-way flights from Burnie/Wynyard to either Devonport or King Island cost $160. Tasair also flies to Burnie/Wynyard from Hobart on weekdays for $160 one way.

BUS

During the week, **Metro Burnie** (☎ 6431 3822) runs regular local buses from Burnie to Wynyard for $3.40. The main bus stop is on Jackson St.

BOAT HARBOUR BEACH

☎ 03 / pop 400

Located just 14km northwest of Wynyard and 3km off the Bass Hwy, this holiday resort has a beautiful cliché of a bay, with white sand and crystal-blue water, and is a lovely spot for exploring rock pools and snorkelling.

The town consists of a single street, the Esplanade, which is the continuation of the steep access road. As you descend the views across the water are breathtaking – a sudden short path on the left as you descend leads to a timber platform where you can stop for a Kodak moment.

Sleeping

Boat Harbour Beach Resort (☎ 6445 1107; Esplanade; motel r $79-109, motel f $120, executive spa unit $175;) This sociable place has accommodation ranging from tiny 'economy' motel rooms to larger rooms nearer the beach and self-contained executive spa units. Also lurking enticingly on the premises are an indoor heated pool, sauna and spa, which are available for all guests.

Seaside Garden Motel (☎ 6445 1111; Esplanade; motel s/d $70/75, unit d $104;) This motel is directly opposite the beach and has nice, compact holiday units in a large garden, including a two-bedroom structure. Guests have access to the heated swimming pool, spa and sauna of the Boat Harbour Beach Resort next door, which is run by the same people. B&B packages are available.

Country Garden Cottages (☎ 6445 1233, 0419 792 663; fax 6445 1019; 15 Port Rd; s/d from $95/105) It may be back near the highway, but this arc of snug, timber-lined cottages fronts two rambling hectares of gardens and is run by the charming Richard and Jacqui – Mr and Mrs 'Have a Chat'. These cottages are a friendly, hospitable and comfortable option.

Killynaught Cottages (☎ 6445 1041; fax 6445 1556; 17266 Bass Hwy; ste/d from $120/160) On the highway back towards Wynyard, Killynaught has attractive, rural views to the rear. The cottages are fully self-contained and lavishly decorated in Federation style. There are open fireplaces in the lounge rooms, spas in the bathrooms and ingredients for cooked breakfasts in the kitchens.

Harbour Houses (☎ 6442 2135; www.harbourhouse.com.au; Esplanade; d $185-200) This place is dressed to impress in ultramodern style. The self-contained retreat has open-plan living, floor-to-ceiling views of the coast, and the sandy shores are a skip away. It accepts cash or cheque only.

Eating

Jolly Rogers (☎ 6445 1710; Esplanade; mains $10-25; breakfast, lunch & dinner Sep-May) This is a laid-back beachside café serving real hunger solutions, such as focaccias and garlic tiger prawns, pasta and stuffed scotch fillets for more-evening fare, and drinks and snacks in between. In the vicinity is a fenced play area where you can stow the little ones.

Jetty Bar & Cafe (mains $13-20; breakfast, lunch & dinner) Offering counter bistro-style meals, this is a good option if you prefer to chow down and drink a tad more informally, either inside or alfresco.

Jacobs Restaurant (☎ 6445 1107; Esplanade; mains $16.50-35; dinner) Jacobs is an à la carte eatery at the Boat Harbour Beach Resort (left). There's a wide range of international cuisine, and good vegetarian and seafood options. Those with special dietary requirements can be catered to. Desserts include wild-berry pancakes and the somewhat intriguing bourbon and vanilla-bean ice cream.

Getting There & Away

You'll need your own transport. If driving from Wynyard, the best route from the cape is to follow Tollymore Rd northwest; there are some great views of the cliffs and rocky coast along this road. By bus, the twice-daily (weekdays only) Redline service from Burnie will drop you at the turn-off to Boat Harbour (3km) and Sisters Beach (8km) for $6.

ROCKY CAPE NATIONAL PARK

This is Tasmania's smallest national park, stretching for 12km along the Bass Strait shoreline. Its major features are rocky headlands, heath-covered hills and caves once occupied by Aborigines (the park's Aboriginal name is Tangdimmaa) – the caves were used from 8000 years ago up until European occupation in the 19th century. The coast here is mostly rugged quartzite and the park is believed to contain the only stands of *Banksia serrata* in the state.

There are a couple of beaches within the park, the best known being **Sisters Beach**, an 8km expanse of bleached sand. It's a good place for swimming and fishing. On the eastern side of the creek there are picnic tables and a shelter; a foot-bridge crosses the creek, providing access to the beach.

The Sisters Beach village, reached by following the side road from the Bass Hwy that passes the turn-off to nearby Boat Harbour, is a popular resort surrounded by the national park. The park has a rugged coastline, and wildflowers and orchids bloom throughout the park in spring and summer.

On Rocky Cape, you can drive out to a stunted **lighthouse** (more the size of an outhouse), with the Nut (p256) floating distantly on the horizon.

Bushwalking

From Sisters Beach, the walk to **Wet Cave**, **Lee Archer Cave** and **Banksia Grove** takes 45 minutes; to reach the start of this walk, follow the signs to the boat ramp. You can continue further along the coast to Anniversary Point (three hours return). It's also possible to follow the coast to Rocky Cape and return along the **Inland Track** (eight hours return).

From the western end of the park at Rocky Cape Rd (accessed from a separate entrance off the Bass Hwy, west of the turn-off to Sisters Beach), you can visit two large Aboriginal caves, the South and North Caves, the latter off the road to the lighthouse. Both caves involve a 30-minute return walk, but take note: the caves are significant Aboriginal sites, so visitors are encouraged *not* to enter them. There's also a good circuit of the cape itself – allow 2½ hours.

Sleeping & Eating

There are no camping facilities inside the national park itself, only on the highway near the entrance to Western End (right).

DETOUR

In the hills south of the Rocky Cape National Park, a couple of waterfalls worth visiting include **Detention Falls**, 3km south of Myalla on the C229, and **Dip Falls**, near Mawbanna (jump on the C225 east of Black River and follow the signs). A short but steep walk will get you to the base of Dip Falls; alternatively, there's a viewing platform across the river. About 1km from the car park, you'll find the Big Tree, its circumference measuring 16m.

SISTERS BEACH

Birdland Cottages (☎ 6445 1471, 0418 160 080; 7 Banksia Ave; s & d $85, per week $450) Old-style, tranquil and good-value bushy abodes are on offer here. Linen is provided.

Beach Houses Holiday Apartments (☎ 6445 1147; Kenelm Ave; d $90-110, per week $540-660) These self-contained three-bedroom units are attractive timber cottages lying amid some large *Banksia serrata*. Inquire at the **Sisters Beach General Store** (☎ 6445 1147; Honeysuckle Ave; 🕑 7.30am-8.30pm summer, 7.30am-7.30pm winter), which also sells takeaway and park passes.

Holiday shacks in the area can sometimes be rented short-term, but the owners generally prefer occupancies of at least a week, so definitely do not rely on this possibility for overnight accommodation. Ask about the shacks at the general store.

WESTERN END

Rocky Cape Tavern & Caravan Park (☎ 6443 4110; Bass Hwy; unpowered/powered sites $10/15, on-site vans $25-30, motel d $55) Conveniently located on the highway just near the entrance to the western end of the national park, this place has clean and tidy facilities. There's also an on-site tavern serving counter meals daily. Site prices are for up to two people.

Sunrise Resort (☎ 6443 4197, 0409 661 329; dm $20, unit s/d/f $45/60/80) Some 2km west of the park and 27km from Stanley is this scruffy-looking roadside enclave, with four self-contained family units, two each sleeping six/seven people.

Rainbow Gardens & Tearooms (☎ 6443 4187; 19469 Bass Hwy; 🕑 by appointment) Rainbow Gardens is naturally decorated with a colourful garden and bird life. It sells a selection of light meals and local arts and crafts.

CRAYFISH CREEK TO BLACK RIVER

This part of the coastline is a series of pretty little beaches and rocky coves marred by the heavy-industry complex at Port Latta, the terminus for the 85km iron-ore pipeline from Savage River. Fortunately there's only one factory located here, and away from the busy smokestack the coast is pleasant.

Gateforth Cottages (☎ 6458 3230; gateforthcottages@tassie.net.au; 179 Mengha Rd; d with/without spa $155/140) Offering comfortable and very relaxed self-contained cottage accommodation, and with fantastic views of Circular Head, Gateforth is also a terrific place to view the milking, watch the farm animals and go fishing. Kids are most welcome. It's located about 6km west of the Port Latta-to-Black River turn-off.

Crayfish Creek Caravan Park (☎/fax 6443 4228, 0419 302 354; 20049 Bass Hwy; unpowered/powered sites $12/16, on-site vans $30, cabins $65-85) Set beside the bushland-lined Crayfish Creek, 2km east of Port Latta. Besides wild secluded sites, a small on-site store and a beach a short walk away, the park also has a fine multilevel 'tree house' (doubles from $135, and with spa) for those who prefer lofty accommodation. Site prices are for up to two people.

Two kilometres west of Port Latta, on the Stanley side near Black River, is the **Peggs Beach Conservation Area** (camp sites per adult/child $2.50/1.50), with toilets, tables, fireplaces, water and an on-site caretaker with whom you register. This area is very popular for fishing and is prime Australian salmon territory (October to March).

STANLEY

☎ 03 / pop 600

Nestled snugly like a collar at base of the isthmus (known as the Neck), under the auspicious protection of the monolithic Circular Head (better known as the Nut), the town's major tourist drawcard. With its congenial atmosphere, numerous B&Bs and souvenir shops, there's only a slight hint that most of the town seems to hang on desperately to the skirts of the tourist

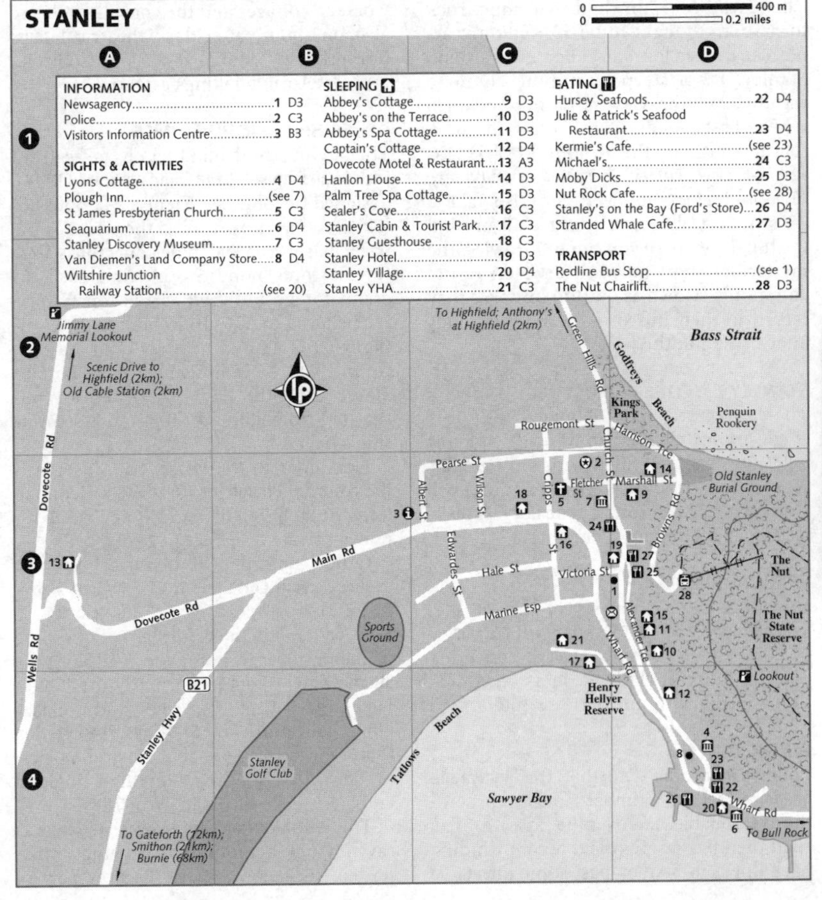

seasons in order to face the onslaught of the Roaring 40s and winter chill.

Information

There's an ATM located inside the town's minimart.

Newsagency (☎ 6458 1372; 17 Church St) You can make eftpos withdrawals here.

Post office Also a Commonwealth Bank/National Bank agent.

Visitors centre (☎ 6458 1330; stanley@tasvisinfo.com.au; 45 Main Rd; 9am-5pm Mon-Fri, 10am-4pm Sat & Sun) Friendly and knowledgeable staff with extensive regional advice. Also offers Internet access ($2 per 15 minutes) and laptop connections.

Sights & Activities

THE NUT

This striking 152m-high volcanic rock formation, thought to be 13 million years old, can be seen for many kilometres around Stanley. It's a steep 20-minute climb to the top, but the view is definitely worth it. The best lookout is a five-minute walk to the south of the **chairlift** (☎ 6458 1286; adult/child/family $9/7/25; 9.30am-5.30pm Oct-May, 10am-4pm Jun-Sep), and you can also take a 35-minute walk (2km) on a path around the top. From here you can wait to view the mysterious short-tailed shearwaters (more commonly known as mutton birds) as they return to their burrows by the thousands after fishing in the ocean.

STANLEY DISCOVERY MUSEUM

To learn more about Stanley, visit this single-room **folk museum** (Church St; adult/child $3/50¢; 10am-4pm), filled with old Circular Head photos and artefacts, including marine curios. It also runs a genealogical service ($5, including museum entry).

SEAQUARIUM

Providing a great display of marine life, **Seaquarium** (☎ 6458 2052; Fisherman's Dock; adult/child/family $8/5/23; 9.30am-4.30pm) is a great place to bring the kids. It offers an educational forum with interactive exhibits.

SCENIC DRIVE

Follow Dovecote Rd north to the **Jimmy Lane Memorial Lookout**, a timber platform providing a reasonable view over the cape area. The road then passes Highfield before winding back down to Stanley past some attractive hillside scenery with views of the Nut and across the coastline and township.

HIGHFIELD

This impressive **homestead** (☎ 6458 1100; Green Hills Rd; adult/child/family $6/4/14, grounds only $2; 10am-4pm) was built in 1835, on the high land north of Stanley, to serve as the headquarters of VDL, a wool-growing venture launched in 1824 that was granted 1000 sq km of unexplored territory. The Ford family, who purchased Highfield post-VDL and lived there through two generations, has returned around 100 pieces of original furniture to the site. Guided tours of the Regency-style house take place on weekdays; on weekends tours are self-guided. The grounds include stables, grain stores, workers' cottages and the chapel. There are also one-hour, after-dark theatrical **tours** (adult/child/family $10/5/25) at 8.30pm from October to April; bookings essential.

OTHER HISTORIC BUILDINGS

The old bluestone building on the seafront is the **Van Diemen's Land Company Store** (1844), designed by John Lee Archer, a famous colonial architect. Also near the wharf is the particularly fine old bluestone **Ford's Store** (or Customs Bond Store), first used for grain storage and then as a bacon factory. It's believed to have been built in 1859, although the plaque near its door dates it from 1885. Now housing the restaurant Stanley's on the Bay (p259), it was constructed from stones brought to Stanley as ship's ballast.

Next door to the Discovery Museum is the restored **Plough Inn** (Church St), a Georgian terrace that began life in 1854 as a hotel. It's now a private residence.

Other buildings of historical interest include **Lyons Cottage** (☎ 6458 1145; 14 Alexander Tce; admission by donation; 10am-4pm Nov-Apr, 11am-3pm May-Oct), the birthplace of one-time prime minister Joseph Lyons (b 1879); the **Stanley Hotel** (Church St), formerly the Union Hotel and dating from 1849; and the dazzling whitewash of **St James Presbyterian Church** (Fletcher St), probably Australia's first prefabricated building, bought in England and transported to Stanley in 1885.

The **Wiltshire Junction Railway Station** was saved from demolition by being transported to Stanley, where it's now part of the Stanley Village accommodation complex (right).

DOCKSIDE FESTIVAL

On the weekend before the Melbourne Cup (late October/early November), Stanley hosts the **Dockside Festival**, an annual feast of food, entertainment and jazz music celebrating the culmination of the Melbourne-to-Stanley yacht race (the precursor to the Sydney-to-Hobart yacht race).

Tours

Stanley Seal Cruises (☎ 0419 550 134; www.users.bigpond.com/staffordseals) Provides a 75-minute cruise to see around 200 Australian fur seals sunning themselves on Bull Rock, near Stanley. The cruises usually take place at 10am, 1.30pm and 4.30pm (3.30pm April to September), weather permitting, and cost $40/17 per adult/child. There are also combined platypus and penguin tours for $45/15.

Wilderness to West Coast Tours (☎ 6458 2038; www.wildernesstasmania.com) Based in Stanley, and has platypus-spotting excursions (adult/child $30/15) and penguin-viewing tours ($15/5), when the birds appear at either end of Godfreys Beach from late September until February. Its full-day four-wheel-drive wilderness tours ($225/195 per one/three or more people) leave from the centre of town to take in rainforest and Edge of the World areas (includes gourmet lunch), or you can join a tag-along tour in your own four-wheel drive for $99 per person.

Sleeping

TOWN CENTRE

Stanley Cabin & Tourist Park (☎ /fax 6458 1266; www.stanleycabinpark.com.au; Wharf Rd; unpowered sites $18-22, powered sites $20, on-site vans from $40, cabins $55-100) Located on a great site right on Sawyer Bay, this park is loaded with amenities and has well-serviced vans and cabins (site prices are for up to two people; you pay extra for waterfront camp sites). Guests can use the YHA kitchen.

Stanley YHA (☎ /fax 6458 1266; www.stanleycabinpark.com.au; Wharf Rd; dm $20) This no-frills place is at the Stanley Cabin & Tourist Park.

Stanley Hotel (☎ 6458 1161; 19 Church St; s with/without bathroom $35/55, d from $55/80) Refurbished to within an inch of its life, this pub (formerly the Union Hotel; opposite) provides comfortable, spacious and modern accommodation. The shared bathroom facilities have been updated and are so clean they shine. The rooms with views to the Nut or beach are good value.

Stanley Guesthouse (☎ 6458 1488; 27 Main Rd; d $135) Well managed and pleasant, this antique-furnished, Federation-style (Queen Anne) B&B is comfortable enough, and prices include full cooked breakfast. Not suitable for children under 12.

Sealer's Cove (☎ 6458 1414; fax 6458 2076; 2-4 Main Rd; d $95-110) Run by the same folk that cook the best pizza in town (p258) is this decent, modern comfortable B&B. You can opt for continental or a full cooked breakfast. We suggest the cooked brekky.

Stanley Village (☎ 6458 1404; fax 6458 1403; 15 Wharf Rd; d with/without spa $140/130) On the edge of the rock-strewn bay shore, not far from the action. The motel-style rooms include en suites and terrific views over the beach.

Hanlon House (☎ 6458 1149; www.tassie.net.au/hanlonhouse; 6 Marshall St; s $110, d from $160) Hanlon House, originally a Catholic presbytery, has comfortably old-fashioned en suite rooms ('Mary Ellen' is the spa suite) accompanied by generous breakfasts. A nice spot to enjoy the seaside views, with vittles and vino in front of the log fire.

Captain's Cottage (☎ 6458 3230, 0419 871 581; fax 6458 3237; 30 Alexander Tce; d $160) This heritage-listed, upmarket B&B has incredible water views, making it a great choice. Built in 1838, this character-filled stone cottage has a double shower, claw-foot bath, cosy wood fires and more-conventional electric heating. Evening meals can be arranged.

There's a collective of 'Abbey' accommodation in town, all of which can be booked at the **Nut Rock Cafe** (☎ 1800 222 397, 6458 1186; fax 6458 1290; The Nut State Reserve, Brown Rd). There's the period-style **Abbey's Cottage** (1 Marshall St; d $150), across the road from Hanlon House; the more modern **Abbey's on the Terrace** (34 Alexander Tce; d $150); and the light-and-bright **Abbey's Spa Cottage** (46 Alexander Tce; d $160). Managed by the same people and also on Alexander Tce (a hillside thoroughfare that yields some fine views of the water) is the plush **Palm Tree Spa Cottage** (48 Alexander Tce; d $170).

OUT OF TOWN

Dovecote Motel & Restaurant (☎ 6458 1300; www.dovecote.com.au; 58 Dovecote Rd; tw $90-110, d $120-130, apt $135-150) With million-dollar views of the Nut and township, this welcoming option has a selection of motel rooms and self-contained accommodation. The restaurant has a satisfying menu selection.

Old Cable Station (☎ 6458 1312; stafford.seals@bigpond.com; West Beach Rd; d with/without spa $140/110, self-contained d $180-220) Having maintained a telephonic link with the mainland for over 30 years from 1935, it now upholds a modern B&B. Comprising private en suite accommodation (self-contained cottages include spa), continental breakfast and sea views from all rooms, this is a fabulous option if you're after a peaceful and secluded location.

Anthony's at Highfield (☎ 6458 1245; Green Hills Rd; s/d $60/100) This large cottage, built for the VDL in 1828, is directly opposite Highfield homestead, has incredible views of the Nut, and sleeps up to six people. Anthony's is gay- and lesbian-friendly, and the rate includes continental breakfast.

Gateforth (☎ 6458 3230, 0419 871 581; stay@gateforthcottages.com; 40 Medwins Rd, Black River; d $130-160) Twelve kilometres east on the Bass Hwy, Gateforth is a vegetable, cattle and sheep farm located east of town overlooking Stanley with three attractive self-contained cottages, two with spas and all with porches from which to look across expansive pastureland to the distant Nut. This place is private and attentive to guests, provides hearty breakfast provisions, welcomes children, and prepares dinners utilising farm-fresh produce (with prior notice).

Eating

Moby Dicks (☎ 6458 1329; 5 Church St; mains $8-16; ⌚ breakfast) This new breakfast bar is a unique and charming take on the humble breaking of the fast. Until 11am you can have your eggs done pretty much any way you like, or you can choose a mixed grill or Canadian-style waffles (bacon and eggs with maple syrup; $10). It also does sandwiches, rolls and some of the more traditional, grainy porridge fare.

Sealer's Cove (☎ 6458 1414; mains $10-18.50; ⌚ dinner Tue-Sun) Not just a B&B, but also an Italian restaurant with a large selection of reasonably priced salads, pasta and pizzas. The sweet pizza seafood toppings were so fresh and succulent, we ordered the same again (veggie options include the Sassafras pizza – superb).

Michaels (☎ 6458 1144; 25 Church St; lunch $7-13, dinner $19-25; ⌚ lunch & dinner Nov-Apr, dinner Thu-Sun May-Oct) Using the freshest local produce for it's à la carte menu, Michael's is a quality restaurant serving salads, pita rolls and the odd steak for lunch, and dishes like Thai chicken and roulades for dinner. An adjoining room is conveniently devoted to sales of Tasmanian wines.

Stanley Hotel (☎ 6458 1161; 19 Church St; meals from $15; lunch & dinner) This pub serves better-than-average bistro-type fare, including year-round fresh seafood and servings the size of the Nut itself. The burgers are supreme: the beef bred round these parts is grass-fed.

Stranded Whale Cafe (☎ 6458 1202; 6 Church St; mains $4-8; ⌚ breakfast & lunch, dinner Fri Sep-May) Just down from the Town Hall, the Stranded Whale serves excellent homemade meals, including filling soups and good bread.

Nut Rock Cafe (☎ 1800 222 397, 6458 1186; fax 6458 1290; The Nut State Reserve, Brown Rd; mains $6-15; ⌚ breakfast & lunch) This cheery café, at the base of The Nut, specialises in lobster and has a good range of breakfasts and light lunches, from pancakes to smoked salmon.

DETOUR

As you head south on the B22 leading out of Smithton, just 3km north of Edith Creek you'll come upon **Allendale Gardens & Rainforest** (☎ 6456 4216; fax 6456 4223; Edith Creek; adult/child 5-16 years $7.50/3.50; ⌚ 9am-6pm Oct-Apr), over two hectares of bird-filled exotic and native gardens. No less than six bridges cross Allen Creek as it meanders through the gardens.

Restore your spirit by taking a lengthy walk through the cool-temperate rainforest, which has towering 300- to 500-year-old Stringy Barks with girths of over 15m, dense blackwood and dogwood forests, the rare creeping fern, enormous man-fern groves, and endangered land crayfish. A charming café serves Devonshire teas (Max's home-made jam is superb), and you can stay in one of two self-contained **mudbrick cottages** (ste d with/without bathroom $130/100).

To head back to Stanley, take the picturesque route (30 minutes) south through Edith Creek, along the C219 towards Nabageena, which then traverses gravel back roads through Lileah, Alcomie, Mengha, Forest and South Forest. The farmlands are quite pretty and the view of the Nut as you approach Stanley is unforgettable.

Stanley's on the Bay (☎ 6458 1404; 15 Wharf Rd; mains $21-28; ⌚ dinner Mon-Sat Sep-Jun) Set inside the historic and atmospheric old Ford's Store (p256) down on the wharf, this fine-dining establishment is incredibly popular so book ahead. Try the fabulous steak creations and the seafood – seems so fresh, like it's just been fished out of the wharf.

Hursey Seafoods (☎ 6458 1103; 2 Alexander Tce; ⌚ 9am-6pm) is awash with tanks filled with live sea creatures – including fish, crayfish, crabs and eels – for the freshest of seafood takeaways. The Hursey complex includes **Kermies Cafe** (mains $10-18; ⌚ 9am-8pm summer, to 6pm winter), a café-takeaway serving battered prawns, crayfish salad and abalone patties, and upstairs, the licensed **Julie & Patrick's Seafood Restaurant** (mains $19-28; ⌚ dinner), where you can dine on marinated octopus and abalone steaks. Both eateries have ankle-biter menus.

Getting There & Around

BUS

Redline offers an evening service into Stanley (arriving 5pm) from Burnie, but the next service out is in the morning departing 7.15am (heading to Burnie again). See p246 for other details.

SMITHTON & AROUND

☎ 03 / pop 3320

Located 22km southwest of Stanley, Smithton serves one of Tasmania's largest forestry areas and is also the administrative centre for Circular Head. It has some pretty aspects and is a nice place to take in the rural community charm; it's also a good place to stock up before you head off down south.

For an insight into the European history of Circular Head, visit the **Circular Head Heritage Centre** (☎ 6452 3296; cnr Nelson & King Sts; adult/child $2/1; ⌚ 10am-3pm Mon-Sat, 12.30-3pm Sun).

You'll find all the major banks here and there are two ATMS on Emmett St.

Sights & Activities

WOOLNORTH

About 25km from Smithton, and sprawling across the northwestern tip of Tasmania, is the 220-sq-km cattle and sheep property of **Woolnorth**, the only remaining holding of the VDL. Today it remains one of Tasmania's most historic farming properties, and its commercial operation comprises thousands of dairy cattle (its 80-bail rotary operation can milk 1800 cows a day) and 1500 merino mews.

The property and surrounding areas, such as Woolnorth Point and Cape Grim, include some new Hydro Tasmanian wind farms (harnessing the power of the Roaring 40s) and are only accessible through private land at Woolnorth. You can access a public road to see the turbines from a distance but you'll need to take a tour to visit the farm ($95 per adult). Contact the Stanley visitors centre (p256) for details.

The road heading from Smithton towards Woolnorth passes through farmlands with views over the narrow waterways that separate Perkins and Robbins Islands.

LACRUM

Located 6km west of Smithton, this **dairy** (☎ 6452 2653; lacrumcheese@tassie.net.au; Hardmans Rd; adult/child $5/2.50; ⌚ 3-5pm Nov-Jun) uses non-animal rennet to produce a range of tasty farm cheeses, including brie, camembert and the powerful Limburger. The factory is no longer in operation but you can still taste some Lactos and King Island varieties here.

MILKSHAKES HILLS FOREST RESERVE

Temperate rainforest and some buttongrass moorland can be found at this forest reserve, 45km south of Smithton – the perfect place for a date with a picnic hamper. There are several short walking tracks around the picnic grounds and a longer track (one hour return) to the top of one of the 'Milkshakes'.

LAKE CHISHOLM

Even further south of Smithton is this tranquil lake, actually a flooded limestone or dolomite sinkhole. You can take a 30-minute return walk from the car park, which will lead you through a beautiful old myrtle rainforest to the lake itself. The gravel roads leading to the lake may be closed after heavy rain.

DISMAL SWAMP

Thirty kilometres southwest of Smithton (just off the A2), Forestry Tasmania has set up the alluringly named **Dismal Swamp** (☎ 6456 7199; www.tasforestrytourism.com.au/pages/site_nw_dismal.html; adult/child 13-16 years $10/7;

9am-5pm), essentially a 110m-long slide providing a thrilling descent into a blackwood sinkhole (unsuitable for those under 13 years; open-backed shoes not advised). It incorporates a treetop interpretation centre constructed mostly of blackwood, and gives visitors the opportunity to wander through the swamp floor along a boardwalk maze, with contemporary sculptures planted among the man ferns. The view from inside the toilet cubicles across the tree-top canopy is superb. There's a café and small gift shop.

Sleeping & Eating

Montagu Camping Ground (Old Port Rd; camp sites $10; Nov-Apr) This ground is just east of the diminutive Montague township, which is 16km west of Smithton. Site prices are for up to two people.

Bridge Hotel/Motel (6452 1389; bridgehotel@our.net.au; 2 Montagu Rd; hotel s/d $40/50, motel s/d $70/85) On the road heading out to Montagu, this place has comfortable rooms with shared facilities in the hotel proper and several dozen with en suite motel units round the back. Lamb's fry and seafood platters are available nightly in the Colloboi restaurant.

Tall Timbers Hotel/Motel (1800 628 476; www.talltimbershotel.com.au; Scotchtown Rd; motel s/d/tr from $100/115/130, spa s/d/tr $110/125/155, 1-/2-bedroom units $145/175) Some 2km south of Smithton, this option has been impressively hammered together using blackwood and celery-top cuttings. It hosts live bands and has a good bistro (open for lunch and dinner) serving plenty of grilled meat dishes, and also caters to noncarnivores.

Rosebank Cottages (6452 2660; www.rosebankcottages.com; d with/without spa $140/150) Comprises two charming and quaint B&B cottages (surprisingly called 'Rosebud' and 'Rosies'), one in Smithton (42 Goldie St) and the other (with a spa) 6km east of town at Sedgy Creek (46 Brooks Rd), 500m off the highway. Breakfast is provided.

Getting There & Away

See p246 for details.

MARRAWAH

03 / pop 370

Marrawah, an untrammelled delight, is where the wild Southern Ocean occasionally throws up the remains of ships wrecked on the dangerous and rugged west coast. Marrawah's nearby beaches and rocky outcrops can be hauntingly beautiful, particularly at dusk, and the seas are often huge. It's at Green Point beach that the annual West Coast Classic, a notable surfing competition, is held. The beach is also one of the world's consistent spots for sideshore wind, hence its popularity as a windsurfing mecca, too.

Marrawah General Store (6457 1122; 800 Comeback Rd; 7.30am-7pm Mon-Fri, 8am-7.30pm Sat & Sun) sells supplies and petrol, is an agent for Australia Post and Commonwealth Bank, and operates the Swell Café in the summer months. There's no regular public transport to Marrawah, but note that the drive into town is very scenic. As the northern gateway for the Western Explorer to Corinna (p263), fill up on fuel here if you're planning to take that route, as there are no other petrol outlets for around 200km until Zeehan or Savage River.

Activities

SURFING

One of Marrawah's major attractions is its enormous surf. The **West Coast Classic**, that most excellent round of the state's surfing

GETTING AWAY FROM IT ALL

The northern coastal route is often packed with beachcombing tourists. If you need to find some peace from the throngs, head south on the B22 and veer west on C214 at Roger River. The 15km-long drive along this minor road, between Roger River and Kanunnah Bridge, skirts the South Arthur Forests and is truly isolated. Once you've reached Kanunnah Bridge, you can decide whether you'd like to ditch the car and launch a raft or kayak to Arthur River (medium rapids), or keep driving by veering southeast on the C218 where you'll start passing through several reserves with good picnic facilities and interesting walks, including Julius River Forest (two hours return), Lake Chisholm and Milkshakes Hills Forest Reserves. Take extra care during weekdays when forestry traffic also uses this road.

TASMANIAN ABORIGINAL SITES

The Marrawah area, with its isolated west-coast beaches and cliffs, has seen minimal disturbance from European development, in direct contrast to the maximal disturbances visited by Europeans upon the area's former Aboriginal inhabitants – these include the massacre of an estimated 30 Aborigines in 1827 at the aptly named Cape Grim to the north, apparently in response to the slaughter of a flock of sheep. Particular areas have now been proclaimed reserves to protect the relics, including rock carvings, middens and hut depressions.

There's a significant Aboriginal site along the road to Arthur River at West Point (it's best to get the latest report on road conditions by contacting the Stanley visitors centre (p256), and another beyond the township at Sundown Point, the latter with several dozen mudstone slabs engraved with mainly circular motifs. There are also innumerable important traditional sites in the Arthur Pieman Conservation Area further south, and several impressive cave sites at Rocky Cape National Park (know to Indigenous people as Tangdimmaa) to the northeast. But arguably the most important Aboriginal art site in the area, if not the state, can be found 7km north of Marrawah at Preminghana (formerly known as Mt Cameron West) – drive along the gravel road north of the Marrawah General Store and take the first turn left.

Three kilometres beyond Preminghana, at the northern end of the beach, are low-lying slabs of rock encrusted with geometric motifs that are believed to date back at least two millennia. Also in this area are remnants of stone tools, the quarries from which these were dug, and middens. There are also natural links with Tasmanian Aboriginal culture, such as boobialla, honeysuckle and tea-tree clusters – plants used to prepare food and traditional medicines.

Preminghana was returned to the Aboriginal people in 1995 – you can't visit the area independently. If you'd like to be authoritatively guided around this and other significant Aboriginal sites, contact the **Tasmanian Aboriginal Land Council** (TALC; ☎ 6231 0288; fax 6231 0298; 4 Lefroy St, Nth Hobart), which keeps a list of heritage officers who can accompany you to the sites for a set group fee.

championships, is regularly decided here, as is a round of the state's windsurfing championships. Green Point, 2km from the town centre, has a break that's impressive in southerly conditions, and there's also good surfing further along the road at Nettley Bay.

South of Marrawah, there's good surfing in an easterly at Lighthouse Beach (at West Point) and great reef surfing in similar conditions at Bluff Hill Point. West Point surf beach is reached by taking the left-hand branches of the road from the turn-off on the C214, while Bluff Hill Point surf beach is to the right of the lighthouse at the end of another side road further south.

BUSHWALKING

There's a beach walk from Bluff Hill Point to West Point that takes four hours one way, and a coastal walk from Bluff Hill Point to the mouth of the Arthur River that takes two hours one way. There's also a highly scenic walk of around three hours return north along the beach from Green Point to Preminghana (see above, for details of the indigenous significance of these areas).

FISHING

The whole region is good for fishing. In winter you can catch Australian salmon at Nettley Bay or off the rocks at West Point, while in summer you can catch black-backed salmon in the general bay area and at the mouth of the Arthur River. Estuary perch can be caught in the Arthur River.

Tours

Geoff King (☎ 6457 1191; jonesking@tassie.net.au), the owner of Glendonald Cottage, conducts a range of wildlife tours in the area, including a twilight trip out to an old fishing shack on his 300-hectare property to see some voracious Tasmanian devils tuck in to a buffet dinner (devil trip from $40 per person).

Sleeping & Eating

Camping is possible for free at beautiful Green Point, where there are toilets, water and an outdoor cold shower. You must pitch your tent by the toilets back from the beach, not on the foreshore.

Glendonald Cottage (☎/fax 6457 1191; 79 Arthur River Rd; s/d from $60/85) Just down the C214 towards Arthur River, this is a fully self-contained, spacious and comfortable two-bedroom rural place with plenty of reading material on Aboriginal history and the ecology of the area. The owner also runs excellent wildlife tours (p261).

Marrawah Beach House (☎ 6457 1285; 19 Beach Rd; s/d from $90/110) On the short road to Green Point beach, this house sleeps four adults and one child and has an unobstructed view to the ocean. Ring ahead, as the managers live off-site.

Ann Bay Cabins (☎/fax 6457 1361; annbaycabins@southcom.com.au; Green Point Rd; d $115) This is a pair of superb, soporific, spa-equipped beach cabins, both filled with handcrafted furniture, and with views to the water from their front decks. Continental brekky is provided.

Arties (☎ 6547 1144; artiesmarrawah@bigpond.com; d $130) Set back from the road about 3.5km south of Marrawah and sitting on three acres of native bushland, this private, fully self-contained accommodation offers a comfortable stay for up to six people and proximity to the Arthur Pieman Conservation Area.

Marrawah Tavern (☎ 6457 1102; Comeback Rd; mains $9-17; lunch & dinner) This pub doesn't have accommodation but serves big, excellent counter meals – the steaks are a real feast.

ARTHUR RIVER

☎ 03 / pop 110

The sleepy town of Arthur River, 14km south of Marrawah and mainly a collection of holiday houses for people who come here to fish, is unserviced by regular public transport. There's a **Parks & Wildlife Service ranger station** (PWS; ☎ 6457 1225) on the northern side of the river, where you can get camping information and permits for off-road vehicles.

> **QUICKSAND WARNING**
>
> Note that some sandy beaches at Arthur Beach have more than wild beauty – they are dotted with areas prone to quicksand, so please seek advice at the local **Parks & Wildlife Service ranger station** (PWS; ☎ 6457 1225) when you inquire about permits for designated off-road driving.

Gardiner Point, signposted off the main road on the southern side of the old, timber (but partly tarred) bridge, has been christened the **Edge of the World** by locals because the sea here stretches uninterrupted all the way to Argentina. There's a plaque at the point and a great view of some rocky coastline. It also has an amazing picnic shelter overlooking the ocean break, including a fireplace, seating and protection from pesky seagulls out to relieve you of your sandwich. No camping is allowed.

Activities

CANOEING

You can explore 15km of river scenery on your own via **Arthur River Canoe & Boat Hire** (☎ 6457 1312, 6457 1158). This place offers information on river conditions and storage for your gear, and hires boats for $18/110 per hour/day, canoes or dinghies from $60 per day (depending on the craft), and kayaks for $8/40 per hour/day. You can also be transported upriver for a 40km downriver paddle from Kanunnah Bridge to Arthur River bridge, which takes two days.

CRUISES

Arthur River Cruises (☎ 1800 151 509, 6457 1158; http://arthurrivercruises.com) has been operating for around 20 years and offers a comfortable, scenic day cruise departing at 10am and returning at 3pm, available most days as long as a minimum of eight people have booked. Its boat, the spacious MV *George Robinson*, motors upriver to the confluence of the Arthur and Frankland Rivers, where you can see bird life including sea eagles and azure kingfishers, and enjoy a BBQ and an interesting rainforest walk. The cost is $50/16.50 per adult/child and cruises must be booked at least a day in advance.

An alternative cruise is offered by **AR-Reflections River Cruises** (☎/fax 6457 1288; 4 Gardiner St). Its attractive MV *Reflections* departs at 10.15am daily for a 5½-hour return trip to Warra Landing, where you also get a guided rainforest walk; a morning luncheon and BBQ lunch is provided back at the kiosk. The cruise costs $60/25 per adult/child.

Sleeping & Eating

Camping grounds (unpowered sites per adult/pensioner/family $4/3.60/12, per week $15/14/50) in the area include Manuka, Peppermint and Prickly Wattle, the latter on the road to Couta Rocks. All grounds have taps, cold showers and toilets but no bins – take your rubbish out with you. Self-register at the PWS office. Prices are for up to two people.

Arthur River Holiday Units (☎/fax 6457 1288; 2 Gardiner St; s/d from $70/90) These units are self-contained and range in size from one to three bedrooms. There are log fires and laundry facilities, and a continental breakfast costs extra. It also offers accommodation/cruise packages, but no credit-card facilities are available. There's a shop located nearby.

Ocean View Holiday Cottage (☎ 6457 1100, 0419 537 500; Lot 80 Gardiner St; d $80) This is a pleasant three-bedroom house sleeping up to six people. With views of the river mouth, it also offers a cosy wood fire, electric blankets and satellite TV. Inquire at the house opposite.

Sunset Holiday Villas (☎/fax 6457 1197; 23 Gardiner St; d $85) This option has two self-contained units sleeping six people comfortably and sharing a balcony and views of the beach, which can be stunning at sunset. Continental brekky is available on request for $6.50 per person.

The town has a **kiosk** with limited supplies, but there are also **fresh crayfish** (☎ 6457 1197; 21 Gardiner St) available.

WESTERN EXPLORER & ARTHUR PIEMAN CONSERVATION AREA

The Western Explorer is the name of the road linking Smithton to the Pieman River. Because there's a barge to carry cars across the Pieman at the tiny settlement of Corinna, it's possible to use this route to

TARKINE WILDERNESS

The Tarkine is a 3500-sq-km wilderness between the Arthur River in the north and the Pieman River in the south.

Over a decade ago, conservationists tried unsuccessfully to prevent the development of what they called the 'the road to nowhere' between Corinna and Balfour, a road that now runs close to – and at times within – the eastern border of a section of the Tarkine called the Arthur Pieman Conservation Area (above). Conservation groups are still seeking World Heritage area protection for this diverse region, beyond the small section declared the Savage River National Park (p265) several years ago. Described as one of the world's great archaeological regions due to its Indigenous heritage values, this area in fact contains a myriad of buttongrass, towering sand dunes, expansive middens, pristine eucalypt forests, a beautiful myrtle rainforest corridor (which the Tasmanian government has given the OK to log) wild rivers, heathland, moorlands and pounded coastal landscapes that face the full might of the Roaring 40s.

Not everyone agrees it's a wilderness area though – former Tasmanian premier Tony Rundle once said that the Tarkine 'has no more wilderness than Battery Point'. And the state's forestry industry would seem to prefer fewer restrictions on logging in order to allow the exploitation of the Tarkine's 2000 sq km of rainforest.

Tiger Trails (☎ 6234 3931, 0427 397 815; www.tasmaniawalks.com) offers adventurous and comprehensive guided tours of the Tarkine (six/seven days $849/1299), but if you'd like a self-drive flyer or detailed track notes contact the **Tarkine National Coalition** (☎ 6431 2373; www.tarkine.org; PO Box 218 Burnie 7320), which is working with the Wilderness Society, the World Wide Fund for Nature, the Australian Conservation Foundation and other conservation groups to protect this Gondwanic area. There's also a leaflet published by the **Wilderness Society** (☎ 6234 9366; 130 Davey St, Hobart) that details a self-guided tour of the northern reaches of what constitutes Australia's (and arguably the world's) largest temperate rainforest (also Australia's largest contiguous rainforest), beginning from the highway township of Sisters Creek and heading off on a network of dirt forestry roads (suitable for two-wheel drives), emerging onto the Murchison Hwy at Henrietta. The scenic lows and highs of the drive respectively include logging coupes and a walk to the stunningly tranquil Myrtle Reach on the Arthur River. Allow at least a half-day for the trip, fill up your car's tank before setting off, drive carefully and check road conditions after heavy rain.

For some snapshots of this profoundly beautiful region, buy the pictorial *The Tarkine: Endangered Wilderness,* published by the Wilderness Society.

the west coast as an alternative to the Murchison Hwy. More significantly, though, the road is an attraction in its own right, running through or close to the eastern boundary of the Arthur Pieman Conservation Area.

The condition of the C249 – the 53km section from the C214 to Corinna that was upgraded from a four-wheel-drive track in 1995 – varies from season to season, if not month to month. Although this road is regularly negotiated by vehicles without four-wheel drive and is promoted as a tourist route, it's remote, mostly unsealed, narrow, at times very rough and rocky, and has steep ascents and descents, all of which well justifies its 50km/h speed limit. The road should probably not be attempted in bad weather or at night. For an up-to-date assessment on track conditions try asking Corinna's **barge operator** (☎ 6446 1170), or a **ranger** (PWS; ☎ 6457 1225) at Arthur River, or you can contact the **Stanley visitors centre** (☎ 6458 1330).

Another hazard is the bleak, rugged terrain you pass at its southern end: in places the view is so seductive that despite the challenging nature of the drive, you just won't be able to help snatching the occasional glance. The northern end, however, is far less scenic and therefore not such a hazard.

Make sure you remember to fill your car's fuel tank at Zeehan, Tullah or Waratah (in the south) or at Marrawah (in the north), because petrol is unavailable between these points (you should probably fill up with food supplies, too). For more information about the barge across the Pieman, see p263. For a map of the southern region of the Western Explorer, see Map p267.

The remote features of the 1000-sq-km **Arthur Pieman Conservation Area**, part of the outstanding Tarkine Wilderness (see the boxed text, p263), include magnificent **ocean beaches** with some of the wildest swells in the state, **waterfalls** on the Nelson Bay River, **Rebecca Lagoon**, **Temma Harbour**, the old mining town of **Balfour**, the **Pieman River** and the **Norfolk Ranges**. Bird-watchers will relish the chance to see three **rare birds** in this region: the ground parrot, the orange-bellied parrot and the hooded plover. A management plan for the Arthur Pieman, which attempts to address local commercial issues (fishing, wind farms, bull-kelp collection), recreational issues (camping, off-road driving) and the area's highly significant Aboriginal heritage, was finally produced by the state government in early 2002.

CORINNA & PIEMAN RIVER

☎ 03

The small vehicular ferry across the Pieman River at the tiny settlement of Corinna (the Aboriginal word for Tasmanian tiger), on the river's northern bank, makes this one-time gold-mining settlement a connector between the west and northwest coasts. The other main reason to visit Corinna's somewhat idyllic, forested surrounds is to take the **Pieman River Cruise** (☎ 6446 1170), a laidback, far more rustic alternative to the crowded, mass-produced Gordon River cruises out of Strahan. Costing $40/20 per adult/child, the tour on the MV *Arcadia II* departs at 10.30am and returns at 2.30pm daily. It's best to book 24 hours in advance, as during summer it can be booked out and in winter it only runs if there are bookings.

Sleeping & Eating

The **concessionaire** (☎ 6446 1170) in Corinna provides only a limited supply of snacks and refreshments. It also runs a small **camping ground** (unpowered sites $8) and **Pieman Retreat Cabins** (s & d $80), large self-contained units sleeping up to six people (these can get a bit musty but are fine for an overnight stop). There's a small charge for linen, and site prices are for up to two people.

Getting There & Away

There isn't regular public transport available to Corinna. From the south, it's approximately a 45-minute drive from Zeehan and a 1½-hour drive from Strahan, while from the north it will take a three- to four-hour drive from Smithton. See p263 for more details.

As well, the *Fatman* **ferry** (☎ 6446 1170; motorcycles & bicycles/standard vehicle/caravan $11/20/25; 9am-5pm Apr-Sep, to 7pm Oct-Mar) slides across the Pieman on demand (allow about 15 minutes). Note there's a length limit on caravans: front-wheel base of car to rear-wheel base of caravan must not exceed 9m (maximum body width is 2.5m).

JASON EDWARDS

Lavender farm (p190) outside Nabowla

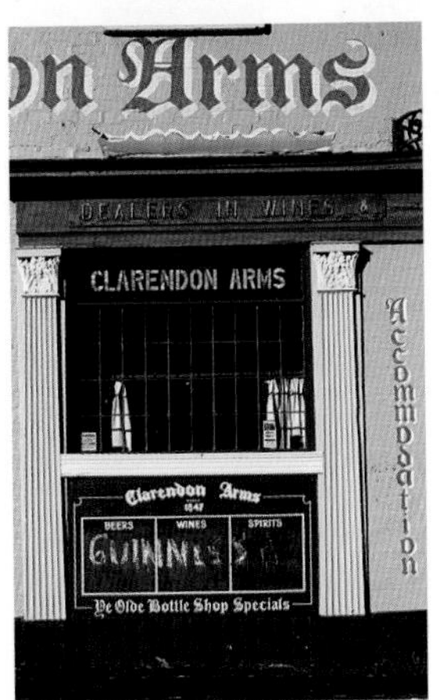

ROSS BARNETT

The historic Clarendon Arms Hotel (p220) in Evandale

Bay of Fires Lodge on the Bay of Fires Walk (p187)

HOLGER LEUE

GRANT DIXON

Opium poppy field (p214) near Devonport

ROB BLAKERS

Rainforest in the Tarkine Wilderness (p263)

John Lendis' *The Old Grocer's Shop*, one of Sheffield's many murals (p232)

CHRIS KLEP

The Nut (p256), Stanley

ROSS BA

HELLYER GORGE

Seven kilometres west of Burnie is Somerset, at the junction of the Murchison and Bass Hwys. Forty kilometres south of Somerset, the Murchison Hwy winds its way through the impressive Hellyer Gorge, which is on the banks of the Hellyer River. The picnic area makes for a pleasant roadside repose with two short walks along the river: there are toilet facilities, a children's playground and water taps (undrinkable).

Connecting Burnie with the Waratah area is route B18, an alternative road that's faster but less scenic, passing through Ridgley and Hampshire, avoiding the stunningly peaceful winding road through Hellyer Gorge.

About 40km south of Hellyer Gorge is the CI32 turn-off to Cradle Mountain. This major highway is a link from the west coast to the northern end of Cradle Mountain–Lake St Clair National Park.

WARATAH

☎ 03 / pop 230

Waratah has two claims to fame. It was once home to the world's richest tin mine at nearby Mt Bichoff, and the last verifiably breathing Tasmanian tiger was trapped nearby and shipped off to die in a Hobart zoo in 1936.

Waratah is built on both sides of the narrow Lake Waratah (popular for trout fishing in season) and parts of town look on to encroaching ravines and engagingly wild hillsides. The local **museum** (☎ 6439 1252; Smith St; 10am-4pm Oct-May, noon-3pm Mon-Fri Jun-Sep) preserves assorted relics and records of the boom days. If you find it unstaffed, inquire at the post office across the road or at the nearby roadhouse.

Next door to the museum is **Philosopher Smith's Hut**, a reconstruction of the abode of one James Smith, the prospector who discovered tin at Mt Bischoff.

There are also some signposted **walking tracks** around town, including the recommended two-hour return journey to the Power House.

Behind the post office, **Waratah Camping & Caravan Lakeside Park** (☎ 6439 7100; Smith St; unpowered sites per person $6, powered sites incl amenities $11) consists of a gravelled area for caravans and lakeside lawns for tent-pitchers (facilities cost $5). Keys to the amenities block are available at the post office or after hours at the **Bischoff Hotel** (☎ 6439 1188; Main St; s/d from $25/55), opposite a gully with a small waterfall. At the Bischoff, the town's main remnant from the old mining days, try for the more spruced up, slightly more expensive room with water views. Counter **meals** (mains $8.50-13; lunch & dinner) are served.

SAVAGE RIVER NATIONAL PARK

A remote area of 180 sq km, this park sits in Australia's largest area of cool-temperate rainforest and contains a swathe of buttongrass on its central Baretop Ridge; Savage River was initially worked over for its alluvial gold and subsequently for its iron ore. Prior to the park's creation, the Public Land Use Commission recommended it should be 350 sq km (twice its current size) and that its location within the sizable Tarkine Wilderness (see p263) may have affected its ultimate size.

There are no roads into Savage River National Park, though highways pass by about 5km to 10km from the park's southern and eastern boundaries.

The West

The wild West is the perfect region to play the weekend warrior with the four-wheel drive and motor through pristine scenery, or to cut through the silent mirrored waters of the King River on a cruise, or to get the hell out of Dodge and go take a hike, literally.

You'll see thousands of millions of years captured in the ancient rocks, wrought in volcanic fire and scraped clean by ice; glaciers melted 10,000 years ago to dig Lake St Clair's bed and shape the nearby crags. Formidable mountains, buttongrass plains, tranquil lakes, dense rainforests and a treacherous coast are all compelling features of this beautiful region, much of which is now part of the Tasmanian Wilderness World Heritage Area. For thousands of years the west was home to indigenous folk who lived through the last ice age.

It was over the West's wild rivers, beautiful lakes and serene valleys that battles between environmentalists and governments have raged. In the 1980s, the proposed damming of the Franklin and lower Gordon Rivers caused one of the greatest, longest-running environmental debates in Australia's history. Strahan has subsequently profited from an ecotourism bonanza, and mining strongholds and authentic, rugged towns like Rosebery and Zeehan have rich industrial heritage.

HIGHLIGHTS

- Wending through dense forest and crossing wild rivers on the historic **West Coast Wilderness Railway** (p280)
- Paying homage to the bushwalker's Mecca, the **Overland Track** (p285) at Cradle Mountain–Lake St Clair National Park
- Rafting the wild, utterly sensational **Franklin River** (p283)
- Inspecting Tasmania's national mineral emblem at the **West Coast Pioneers Memorial Museum** (p270) in Zeehan
- Tumbling down 30m-high sandy skyscrapers at **Henty Dunes** (p274)
- Soaring through the air on a scenic flight over the white-quartzite headgear of **Frenchmans Cap** (p275)
- Taking a moment to savour the rugged beauty and frontier spirit of **Queenstown** (p278)
- Cutting through the tannin-rich waters on a cruise of the spectacularly serene **Gordon River** (p274) from Strahan

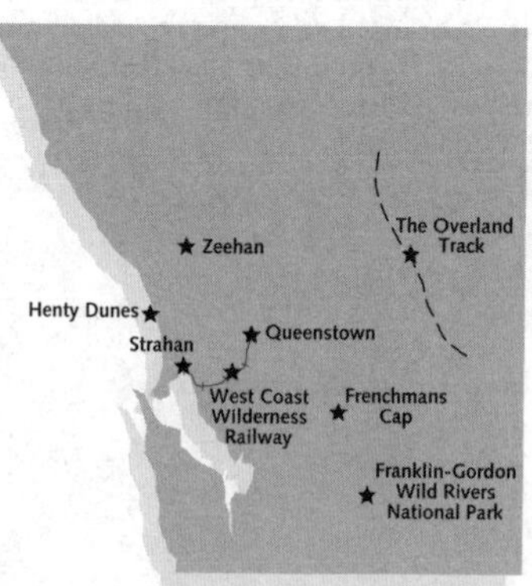

Getting There & Around

TassieLink (☎ 6272 7300, 1300 300 520; www.tassielink.com.au) runs one bus a day – from Tuesday to Friday and on Sunday – from Hobart to Bronte Junction ($29.20, 2½ hours), Derwent Bridge ($34.90), Lake St Clair ($40.60, three to 3½ hours), the start of the Frenchmans Cap walk ($42.10, four hours), Queenstown ($51.20, five to 5½ hours) and Strahan ($59.20, 6½ to 8½ hours, times varying due to Queenstown stopover); there are return services on the same days. From Launceston, TassieLink buses run once-daily on Monday, Tuesday, Thursday and Saturday to Sheffield ($19.80, 2½ hours), Gowrie Park ($23.40), Cradle Mountain ($46.60, 3½ hours), Tullah ($40.30, 4¼ hours), Rosebery ($42), Zeehan ($48.80, 5½ hours), Queenstown ($56.50, 6½ hours) and Strahan ($64.50, eight hours); again, there are return services on the same days. TassieLink also has a twice-weekly service (on Wednesday and Friday) that picks up passengers from the ferry terminal in Devonport in the morning and runs them to Burnie ($10, one hour), Tullah ($25.40, 2¼ hours), Rosebery ($27.30, 2½ hours), Zeehan ($34.40, three hours), Queenstown ($42.50, 3¾ hours) and Strahan ($50.50, 4¾ hours) – the route is also run in reverse on the same days in time for the nightly ferry sailing.

For information about additional services for those walking the Overland Track see p293.

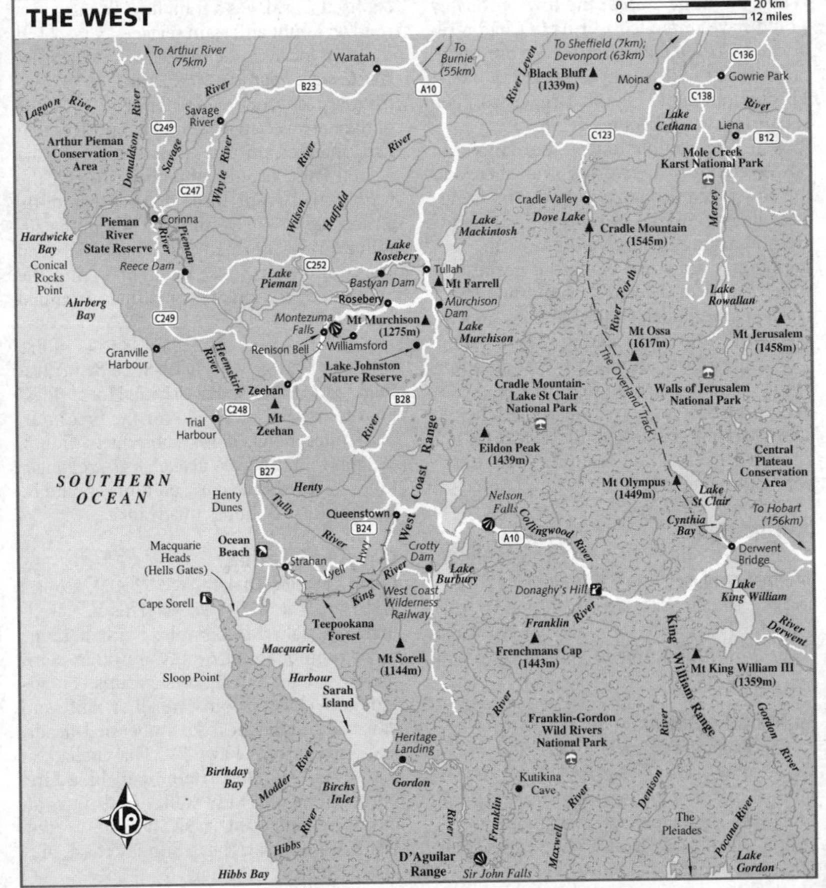

Drivers heading north up the Western Explorer Rd should fill up at Zeehan, Tullah or Waratah, as there's no fuel at either Savage River or Corinna, only at distant Marrawah.

TULLAH

☎ 03 / pop 270

This old mining town has had its fair share of isolation to endure – for a long time, the only access was on foot or, later, by train. The town was established in 1892 when a lead-zinc-copper-silver-ore body was discovered on Mt Farrell, the mining of which continued until the early 1970s.

In 1962, the construction of the Murchison Hwy from Burnie to Queenstown linked Tullah with the rest of Tasmania. When the mine closed, the town probably would have imploded if it hadn't had a reprieve by being chosen as the accommodation site for hydroelectric-scheme workers. Throughout the 1970s and early 1980s, 2000 construction workers resided here.

With the completion of the dams and power stations, the workers vanished and the town emptied; many of the buildings were also removed. The remaining residents are now trying to survive on tourism, with the biggest drawcard being the impressive trout caught in the lakes around town.

The name Tullah comes from an Aboriginal word meaning 'meeting of two rivers', a definition now muddied by the flooding of the rivers in question to form Lake Rosebery, part of a large hydroelectric scheme. The town has great views of Mt Murchison and Mt Farrell, while beautiful Lake Rosebery laps at the edges of town.

Information

At the jerry-built Tullah Village is a **visitors information room** (☎ 6473 4264; Farrell St; ⌚ 10am-noon & 1-3pm peak holiday periods), staffed by volunteers. The café here is also an Australia Post and Commonwealth Bank agency, and has public toilets.

Sights & Activities

At the **Radford Woodcrafts** gallery and workshop (☎ 6473 4344; ⌚ 9am-5pm), opposite the pub, you can watch the wood-turner at work on Tassie timbers, and buy good-quality lamps, clocks, bowls and wine racks, plus other souvenirs.

There are several scenic drives passing the major hydroelectric dams and lakes. Three kilometres north of town you can follow a road west for 55km to **Reece Dam**. The road crosses the dam wall and continues a further 29km to Zeehan. The other main scenic road starts 5km south of town and heads over the flanks of Mt Murchison towards Queenstown – known as the **Anthony Rd**, it provides good views as it crosses the West Coast Range. From town, a very scenic minor road also leads to **Murchison Dam**.

The area's best **walks** include **Mt Farrell** (three hours return), which gives glorious views of peaks near and far, and **Mt Murchison** (six hours return).

From 1908 until the 1960s, Tullah's only transport link with the rest of the allegedly civilised world was a train line. Eventually a road was built and train services ceased, but in 1977 local residents decided to restore **Wee Georgie Wood** (☎ 6473 2228, 0417 147 015; Murchison Hwy; adult/pensioner/child/family $5/3/2/10), one of the narrow-gauge steam locomotives that had operated on the railway. It's opposite Farrell Park. From September to April the train runs two or three days each month, almost always on a Sunday. Though the 20-minute rides normally take place between 10am and 4pm, over daylight saving the hours of operation are sometimes extended until 9pm.

One way to see the region is to go horse riding or boating with **Tullah Horse-Back & Boat Tours** (☎ 6473 4289; Mackintosh Track). Horse rides/boat tours start at $35/20 for the first hour, with rates reduced for subsequent hours. Wagon tours are also available as are longer tours for two/three days; all tours should be book at least 24 hours in advance.

Sleeping & Eating

Tullah Lakeside Chalet (☎ 6473 4121; fax 6473 4130; Farrell St; dm $21, r from $60) This is a well-managed lakeside complex with a range of accommodation; rooms are often completely booked out by tour groups. 'Standard' and 'chalet' rooms are all en suite and have natural touches like timber bed-heads, and some rooms have TV. The chalet can advise on canoe/boat/mountain bike hire, horse riding and local walks. It also has an attractive **restaurant** (mains $10-25; ⌚ breakfast, lunch & dinner) with a cheap Sunday roast, plus a well-stocked wine bar.

Tullah Village Café (☎ 6473 4377; Farrell St; mains around $12; ⌚ breakfast, lunch & dinner) At the time of writing there were plans for this place to be extended and to provide caravan park/cabin-type accommodation. (This place also handled bookings for rooms in a few houses around town). The café serves breakfasts, takeaway and heavier fare (hamburgers, tuna patties, schnitzels), and kids' meals.

Tullah Tavern (☎ 6473 4141; Murchison Hwy; units $80) This welcoming pub offers two very tidy and adequate self-contained units. The tavern also dishes up some good-value counter **meals** (mains $10-22; ⌚ breakfast summer, lunch & dinner year-round). Here you can tear into a tender beef scotch fillet ($22) or rump steak ($19) and then join in with the locals for karaoke some nights, or be entertained by a live-music band.

Getting There & Away

See p267 for information. Buses arrive at and depart from the BP service station.

ROSEBERY

☎ 03 / pop 1600

Rosebery sits in a picturesque valley, surrounded by lush greenery (on its eastern boundary lies the imposing Murchison Range, to the north sits 950m-tall Mt Black). While most visit Rosebery for its rich mining heritage (mining still continues to employ several hundred people and supports the town's economy) and splendid natural surrounds, it is also worthwhile spending some time getting to know the incredibly friendly townsfolk: they're of the ilk where the men are tough and the women even bolder.

Information

Newsagency (☎ 6473 1142; Agnes St; ⌚ 6am-7.30pm Mon-Fri, until 1pm Sat & Sun) Also handles ANZ transactions and has a 24-hour ATM.

Online access centre (☎ 6473 1938; Morrisby St)

Post office (Agnes St) Also a Commonwealth Bank agent.

Sights & Activities

The high school has some interesting old **mine remnants** (Propsting St) along its front fence, including a water wheel and railway carriage for steep inclines. The school also contains a small **mining museum** (admission free) that displays artefacts and old photos; ask at the school's reception. There's also a **heritage centre** next to the Pasminco Mine site containing pictures and other memorabilia of the town's history; access to the centre is via a public gate (opposite the BP service station), which accesses the road leading to the mine and centre.

The picnic area at the southern entrance to town is the start of a short walk along the Stitt River and over Park Rd to **Stitt Falls**, which are good after recent rainfall.

The two-day **Rosebery Irish Festival** takes place yearly in mid-March, with heaps of live music, wood-chopping and billycart races, and kids' activities like face-painting.

Sealed roads lead to Williamsford, 8km south of Rosebery, the site of an abandoned mining town and also the start of an excellent walk to the impressively tall **Montezuma Falls** (at 104m they are Tasmania's highest). The easy return walk along an abandoned railway line takes about three hours. You can explore the adit (horizontal mine shaft) at the end of the walk, but it's best to bring a torch.

If you prefer a guided walk to Montezuma Falls, **Hay's** (☎ 6473 1247; 10-12 Esplanade; www.haystour.com) runs four-hour trips for $45 per person, which include lunch. Another option with Hay's is a two-hour surface tour of the **Pasminco Zinc Mine**; the first tour departs at 9.30am (times vary according to season) and costs $15/10 per adult/child. Hay's also runs trips to see an extraordinary 10,000-year-old stand of Huon pine in the **Lake Johnston Nature Reserve** ($77 per person, 1½ to two hours) – only licensed tour operators are permitted to take the public into this reserve. Additionally, Hay's offers trout fishing tours on any of the lakes that are part of the hydroelectric schemes.

Sleeping & Eating

Mount Black Lodge (☎ 6473 1039; mountblacklodge@hotmail.com; Hospital Rd; with/without bathroom s $77/30, d $88/40) This is a great place to stay, with sizeable rooms, a wood-heated lounge, a thoroughly relaxing atmosphere and fine views of Murchison Range from its en-suite rooms. The excellent food at its **Blue Moon Restaurant & Gallery** (mains $14-20; ⌚ dinner) includes Atlantic salmon and char-grilled Scotch fillet; vegetarians should identify themselves and will be amply catered for. It's occasionally open for lunch, too.

Rosebery Caravan Park (☎ 6473 1366; Park Rd; unpowered/powered sites $16/19, dm $21, on-site vans $40, cabins $60-75) This park is surrounded by hills and has a small, grassy camping area, a gravel caravan area and a functional budget lodge. Prices are for two people.

Donlene Bed & Breakfast (☎ 6473 1634; 3 Morrisby St; r from $85) This accommodation option features basic accommodation with breakfast and dinner provided (or BBQ for the evening meal), including picnic lunches. Pets are welcome.

There are also a number of snack bars and a large bakery on the main street.

Getting There & Away

Buses arrive at and depart from Mackrell's Milkbar at 24 Agnes St. There are no services from Rosebery to Burnie.

See p267 for information.

ZEEHAN

☎ 03 / pop 1120

Zeehan has experienced its fair share of highs and lows over the last century, with its fortunes intrinsically linked to those of local mining. By the late 19th century Zeehan had become a booming silver mining centre known as Silver City, with a population that peaked at nearly 10,000. In its heyday Zeehan had 26 hotels and its Gaiety Theatre seated 1000 people, and for a time it even had its own stock exchange.

The town began a slow decline, however, after the mines began to fail, but with the expansion of the Renison Tin Mine at Renison Bell in the late 1960s, 17km towards Rosebery, Zeehan revived when it became the housing base for Renison Ltd.

Zeehan is a convenient place to spend the night if you're planning on driving the 50km to the Pieman River (p264) to take a cruise or go boating on the beautiful watercourse, or continue along the Western Explorer Rd to the northwestern corner of the state.

Today it's mainly a sleepy town where if you get here on a Saturday or Sunday afternoon you could be forgiven for believing you just saw some tumbleweed roll down the main street.

GETTING AWAY FROM IT ALL

Avoid the tourist hoards during peak season and head out to remote **Granville Harbour** (above). Located northwest of Zeehan, a gravel road leads to this tranquil seaside haven, making it the perfect respite from the hectic touring routes. Make sure you check the road conditions before you go.

Orientation & Information

Zeehan is a tiny place but it's worth noting that the historic part of Main St is at the northern end of town, not the bit you see when entering from Strahan or Queenstown. The town is the administrative centre for the region and has branches of the ANZ and Commonwealth Banks (none with ATMS), and a library with public Internet access. The **online access centre** (☎ 6473 1938; Zeehan Primary School, Belstead St; 9am-noon Mon, Tue & Fri, 2-5pm Wed) also provides Net use for $2 per 15 minutes. Tourist information can be obtained at the impressive West Coast Pioneers Memorial Museum (below).

November sees the **Zeehan Gem & Mineral Fair** (adult/child $2/1), which features gems, jewellery, minerals, crystals, fossils and activities, such as rides, gem-panning and crystal hunts.

Sights & Activities

WEST COAST PIONEERS MEMORIAL MUSEUM

This excellent **museum** (☎ 6471 6225; Main St; adult/senior & student/family $9/8/20; 9am-5pm) is in the 1894 School of Mines building. Nationally acknowledged as one of Australia's best regional mining museums, it also includes displays on the west's rail and shipping heritage. The ground floor features an interesting mineral collection, a fauna display and a mining gallery. Upstairs are photographs of old mining towns and their inhabitants. To one side of the museum is an exhibit of steam locomotives and carriages used on the early west-coast railways, while downstairs from here is a crocoite 'cavern', filled with specimens of the rare mineral (Tasmania's official mineral emblem).

GAIETY GRAND

The Gaiety Theatre and the Grand Hotel are a single building known as the Gaiety Grand, a short distance up Main St from the museum.

WARNING

If walking off marked tracks in the bush close to Zeehan or at Trial Harbour, beware of abandoned mine shafts hidden by vegetation.

The Gaiety was one of the biggest, most modern theatres in the world when it opened in February 1899, and what a bonus it must have been for the miners to be able to move between the pub and the theatre through connecting doors. In his book *The Peaks of Lyell,* historian Geoffrey Blainey notes that to mark the Gaiety's opening a Melbourne troupe of 60 was brought to town, where it played to a house of 1000 every night for a week, pulling audiences from as far afield as Queenstown, then a six-hour journey away. It also attracted performances by such luminaries as Dame Nellie Melba.

After being subjected to appalling renovations over the years, the Gaiety Grand is slowly being restored using donations given to the Pioneers Museum, whatever government grants can be secured, and any proceeds from sales in the volunteer-run gallery at the front of the building. Tours are available (see below).

HISTORIC WALK

An excellent way to see Zeehan is to take this circuit walk. Starting at the museum, follow Main St west, turn left down Fowler St towards the golf course and walk through **Spray Tunnel**, a former railway tunnel. Turn left again to follow the Comstock track (an old tramway) south to **Florence Dam**. Follow the right track at the fork, winding around Keel Ridge, then descend to the southern end of Main St. The walk takes two to three hours and passes a lot of old mine sites.

More detailed notes on this walk and others around the mining sites of the west coast are detailed in *Historic Mines of Western Tasmania* by Duncan How, available at the museum for $10. Alternatively, take the Spray Tunnel scenic drive suggested by the museum (all the way or as far as the tunnel, from where you can continue on foot).

TOURS

Tours of the Gaiety Grand are available from **Silver City Info/Tours** (☎ 6471 5095, 0438 716 389; silvercitytours@our.net.au; 129 Main St), who can guide you on a 30-minute tour of the theatre or a one-hour tour of the entire building from $6.50/4.50 per adult/concession (tour times by arrangement). Silver City also offers informative guided tours of the Pioneers Museum and of Zeehan township.

OTHER ATTRACTIONS

There are plenty of old mining relics outside town. Four kilometres south of Zeehan you'll find some **old smelters** beside the highway. For panoramic views you can follow the track starting near the smelters to the top of **Mt Zeehan**; the walk takes three hours return.

At Renison Bell, 17km northeast of Zeehan, there's a signposted **Battery Mill Walk** starting 300m west of the mine entrance. This visits the old mill site where rock from the mine was crushed. A locomotive, railway sidings and old workings are described with the aid of photographic plaques beside the track. Allow about 45 minutes return for a visit.

Northwest of Zeehan, a quiet sealed road leads to **Reece Dam** on the Pieman River, part of the Pieman hydroelectric scheme. This road allows access to some rarely visited places like **Granville Harbour** (opposite), a small coastal holiday place down a side road where you can camp, and Corinna, the departure point for the Pieman River Cruise (p264). The road to Reece Dam also provides a view of **Heemskirk Falls**; a one-hour, signposted return walk leads to the base of the falls. For **fishing** enthusiasts, Granville Harbour is a good place for crayfish and Lake Pieman, behind Reece Dam, has some fine trout.

A gravel road heads west from Zeehan to **Trial Harbour**, the town's original port and now a collection of holiday homes and a few permanent residences; there are no shops or other facilities. You can do a few short and long walks around here and there are some great fishing spots, plus it's a beautiful place to camp – pick up the brochure on Trial Harbour from Zeehan's Pioneers Museum. Another feature is the **local history room**, with old photos and other memorabilia. It's open most days.

To sample a bit of local entrepreneurialism, visit **Shorty's** (☎ 6471 6595; 22 Shaw St; admission by gold-coin donation; 🕒 10am-5pm) for an unusual collection of minerals, mining odds and ends, and 'bushcraft oddities'. Shaw St runs off Main St at the northern end of town. At this end of town you'll also find the eccentric **Dr Frankensteins Museum of Monsters** (☎ 6471 6580; 12 Whyte St; entry by donation). This local funhouse (opposite the 'Farque Ranch') is open in the afternoon; just ring the doorbell to alert the monster to your arrival.

From Zeehan, you can take Henty Rd (B27) to **Henty Dunes** (p274).

Sleeping & Eating

Treasure Island Caravan Park (☎ 6471 6633; tiz@dodo.com.au; Hurst St; unpowered/powered sites $15/19, on-site vans $35-50, cabins $55-80) This park is spread out alongside the Zeehan Rivulet on the northern edge of town. It has friendly management and plenty of greenery surrounding the accommodation options.

Hotel Cecil (☎ 6471 6221; fax 6471 6599; Main St; s $40, d with/without bathroom $55/65, cottages $85) This hotel has small but ultraclean hotel rooms and, on an adjacent block, three very comfortable, cosy self-contained miners' cottages. It also serves **pub meals** (mains $12-20; dinner), such as tasty rissoles, garlic prawns and hearty steak and pasta dishes.

Heemskirk Motor Hotel (☎ 6471 6107, 1800 639 876; fax 6471 6694; Main St; r $85-100) At the eastern entrance to town, this motel won't win any architectural design awards, but it does have decent-sized motel rooms and includes the friendly **Abel Tasman Bistro** (mains $12-19; lunch & dinner), which serves Mongolian lamb, salmon patties and chilli chicken; there's an occasional mealtime floorshow to entertain the occasional coach group.

Mt Zeehan Retreat (☎ 6471 6424; fax 6471 6430; 12 Runcorn St; d with shared bathroom $80, with en suite $95-110) This is a friendly modern house run by charming owners, with a couple of en-suite rooms, the upstairs one with good views. There are no credit-card facilities but a hearty continental breakfast is included in the tariff.

Zeehan Motor Inn & Lodge (☎ 6471 6107; Main St; dm $65, d from $80) This motel has brick motel units with standard but basic utilities, including hair dryers. It also has a range of accommodation in a nearby hostel with shared facilities.

Museum Coffee Lounge (☎ 6471 6225; Main St; 9am-5pm) You don't need to pay the museum entry fee to have a coffee here. This café offers inventive, cheap, light lunches, such as sandwiches, filling rolls, soup and savoury croissants.

Coffee Stop (☎ 6471 6709; 110 Main St; breakfast & lunch Mon-Wed, breakfast, lunch & dinner Thu-Sat) This place serves light meals, such as quiche, sandwiches and takeaway snacks, and has local crafts on display.

Getting There & Away

Buses arrive at and depart from Marina's Coffee Shop, on the main street.

See p267 for more information.

STRAHAN

☎ 03 / pop 700

Strahan is 40km southwest of Queenstown on Macquarie Harbour and is the only sizeable town on the rugged west coast. The town unpredictably shot to fame in the 1980s as the centre for the Franklin River Blockade (see p282 for details) and since then has exploited its proximity to wilderness by offering a variety of tours on the Gordon River. Several developers have aggressively transformed its harbourside main street into what is now euphemistically called Strahan Village – it's more an expensive, self-aggrandising shopping strip than a true community – but the town's true appeal ironically lies in the natural and historical attractions around it rather than in the town itself, which has been overcommercialised.

There's no denying Strahan's popularity as a tourist destination, reputedly one of the most popular in the state, a statistic easily believed by anyone who has been packed into a peak-season Gordon River cruise. So if you like a bit of luxury, you may find the polish of this developing commercial settlement the perfect foil for the harsh landscape and uncompromising authenticity of the surrounding mining towns.

Information

ATM Outside the Fish Café.

Azza's general store (Innes St; 6.30am-9pm) Has a multicard ATM.

Online access centre ($3 per 30 min) In the Parks & Wildlife Service office.

Parks & Wildlife Service (PWS; ☎ 6471 7122; 9am-5pm Mon-Fri) In the old Customs House, a fine Federation structure adorning the foreshore. This building also houses a branch of the State Library of Tasmania.

Post office Also in the PWS building; a Commonwealth Bank agent.

Strahan Clinic (☎ 6471 7152; Bay St) For health-related matters.

Strahan visitors centre (☎ 6471 7622; strahan@tasvisinfo.com.au; Esplanade; 🕑 10am-8pm) Architecturally innovative; almost a tourist attraction in its own right. Its friendly staff can find you accommodation or issue a national park pass. See below and p278 for more information on the centre's diverse offerings.

Supermarket/newsagent (Reid St) Also handles ANZ accounts.

Sights

MUSEUMS & GALLERIES

West Coast Reflections (☎ 6471 7622; Esplanade; adult/child/concession/f $4.50/free/3/9; 🕑 10am-8pm summer, 10am-6pm winter) is the museum section of the Strahan visitors centre, installed beyond the Huon-pine reception desk. It's a creative and thought-provoking display on the history of the west coast, with a refreshingly blunt appraisal of the region's environmental disappointments and achievements, including the Franklin Blockade.

Nearby is **Strahan Woodworks** (☎ 6471 7244; 12 Esplanade; 🕑 8.30am-5pm), where you can see Huon pine, sassafras and myrtle being turned and then buy the end results, mainly kitchen knick-knacks, platters and ornamental objects. For more arts and crafts, check out the **Cove Gallery** (☎ 6471 7572; Esplanade; 🕑 8am-6pm summer, 10am-4pm winter), around the bay in the Risby Cove complex.

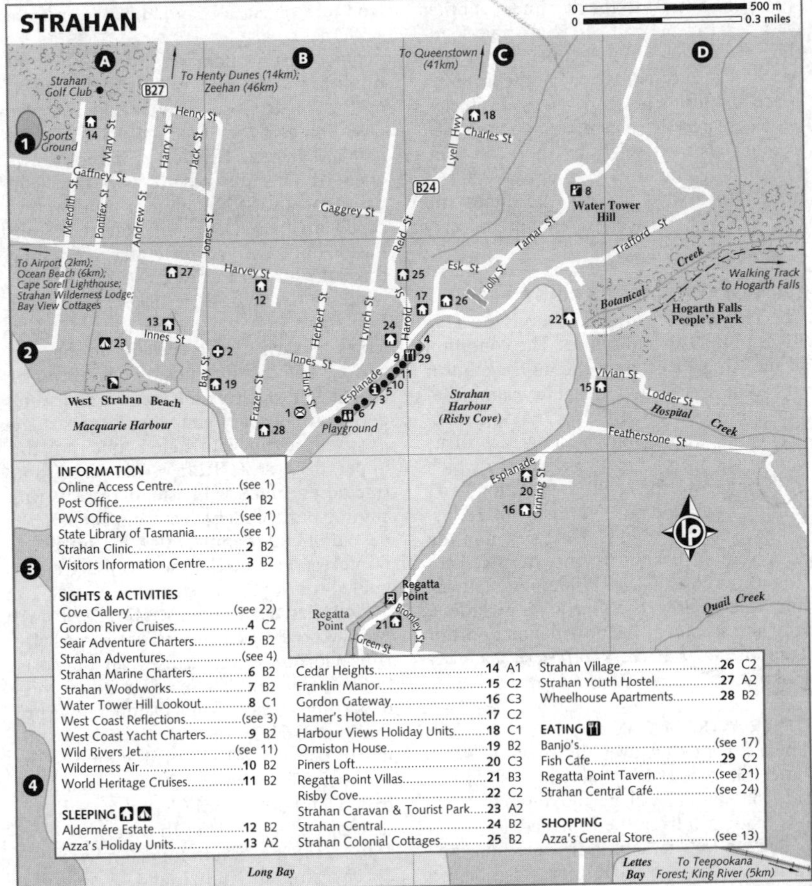

OCEAN BEACH & HENTY DUNES

Six kilometres from town is the impressive Ocean Beach, a 33km stretch of sand from Trial Harbour in the north to Macquarie Heads in the south – the sunsets here have to be seen to be believed. Due to rips and undertows, swimming at this beach is *not* recommended nor advised. The dunes behind the beach become a **mutton bird rookery** from October, when the birds return from their 15,000km winter migration – they remain here until April, providing an evening spectacle as they return to their nests at dusk.

Fourteen kilometres along the road from Strahan to Zeehan are the spectacular Henty Dunes, a series of 30m-high white sand dunes on Ocean Beach. They're a soothing contrast to the harshness of other west-coast scenery and an irresistible sandslide to any children. Unfortunately, the peaceful beauty is marred by the strident, peace-shattering noises of off-road vehicles, which are permitted here, though the beach is often claimed solely by those on foot. From the picnic area you can take a 1½-hour return walk through the dunes and out to Ocean Beach; remember to carry drinking water.

TEEPOOKANA FOREST & KING RIVER

The Teepookana Forest surrounds the King River to the east of Strahan. The condition of the King River is on the improve but it has long served as a graphic example of that other west-coast feature, environmental degradation: a fixture along each of its banks has been a band of sludge in which nothing grows, the result of pollution from mining operations in Queenstown. Yet incongruous as it sounds, the forest and the river remain beautiful. An extensive section of the West Coast Wilderness Railway line which follows the King River includes a stop at a station at the now-defunct port of Teepookana and access to **Teepookana Tower** lookout.

OTHER ATTRACTIONS

There's a lookout over the town at **Water Tower Hill**, accessed by following Esk St beside the Strahan Village booking office; it's less than 1km from the Esplanade.

Hogarth Falls is a pleasant one-hour return walk through the rainforest beside the platypus-inhabited Botanical Creek. The track starts at People's Park.

The 45m-high **Cape Sorell Lighthouse**, at the harbour's southern head, is purportedly the second-highest in Australia. You'll need a boat to cross the heads unless you can find an accommodating fisher to take you over. A return walk of two to three hours along a vehicle track from the jetty at Macquarie Heads leads to the lighthouse.

Activities

RIVER & HARBOUR CRUISES

Both the following companies offer popular river cruises that include a rainforest walk at Heritage Landing, views of or passage through Hells Gates (the narrow entrance to Macquarie Harbour), and a one-hour land tour of Sarah Island, the former penal settlement.

Operating a catamaran purpose-built to minimise wake and any subsequent effects on the fragile Gordon riverbanks is **Gordon River Cruises** (☎ 6471 4300, 1800 628 286; www.strahanvillage.com.au; Esplanade). This outfit offers 5½-hour cruises that depart at 8.30am daily, and also at 2.30pm over summer (except Christmas Day), but note that from Easter until the end of winter, a booking through Gordon River Cruises will see you wind up on a World Heritage Cruises boat (see following) – Gordon River Cruises leases its own craft elsewhere during that period. The cost depends on where you sit (you'll find most people get up and wander about anyway) and whether meals are involved: a trip with buffet lunch on the upper deck costs from $175 per person (including wine), while standard seats (including buffet lunch) cost from $80/45/190 per adult/child/family. All trips involve a rainforest walk at Heritage Landing and a guided tour of Sarah Island.

World Heritage Cruises (☎ 6471 7174, 1800 611 796; www.worldheritagecruises.com.au; Esplanade) also runs Gordon River cruises on purpose-built catamarans. There's a six-hour cruise departing at 9am from October to April that costs $65/25/165 per adult/child/family, and also at 2pm returning 8pm in the summer. There are half-day cruises offered from October to April (departing 9am, returning 1.30pm). This shorter tour costs $60/22/145 per adult/child/family but it doesn't stop at Sarah Island. A smorgasbord is available on board (adult/child $15/6) for those who don't pack their own lunchboxes.

Six hours on the river not enough? A new offering from World Heritage Cruises is a two-night cruise on the Gordon River, operating two to three times a week from October to April. A maximum of 24 passengers are accommodated in a purpose-built, 12-cabin vessel; the price of $1995 per person includes all meals, shore excursions and activities such as kayaking and guided bird-watching.

West Coast Yacht Charters (☎ 6471 7422; Esplanade; 🕑 8.30am-5pm Apr-Nov, 8.30am-6pm Dec-Mar) has a 2½-hour cruise on the *Stormbreaker* around Macquarie Harbour, including a crayfish dinner (seasonal) or your choice of salmon or steak. The cruise costs $60/45 per adult/child and departs daily at 5pm (6pm in summer). The 'two day–two night cruise' up the Gordon River costs $400/200 per adult/child, but note the first night is spent moored at Strahan Wharf; also note that dinner is provided the second night but not the first. You can also arrange a B&B bunk on the water (p276).

Strahan Marine Charters (☎ 6471 7353, 0418 135 983), at the end of Strahan Wharf, is another option for fishing or sightseeing charters, which can be arranged from $55 per person (minimum four people).

SEA KAYAKING

Experienced or inexperienced paddlers can take sea-kayak tours with **Strahan Adventures** (☎/fax 6471 7776; Esplanade), which operates from the Gordon River Cruises building. Tours from Risby Cove along the waterfront and back cost $50 per person, while twilight tours of Henty River cost $80 per person. Hardier trips to the Franklin or Gordon Rivers or to Sarah Island can also be arranged.

JET-BOAT RIDES

Wild Rivers Jet (☎ 6471 7174; www.wildriversjet.com.au; Esplanade) runs exhilarating 50-minute jet-boat rides on the hour from 9am to 4pm up the rainforest-lined gorges of the tannin-rich King River. Departing from the Strahan Wharf, this wet experience costs $55/33/155 per adult/child/family and there's a minimum of two people per ride. Bookings are recommended.

FOUR-WHEEL MOTORBIKE RIDES

Dune Buggy Tours (☎ 6471 7622, 0419 508 175; $40) offers 35- to 40-minute controlled guided hooning over the Henty Dunes with four-wheeled motorbikes (with automatic clutch). There's a 12km/h speed limit and participants must have a full drivers licence.

SCENIC FLIGHTS

The following companies offer daily flights (weather permitting); trips should be booked ahead.

Seair Adventure Charters (☎ 6471 7718; www.adventureflights.com.au; Strahan Wharf; 🕑 8.30am-5pm Sep-Jul) conducts light-plane and helicopter flights over the region. Flight details include 45-minute light-plane flights over Frenchmans Cap, the Franklin and Gordon Rivers, and Sarah Island ($160/90 per adult/child), 65-minute light-plane flights over the Cradle Mountain region ($175/90), as well as 60-minute helicopter flights over the Teepookana Forest ($165/90). Or you can have a quick flutter on a 15-minute helicopter ride over Hells Gates, Henty Dunes and Macquarie Harbour ($95/60). Fixed-wing flights take off from Strahan airport while the helicopters take off from a the wharf.

Wilderness Air (☎ 6471 7280; wildair@tassie.net.au; Strahan Wharf; 🕑 8.30am-5pm Sep-May) has seaplanes departing the wharf area roughly every 90 minutes from 9am until 5pm, flying upriver to land at Sir John Falls, where you get to walk in the rainforest; the 80-minute flights cost $150/90 per adult/child.

SWIMMING

Next to the caravan park is **West Strahan Beach**, with a gently shelving sandy bottom that provides safe swimming.

Sleeping

Much of the accommodation in the centre of town is run by **Strahan Village** (☎ 6471 4200, 1800 628 286; www.strahanvillage.com.au; 🕑 7am-7pm May-Oct, 7am-9pm Nov-Apr), which has its booking office under the clock tower on the Esplanade. Another chunk of the town's accommodation is handled by the booking office of **Strahan Central** (☎ 6471 7612; strahancentral@trump.net.au; 1 Harold St; 🕑 noon-4pm), which doubles as a posh café.

Strahan's popularity means it's inevitably a good idea to book ahead, particularly over the peak seasons.

BUDGET

Strahan Youth Hostel (☎ 6471 7255; 43 Harvey St; dm $20, 2-bed dm $25, d $50, cottages $75) Don't be fooled by the old YHA signage, it's not affiliated with YHA any longer. This place may be in a nice bush setting around 15 minutes' walk from the town centre, but it has very plain bunks and doubles, and tiny, ordinary A-frame cabins; the cottages are self-contained. The shared facilities could do with a decent scrub, too.

Strahan Caravan & Tourist Park (☎ 6471 7239; cnr Jones & Andrew Sts; unpowered/powered sites $20/25, on-site vans $50) A well-maintained beachfront park that's only a short distance from the heart of the village and offers good-value accommodation and facilities, including cabins (see right). Site prices are for up to two people.

West Coast Yacht Charters (☎ 6471 7422, 0419 300 994; Esplanade; dm adult/child $40/20, d $80) If you're hankering to sleep in a floating bunk on a wharf-moored yacht, then this is a great option. Because the yacht is used for charters, it has late check-in and early check-out (be prepared to check in after 7.30pm and disembark before 9am). The yacht isn't moored every night (overnight cruises on Gordon River are available), so you'll need to book ahead. Prices include continental breakfast and linen is supplied.

Strahan Wilderness Lodge (☎ 6471 7142; Ocean Beach Rd; d with/without bathroom $65/50;) A kilometre or two north of town, you can exchange the street traffic for birdsong among 28 peaceful acres of coastal vegetation. This old-style, laid-back place has spacious rooms and great views of gardens and harbour; prices include continental breakfast. There's also a heated indoor pool and spa housed in a conservatory-style building.

Camping is possible at the basic **camping ground** (unpowered sites $5) at Macquarie Heads, 15km southwest of Strahan; follow the signs to Ocean Beach and see the caretaker. Prices are for up to two people.

MIDRANGE

Guesthouses & B&Bs

Bay View Cottages (☎ 6471 7142; Ocean Beach Rd; d $75-95) The same people who manage Strahan Wilderness Lodge run these private, one-, two- or three-bedroom self-contained cottages. Each includes linen, tea- and coffee-making facilities, TV and heating.

Harbour Views Holiday Units (☎ 6471 7143; 0438 584 143; 1 Charles St; d $85-100) On the road into Strahan from Queenstown, this place offers roomy and comfortable family-style accommodation which includes a pair of motel-style, self-contained one- and two-bedroom B&B rooms in a bushland setting. While the kids can be entertained with jigsaws and board games, the oldies can check out the views or fill in some time watching the video of Tassie to help keep the holiday itinerary up to speed.

Self-Contained Apartments

Azza's Holiday Units (☎ 6471 7253; 7 Innes St; d from $80) At the back of the general store, what looks like a set of plain self-contained tin cubicles hides fairly comfortable lodgings with basic cooking facilities, TV, and a short walk to West Strahan Beach.

Strahan Caravan & Tourist Park (☎ 6471 7239; cnr Jones & Andrews Sts; cabins $90) This beachfront park offers standard prefabricated cabins, which are basic but comfortable. Its close proximity to the village and beach makes it a good option. Pets are not welcome.

Cedar Heights (☎ 6471 7717; cedarheights@vision.net.au; 7 Meredith St; s/d from $85/100) These timber cabins with private courtyards are set back in a quiet street away from the hustle and bustle; the most you'll hear are the sounds of a golf ball being thwacked at the nearby golf course or a game of footy at the oval opposite. One apartment has a spa.

Regatta Point Villas (☎ 6471 7103; fax 6471 7366; Esplanade; d from $120) Near the West Coast Wilderness Railway station at Regatta Point and managed by the local tavern, this place offers eight roomy, self-contained units with fair views.

Gordon Gateway (☎ 6471 7165; 1300 134 425; ggc@tassienet.au; Grining St; studios/chalets/ste $135/210/220) In a scenic hillside location on the way to Regatta Point, this place has 10 modern, well-outfitted, fully self-contained studio units (including a barrier-free room) and several larger A-frame chalets (with spa); all units have excellent views out to Macquarie Harbour and the township. Breakfast is available.

TOP END

Hotels, Guesthouses & B&Bs

Hamers Hotel (☎ 6471 4200, 1800 628 286; fax 6471 4389; Esplanade; s & d $170, apt $200-300) The heritage-listed Hamers offers stylishly enhanced en-suite accommodation, including a balcony room with superb views across the harbour.

Strahan Colonial Cottages (☎ 6471 7077; 1800 777 455; 7 Reid St; d $175-200) Managed by Strahan Central (p275), this is a hillside row of plushly renovated old cottages dating from 1870; there's lots of frill, plaid, gingham and florals thrown in with the comfy furniture. Breakfast provisions are included.

Franklin Manor (☎ 6471 7311; www.franklinmanor.com.au; Esplanade; standard d $185, stables d $220, deluxe d $240) On the foreshore across Risby Cove from the town centre is this especially charming, century-old boutique hideaway with a relaxed ambience and set in lovely grounds on a hillside. There are 14 stylish en suite rooms and four deluxe stables/cottages. Extras you'll appreciate are king-size beds and spa en suite in the deluxe rooms, roaring log fires in winter, a formidably stocked underground cellar and a fine on-site restaurant (p278).

Piners Loft (☎ 6471 7036, 1300 134 425; www.pinersloft.com.au; Grining St; d from $250) This is a good-looking two-storey self-contained lookout (sleeping seven) atop poles of King Billy and celery-top pine. Replete with modern facilities and great water views; breakfast provisions are supplied.

Ormiston House (☎ 6471 7077, 1800 777 455; www.ormistonhouse.com.au; Esplanade; d $200-270) Off West Strahan Beach is this opulent but not overly formal Federation manor and guesthouse with well-appointed rooms and great views. Rich furnishings extend through to the living quarters and there's a great log fire to sit by as you sip on a red. The original scullery is now a bathroom with a deep claw-foot bath. Breakfast is included.

Motels

Strahan Central (☎ 6471 7612; fax 6471 7513; 1 Harold St; d $165-180) This company offers a number of modern, attractive, split-level suites located above its booking office/café. This option offers great views over the township and the price includes continental breakfast.

Risby Cove (☎ 6471 7572; www.risby.com.au; Esplanade; d with/without spa $200/195) This eye-catchingly modern yet rustic (corrugated-iron look) complex on the foreshore, 500m east of the town centre, has lodgings in a large house with great one- and two-bedroom suites (sleeping seven; child-friendly), some overlooking the marina. There are bikes and dinghies for hire, plus a gallery and a high-quality restaurant on-site (p278).

Self-Contained Apartments

Wheelhouse Apartments (☎ 6471 7777; www.wheelhouseapartments.com.au; 4 Frazer St; d $250) Architecturally innovative Wheelhouse's luxuriously appointed apartments (with spa) offer fantastic floor-to-ceiling views of the harbour from their cliff-top perch. Breakfast provisions are supplied and there's wheelchair access.

Strahan Village (☎ 6471 4200, 1800 628 286; fax 6471 4389; Esplanade; d $140-290) This conglomerate runs a group of self-contained cottages and terraces on the waterfront near the booking office, built in various colonial styles and with varying degrees of luxury; some include spa. Breakfast is available and there's access for those in wheelchairs.

Aldermère Estate (☎/fax 6471 7418; aldermereonharvey@bigpond.com; 27 Harvey St; cottage $180, apt with/without spa $250/200) Aldermère has several stylish and luxuriously modern fully self-contained two-storey apartments, with one- or two-bedroom configurations and a self-contained cottage. The apartments are serviced daily and include gas log fires and a hearty continental brekky.

Eating

Banjo's (☎ 6471 7794; Esplanade; pizzas from $10; 🕑 6am-8.30pm) This popular central bakery next to Hamers Hotel serves a wonderful breakfast menu along with snacks such as sandwiches, hot chunky pies and other savouries and pastries. You'll have to wait until after 6pm for its glorious oven-baked pizzas. Nice strong coffee, too.

Hamer's Hotel (☎ 6471 7191; Esplanade; meals $13-25; 🕑 lunch & dinner) This family-friendly joint serves commendable counter meals and grill options, including vegetarian dishes. Carnivores can enjoy unique meals, such as wallaby sirloin, or tuck into some seafood feasts. Other dishes include a selection of pastas and salads. Its public bar is a good spot to down a couple of beers with good views of pavement traffic and the harbour.

Fish Café (☎ 6471 4386; Esplanade; meals $5-10; 🕑 breakfast, lunch & dinner) If you were to survive on takeaway then you've hit the jackpot. This bustling café does a good trade in fresh, succulent seafood, chips, burgers, pies and rolls. Good options include the generous fisherman's box (a medley of seafood and chips; $10), a Strahan souvlaki with chicken ($6), the crumbed flounder ($4) and battered Tasmanian scallops ($1.80 each); eat in or prepare for battle with the seagulls.

Regatta Point Tavern (☎ 6471 7103; Esplanade; mains $16-18; lunch & dinner) If you want to eat with the locals away from the glitz, make your way to this pub, near the railway terminus 2km around the bay from Strahan's centre. It serves good hearty seafood and steak meals in its bistro; there's also a kiddies' menu. Prices are very reasonable.

Strahan Central Café (☎ 6471 7612; 1 Harold St; noon-4pm) This is an unpretentious, licensed place with smoked salmon salad, focaccias and soup for around $10 to $14, plus distinctive daily blackboard specials. It also offers fine scones with jam ($6.40).

Franklin Manor (☎ 6471 7311; Esplanade; mains $30-35; breakfast & dinner) Franklin Manor makes for a deliciously grand dining space. The mod-Oz menu features local produce and changes seasonally, though ocean trout is a fixture, and meals for vegetarians, vegans and coeliac sufferers are easily prepared with advance notice. Wine fanciers will love the huge wine list and the house sommelier is spot on. Bookings are recommended.

Risby Cove (☎ 6471 7572; Esplanade; mains $20-25; lunch & dinner) Risby Cove serves great lunches, teas and dinners top-heavy with seafood in its licensed, innovative water-edged surrounds. Excellent contemporary dishes include pasta, hearty beef meals and a couple of classy vegetarian options, including game and the use of bush herbs.

Entertainment

The Ship That Never Was (☎ 6471 7622; Esplanade; adult/concession/child $13/10/2.50) The Strahan visitors centre stages this play in its amphitheatre. It's the entertainingly theatrical story of some convicts who escaped from Sarah Island in 1834 by building their own ship, and pleases all age groups. Performances are held at 5.30pm year-round, and also at 8.30pm in January.

Risby Cove (☎ 6471 7572; risbycove@bigpond.com; Esplanade; adult/child $8.50/5.50) New release flicks are shown on a big video screen at the Risby Cove Theatrette at 7pm nightly, plus 1pm on Sunday. Ring for details of which movies are playing.

Hamer's Hotel (☎ 6471 4200; Esplanade) This pub sometimes stages live music entertainment. Watch the billboards for what's on.

Getting There & Around

Buses arrive at and depart from the visitors centre. **Strahan Taxis** (☎ 0417-516 071) has services to surrounding attractions like Henty Dunes ($25 per taxi, maximum four people). **Risby Cove** (☎ 6471 7572) rents out bicycles ($15/hr, $10/20 per half/full day).

Those embarking on a cruise can park for free at the wharf car park. Spaces in front of the main shopping area have 30- to 60-minute time limits.

QUEENSTOWN

☎ 03 / pop 3400

The final, winding descent into Queenstown from the Lyell Hwy is unforgettable for its denuded 'moonscape' hills and deep, eroded gullies testifying to the destruction of the local environment by mining. These days mining activities are monitored and sulphur emissions are controlled, and in recent years patches of green have begun appearing on the slopes.

Queenstown is now very busy occupying itself with tourism. Unlike its overcommercialised sister town, Strahan, Queenstown has more of an authentic pioneer village atmosphere popular with visitors for its rich social and industrial history, augmented by the completion of the West Coast Wilderness Railway, which is breathing new life into the township. Just like the surrounding vegetation, the town is making a comeback.

Orientation & Information

Orr St, which meets Driffield St almost directly opposite the West Coast Wilderness Railway station, is the subdued heart of the town. Most shops, hotels and businesses are either on this street or very close by.

The Eric Thomas Galley Museum now houses the **Queenstown visitors centre** (☎ 6471 1483; 1-7 Driffield St), a veritable treasure trove of social and industrial history and run by volunteers with comprehensive information on the region. There's a Commonwealth Bank with ATM on Orr St.

The local **PWS** (☎ 6471 2511; Penghana Rd; 🕑 8am-5pm Mon-Fri), next door to the mine entrance, is the place to find out about nearby walking tracks and to buy national park passes. If you intend to use the Mt McCall Rd, a controversial four-wheel-drive track from the southern end of Lake Burbury to the Franklin River, ask the ranger to issue you with a free permit and a key to the gate. See p43 about the impact of four-wheel driving. There's an after-hours number for permit requests (☎ 6471 2533).

Sights & Activities

ERIC THOMAS GALLEY MUSEUM

This **museum** (☎ 6471 1483; 1-7 Driffield St; adult/pensioners/concession/family $4/3/2.50/10; 🕑 9.30am-6pm Mon-Fri, 12.30-6pm Sat & Sun Oct-Mar, 10am-5pm Mon-Fri, 1-5pm Sat & Sun Apr-Sep) started life as the Imperial Hotel in 1898 and features an intriguing jumble of old photographs, mining equipment, household goods and clothing from Queenstown's past. Particularly impressive are the 800-plus B&W photographs collected by local Eric Thomas and displayed on the walls of seven rooms – most date from before 1940 and have wonderfully idiosyncratic captions written by Mr Thomas. There's wheelchair access to the ground floor.

MINER'S SIDING

Opposite the museum is the Miner's Siding, a public park that features an elevated

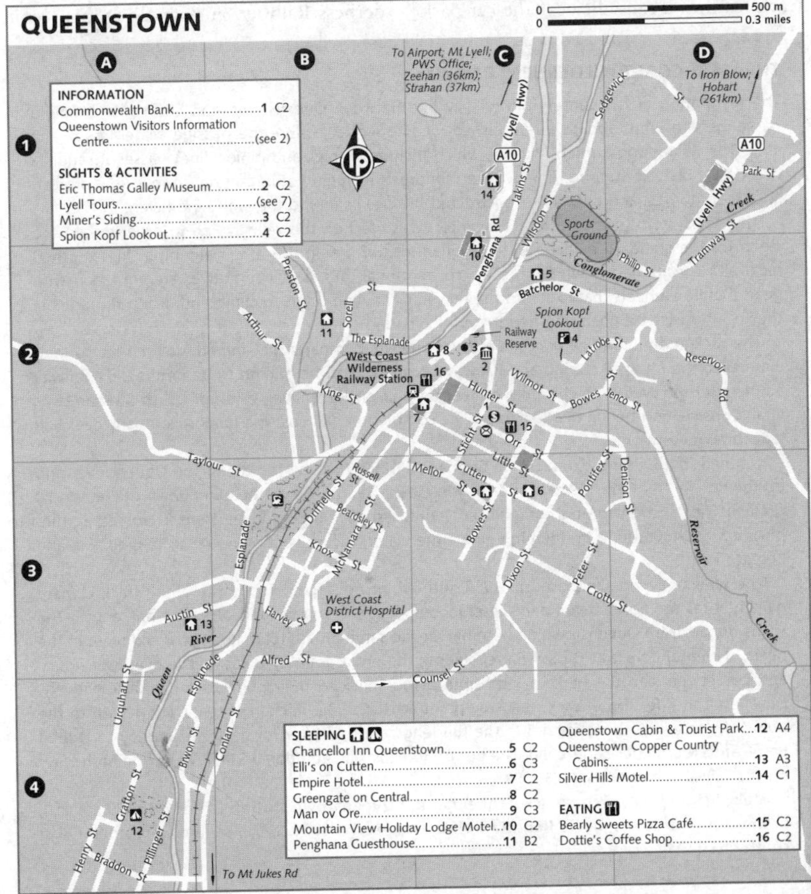

length of railway track and various rock, bronze and Huon-pine sculptures – up until the recommissioning of the Abt Railway, a restored Abt locomotive was parked here. This was Queenstown's centenary project and the sculptures tell the story of the Abt Railway's journey to Strahan and a hundred years of mining. Fittingly, the siding is located where the original train station used to be.

SPION KOPF LOOKOUT

Follow Hunter St uphill, turn left onto Bowes St, then do a sharp left onto Latrobe St to a small car park, from where a short, steep track leads to the summit of Spion Kopf (named by soldiers after a battle in the Boer war). The rhododendron-lined track features a rail adit near the car park and the top of the hill has a pithead on it. The panoramic views of town are excellent, particularly at sunset.

IRON BLOW

On top of the pass on the Lyell Hwy at Gormanston Hill, just before the final descent along hairpin bends into Queenstown, is a sealed side road leading to a lookout over the geological wound of Iron Blow. This is the now-deserted and flooded open-cut mine where the town's illustrious mining career began in 1883.

MT JUKES RD

Continue south along Conlan St to Mt Jukes Rd, which will take you to side roads leading to sections of the West Coast Wilderness Railway. Further along this scenic

THE WEST COAST WILDERNESS RAILWAY

The restoration of the century-old railway line between Queenstown and Strahan is enabling passengers to jump aboard a refurbished locomotive to explore the pristine wilderness of the area. The 35km-long stretch (8km of which includes a rack-and-pinion line) passes through a half-dozen historic stations, immaculate rainforest (including stunning dense myrtle rainforest) and deep gorges, and over 40 reconstructed bridges spanning the wild King River.

The Abt system (named after its inventor) was used on this railway line to cover terrain too steep for the standard haulage of large quantities of ore. In this arrangement, a third toothed rack rail is positioned between the two conventional rails, and locomotives are equipped with geared pinion wheels that lock into the rack rail, allowing trains to climb and descend gradients they'd otherwise be unable to negotiate fully loaded.

The rack-and-pinion line was the reason why the company that mined Mt Lyell for so long was called the Mt Lyell Mining and Railway Company. For the mining to be profitable, a railway connecting Mt Lyell with the port of Teepookana on King River, and later with Strahan, was vital. Construction began in 1894 and by its completion had cost the mining company over half its capital investment.

Opened in 1896 and extended to Strahan in 1899, the line ran along the Queen River and up the one-in-16 gradient Abt section to Rinadeena Saddle, before heading down the one-in-20 gradient Abt section through magnificent rainforest to the King River. Here it crossed a stunning, curved 400m-long bridge high above the water, before continuing on to Teepookana and Regatta Point.

The railway eventually closed in 1963 and fell into disrepair. Today the entire track is magnificently restored and steam and diesel locomotives take passengers along its full length. The trains depart from Queenstown and Strahan at the same times (10am and 3pm) and meet in the heart of the rainforest at Dubbil Barrel station; the entire journey takes a little over four hours, and passengers can then take a later train or bus back to their point of origin. Alternatively, travellers can ride to the track's halfway point at Dubbil Barril, change trains and return to the point of departure. Costs for riding the full length one way, or for a return journey to Dubbil Barril, are $100/55 per adult/child. The bus option costs an additional $14/7, or to ride both ways on the railway costs $195/110.

Make inquiries or purchase tickets at either the **Queenstown station** (☎ 6471 1700; Driffield St), in the centre of town, or the **Regatta Point station** (☎ 1800 628 288), on the waterfront 1.5km south of Strahan's centre.

road (9km south of Queenstown) is **Newall Creek**, where a platform provides access to a patch of superb King Billy and Huon-pine rainforest. The bitumen section of the road ends at **Lake Burbury**, a mountain-surrounded Hydro Tasmania lake that can be seen to magnificent effect from a lookout on the descent to its shores (see also p282). All roads past the dam wall are for four-wheel drive only – the best way to visit the places further south is with Lyell Tours (below).

Tours

MINE TOURS

The open-cut section of the Mt Lyell Mine is no longer worked, but mining continues deep beneath the massive West Lyell crater.

Douggies Mine Tours (☎ 6471 1472) An underground mine tour ($58 per person; 2½ hours). Tours leave at 8.15am, 10.15am and 1.15pm (and 7.30pm by demand) with a minimum of two people and maximum of eight. You're able to view the working machinery and get to chat with the miners themselves. Children under 12 years are not allowed and bookings are essential.

Lyell Tours (☎ 6471 2388) A one-hour surface tour departs from outside the Empire Hotel daily at 9.15am and 4.30pm (4pm daily June to August) and costs $18/9 per adult/child. The underground tour takes 2½ hours and costs $55 per adult (children under 12 not admitted); ring to ask about departure times. Bookings are essential and participants must wear long sleeves, long pants and enclosed shoes.

Sleeping

BUDGET

Lake Burbury camping ground, a 15-minute drive from Queenstown, is a scenic alternative to accommodation in town (for details see p282).

Queenstown Cabin & Tourist Park (☎ 6471 1332; fax 6471 1125; 17 Grafton St; unpowered/powered sites $18/22, dm $15, on-site vans $45, cabins $75) About 500m south of the town centre, this park is an adequate option, with communal kitchen and sheltered barbecue area. It has an ultra-budget lodge with basic rooms sleeping two to four people, spotless vans and cabins, and also manages the simple timber **Jukes Cottage** and **Owen Cottage** (d/q from $100/150).

Empire Hotel (☎ 6471 1699; empirehotel@tassie.net.au; 2 Orr St; s $30, d with/without bathroom $50/40) This is a majestic, century-old hotel that dominates the town centre. Constructed from timbers that were sent to England to be wood-turned and then shipped back to Queenstown, it contains an imposing Blackwood staircase classified by the National Trust, and fair budget rooms.

Mountain View Holiday Lodge Motel (☎ 6471 1163; fax 6471 1306; 1 Penghana Rd; dm/s/d from $15/65/75) This motel has shared accommodation in four-bed rooms, each with its own toilet and shower, and small one- and two-bedroom motel units. There's an adequate campers kitchen available and an on-site bistro/restaurant serving breakfast and dinner.

Queenstown Copper Country Cabins (☎ 0417 398 343; fax 6471 1086; 13 Austin St; s $65-75, d $70-95) This is a compact collection of modern, self-contained timber cabins, one of which is equipped for disabled travellers. The cabins are incredibly neat and tidy and there are laundry facilities nearby.

MIDRANGE

Greengate on Central (☎ 6471 1144, fax 6471 2507; 7 Railway Reserve; apt from $90) Greengate is a charming home offering very comfy self-contained lodgings just a hop, skip & jump across the railway tracks behind the railway station.

Silver Hills Motel (☎ 6471 1755; Penghana Rd; tw $95, d $105-115) This silvery gem has lots of refurbished motel shackettes, but the views from the top floors of the brick units at the back are pretty good. The rooms include electric blankets, TV, fridge and tea- and coffee-making facilities. If you can't be bothered fending for yourself then head to its à la carte restaurant (p282).

Elli's on Cutten (☎ 0407 712 285; samarah@our.net.au; 55 Cutten St; d $120) This option is a spacious self-contained two-bedroom holiday home. It sleeps up to six people comfortably, providing a unique bathtub to soak in and a cosy wood fire to snuggle up to. There's also a fully equipped kitchen with continental breakfast provisions, a full sized fridge, TV, VCR and electric blankets. All linen is supplied, there's a washing machine and drier, and weekly tariffs are also available.

Man ov Ore (☎ 6471 1210; www.manovore.com; cnr Cutten & Bowes Sts; d $120-140) Built in 1897, this stately Victorian home is like staying within the confines of indulgent pleasure. This colonial option has a 'boudoir' atmosphere with rich, red painted décor and antique furniture. It includes a fully equipped kitchen with breakfast provisions and four very comfortable and spacious bedrooms; there's an en suite in the main bedroom.

TOP END

Penghana (☎ 6471 2560; fax 6471 1535; 32 The Esplanade, access via Preston St; d with/without bathroom from $150/110) This National Trust listed mansion was built in 1898 for the first general manager of the Mt Lyell Mining & Railway Co, and, as befits its managerial stature, is located on a hill above town amid a rare number of trees. The B&B accommodation here is first-rate and includes a billiards room and a grand dining room to enjoy chef-prepared à la carte meals (Wednesday to Sunday).

Eating

Dotties Coffeeshop (☎ 6471 1700; Queenstown Station, Driffield St; 🕑 breakfast, lunch & dinner) Dotties is a good option if you're a bit of a train spotter. Serving smooth, creamy coffee and a selection of café delights, such as gourmet pies, pastries, cakes and biscuits, you can also sit alfresco on the train platform itself.

Empire Hotel (☎ 6471 1699; 2 Orr St; mains $12-17; 🕑 lunch & dinner) This old miner's pub has survived the ages and includes an atmospheric heritage dining room serving a changing menu of hearty pub standards, including well-priced lamb rissoles, pasta and other more exotic favourites, such as *rogan josh*.

Silver Hills Motel (☎ 6471 1755; Penghana Rd; mains from $10; breakfast & dinner) Don't let the bunker-style look of this motel's exterior scare you, the fully licensed à la carte restaurant here is enormous with inviting décor and friendly service. It serves up a range of familiar dishes, such as steaks, grills, roasts and rice dishes, and there's also a separate children's menu.

Bearly Sweets Pizza Café (☎ 21 Orr St; pizzas $10-19; 🕑 dinner) This friendly place suggests over 20 different takes on the humble pizza – if you need to get a filling meal you can't go wrong with this fab option. The family-sized *capricciosa* is terrific value.

DETOUR

Heading south out of Queenstown along Conlan St to Mt Jukes Rd for about 15 minutes you'll come to the end of the bitumen road, which will lead you straight to **Lake Burbury**. Built as a large hydroelectric dam, its construction flooded 6km of old Lyell Hwy. Situated within the Princess River Conservation Area, the scenery around the lake is magnificent, especially when there's snow on the nearby peaks. There are impressive vistas from the attractive shoreline **camping ground** (unpowered sites $5) just east of Bradshaw Bridge (there's a caretaker; site price includes up to two people), there's a public picnic area with sheltered electric barbecues and a children's playground. The lake is also a trout fishing Mecca. You can also camp for free on the other side of the lake but the environment is less salubrious: dirt sites, no facilities.

Getting There & Away

Buses arrive at and depart from the milk bar at 65 Orr St.

See p267 for more information.

FRANKLIN-GORDON WILD RIVERS NATIONAL PARK

This environmentally awesome park is part of the Tasmanian Wilderness World Heritage Area and includes the catchments of the Franklin, Olga and Gordon Rivers. The park was proclaimed in 1981 thanks to the lobbying efforts of the Tasmanian Wilderness Society (TWS), the organised conservation group that emerged in the aftermath of the failed campaign to stop the Hydro Electric Commission (HEC; now Hydro Tasmania) from flooding Lake Pedder.

The TWS, trying to prevent the HEC from building more dams on the lower Gordon and Franklin Rivers, pushed for World Heritage listing for the area, a nomination duly made in 1981 by the federal government. In the same year, the Tasmanian government held a referendum asking the public to choose between two different dam schemes. Despite being told that writing 'No Dams' on their ballot papers would render their votes informal, 46% of voters did just that, a big indication of public dissatisfaction with *any* dam scheme.

While this referendum was being conducted, state parliament was in turmoil, with both the premier and the opposition party leader being dumped over the issue. A state election was forced that resulted in a change of government, but the new governing party also supported the HEC dam project. When the World Heritage Committee eventually announced the area's World Heritage listing and expressed concern over the proposed dam, the new premier attempted to have the listing withdrawn.

The TWS and other conservation groups turned their attention to federal politics. In May 1982, at a Canberra by-election, 41% of voters wrote 'No Dams' on their ballot papers, but the federal government still refused to intervene.

Dam construction began in 1982, and almost immediately, protesters set off from Strahan to stage what became known as the 'Franklin River Blockade'. They protested peacefully, but even so, the Tasmanian government passed special laws allowing protesters to be arrested, fined and jailed: in the summer of 1982–83, 1400 people were arrested in a confrontation so intense it received international news coverage.

The Franklin River became a major issue in the 1983 federal election, in which the reigning party was defeated and the country's new political supervisors stepped in to fully implement the Franklin and Gordon Rivers' World Heritage assignation. After its victory, the TWS changed its name to the Wilderness Society and remains involved in conservation issues Australia-wide.

The national park's most significant peak is **Frenchmans Cap** (1443m), with a magnificent white-quartzite top that can be seen from the west coast and from the Lyell Hwy. The mountain was formed by glacial action and has Tasmania's tallest cliff face.

The park also contains a number of unique plant species and major Aboriginal sites. The most significant is **Kutikina Cave**, where over 50,000 artefacts have been found, dating from the cave's 5000-year-long occupation between 14,000 and 20,000 years ago. The only way to reach the cave, which is on Aboriginal land in remote forest, is by rafting down the Franklin.

Much of the park consists of deep river gorges and impenetrable rainforest, but the Lyell Hwy traverses its northern end. Along this road are a number of signposted features of note, including a few short walks that you can take to see just what this park is all about.

Collingwood River This is the usual starting point for rafting the Franklin River, of which the Collingwood is a tributary. You can camp for free here; there are pit toilets and fireplaces.

Donaghys Hill Located 4km east of the bridge over the Collingwood River, this 40-minute return walk leads to the top of the hill above the junction of the Collingwood and Franklin Rivers. It has spectacular views of the Franklin and Frenchmans Cap.

Franklin River Nature Trail From the picnic ground where the highway crosses the river, a 25-minute return nature trail has been marked through the forest.

Frenchmans Cap Six kilometres further east is the start of the three- to five-day walk to Frenchmans Cap, the park's best known bushwalk. It has two shelter huts along the way and lots of lovely, deep mud. Even if you don't intend doing the whole bushwalk, you'll enjoy the initial 15-minute walk along the banks of the Franklin River. You can take a TassieLink-scheduled service to the beginning of this walk – see p267 for details.

Nelson River Just east of Lake Burbury, at the bottom of Victoria Pass, is an easy 20-minute return walk through rainforest to the excellent, 35m-high Nelson Falls. Signs beside the track highlight common plants of the area.

Rafting the Franklin

Rafting the very wild Franklin River makes for an utterly sensational but hazardous journey. Experienced rafters can tackle it if they're fully equipped and prepared. For the inexperienced (who make up about 90% of all Franklin raftees), there are tour companies offering complete rafting packages. Whether you go with an independent group or a tour operator, you should contact the park rangers at the **Lake St Clair visitors centre** (☎ 6289 1172; Cynthia Bay; 🕑 8am-5pm winter, to 7pm or 8pm summer), which also has the latest information on permits and regulations, or the **Queenstown PWS office** (☎ 6471 2511; Penghana Rd) for current information on permits, regulations and environmental considerations. You should also check out the detailed Franklin rafting notes on the PWS website www.parks.tas.gov.au.

All expeditions should register at the booth at the junction of the Lyell Hwy and the Collingwood River, 49km west of Derwent Bridge. The trip down the Franklin, starting at Collingwood River and ending at Sir John Falls, takes between eight and 14 days. Shorter trips on certain sections of the river are also possible. From the exit point, you can be picked up by a **Wilderness Air** (☎ 6471 7280; wildair@tassie.net.au) seaplane or paddle a further 22km downriver to a Gordon River cruise boat.

You can also just do half the river. The upper Franklin takes around eight days from Collingwood River to the Fincham Track – it passes through Irenabyss Gorge and you can scale Frenchmans Cap as a side trip. The lower Franklin takes seven days from the Fincham Track to Sir John Falls and passes through Great Ravine. These trips are really only practical for tour groups, as the Fincham Track requires a four-wheel-drive vehicle and is a long way from the main highways.

These tour companies offer complete rafting packages:

Rafting Tasmania (☎ 6239 1080; raftingtas@ozemail.com.au) Has five-/seven-/10-day trips costing $1400/1650/2150.

Tasmanian Expeditions (☎ 6334 3477, 1800 030 230; www.tas-ex.com) Another operator with nine-/11-day trips for $2190/2450.

Water By Nature (☎ 1800 111 142, 0408 242 941; www.franklinrivertasmania.com) This new operator (formerly Peregrine) provides five-/seven-/10-day trips for $1390/1690/2250.

MAPS

You'll need Tasmap's 1:100,000 *Olga and Franklin* and 1:25,000 *Loddon* maps, available from the Tasmanian Map Centre and Service Tasmania in Hobart (p68). A laminated Wilderness Guides map may also be available from outdoor-equipment shops.

CRADLE MOUNTAIN–LAKE ST CLAIR NATIONAL PARK

☎ 03

Tasmania's best-known national park is the superb 1262-sq-km World Heritage area of Cradle Mountain–Lake St Clair. Its spectacular mountain peaks, deep gorges, lakes, tarns and wild moorlands extend from the Great Western Tiers in the north to Derwent Bridge on the Lyell Hwy in the south. It was one of the most glaciated areas in Australia and includes Mt Ossa (1617m), Tasmania's highest peak, and Lake St Clair, Australia's deepest (over 200m) natural freshwater lake.

The preservation of this region as a national park was due in part to Gustav Weindorfer, an Austrian who fell in love with this area and felt that everyone should be able to enjoy it. See p290.

There are plenty of day walks in Cradle Valley and at Cynthia Bay (Lake St Clair; Leeawuleena to the indigenous people, which means 'sleeping water'), but it's the spectacular 80.5km-long Overland Track between the two that has turned this park into a bushwalker's Mecca. At the time of writing the conditions for walking the track were under review; see p288 for more details.

INFORMATION

All walking tracks in the park are signposted, well defined and easy to follow, but it's still advisable to carry a map, which can be purchased at the park's visitors centres.

Cradle Valley

There are now two visitor information centres. Immediately opposite the Cradle Mountain Tourist Park and 3km north of the park's boundary is the new **Cradle information centre** (☎ 6492 1110; Cradle Mountain Rd; 🕒 8.30am-4.30pm) with its vast car park. This is the starting point for the bus shuttle service (p293) into the national park; here you can purchase park passes, bushwalking information, food and fuel. Within the park boundaries itself lies the PWS-run **Cradle Mountain visitors centre** (☎ 6492 1133; www.parks.tas.gov.au; 🕒 8am-5pm Jun-Aug, 8am-6pm Sep-May), which provides extensive bushwalking information, reference videos, a PWS shop and interesting displays about the flora, fauna and history of the park. The centre is staffed by rangers who can advise you on weather conditions, walking gear, and bush safety and etiquette. The static and audiovisual displays on the region are worth spending some time on and, in summer, the rangers run many free informative and educational activities. The centre has a public telephone, toilets, drinking water and eftpos (maximum withdrawal $50). It's also wheelchair accessible and accepts major credit cards.

Dove Lake has flushing toilets but no drinking water, while Waldheim has composting toilets, drinking water and a very good day-use hut with gas heaters.

Attention all food and wine devotees: mid-June sees the popular **Tastings at the Top**, usually held at Cradle Mountain Lodge (p291). This is three days of tasting gastronomic delights, sampling a bevy of wine, and attending workshops by food and wine specialists.

Whatever time of the year you visit, be prepared for cold, wet weather in the Cradle Valley area: it rains on seven days out of 10, is cloudy on eight days out of 10, the sun shines all day only one day in 10, and it snows on 54 days each year (see also right).

Cynthia Bay

Occupying one wing of a large building at Cynthia Bay, on the southern boundary of the park, is the **Lake St Clair visitors centre** (☎ 6289 1172; 8am-7pm Dec & Jan, to 8pm Feb, to 5pm Mar-Nov). Apart from providing all the necessary information on the Cradle Mountain–Lake St Clair National Park (as well as on the Franklin-Gordon Wild Rivers National Park), the centre also has displays on the area's geology, flora and fauna, bushwalkers and Tasmanian Aborigines. There's fibre-work by three indigenous artists, which acknowledges the island's nine Aboriginal nations (see p289 for details of the indigenous cultural walk at Cynthia Bay).

At the adjacent, separately run **Lakeside St Clair Wilderness Park** (☎ 6289 1137; www.lakestclairwildernessholidays.com.au; 8am-5pm winter, to 7pm or 8pm summer), you can book a range of accommodation (see p292), a seat on a ferry or cruise (p293), which is also available for charter, or hire dinghies.

THE OVERLAND TRACK

Information

A handy pocket-sized reference for the walk is *The Overland Track – A Walkers Notebook*, published by the PWS and detailing all sections of the track and the flora and fauna that live there. A good website is www.overlandtrack.com.au.

The best time to walk the Overland Track is during summer, when flowering plants are most prolific (also December to April sees longer daylight hours and warmer average temperatures), although spring and autumn also have their attractions. You can walk the track in winter, but only if you're very experienced.

The Track

The track can be walked in either direction, but most people walk from north to south. Walkers sometimes start at Dove Lake, but the recommended route actually begins at Ronny Creek, a walk of around 5km from the visitors centre. The start of the track was shifted here from Waldheim Chalet a few years ago, adding 500m of easy boardwalk to the route.

The trail is well marked for its entire length and, at an easy pace, takes around five or six days to walk. Along the track are numerous secondary paths leading up to features like **Mt Ossa**, so the length of time you take is only limited by the amount of supplies you carry. Although the track takes you through wilderness, it's so well used that you can expect to meet many walkers each day – each year approximately 9000 people hike this path. Concerns are mounting, however, for the environmental degradation and overcrowding of the track; see p288 for changes introduced to the way the Overland Track is managed.

There are unattended huts along the track that you can use for accommodation, but in summer they fill up quickly so make

WEATHER WARNING

In summer the weather is often fine, but snowfalls, howling winds, sleet, relentless rain and a blazing sun are also regular features. You must be prepared to walk in cold, wet conditions and, if necessary, to camp in snow. A significant number of those who walk the track for the first time have inadequate clothing and equipment – be warned that when very cold or stormy weather occurs, the walk can transform from an adventure to, at best, a highly uncomfortable experience or, at worst, a serious health-threatening venture.

The most dangerous part of the walk is the northern half, along the exposed high plateau between Waldheim and Pelion Creek, particularly near Mt Pelion West. The southwest wind that blows across here can be dangerously cold and sometimes strong enough to knock you off your feet.

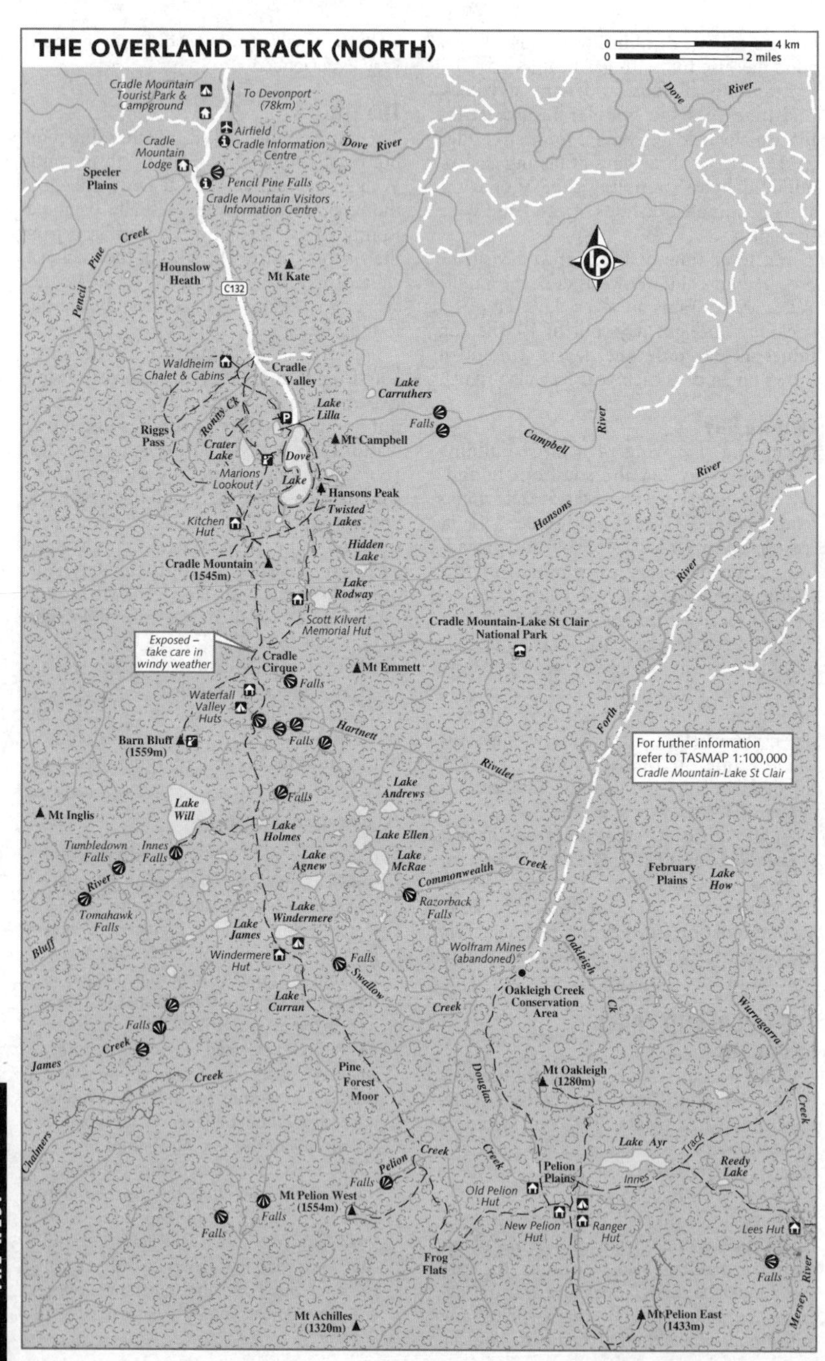
THE OVERLAND TRACK (NORTH)
0 4 km
0 2 miles
Cradle Mountain Tourist Park & Campground
To Devonport (78km)
Airfield
Cradle Information Centre
Dove River
Cradle Mountain Lodge
Speeler Plains
Pencil Pine Falls
Cradle Mountain Visitors Information Centre
Pencil Pine Creek
Hounslow Heath
Mt Kate
C132
Waldheim Chalet & Cabins
Cradle Valley
Lake Carruthers
Lake Lilla
Falls
Riggs Pass
Ronny Ck
Crater Lake
Dove Lake
Mt Campbell
Campbell River
Marions Lookout
Hansons Peak
Twisted Lakes
Hansons River
Kitchen Hut
Hidden Lake
Cradle Mountain (1545m)
Lake Rodway
Scott Kilvert Memorial Hut
Cradle Mountain-Lake St Clair National Park
Exposed – take care in windy weather
Cradle Cirque
Mt Emmett
Waterfall Valley Huts
Hartnett Rivulet
Barn Bluff (1559m)
Forth River
For further information refer to TASMAP 1:100,000 Cradle Mountain-Lake St Clair
Lake Andrews
Mt Inglis
Lake Will
Lake Holmes
Lake Ellen
Tumbledown Falls
Innes Falls
Lake Agnew
Lake McRae
Commonwealth Creek
February Plains
Lake How
Bluff River
Tomahawk Falls
Razorback Falls
Lake Windermere
Lake James
Windermere Hut
Wolfram Mines (abandoned)
Oakleigh Ck
Swallow Creek
Lake Curran
Oakleigh Creek Conservation Area
Wurragarra Creek
James Creek
Chalmers Creek
Pine Forest Moor
Douglas Creek
Mt Oakleigh (1280m)
Lake Ayr
Pelion Creek
Innes Track
Reedy Lake
Pelion Plains
Old Pelion Hut
Mt Pelion West (1554m)
New Pelion Hut
Ranger Hut
Lees Hut
Frog Flats
Mersey River
Mt Achilles (1320m)
Mt Pelion East (1433m)

THE WEST

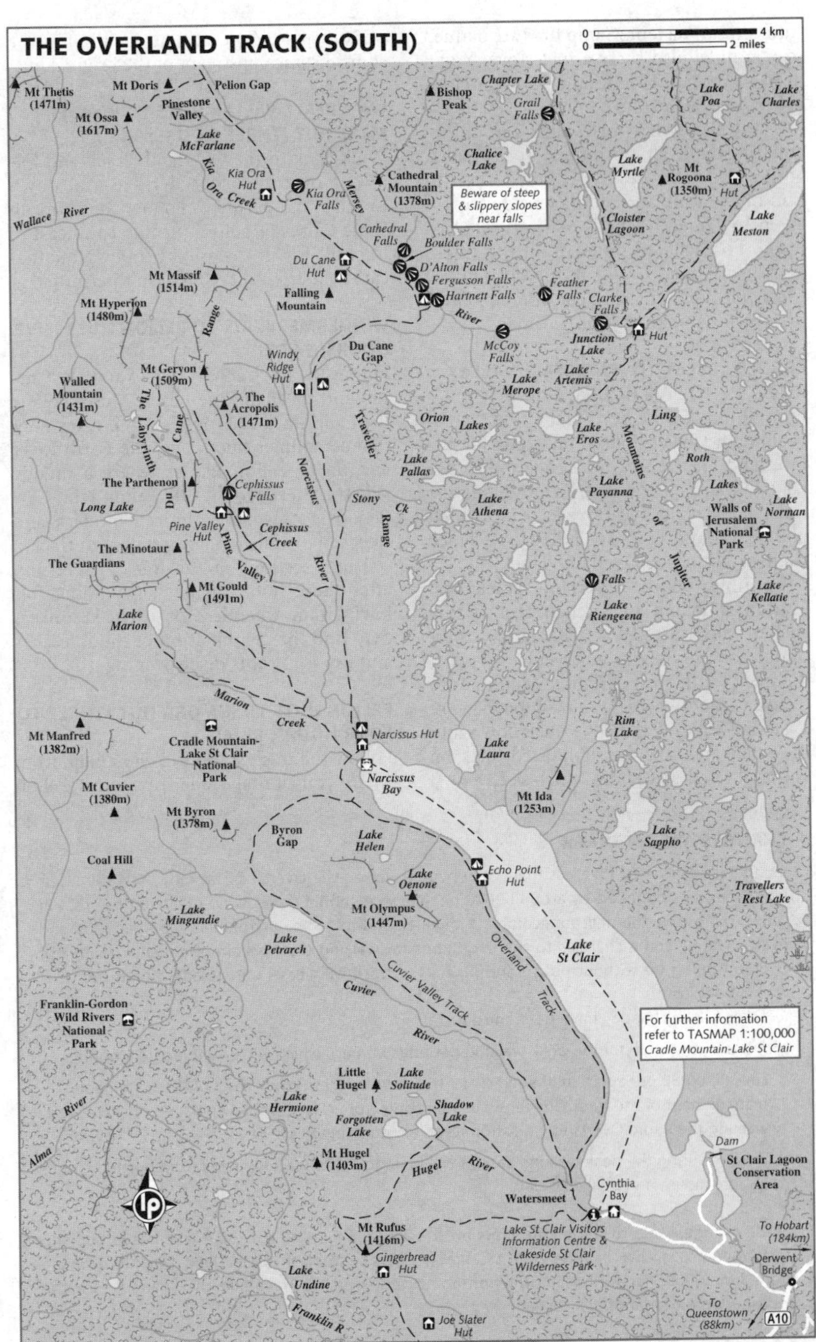
THE OVERLAND TRACK (SOUTH)
0 4 km
0 2 miles
Mt Thetis (1471m)
Mt Doris
Pelion Gap
Mt Ossa (1617m)
Pinestone Valley
Lake McFarlane
Kia Ora Creek
Kia Ora Hut
Kia Ora Falls
Mersey
Bishop Peak
Chapter Lake
Grail Falls
Chalice Lake
Lake Poa
Lake Charles
Lake Myrtle
Mt Rogoona (1350m)
Hut
Lake Meston
Cathedral Mountain (1378m)
Beware of steep & slippery slopes near falls
Cloister Lagoon
Wallace River
Cathedral Falls
Boulder Falls
D'Alton Falls
Fergusson Falls
Hartnett Falls
Du Cane Hut
Mt Massif (1514m)
Falling Mountain
Feather Falls
Clarke Falls
Mt Hyperion (1480m)
River
McCoy Falls
Junction Lake
Hut
Du Cane Gap
Windy Ridge Hut
Range
Mt Geryon (1509m)
Lake Merope
Lake Artemis
Walled Mountain (1431m)
The Acropolis (1471m)
The Labyrinth
Du Cane
Traveller
Orion Lakes
Ling
Lake Eros
Mountains of Jupiter
Roth
Lake Pallas
Narcissus
The Parthenon
Cephissus Falls
Stony Ck
Lake Payanna
Lakes
Long Lake
Lake Athena
Walls of Jerusalem National Park
Lake Norman
Pine Valley Hut
Cephissus Creek
Range
The Minotaur
Pine Valley
The Guardians
River
Mt Gould (1491m)
Falls
Lake Kellatie
Lake Riengeena
Lake Marion
Marion Creek
Rim Lake
Mt Manfred (1382m)
Cradle Mountain-Lake St Clair National Park
Narcissus Hut
Lake Laura
Narcissus Bay
Mt Cuvier (1380m)
Mt Ida (1253m)
Mt Byron (1378m)
Byron Gap
Lake Helen
Lake Sappho
Coal Hill
Echo Point Hut
Lake Oenone
Travellers Rest Lake
Lake Mingundie
Mt Olympus (1447m)
Lake Petrarch
Overland Track
Lake St Clair
Cuvier Valley Track
Cuvier River
Franklin-Gordon Wild Rivers National Park
For further information refer to TASMAP 1:100,000 Cradle Mountain-Lake St Clair
Little Hugel
Lake Solitude
Lake Hermione
Shadow Lake
Alma River
Forgotten Lake
Dam
St Clair Lagoon Conservation Area
Mt Hugel (1403m)
Hugel River
Watersmeet
Cynthia Bay
Mt Rufus (1416m)
Lake St Clair Visitors Information Centre & Lakeside St Clair Wilderness Park
To Hobart (184km)
Gingerbread Hut
Derwent Bridge
Lake Undine
Franklin R
Joe Slater Hut
To Queenstown (88km)
A10

THE WEST

sure you carry a tent. Camp fires are banned so you must also carry a fuel stove. You'll need a park pass to enter the park, purchasable from the visitors centres.

The walk itself is extremely varied, negotiating high alpine moors, rocky scree, gorges and tall forest. A detailed description of the walk and all major side trips is given in Lonely Planet's *Walking in Australia*. For detailed notes of all the tracks in the park, read *Cradle Mountain-Lake St Clair and Walls of Jerusalem National Parks* by John Chapman & John Siseman.

CRADLE VALLEY TO WATERFALL VALLEY HUTS (3½ TO FIVE HOURS; 13KM)

From Ronny Creek, beyond the side road to Waldheim Chalet, follow the signs for the Overland Track past Crater Falls and Crater Lake to Marions Lookout. Avoid taking the track to Lake Lilla and Dove Lake (to the left of the Overland Track) and the Horse Track (to the right of the Overland Track).

Continue on the Overland Track past Marions Lookout to Kitchen Hut, a tiny shelter with no toilet/water facilities, permitted for use only in emergencies. Follow the track to the west of Cradle Mountain to Cradle Cirque, where there are good views of Waterfall Valley. Follow the track down into the valley and take the signposted track on your right to the two huts, which sleep a total of 28 people. Tent sites are in the forest a short distance upstream of the original hut.

WATERFALL VALLEY HUTS TO WINDERMERE HUT (THREE HOURS; 9KM)

Walk back to the Overland Track and follow it over an exposed ridge and down to Lake Windermere. Follow the shore to some tent sites before turning southeast to the hut, which sleeps 40 people. Note that camping around the lake isn't permitted.

WINDERMERE HUT TO PELION HUTS (FIVE HOURS; 14KM)

Follow the track across a creek to Lake Curran and through Pine Forest Moor. Follow the main track to Frog Flats and camp sites that sometimes flood, over the Forth River and on to Pelion Plains, where a muddy side track leads to the Old Pelion Hut. New Pelion Hut, which is indeed modern and sleeps 60, is further along the main track.

Large sections of the track before and after these huts can be heavy-going following rain, when less experienced walkers may find the combination of mud, leeches and exposed roots disheartening.

PELION HUTS TO KIA ORA HUT (THREE TO FOUR HOURS; 8KM)

Follow the track south to Pelion Gap, from where you can take side trips to Mt Pelion

CHANGES ARE ON TRACK

In 1953 it's estimated that less than 1000 people walked the Overland Track; by 2004 the Overland Track was pounded by around 9000 people, so it should come as no great surprise that in order to preserve the delicate ecology of the area and to avoid environmental degradation and overcrowding, some changes to the conditions for walking the track are required. The idea of people turning up without notice and hiking the track will cease, particularly during the peak walking season.

Three major changes have been introduced:

- A booking system for the peak walking period (summer), which will be subject to a quota.
- Fees ($100/80 per adult/child aged six to 16 & pensioner) to cover costs of the sustainable management of the track. The fees will only apply from November to April, and only to those walking the entire Overland Track from Cradle Mountain to Lake St Clair.
- Visitors during the peak walking season will be required to walk the track from north to south (Cradle Mountain to Lake St Clair).

These changes were to come into effect for the 2005–06 walking season. A web-based booking system was to go live in June 2005 to allow walkers to book their Overland Track hike online from June 2005. For further information about the Overland Track and the changes visit the website www.overlandtrack.com.au.

East (1½ hours return) and Mt Ossa (three hours return), the highest point in Tasmania. From Pelion Gap, follow the track into Pinestone Valley, where you'll cross Pinestone Creek. Continue on to Kia Ora Hut, which sleeps 24 people. Limited tent sites are nearby.

KIA ORA HUT TO WINDY RIDGE HUT (THREE TO FOUR HOURS; 11KM)

Follow the track across Kia Ora Creek and on to Du Cane Hut, which is National Trust registered and no longer used, except in emergencies. Some good camp sites are available in the hut's vicinity. Continue about 2.5km to the signposted turn-off to Hartnett Falls, an excellent side trip that takes about one hour return. If you do take this track, make sure you continue from the top of the falls (where there are tent sites) down to the river and upstream to the gorge at the falls' base.

Return to the Overland Track and climb to Du Cane Gap, then descend to Windy Ridge Hut, which sleeps 24. Poor camp sites are available a little to the north, near what's left of an earlier hut.

WINDY RIDGE HUT TO NARCISSUS HUT (THREE HOURS; 9KM)

Follow the track across substantial sections of boardwalk and a bridge to Narcissus Hut. About halfway along, there's a track on the right leading to Pine Valley and onward to The Labyrinth and The Acropolis (1471m), a highly recommended side trip. To reach Pine Valley Hut takes 1½ hours and from there you should allow another three to five hours to ascend The Acropolis summit, where the views on a clear day are magnificent.

From Narcissus Hut, simply complete the track on foot via the Overland Track. A longer and more scenic route is the Cuvier Valley Track (seven hours; 19km), which branches off to the right of the main track 1km from the raised bridge at Hamilton Creek. This route is more suited to the experienced walker since it's significantly more difficult than other routes: there's little or no track to follow, rather a series of not always easily seen markers. In addition, part of the route follows a water course (read: knee-high mud) and thus should only be walked in very dry conditions.

Alternatively, you can radio Lakeside St Clair Wilderness Park from Narcissus Hut to get one of their ferries to come and pick you up; this will save you a five-hour (17km) walk. See p293 for details.

It can occasionally be an ordeal to get a seat on the ferry: bookings are unreliable (book before you begin the trek, and *always* reconfirm by radio when you arrive at the hut); seats on the ferry are limited (if you miss out on a seat, you'll have to wait for the next scheduled service); and the batteries in the radio may be flat (not unheard of), in which case you may be stuck at Narcissus until a boat turns up of its own accord.

OTHER BUSHWALKS

Cradle Valley

The visitors centre features an easy but quite spectacular 10-minute circular boardwalk through the adjacent rainforest called the **Rainforest Walk**; it's more than suitable for wheelchairs and prams. There's another boarded path nearby leading to **Pencil Pine Falls** and on to **Knyvet Falls** (25 minutes return), as well as the **Enchanted Nature Walk** alongside Pencil Pine Creek (25 minutes return). The boardwalk running the 8.5km-long **Cradle Valley walk** between the visitors centre and Dove Lake is also wheelchair-friendly.

Crater Lake is a popular two-hour return walk from Ronny Creek. You can also climb **Cradle Mountain**, but this takes a full day to complete: allow seven hours return.

Walks also start from **Dove Lake**. The best walk in the area is the circuit of the lake itself, which takes two to three hours to complete. All other walks involve steep climbs – the four-hour return walk to **Mt Campbell** and the **Twisted Lakes** provides great views of Cradle Mountain and nearby lakes.

Cynthia Bay

The **Larmairremener tabelti** is an Aboriginal culture walk that winds through the traditional lands of the Larmairremener, the indigenous people of the region. The walk (one hour return) starts at the visitors centre and loops around through Watersmeet before leading along the lake's shoreline back to the centre. From Watersmeet, you can also take the **Platypus Bay Circuit** (30 minutes return). Most other walks are fairly long: the circuit of **Shadow Lake** takes four hours return, while the **Mt Rufus** circuit is seven hours return.

One way to do some good walking is to catch the ferry service to either Echo Point Hut or Narcissus Hut and walk back to Cynthia Bay along the lake shore. From Echo Point it's about three to five hours' walk back, and from Narcissus Hut it's about five to six hours.

TOURS

Bushwalking

Craclair (☎ 6339 4488; www.craclair.com.au) This is the most experienced company at running guided bushwalking tours in this national park. It runs eight-day tours along the Overland Track for $1485 per person. This is a good way to walk the track because all packs, sleeping bags, tents, jackets and over-trousers are supplied. The company also runs shorter trips, like three-/four-day Cradle Mountain circuits for $580/770 per person.

Cradle Mountain Huts (☎ 6391 9339; www.cradlehuts.com.au) If camping isn't for you, then from November to May you can take a six-day guided walk in a small group (four to 10 people) along the Overland Track which includes accommodation in private huts. The $1995 fee per person also includes meals, national park entry fees and transfer to/from Launceston, and you can also hire bushwalking gear (eg backpacks, Gore-Tex gear, $40 per item).

Tasman Bush Tours (☎ 6423 2335; www.tasmanbushtours.com) Offers a six-day package for $980. This includes camping gear, park pass, food, ferry tickets to Lake St Clair and transport to/from Devonport.

Tasmanian Expeditions (☎ 6334 3477, 1800 030 230; www.tas-ex.com) Does an eight-day trip for $1240 (November to April) combining Cradle Mountain and the Walls of Jerusalem (p228).

Taz Tours (☎ 6492 1181, 0408 261 705; highlandrangers@bigpond.com) Conducts a number of activities, including hiking the Waterfall Valley (two days/two nights costing $275), taking a lakes fishing expedition (four days/four nights for $995) or hiking the Overland Track (six days/six nights for $1175). All treks include accommodation on the final night at Cradle Mountain. It also offers canoeing, wildlife and mountain bike tours.

TigerLine (☎ 6271 7333, 1300 653 633) Offers a day tour (adult/child $113/68), for the less energetic, to Cradle Mountain from Launceston via Sheffield on Tuesday, Thursday and Saturday, which includes morning tea.

THE WEINDORFERS' LEGACY

In 1910 Gustav Weindorfer climbed to the top of Cradle Mountain, looked across the rugged terrain and announced, 'This must be a national park for all the people for all time. This is magnificent, and people must know about it and enjoy it.'

Gustav Weindorfer is most famous for building the alpine chalet, Waldheim (German for 'Forest Home'), in 1912 on top of this rugged and isolated wonderland. Born in Austria in 1874, Gustav Weindorfer came to Australia in 1900 where he met Kate Cowle (b 1864). They were married in 1906 and spent their honeymoon on Mt Roland. They bought a 100-acre farm at Kindred (southwest of Devonport) and settled down to farming.

What has captured the imagination of generations is the fact that Gustav had the incredible foresight to identify the mountain's natural significance a century ago, and together with the help of friends Gustav began to lobby successive governments to have the area preserved.

What is less well known is that his wife, Kate, also played a key role in the preservation of this area. Her passion extended to flora and botany and by becoming a member of a field naturalists club she learned about the unique nature of the mountain's bushland and flora, encouraging Gustav's appreciation of the landscape. The Weindorfers shared their time between Cradle Mountain and Kindred. Their spirit was tenacious – in those days a horse and cart could only get within 15km of Cradle Mountain, and from there it was a choice between pack horse or walking in order to carry in supplies. It was Kate who purchased some 60 acres of land in 1912, covering the present entrance to the park, where Gustav was able to build Waldheim. Both Gustav and Kate encouraged visitors to come to their remote home to share in the marvels of Cradle Mountain.

In 1916 Kate died from a long illness, and Gustav lived there permanently, devoting his life to preserving the mountain he loved. He died in 1932, but it wasn't until half a century later that Cradle Mountain was finally declared a national park, and a World Heritage Area sometime after that.

The original chalet burnt down in a bushfire in 1974, but it was rebuilt using traditional bush carpentry techniques and stands proudly as a humble legacy to potent insight. Just inside the doorway Gustav inscribed 'This is Waldheim/Where there is no time/And nothing matters'.

Scenic Flights

An entirely sedentary way to see the region's sights is to take a helicopter flight with **Seair Adventure Charters** (☎ 6492 1132; www.adventureflights.com.au; Cradle Mountain Rd; flights Sep-Jun). Helicopter flights leave from the airstrip next to Cradle Wilderness Cafe, about 1.5km northeast of Cradle Mountain Lodge, and pass over Crater Lake, Mt Emmett and Lake Will into Fury Gorge (Australia's deepest). Flights lasting 50 minutes cost $185/110 per adult/child.

SLEEPING & EATING

Cradle Valley

The Cradle Valley has heaps of accommodation options, but if you find yourself unable to secure a booking you could always try Gowrie Park (p229), Waratah (p265) or Tullah (p268). A lot of the accommodation here is self-catering; some of the grocery stores stock some tinned goods and basic supplies such as frozen bread and milk.

Waldheim Chalet & Cabins (☎ 6492 1110; cradle@dpiwe.tas.gov.au; cabins from $70) Some 5km into the national park is this bunch of basic four-, six- and eight-bunk huts containing gas stoves, a small fridge, cooking utensils and wood or gas heaters; bring your own bedding. Bookings are handled by Cradle Mountain visitors centre (p284).

Cradle Mountain Tourist Park & Campground (☎ 6492 1395, 1800 068 574; www.cosycabins.com/cradle; Cradle Mountain Rd; unpowered/powered sites $20/25, dm $25, cabins $95-125) This is a bushland complex situated 2.5km outside the national park. It has well-separated sites (prices are for up to two people), a YHA hostel with four- and six-bunk dorms, and self-contained cabins.

Cradle Mountain Highlanders Cottages (☎ 6492 1116; www.cradlehighlander.com.au; Cradle Mountain Rd; cabins $105-180) This genuinely hospitable place has a rustic collection of self-contained, different-sized timber cottages with wood or gas fires, queen-sized four-poster bush pole beds, electric blankets, TV, mineral water on tap and hearty continental breakfast provisions. Two cabins include a spa and beer and wine is available; all cabins include linen and are serviced daily.

Cradle Mountain Wilderness Village (☎ 6492 1018; www.cradlevillage.com.au; Cradle Mountain Rd; cottages $170, chalets $180, villas $190; 💻) Less than 500m from the national park boundary and nestled in bushland off the main road, this impressive hilltop resort offers private, fully equipped cabins and chalets, which include get-away-from-it-all accessories like phones, satellite TVs and data points. Views stretch all the way to Cradle Mountain.

Cradle Mountain Lodge (☎ 6492 1303, 1800 737 678; bookings@voyages.com.au; Cradle Mountain Rd; tw per person from $115, d $200-330; 💻) This should by all rights be designated a township, seeing as there are around 100 cabins surrounding the main lodge. The cabins are well appointed (all have a log fire) and spaced so you see very little, if anything, of your neighbours; an absence of phones and TVs reinforces the solitude. In the lodge proper, you can eat Caesar salad and gourmet pizzas in the informal **Tavern Bar** (mains $12-19; meals 🕑 lunch & dinner) or veal loin and spinach-and-ricotta tortellini in the more formal **Highland Restaurant** (mains $19-26; 🕑 dinner). There's also a plethora of activities (guided and self-guided) to keep you busy. This is also the venue for the renowned winter event, Tastings at the Top (p285).

Cradle Mountain Chateau (☎ 6492 1404; bookings@cradlemountainchateau.com.au; Cradle Mountain Rd; standard r with/without breakfast $280/240, King spa r $320/280, ste $360/320; 💻) Formerly run by Dohertys, this resort sits on the road to the national park entrance. Accommodation is comfortable, guests have all the standard amenities, including bar fridge, TV, luxurious private bathroom and some rooms include a private balcony. Some of the more standard rooms have terrific views of the car park. There's a fine-dining restaurant and bistro here serving high-quality cuisine, with excellent views of the surrounding plateau. Here you'll also find the impressive **Wilderness Gallery** (☎ 6492 1404; www.wildernessgallery.com.au; Cradle Mountain Rd; admission $5; 🕑 10am-5pm) showcasing incredible environmental photography; there's a well-stocked gift shop.

Cradle Wilderness Cafe (☎ 6492 1400; Cradle Mountain Rd; mains $7-20; 🕑 9am-5pm Mar-Nov, 9am-8pm Dec-Feb) This café has a good range of satisfying mains, including roasted vegetable risotto, plus takeaways.

Road to Cradle Mountain

Cradle Chalet (☎ 6492 1401; www.cradlechalet.com.au; 1422 Cradle Mountain Rd, Moina; d $180-240) This boutique luxury lodge offers private forest chalets/suites that are well appointed, clean and comfortable, with great forest vistas. The rooms include continental breakfast and evening meals (around $25) by arrangement. The hosts are very friendly and can offer lots of regional advice.

Lemonthyme Lodge the Chancellor (☎ 6492 1112; www.lemonthyme.com.au; Dolcoath Rd, Moina; lodge from $110, cabins $250-340) Off Cradle Mountain Rd is this luxurious Ponderosa pine–built mountain retreat. You can stay in self-contained cabins, some with spa, or in cheaper rooms in the main lodge (shared facilities), and eat in the lodge's reputable **restaurant** (2-/3-course mains $45/55; breakfast & dinner for guests only), serving marinated quail, paddock-fed beef dishes, hearty pumpkin, parsnip and apple soup and grilled vegetable terrine. If driving to Cradle Mountain from Devonport (65km), turn onto the gravel Dolcoath Rd 3km south of Moina and follow it for a scenic 8km; it's a fair way to drive and then find out there are no spare rooms, so book ahead.

Cynthia Bay

Lakeside St Clair Wilderness Park (☎ 6289 1137; www.view.com.au/lakeside; unpowered/powered sites $12/15, dm $25; cabins $196) You can choose between camp sites (site prices are for up to two people; note there are no powered tent sites), Spartan two- to four-bunk rooms in a budget lodge (there are kitchen facilities available), or self-contained alpine cabins. The camping ground has little grass cover, so pack a groundsheet. The well-maintained cabins include continental breakfast. You'll find a booking counter, a gift shop that also has a small selection of toiletries and a **café** (mains $4-10; 8am-5pm, to 6pm summer), serving light meals like toasted sandwiches or more substantial fare, such as burgers. There are also a couple of vegetarian options, including a massive dose of sour cream and wedges ($6.50) and bottomless cups of strong, creamy coffee – yay!

You can camp for free at Fergy's Paddock, 10 minutes' walk back along the Overland Track, though bear in mind it only has pit toilets and no fires are allowed.

Derwent Bridge & Bronte Park

These small villages offer a variety of options and make a good base for trout fishing in nearby lakes.

Derwent Bridge Wilderness Hotel (☎ 6289 1144; fax 6289 1173; Derwent Bridge; dm $25, d with/without bathroom $105/85) An impressive high-beamed roof is the centrepiece of the chalet-style pub, giving the lounge bar a warm, expansive atmosphere in which many people enjoy a beer or a feed; the warmth is aided by a massive log fire. The hostel and hotel accommodation is plain but comfortable. You can also get reasonable food at its **restaurant** (mains $13-25; breakfast, lunch & dinner) like ostrich and game sausages, a descent scotch fillet or eye rump to fill the belly. The hotel also has backpacking and hiking gear available, spinning rods and fishing licences, dingy and canoe hire, and Telstra phone cards for sale.

Bronte Park Highland Village (☎ 6289 1126; www.bronteparkhighlandvillage.com.au; 378 Marlborough Hwy, Bronte Park; unpowered/powered sites $12/14, dm from $20, chalet d $95-105, cottage d $90-160) Just off the Lyell Hwy 30km east of Derwent Bridge, this place has a wide variety of accommodation (site prices are for up to two people), plus a bar, a bistro **restaurant** (mains $15-20; breakfast, lunch & dinner) dishing up a seasonal menu of pastas, steaks, salads and blackboard daily specials, and large communal areas with log fireplaces to enjoy an ale or two. There are also hour-long four-wheel-drive wildlife tours available; they depart at 9pm and cost $20/10 per adult/child. The village has petrol, diesel and gas available, and there's a general store. You can arrange transport from Lake St Clair with **Maxwells** (☎ 6289 1125; $7 per person one way).

Derwent Bridge Chalets (☎ 6289 1000; fax 6289 1230; www.troutwalks.com.au; Lyell Hwy, Derwent Bridge; d $155-200) Just 5km from Lake St Clair (500m east of the turn-off), this gay-and lesbian-friendly place has several one-, two- and three-bedroom self-contained roomy cabins, some with spa but all with full kitchen and laundry facilities and back-porch bush views. The same people run **Travellers Rest Cabins** (d from $115), which are comfortable lodgings in neat, self-contained cabins.

Hungry Wombat Café (☎ 6289 1125; Lyell Hwy, Derwent Bridge; mains $8; 8am-6.30pm) Part of the Caltex service station, this friendly, clean and well-managed café is well placed to feed the famished, serving breakfasts to keep you going all day, life-sized succulent burgers, pies and pastries, and other hearty fare like chunky soups and filling sandwiches.

GETTING THERE & AWAY

See p267 for details of year-round services to Cradle Mountain and Lake St Clair. During summer, there are extra services.

TassieLink (☎ 6271 7320, 1300 300 520; www.tassielink.com.au) has additional 'Wilderness' services to Cradle Mountain (Dove Lake) from Launceston, which means that there's a bus running from either end once every day ($45 one way, three to 3½ hours). This service travels to Cradle Mountain via the Devonport ferry terminal on Tuesday, Thursday and Saturday (the fare from Devonport is $31). Bookings for the service are essential.

TassieLink also has additional 'Wilderness' services to Lake St Clair – from Hobart buses run once a day ($45, three hours), while from Launceston there's one bus on Monday, Wednesday and Saturday ($80, three hours).

TassieLink can also drop you off at one end of the Overland Track and pick you up at the other end. There are various options depending on where you're coming from and going to, so call TassieLink for prices (packages must be pre-booked). While you don't have to pay to have your luggage transported, you do have to pay around $5 per bag for it to be stored until you're ready to collect it.

Maxwells (☎ 6492 1431, 0418 584 004) runs services on demand from Devonport to Cradle Mountain (one to four passengers $160, five or more $40 per passenger), Launceston to Cradle Mountain ($240/60) via Walls of Jerusalem (p229), Devonport and Launceston to Lake St Clair ($280/70), and Lake St Clair to Bronte Park and Frenchmans Cap ($65/15).

It's possible that you might be able to find a more convenient or cheaper transport option by talking to staff at bushwalking shops or hostels. If driving, you'd best fill up with petrol before heading out to Cradle Mountain, prices are significantly higher than outside the national park. From Bronte Park, if you're heading north on Marlborough Rd towards the Great Lake (35km), most of the road is gravel; it's in good nick if there are dry conditions but it's best to check with the locals for road conditions during winter.

GETTING AROUND

Cradle Valley

Immediately opposite the Cradle Mountain Tourist Park is the new Cradle information centre. From here free shuttle buses leave at 15-minute intervals (mid-September to late May), stopping at the park's Cradle Mountain visitors centre, Snake Hill, Ronny Creek (near Waldheim Chalet) and then on to Dove Lake. Visitors can alight at any bus stop along the way. Note that despite the frequency of shuttle buses there may be substantial queues at peak times. Contact the Cradle Mountain visitors centre (p284) for the shuttle's reduced winter timetable.

Maxwells (☎ 6492 1431, 0418 584 004) also provides an on-demand year-round shuttle service for $9 per person (one way), picking up passengers from the camping ground and other accommodation venues. Bookings are essential.

Cynthia Bay

Also run by **Maxwells** (☎ 6289 1125, 0418 328 427) is an on-demand service between Cynthia Bay/Lake St Clair and Derwent Bridge ($7 per person one way).

Lakeside St Clair Wilderness Park (☎ 6289 1137; www.lakestclairwildernessholidays.com.au) currently runs a ferry service which does one-way (adult/child $20/15) and return (adult/child $25/20) trips from Cynthia Bay to Narcissus Hut at the northern end of Lake St Clair, taking around 45 minutes one way and departing at least three times daily (usually 9am, 1pm and 3pm); bookings are essential and you can expect to pay more if there are fewer than four people on board. You can also alight about halfway to Narcissus Hut at Echo Point ($15 per person one way). If you're using the ferry service at the end of your Overland Track hike, you *must* radio the ferry operator when you arrive at Narcissus Hut (the ferry collects bushwalkers at 9.30am, 1pm and 3.30pm).

At the time of research some changes to the ferry system were to include a new cruise boat, the *Leeawuleena*, due to start operating two-hour cruises of the lake, while the taxi ferry would provide a service for bushwalkers only. Contact the Lakeside St Clair Wilderness Park for details.

The Southwest

The southwest is a gloriously wild area covering almost a quarter of Tasmania, with very few signs of human intervention. A single main road penetrates as far as the hydroelectric power scheme, built when there were only two small national parks: Frenchmans Cap, and Lake Pedder (ultimately flooded despite its supposedly protected status).

Since Lake Pedder was destroyed, the regional map has changed drastically, with the whole area now contained within national parks. Every summer, thousands of bushwalkers follow the better-known wilderness tracks. While some short walks can be done from the access road, most walks require you to carry all your gear and camp for at least a week.

The area's sole sealed road starts from Westerway, west of New Norfolk. It passes the entrance to Mt Field National Park (p106) before continuing to Maydena. From here the road becomes narrow and winding, passing through tall forests then traversing open country to Strathgordon; the final stretch has wonderful views of rugged mountain ranges.

From Maydena you can detour south into the magnificent, tall-timbered Styx Valley. Halfway to Strathgordon is a gravel sideroad to excellent views of the major mountains of the Southwest National Park.

HIGHLIGHTS

- Driving through the **Styx Valley** (p297) to see the earth's tallest hardwoods, then adding your voice to the campaign to protect them
- Donning a backpack and getting back to nature on the **South Coast Track** (p299)
- Swallowing any fear of heights and **abseiling** (p298) down the massive Gordon Dam wall
- Escaping the rest of the world by camping and bird-watching at tiny, remote **Melaleuca** (p300)
- Taking the soft option and doing a day trip into the **southwest by air** (p299) from Hobart
- Getting in touch with your inner child to follow the fun **Creepy Crawly Nature Trail** (p298)
- Enjoying the splendour and peacefulness of Port Davey and Bathurst Harbour from a **kayak** (p299)

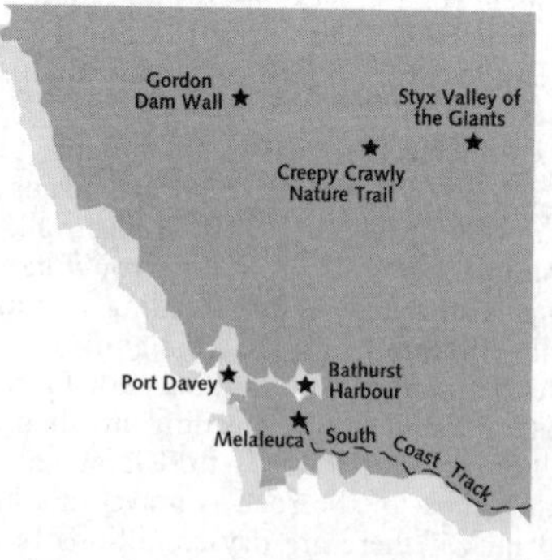

- www.parks.tas.gov.au/natparks/southwest/

History

The southwest's original inhabitants were the Tasmanian Aborigines, who arrived at least 35,000 years ago. Evidence of Aboriginal habitation has been found in many local caves. At that stage, the world was enduring an ice age and the southwest was covered with open grasslands that were ideal for hunting animals. Between 18,000 and 12,000 years ago, the ice retreated and, with the warmer climate, thick forests began growing across the region. The Aboriginal people regularly burned the grassy plains, but this only delayed the inexorable advance of the forests. By the time Europeans arrived, the only indigenous people left in the area lived around the coastline.

European explorers were at first appalled by the landscape. Matthew Flinders, the first to circumnavigate Tasmania, described the southwest thus: 'The mountains are the most dismal that can be imagined. The eye ranges over these peaks with astonishment and horror.' Other reports from those who climbed the peaks aptly described the interior as a series of rugged ranges that extended to the horizon.

Most of the early explorers were surveyors who measured the land and cut tracks across the area under great hardship. The tracks were to provide access to the west coast and (optimistically) open the region for development. A road was eventually laid from the north to Gordon Bend and

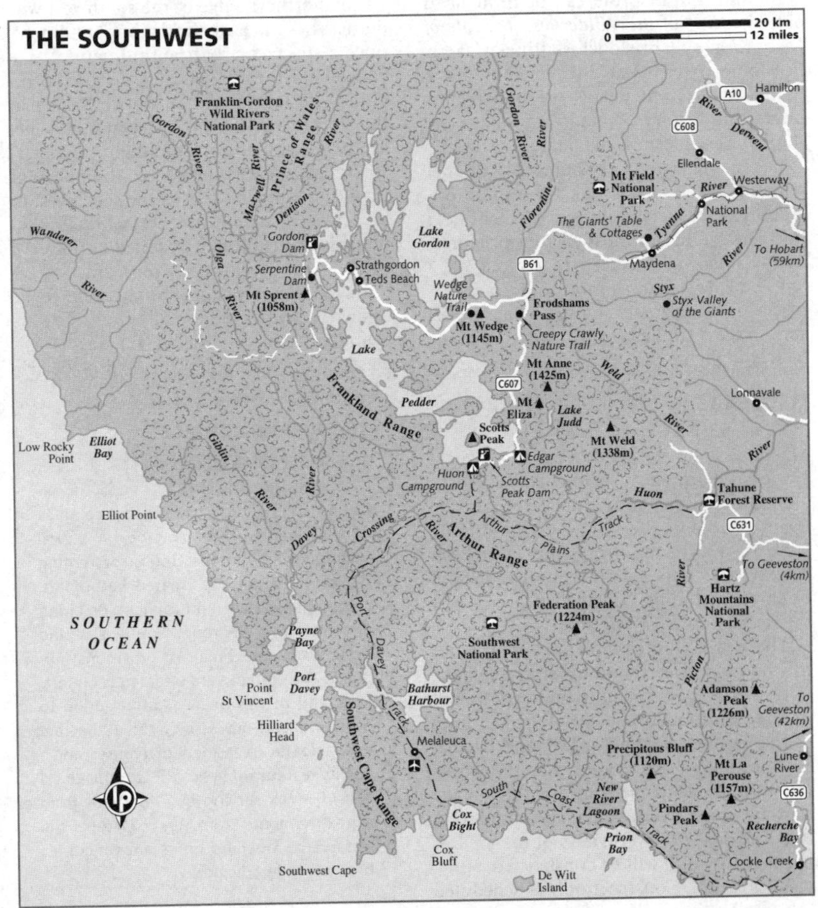

in the 1880s the government seriously considered digging a railway tunnel underneath Mt Anne to Port Davey. However, the anticipated mineral deposits and good farming lands were few and far between. Huon pine was logged around Port Davey, osmiridium was mined at Adamsfield, tin was mined at Melaleuca and a tiny farm existed at Gordonvale, but overall there was little potential for exploitation and the few tracks vanished under encroaching scrub and forest. The southwest was then left pretty much alone, with most Tasmanians regarding it as uninhabitable. The trials of early explorers make for interesting reading in *Trampled Wilderness: The History of South-West Tasmania* by Ralph & Kathleen Gowlland (out of print; can be difficult to obtain). *King of the Wilderness: the Life of Deny King* by Christobel Mattingley sacrifices objectivity for at-times melodramatic hero worship, but details the nonetheless interesting history of a man who made the southwest wilderness his home.

Of all the early developments, all that remains is the small-scale tin-mining operation at Melaleuca, a tiny settlement near Port Davey. But for most visitors, predominantly bushwalkers keen to set out on a long hike, Melaleuca's most important feature is its small gravel airstrip, which allows aerial access to the area by chartered plane or scenic flight.

MAYDENA

☎ 03 / pop 380

Maydena is on the road between Mt Field National Park and Strathgordon. North along Junee Rd, a 10-minute drive past the Giant's Table, is the start of a five-minute walk to a cave-mouth of the **Junee River karst system**. This system comprises 30km of caves, including Niggly Cave, reputedly the deepest in Australia at 375m.

There are big things planned to attempt to woo more tourists to this stunning area: Forestry Tasmania plans to build another of its tourist attractions here (along the lines of the Tahune AirWalk, p138, and Dismal Swamp, p259). The project has the working title the **Maydena Hauler**, a three-stage railway which will journey up a mountain to a lookout with 360° views of the area. A heritage saw mill will be constructed, and a visitors centre. Construction was scheduled to begin in early 2005, with completion due some 12 to 18 months later.

Sleeping & Eating

The Wren's Nest (☎ 6288 2280; 8 Junee Rd; d $120, extra adult/child $25/15) A well-equipped and homey three-bedroom cottage with all self-contained necessities (including laundry, wood heating and breakfast provisions).

Roydon Alpaca Stud & Accommodation (☎ 6288 2212; 40 Junee Rd; r/cottage d $75/95, extra person $20) Enjoy the lovely mountain views and warm hospitality at this alpaca stud, which offers an in-house B&B room, or a self-contained cottage that sleeps up to six.

LAKE PEDDER IMPOUNDMENT

At the northern edge of the southwest wilderness lies the Lake Pedder impoundment, once a spectacularly beautiful natural lake considered the ecological jewel of the region. The largest glacial outwash lake in the world, it covered 3 sq km and its wide, sandy beach made an ideal light-plane airstrip. The lake was considered so important that it was the first part of the southwest to be protected within its own national park, but this status ultimately failed to preserve the original, glorious environment.

In the early stages of what came to be known as 'hydro-industrialisation', the government body responsible for Tasmania's electricity production – the Hydro-Electric

THE AUTHOR'S CHOICE

The Giants' Table & Cottages (☎ 6288 2293; www.giantstable.com; Junee Rd; r s/d $50/70, cottage d $120-135, extra person $30) This complex of revamped workers' cottages in a rural setting gives you the option of renting a room in a cottage (shared bathrooms, communal kitchen and lounge), or hiring an entire four-bedroom house (sleeping up to 10 people; breakfast provisions supplied). The cottages are clean and comfortable, and there's been great attention to detail in the fit-out. Also on this 10-hectare river-side site are resident platypuses, and a quality **restaurant** (mains $17-22; lunch and dinner Nov-Apr) serving huge portions from a creative menu. From May to October the restaurant's opening hours are varied; it's best to call in advance.

CHRIS KLEP

Strahan (p272)

Winter dawn at Cradle Mountain–Lake St Clair National Park (p284)
ROB BLAKERS

CHRIS KLEP

Effects of mining, Queenstown (p278)

Scoparia and cushion plants, Cradle Mountain–Lake St Clair National Park (p284)
CHRIS BELL

Columnar dolerite cliffs, Cradle Mountain–Lake St Clair National Park (p284)
GRANT DIXON

GARETH MCCORMACK

The Lake Pedder impoundment (p296) in Southwest National Park

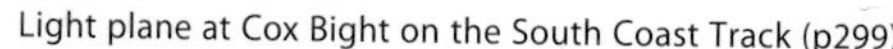

Light plane at Cox Bight on the South Coast Track (p299)

GRANT DIXON

CHRIS KLEP

Gordon Dam (p298), Strathgordon

Boats in the harbour on King Island (p302)

OLIVER ST

Commission (HEC), now Hydro Tasmania – built dams, power stations and pipelines on the Central Plateau and Derwent River. These activities went largely unchallenged until the 1960s, when the HEC proposed flooding Lake Pedder, at that stage the only national park in the southwest, to create a much larger lake for electricity generation. There were immediate protests from people who had begun to realise the cost to Tasmania's natural environment, particularly the wilderness areas, of the HEC's all-consuming industrial agenda; this was inflamed by the revelation that the flooding of Lake Pedder was not even necessary for the viability of the larger scheme it was part of.

The protests were to no avail, however, as Lake Pedder was flooded in 1972, and the HEC turned its developmental attention to the lower Gordon and Franklin Rivers. For details of the ensuing conservation-movement struggle to prevent these new dams, which had a markedly different result to the Lake Pedder campaign, see p282.

Together with nearby Lake Gordon, the Lake Pedder impoundment holds 27 times the volume of water in Sydney Harbour and is the largest inland freshwater catchment in Australia. The Gordon Power Station is the largest hydroelectric power station in Tasmania.

Trout fishing is popular and boats are allowed on the Lake Pedder impoundment. The fish caught range from 1kg to 20kg in size. Small boats or dinghies are discouraged because the lake is 55km long and frequent storms generate sizeable, potentially dangerous waves. Boat ramps exist at Scotts Peak Dam in the south and near Strathgordon in the north. Given the scale of the controversy surrounding the inundation of Lake Pedder, you'll be surprised at just how puny the dams on this lake appear, especially when compared with the massive Gordon Dam.

There are two free camping grounds near the southern end of the lake. The **Edgar Campground** has pit toilets, water, fine views of the area and usually a fisherman or two – in wet weather it's less attractive as it's exposed to cold winds. A better place to camp

STYX VALLEY OF THE GIANTS

The valley lying to the south of the Maydena Range was carved out by the Styx River on its way to joining the Derwent River. It is known evocatively as the 'Valley of the Giants', because it contains white-trunked specimens of eucalyptus (*Eucalyptus regnans* to be precise) that are the tallest trees in the southern hemisphere, and the highest-standing hardwoods in the world, with heights of up to 95m recorded in the valley.

The region is the subject of an ongoing tussle between the state-government-managed forestry industry and conservationists. Logging companies, which are already very active in the area, appear determined to clear-fell most of the remaining old-growth forest in the Styx (bar a small portion set aside in reserves) in the coming years, primarily for wood-chipping.

Conservationists, on the other hand, argue for the preservation of the upper Styx River Valley's record-breaking environment and have called for the establishment of a 150-sq-km national park, to be incorporated into the Tasmanian Wilderness World Heritage Area. The stated rationale for the Styx Valley of the Giants National Park is not just the protection of the tall trees and the surrounding wilderness, but also the creation of an economically significant tourist attraction.

If you want to experience the Styx for yourself, including the awesome Big Tree Reserve and the magical short walk to Shingle Bend, embark on the self-drive tour detailed in the Wilderness Society's *Styx Valley of the Giants* brochure and map, available from many businesses in the area (pop into the Maydena Trading Post, a general store on the main road through town) or online at www.wilderness.org.au/campaigns/forests/tasmania/styx/styx_selfdrive/. Please heed the warnings in this brochure too, about directions, log trucks and road conditions (the unsealed roads can be managed in two-wheel-drive vehicles, but roads get very slippery in the wet). The Wilderness Society is also planning to build a walking track linking features of significance in the valley, called the Styx Giants Trail. The aim is to increase the number of tourists – the more people who visit, understand and appreciate this unique part of the state, the more voices can be added to the campaign to protect it.

is the nearby **Huon Campground**, hidden in tall forest near Scotts Peak Dam and with identical facilities to Edgar.

STRATHGORDON

☎ 03 / pop 75

Built to service HEC employees during construction of the Gordon River Power Scheme, the tiny 'township' of Strathgordon is becoming a popular bushwalking, trout fishing, boating and water-skiing destination.

About 2km past the township is the turn-off to the **Lake Pedder Lookout**, with lovely views and interesting information boards. A further 10km west is the **Gordon Dam lookout and visitors centre** (☎ 6280 1134; 10am-5pm Nov-Apr, 11am-3pm May-Oct), located at the 140m-high Gordon Dam and providing information on the scheme. Tours of the underground Gordon Power Station no longer operate, but as an alternative, Hobart-based **Aardvark Adventures** (☎ 6273 7722, 0408 127 714; www.aardvarkadventures.com.au) organises abseils down the dam wall ($160, suitable for beginners, minimum four people). This is one to brag about to your mates – it's the world's highest commercial abseil.

Accommodation-wise, your only options are the free **Teds Beach Campground** beside the Lake Pedder impoundment (toilets and electric barbecues; no fires permitted), or the newly renovated **Lake Pedder Chalet** (☎ 6280 1166; www.lakepedderchalet.com.au; d $50-100). There are three standards of rooms here; the cheapest rooms have shared bathroom facilities and are excellent value and the top-priced rooms have great lake views. Also here is a **restaurant** (lunch $7-11, dinner mains $14-21; breakfast, lunch, dinner) serving well-priced meals in a dining room with excellent lake views. To help you better explore the area, the Chalet offers bike and boat hire, rod and tackle rental, and fishing, lake and wildlife-spotting tours.

SOUTHWEST NATIONAL PARK

There are few places left in the world that are as isolated and untouched as Tasmania's southwest wilderness. The state's largest national park is home to some of the world's last tracts of virgin temperate rainforest, which contribute much to the grandeur and extraordinary diversity of this ancient area.

The southwest is the habitat of the endemic Huon pine, which lives for more than 3000 years, and of the swamp gum, the world's tallest hardwood and flowering plant. About 300 species of lichen, moss and fern – some very rare – festoon the dense rainforest, glacial tarns are seamless silver mirrors on the jagged mountains, and in summer the alpine meadows are picture-perfect with wildflowers and flowering shrubs. Through it all run the wild rivers, with rapids tearing through deep gorges and waterfalls plunging over cliffs.

Each year more people venture into the heart of this incredible part of the Tasmanian Wilderness World Heritage Area, in search of the peace, isolation and challenge of a region virtually untouched since the last ice age.

To walk across this region is something suggested only for fit, experienced bushwalkers. You can see a small part of it by following the gravel road from Frodshams Pass on the Strathgordon Rd (30km past Maydena) to Scotts Peak. About 2km along the road to Scotts Peak is the **Creepy Crawly Nature Trail**, an easy 20-minute walk through rainforest, with child-friendly interpretive signs dealing with the insects of the area. Further south, the road leaves the forest near Mt Anne, revealing wonderful views of the surrounding mountains in fine weather. To the west lies the Frankland Range, while to the south is the jagged crest of the Western Arthur Range. The road ends at Scotts Peak Dam and nearby are several free camping grounds (see p297).

The **visitors centre** (☎ 6288 1149) at Mt Field National Park, staffed by the Parks & Wildlife Service, is the place to get your national parks pass and information about the southwest. Park fees apply even if you're just driving on the Strathgordon-bound road through the park.

Day Walks

From Scotts Peak Rd you can climb to **Mt Eliza**, a steep, five-hour return walk. Using the same track, you can walk further to climb **Mt Anne**, a challenging trip of around eight to ten hours return. Another challenging eight-hour walk for experienced hikers is from Red Tape Creek (29km south of the main road, B61, along Scotts Peak Rd) to **Lake Judd**.

From the Huon Campground, the best short walk follows the start of the **Port Davey Track** as it passes through a forest and across the buttongrass plain. At the end of the forest, about 1km along the track, the tracks starts to deteriorate, making this a good point to turn around and head back.

Mt Wedge is a popular five-hour return walk (signposted off the main road) and, being located between the Lake Pedder impoundment and Lake Gordon, has sweeping views. If you're not up to that, from the carpark is the 15-minute **Wedge Nature Trail** that takes you past a number of native trees.

Long Bushwalks

The best-known walks in the park are the 70km **Port Davey Track** used by walkers between Scotts Peak Rd and Melaleuca (four or five days' duration), and the considerably more popular, 85km **South Coast Track** between Cockle Creek and Melaleuca (see p142 to get some information about Cockle Creek).

The South Coast Track takes six to eight days to complete and hikers should be well prepared for the often vicious weather conditions. Light planes are used to airlift bushwalkers into or out of the southwest, landing at Melaleuca, and there's vehicle access to Cockle Creek at the park's southeastern edge (see below). Detailed notes to the South Coast Track are available in Lonely Planet's *Walking in Australia*, and detailed information is available on the website of the **Parks & Wildlife Service** (www.parks.tas.gov.au/recreation/tracknotes/scoast.html).

There are many other walks in the park, but you should first complete one of the better-known walks. Contrary to what you might think, the South Coast Track actually makes good preparation for the more difficult walks in the area involving unmarked tracks – these require a high degree of bushwalking skill to complete safely and enjoyably. The shortest of these is the three-day circuit of the **Mt Anne Range**. Scaling **Federation Peak**, which has earned a reputation as the most difficult walk in Australia, will take a highly experienced walker around seven days. The **Western Arthur Range** is another extremely difficult traverse, for which seven to 11 days are recommended.

Getting There & Away

From December through March, **TassieLink** (☎ 1300 300 520; www.tassielink.com.au) operates

TOURS IN THE SOUTHWEST

There are a few tours available for those who'd like to tackle the southwest in a small group, with an experienced guide and someone else organising much of the gear and logistics!

Tasmanian Expeditions (☎ 1300 666 856, 6334 3477; www.tas-ex.com) offers two walking tour options (graded 5 on a scale from 1 to 5, classified as 'self-supported very strenuous activities'). The first option is a nine-day trek on the South Coast Track ($1790), flying in to Melaleuca and walking east; for hard-core trekkers there's a 16-day trek along both the Port Davey and South Coast Tracks ($2990). **Tiger Trails** (☎ 6234 3931; www.tigertrails.green.net.au) offers a 10-day tour along the South Coast Track ($1599).

If you're seeking a somewhat easier option, you might like to consider a kayaking trip. From December to March, **Roaring 40s Ocean Kayaking** (☎ 6267 5000, 1800 653 712; www.roaring40skayaking.com.au), based at Kettering on Tasmania's southeast coast, offers kayaking trips exploring Port Davey and Bathurst Harbour. Access to the area is by light plane to and from Hobart, and the cost is $1300/1995 for a three-/seven-day trip.

Sounds too hard? Well, for those of you who like your creature comforts, there is a soft option – scenic flights out of Hobart taking in the sights of the southwest, with time spent on the ground. **Par Avion** (☎ 6248 5390; www.paravion.com.au) has three options, starting from a basic scenic flight (no landing) for $150. You're better off spending a little extra and taking the four-hour option ($170), which includes a landing at Melaleuca and a short boat trip here. You can also choose the $275, eight-hour option, 'A Day in the Wilderness', which includes a Melaleuca landing, lunch and a cruise to Celery Top Islands. **Tasair** (☎ 6248 5088; www.tasair.com.au) also offers flights; its speciality is a 2½-hour flight ($176) that includes 30 minutes on the ground, with a beach landing at Cox Bight (if weather conditions are right) or at Melaleuca.

an early-morning bus on Tuesday, Thursday and Saturday from Hobart to Mt Anne ($60.50, 3¼ hours), the end of the Mt Anne circuit at Red Tape Creek ($60.50, 3½ hours), and Scotts Peak ($64, four hours). TassieLink also departs Hobart for Cockle Creek ($57, 3½ hours) at 9am Monday, Wednesday and Friday from December through March. Bookings are essential.

If you're tackling both the Port Davey and South Coast Tracks, and plan on catching TassieLink buses to/from the Scotts Peak and Cockle Creek ends, you pay $100 for all transport and can arrange for extra luggage to be stored at the company's Hobart or Launceston depots for $5 per bag during your walk.

MELALEUCA

This is a tiny location deep in the southwest near Port Davey, where a few people mine alluvial tin on the buttongrass plain and the PWS keeps a semi-resident team. The only access to the area is by sea or light plane, or by following walking tracks for at least five days. There are no shops or any facilities apart from two walkers huts; you can also camp in a nearby tea-tree grove. The major attraction for visitors is the excellent bird-hide, a substantial building from where you might see the rare orange-bellied parrot.

Flights operate to Melaleuca's gravel runway on demand from Hobart. One of the most regular services is a daily flight by **Par Avion** (☎ 6248 5390; www.paravion.com.au) from Hobart to Melaleuca ($145 one-way, 45 minutes). **Tasair** (☎ 6248 5088; www.tasair.com.au) also provides a service for bushwalkers, available to or from Melaleuca or Cox Bight ($150 one-way). Both companies offer scenic flights of the wilderness area, which may include landings (see p299).

Bass Strait Islands

You might well feel that Tasmania moves at a slow pace compared to the mainland states and offers a welcome chance to relax and get back to nature and close to wildlife – but there are two island groups in Bass Strait that offer the chance to drop back a few more gears and enjoy all of the above, plus the peace and solitude of island life.

Even if you visit King Island or Flinders Island in January, the busiest month, you're unlikely to encounter many other cars on your explorations – and the drivers of cars you do pass will give you a friendly wave of greeting. You'll dine well on the local produce (King Island's dairy products are justifiably ranked highly by cheese connoisseurs, and there's excellent seafood, beef and lamb, too). You can walk these off on great walking tracks, and you're almost guaranteed a beach to yourself.

King Island is the largest island in the Hunter Group, planted at the western end of Bass Strait, and Flinders Island is the largest of the Furneaux Group in Bass Strait's east. These two main islands have served as the transient homes of prospectors, sealers and sailors, and also as a long-term destination for Tasmanian Aborigines who were 'resettled' from the Tasmanian mainland. Today, King and Flinders Islands are mainly rural communities that offer visitors the opportunity to delve into natural coastal beauty rich in marine and other wildlife. Both are easily accessed by air from Melbourne and northern Tasmania and offer a battery-recharging break. You'll find that a weekend visit is barely enough time to enjoy all that each island has to offer.

HIGHLIGHTS

- Say cheese! Sampling the heavenly, award-winning cheeses at **King Island Dairy** (p302)
- **Surfing** (p303) some of Australia's best, most remote waves at British Admiral Beach
- Unwinding on the stunning, empty **Trousers Point beach** (p307), with the mountains looming in the background
- Leaving all your stresses behind by checking in at **Healing Dreams** (p309) on Flinders Island
- Going diving to explore **shipwrecks** (p303) and get a sense of Bass Strait's awesome power
- Catching your breath atop **Mt Strzelecki's peak** (p307) and taking in the magnificent views

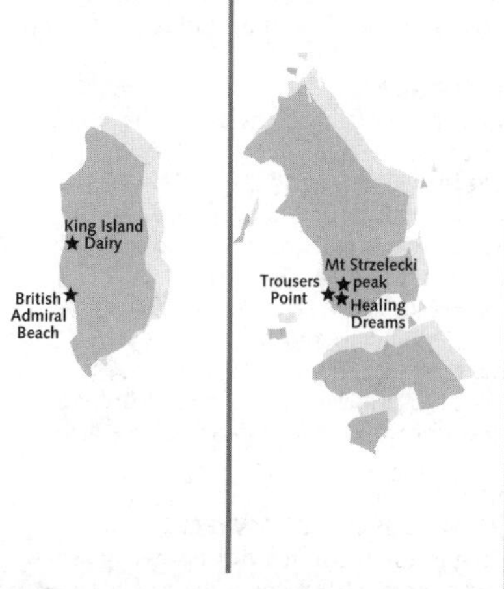

KING ISLAND

☎ 03 / pop 1765

King Island guards the western end of Bass Strait. Only 64km long and 27km across at its widest point, this small island's beautiful beaches, rocky coastline, seafood and dairy fare, and rustic atmosphere more than compensate for its size.

Europeans first encountered the island in 1798 and named it after Governor King of New South Wales. It gained a reputation as a breeding ground for seals and sea elephants, but soon the animals were hunted close to extinction by sealers and sailors known collectively as Straitsmen.

Over the years, the stormy seas of Bass Strait have claimed many ocean-going vessels – there are at least 57 shipwrecks in the waters around King Island. The island's worst shipwreck occurred in 1845 when the *Cataraqui*, an immigrant boat, went down with 399 people aboard; all lives were lost.

King Island is best known for its dairy produce, although kelp and large crayfish are also valuable exports. Another main industry was the production of scheelite – used in the manufacture of armaments – until the mine and factory at Grassy closed in 1990. After practising being a ghost town for several years, Grassy began re-enlivening itself with tourist accommodation.

King Island's main township is Currie, which is also the local harbour. It's close to the airport and most of the island's facilities are located here. Other notable settlements on the island are Naracoopa on the east coast and Grassy to the southeast.

Information

Most businesses on the island have eftpos facilities.

King Island Tourism (☎ 1800 645 014, 6462 1313; www.kingisland.org.au; PO Box 269, Currie 7256) Providing information in person or via its comprehensive website.
Main post office (Main St, Currie)
Online Access Centre (☎ 6464 1778; 5 George St, Currie; ⌚ closed Tue & Sun)
Trend (☎ 6462 1360; Edward St, Currie; ⌚ 9am-6.30pm) For tourist information once you reach the island.
Westpac bank (Cnr Main & Edward Sts, Currie) ATM.

Sights

LIGHTHOUSES & SHIPWRECKS

King Island has four lighthouses to guard its treacherous coasts. The one at Currie was built in 1880, while the one at Cape Wickham was built in 1861 and is the tallest in the southern hemisphere. Neither is open, but the latter is surrounded by attractive coastal scenery, and there is a cairn there to commemorate the lighthouse keepers. There's another lighthouse at Stokes Point, the southernmost point of the island, while Cumberland lighthouse is south of Naracoopa on the eastern side of the island.

Those interested in the island's maritime history should track down a copy of *The King Island Maritime Trail: Shipwrecks & Safe Havens*, a booklet with information on a dozen shipwreck sites around the island, complete with simple maps and details of the relevant coastal memorial cairns. Alternatively, get information online from www.kingisland.net.au/~maritime/.

KING ISLAND HISTORICAL MUSEUM

The island's **museum** (☎ 6462 1698; Lighthouse St, Currie; adult/child $4/1; ⌚ 2-4pm Sep-Jun), staffed by volunteers and located in the cottage that once housed the chief light-keeper, features many local-history displays but is particularly fond of the remnants of maritime disasters.

KING ISLAND DAIRY

Visiting King Island inevitably entails a visit to the fromagerie of the **King Island Dairy** (☎ 6462 1348; www.kidairy.com.au; North Rd, Loorana; ⌚ 12.30-4.30pm, closed Sat Oct-Apr, closed Wed & Sat May-Sep), 8km north of Currie, just beyond the airport. Here you can learn about the local dairying activities and sample and buy the award-winning brie, cheddar or thick cream for which the island is renowned.

KELP INDUSTRY

Kelp Industries Pty Ltd (Netherby Rd) was established in 1975 to commercially harvest the masses of bull kelp that wash up onto the island's rocks and beaches. The factory is the only kelp-processing plant in Australia. From the roadway next to Currie Golf Course you can see the kelp being air-dried on racks. It's left on the racks for about two weeks, kiln-dried, crushed, then shipped to Scotland where it's blended with kelp from other countries to create alginates, which are used in the manufacture of a variety of products including sauces, lotions and detergents.

CALCIFIED FOREST

From Currie, head south to the **Seal Rocks Reserve** (off South Rd) to visit the impressive Calcified Forest. A walk of 1km from the car park leads to a viewing platform from where the ancient petrified tree trunks can be seen. Some experts believe them to be up to 30 million years old. The place has a sombre, almost eerie feel, like a geological graveyard.

Activities

WATER SPORTS

Surf and freshwater **fishing** are popular here, as is **surfing** at the southern end of British Admiral Beach, Currie's main sandy stretch. You can **swim** at many of the island's unpopulated beaches and freshwater lagoons.

Diving among the local marine life and shipwrecks is recommended. **King Island Dive Charters** (☎ 6461 1133; www.kingislanddivecharter.com.au) provides single boat dives for $75, as well as good-value three- to seven-day packages.

OTHER ACTIVITIES

Golfing is popular on the island. So is **bushwalking**, particularly in the fern gullies of Yarra Creek Gorge, where you can see some of the island's 78 bird species.

There's plenty of **wildlife** to observe, such as quails, wallabies, platypuses and seals. Tiger and brown snakes also inhabit the island, and you'll see feral pheasants and flocks of wild turkeys. In the summer months, a colony of little (fairy) penguins comes ashore at dusk at the end of the breakwater at Grassy – take care not to disturb them or dazzle them with bright lights.

Tours

King Island Coaches (☎ 1800 647 702, 6462 1138; www.kingislandgem.com.au; 95 Main St, Currie), based at the King Island Gem Motel (see p304), offers various half-/full-day island explorations ($40/80), as well as an evening tour to view little penguins ($40).

Sleeping

CURRIE

Bass Caravan Park & Cabins (☎ 6462 1260; www.kingislandgem.com.au; 100 Main St; on-site van $45, cabin $100) A few kilometres from the beach, this small park offers a handful of on-site caravans with en suite, plus two-bedroom cabins with full kitchen and bathroom. Prices are based on two people.

Boomerang by the Sea (☎ 6462 1288; www.bythesea.com.au; Golf Club Rd; s/d $100/120) Boomerang has decent, well-equipped motel rooms that all enjoy superb ocean views across the golf course. It's only a short stroll into town, and there's a high-quality restaurant on site (see p304).

King Island A-Frame Holiday Homes (☎ 6462 1260; www.kingislandgem.com.au; 95 Main St; d $130, 3-6 people $190) This complex of three A-frame units is 2km north of Currie. Each two-storey, three-bedroom unit sleeps six in self-contained comfort, with the bonus of sea views.

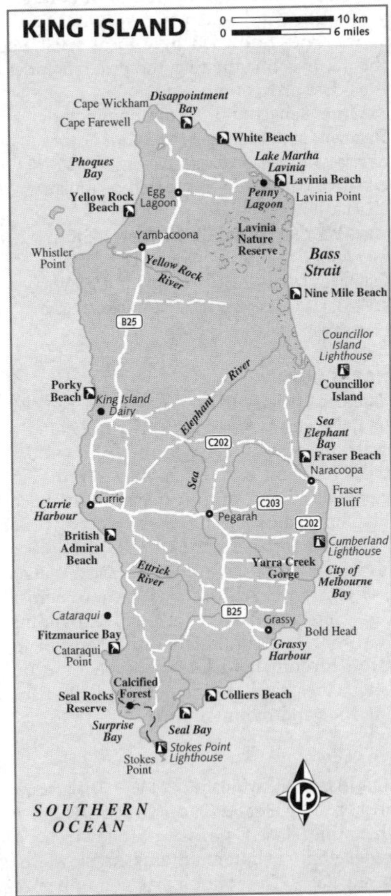

King Island Gem Motel (☎ 6462 1260; www.kingislandgem.com.au; 95 Main St; s/d/tr $105/125/145) This motel is managed by the aforementioned A-frame owners and has well-equipped, but plain, brick motel rooms. Continental breakfast is included; room-service meals are available.

Parers King Island Hotel (☎ 6462 1633; parers@kingisland.net.au; 7 Main St; s $70-80, d $90-110) In the centre of Currie, this pub has good motel-style suites in its double-storey structure and the main bar has a large open fireplace. The hotel provides easy access to shops, harbour and golf course.

Devil's Gap Retreat (☎ 6462 1180; devilsgap@kingisland.net.au; Charles St; d $130) On the foreshore 1km northwest of Currie are these two self-contained, one-bedroom cottages with open fires, spas and sweeping ocean views. They're owned by a local artist, so the décor is imaginative; the price includes breakfast provisions.

Other self-contained options include:

Shannon Coastal Cottages (☎ 6462 1370; www.shannoncoastalcottages.com.au; Charles St; d $150-160, extra adult $30) Two well-equipped cottages northwest of Currie.

Wave Watcher Holiday Units (☎ 6462 1517; wavewatcher@bigpond.com; 16 Beach Rd; d $150)

Gullhaven (☎ 6462 1560; 11 Huxley St; d $80, extra adult $35) Large, modest, central four-bedroom house (sleeps eight).

NARACOOPA

Naracoopa Holiday Units (☎ 6461 1326; Beach Rd; s/d $70/90, extra adult/child $22/14) If you're after a seafront location close to the fishing jetty, try here. These two self-contained units are nestled in their own private gardens on Sea Elephant Bay.

Baudins Cottages (☎ 6461 1110; baudins@kingisland.net.au; The Esplanade; d $125-155, additional person $40) On the beachfront, with views across Sea Elephant Bay, the attractive Baudins has four self-contained units (one- and two-bedroom) and lots of beach time on offer. Guest facilities include the use of fishing rods and mountain bikes.

GRASSY

King Island Holiday Village (☎ 6461 1177; kiholiday@kingisland.net.au; Blue Gum Drive; units $135-180) Since the mine closed, Grassy has slowly been redeveloping, but maintains its slow, relaxed pace. This option has a number of houses and units in town, of varying sizes, some spa-equipped; prices include breakfast provisions.

Eating

CURRIE

There are good eating options in Currie within walking distance of most accommodation. There are also two supermarkets on Main St; both are open daily.

Nautilus Coffee Lounge (☎ 6462 1868; Edward St; meals $4-12; 🕑 daily) In a courtyard beside the roundabout, Nautilus offers Devonshire tea, crayfish rolls, soup, burgers and other light meals, plus some local art and craft goods for sale.

King Island Bakery (☎ 6462 1337; 5 Main St; snacks $3-6; 🕑 from 6am) An excellent spot for picnic supplies, selling lots of freshly baked goods, including raved-about gourmet pies with fillings like crayfish, Camembert and asparagus, and King Island beef.

Boomerang by the Sea (☎ 6462 1288; Golf Club Rd; mains from $22; 🕑 dinner nightly Sep-Apr, closed Sun May-Oct) Recognised as one of the island's best eating options, this roomy restaurant has spectacular ocean views and serves up delicious, locally sourced produce. Beef, cheese and seafood make it a sure bet.

Parers King Island Hotel (☎ 6462 1633; 7 Main St; mains $13-20; 🕑 lunch & dinner) The hotel's bistro also serves lots of the exemplary local produce and has regular, good-value lunch specials.

For something different, head to the charming, novel **Boathouse** (🕑 24hr) on the harbour – a 'restaurant without food', where you can have a picnic (BYO everything!). It's been decorated by a local artist and is always open.

NARACOOPA

Baudins (☎ 6461 1110; The Esplanade; mains $20-25; 🕑 dinner) On the eastern side of the island is the colonial-style Baudins, serving beef, seafood and other well-prepared local edibles in its restaurant on the bay.

Seashells (☎ 6461 1033; The Esplanade; 🕑 daily) Grab fish and chips from this, the local takeaway food specialist, and head for the beach. Some groceries available.

GRASSY

There's a supermarket in the town, and the refurbished **Grassy Club** (☎ 6461 1341; Currie Rd;

lunch Thu-Sun, dinner Wed-Mon, bar open daily) has a bar and a bistro with a new owner-chef, and an appealing modern menu of tapas and main dishes showcasing the local gourmet goodies.

Getting There & Away

Flying is your only option for visiting King Island.

King Island Airlines (☎ 9580 3777; www.kingislandair.com.au) flies to King Island daily from Melbourne's Moorabbin airport, with full economy fares costing $150/295 one way/return; booking at least seven days in advance will reduce the return fare to $250.

Regional Express (REX; ☎ 13 17 13; www.regionalexpress.com.au) flies from Tullamarine airport (Melbourne) to King Island, with return fares around $400.

Tasair (☎ 6248 5088; www.tasair.com.au) flies daily from Devonport and Burnie/Wynyard to King Island (costing $363 return from both destinations). Connecting flights from Hobart to Burnie are usually available, but this brings the fare to a whopping $726 return.

You can usually save yourself some money through an airline package deal. King Island Airlines has deals starting at around $350 per person for two nights' accommodation and air fares (car hire is extra). REX also has package deals.

Getting Around

There's no public transport on the island. Hire-car companies will meet you at the airport and bookings are highly recommended.

Most of King Island's 500km of roads are not sealed, so drive carefully. Unless you have a four-wheel drive, take extra care choosing which roads or tracks you take, or be prepared to dig yourself out of some sandy or muddy situations.

In Currie, you can rent cars from **Cheapa Island Car Rental** (☎ 6462 1603; kimotors@kingisland.net.au; 1 Netherby Rd) from around $70 per day; you can reduce your excess from $800 to $330 by paying an extra $6 per day. **King Island Car Rental** (☎ 1800 777 282, 6462 1282; kicars@bigpond.com; 2 Meech St, Currie) has cars from $62 to $110 per day; you can reduce the excess from $1100 to $330 by paying an extra $8.80 per day.

The island's light traffic and flat roads make it straightforward for cycling. You can hire mountain bikes from **The Trend** (☎ 6462 1360; Edward St, Currie).

The island's **taxi service** (☎ 6462 1138) might also prove useful.

FLINDERS ISLAND

☎ 03 / pop 925

Flinders Island (about 60km long and 20km wide) is the largest of the 52 islands that make up the Furneaux Group, and the richest in natural attractions. There are beautiful beaches (especially on the western side), plus outstanding fishing and scuba diving – there's no shortage of shipwrecks around this island group. There are also some great bushwalks, the most popular being the track to the granite Strzelecki Peaks in the Strzelecki National Park – your efforts will be rewarded with superb views of the surrounding area.

First charted in 1798 by the British navigator Matthew Flinders, the Furneaux Group became a base for the Straitsmen, who not only slaughtered seals in their tens of thousands, but also indulged in piracy. Of the 120 or so ships wrecked on the islands' rocks, it's thought that more than a few were purposely lured there by sealers displaying false lights.

The most tragic part of Flinders Island's history, however, was its role in the dismal treatment of Tasmanian Aborigines. Between 1829 and 1834, the Indigenous people who had survived the state's martial law (which gave soldiers the right to arrest or shoot any Aboriginal person found in a settled area) were brought to the island to be resettled. Of the 135 survivors who were transported to Wybalenna (an Aboriginal word that means 'Black Man's Houses') to be 'civilised and educated', only 47 survived to make the journey to Oyster Cove, near Hobart, in 1847. See p21 for more of this sorry tale.

The island's abundant vegetation supports a wide variety of wildlife, including more than 150 bird species. One of the most well known is the Cape Barren goose – its protected habitat and increasing numbers mean that it's no longer close to extinction. The other well-known species is the mutton bird, which was once hunted in large numbers. Drive slowly on the roads at night to avoid hitting nocturnal wildlife.

Whitemark is the main administrative centre for the island, while Lady Barron,

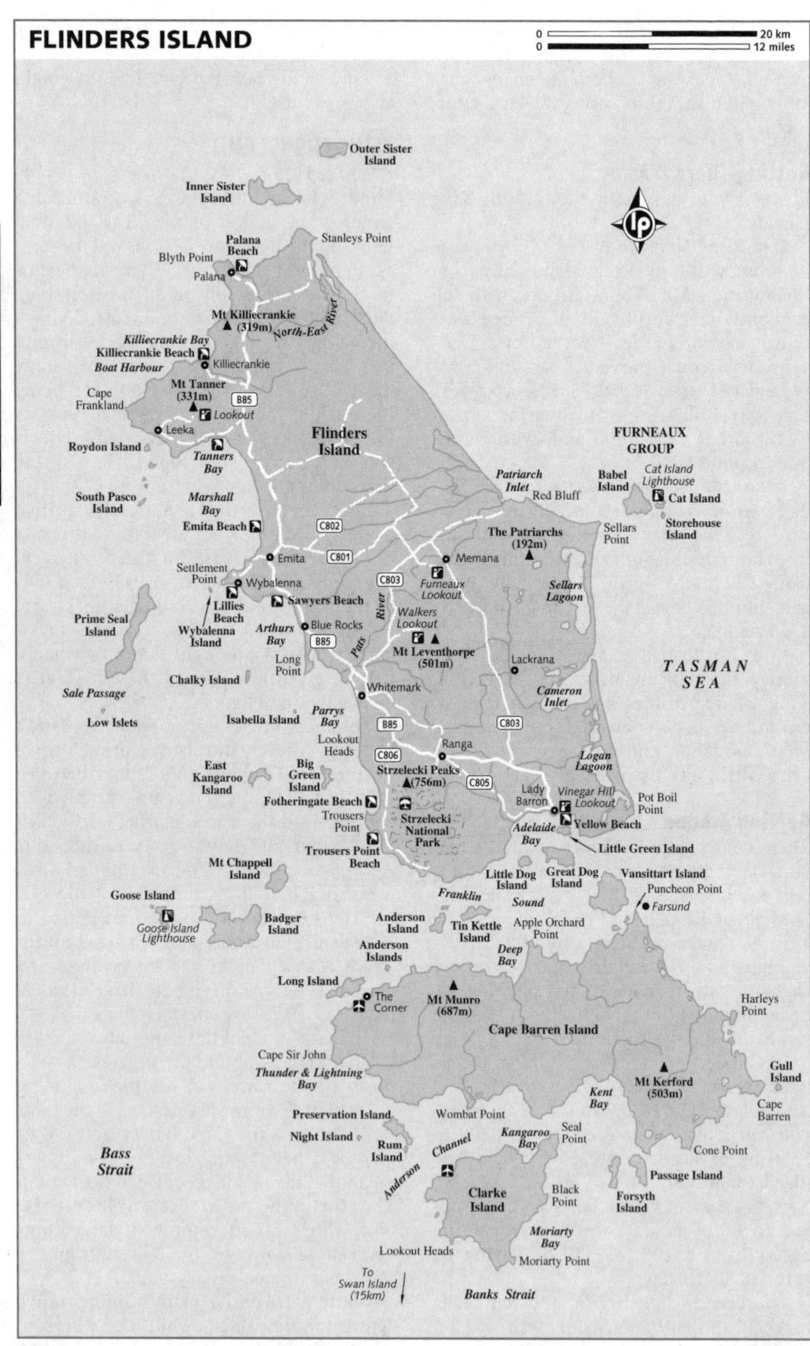

FLINDERS ISLAND
0 20 km
0 12 miles
Outer Sister Island
Inner Sister Island
Palana Beach
Stanleys Point
Blyth Point
Palana
Mt Killiecrankie (319m)
North-East River
Killiecrankie Bay
Killiecrankie Beach
Boat Harbour
Killiecrankie
Cape Frankland
Mt Tanner (331m)
B85
Lookout
Leeka
Flinders Island
Roydon Island
Tanners Bay
FURNEAUX GROUP
Patriarch Inlet
Red Bluff
Babel Island
Cat Island Lighthouse
Cat Island
South Pasco Island
Marshall Bay
Emita Beach
C802
The Patriarchs (192m)
Sellars Point
Storehouse Island
Emita
C801
Memana
Settlement Point
Wybalenna
C803
Furneaux Lookout
Sellars Lagoon
Lillies Beach
Sawyers Beach
River
Walkers Lookout
Prime Seal Island
Wybalenna Island
Arthurs Bay
Blue Rocks
B85
Pats
Mt Leventhorpe (501m)
Lackrana
Long Point
TASMAN SEA
Chalky Island
Whitemark
Cameron Inlet
Sale Passage
Parrys Bay
Low Islets
Isabella Island
B85
C803
Lookout Heads
Ranga
Logan Lagoon
East Kangaroo Island
Big Green Island
C806
Strzelecki Peaks (756m)
C805
Lady Barron
Vinegar Hill Lookout
Pot Boil Point
Fotheringate Beach
Trousers Point
Strzelecki National Park
Yellow Beach
Adelaide Bay
Little Green Island
Trousers Point Beach
Mt Chappell Island
Little Dog Island
Great Dog Island
Vansittart Island
Goose Island
Franklin
Sound
Puncheon Point
Farsund
Goose Island Lighthouse
Badger Island
Anderson Island
Tin Kettle Island
Apple Orchard Point
Anderson Islands
Deep Bay
Long Island
The Corner
Mt Munro (687m)
Harleys Point
Cape Barren Island
Cape Sir John
Thunder & Lightning Bay
Gull Island
Mt Kerford (503m)
Kent Bay
Cape Barren
Preservation Island
Wombat Point
Night Island
Rum Island
Channel
Kangaroo Bay
Seal Point
Cone Point
Bass Strait
Anderson
Clarke Island
Black Point
Passage Island
Forsyth Island
Moriarty Bay
Lookout Heads
Moriarty Point
To Swan Island (15km)
Banks Strait

in the south, is the main fishing area and deepwater port. Industries on the island include farming, fishing and seasonal muttonbirding.

Information

Local tourism operators, shop managers and others on the island are the best sources of information. A helpful website is www.focusonflinders.com.au. Note that regular mobile phones don't work on the island. Petrol can be purchased only in Whitemark and Lady Barron. There are no ATMs, but most businesses have eftpos facilities.

Flinders Island Area Marketing & Development Office (☎ 1800 994 477, 6359 2380; www.flindersislandonline.com.au; PO Box 103, Whitemark 7255) Can help you with pre-planning.

Main post office (Patrick St, Whitemark)

Online Access Centre (☎ 6359 2396; Lagoon St, Whitemark; 🕑 10am-4pm Mon-Fri) Inside the Service Tasmania building.

Sights

WYBALENNA HISTORIC SITE

The Wybalenna Historic Site is all that remains of this unfortunate settlement set up to 'care for' the Aboriginal people. In truth, the opposite was achieved, with most of the people sent here succumbing to disease. This site is rated as one of the most important historic sites in the state. Close by are the cemetery and memorial chapel. In 1999 Wybalenna was returned to the descendants of the Indigenous people who lived there.

FURNEAUX MUSEUM

Not far from Wybalenna, at Emita, is the **Furneaux Museum** (☎ 6359 2010; adult/child $4/free; 🕑 1-5pm daily late Dec-Jan, 1-5pm Sat & Sun rest of year), housed in what was the first government school on the island. The volunteer-staffed museum displays a variety of Aboriginal artefacts (including beautiful shell necklaces) as well as old sealing and sailing relics, and also has a display on the muttonbird industry.

TROUSERS POINT

Located on the island's southwestern tip, the intriguingly named Trousers Point is well worth a visit to explore its spectacular rocks and beaches. There are picnic tables, barbecues and toilets in the camping ground under the drooping she-oaks. The colourful rocks surrounding the point are easily accessible and are the perfect place to drop a fishing line and enjoy great views of the Strzelecki peaks. It's a beautiful spot from which to watch the sunset.

Activities

BUSHWALKING & LOOKOUTS

Bushwalking is a popular activity for visitors. *A Walking Guide to Flinders Island and Cape Barren Island*, by Doreen Lovegrove and Steve Summers (about $12, available from various shops on the island) gives information on a number of walks of varying length and difficulty. Walks along beach and coastal-heath trails can be linked with hinterland and mountain tracks throughout the island.

The 4km-long **Strzelecki Peaks Track**, a key route into the Strzelecki National Park, starts about 12km south of Whitemark on Trousers Point Rd. This well-signposted track ascends Mt Strzelecki to spectacular views at a height of 756m. It's about a four- to five-hour return walk, and it's essential that you carry warm clothing, wet-weather gear, food and water at any time of the year.

The 1½- to two-hour return circuit walk of Trousers Point exposes you to some of the national park's coastal splendour.

There are also a number of lookouts on the island, including **Furneaux Lookout** and **Walkers Lookout**, almost in the centre of the island, plus **Vinegar Hill** in the south and **Mt Tanner** in the north.

ROCK CLIMBING

Rock climbers will find some challenging rock stacks or granite walls on Flinders Island. Mt Killiecrankie has some very steep granite faces rising from sea level. The rock climbs within Strzelecki National Park and the ridge walk along the Strzelecki peaks should be attempted only by experienced walkers and climbers.

FOSSICKING

Rock hounds of another variety can find various localities in which to fossick for the elusive Killiecrankie 'diamond' – actually the semi-precious stone topaz. Most are clear, but some have are pale blue or pink. **Killiecrankie Enterprises** (Killiecrankie ☎ 6359 8560;

Killiecrankie Bay Rd; Whitemark (☎ 6359 2130; Patrick St) can advise lapidaries on good spots to spend some time.

SCUBA DIVING

There are several good scuba-diving locations in the local waters, with abundant sea life and shipwrecks to explore. In many places you can enter from the beach or shelving rocks. **Flinders Island Dive** (☎ 6359 8429; flindersdive@yahoo.com) offers half-/full-day diving charters from $100/160 per person. Mike, the owner, can also arrange fishing charters.

FISHING

Rock fishing along the southern, northern and northwestern coasts is good all year. Bait is easily obtained from the rocks and fishing tackle can be purchased from stores; however, you need to bring your own rod. Beach fishing is popular on the eastern coast and from Red Bluff. The North-East River also has good fishing.

A number of local operators can arrange charter boats and fishing trips:

Flinders Island Adventures (☎ 6359 4507; jamesluddington@bigpond.com) Full-day charter costs $995 for a group of up to eight people, with gear and bait supplied.

Flinders Island Dive (☎ 6359 8429; flindersdive@yahoo.com) Half-/full-day charter from $440/660; all gear supplied.

Killiecrankie Enterprises (☎ 6359 8560; Killiecrankie Bay Rd) Charters its 10-seater boat for fishing or sightseeing for $125 per hour (minimum two hours), $550 per half day or $800 per full day; rods, lines and bait included.

MUTTON BIRDS

Each September, mutton birds (also called shearwaters) return to Flinders and other Bass Strait islands after a summer in the northern hemisphere, to clean out and repair their burrows from the previous year. They then head out to sea again before returning in November for the breeding season, which lasts until April. Eggs are laid in a three-day period and the parents take it in turns (two weeks at a time) to incubate the egg.

Once the single chick has hatched, the parents feed the fledgling until mid-April, when all the adult birds depart, leaving the young to fend for themselves and hopefully to follow their parents north.

Unfortunately for the well-fed mutton birds, they are central to a local industry that commercially values their meat – once the adults leave their nests, the 'birders', or mutton-bird hunters, move in.

Tours

Flinders Island Adventures (☎ 6359 4507; jamesluddington@bigpond.com) Can help you explore the island in a number of ways, including fishing charters (see left), half- or full-day four-wheel-drive tours ($90/156 per person), cruises around the outer islands, and other customisable touring options. It also runs evening tours for $30 a head (late October to late April) from Lady Barron to view the awesome spectacle of thousands of mutton birds (see left returning at sunset to the small islands in Adelaide Bay).

Resolution Adventures (☎ 0408 516 113; www.resolution.org.au) Offers trips aboard a 50ft sailing catamaran out of Lady Barron. Take a half-day cruise ($80 per person, minimum two passengers), full-day outing ($150 per person, minimum four) or sunset cruise ($55), or opt to get away for a few days (from $990 per person for three nights, including all meals; boat sleeps six).

Sleeping

There is a good spread of accommodation on the island – everything from laid-back camping to motel rooms, holiday houses and a retreat offering guaranteed rest and relaxation. The bulk of the options are in the island's south.

WHITEMARK

Interstate Hotel (☎ 6359 2114; interstatehotel@trump.net.au; Patrick St; s $22-60, d $38-90) In the centre of Whitemark is this pub, built in 1911 and renovated in heritage style. It's a comfortable place offering an array of rooms and facilities, from no-frills budget options to better-standard rooms with private shower and TV.

Flinders Island Cabin Park (☎ 6359 2188; fi_cabinpark@yahoo.com.au; Bluff Rd; camp sites $7 per person, cabin d $50-95, extra person $15) This park is about 4km north of Whitemark, close to the airport. On offer are a handful of affordable, family-sized brick cabins, some with private bathroom. The helpful owner also has cars and bikes for rent. The park isn't signposted from the main road – go down the road for Bluff Point, and it's the first property on the left.

LADY BARRON

Furneaux Tavern (☎ 6359 3521; potboil@bigpond.com; Franklin Pde; s/d $80/110, extra person $30) The tavern has 10 comfortable, spacious motel units set in native gardens behind the bar-restaurant. Each unit is equipped with TV, fridge, kettle and toaster (continental breakfast provisions cost extra). Note that some road signage still refers to this place as the Flinders Island Lodge.

Silas Beach (☎ 6359 3521; Franklin Pde; d $130, extra person $35) In an absolute waterfront location and enjoying great views is this modern, three-bedroom holiday house, sleeping six and providing all the comforts of home. Book through the tavern.

Other holiday homes for rent here (usually with a two-night minimum stay) include:

Bucks at Lady Barron (☎ 6359 3535; buckmd@ozemail.com.au; Franklin Pde; d/tr/q $122/126/140) Three bedrooms, sleeps six.

Lady Barron Holiday Home (☎ 6359 3555; mastersflinders@trump.net.au; Franklin Pde; d $82, extra adult/child $16/8) Also with three bedrooms, sleeping six.

TROUSERS POINT AREA

There is free camping in a lovely campground on Trousers Point, where facilities include toilets and gas barbecues (no powered sites, no showers).

THE AUTHOR'S CHOICE

Healing Dreams Retreat (☎ 1800 994 477, 6359 4588; www.healingdreams.com.au; Trousers Point Rd; r $260) Check in to this small retreat (maximum 14 guests) and you can rest assured you'll leave relaxed and revitalised. It's in a great location, at the foot of the Strzelecki Peaks, and with Trousers Point beach close by. Winning features include spacious, well-equipped rooms with eclectic décor, a lovely communal lounge and dining area, small gym, outdoor spa, sauna, massage rooms, and loads of wildlife-rich grounds to explore. The rate listed here is for bed and breakfast only; there are also deals which include treatments, activities and all meals (made from organic produce grown on the property) – see the website for more. And even if you're not staying here, you can get a small group together for an afternoon of massage and hot-tub action – call for details.

Mim's Seaside Shack (☎ 6359 4526; Big River Rd; d $60) About 3km past the turn-off to Trousers Point is this spruced-up beach shack, in a great bush location and fronted by a secluded beach. It's a simple but comfy set-up, and has all the necessary self-catering facilities.

KILLIECRANKIE

Killiecrankie Bay Holiday House (☎ 6359 8560; Killiecrankie Bay Rd; d $110, extra adult/child $20/10) This two-storey, self-contained house is in the island's north, close to lovely Killiecrankie Bay. It's perfect for groups and extended families, with five bedrooms which sleep up to 10 people, including two bathrooms, two kitchens, laundry and barbecue.

Killiecrankie also has a very basic **camping** ($5 per site) area with barbecues, toilets and cold showers (look for the small sign on the main road).

Eating

WHITEMARK

Walkers Supermarket (☎ 6359 2010; Patrick St; 9am-5.30pm Mon-Fri, 9am-12.30pm Sat) Flinders Island's main store has a good range of groceries, as well as fuel.

Flinders Island Bakery (☎ 6359 2105; Lagoon Rd; sandwiches & pies approx $4; 8.30am-5pm Mon-Fri) For lunch, how about a salad roll or chunky lamb curry pie, followed by decent coffee and a slice of lemon tart? The bakery opens on weekends in summer.

Sweet Surprises (☎ 6359 2138; Lagoon Rd; snacks & meals $3-9; 8am-5.30pm Mon-Fri, 9am-1pm Sat) Opposite the bakery is this friendly, low-key coffee shop, serving standard light meals and takeaways.

Interstate Hotel (☎ 6359 2114; Patrick St; lunch $10, dinner mains $16-25; lunch Mon-Fri, dinner Mon-Sat) Drop into this gracious old pub in the centre of Whitemark, the hub of island life. Its dining room serves a range of well-priced lunches and dinners, with the usual array of pub dishes on offer and a welcome emphasis on local seafood.

LADY BARRON

This township's **multi store** (☎ 6359 3503; Henwood St; 9am-5pm daily) has a good range of supplies, plus fuel.

Furneaux Tavern (☎ 6359 3521; Franklin Pde; bar meals $8-12, restaurant mains $22-32; bar meals lunch & dinner daily, restaurant meals lunch & dinner

Wed-Sun) This is your only option for meals in Lady Barron, but the tavern looks after everyone with its great views; social bar; cheap, filling bar meals such as burgers or fish and chips; and a restaurant menu featuring the star players of the local produce scene (including lamb, beef, scallops and fresh fish).

KILLIECRANKIE

The only place to buy food here is at **Killiecrankie Enterprises** (☎ 6359 8560; 527 Killiecrankie Bay Rd; 9am-5pm daily), which has limited supplies, snacks and various hot and cold drinks (and seasonal crayfish, if you order ahead).

Getting There & Away

AIR

Airlines of Tasmania (☎ 1800 144 460, 6359 2312; www.airtasmania.com.au) offers daily scheduled services between Launceston and Flinders Island ($281 return), as well as services to Moorabbin in Victoria three times a week ($395 return). There are additional services according to demand, especially in the peak summer season.

Flinders Island Travel (☎ 1800 674 719, 6224 0444; www.flindersislandtravel.com.au) can help arrange tailor-made package deals (including flights, accommodation and car rental).

FERRY

Southern Shipping Company (☎ 6356 1753; www.focusonflinders.com.au/sship.htm;southernshipping@bigpond.com) operates a ferry once a week (departing Monday) from Bridport in Tasmania's northeast to Flinders Island; the ferry continues to Port Welshpool in Victoria on demand (usually once a month). A return trip to Flinders Island costs $90/50 per adult/child (transporting a vehicle costs from $484 to $870, depending on the vehicle size). The journey takes eight hours. The ferry can carry up to 12 passengers; there is a lounge but no meals or sleeping quarters. Bookings must be made at least a month in advance; phone the shipping company for schedule details.

Getting Around

There is no public transport on the island. Hire-car companies will meet you at the airport and bookings are essential. **Bowman-Lees Car Hire** (☎ 6359 2388), based in Whitemark, rents a mixture of early- and late-model vehicles for between $60 and $80 per day. The Flinders Island Cabin Park (see p308) has cars for similar rates, as well as bikes.

There are a good many unsealed roads on the island, so you'll need to drive carefully, particularly around the more remote areas.

PADDLING STRAIT

Remarkably, the stormy, bitterly cold, often treacherous waters of Bass Strait have proved an irresistible attraction to occasional parties of the very hardiest sea kayakers, battling strong currents and stronger winds to cross between the mainland and Tasmania. The first successful crossing was made, it's thought, in 1971 by a trio of Victorians in slalom kayaks. Since then a number of parties have attempted the crossing, although only about 50 kayakers (so far) have successfully made it across.

It's 'only' a 250km trip measured on the map, but currents, tides and wind drift mean that the kayakers travel much further than that. Bass Strait crossings involve a two-week, or longer, itinerary with entire days often lost to bad weather. Overnight, kayakers stay huddled in tents on the bleak, windswept rocks that pass for islands in the Bass Strait. After a full day's paddling through often 3m-high waves, exhausted paddlers, who just want to crawl into a tent and collapse, are sometimes required to scour rugged island coasts for a safe landing spot where their kayaks won't be dashed to pieces against the rocks. This is the Mt Everest of sea kayaking!

If you trace the usual route south on a map, kayakers run from Wilsons Promontory, the southernmost tip of the Australian mainland, to Hogan Island, Erith Island (Kent Group), Flinders Island, Preservation Island and Clarke Island. Landfall on Tasmanian terra firma is usually at Little Musselroe Bay in Tasmania's northeast.

At the time of research there were no tour operators offering this passage as an organised trip; if you're a very experienced kayaker and really keen, contact one of the main kayaking associations in mainland states to investigate any parties who might be tackling the journey.

Unless you have a four-wheel drive, try not to end up in sandy or slippery places.

There is one **taxi** (☎ 6359 2112) for hire on the island.

OTHER ISLANDS

Cape Barren Island

Cape Barren Island is around 10km to the south of Flinders Island and is the only other island in the Furneaux Group to have a permanent settlement. Kent Bay, on its southern side, was the first settlement south of Sydney. For experienced bushwalkers, the circuit walk of the shoreline offers great coastal views, including the wreck of the *Farsund,* lovely beaches and interesting rock formations.

The main settlement on Cape Barren Island, known as **The Corner**, has a small school, church and medical centre. This was the area given over for the resettlement of the Straitsmen from Flinders Island in 1881. Today's islanders number about 70; the majority of these are Aboriginal, and there are plans for the government to transfer Crown land on the island to the Aboriginal Land Council of Tasmania. The Aborigines here have strong traditions of mutton-birding and shell-necklace making.

Flights to Cape Barren Island are infrequent and it would be better to arrange a charter flight from Melbourne or Launceston if you have the numbers. Alternatively you can fly to Flinders Island and then arrange a boat charter to take you across, allowing you to cache supplies on the way to your drop-off point. You should be able to charter a boat from Flinders Island Adventures (see p308) for this purpose.

Kent Group National Park

In 2001, the half-dozen tiny land masses of the Kent Group, located 55km northwest of Flinders Island, and with only Deal, Dover and Erith big enough to qualify as islands (the other three are islets), became Tasmania's 19th national park. Named by Matthew Flinders after a fellow naval officer in 1798, this 27.5-sq-km region qualified for park status partly due to its cultural heritage, which includes human occupation dating back at least 8000 years, the presence of seal hunters in the 19th century and an old lighthouse on Deal Island. It also qualified because of its outstanding wildlife, such as the sizable fur seal colony at Judgement Rocks and roosting sea birds in the form of short-tailed shearwaters, oystercatchers, petrels and penguins. The waters surrounding the islands are a marine reserve.

Swan Island

There are not many islands where you can be the sole renter, and at reasonably low prices to boot. Swan Island is one of the exceptions. The owners live in one house here and rent the other house on the island.

Just 3km off the northeast coast of Tasmania, this island is 3km long and is dominated by its lighthouse, built in 1845 and automated in 1986 when the government sold the island. The main attraction is a get-away-from-it-all experience. Many sea birds nest in its environs and you can watch the mutton birds and penguins returning to their nests around sunset. The island has several beaches and the immediate area has decent fishing and scuba diving.

The island's self-contained accommodation, **Swan Island Retreat** (☎/fax 6357 2211; s/d $55/77, extra adult $55), is in the old lighthouse keeper's quarters and sleeps up to six. You can also opt for a fully catered stay ($110/187 for a single/double).

There's an airstrip for light planes – discuss charter flight possibilities with the owners when making your booking.

Three Hummock Island

In a similar get-away vein to Swan Island, but at the other end of Bass Strait, is the 29-sq-km Three Hummock Island, 25km off Tasmania's northwestern tip. The sole resident family moved here in 1951 and runs the **Eagle Hill Lodge** (☎ 6452 1405; www.threehummockisland.com.au; $65 per person), which sleeps up to 10 people and has a fully equipped kitchen, lounge and ocean views. Bring your own food if self-catering (arrange this with the owners). Boat hire, guided walks and four-wheel-drive tours are available.

Charter flights to Three Hummock Island are possible leaving from Burnie/Wynyard airport in Tasmania, and from Melbourne's Moorabbin airport. Roaring 40s Ocean Kayaking (p125), basing itself at Kettering in Tasmania's southeast, organises an annual five-day trip to Three Hummock Island, which involves circumnavigating the island by kayak.

Directory

CONTENTS

ACCOMMODATION

It's not difficult to get a good night's sleep in Tasmania, which offers everything from the tent-pegged confines of camping grounds and the communal space of hostels to gourmet breakfasts in guesthouses and at-your-fingertip resorts, plus the gamut of hotel and motel lodgings. But despite the variety of places to stay, Tasmania's main tourist centres are often fully booked in summer, at Easter and during other public holidays, so it's wise to book ahead.

The listings in the Sleeping sections of this guidebook are ordered from budget to midrange to top-end. We generally treat any place that charges up to $40/80 per single/double as budget accommodation. Midrange facilities are $80 to $150 per double, while the top-end tag is applied to places charging more than $150 per double.

In most areas you'll find seasonal price variations. Over summer (December to February) and at other peak times, particularly school and public holidays, prices are usually at their highest. The weekend escape is a notion that figures prominently in the Australian psyche and mainlanders are discovering the joys of a weekend break in Tassie, which means that accommodation from Friday night through Sunday can be in greater demand (and pricier) in major tourist centres. The cooler winter months (June to August) experience significantly less tourist traffic and there can often be decent savings on accommodation prices.

High-season prices are quoted in this book unless otherwise indicated. Use our prices as a guide and remember that stand-by (walk-in) rates and low-season rates (not to mention weekend specials and the like) can be lower than anything quoted in

PRACTICALITIES

- If you're after news, check the main local newspapers: *The Mercury* (www.themercury.com.au) covering Hobart and the south; and *The Examiner* (www.examiner.com.au) in Launceston and the north.
- *40° South* is a glossy quarterly magazine ($10) packed with articles about the state.
- On TV, watch the ad-free ABC, the government-sponsored and multicultural SBS, or one of two commercial stations, namely WIN (the equivalent of Channel Nine on the mainland), or Southern Cross (broadcasting programs from the mainland's Channels Seven and Ten).
- Videos you buy or watch will be based on the PAL system.
- Plugs have angled pins; the electricity supply is 220-240V AC, 50Hz.
- For weights and measures, the metric system is used.

this book. Walk-in rates are best queried late in the day; travellers should also check websites such as www.wotif.com for last-minute deals.

Most accommodation in Tasmania offers nonsmoking rooms (many places, especially hostels and guesthouses, are entirely non-smoking). Air conditioning is rare outside of big-city hotels – but standards of heating may be of more interest to travellers (see right). If you have a car, ask about parking when booking accommodation for central Hobart and Launceston.

For comprehensive listings, the **Royal Automobile Club of Tasmania** (RACT; ☎ 13 27 22; www.ract.com.au) has a statewide directory (updated annually) of accommodation to suit all budgets in almost every town. It's available from the club (and its affiliates, such as the RACV in Victoria or NRMA in NSW) for a nominal charge. Alternatively, check the listings in the free, bimonthly *Tasmanian Travelways* newspaper (available in hard-copy format from visitors centres and other tourist establishments, or online at www.travelways.com.au). Another general option is the website of **Tourism Tasmania** (www.discovertasmania.com), which has comprehensive coverage of accommodation possibilities (click on Where to Stay).

Camping & Caravan Parks

There's an abundance of places in Tasmania where you can camp for free or little cost, many magical in their serenity. For details of the reserves, conservation areas and roadside bays where you can lay your sleeping bag, check out the *Camping Guide to Tasmania*, compiled by Craig Lewis and Cathy Savage (about $10), or go online to the website of the **Parks & Wildlife Service** (www.parks.tas.gov.au) – click on Outdoor Recreation, then Camping & Caravaning. Camping in most national parks requires you to purchase a park pass and then pay a small site fee (up to $6/4 per adult/child), but quite a few parks don't have site fees – though of course this often means minimal facilities.

Tasmania has a large number of camping and caravan parks (sometimes calling themselves 'tourist parks') that generally comprise the state's cheapest form of accommodation, with nightly costs for two campers being anywhere between $12 and $20, slightly more for a powered site. Most towns in Tasmania have camping and caravan parks conveniently close to the city centre (with the notable exception of Hobart). In general, caravan parks are well maintained and represent good value, with almost all of them equipped with hot showers, kitchens and laundry facilities. Some parks offer cheap dormitory-style accommodation, and many have old on-site vans that you can rent for the night, though there is a trend to phase these out in favour of on-site cabins. Cabin sizes and facilities vary, but expect to pay $50 to $90 for two people in a cabin with a kitchenette.

If you intend to do a lot of caravanning/camping, consider joining one of the major chains such as **Big 4** (☎ 9811 9300, 1800 632 444; www.big4.com.au), which offers discounts at member parks.

A good general resource for campers and caravanners is the free *Caravan and Camping in Tasmania* brochure (available from most large visitors centres), and the website www.caravantasmania.com.au.

Guesthouses & B&Bs

Tasmania is like a giant incubator for B&Bs and guesthouses, so numerous are these places. New places are opening all the time and include everything from restored convict-built cottages, rambling old houses, upmarket country manors and beachside bungalows to a simple bedroom in a family home. Note that some places advertise

BRRRRR

If you're travelling around Tasmania in the cooler months (May to September), you may find your accommodation very cold when you arrive, particularly if you're staying in a cottage or self-contained unit. Ask about heating when you make your booking, and if you know your arrival time, ask your hosts to light a fire or turn on the heating in advance.

The heating in cheap hotel rooms, cabins and hostels can sometimes be plain inadequate; if you have your own transport and intend to stay in such accommodation, consider packing a small heater of your own as a back-up. The good news is that many establishments have electric blankets on their beds.

themselves as B&Bs but are in actual fact self-contained cottages with breakfast provisions supplied.

Only in the cheaper B&Bs are you likely to have to share the bathrooms and the toilets – sometimes the lack of an en suite simply means the exclusive use of a separate bathroom across the hall. Breakfast is cooked or continental and is often supplied in the form of provisions that you must cook or serve yourself. Some B&B hosts, especially in isolated locations or in small towns where restaurants are limited, may cook dinner for guests (usually 24 hours' notice is required). Rates usually range from $70 to $160 a double, although there is a lack of B&B accommodation at the lower end of this price range, and rooms in top-end places can go for much more.

The best online information is at **Bed & Breakfast and Boutique Accommodation of Tasmania** (www.tasmanianbedandbreakfast.com), with links to over 140 B&Bs.

Hostels

Though not as prolific as on the mainland, youth hostels and/or backpacker facilities can be found in major towns (although the YHA network in Tasmania is shrinking).

To stay in a hostel you often need to supply your own bed linen – for hygiene reasons, a regular sleeping bag will not do. If you haven't got sheets they can be rented at many hostels (for around $3 to $5).

INDEPENDENT HOSTELS

Tasmania has plenty of independent hostels. The standard of these can vary enormously: some places are run-down hotels trying to fill empty rooms (the unrenovated ones are often gloomy and depressing); others are converted motels where each four-to-six-bed unit has a fridge, TV and bathroom, but communal areas and cooking facilities may be lacking. There are also purpose-built hostels, often with the best facilities. The best places tend to be smaller, more intimate hostels where the owner is also the manager, and this is the norm in Tasmania.

Independent backpacker establishments typically charge $19 to $26 for a dorm bed and $40 to $60 for a twin or double room (usually without bathroom).

YHA HOSTELS

At the time of research, Tasmania has 14 hostels as part of the **Youth Hostels Association** (YHA; www.yha.com.au). The YHA is part of the **International Youth Hostel Federation** (IYHF; www.hihostels.com), also known as Hostelling International (HI), so if you're already a member of that organisation in your own country, your membership entitles you to YHA rates in the relevant Tasmanian hostels.

The annual *YHA Accommodation & Discounts Guide* booklet is available from any Australian YHA office and from some offices overseas, and gives details of all the YHA hostels in Australia (including prices), plus any membership discount entitlements (transport, activities etc).

The **Tasmanian YHA office** (Map p70; ☎ 6234 9617; yhatas@yhatas.org.au; 1st fl, 28 Criterion St, Hobart) hands out information to travellers and also conducts an Australia-wide hostel-to-hostel booking service.

Nightly charges are between $10 and $30 for members; most hostels also take non-YHA members for an extra $3.50. Visitors to Australia should purchase a HI card preferably in their country of residence, but can also buy one at major local YHA hostels at a cost of $35 for 12 months; see the HI website for further details. Australian residents can become full YHA members for $52/85 for one/two years; join online, at the Hobart or any state office, or at any YHA hostel.

YHA hostels provide basic accommodation, usually in small dormitories (bunk rooms), and often also have twin and double rooms. They usually have 24-hour access, cooking and laundry facilities, and a communal area with a TV. Many have informative noticeboards and lots of brochures.

Hotels & Motels

Except for pubs (see opposite), hotels in cities or places visited by lots of tourists are generally of the business or luxury variety where you get a comfortable, anonymous and mod-con filled room in a multistorey block. These places tend to have a restaurant-café, room service and various other facilities. We quote 'rack rates' (the official advertised rates) throughout this book; often hotels and motels offer discounts.

For comfortable midrange accommodation, motels (or motor inns) are the places to stay. Prices vary and there's rarely a cheaper rate for singles, so they're better if you are travelling as a couple or a group of three. Motels in Tasmania tend to be squat structures that congregate just outside the CBD or on the highways at the edge of town. Most are modern-ish (though the décor in many seems stuck in a 1970s time warp) and have similar facilities (tea- and coffee-making, fridge, TV, bathroom) but the price will indicate the standard. You'll mostly pay between $60 and $120 for a room.

Not many of the familiar hotel chains have a presence in Tasmania, but following are some useful accommodation groups and websites:

Best Western (☎ 13 17 79; www.bestwestern.com.au) A midrange chain with 17 properties (predominantly motels) throughout the state

Federal Hotels & Resorts (☎ 1800 130 002; www.federalresorts.com.au) Upmarket hotels and resorts in Hobart, Launceston, Strahan, Cradle Mountain and Freycinet National Park.

Grand Hotels International (www.ghihotels.com) Operates the swish Hotel Grand Chancellor in Hobart and Launceston; also has less ritzy Chancellor Inns in places like Scamander, Port Arthur, Burnie and Queenstown.

The Innkeepers Collection (☎ 6224 3579, 1300 130 269; www.innkeeper.com.au) Large, Tasmania-wide accommodation group that includes hotels, motels, lodges and apartments.

Pubs

Hotels in Australia are the places that serve beer – commonly known as pubs (from the term 'public house'). Pub rooms are invariably cheap, upstairs, small, older in style and plain, with a long amble down the hall to the (shared) bathroom. That said, plenty of aging hotels have been renovated in recent times. In many smaller towns, staying at a pub means that you'll be in the social heart of the community.

You can sometimes rent a single room at a pub for not too much more than you'd pay for a bed in a hostel dorm. Standard pubs have singles/doubles with shared facilities starting from prices of around $25/50; a continental breakfast is often included in the price. Few pubs have a separate reception area – just ask in the bar whether there are rooms available. But if you're a light sleeper, never book a room above the bar, especially on Friday and Saturday nights.

The useful website www.tassiepubs.com.au has details of hotels offering pub accommodation.

Self-Contained Apartments & Cottages

Holiday units are predominantly self-contained, with many rented on either a daily or weekly basis. They often have two or more bedrooms, making them cost-effective for groups. The prices given in this guide are for single-night stays and are mostly in the range of about $65 to $100 a double – the larger units (which are often referred to as 'villas' or 'chalets') regularly cost over $100 per double, while historic cottages can be anything up to about $150 a double, higher in the pricier parts of Hobart or historic towns like Richmond. Unlike prices for holiday units, prices for historic cottages usually include breakfast (with cook-your-own provisions provided).

TasVillas (☎ 6344 3222, 1800 030 111; www.tasvillas.com.au) is a network of self-contained, self-catering accommodation throughout the state. **Cottages of the Colony** (www.cottagesofthecolony.com.au) has links to self-contained historic cottages.

Other Accommodation

There are also less-conventional accommodation possibilities. Farmers may be willing to rent out a room in exchange for some labour, or just to supplement their income.

Back in city limits, it's sometimes possible to stay in the hostels and halls of residence normally occupied by university students, though you'll need to time your stay to coincide with the longer uni holiday periods (from November to February).

If you want to spend a bit longer in Tasmania, the first place to look for a shared flat or a room is in the classifieds advertisements section of the daily newspapers – Wednesday and Saturday are usually the best days. Noticeboards in universities, hostels, bookshops and cafés are also good to check out.

ACTIVITIES

See the Tasmania Outdoors chapter on p44.

BUSINESS HOURS

Most shops and businesses are open from 9am to 5pm or 5.30pm Monday to Friday, and to either noon or 5pm on Saturday.

Sunday trading is becoming more common but it's currently limited to the major cities. Also in most large towns there is usually one late shopping night each week (normally Friday) when traders keep their doors open until 9pm. You'll find milk bars (general stores) and also convenience stores often open until late and usually open over the weekend.

Banks are normally open 9.30am to 4pm Monday to Thursday, and until 5pm Friday. The exception is in small towns where they may open only one or two days a week.

Post offices are generally open 9am to 5pm weekdays, but you can also buy stamps from newsagencies.

Restaurants typically open at noon for lunch and between 6pm and 7pm for dinner; most dinner bookings are made for 7pm or 7.30pm. Restaurants are typically open until at least 9pm but tend to serve food until later on Friday and Saturday. That said, the main restaurant strips in large cities keep longer hours throughout the week. Cafés tend to be all-day affairs that either close around 5pm or continue their business into the night (often to around 8pm). Pubs usually serve food from noon to 2pm and from 6pm to 8pm. Pubs and bars often open for drinking at lunchtime and continue well into the evening, particularly from Thursday to Saturday.

Keep in mind that nearly everything is closed on Christmas Day.

CHILDREN

Practicalities

Hobart and most major towns have centrally located public rooms where mothers (and sometimes fathers) can go to nurse their baby or change its nappy; check with the local visitors centre or city council for details. While many Australians have a relaxed attitude about breast-feeding or nappy changing in public, others frown on it.

Most motels and the better-equipped caravan parks will be able to supply cots and baby baths. Some also have playgrounds, games rooms or swimming pools. Top-end and some midrange hotels are well versed in the needs of guests who have children; some may also have in-house children's videos and child-minding services. B&Bs, on the other hand, often market themselves as sanctuaries from all things child-related.

Some cafés and restaurants make it difficult to dine with small children, lacking a specialised children's menu, but many others do have kids' meals, or will provide small serves from the main menu. Some also supply high chairs.

Child concessions (and family rates) often apply for such things as accommodation, tours, admission fees, and air and bus transport, with discounts as high as 50% of the adult rate. However, the definition of 'child' can vary from under 12 to under 18 years. Accommodation concessions generally apply to children under 12 years sharing the same room as adults. On the major airlines, infants travel free provided they don't occupy a seat – child fares usually apply between the ages of two and 11 years.

Items such as baby food formula and disposable nappies are widely available in urban centres. Major hire-car companies will supply and fit booster seats for you, for which you'll be charged around $16 for up to three days' use, with an additional daily fee for longer periods.

Lonely Planet's *Travel with Children* contains plenty of useful information for travel with ankle-biters.

Sights & Activities

Tasmania is a place where kids can't complain about a lack of nature-based activities, because there's almost always a forest, national park trail or beach in the immediate vicinity. There's also an array of active pursuits available (cruises, kayaking, quad-biking), although such activities may well mean a bit more financial expenditure from parents.

Nearly all tourist attractions offer significant discounts for children, with the very young often admitted free. Not all of Tasmania's historic buildings and museums will hold the interest of kids, but there are still plenty of historical, natural or science-based exhibits to get them thinking – these range from wildlife parks and aquariums to ghost tours.

CLIMATE

Tasmania is in the path of the Roaring 40s, a notorious current of wind that encircles the globe and produces very changeable weather. It's not surprising, then, that the west and southwest can be blasted by strong

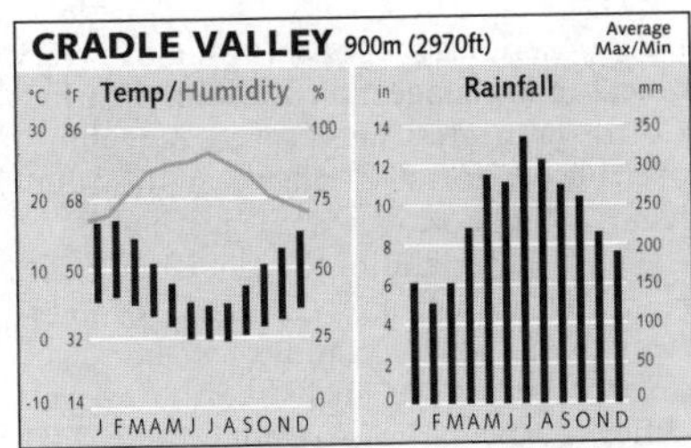

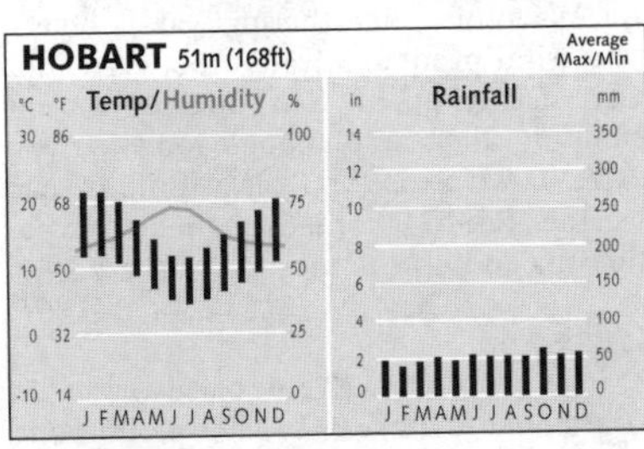

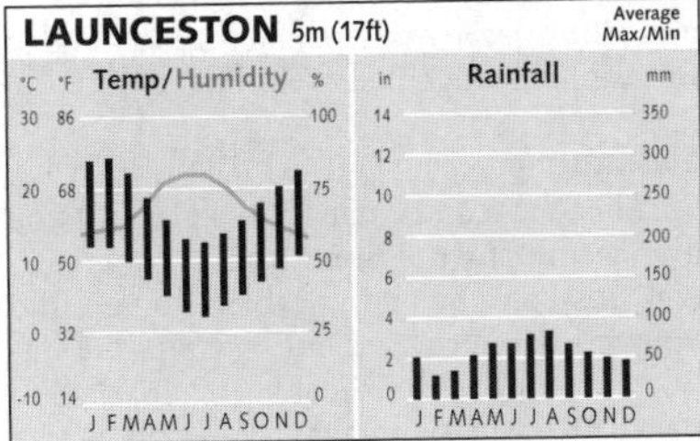

winds and drenched by heavy rain. Nevertheless, because the state is small and also an island, it enjoys a maritime climate, which means that it's rarely extremely cold or extremely hot. The east coast is nearly always warmer and milder than anywhere else in the state. Hobart is Australia's second-driest capital after Adelaide.

Tasmania experiences four distinct seasons, although storms can deposit wintry conditions any time of year. Summer (December to February), with its generally warm days and mild nights, is the most pleasant time of year.

See p13 for more information on the seasons.

CUSTOMS & QUARANTINE

For comprehensive information on customs regulations, contact the **Australian Customs Service** (☎ 1300 363 263, 02-6275 6666; www.customs.gov.au).

> **INTERSTATE QUARANTINE**
>
> There are stringent rules in place to protect the 'disease-free' status of the agriculture of this island state, and fresh fruit, vegetables and plants cannot be brought into Tasmania. Tourists must discard all items prior to their arrival (even if they're only travelling from mainland Australia). There are sniffer dogs at Tasmanian airports, and quarantine inspection posts at the Devonport ferry terminal; while quarantine control here often relies on honesty, officers are entitled to search your car for undeclared items.

When entering Australia you can bring most articles in free of duty provided that they are for personal use and you'll be taking them with you when you leave. There's a duty-free quota per person of 1125mL of alcohol, 250 cigarettes and dutiable goods up to the value of A$400.

When it comes to prohibited goods, there are a few things you should be particularly conscientious about. The first is drugs, which customs authorities are adept at sniffing out; the second is all food, plant material and animal products.

DANGERS & ANNOYANCES

Animal Hazards

Judging by Australia's remarkable profusion of dangerous creatures, Mother Nature must have been really pissed off when she concocted the local wildlife. Travellers don't need to be in a constant state of alarm, however – you're unlikely to see many of these creatures in the wilds of Tasmania, much less be attacked by one.

INSECTS

For four to six months of the year you'll have to cope with those two banes of the Australian outdoors: the fly and the mosquito (mozzie). Flies aren't too bad in the cities but they can get out of hand in the bush. Mosquitoes get active around sunset; insect repellents go some way towards deterring these pests, and calamine lotion can soothe the bites, but it's best to cover up.

LEECHES

Leeches may be present in damp rainforest conditions; they attach themselves to your skin to suck your blood. Trekkers often get them on their legs or in their boots. Salt or a lighted cigarette end will make them fall off. Do not pull them off, as the bite is then more likely to become infected. Clean and apply pressure if the point of attachment is bleeding. An insect repellent may keep them away.

SNAKES

The dangerous animal that captures visitors' imaginations the most is the snake. Although all snakes in Tasmania are venomous, they are not aggressive and, unless you have the bad fortune to stand on one, it's unlikely you'll be bitten. February is the month when snakes are at their most active.

To minimise your chances of being bitten, always wear boots, socks and long trousers when walking through undergrowth where snakes may be present. Don't put your hands into holes and crevices, and be careful when collecting firewood. Most importantly, if you see a snake, leave it alone.

For information on treating snake bites, see p344.

SPIDERS

One eight-legged critter to stay away from is the black one with a distinctive red stripe on its body, called (strangely) the redback spider; for bites, apply ice and seek medical attention. The white tail is a long, thin, black spider with, you guessed it, a white tail, and has a fierce bite that can lead to local inflammation. The disturbingly large huntsman spider, which often enters homes, is harmless, though seeing one for the first time can affect your blood pressure.

Bushfires & Blizzards

Bushfires are a regular occurrence in Australia. In hot, dry and windy weather, be extremely careful with any naked flame – cigarette butts thrown out of car windows have started many a fire. On a total fire ban day it's forbidden to use even a camping stove in the open. Locals will not be amused if they catch you breaking this particular law; they'll happily dob you in, and the penalties are severe.

When a total fire ban is in place, bushwalkers should delay their trip until the weather improves. If you're out in the bush and you see smoke, even a long way away, take it seriously – bushfires move very quickly and change direction with the wind. Go to the nearest open space, downhill if possible. A forested ridge, on the other hand, is the most dangerous place to be.

At the other end of the elemental scale, blizzards can occur in Tasmania's mountains at any time of year. Bushwalkers need to be prepared for such freezing eventualities, particularly in remote areas. Take warm clothing like thermals and jackets, plus wind-proof and waterproof garments. Carry a high-quality tent suitable for snow camping and carry enough food for two extra days, in case you get held up by bad weather. See p344 for information on hypothermia and how to minimise its risk.

Crime

Tasmania is a relatively safe place to visit but you should still take reasonable precautions. Don't leave hotel rooms or cars unlocked, and don't leave your valuables unattended or visible through a car window.

Swimming

Surf beaches can be dangerous places if you aren't used to the conditions. Undertows (or 'rips') are the main problem. If you find yourself being carried out by a rip, the important thing to do is just keep afloat; don't panic or try to swim against the rip, which will exhaust you. In most cases the current stops within a couple of hundred metres of the shore and you can then swim parallel to the shore for a short way to get out of the rip and make your way back to land.

DISABLED TRAVELLERS

Disability awareness in Tasmania is pretty high and getting higher. Legislation requires that new accommodation meet accessibility standards, and discrimination by tourism operators is illegal. Many key attractions provide access for those with limited mobility and a good number of tour operators also have the appropriate facilities – it's still a good idea, though, to call ahead and confirm this. There are also a number of local agencies that provide information and/or assistance to disabled travellers.

The best source of reliable information is the **National Information Communication and Awareness Network** (Nican; ☎/TTY 02-6285 3713, TTY 1800 806 769; www.nican.com.au). It's an Australia-wide directory providing information on access issues, accessible accommodation, sporting and recreational activities, transport and specialist tour operators.

Tourism Tasmania (☎ 6230 8235, 1800 806 846; www.discovertasmania.com) has details of disability-friendly accommodation, attractions and services. Other recommended sources include the **Paraplegic & Quadriplegic Association Tasmania** (☎ 6272 8816; www.paraquadtas.org.au), with information about accommodation, accessible toilets, mobility maps and attractions; and the **Aged & Disability Care Information Service** (☎ 6234 7448; www.adcis.org.au).

The **Parks & Wildlife Service** (☎ 1300 135 513; www.parks.tas.gov.au) publishes a useful brochure, *Parks for all People*, which outlines access for mobility-impaired visitors to Tasmania's national parks and reserves. This information is also available online at www.parks.tas.gov.au/recreation/disabled/disabled.html.

One recent initiative of great interest to disabled travellers is the **Devils Playground** (☎ 6343 3119; www.thedevilsplayground.com.au), a planned touring circuit of the state, with affordable accommodation and barrier-free facilities at many locations. The website gives details.

DISCOUNT CARDS

The **International Student Travel Confederation** (ISTC; www.istc.org) is an international collective of specialist student travel organisations. It's also the body behind the internationally recognised International Student Identity Card (ISIC), which is issued to full-time students aged 12 years and over, and gives the bearer discounts on accommodation, transport and admission to various attractions.

Senior travellers and travellers with disabilities who reside in Australia are eligible for concession cards; most states and territories issue their own version and these can be used Australia-wide. Senior and disabled travellers who live overseas will generally find that the cards issued by their respective countries are not 'officially' recognised in Australia, but that most places (though not all) will still acknowledge such a card and grant a concession where one applies.

See Tasmania Card

A recent initiative is the **See Tasmania 'Smartvisit' Card** (☎ 1300 661 711; www.seetasmaniacard.com), which might be of interest to short-term visitors. Purchase of the card allows free or discounted entry to some 60 attractions and activities around the state (including national parks, National Trust properties and big-ticket drawcards like the Port Arthur Historic Site and the Tahune Forest AirWalk), plus a book and maps to help you plan your travels. The card is not cheap, however ($129/69 per adult/child for three days, $189/119 for seven days, and $269/169 for 10 days), and it's worth noting that it can only be used on consecutive days. Before purchasing, do some research to determine if it's a worthwhile investment – you should be intending to do a lot of sightseeing in a relatively short time. Cards can be purchased online, from many travel agents, and from Thrifty car-rental outlets in Tasmania.

EMBASSIES & CONSULATES

Australian Embassies & Consulates

The website of the **Department of Foreign Affairs & Trade** (www.dfat.gov.au) provides a full listing of all Australian diplomatic missions overseas. They include:

Canada Ottawa (☎ 613-236 0841; www.ahc-ottawa.org; Suite 710, 50 O'Connor St, Ottawa, Ontario K1P 6L2) Also in Vancouver and Toronto.

France Paris (☎ 01-40 59 33 00; www.austgov.fr; 4 Rue Jean Rey, 75724 Cedex 15, Paris)

Germany Berlin (☎ 030-880 0880; www.australian-embassy.de; Friedrichstrasse 200, 10117 Berlin) Also in Frankfurt.

Ireland Dublin (☎ 01-664 5300; www.australianembassy.ie; 2nd fl, Fitzwilton House, Wilton Tce, Dublin 2)

Japan Tokyo (☎ 03-5232 4111; www.australia.or.jp; 2-1-14 Mita, Minato-Ku, Tokyo 108-8361) Also in Osaka, Nagoya and Fukuoka City.

Netherlands Hague (☎ 070-310 82 00; www.australian-embassy.nl; Carnegielaan 4, The Hague 2517 KH)

New Zealand Wellington (☎ 04-473 6411; www australia.org.nz; 72-78 Hobson St, Thorndon, Wellington); Auckland (☎ 09-921 8800; Level 7, Price Waterhouse Coopers Bldg, 186-194 Quay St, Auckland)

UK London (☎ 020-7379 4334; www.australia.org.uk; Australia House, The Strand, London WC2B 4LA) Also in Edinburgh and Manchester.

USA Washington DC (☎ 202-797 3000; www.austemb.org; 1601 Massachusetts Ave NW, Washington DC 20036) Also in Los Angeles, New York and other major cities.

Embassies & Consulates in Australia

The principal diplomatic representations to Australia are in Canberra. There are also representatives in other major cities, particularly from countries which have strong links with Australia like the USA, the UK and New Zealand.

Consulates in Hobart include the following. For a complete listing, look in the Tasmanian **Yellow Pages** (www.yellowpages.com.au).

Germany (☎ 6223 1814; 348 Sandy Bay Rd)

Netherlands (☎ 6225 3951; 439A Sandy Bay Rd)

FESTIVALS & EVENTS

The events pages of the website of **Tourism Tasmania** (www.discovertasmania.com/events/) have comprehensive coverage of goings-on in the state.

Details of festivals grounded in a single town or area are provided throughout this book – see especially the Festivals & Events sections of the Hobart (p82) and Launceston (p199) chapters.

Major state-wide or region-specific festivals includen the following:

March

Taste of the Huon Two-day festival in mid-March celebrating the food, wine, music and crafts of the Huon Valley, D'Entrecasteaux Channel area and Bruny Island.

Ten Days on the Island (www.tendaysontheisland.com) Biennial event (odd-numbered years) which usually runs from late March until early April and is Tasmania's premier cultural festival.

Three Peaks Race (www.threepeaks.org.au) Crazy four-day event where competitors have to sail their yachts and also run up three of Tasmania's higher mountains (Mt Strzelecki, Mt Freycinet and Mt Wellington). It starts from Beauty Point north of Launceston every Easter (March-April).

April

Anzac Day National public holiday (25 April) commemorating the landing of Anzac troops at Gallipoli in 1915. Memorial marches by returned soldiers are held all over the country.

Targa Tasmania (www.targa.org.au) Six-day rally for exotic cars that runs around the entire state, appropriating 200km of roads as it goes.

September

Blooming Tasmania Beginning in spring and lasting over six months, this is a coordinated set of festivals, displays and open gardens around the state. A special brochure is produced every year detailing when each festival occurs and when gardens are open to the public (available online at www.discovertasmania.com – click on Things to See & Do, Island Lifestyle & Culture, then Gardens).

October

Royal Shows The royal agricultural and horticultural shows of Hobart, Burnie and Launceston are held during this month.

FOOD

The innovative food that is offered in top-quality Tasmanian eateries doesn't always cost a fortune. Best value are the modern cafés, where you can get a good meal in casual surroundings for under $20. A full cooked breakfast at a café costs around $10. Some inner-city pubs offer upmarket restaurant-style fare, but most pubs serve standard (often large-portion, meat-heavy) bistro meals, usually in the $10 to $19 range, and these are served in the dining room or lounge bar. Bar (or counter) meals, which are eaten in the public bar, usually cost between $6 and $10. Top restaurants have main meals (generally showcasing the state's fantastic produce) in the $20 to $30 price range.

For general opening hours consider that breakfast is normally served between 6am and 11am, lunch starts around noon till 2pm or 3pm and dinner usually starts after 6pm.

See the Food & Drink chapter (p58) for more information.

GAY & LESBIAN TRAVELLERS

On 1 May 1997, after a nine-year law-reform campaign, the Tasmanian parliament repealed Tasmania's anti-gay laws, thereby complying with the 1994 UN ruling on this issue and eliminating Australia's only remaining state law banning same-sex relations. Tasmania is now considered by gay- and lesbian-rights groups to have greater equality in criminal law for homosexual and heterosexual people than most of the other Australian states. The website of **Tourism Tasmania** (www.discovertasmania.com – click on About Tas, then Gay & Lesbian) has background information, and testimonials to assure travellers that the bad old days are well and truly over. Rodney Croome is the high-profile Tasmanian gay advocate who fronted the long campaign to decriminalise homosexuality in Tassie. His website (www.rodneycroome.id.au) has some great reading on gay life in the island state, among other subjects.

There are small but proud gay and lesbian communities in Tasmania. The **Gay and**

Lesbian Community Centre (GLC Centre; www.glctas.org), based in Hobart but with Tasmania-wide links, is a good source of information on issues and events involving the gay and lesbian community. It has a regular stand at Hobart's Salamanca Market and produces a few useful publications, including a monthly newsletter and annual business directory. There is a **gay information line** (☎ 6234 8179) with a host of contact numbers for support groups, plus details of coming events and gay-friendly bars and restaurants. The Venues page of the **Queer Society** (www.queertas.com) at the University of Tasmania is also a good source of information.

Be sure to pick up at copy of the free GayTas map (available at most visitors centres), updated regularly and listing gay-owned and gay-friendly businesses throughout the state. There's a growing number of high-quality gay-owned accommodation in Tasmania, including Corinda's Cottages in Hobart (p87); Riseley Cottage, south of Dover (p140); Kabuki by the Sea, south of Swansea (p166); Meredith House & Mews in Swansea (p165); and Oatlands Lodge in Oatlands (p146).

Gay and lesbian travellers should also check out the Tasmania pages on the website of the **Gay Australia Guide** (www.gayaustraliaguide.com), although some of the listings for dining and nightlife are out of date.

HOLIDAYS

Public Holidays

The holidays listed are statewide unless indicated:

New Year's Day 1 January
Australia Day 26 January
Hobart Regatta Day2nd Monday or Tuesday in February (southern Tasmania)
Launceston Cup Last Wednesday in February (Launceston only)
Eight Hour Day 2nd Monday in March
Easter March/April (Good Friday to Easter Tuesday inclusive)
Anzac Day 25 April
Queen's Birthday 2nd Monday in June
Burnie Show 1st Friday in October (Burnie only)
Launceston Show 2nd Thursday in October (Launceston only)
Hobart Show 3rd Thursday in October (southern Tasmania)
Recreation Day 1st Monday in November (northern Tasmania)
Devonport Show Last Friday in November (Devonport only)
Christmas Day 25 December
Boxing Day 26 December

School Holidays

The Christmas holiday season, from mid-December to late January, is part of the summer school vacation and is the time when accommodation often books out. There are three shorter school holiday periods during the year, but they vary by a week or two from year to year, falling from early to mid-April, late June to mid-July, and late September to early October. For a useful list of school holidays in all Australian states, see www.dest.gov.au/schools/dates.htm.

INSURANCE

Don't underestimate the importance of a good travel-insurance policy that covers theft, loss and medical problems. Most policies offer lower and higher medical-expense options; the higher ones are chiefly for countries that have extremely high medical costs, such as the USA. There is a wide variety of policies available, so compare the small print.

Some policies specifically exclude designated 'dangerous activities' such as scuba diving, motorcycling, skiing and even bushwalking. If you plan on doing any of these things, make sure the policy you choose fully covers you.

You may prefer a policy that pays doctors or hospitals direct rather than you having to pay on the spot and claim later. If you have to claim later make sure you keep all documentation. Check that the policy covers ambulances and emergency medical evacuations by air.

See also Predeparture (p342) in the Health chapter. For information on insurance matters relating to rental cars, see p338.

INTERNET ACCESS

Whether you use Internet cafés or bring along your own computer, it's easy to get connected in Tasmania. You'll find cybercafés in the main towns, and Internet kiosks or terminals at many hostels and hotels. As part of a government-funded telecommunications scheme, online access centres have been set up in around 65 of the state's towns. They are intended primarily for rural Tasmanians, but also provide Internet access for visitors. For a complete listing of these centres, which charge reasonable rates and are located primarily (but not exclusively) in libraries and schools, pick up the *Tasmanian Communities Online* brochure at many visitors centres, or visit the scheme's website at www.tco.asn.au.

LEGAL MATTERS

Most travellers will have no contact with the Australian police or any other part of the legal system. Those that do are likely to experience it while driving. There is a significant police presence on the country's roads, with the power to stop your car and ask to see your licence (you're required to carry it), check your vehicle for roadworthiness, and also to insist that you take a breath test for alcohol. Needless to say, drink-driving offences are taken seriously here.

If you are arrested, it's your right to telephone a friend, relative or lawyer before any formal questioning begins. Legal Aid is available only in serious cases and only to the truly needy (for links to Legal Aid offices see www.nla.aust.net.au). However, many solicitors do not charge for an initial consultation.

MAPS

The selection of maps available is wide, but many are of average quality. One of the best road maps of the state (1:500,000) is produced by the **Royal Automobile Club of Tasmania** (RACT; ☎ 13 27 22; www.ract.com.au) and is on sale in the organisation's offices around the island. This sheet map includes detail of main city centres.

For more detail, including contours, the maps (1:250,000) published by the state government's Department of Primary Industries, Water & Environment (DPIWE), more specifically its map publication arm TASMAP, are recommended. The state is covered in four sheets, which are available from map retailers.

The best atlas is the *Tasmania Country Road Atlas* (around $30), published by UBD. The 16th edition was published in 2004 and contains clear, detailed maps of over 45 significant towns in the state. It's available from various newsagencies, bookshops and visitors centres, at **Service Tasmania** (☎ 1300 135 513; www.service.tas.gov.au; 134 Macquarie St, Hobart) and the **Tasmanian Map Centre** (☎ 6231 9043; www.map-centre.com.au; 100 Elizabeth St, Hobart).

DPIWE also produces 1:25,000 topographic sheets appropriate for bushwalking, ski-touring and other activities requiring large-scale maps. Many of the more popular sheets, including day walks and bushwalks in national parks, are usually available over the counter at shops specialising in bushwalking gear and outdoor equipment, and also at urban and national park visitors centres, Service Tasmania or the Tasmanian Map Centre.

MONEY

Australia's currency is the Australian dollar, made up of 100 cents. There are 5c, 10c, 20c, 50c, $1 and $2 coins, and $5, $10, $20, $50 and $100 notes. Although the smallest coin in circulation is 5c, prices are often still marked in single cents and then rounded to the nearest 5c when you come to pay.

See p15 to get an idea of expenses in Tasmania.

ATMs, Eftpos & Bank Accounts

Banks exist in most sizeable Tasmanian towns, but in the smaller centres are often open only two or three days a week. Post offices act as agents for the Commonwealth Bank, although like banks, post offices in many of the smaller towns are open only restricted weekday hours. Even the 24-hour ATMs, most of which accept cards from other banks and can be used to withdraw up to $1000 a day (cash amount varies depending on the bank), can be few and far between outside the state's largest centres. However, there's usually at least one pub, general store, petrol station or newsagent in town that offers an Electronic Funds Transfer at Point Of Sale (eftpos) service. This means that you can use your credit or debit card to pay for purchases and, in the case of debit cards, simultaneously make small cash withdrawals (you'll need your PIN).

Credit Cards

Perhaps the best way to carry most of your money is in the form of a plastic card, especially if that's the way you do it at home. Australia is well and truly a card-carrying society – credit cards such as Visa and MasterCard are widely accepted for everything from a hostel bed or a restaurant meal to an adventure tour, and a credit card is pretty much essential (in lieu of a large deposit) if you want to hire a car. They can also be used to get cash advances over the counter at banks and from many ATMs, depending on the card, but be aware that these incur immediate interest. Charge cards such as Diners Club and American Express (Amex) are not as widely accepted.

Apart from losing them, the obvious danger with credit cards is maxing out your limit and going home to a steaming pile of debt and interest charges. A safer option is a debit card with which you can draw money directly from your home bank account using ATMs, banks or Eftpos machines around the country. Any card connected to the international banking network – Cirrus, Maestro, Plus and Eurocard – should work, provided you know your PIN. Fees for using your card at a foreign bank or ATM vary depending on your home bank; ask before your leave.

The most flexible option is to carry both a credit and a debit card.

Exchanging Money

Changing major forms of foreign currency or travellers cheques is usually no problem at banks throughout Australia or at licensed moneychangers such as Thomas Cook or Amex in the major cities.

See the table on the inside back cover of this book for exchange rates at the time of publication.

Taxes & Refunds

The Goods and Services Tax (GST), introduced by the federal government in 2000 amid much controversy, is a flat 10% tax on all goods and services – accommodation, eating out, transport, books, furniture, clothing and so on. There are, however, some exceptions, such as basic foods (milk, bread, fruits and vegetables etc). By law the tax is included in the quoted or shelf prices, so all prices in this book are GST-inclusive. International air and sea travel to/from Australia is GST-free, as is domestic air travel when purchased outside Australia by nonresidents.

If you purchase goods with a total minimum value of $300 from any one supplier no more than 30 days before you leave Australia, you are entitled under the Tourist Refund Scheme (TRS) to a refund of any GST paid. The scheme only applies to goods you take with you as hand luggage or wear onto the plane or ship. For more details, contact the **Australian Customs Service** (☎ 1300 363 263, 02-6275 6666; www.customs.gov.au).

Travellers Cheques

If your stay is short, then travellers cheques are safe and generally enjoy a better exchange rate than foreign cash in Australia. Also, if they are stolen (or you lose them), they can readily be replaced. There is, however, a fee for buying travellers cheques (usually 1% of the total amount) and there may be fees or commissions when you exchange them.

Amex, Thomas Cook and other well-known international brands of travellers cheques are easily exchanged. You need to present your passport for identification when cashing them. Fees per transaction for changing foreign-currency travellers cheques vary from bank to bank.

Buying travellers cheques in Australian dollars is an option worth looking at. These can be exchanged immediately at banks without being converted from a foreign currency and aren't subject to commissions, fees and exchange-rate fluctuations.

POST

Australia's postal services are efficient and reasonably cheap. It costs 50c to send a standard letter or postcard within the country. **Australia Post** (www.auspost.com.au) has divided international destinations into two regions for letters: Asia-Pacific and Rest of the World; airmail letters up to 50g cost $1.20/1.80, respectively. The cost of a postcard (up to 20g) is $1.10 across the board.

There are four international parcel zones and rates vary by distance and class of service.

Sending & Receiving Mail

Post offices are usually open from 9am to 5pm Monday to Friday. There are also many post office agencies lurking within general stores and newsagencies.

All post offices will hold mail for visitors, and some city GPOs (main or general post offices) have busy poste restante sections.

You need to provide some form of identification (such as a passport) to collect mail.

SOLO TRAVELLERS

People travelling alone in Tasmania face the unpredictability that is an inherent part of making contact with entire communities of strangers: sometimes you'll be completely ignored as if you didn't exist, and other times you'll be greeted with such enthusiasm it's as if you're a long-lost relative.

Solo travellers are quite a common sight throughout the state and there is certainly no stigma attached to lone visitors. Women travelling on their own should exercise caution when in less-populated areas, and might find that guys get annoyingly attentive in some drinking establishments; see also Women Travellers (p327).

TELEPHONE

There are a number of telecommunications providers offering various services in Australia. The two main players are the mostly government-owned **Telstra** (www.telstra.com.au) and the fully private **Optus** (www.optus.com.au). Both are also major players in the mobile (cell) market, along with **Vodafone** (www.vodafone.com.au).

Information & Toll-Free Calls

Numbers starting with ☎ 190 are usually recorded information services, charged at anything from 35c to $5 or more per minute (more from mobiles and payphones).

Toll-free numbers beginning with ☎ 18 00 can be called free of charge from anywhere in the country, though they may not be accessible from certain areas or from mobile phones. Calls to numbers beginning with ☎ 13 or ☎ 1300 are charged at the rate of a local call – the numbers can usually be dialled Australia-wide, but may be applicable only to a specific state or STD district. Telephone numbers beginning with either ☎ 1800, ☎ 13 or ☎ 1300 cannot be dialled from outside Australia.

To make a reverse-charge (collect) call from any public or private phone, just dial ☎ 1800-REVERSE (1800 738 3773), or ☎ 12550.

International Calls

Most payphones allow ISD (International Subscriber Dialling) calls, the cost and international dialling code of which vary depending on the service provider. International calls from Australia are cheap and subject to specials that reduce the rates even more, so it's worth shopping around – look in the *Yellow Pages* for a list of providers.

The **Country Direct service** (☎ 1800 801 800) connects callers in Australia with operators in nearly 60 countries to make reverse-charge (collect) or credit-card calls.

When calling overseas you need to dial the international access code from Australia (☎ 0011 or ☎ 0018), the country code and the area code (without the initial 0). So for a London number you'd dial ☎ 0011-44-171, then the number. Also, certain operators will have you dial a special code to get access to their service.

If calling Australia from overseas, the country code is ☎ 61 and you need to drop the 0 (zero) in the state/territory area codes.

Local Calls

Calls from private phones cost 15c to 25c while local calls from public phones cost 40c; both involve unlimited talk time. Calls to mobile phones attract higher rates and are timed. Blue phones or gold phones that you sometimes find in hotel lobbies or other businesses usually cost a minimum of 50c for a local call.

Long Distance Calls & Area Codes

For long-distance calls, Australia uses four STD (Subscriber Trunk Dialling) area codes. STD calls can be made from virtually any public phone and are cheaper during off-peak hours, generally between 7pm and 7am. Long-distance calls (ie to more than about 50km away) within these areas are charged at long-distance rates, even though they have the same area code.

Broadly, these are the main area codes:

State/territory	Area code
ACT	☎ 02
NSW	☎ 02
NT	☎ 08
QLD	☎ 07
SA	☎ 08
TAS	☎ 03
VIC	☎ 03
WA	☎ 08

When calling from one area of Tasmania to another, there's no need to dial 03 before the local number (and you don't need to add the 03 when calling Victoria either). Local numbers start with the digits 62 in Hobart and southern Tasmania, 63 in Launceston and the northeast, and 64 in the west and northwest.

Mobile (Cell) Phones

Local numbers with the prefixes ☎ 04 belong to mobile phones. Australia's two mobile networks – digital GSM and digital CDMA – service more than 90% of the population but leave vast tracts of the country uncovered. Major towns get good reception, but elsewhere it's haphazard or nonexistent (see the boxed text, right).

Australia's digital network is compatible with GSM 900 and 1800 (used in Europe), but generally not with the systems used in the USA or Japan. For overseas visitors, GSM 900 and 1800 mobiles can be used in Australia if set up at home first – contact your service provider before you travel.

It's easy and cheap enough to get connected short-term, though, as the main service providers (Telstra, Optus and Vodafone) all have prepaid mobile systems. Just buy a starter kit, which may include a phone or, if you have your own phone, a SIM card (around $15) and a prepaid charge card. The calls tend to be a bit more expensive than with standard contracts, but there are no connection fees or line-rental charges and you can buy the recharge cards at convenience stores and newsagents. Don't forget to shop around between the three carriers as their products differ.

MOBILE PHONE RA(N)GE

Many mainland visitors to Tasmania take their mobile phone along for the journey, figuring it will be useful for staying in contact with folks back home, phoning ahead to secure accommodation, or making all-important dinner reservations at Tassie's finest restaurants. And they're right – a mobile phone would prove useful in Tasmania for all those reasons, but if you're not on the Telstra mobile network, forget it! Optus and Vodafone coverage is all but non-existent outside of Hobart, Launceston, Burnie and Devonport. If you plan to spend some time touring Tasmania, it might be worth purchasing a Telstra pre-paid SIM card for your mobile phone – you'll still struggle to find a signal in the more remote parts of the state, but overall coverage will be a vast improvement over that of Optus or Vodafone.

Phonecards

A wide range of phonecards is available. These can be bought at newsagents and post offices for a fixed dollar value (usually $10, $20, $30 etc) and can be used with any public or private phone by dialling a toll-free access number and then the PIN on the card. Once again, it's well worth shopping around, as call rates vary from company to company. Some public phones also accept credit cards.

TIME

Australia is divided into three time zones: Western Standard Time (GMT/UTC plus eight hours) applies in WA; Central Standard Time (GMT/UTC plus 9½ hours) covers the NT and SA; and Eastern Standard Time (GMT/UTC plus 10 hours) covers Tasmania, Victoria, NSW and Queensland.

During the summer things get slightly screwed up, as daylight saving time (when clocks are put forward an hour) does not operate in WA, Queensland or the NT, and in Tasmania it starts a month earlier than in the other states (see p326).

TOURIST INFORMATION

The main tourism authority for the state is **Tourism Tasmania** (☎ 6230 8235, 1800 806 846; www.discovertasmania.com; GPO Box 399, Hobart 7001) which disseminates loads of information about Tasmania and has a comprehensive website.

Local Tourist Offices

Tasmania's visitors centres, sometimes referred to as TTICs (Tasmanian Travel & Information Centres), are privately run. The key ones are located in Hobart, Launceston, Devonport and Burnie (see the relevant chapters for contact details). As well as supplying brochures, maps and other information, they will often book transport, tours and accommodation. They are generally open from around 8.30am or 9am to 5pm or 5.30pm weekdays and slightly shorter hours on weekends.

DAYLIGHT SAVING

Daylight saving in Tasmania begins on the first Sunday in October and ends on the last Sunday in March (note that daylight saving in Victoria, NSW and SA begins the *last* Sunday in October).

Other centres belonging to the Tasmanian Visitor Information Network are scattered in many smaller towns across the island. The standard of service provided varies enormously from place to place, and some centres are staffed by volunteers (resulting in irregular opening hours).

At visitors centres throughout the state you can pick up the invaluable free, bimonthly newspaper, *Tasmanian Travelways* (online at www.travelways.com.au). It's packed with information, including comprehensive listings of accommodation, activities, public transport and vehicle hire, all with an indication of current costs throughout the state.

The visitors centres also stock a host of other free tourist literature, including *This Week in Tasmania* (an odd name given that it's published seasonally), the monthly newspaper *Treasure Island,* and *Tasmania: The Visitors Guide,* published twice a year.

Interstate Tourist Offices

On the mainland, there are government-operated **Tasmanian Travel Centres** (☎ 1300 655 145; www.tastravel.com.au; Sydney ☎ 02-9202 2055; 60 Carrington St; Melbourne ☎ 03-9206 7947; 259 Collins St) in Sydney and Melbourne. These travel centres provide information on all things Tasmania, and can also book accommodation, tours and transport.

TOURS

A number of operators offer tours both to and within Tasmania. Many travel agents can arrange package deals from the mainland that include transport to Tasmania (either by air or sea), car rental and accommodation. Contact Tourism Tasmania or the Tasmanian Travel Centres in Sydney and Melbourne (see above), **Qantas Holidays** (☎ 13 14 15; www.qantas.com) or **TasVacations** (☎ 1800 030 160; www.tasvacations.com) to get some ideas.

Once you're in Tasmania, there are operators who can guide you to the highlights (or off the beaten track), and many more who can offer a wilderness experience or activity-based tour. Most trips depart from Hobart or Launceston, but some operators have tours out of Devonport.

Many businesses are listed in the relevant sections of this chapter; other suggestions include the following:

Adventure Tours (☎ 1300 654 604, 08-8309 2277; www.adventuretours.com.au) An Australia-wide company offering three- to seven-day tours in Tasmania. Participants can choose between hostel or motel-style accommodation; prices for a three-day tour start at $355.

Bottom Bits Bus (☎ 1800 777 103, 6229 3540; www.bottombitsbus.com.au) Has a program of day-trips out of Hobart from $89, or a three-day tour ($345) taking in the far south, including Bruny Island, Hastings Caves, adventure caving and Cockle Creek. Small groups (maximum 12).

Craclair Tours (☎ 6424 7833; www.craclair.com.au) Based in Devonport; offers guided walking tours (four- to 10-day trips) in national parks and wilderness areas, including the Overland Track. A three-day cabin-based Cradle Mountain trip costs $580.

Island Cycle Tours (☎ 1300 880 334, 6234 4951; www.islandcycletours.com) Offers a great range of guided cycling trips – day-trips from Hobart (including a descent of Mt Wellington), budget-minded walking and cycling tours (from one to 10 days), and 'indulgence' trips (three to seven days) with more creature comforts.

Island Escape Tours (☎ 1800 133 555, 6344 9799; www.islandescapetours.com) A Launceston-based company offering day-trips ($75-110) as well as three- to seven-day tours. Encourages 'active participation', plus offers participants the chance to break a tour and rejoin the next bus.

TASafari (☎ 1300 882 415; www.tasafari.com.au) Offers three-, five- and nine-day four-wheel-drive tours that visit the well-known and more remote parts of the state. There's bushwalking, bush camping and off-road driving – a three-day tour of the state's east is $470; five days in the west is $790.

Tasmanian Expeditions (☎ 1300 666 856, 6334 3477; www.tas-ex.com) Offers an excellent range of activity-based tours out of Hobart and Launceston, ranging in length from half a day to 16 days, with a choice of bushwalking, river-rafting, rock-climbing, cycling and kayaking in remote locations such as the Franklin River or the southwest wilderness.

Tigerline Coaches (☎ 1300 653 633, 6271 7333; www.tigerline.com.au) A program of coach tours (half- and full-day trips) to major attractions in and around Hobart and Launceston. A half-day trip from Hobart to Richmond is $52; a full day to Port Arthur is $77.

Tiger Trails (☎ 6234 3931; www.tigertrails.green.net.au) Green eco-tour company offering guided walks – one-day and multi-day – in pristine areas such as the Tarkine forest, Styx Valley, Maria Island and along the South Coast Track, ranging from easy to challenging. Day trips are $99.

Under Down Under (☎ 1800 064 726, 6362 2237; www.underdownunder.com.au) Offers nature-based, backpacker-friendly trips, with a pro-green leaning. There are tours from two to eight days, including a two-day tour into the Tarkine forest ($259).

VISAS

All visitors to Australia need a visa – only New Zealand nationals are exempt, and even they receive a 'special category' visa on arrival. Visa application forms are available from Australian diplomatic missions overseas, travel agents or the website of the **Department of Immigration & Multicultural & Indigenous Affairs** (☎ 13 18 81; www.immi.gov.au). There are several types of visa.

Electronic Travel Authority (ETA)

Many visitors can get an ETA through any International Air Transport Association (IATA) registered travel agent or overseas airline. They make the application when you buy a ticket and they issue the ETA, which replaces the usual visa stamped in your passport. It's common practice for travel agents to charge a fee for issuing an ETA (usually around US$15). This system is available to passport holders of 33 countries, including the UK, the USA and Canada, most European and Scandinavian countries, Malaysia, Singapore, Japan and Korea.

You can also make an online ETA application at www.eta.immi.gov.au, where no fees apply.

Tourist Visas

Short-term tourist visas have largely been replaced by the free Electronic Travel Authority (ETA; see earlier). However, if you are from a country not covered by the ETA, or you want to stay longer than three months, you'll need to apply for a visa. Standard visas (which cost A$65) allow one (in some cases multiple) entry, stays of up to three months, and are valid for use within 12 months of issue. A long-stay tourist visa (also A$65) can allow a visit of up to a year.

Visa Extensions

Visitors are allowed a maximum stay of 12 months, including extensions. Visa extensions are made through the Department of Immigration & Multicultural & Indigenous Affairs and it's best to apply at least two or three weeks before your visa expires. The application fee is A$170. It's nonrefundable, even if your application is rejected.

Working Holiday Maker (WHM) Visas

Young (aged 18 to 30), single visitors from Canada, Cyprus, Denmark, Finland, Germany, Hong Kong, Ireland, Japan, Korea, Malta, the Netherlands, Norway, Sweden and the UK are eligible for a WHM visa, which allows you to visit for up to two years and gain casual employment.

The emphasis of this visa is on casual and not full-time employment, so you're only supposed to work for any one employer for a maximum of three months. This visa can only be applied for in Australian diplomatic missions abroad and you can't change from a tourist visa to a WHM visa once you're in Australia. You can also apply for this visa online (www.immi.gov.au/e_visa/visit.htm).

You can apply for this visa up to a year in advance, which is worthwhile as there's a limit on the number issued each year. Conditions include having a return air ticket or sufficient funds for a return or onward fare, and an application fee of A$170 is charged.

WOMEN TRAVELLERS

Tasmania is generally a safe place for women travellers, although the usual sensible precautions apply. It's best to avoid walking alone late at night in major towns. The same applies to rural towns where there are often a lot of unlit, semideserted streets between you and your temporary home. When the pubs close and there are inebriated people roaming around, it's not a great time to be out and about.

Lone women should also be wary of staying in basic pub accommodation unless it looks safe and well managed. Stereotypically, the further you get from 'civilisation' (ie the big cities), the less enlightened your average Aussie male is probably going to be about women's issues. Having said that, many women travellers say that they have met the friendliest, most down-to-earth blokes in small-town pubs.

Lone female hitchers are tempting fate – hitching with a male companion is safer.

WORK

Casual work can usually be found in the high season (summer) at the major tourist centres. Seasonal fruit-picking is another prime possibility, though be warned that it's a tough way to earn a few dollars and pay is proportional to the quantity and quality of fruits picked. In Tasmania the main harvest times are December to April, and the main areas are the Huon and Tamar Valleys. Grape-picking jobs are sometimes available in late autumn and early winter, as a number of wineries still hand-pick their crops. The best source for information on fruit-picking work is on the website of **Australian Job Search** (www.jobsearch.gov.au), a Commonwealth government agency – click on Harvest Trail for lots of practical info.

Volunteer Work

The not-for-profit **Conservation Volunteers Australia** (☎ 1800 032 501, 03-5330 2600; www.conservationvolunteers.com.au) organises practical conservation projects for volunteers (including overseas visitors) such as tree planting, walking-track construction and flora and fauna surveys. It's an excellent way to get involved with conservation-minded people and visit some interesting areas of the country, with a number of worthy projects in Tasmania. Most projects are either for a weekend or a week and all food, transport and accommodation is supplied in return for a small contribution to help cover costs (about $30 per day).

Willing Workers on Organic Farms (WWOOF; ☎ 03-5155 0218; www.wwoof.com.au) is a well-established program, with a number of host farm and businesses in Tasmania. The idea is that 'wwoofers' do a few hours' work each day on a farm or cottage business in return for bed and board, often in a family home. Some places have a minimum stay of a couple of days but many will take you for just a night. See the website for information on becoming a 'wwoofer'.

Transport

CONTENTS

GETTING THERE & AWAY

They don't call Australia the land 'down under' for nothing. It's a long way from just about everywhere, and getting here usually means a long-haul flight.

There are no direct international flights available to or from Tasmania. Overseas visitors to the island state will need to fly to one of Australia's mainland cities and connect to a Tassie-bound domestic flight. Melbourne and Sydney airports have the most frequent direct air links to Hobart and Launceston.

ENTERING THE COUNTRY

Disembarking from your aeroplane in Australia is generally a straightforward affair, with only the usual customs declarations and the fight to be first to the luggage carousel to endure.

Recent global instability has resulted in conspicuously increased security in Australian airports, both in domestic and international terminals, and you may find that customs procedures are now more time-consuming.

See p317 for more information on customs and quarantine.

> **THINGS CHANGE...**
>
> The information in this chapter is particularly vulnerable to change. Check directly with the airline or a travel agent to make sure you understand how a fare (and ticket you may buy) works and be aware of the security requirements for international travel. Shop carefully. The details given in this chapter should be regarded as pointers and are not a substitute for your own careful, up-to-date research.

Passport

There are no restrictions when it comes to citizens of foreign countries entering Australia. If you have a visa (p327), you should be fine.

INTERNATIONAL AIR TRAVEL

There are many competing airlines and a wide variety of air fares if you're flying in from Asia, Europe or North America, but you'll still pay a lot for a flight. Any time of the year can turn out to be busy for inbound tourists – if you plan to fly at a particularly popular period (Christmas is a notoriously difficult time to get into Sydney or Melbourne) or on a particularly popular route (such as Hong Kong, Bangkok or Singapore to Sydney or Melbourne), ensure that you make your arrangements well in advance.

Airlines

The east coast of Australia is the most common gateway for international travellers. Airlines that visit Australia follow (note that all phone numbers mentioned here are for dialling from within Australia):

Air Canada (☎ 1300 655 757; www.aircanada.ca; airline code AC) Flies to Sydney.

Air New Zealand (☎ 13 24 76; www.airnz.com.au; airline code NZ) Flies to Melbourne, Sydney, Perth.

Air Paradise International (☎ 1300 799 066; www.airparadise.co.id; airline code AD) Flies to Melbourne, Sydney, Perth.

Australian Airlines (☎ 1300 799 798; http://australianairlines.com.au; airline code AO) Flies to Melbourne, Sydney, Cairns.

British Airways (☎ 1300 767 177; www.britishairways.com.au; airline code BA) Flies to Sydney.
Cathay Pacific (☎ 13 17 47; www.cathaypacific.com; airline code CX) Flies to Melbourne, Sydney, Brisbane, Cairns, Perth, Adelaide.
Emirates (☎ 1300 303 777; www.emirates.com; airline code EK) Flies to Melbourne, Sydney, Brisbane, Perth.
Freedom Air (☎ 1800 122 000; www.freedomair.com; airline code SJ) Flies to Melbourne, Sydney, Brisbane.
Garuda Indonesia (☎ 1300 365 330; www.garuda-indonesia.com; airline code GA) Flies to Melbourne, Sydney, Brisbane, Perth.
Gulf Air (☎ 13 12 23; www.gulfairco.com; airline code GF) Flies to Melbourne, Sydney.
Japan Airlines (☎ 02-9272 1100; www.jal.com; airline code JL) Flies to Melbourne, Sydney, Cairns, Brisbane.
KLM (☎ 1300 303 747, 02-9231 6333; www.klm.com; airline code KL) Flies to Melbourne, Sydney.
Malaysia Airlines (☎ 13 26 27, 02-9364 3500; www.malaysiaairlines.com.au; airline code MH) Flies to Sydney, Brisbane, Perth, Adelaide, Cairns.
Qantas (☎ 13 13 13; www.qantas.com.au; airline code QF) Flies to Melbourne, Sydney, Brisbane, Perth.
Royal Brunei Airlines (☎ 08-8941 0966; www.bruneiair.com; airline code BI) Flies to Brisbane, Perth, Darwin.
Singapore Airlines (☎ 13 10 11; www.singaporeair.com.au; airline code SQ) Flies to Melbourne, Sydney, Brisbane, Perth, Adelaide.
South African Airways (☎ 1800 099 281, 08-9216 2200; www.flysaa.com; airline code SA) Flies to Sydney, Perth.
Thai Airways International (☎ 1300 651 960; www.thaiairways.com.au; airline code TG) Flies to Melbourne, Sydney, Brisbane, Perth.
United Airlines (☎ 13 17 77; www.unitedairlines.com.au; airline code UA) Flies to Melbourne, Sydney.

Tickets

Be sure you research the options carefully to make sure you get the best deal. The Internet is an increasingly useful resource for checking airline prices.

Automated online ticket sales work well if you're doing a simple one-way or return trip on specified dates, but are no substitute for a travel agent with the low-down on special deals, strategies for avoiding stopovers and other useful advice.

> **DEPARTURE TAX**
>
> There is a A$38 departure tax when leaving Australia. This is included in the price of airline tickets.

Paying by credit card offers some protection if you unwittingly end up dealing with a rogue fly-by-night agency in your search for the cheapest fare, as most card issuers provide refunds if you can prove you didn't get what you paid for. Alternatively, buy a ticket from a bonded agent, such as one covered by the **Air Travel Organiser's Licence** (ATOL; www.atol.org.uk) scheme in the UK. If you have doubts about the service provider, at the very least call the airline and confirm that your booking has been made.

Round-the-world tickets can be a good option for getting to Australia.

For online bookings, start with the following websites:

Airbrokers (www.airbrokers.com) This US company specialises in cheap tickets.
Cheap Flights (www.cheapflights.com) Very informative site with specials, airline information and flight searches from the USA and other regions.
Cheapest Flights (www.cheapestflights.co.uk) Cheap worldwide flights from the UK; get in early for the bargains.
Expedia (www.expedia.msn.com) Microsoft's travel site; mainly US-related.
Flight Centre International (www.flightcentre.com) Respected operator handling direct flights, with sites for Australia, New Zealand, the UK, the USA and Canada.
Flights.com (www.tiss.com) Truly international site for flight-only tickets; cheap fares and an easy-to-search database.
Roundtheworld.com (www.roundtheworldflights.com) This excellent site allows you to build your own trips from the UK with up to six stops. A four-stop trip including Asia, Australia and the USA costs from £800.
STA (www.statravel.com) Prominent in international student travel but you don't have to be a student; site linked to worldwide STA sites.
Travel Online (www.travelonline.co.nz) Good place to check worldwide flights from New Zealand.
Travel.com (www.travel.com.au) Good Australian site; look up fares and flights into and out of the country.
Travelocity (www.travelocity.com) US site that allows you to search fares (in US$) to/from practically anywhere.

Asia

Most Asian countries offer fairly competitive air fare deals, with Bangkok, Singapore and Hong Kong being the best places to shop around for discount tickets.

Flights between Hong Kong and Australia are notoriously heavily booked. Flights to/from Bangkok and Singapore are often part of the longer Europe-to-Australia route so they are also sometimes full. The moral of the story is to plan your preferred itinerary well in advance.

Typical one-way fares to Sydney are US$350 leaving from Singapore, US$340 from Penang or Kuala Lumpur, and about US$330 from Bangkok. From Tokyo, fares start at US$650.

There are several good local agents in Asia:

Hong Kong Student Travel Bureau (☎ 2730 3269)

STA Travel Bangkok (☎ 02-236 0262; www.statravel.co.th)

STA Travel Singapore (☎ 65-6737 7188; www.statravel.com.sg)

STA Travel Tokyo (☎ 03-5391-3205; www.statravel.co.jp)

Canada

The air routes from Canada are similar to those from mainland USA, with most Toronto and Vancouver flights stopping in one US city such as Los Angeles or Honolulu before heading on to Australia. Air Canada flies from Vancouver to Sydney via Honolulu and from Toronto to Melbourne via Honolulu.

Canadian discount air ticket sellers' (consolidators') air fares tend to be about 10% higher than those sold in the USA. **Travel Cuts** (☎ 800-667-2887; www.travelcuts.com) is Canada's national student travel agency and has offices in all major cities.

Fares out of Vancouver to Sydney or Melbourne cost from C$1650/2100 in the low/high season via the US west coast. From Toronto, fares go from around C$1800/2200.

Continental Europe

From the major destinations in Europe, most flights travel via one of the major Asian cities such as Singapore, Bangkok, Hong Kong or Kuala Lumpur. Some flights are also routed through London before arriving in Australia.

Fares from Paris in the low/high season cost from €1000/1200. Here are some agents in Paris:

Nouvelles Frontières (☎ 08 25 00 08 25; www.nouvelles-frontieres.fr) Also has branches outside of Paris.

OTU Voyages (☎ 01 40 29 12 12; www.otu.fr) Student/youth oriented, with offices in many cities.

Usit Connect Voyages (☎ 01 43 29 69 50; www.usitconnections.fr) Student/youth specialists, with offices in many cities.

A good option in the Dutch travel industry is **Holland International** (☎ 070-307 6307; www.hollandinternational.nl). From Amsterdam, return fares start at around €1500.

In Germany, good travel agencies include the Berlin branch of **STA Travel** (☎ 030-311 0950; www.statravel.de). Fares start at around €900/1000 in the low/high season.

New Zealand

Air New Zealand and Qantas operate a network of flights linking Auckland, Wellington and Christchurch in New Zealand with most major Australian gateway cities. Fares from New Zealand to Sydney cost around NZ$350/700 one-way/return.

Other trans-Tasman options include the following:

Flight Centre (☎ 0800 243 544; www.flightcentre.co.nz) Has a large central office in Auckland and many branches throughout the country.

Freedom Air (☎ 0800 600 500; www.freedomair.com) Air New Zealand subsidiary that operates direct flights and offers excellent rates year-round.

STA Travel (☎ 09-309 0458; www.statravel.co.nz) Has offices in various cities.

UK & Ireland

There are two routes from the UK: the western route via the USA and the Pacific, and the eastern route via the Middle East and Asia. Flights are usually cheaper and more frequent on the latter. Some of the best deals around are with Emirates, Gulf Air, Malaysia Airlines, Japan Airlines and Thai Airways International. British Airways, Singapore Airlines and Qantas generally have higher fares but may offer a more direct route.

A popular agent in the UK is the ubiquitous **STA Travel** (☎ 0870-160 0599; www.statravel.co.uk).

Typical direct fares from London to Sydney are UK£400/650 one-way/return during the low season (March to June). In September and mid-December fares go up by as much as 30%, while the rest of the year they're somewhere in-between. High-season fares start at around UK£450/750 one-way/return.

From Australia you can expect to pay around A$900/1650 one-way/return in the low season to London and other European capitals (with stops in Asia on the way) and A$1100/2050 in the high season.

USA

Airlines directly connecting Australia across the Pacific with Los Angeles or San Francisco include Qantas, Air New Zealand and United Airlines. There are also numerous airlines offering flights via Asia, with stopover possibilities including Tokyo, Kuala Lumpur, Bangkok, Hong Kong and Singapore; and via the Pacific with stopover possibilities like Nadi (Fiji), Rarotonga (Cook Islands), Tahiti (French Polynesia) and Auckland (NZ). In most cases, you will need to purchase an additional fare to Hobart.

As in Canada, discount travel agents in the USA are known as consolidators. San Francisco is the ticket consolidator capital of America, although some good deals can be found in Los Angeles, New York and other big cities.

STA Travel (☎ 800-777 0112; www.statravel.com) has offices around the country, and can assist with tickets.

Typically you can get a return ticket to Melbourne or Sydney from the west coast for US$1300/1700 in the low/high season, or from the east coast for US$1600/1900. To Perth it's a little more expensive and often involves a flight change in Asia, New Zealand or the east coast of Australia.

Return low/high-season fares from Australia to the US west coast cost around A$1750/1850, and to New York A$1800/1950.

DOMESTIC AIR TRAVEL

There are major airports located at Hobart and Launceston, as well as smaller operations at Burnie/Wynyard and Devonport. (Burnie/Wynyard airport is officially known as Burnie airport but is actually located 20km west of Burnie near the town of Wynyard. Due to the fact that some Tasmanians call the airport 'Burnie' and others call it 'Wynyard', we refer to the airport throughout this book as 'Burnie/Wynyard'.)

Airlines with services between Tasmania and the Australian mainland are:

Jetstar (☎ 13 15 38; www.jetstar.com.au) Qantas' new low-cost airline. Direct flights from Melbourne, Sydney, Brisbane and Adelaide to Hobart; also from Melbourne, Sydney and Brisbane to Launceston.

Qantas (☎ 13 13 13; www.qantas.com.au) Direct flights from Sydney and Melbourne to Hobart, and from Melbourne to Launceston. QantasLink (the regional subsidiary) offers flights from Melbourne to Burnie and Devonport.

Regional Express (REX; ☎ 13 17 13; www.regionalexpress.com.au) Flies from Melbourne to Devonport, Burnie/Wynyard and King Island.

Virgin Blue (☎ 13 67 89; www.virginblue.com.au) Direct flights from Melbourne, Sydney, Brisbane and Adelaide to Hobart, and from Melbourne and Sydney to Launceston.

Qantas and Virgin Blue have connecting flights from most other mainland capitals.

See p305 and p310 for information on airlines servicing King and Flinders Islands respectively.

Fares

Few people pay full fare on domestic travel, as the airlines offer a wide range of discounts. These come and go and there are regular special fares, so keep your eyes open and check the airlines' websites. Air fares to Tasmania are constantly changing and you can get some good deals, especially if you book well in advance or if you're planning a wintertime trip. Regular one-way and return domestic fares are similar on Qantas and Virgin Blue, while Jetstar offers some very good bargains, usually (but not always) cheaper than the two major airlines. Lowest one-way prices from Melbourne to Tasmania are in the $69 to $150 range; Sydney to Tassie costs $89 to $160, from Brisbane costs from $149 to $200, and from Adelaide costs from $129 to $155.

Advance-purchase deals provide the cheapest air fares. Some advance-purchase fares offer up to 33% discount off one-way fares and up to 50% off return fares. You have to book one to four weeks ahead, and you often have to stay away for at least one Saturday night. There are restrictions on changing flights and you can lose up to 100% of the ticket price if you cancel,

QUARANTINE

There are stringent rules in place to protect the disease-free status of the agriculture of this island state, and plants, fruit and vegetables cannot be brought into Tasmania. Tourists must discard all items prior to their arrival (even if they're only travelling from mainland Australia).

although you can buy health-related cancellation insurance.

There are also special deals available only to foreign visitors (in possession of an outbound ticket). If booked in Australia these fares offer a 40% discount off a full-fare economy ticket. They can also be booked from overseas (which usually works out a bit cheaper).

SEA

Cruise Ship

Just about the only way to see firsthand the spectacular diversity of wildlife on remote, sub-Antarctic Macquarie Island, which was proclaimed Tasmania's second World Heritage area in 1997 (see p55), is to take one of the sub-Antarctic islands cruises scheduled by New Zealand–based **Heritage Expeditions (NZ)** (☎ 1800 143 585; www.heritage-expeditions.com). At the time of research the company offered a couple of wonderful options – choose a 19-day birding tour, or a 27-day trip to Antarctica, taking in various sub-Antarctic islands and both incorporating two days on Macquarie Island. These cruises usually take place once or twice a year; prices per person for the shorter cruise range from around US$7000 for twin share (shared facilities) to US$9400 for a suite, plus US$250 for landing fees. Check the comprehensive website for more information.

Ferry

There are three high-speed *Spirit of Tasmania* ferries operated by **TT-Line** (☎ 13 20 10; www.spiritoftasmania.com.au); two cruise nightly in either direction between Melbourne and Devonport on northern Tasmania's coast, the third sails twice a week between Sydney and Devonport. The terminal details are as follows:

Devonport (Esplanade, East Devonport)
Melbourne (Station Pier, Port Melbourne)
Sydney (47-51 Hickson Rd, Gate D8N, Darling Harbour)

For all ferry crossings there are limited, discounted apex (advance purchase) fares available for return journeys – inquire when booking.

MELBOURNE–DEVONPORT

The two ferries plying Bass Strait nightly between Melbourne and Devonport can each accommodate 1400 passengers and around 650 vehicles. With their restaurants, bars and games facilities, each vessel more closely resembles a floating hotel than a ferry. The public areas of the ships have been designed to cater for wheelchair access, as have a handful of onboard cabins.

One ferry departs from Melbourne's Station Pier and the other departs from the terminal in Devonport (departures at 9pm), with both arriving at their destinations across Bass Strait at approximately 7am the next morning. Additional day sailings are scheduled during the peak season (from mid-December to April; call or check the website for schedules) – these day sailings depart at 9am and arrive at 7pm.

Fares depend on whether you're travelling in the peak season (mid-December to late January), shoulder season (late January to April, and September to mid-December) or off-peak season (May to August), and there's a range of seating and cabin options – cruise seats are the cheapest and resemble airline seats. Cabins are available in twin or four-berth configurations, with or without porthole windows, or you can opt for a 'deluxe' cabin (with a queen-size bed and complimentary bottle of sparkling wine). All cabins have private bathroom. Child,

PACKAGE DEALS

Many travel agents can help you arrange a package deal from the mainland that usually includes transport to Tasmania (either by air or sea), car rental and accommodation – these packages can often work out considerably cheaper than purchasing each component separately. As you would expect, the biggest discounts apply in the quieter periods of autumn, winter and spring, whereas in summer the deals rise in price. Most package deals have conditions attached to them, of which the most common is twin share (two people), and sometimes an itinerary is fixed at booking.

Contact **Tourism Tasmania** or Sydney and Melbourne **travel centres** (see p326), **Qantas Holidays** (☎ 13 14 15; www.qantas.com) or **TasVacations** (☎ 1800 030 160; www.tasvacations.com) for ideas.

If you're visiting King or Flinders Islands, package deals are a particularly good idea. See p305 and p310 for details.

student, pensioner and senior discounts apply to all accommodation except for deluxe cabins. Prices do not include meals, which can be purchased on board from an à la carte restaurant or cafeteria.

Prices (per adult) are as follows:

Fare	Peak season	Shoulder season	Off-peak season
cruise seat	$145	$115	$108
inside 4-berth cabin	$215	$196	$187
inside twin cabin	$260	$220	$210
deluxe cabin	$383	$322	$295
standard vehicles & campervans up to 5m length	$55	$10	$10
motorcycles	$38	$5	$5
bicycles	$6	free	free

Daytime sailings have only one type of seating on offer (seats, no cabins) and cost $145 for an adult in the peak season and $99 during the shoulder season (there are no daytime sailings in the off-peak season).

SYDNEY–DEVONPORT

In early 2004 TT-Line began a much-hyped ferry service three times weekly between Sydney and Devonport, with a journey time of 21 to 22 hours. At the time of research, however, the future of the Sydney ferry service was in some doubt, as passenger numbers had proved to be far lower than anticipated (due, in no small part, to the cheap airfares that came about with the birth of Qantas' low-cost airline, Jetstar). In November 2004 the ferry service was cut back to two sailings a week (with three trips in the peak season from mid-December to mid-January), but further changes may be on the cards – it's best to check TT-Line's website for up-to-date information.

The ferry departs Devonport at 3pm Thursday (arriving Sydney 1pm Friday) and 4pm Saturday (arriving Sydney 2pm Sunday). In the opposite direction, the boat leaves Sydney at 4pm Friday (arriving Devonport 1pm Saturday) and 5pm Sunday (arriving Devonport 2pm Monday).

As with the Melbourne ferries, there is a range of accommodation options, including budget accommodation in dormitories, plus four-berth, twin or double cabins. Fares are based on the same seasonal structure, with discounts for children, students, pensioners and seniors (except for the hostel beds). Unlike the Melbourne ferries, Sydney fares include a buffet dinner and brunch.

Fare	Peak season	Shoulder season	Off-peak season
hostel	$270	$255	$230
inside 4-berth cabin	$420	$400	$360
inside twin cabin	$490	$465	$420
porthole double cabin	$520	$495	$445
standard vehicles & campervans up to 5m length	$55	$10	$10
motorcycles	$38	$5	$5
bicycles	$6	free	free

WARNING TO WEAK STOMACHS!

Bass Strait is known as one of the roughest shipping channels in the world, so travellers prone to seasickness should prepare themselves (just in case).

Yacht

Every year hopeful adventurers head to Sydney to try to find a berth on a yacht in the late-December Sydney to Hobart Yacht Race, but they nearly always luck out, as the yachts use their regular crews. You'll have far more luck crewing a boat from Hobart back to its home port after the race has been completed, when many of the regular crew fly home.

GETTING AROUND

Tasmania is decentralised and its population very small. While public transport is adequate between larger towns and popular tourist destinations, visiting remote sights might prove frustrating due to irregular or, in some cases, nonexistent services. There are, however, plenty of car-rental companies offering decent rates for early-model vehicles, an option you should seriously consider when planning your itinerary, particularly if your time is limited and the places you want to visit are far-flung.

AIR

As distances within Tasmania are not so huge, air travel within the state is not very common. Of more use to travellers are the air services for bushwalkers in the southwest, and links between major towns and King and Flinders Islands.

There are a few small regional airlines within the state:

Airlines of Tasmania (☎ 6248 5490, 1800 144 460; www.airtasmania.com.au) Flies daily between Launceston and Flinders Island (adult fare $140.30 one-way). Also three times a week between Hobart and Strahan on the west coast ($148 one-way).

Par Avion (☎ 6248 5390; www.paravion.com.au) Flies from Hobart to Melaleuca in the southwest wilderness (adult fare $145 one-way). Good for scenic flights and bushwalker pick-ups or drop-offs.

Tasair (☎ 6248 5088, 1800 062 900; www.tasair.com.au) Flies daily to King Island from Devonport and Burnie/Wynyard (adult fare $181.50 one-way), and also flies weekdays between Burnie/Wynyard and Hobart (also $181.50 one-way). Also offers charters and scenic flights, plus a bushwalkers' service to Cox Bight and Melaleuca ($150 one-way).

BICYCLE

Tasmania's compact size makes it a tempting place to cycle around. It's a great way to get close to nature (not to mention, it has to be said, to log trucks, rain and roadkill), and provided you're prepared for steep climbs and strong headwinds in certain sections, you should enjoy the experience immensely.

If you're coming specifically to cycle, it's worth bringing your own bike or considering buying a bike and reselling it at the end (it's best to buy from a store in a larger city such as Hobart or Launceston). Note that bicycle helmets are compulsory in Tasmania (and all other states and territories of Australia), as are white front lights and red rear lights for riding at night.

To bring a bike over on one of the *Spirit of Tasmania* ferries costs $6 each way in the peak season, but is free at other times. If you're bringing your own bike, check with the airline for costs and the degree of dismantling and packing required.

While the same road rules that apply to cars also apply to bicycles, riders should also follow another rule – if in doubt either give way or get out of the way. Even if you're in the right, you will almost certainly come off second best in any collision. When cycling on the state's many narrow, winding roads, always keep your eyes and ears open for traffic. Also watch out for wooden bridges with gaps between the slats that can trap bicycle wheels, and try not to cycle at night. Full notes and lots of practical advice for cycling around the state can be found in *Bicycling Tasmania* by Ian Terry & Rob Beedham, or visit http://dmurphy.customer.netspace.net.au/giro2.htm for an excellent online guide.

Bike rental is available in the larger towns, and there are also a number of operators offering multi-day cycling tours or experiences such as mountain-biking down Mt Wellington in Hobart. See p47 for more information.

BOAT

A car ferry runs at least eight times a day from Kettering to Bruny Island in Tasmania's southeast. To effectively explore this rather long (and rather beautiful) island, you'll need your own car or bicycle. See p131 for details.

At the time of research there were two boat services running from the east coast to small Maria Island, which is a national park. These services also operate daily, carrying only passengers and bicycles, as vehicles aren't allowed on the island. See p162 for details.

There is also a small weekly passenger and car ferry from Bridport in Tasmania's northeast to Flinders Island (the ferry continues on to Port Welshpool in Victoria on demand). See p310 for more information.

BUS

Tasmania has a reasonable bus network connecting major towns and centres, but weekend services are infrequent and this can be inconvenient for travellers with limited time. There are more buses in summer than in winter, but smaller towns are still not serviced terribly frequently.

The main bus lines are **Redline Coaches** (☎ 6336 1446, 1300 360 000; www.tasredline.com.au) and **TassieLink** (☎ 6271 7320, 1300 300 520; www.tassielink.com.au), and between them they cover most of the state. TassieLink is owned by Tasmanian Tours & Travel, which also has a tours/charters arm called **Tigerline Travel** (☎ 6271 7333, 1300 653 633; www.tigerline.com.au).

Buses run along most major highways year-round. TassieLink runs from both Hobart and Launceston to the state's west (Cradle Mountain, Strahan, Queenstown, Lake St Clair) and to the east coast (St Helens, Bicheno, Swansea), from Hobart to Port Arthur, and south from Hobart down the Huon Valley. It also runs the 'Main Road Express', express services that connect Bass Strait ferry arrivals/departures in Devonport to Launceston, Hobart and Burnie.

Redline services the Midland Hwy between Hobart and Launceston, the north coast between Launceston and Smithton, north from Launceston to George Town, and to the east coast.

Additionally, **Hobart Coaches** (☎ 13 22 01; www.hobartcoaches.com.au) runs regular services from the capital south as far as Woodbridge and Cygnet, and north to Richmond and New Norfolk. See the relevant chapters for details of these and other regional services.

Over summer, TassieLink buses also run along numerous minor roads to popular bushwalking destinations. Special fares that enable you to be dropped off at the start of a walk and picked up at the end are offered. Buses take the link road from Devonport past Cradle Mountain to the Lyell Hwy, and services also run from Hobart past Mt Field and Maydena to Scotts Peak, and from Hobart past Dover to Cockle Creek in the south. See these destinations in the relevant chapters for more information.

There are smaller transport operators offering useful bus services on important tourist routes (eg between Bicheno and Coles Bay, or within the Cradle Mountain–Lake St Clair region); details of these are given in the relevant sections of this book.

Note that all bus fares and conditions quoted throughout this book are subject to change and should be used as a guide only.

Bus Passes

TASSIELINK

TassieLink offers an Explorer Pass valid on all scheduled services for unlimited kilometres (see right). The pass can be bought from mainland Tasmanian travel centres, YHA and STA Travel offices, most other travel agents, or directly from TassieLink. Explorer Pass holders are also entitled to discounts for Tigerline sightseeing tours from Hobart and Launceston. If you intend to buy an Explorer Pass, ask for TassieLink's timetables in advance or check the company's website and plan your itinerary carefully before making your purchase – this is the best way to ensure you'll be able to get where you want to go within the life of the pass. The free bimonthly newspaper *Tasmanian Travelways* (available at visitors centres within and outside the state) also has timetables and fares for major routes, but you're better off using one of the company's own printed timetables.

Explorer Pass	Valid for	Cost
7-day pass	travel in 10 days	$172
10-day pass	travel in 15 days	$205
14-day pass	travel in 20 days	$237
21-day pass	travel in 30 days	$280

REDLINE COACHES

Redline offers its own form of bus pass, the Tassie Pass, with unlimited travel on its services but no extended validity beyond the specified number of days (in contrast to the Explorer Pass). As the Redline bus network is not nearly as comprehensive as that of TassieLink, it's especially worth checking Redline's websites and timetables to ascertain its worth to you before you purchase.

Tassie Pass	Cost
7-day pass	$135
10-day pass	$160
14-day pass	$185
21-day pass	$219

YHA PASSES

Available from the office of the **Tasmanian YHA office** (☎ 6234 9617; yhatas@yhatas.org.au; 1st fl, 28 Criterion St, Hobart; 🕒 9am-5pm Mon-Fri) is the Tasmania Coach Pass and Accommodation deal, whereby you purchase a TassieLink Explorer bus pass (see above) and YHA hostel accommodation package for either seven, 10, 14 or 21 days. Seven nights' dorm-style accommodation and a seven-day bus pass costs $332; a 21-day package costs $720. It's possible to upgrade to twin or double accommodation at additional cost. While these packages might appear to offer reasonable value, it's important to remember that YHA hostels are not widespread in Tasmania – there are no YHA hostels on the west coast, for example, or south of Hobart, or along the Midland Hwy, or in the popular east-coast towns of Swansea or Bicheno. Our advice is to pay your accommodation as you go and not commit yourself to any one form of accommodation. There may not be a YHA hostel at your destination of choice, but there may well be an independent hostel, cheap pub room or budget cabin you can stay in.

Costs

Fares are quite reasonable for bus travel within Tasmania. To give some idea of the fares and travel times, a one-way trip between Devonport and Launceston is around $18 and takes 1½ hours; Hobart–Launceston is $26.50 (2½ hours); Hobart–Queenstown is $51.20 (five to 5½ hours); Hobart–Dover is $17 (1¾ hours); and Launceston–Bicheno is $26 (2½ hours).

Reservations

If you want a seat on either Redline Coaches or TassieLink, it is advisable to make a booking.

CAR & MOTORCYCLE

There is no doubt that travelling by car is the best option in Tasmania, as it gives you the freedom to explore according to your own timetable. Although you can bring cars from the mainland to Tasmania, renting may be cheaper, particularly for shorter trips. Tasmania has many international, national and local car-rental agencies, and rates are considerably lower here than on the mainland.

Motorcycles are another popular way of getting around, and the climate is OK for bikes for a large part of the year. You can bring your own motorbike across on the ferry from the mainland for a small fee, or hire one once you get here.

Automobile Associations

The **Royal Automobile Club of Tasmania** (RACT; ☎ 13 27 22; www.ract.com.au; Hobart cnr Patrick & Murray Sts; Launceston cnr York & George Sts) provides an emergency breakdown service to members and has reciprocal arrangements with services in other Australian states and some from overseas. It also provides tourist literature, excellent maps and detailed guides to accommodation and camping grounds. The roadside assistance number is ☎ 13 11 11.

Bring Your Own Vehicle

It's easy to bring your own vehicle across from the mainland on the ferries operating out of Melbourne and Sydney. Before you book a ferry ticket, however, it's worth doing some calculations to determine whether it's the most economical option for your intended trip. Two cheap Sydney-Hobart flights plus two weeks' car rental may work out cheaper than two berths on the Sydney-Devonport ferry.

Driving Licence

You can generally use your own home-country's driving licence in Australia, as long as it's in English (if it's not, a certified translation must be carried) and has an identifying photograph. Alternatively, it's a simple matter to arrange an International Driving Permit (IDP), which should be supported by your home licence. Just go to your home country's automobile association and it can issue one on the spot. The permits are valid for 12 months.

WHAT'S THE RUSH?

Driving around Tasmania is the easiest, most flexible way to see the state. If you do drive, don't make the mistake of drawing up exhaustive itineraries with carefully calculated driving times between each and every destination. Though this is sometimes necessary to catch a particular tour on a particular day or to check in at a prebooked B&B, it runs contrary to the real idea behind driving around Tasmania – that you can stop for a spontaneous photo or a leisurely browse, or divert down a side-road to explore the unfamiliar whenever you feel like it. Too many people make the mistake of thinking they can see all of Tasmania's top attractions in one week, madly dashing from the west coast to the east (via Cradle Mountain, Hobart and Port Arthur), and they end up going home in desperate need of a holiday!

Fuel

Fuel (super, diesel and unleaded) is available from service stations sporting the well-known international brand names. In small towns there's often just a pump outside the general store, while the larger towns and cities have conventional service stations and garages. Most are open from 8am to 6pm weekdays, but fewer are open on weekends, and fewer still are open late at night or 24 hours a day, something to keep in mind if you intend travelling long distances at night.

Fuel prices vary from place to place and from price war to price war, but basically fuel is heavily taxed and continues to hike up, much to the shock of Australian motorists. Unleaded petrol (used in most new cars) is now hovering around $1.10 a litre in Tasmanian cities and large towns. Once you get out into the small rural towns, prices rise (up to about $1.20 a litre at the time of writing).

Insurance

In Australia, third-party personal injury insurance is always included in the vehicle registration cost. This ensures that every registered vehicle carries at least minimum insurance. You'd be wise to extend that minimum to at least third-party property insurance as well – minor collisions with other vehicles can be amazingly expensive.

When it comes to hiring cars from a hire company, know exactly what your liability is in the event of an accident. Rather than risk paying out thousands of dollars if you do have an accident, you can take out your own comprehensive insurance on the car, or (the usual option) pay an additional daily amount to the rental company for an 'insurance excess reduction' policy. This brings the amount of excess you must pay in the event of an accident down from between $2000 and $5000 to a few hundred dollars.

Be aware that if you're travelling on dirt roads you will not be covered by insurance unless you have a four-wheel drive – in other words, if you have an accident you'll be liable for all the costs involved. Also, most companies' insurance won't cover the cost of damage to glass (including the windscreen) or tyres. Always read the small print.

Purchase

If you're planning a stay of several months that involves lots of driving, buying a second-hand car will be much cheaper than renting. But remember that reliability is all-important.

You'll probably get any car cheaper by buying privately through a local newspaper rather than through a car dealer. Buying through a dealer does have the advantage of some sort of guarantee, but this is not much use if you're buying a car in Sydney for a trip to Tasmania.

When you come to buy or sell a car, there are usually some local regulations to be complied with. The website www.justice.tas.gov.au/newca/trading/mvehicles.htm offers advice on how to make buying a car simpler and safer. To avoid buying a lemon, you might consider forking out some extra money for a vehicle appraisal before purchase – the **RACT** (☎ 13 27 22; www.ract.com.au) offers this kind of inspection (for a fee).

Rental

Tasmania has many international, national and local car-rental agencies, and rates are considerably lower here than on the mainland. The free, bimonthly *Tasmanian Travelways* newspaper (available in hard-copy format from many visitors centres and other tourist establishments, or online at www.travelways.com.au) lists many of the rental options.

Before you decide on a company, ask about any kilometre limitations and find out what the insurance covers – ensure there are no hidden seasonal adjustments. It is, however, quite normal for smaller rental companies to ask for a bond of $300 or more. Also remember that most companies do not cover accidents that occur on unsealed roads, and hike up the excess in the case of damage or an accident on such a road – which is a considerable disadvantage in a state where so many of the best destinations can only be reached via unsealed roads.

Larger international firms have booking desks at airports and offices in major towns. They have standard rates from about $70 to $80 for high-season, multi-day hire of a small car – the deal should include unlimited kilometres and no bond. By booking in advance and choosing smaller cars, rates can be as low as $60 per day for one week's hire (outside the high season). Companies include the following:

AutoRent-Hertz (☎ 1800 030 222, 6237 1111; www.autorent.com.au)
Avis (☎ 13 63 33, 6234 4222; www.avis.com.au)
Budget (☎ 13 27 27; www.budget.com.au)
Europcar (☎ 1800 030 118; www.europcar.com.au)
Thrifty (☎ 1800 030 730; www.tasvacations.com.au)

Savings can be made by going to the smaller operators but this must be weighed against the rental conditions and general condition of the vehicle – make sure you're familiar and confident with both before you sign. Small local firms rent older cars for as little as $30 to $35 a day, depending on the length of time and season. Prices then increase according to the model and age of the cars. The smaller companies don't normally have desks at arrival points but can usually arrange for your car to be picked up at airports and the ferry terminal in Devonport. Operators include the following:

Lo-Cost Auto Rent (www.locostautorent.com) Hobart (☎ 6231 0550); Launceston (☎ 6334 6202); Devonport (☎ 6427 0796)
Rent-a-Bug (www.rentabug.com.au) Hobart (☎ 6231 0300); Launceston (☎ 6334 3427); Devonport (☎ 6427 9444) Offering cheap Volkswagen Beetles, plus older-model vehicles.
Selective Car Rentals (☎ 6234 3311; www.selectivecarrentals.com.au) Office in Hobart.

CAMPERVANS

Tasmanian Travelways also has a listing of campervan rental companies. **Autorent-Hertz** (☎ 1800 030 500; www.autorent.com.au) has three-berth campervans for around $640 per week from May to mid-September, rising in stages to a hefty $1300 in the peak period from Christmas to mid-January. Other companies offer campervan rental:

Britz (☎ 1800 331 454, 6248 4168; www.britz.com)
Cruisin' Tasmania (☎ 1800 772 758, 6264 3185; www.cruisin-tasmania.com.au).
Maui (☎ 1300 363 800, 6248 4168; www.maui-rentals.com)
Tasmanian Campervan Hire (☎ 1800 807 119, 6248 9623; www.tascamper.com)

MOTORCYCLES

Tasmanian Motorcycle Hire (☎ 6391 9139; www.tasmotorcyclehire.com.au; 17 Coachmans Rd, Evandale) has a range of touring motorbikes for rent from $175 per day (cheaper rates for longer rentals); full pricing details are listed on the website. Evandale is south of Launceston, not far from the airport.

PACKAGES

Another popular option is to invest in an accommodation and car-rental package. These can be arranged on the mainland or in Tasmania by travel agents or Tasmanian visitors centres and often work out to be very economical.

For backpackers who don't want to rely on buses, there's the Tasmania Freedom Car Pass & Accommodation package, available from the office of the **Tasmanian YHA office** (☎ 6234 9617; yhatas@yhatas.org.au; 1st fl, 28 Criterion St, Hobart; 9am-5pm Mon-Fri), which offers various combinations of YHA hostel accommodation and rental of a medium-sized car including insurance (with a large excess) and unlimited kilometres. Seven nights' dorm-style accommodation and seven days' car rental is $343; the same package over 21 days costs $962. It's possible to upgrade to twin or double accommodation at additional cost. If you're considering purchasing one of these packages, it's important to remember that YHA hostels are not widespread in Tasmania – there are no YHA hostels on the west coast, for example, or south of Hobart, or along the Midland Hwy, or in the popular east-coast towns of Swansea or Bicheno. Our advice is to pay your accommodation as you go and not commit yourself to any one form of accommodation. There may not be a YHA hostel at your destination of choice, but there may well be an independent hostel, cheap pub room or budget cabin.

Road Conditions & Hazards

Distances may appear short when looking at a map of Tasmania (especially in relation to distances on the mainland), but roads are often narrow and winding, making trip durations considerably longer than anticipated. There are also many unsealed roads throughout the state leading to sites of interest – bear this in mind when renting a car, as many insurance policies won't cover you for damage or accidents incurred while driving on such roads.

Watch out for wildlife while you're driving around the island – the huge number of carcasses lining main roads is sad testimony to the fact that many drivers don't use enough caution. Many local animals are nocturnal and often cross roads around dusk, so try to avoid driving in rural areas when darkness falls; if it's unavoidable, then slow down. And be warned that hitting a wombat not only kills the unfortunate animal, but can also make a mess of your car.

Many roads, including some highways, are fairly narrow with many sharp bends and, occasionally, one-lane bridges that aren't clearly signposted. Cycling is popular on some roads (particularly on the east coast) and when encountering bicycles you should wait until you can pass safely. Log-trucks piled high and speeding around sharp corners also demand caution. Finally, in cold weather be wary of 'black ice', an invisible layer of ice over the bitumen, especially on the shaded side of mountain passes. It's wise to drive a little more slowly and allow more time to react to these hazards.

Anyone considering travelling on four-wheel-drive tracks should read the free publication *Cruisin' Without Bruisin'*, available and at visitors centres around the state or online from the Parks & Wildlife Service website (www.parks.tas.gov.au/recreation/4wd/4wd.html). It details over 20 tracks (graded easy to hard) and explains how to minimise your impact on the regions you drive through.

Road Rules

Driving in Tasmania holds few surprises, other than the odd animal caught in your headlights. Cars are driven on the left-hand side of the road (as they are in the rest of Australia). An important road rule is 'give way to the right' – if an intersection is unmarked (which is unusual), you must give way to vehicles entering the intersection from your right.

In towns and cities, the general speed limit is 50km/h, while on the open road the general limit is 100km/h, although on major highways such as the Midland it's 110km/h. Speed cameras operate in Tasmania and are usually carefully hidden.

Wearing a seat belt is compulsory – you'll be fined if you don't use them. Children

ROAD DISTANCES (KM)

	Burnie	Deloraine	Devonport	Geeveston	Hobart	Launceston	New Norfolk	Oatlands	Port Arthur	Queenstown	St Helens	Scottsdale	Smithton	Sorell	Swansea
Deloraine	100														
Devonport	50	50													
Geeveston	381	281	331												
Hobart	328	228	278	53											
Launceston	137	51	87	254	201										
New Norfolk	290	190	240	91	38	197									
Oatlands	246	146	196	136	83	118	79								
Port Arthur	386	286	336	148	95	258	133	140							
Queenstown	148	204	198	312	259	251	221	261	354						
St Helens	293	207	243	304	251	156	247	168	299	407					
Scottsdale	197	111	147	314	261	60	257	178	318	311	96				
Smithton	88	188	138	469	416	225	378	334	474	236	381	285			
Sorell	316	216	266	78	25	188	63	70	70	284	229	248	404		
Swansea	264	164	214	189	136	136	174	114	181	395	118	214	352	111	
Triabunna	314	214	264	139	86	186	124	131	131	345	168	264	402	61	50

These are the shortest distances by road; other routes may be considerably longer.
For distances by coach, check the companies' leaflets.

must be strapped into an approved safety seat. Talking on a hand-held mobile phone while driving is illegal.

The other main law applies to drinking and driving: a strict limit of 0.05% blood alcohol content applies. There are heavy penalties if you break this law – your licence will be cancelled and jail sentences are imposed on offenders with multiple convictions. Random breath tests are also regularly conducted by police. All in all, the best policy is not to get behind the wheel if you've been drinking.

HITCHING

Travel by thumb in Tassie is generally good, but wrap up in winter and keep a raincoat handy. Many of the state's minor roads are still unsurfaced and traffic on them can be very light, so although some of these roads lead to interesting places, you'll probably have to give them a miss if you're hitching.

That being said, hitching is never entirely safe in any country in the world and we don't recommend it. Travellers who decide to hitch should understand that they're taking a small but potentially serious risk. People who do choose to hitch will be safer if they travel in pairs and let someone know where they are planning to go.

People looking for travelling companions for car journeys around the state often leave notices on boards in hostels and backpacker accommodation. The website www.needaride.com.au is a good resource.

LOCAL TRANSPORT

Metro (☎ 13 22 01; www.metrotas.com.au; information line 5am-11.30pm Mon-Thu, 5am-1.30am Fri, 6.30am-1am Sat, 8am-10.30pm Sun) operates bus networks in Hobart, Launceston and Burnie, offering visitors inexpensive services enabling them to reach some out-of-the-way attractions. For schedules and price lists of the Hobart services, stop by the main post office at the corner of Elizabeth and Macquarie Sts.

Taxis are available in all major towns and can be a handy way of getting to places otherwise not easily reached. Outside the major towns, local transport is limited.

TRAIN

For economic reasons there are no longer any passenger rail services in Tasmania, which probably accounts for the number of model railways and train exhibitions throughout the state.

Health

Dr David Millar

CONTENTS

Australia is a healthy country in which to travel. Diseases of insanitation such as cholera and typhoid are unheard of. Thanks to Australia's isolation and quarantine standards, even some animal diseases such as rabies and foot-and-mouth disease have yet to be recorded.

Few travellers to Australia will experience anything worse than an upset stomach or a bad hangover, and if you do fall ill the standard of hospitals and health care is high.

PREDEPARTURE

Since most vaccines don't produce immunity until at least two weeks after they're given, visit a physician four to eight weeks before departure. Ask your doctor for an International Certificate of Vaccination (otherwise known as 'the yellow booklet'), which will list all the vaccinations you've received. This is mandatory for countries that require proof of yellow fever vaccination upon entry (sometimes required in Australia, see right), but it's a good idea to carry a record of all your vaccinations wherever you travel.

Bring medications in their original, clearly labelled, containers. A signed and dated letter from your physician describing your medical conditions and medications, including generic names, is also a good idea. If carrying syringes or needles, be sure to have a physician's letter documenting their medical necessity.

Insurance

Health insurance is essential for all travellers. While health care in Australia is of a high standard and is not overly expensive by international standards, costs can build up and repatriation is extremely expensive.

If your health insurance doesn't cover you abroad, consider getting extra insurance. Find out in advance if your insurance plan will make payments directly to providers or reimburse you later for overseas health expenditures. In Australia, as in many countries, doctors expect payment at the time of consultation. Make sure you get an itemised receipt detailing the service and keep contact details for the health provider. See p345 for details of health care in Australia.

Recommended Vaccinations

If you're really worried about health when travelling, there are a few vaccinations you could consider for Australia. The World Health Organization recommends that all travellers should be covered for diphtheria, tetanus, measles, mumps, rubella, chickenpox and polio, as well as hepatitis B, regardless of their destination. The travel-planning period is a great time to ensure that all routine vaccination cover is complete. The consequences of these diseases can be severe, and while Australia has high levels of childhood vaccination coverage, outbreaks of these diseases do occur.

Required Vaccinations

Proof of yellow fever vaccination is required only from travellers entering Australia within six days of having stayed overnight or longer in a yellow fever–infected country. For a full list of these countries visit the websites of the **World Health Organization** (www.who.int/wer) or the **Centers for Disease Control and Prevention** (www.cdc.gov/travel/blusheet.htm).

INFECTIOUS DISEASES

Bat lyssavirus This is related to rabies and some deaths have occurred after bites. Rabies vaccine is effective. The risk is greatest for animal handlers and vets. The risk to travellers is very low.

Dr David Millar is a travel medicine specialist, diving doctor and lecturer in wilderness medicine.

Dengue fever Occurs in northern Queensland, particularly during the wet season (November to April). Also known as 'breakbone fever', because of the severe muscular pains that accompany it, this viral disease is spread by a mosquito that feeds primarily during the day. Most people recover in a few days but more severe forms of the disease can occur, particularly in residents who are exposed to another strain of the virus (there are four types) in a subsequent season.
Giardiasis This is widespread in waterways. Drinking untreated water from streams and lakes is not recommended. Water filters and boiling or treating water with iodine are effective preventatives. Symptoms consist of intermittent bad smelling diarrhoea, abdominal bloating and wind. Effective treatment is available (tinidazole or metronidazole).
Hepatitis C This is still a growing problem among intravenous drug users. Blood transfusion services fully screen all blood before it is used.
HIV Rates of this disease have stabilised in Australia and levels are similar to other Western countries. Clean needles and syringes are widely available through all chemists.
Malaria This is not an ongoing problem in the region, although isolated cases have occurred in northern Queensland. The risk to travellers is low.
Meningococcal disease Occurs worldwide and is a risk with prolonged, dormitory-style accommodation. A vaccine exists for meningococcal A, C, Y and W. No vaccine is presently available for the viral type of meningitis.
Ross River fever This is widespread in Australia. The virus is spread by mosquitoes living in marshy areas. In addition to fever it causes headache, joint and muscular pains and a rash, and resolves after five to seven days.
Sexually transmitted diseases These occur at rates similar to those in most other Western countries. The most common symptoms are pain while passing urine and a discharge. Infection can be present without symptoms so seek medical screening after any unprotected sex with a new partner. You'll find sexual health clinics in all of the major hospitals. Always use a condom with a new sexual partner. Condoms are readily available in chemists and through vending machines in many public places including toilets.
Tick typhus Cases of this have been reported throughout Australia, but are predominantly found in Queensland and New South Wales. A week or so after being bitten, a dark area forms around the bite, followed by a rash and possible fever, headache and inflamed lymph nodes. The disease is treatable with antibiotics (doxycycline) so see a doctor if you suspect you have been bitten.
Viral encephalitis Otherwise known as Murray Valley encephalitis virus, this is spread by mosquitoes and is most common in northern Australia, especially during the wet season (October to March). It is a potentially serious disease, normally accompanied by headache, muscle pains and sensitivity to light. Residual neurological damage can occur and no specific treatment is available. However, the risk to most travellers is low.

TRAVEL-RELATED ILLNESS

Deep Vein Thrombosis

Blood clots may form in the legs (deep vein thrombosis) during plane flights, chiefly because of prolonged immobility. The longer the flight, the greater the risk. Though most blood clots are reabsorbed uneventfully, some may break off and travel through the blood vessels to the lungs, where they could cause life-threatening complications.

The chief symptom of deep vein thrombosis is swelling or pain of the foot, ankle or calf, usually – but not always – on just one side. When a blood clot travels to the lungs, it may cause chest pain and breathing difficulties. Travellers with any of these symptoms should immediately seek medical attention.

To prevent the development of deep vein thrombosis on long flights, you should walk about the cabin, perform isometric compressions of the leg muscles (ie flex the leg muscles while sitting), drink plenty of fluids and avoid alcohol and tobacco.

Jet Lag & Motion Sickness

Jet lag is common when crossing more than five time zones, resulting in insomnia, fatigue, malaise or nausea. To avoid jet lag try drinking plenty of (nonalcoholic) fluids and eating light meals. Upon arrival, expose yourself to natural sunlight and readjust your schedule (for meals, sleep etc) as soon as possible.

Antihistamines such as dimenhydrinate and meclizine are usually the first choice for treating motion sickness. Their main side effect is drowsiness. A herbal alternative is ginger, which works like a charm for some people.

Travellers' Diarrhoea

If you develop diarrhoea, be sure to drink plenty of fluids – preferably an oral rehydration solution containing lots of salt and sugar. A few loose stools don't require treatment but if you start having more than four or five stools a day, you should start taking an antibiotic (usually a quinolone drug) and an antidiarrhoeal agent (such as loperamide). If diarrhoea is bloody, persists for more than 72 hours or is accompanied by fever, shaking, chills or severe abdominal pain you should seek medical attention. See Water (p344) for prevention of this.

ENVIRONMENTAL HAZARDS

Animal Bites

INSECTS

Various insects can be a source of irritation and, in Australia, may be the source of specific diseases (eg dengue fever, Ross River fever). Protection from mosquitoes, sandflies, ticks and leeches can be achieved by a combination of the following strategies:

- putting on loose-fitting long-sleeved clothing
- applying a 30%-DEET insect repellent to all exposed skin and repeating every three to four hours
- impregnating clothing with permethrin (an insecticide that kills insects but is completely safe to humans)

SHARKS

Despite extensive media coverage, the risk of shark attack in Australian waters is no greater than in other countries with extensive coastlines. Great white sharks are now few in number in the temperate southern waters. Check with surf lifesaving groups about local risks.

SNAKES

Australian snakes have a fearful reputation that is justified in terms of the potency of their venom, but unjustified in terms of the actual risk to travellers and locals. Snakes are usually quite timid in nature and in most instances will move away if disturbed. They only have small fangs, making it easy to prevent bites to the lower limbs (where 80% of bites occur) by wearing protective clothing (such as gaiters) around the ankles when bushwalking. The bite marks are very small and may even go unnoticed.

In all confirmed or suspected bites, preventing the spread of toxic venom can be achieved by applying pressure to the wound and immobilising the area with a splint or sling before seeking medical attention. Firmly wrap an elastic bandage (you can improvise with a T-shirt) around the entire limb, but not so tight as to cut off the circulation. Along with immobilisation, this is a life-saving first-aid measure.

SPIDERS

Australia has a number of poisonous spiders. Red-back spiders are found throughout the country. Bites cause increasing pain at the site followed by profuse sweating and generalised symptoms (muscular weakness, sweating at the site of the bite, nausea). First aid includes application of ice or cold packs to the bite, then transfer to hospital.

White-tailed spiders can also give a nasty bite. Clean the wound thoroughly and seek medical assistance.

Hypothermia

Hypothermia is a significant risk especially during the winter months in southern parts of Australia. Despite the absence of high mountain ranges, strong winds produce a high chill factor that can result in hypothermia even in moderately cool temperatures. Early signs include the inability to perform fine movements (such as doing up buttons), shivering and a bad case of the 'umbles' (fumbles, mumbles, grumbles and stumbles). The key elements of treatment include moving out of the cold, changing out of any wet clothing into dry clothes with wind- and water-proof layers, adding insulation and providing fuel (water and carbohydrate) to allow shivering, which builds the internal temperature. In severe hypothermia, shivering actually stops – this is a medical emergency requiring rapid evacuation in addition to the above measures.

Surf Beaches & Drowning

Australia has exceptional surf. Beaches vary enormously in their underwater conditions: the slope offshore can result in changeable and often powerful surf. Check with local surf lifesaving organisations and be aware of your own expertise and limitations before entering the water.

Ultraviolet Light Exposure

Australia has one of the highest rates of skin cancer in the world. Monitor your exposure to direct sunlight closely. UV exposure is greatest between 10am and 4pm so avoid skin exposure during these times. Always use Sun Protection Factor 30+ sunscreen; apply 30 minutes before going into the sun and reapply regularly to minimise damage.

Water

Tap water in Tasmania is usually safe but, surprisingly, there are some small towns (Swansea on the east coast, for example) where it is recommended that you boil tap water before drinking. It's worth asking for advice if you're unsure about the safety of tap water in the area you're visiting.

Increasing numbers of streams and rivers and lakes are being contaminated by bugs that cause diarrhoea, making water purification essential. The simplest way of purifying water is to boil it thoroughly.

Consider purchasing a water filter. It's very important when buying a filter to read the specifications, so that you know exactly what it removes from the water and what it doesn't. Simple filtering will not remove all dangerous organisms, so if you can't boil water it should be treated chemically. Chlorine tablets will kill many pathogens, but not some parasites like giardia and amoebic cysts. Iodine is more effective in purifying water and is available in tablet form. Follow the directions carefully and remember that too much iodine can be harmful.

HEALTH CARE

Australia has an excellent health-care system. It's a mixture of privately run medical clinics and hospitals alongside a government-funded system of public hospitals. The Medicare system covers Australian residents for some health-care costs. Visitors from countries with which Australia has a reciprocal health-care agreement are eligible for benefits specified under the Medicare programme. Agreements are currently in place with New Zealand, the UK, the Netherlands, Sweden, Finland, Italy, Malta and Ireland – check the details before departing these countries. In general the agreements provide for any episode of ill-health that requires prompt medical attention. For further details visit www.health.gov.au/pubs/mbs/mbs3/medicare.htm. You should, however, carry insurance (see p342).

There are excellent, specialised, public health facilities for women and children in Australia's major centres.

Pharmaceutical Supplies

Over-the-counter medications are widely available from privately owned chemists throughout Australia. These include painkillers, antihistamines for allergies and skin-care products.

You may find that medications readily available over the counter in some countries are only available in Australia by prescription. These include the oral contraceptive pill, most medications for asthma and all antibiotics. If you take medication on a regular basis, bring an adequate supply and ensure you have details of the generic name because brand names may differ between countries.

Self-care

In Australia's remote locations it is possible there'll be a significant delay in emergency services reaching you in the event of serious accident or illness. Do not underestimate the vast distances between most major outback towns; an increased level of self-reliance and preparation is essential.

Consider taking a wilderness first-aid course, such as those offered at the **Wilderness**

MEDICAL CHECKLIST

- acetaminophen/paracetamol or aspirin
- adhesive or paper tape
- antibacterial ointment (for cuts and abrasions)
- antibiotics
- antidiarrhoeal drugs (eg loperamide)
- antihistamines (for hay fever and allergic reactions)
- anti-inflammatory drugs (eg ibuprofen)
- bandages, gauze, gauze rolls
- DEET-containing insect repellent for the skin
- iodine tablets or water filter (for water purification)
- oral rehydration salts
- pocket knife
- permethrin-containing insect spray for clothing, tents and bed nets
- scissors
- safety pins
- steroid cream or cortisone (for poison ivy and other allergic rashes)
- sun block
- thermometer
- tweezers

Medicine Institute (www.wmi.net.au); take a comprehensive first-aid kit that is appropriate for the activities planned; and ensure that you have adequate means of communication. Australia has extensive mobile phone coverage but additional radio communication is important for remote areas.

ONLINE RESOURCES

There is a wealth of travel health advice online. **LonelyPlanet.com** (www.lonelyplanet.com) is a good place to start. The **World Health Organization** (www.who.int/ith/) publishes *International Travel and Health,* which is revised annually and is available online at no cost. Another website of general interest is **MD Travel Health** (www.mdtravelhealth.com), which provides travel health recommendations and is updated daily.

TRAVEL HEALTH WEBSITES

It's usually a good idea to consult your government's travel health website before departure, if one is available.

Australia (www.dfat.gov.au/travel/)
Canada (www.travelhealth.gc.ca)
UK (www.doh.gov.uk/traveladvice/)
USA (www.cdc.gov/travel/)

FURTHER READING

Lonely Planet's *Travel with Children* contains advice on travel health for younger children. Also try reading *Traveller's Health* by Dr Richard Dawood (Oxford University Press) and *International Travel Health Guide* by Stuart R Rose, MD (Travel Medicine Inc).

Glossary

arvo – afternoon
Aussie rules – Australian Rules football, a game (vaguely) resembling rugby played by teams of 18

barbie – barbecue
barrack – cheer on team at sporting event, support ('Who do you barrack for?')
battler – struggler, someone who tries hard
beaut, beauty – great, fantastic
bloke – man
blowies, blow flies – large flies
bludger – lazy person, one who refuses to work
blue – argument or fight ('have a blue')
body board – half-sized surfboard
bonzer – great
boogie board – see *body board*
boomerang – a curved, flat, wooden instrument used by Aborigines for hunting
booze bus – police van used for random breath testing of drivers for alcohol
bottle shop – liquor shop, off-licence
brekky – breakfast
bush tucker – native foods
bush, the – country, anywhere away from the city
bushwalking – hiking
BYO – bring your own; a type of restaurant licence that permits customers to drink bottles of wine they have purchased elsewhere; a 'corkage' charge (say, around $5 per bottle) is added to the bill for this privilege

cask wine – wine packaged in a plastic bladder surrounded by a cardboard box (a great Australian invention)
catch ya later – goodbye, see you later
chook – chicken
cobber – (archaic) see *mate*
counter meal – pub meal
crack the shits – lose one's temper
crook – ill or substandard
cut lunch – sandwiches

dag – dirty lump of wool at back end of a sheep; also an affectionate or mildly abusive term for a socially inept person
dead set – true, dinkum
didgeridoo – wind instrument made from a hollow piece of wood, traditionally played by Aboriginal men
digger – (archaic, from Australian and New Zealand soldiers in WWI) see *mate*
dill – idiot
dinky-di – the real thing
dob in – to inform on someone
Dreamtime – complex concept that forms the basis of Aboriginal spirituality, incorporating the creation of the world and the spiritual energies operating around us; 'Dreaming' is often the preferred term as it avoids the association with time
drongo – worthless or stupid person
dunny – outdoor lavatory

earbash – to talk nonstop
Esky – large insulated box for keeping food and drinks cold

fair dinkum – honest, genuine
fair go! – give us a break!
flake – shark meat, often the fish in fish and chips
flat out – very busy or fast

galah – noisy parrot, thus noisy idiot
g'day – good day, traditional Australian greeting
good on ya! – well done!
grog – general term for alcoholic drinks

homestead – residence of a *station* owner or manager
hoon – idiot, hooligan

icy pole – frozen lollipop, ice lolly
iffy – dodgy, questionable

kick the bucket – to die
Kiwi – New Zealander
knackered – broken, tired
knock – to criticise, deride

larrikin – hooligan, mischievous youth
little ripper – extremely good thing; see also *ripper*
lollies – sweets, candy
loo – toilet

mainlander – someone from the mainland states of Australia
mainland refugee – a *mainlander* who has relocated to Tasmania
map of Tassie – aside from its literal meaning, this is also a rather crude term for the pubic hair of a woman (think about it – especially the island's shape...)
mate – general term of familiarity, whether you know the person or not
milk bar – small shop selling milk and other basic provisions

mobile phone – cell phone
mod Oz – modern Australian cuisine influenced by a wide range of foreign cuisines, but with a definite local flavour
mozzies – mosquitoes

no-hoper – hopeless case
no worries! – no problems! That's OK!

ocker – uncultivated or boorish Australian
off-sider – assistant, partner
outback – remote part of the *bush*

paddock – fenced area of land, usually intended for livestock
perv – to gaze with lust
piss – beer
piss turn, piss up – boozy party
piss weak – no good, gutless
pissed – drunk
pissed off – annoyed
plonk – cheap wine
pokies – poker machines
pom – English person

rapt – delighted, enraptured
ratbag – friendly term of abuse
ratshit – lousy
rip – a strong ocean current or undertow
ripper – good; see also *little ripper*
root – to have sexual intercourse
rooted – tired, broken
ropable – very bad-tempered or angry

sanger – sandwich
scrub – *bush*
sealed road – bitumen road
shark biscuit – inexperienced surfer
sheila – woman
she'll be right – no problems, no worries
shonky – unreliable
shout – to buy a round of drinks ('Your shout!')
sickie – day off work ill (or malingering)
smoko – tea break
snag – sausage
sparrow's fart – dawn
squatter – pioneer farmer who occupied land as a tenant of the government
station – large farm
stolen generations – Aboriginal children forcibly removed from their families during the government's policy of assimilation
stroppy – bad-tempered
stubby – 375ml bottle of beer
sunbake – sunbathe (well, the sun's hot in Australia!)

take the piss – deliberately tell someone an untruth, often as social sport
thongs – flip-flops (definitely *not* a g-string!)
too right! – absolutely!
trucky – truck driver
tucker – food
two-pot screamer – person unable to hold their drink

unsealed road – dirt road
ute – utility; a pick-up truck

wag – to skip school or work
weatherboard – timber cladding on a house
whinge – to complain, moan
wowser – someone who doesn't believe in having fun, spoilsport, teetotaller

yakka – work
yobbo – uncouth, aggressive person
yonks – a long time

Behind the Scenes

THIS BOOK

This is the 4th edition of *Tasmania*. The 1st edition was researched and written by John and Monica Chapman back in 1996. Lyn McGaurr updated the 2nd edition, and Paul Smitz researched and wrote the 3rd edition. For this edition, Carolyn Bain (coordinating author) and Gina Tsarouhas covered countless miles in their quest to get the lowdown on all of Tassie's delights. Australia's leading environmental scientist, Tim Flannery, wrote the Environment chapter, and Dr David Millar wrote the Health chapter. Senator Bob Brown wrote the boxed text 'Simple Steps for Saving the Forests' in the Environment chapter, and Tony Wheeler, Lonely Planet founder, wrote the 'Fire Walking' boxed text in The Northeast chapter.

THANKS from the Author

Carolyn Bain Many thanks to Errol and Stefanie at Lonely Planet for giving me the chance to revisit such a great destination, and to all the fine production folk at LPHQ who made this book look so spiffy, especially editor Laura Gibb and cartographer Valentina Kremenchutskaya. Much appreciation goes to Paul Smitz, whose thorough research for the previous edition made my job considerably less stressful, and to my co-author Gina Tsarouhas for being a delight to work with (and for producing such great material). In Tasmania, boundless thanks to all the friendly locals, mainland refugees and fellow travellers who took time out for a chat and a cuppa, and who shared lots of helpful insights and information. Many thanks to Peter Renwick and Greg Wells for helping to organise my fab Flinders Island sojourn. Finally, to my mates who flew south for fun and games (and restaurant visits), much love and thanks: Helen Aucote, Sally O'Keefe, Rosalind Gilsenan and Sally O'Brien (and to Simone Shirkey, although she never quite made it to Tasmania, because she'd kill me if she didn't get a mention!).

Gina Tsarouhas Many thanks to all those people who helped make this an unforgettable journey, notably the lovely staff at the visitors centres who dealt with my questions with good humour and enthusiasm. I'm grateful to all the readers who sent in their recommendations and every friendly, helpful Taswegian (and non-Taswegian) who generously offered information, advice and tips along the way. To the pilot station boatmen, thanks for the impromptu dash across the water for the MV something or other. Bumble-bee, we miss you; safe travels. Afna, Alfy and Marty, you'll be in our hearts always. A heartfelt *efharisto* to Tsoureki for the lovely photo. To Errol, Stefanie and the rest of the fabulous team, *muchos gracias* for your support and dedication. To my co-author, Carolyn, thank you for your generous spirit and wonderful advice. Most of all, my heart sings with thanks to my wonderful travelling companion, Lisa Baas, who kept me sane and grounded when I wished I could take to the hills and howl in the wilderness, never to return.

CREDITS

Commissioning Editors Stefanie Di Trocchio, Errol Hunt, Marg Toohey and Will Gourlay

THE LONELY PLANET STORY

The story begins with a classic travel adventure: Tony and Maureen Wheeler's 1972 journey across Europe and Asia to Australia. There was no useful information about the overland trail then, so Tony and Maureen published the first Lonely Planet guidebook to meet a growing need.

From a kitchen table, Lonely Planet has grown to become the largest independent travel publisher in the world, with offices in Melbourne (Australia), Oakland (USA) and London (UK). Today Lonely Planet guidebooks cover the globe. There is an ever-growing list of books and information in a variety of media. Some things haven't changed. The main aim is still to make it possible for adventurous travellers to get out there – to explore and better understand the world.

At Lonely Planet we believe travellers can make a positive contribution to the countries they visit – if they respect their host communities and spend their money wisely. Every year 5% of company profit is donated to charities around the world.

Coordinating Editor Laura Gibb
Coordinating Cartographer Valentina Kremenchutskaya
Coordinating Layout Designer John Shippick
Managing Cartographer Corinne Waddell
Assisting Editors Simon Sellars, Diana Saad, Piers Kelly, Victoria Harrison, Trent Holden, Suzannah Shwer, Darren O'Connell and Yvonne Byron
Assisting Cartographers Tony Fankhauser
Cover Designer Jane Hart
Project Managers Glenn van der Knijff and Ray Thomson

Thanks to Wayne Murphy, Stephanie Pearson, Jennifer Garrett, Rebecca Lalor, Jennifer Mundy-Nordin, Karen Emmerson, Ben Oquist and Nick Stebbing.

THANKS FROM LONELY PLANET

Many thanks to the travellers who used the last edition and contacted us with helpful hints, advice and interesting anecdotes:

A Julie Alexander, Lilian Andrew, Raymond Ang, Matthew Aquilina, Paul Arrowsmith, Gay Ashcroft, C M Aspinall **B** Dominik Bach, Chris Bailey, Rob & Sarah Bailey, Mark Barber, Lorissa Barrett, Heini Baumgartner, Sam Blum, Michael Brasier, Judy Brewster, Mary Brosnan, Janice Brown **C** Gerard Callinan, Matthew Campbell-Ellis, Brad Carr, Stephen Chadwick, Meena Chawla, Pam Clarke, Lynnette Conder, Sheila Consaul, Christine & Howard Croxton **D** Richard Deimos, Gesine Dyck **E** J Edwards, Catherine Egger, Kathleen Evans **F** Sarah Fethers, R S Finn, Justin Flynn, Wendy Frew, Justin Fritz, Claudia Froeb **G** Allison Garrett, Graeme & Jennifer Gibson, F J Gray, Jacki & Philip Green, Ronalie Green, Joan Greening **H** Keith Hall, Anne Hall-Bowden, Rosemary Hamburger, Jeff Hangled, Justin Harrison, Edgar Harwood, Ilona Haselhoff, William Hempel, Kerry Hennigan, John Hickey, Mary P Hildebrandt, Tony Hill, Richard Holland, Grant Howard, Peter Howard, Gillian Howell, Alan & Chris Hughes, Craig Hughes, Heather Hyland **I** James G Ingles **J** Alice James, Steve James, Clare Jokuszies **K** Dorine van Kampen, Martin Kaye, Matthew Keenan, Amy Kelly, Michael Kelly, Helen Kendall, Sophie Kennett, Karen Knutsen **L** Elsa Le Fevre, Rachel Liley, Geoff & Judith Lomas **M** Mary Machen, Nina Mackay, Daniel Martin, Greg Martin, Patricia Martin, Francesca Massey, Catherine Masters, Michaela Matross, Angela McKay, Stephanie Messanger, Ceciel Meys, Amy Mo, Andrew Morris, Jenny Morris, John Morrow, Jeff Murphy **N** Julian Nolan **O** Karina O'Carroll, Mike Ogden, Roger Oliver, Brian R Orpet, Jurgen Otto **P** Gennet Paauwe, Robert Payne, Daniel Piper, Narelle Poole, Kathleen Pybus **R** Marianne Reimann, Abe Remmo, Corinna Ritter, Angus Robinson, David & Jacqui Ross, Loretta Ryan **S** Tony Schelleman, Mary Lou Sheehan, Ross Sincock, Susanne Skujat, John Smilgin, Ian Smith, Anja & Martin Spohr, Michael Sprod, Ann Syddall, Claire Szabo **T** Lesley Thomas, Owen Thompson, Katerina Tsacalos, Lisa Turner, Paul Turner **U** Olaf Unglaube **V** Martijn Vermunt, Harry Vos **W** Emma Walmsley, Tim Walter, Alexi Welsh, Joyce and Kenneth Why, Bill Williams, Marilyn & Terry Wilsons, Helen de Wolfe **Y** D C Young

SEND US YOUR FEEDBACK

We love to hear from travellers – your comments keep us on our toes and help make our books better. Our well-travelled team reads every word on what you loved or loathed about this book. Although we cannot reply individually to postal submissions, we always guarantee that your feedback goes straight to the appropriate authors, in time for the next edition. Each person who sends us information is thanked in the next edition – and the most useful submissions are rewarded with a free book.

To send us your updates – and find out about Lonely Planet events, newsletters and travel news – visit our award-winning website: **www.lonelyplanet.com/feedback**.

Note: We may edit, reproduce and incorporate your comments in Lonely Planet products such as guidebooks, websites and digital products, so let us know if you don't want your comments reproduced or your name acknowledged. For a copy of our privacy policy visit www.lonelyplanet.com/privacy.

Index

000 Map pages
000 Location of colour photographs

C

000 Map pages
000 Location of colour photographs

D

INDEX

000 Map pages
000 Location of colour photographs

000 Map pages
000 Location of colour photographs

N

O

P

000 Map pages
000 Location of colour photographs

INDEX

V

W

Z

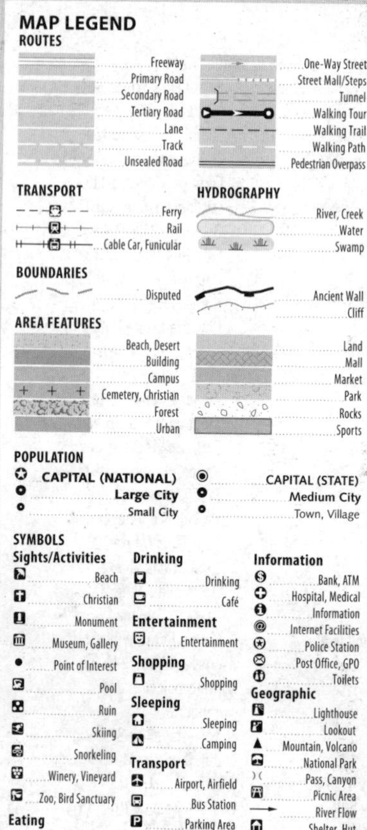

LONELY PLANET OFFICES

Australia
Head Office
Locked Bag 1, Footscray, Victoria 3011
☎ 03 8379 8000, fax 03 8379 8111
talk2us@lonelyplanet.com.au

USA
150 Linden St, Oakland, CA 94607
☎ 510 893 8555, toll free 800 275 8555
fax 510 893 8572, info@lonelyplanet.com

UK
72–82 Rosebery Ave,
Clerkenwell, London EC1R 4RW
☎ 020 7841 9000, fax 020 7841 9001
go@lonelyplanet.co.uk

Published by Lonely Planet Publications Pty Ltd
ABN 36 005 607 983

4th Edition – Oct 2005

First Published – Sep 1996

Cover photographs by Lonely Planet Images: Cradle Mountain and Dove Lake – Cradle Mountain–Lake St Clair National Park, Richard I'Anson (front); Constitution Dock and Franklin Wharf – Hobart, Richard I'Anson (back). Many of the images in this guide are available for licensing from Lonely Planet Images: www.lonelyplanetimages.com.

Printed through Colorcraft Ltd, Hong Kong.
Printed in China.